MAKING MONEY

Coin, Currency, and the Coming of Capitalism

Making Money

Coin, Currency, and the Coming of Capitalism

CHRISTINE DESAN

OXFORD
UNIVERSITY PRESS

OXFORD

UNIVERSITY PRESS

Great Clarendon Street, Oxford, OX2 6DP,
United Kingdom

Oxford University Press is a department of the University of Oxford.
It furthers the University's objective of excellence in research, scholarship,
and education by publishing worldwide. Oxford is a registered trade mark of
Oxford University Press in the UK and in certain other countries

First Edition published in 2014

Impression: 3

Published in the United States of America by Oxford University Press
198 Madison Avenue, New York, NY 10016, United States of America

British Library Cataloguing in Publication Data

Data available

Library of Congress Control Number: 2014935041

ISBN 978–0–19–870957–2

Printed in Great Britain by
CPI Group (UK) Ltd, Croydon, CR0 4YY

To Bob
in another currency altogether

Acknowledgements

I thought that this book had given me the most exciting intellectual journey I'd ever taken; then I realized it was the people in and around the book who made that adventure happen. Some of them lived centuries ago. Fortunately for me, the rest are those who talked, argued, engaged, and helped me throughout the process. Their support came in thousands of ways and these thanks are small change compared to the very large debt I owe. Still, the offering is heartfelt.

This book was informed from the start by critical legal studies and related efforts to understand liberalism as a legal project. It has been a stroke of great fortune (not to mention a lot of fun) to consider capitalism in the company of Mort Horwitz. I thank Lucie White deeply for her vision, teaching, and heart and I am endlessly grateful to Jerry Frug for his guiding wisdom on the process of social change and life more generally. Duncan Kennedy's restless imagination regularly upended my conclusions, an experience that brought more alternatives than I expected into view. Scholars and students from a wide variety of methodologies and disciplines vetted this work at the Institute for Global Law and Policy, a venue made possible by the creative and generous enterprise of David Kennedy. More generally at Harvard Law School and the neighboring law teaching communities, I have benefited enormously from conversations with Betsy Bartholet, Tomiko Brown-Nagin, Dan Danielson, Pnina Lahav, Janet Halley, David Barron, David Grossman, Tammy Lothian, Todd Rakoff, Jim Rogers, Gerry Leonard, and Ken Mack. I thank my colleagues at the HLS Faculty Workshop for a great many insights across the years and I am particularly grateful for the engagement at the very beginning of the project by David Charney.

Many legal historians and fellow travelers nurtured this research. Charlie Donahue shared his tremendous erudition with such goodwill that the medieval became a terrain as inviting as it was intimidating. For their pioneering work on institutions and their invaluable advice, I thank Dirk Hartog, Stan Katz, Tom Greene, and Dan Ernst. For comments and conversations that shaped the project, I am indebted to Paul Brand, Al Brophy, Colleen Dunlavy, Karen Engel, Howard Erlanger, Josh Getzler, Bob Gordon, Sally Hadden, Dan Hamilton, Adam Kosto, Ken Lipartito, Bruce Mann, Bill Nelson, Jeremy Paul, Claire Priest, Jeff Sklansky, Avi Soifer, Rob Steinfeld, and Chris Tomlins. Bill Novak gave me counsel I found extremely productive; I am also grateful to him for a workshop at the University of Michigan. Participants there and at workshops at Boston College Law School, Boston University School of Law, University of Connecticut Law School, University of Minnesota Law School, Newcastle University School of Law, New York University School of Law, Oxford University, the University of Texas at Austin, and Yale Law School were very helpful.

David Fox and Wolfgang Ernst organized a project at Cambridge University on Money in the Western Legal Tradition; their contributions, along with those of Andreas Thier and other participants at the conference were an essential aid. David Seipp, along with Carol Lee, gave expertise both in person and by way of the magnificent Seipp database. Steven Wilf took an amazing eye to the introduction and told me to undertake changes long after I wanted to rethink anything; he was absolutely right. At many points, Barbara Welke graced this project with the intellect and generosity that is her trademark. Malick Ghachem and I began talking about money and finance long ago; I will draw from Malick's acumen for many years to come.

My thanks to Sven Beckert for sharing, in fact *exuding*, his sheer joy in the project of understanding the past; I've benefited enormously from co-teaching with him the Workshop on the Political Economy of Modern Capitalism for the last ten years. The Workshop furnished a forum for discussing this project, both formally and informally, and the work both by students and more senior scholars done there has greatly affected my own. Special thanks to Seth Rockman for his superb insight, both narrative and methodological; to Betsy Blackmar, Barry Cohen, Mike Merrill, and Walter Johnson for discerning commentary at critical moments; and to Jack Womack for his gift for going to the heart of the matter. Alex Keyssar provided the very model of a scholar who unlocks history in order to address its legacies.

I have gained immensely from many others who brought their expertise to bear on this project, including Joanna Gray, Stanley Engermann, Tamar Herzog, George Kenney, Mark Kishlansky, and Vishaal Kishore. Steve Pincus, Justin duRivage, Lucy Kaufman, and others at the Yale University Transitions to Modernity Colloquium improved several chapters of the manuscript. Dan Smail graciously entertained queries that came of the blue, and then organized one of the most exciting seminars I've had the opportunity to attend; I am grateful to the scholars who assembled there including Maryanne Kowaleski, Phillipp Schofield, Michael McCormick, Sally Livingston, and Alan Stahl. Frederick Schnabel was kind enough to share his unparalleled knowledge about the financial world of the 16th century. Bill Sewell read a critical chapter of the manuscript and gave me comments I continue to think about today.

To the people who chase money in history and theory rather than more lucrative places, I am especially beholden. In his scholarship, Nicholas Mayhew decodes a world. He generously illuminated point after point for me. (I also treasure a thrilling trip to the Ashmolean coin room.) With characteristic graciousness, Angela Redish shared an expertise that spans the medieval and the modern; Carl Wennerlind illuminated the early modern age. Perry Mehrling contributed his formidable knowledge about modern "inside money." Randy Wray displayed similar erudition on modern "outside money." A number of theorists and scholars of money and finance gave me comments or read portions of the manuscript that helped greatly, including Martin Allen, Matthew Forstater, Jeffrey Frankel, Geoffrey Ingham, Fadhel Kaboub, Anush Kapadia, Steve Keen, Stephanie Kelton, Marc Lavoie, Gillian Metzger, Jim Millstein, Bill Maurer, and Francois Velde. Steve Marglin approached the project with a gravity and generosity that enabled real exchange, a concept he fundamentally redefines. Chris Fauske, Richard Kleer, and Ivar McGrath organized a series on Money, Power, and Print, where I benefited from commentary by them and others, including Scott Breuninger, Alan Downie, Joyce Goggin, Jim Hartley, Eoin Magennis, Sean Moore, Anne Murphy, Helen Paul, Stephen Timmons, and Patrick Walsh.

One of the best teachers I ever had was a student, now a Ph.D. in economics, Ryan Taliaferro, who guided me through many of the economic models of money (but is not responsible for what I made of them). Lauren Coyle brought amazing knowledge and creativity to the project when she was a J.D. student, now a Ph.D. in anthropology. Helen Lu, now a finance lawyer, brought critical social scientific skills to the project as she collected monetary data and conceptualized the definitional issues it raised. I thank a decade of great research assistants, including Jane Gimian, Stephen Cha-Kim, Meryl Holt, Elizabeth Jensen, Karl Lisberger, Clayton Simmons, Sarah Levin, Sahand Moarefy, Mo Chen, Rose Francis, Christopher Harrington, Pooja Nair, Melanie Griswold, Adejumoke Osha, Christopher Taggart, Luke Appling, Adam Ringguth, David Landau, Aaron Lamb, and Kevin Burke. Iain Frame, Zach Howe, Leia Castaneda, and Mara Caden taught me through their own research. I also benefited from the experience of presenting work to the Modern Money Network, a valuable platform for debate about money created by Rohan Gray and developed by Raul Carrillo.

I am blessed with a money network of my own, a cluster of people without whom this book could not have been written. Farley Grubb engaged conversation at any level from the granular to the abstract; his determination to understand the early American experience animates a great economic imagination. Rowan Dorin combines astonishing erudition and artistry in his approach to all things medieval, including its money. The many-sided dialogue between Morgan Ricks, Nadav Orian Peer, and Roy Kreitner together and separately has been an intellectual joy that was elemental to the manuscript. Here's to Morgan for his analytic drive and eye-opening work and to Nadav for his infectious curiosity and an approach to knowledge that manages to be disciplined and wild at the same time. As for Roy, his rare vision, counsel, and friendship matter more than I can say. He has informed this project from the beginning.

Like the monetary adventure itself, the institutional support for this project comes down to people. Deans Elena Kagan and Martha Minow of Harvard Law School helped the book move forward in many ways, including research time and funds. The Harvard Law School reference librarians, especially Meg Kribble and

Janet Katz, spent hours providing sources and expertise on them. I am extremely grateful to the staff of FRIDA, particularly Louise Ragno along with Melinda Kent, Ashley Pierce, and Heather Pierce. Amanda Cegielski, staff assistant extraordinaire, brought research skills, technical prowess, and an ingenuity that shredded her job description. Sarah Davitt, Jennifer Campbell, Joely Merriman, and Joei Perry also provided critical administrative help. Matt Seccombe, editor with many portfolios, contributed both historical expertise and conceptual wizardry to the work.

Alex Flach at the Oxford University Press brought this book to fruition with an extraordinary blend of advice and support; I am deeply grateful. Matthew Humphrys beautifully steered the production process, and I appreciate the work of Emma Brady, Natasha Flemming, Kathryn Swift, Katherine Marshall, and Jenifer Payne, as well as three anonymous readers who identified important areas for improvement. I thank Carol Oja and Jill Kneerim for good advice about publishing, and Mike Trotman for his ace proof-reading skills. I am indebted to Abelardo Morrell for sharing his stunning photography of bank money.

Finally, I thank the people closest to home. Peg Burhoe, Whit and Susan Larrabee, Amy Parker, Diane Piktialis, Elizabeth Mendizabal, Nina Dwyer, and Carol Smith, along with Laurie Lasky and the entire gang at Emerson Park anchored every day with their friendship. Karen Jacobson, Richard Nasser, and Amy Shapiro treated reports from the medieval and early modern fronts as breaking news; theirs was essential encouragement over a decade-long project.

My family lived the whole enterprise most intimately. I am grateful beyond words to Elizabeth Desan, who moved heaven and earth for this project, and to Wilfrid Desan, whose constant vocation was a better world. Sally Husson, Brenda Husson, Tom Faulkner, "the cousins," and the Desan-Avila clan rooted for the book with great spirit. Barbara Forrest brought inspired judgment to key decisions. I love my brother, Paul, for his combination of clear-eyed critique and loyal advocacy, and my sister, Suzanne, for the brilliant sense of history and narrative that rescued me from a black hole more than once. Though they had my heart from the beginning, David and Jay would have won it all over again given everything they provided, from comic relief to serious support as they grew up with the book. To Bob, who held fast over a thousand years of history and the drama it produced in the present day, I dedicate this work.

Contents Summary

Contents

A note on the text: Capitalization in the sources has been modernized.

List of Figures

Table of Cases

Table of Statutes

* See p. 78, n. 30

Introduction

Perhaps the most powerful revolutions are the ones that deny they ever happened. They install a new approach and erase an earlier practice so successfully that we look at the world through the structures they leave behind. The reinvention of money in early modern England was one such event. This book is about the old ways of making money, the revolution that redesigned that medium, and how that revolution disappeared from view.

At first glance, money seems an odd place for a revolution. According to much of modern thought, money is an instrument, an empty signifier, a function. In economic terminology, it is a unit of account, a mode of payment, and a medium of exchange, more interesting for what it *does* than for what it *is*. But that, in fact, is part of the revolution's vanishing act.

If we look behind the dry labels that sum up what money does, we find the real drama. In order to make a "unit of account," a society must create a measure that everyone will understand as a common value and use when setting a price on objects, labor, even time. The measure must take shape that travels from the center of a society to its margins. Whether it wears, or tears, or is absolutely opaque to those who hold it, it cannot remain abstract but must deliver value immediately, by definition the premier "mode of payment," the best of all credits. It must move hand to hand, a "medium of exchange" for strangers as well as friends, for those without trust or further contact as well as those who can reciprocate at a later time.

Making an entity that can answer demands at once so intimate and so impersonal, so material and so artificial—making money—is a governance project, one of the most penetrating that societies undertake. "Money" is a practice orchestrated among a group to produce the very functions that economists abstract—a way to mark value, maintain it evenly as a means of payment across a real time and place, and pass it among participants. Made by engaging the same people who use it, money is no neutral technology. It is instead a constitutional (small "c") effort in a very particular sense: money is a mode of mobilizing resources, one that communities design for that end and individuals appropriate for their own purposes. It defines authority and distributes material as it operates.

Once we look at money as a constitutional undertaking made by the societies that circulate it, a panorama long obscured by our modern myopia comes into view. The English world has engineered many different moneys over the centuries. Those efforts were critical sites of debate and distribution that configured political economic life, just as they were affected by that environment. Recognizing the way those societies "made money" illuminates the way their inhabitants negotiated value with each other. It documents, yet more specifically, the way their measure—money—defined their exchange.

Silver coin, the paradigmatic money of the early world, at first appears simple—a slug of metal, a natural store of value that passed between people who recognized its worth. In fact, the English penny was a highly contrived product. Set apart by their need for a medium and by their capacity to define it, political authorities directed money's creation. They controlled minting, established coin's count, enforced its use to pay debts, and policed its exclusivity as a medium. They also charged for it at the mint: individuals paid up in extra amounts of silver bullion and came away with coin. "Making money" this way brought sovereign and subject into contact over a matter essential to them both. The price of money was one issue and the pace of minting was another. But the English also debated the power of the penny in relation to the amount of revenue taken in it; they struggled to keep money circulating; they negotiated remedies when coin failed; and they improvised ways around money altogether. They argued over the rights that attached to coin, the political power to manage it, the way to conceptualize it, and more. As they made money, they made the English political economy.

The view to past practice also exposes moments of radical change. The coming of capitalism was one such time, a crucial transformation in modern history. Late in the 17th century, the English broke the pattern they had maintained for centuries. Their government began minting metal into coin for free. Immediately thereafter, the government began paying investors to lend it money in the shape of bank notes that circulated and operated as a public mode of payment. In turn, the government licensed banks to multiply money by lending to individuals on the basis of the coin and public debt the banks held.

The changes went to the heart of the system, where they worked in tandem. First, and in an unprecedented step, the government shared its monopoly over money creation. Reserving responsibility for defining the unit of account, the government granted banks the authority to spread that unit further in paper and at a profit. Second, the government now paid for money instead of selling the liquidity it created. The mechanism that produced liquidity was no longer the calculus made by people who anticipated the cost of making money from metal, coin by coin. It was a grant made by the government that paid for the transmutation and encouraged investors to expand the money supply still further in return for a fee from individuals borrowing from them.

Over the next several centuries, the level of cash irrigating daily exchange in England increased enormously. The money stock that individuals were willing to hold grew something like 65-fold, corrected for inflation.[1] Banks of issue—institutions unknown to the English during the Middle Ages—became structurally essential to the basic activity of the economy. Across that period, approaches to governance shifted; they newly privileged material incentives, productivity, and agency. The legalities that had maintained gold and silver moneys withered to make room for the law that represented and multiplied them in paper form. Other issues, like those many decided in the course of maintaining commodity money, arose and were determined, elaborating a new monetary architecture. At the daily level, a different pattern and culture of exchange emerged. An advocate celebrated banks as "nurseries of national wealth"; a critic condemned the "iron cage" of material striving. And at the global level, nations were increasingly integrated by a monetary-financial code far more exacting than the public norms of international law.[2]

At the same time, money itself became a mystery. The consensus that money was a precious resource produced by the sovereign faded. A world that had been obsessed with the way money was made became a world that denied, just as stubbornly, that project and its importance constituting society. The discipline that claimed the most competence over the subject rejected claims that the way money was made mattered. Macroeconomic textbooks adopted a fable about money's origins that fit within a paragraph and monetary theorists defended the project of imagining money's history in light of its form. "The best models of the economy," one economist noted, "cannot find room" for money at all.[3]

---

[1] This estimate compares money supply per capita corrected for inflation in 1688 and 2009; it is rough, given limits in the data. For 1688 money supply, including specie and bank notes both from the Bank of England and private banks circulating in England and Wales, see Rondo E. Cameron et al., eds., *Banking in the Early Stages of Industrialization: A Study in Comparative Economic History* (New York: Oxford University Press, 1967), 42–46. For 1688 population in England and Wales, see Peter H. Lindert, "English Population, Wages, and Prices: 1541–1913," *Journal of Interdisciplinary History* 15, no. 4 (1985): 633–634. For 2009 money supply, including retail deposits and private sector sterling holdings of notes and coins in the U.K., see Bank of England, Interactive Database, accessed June 26, 2014, <http://www.bankofengland.co.uk/boeapps/iadb/newintermed.asp>. For 2009 population in the U.K., see World Bank, DataBank, accessed June 26, 2014, <http://databank.worldbank.org/data/home.aspx>. The geographic shift in the data is unavoidable, but should be controlled to some extent because it is analyzed per capita for each region, respectively. Price figures are taken from Sally Hills, Ryland Thomas, and Nicholas Dimsdale, "The UK Recession in Context—What Do Three Centuries of Data Tell Us?," *Bank of England Quarterly* Q4 (2010), and the associated online database. Arguably, the comparison should not correct for inflation, since the rise in prices and fall in monetary value has made many more small exchanges possible. Without correcting for inflation, the per capita rise in the money supply is more than 8,000-fold.

[2] Alexander Hamilton, "Report of the Secretary of the Treasury, Dec. 14, 1790," in *Documentary History of the First Federal Congress of the United States of America*, vol. 4, ed. Charlene Bangs Bickford and Helen E. Veit (Baltimore: Johns Hopkins University Press, 1986), 177; Max Weber, *The Protestant Ethic and the Spirit of Capitalism*, trans. Talcott Parsons (London: Routledge Classics, 2001 [1930]), 123.

[3] Frank Hahn, *Money and Inflation* (Oxford: Basil Blackwell, 1982). 1. For a classic example dismissing the importance of the way money is created, see James Tobin, "Money," in *The New Palgrave Dictionary of Economics*, ed. Steven N. Durlauf and Lawrence E. Blume, 2nd ed. (London: Palgrave Macmillan, 2008), 2; for a textbook approach, see N. Gregory Mankiw, *Macroeconomics*, 5th ed. (New York: Worth Publishers, 2003), 157–158; for the proposal of a "conjectural history," see Kevin Dowd, "The Invisible Hand and the Evolution of the Monetary System," in *What Is Money?*, ed. John Smithin (London: Routledge, 2000), 139.

Medieval observers thought that making money was central to political community, a matter that "inheres in the bones of princes."[4] In the modern era, it was an abstraction created by exchange, simply the vocabulary of price. "Real money" was not a matter made by governments, but by the economy. And that was perhaps the point: liquidity was a matter better assumed or left aside. Whether it cost money to make money, who paid and who profited, how constructing money mattered to a society were not questions that anyone asked, despite the fact that reinventing money had reorganized the political economy.

The combination—a medium that was profoundly influential and whose influence was explicitly overlooked—gave the early modern turn even more impact. It diverted attention from the way that money, made and maintained differently, had operated in earlier and other worlds. It introduced a distinctive money, one unmatched in its abundance and penetrating in its reach. It submerged one of the most significant distributive issues of our times. And it constricted understanding of money and the way it operated by locating it as something dismissed by its own experts, who had effectively emptied it of living content.

The events of 2008 demonstrated the tremendous import of money as we have made it—and the radical limits to our knowledge about the way it works. The collapse in the U.S. housing market became a crisis when the short-term money markets froze. While some people understood the way banks multiplied the money supply, very few had mapped the activities of the "shadow banking" sector, or recognized that its operations had extended far further than the dollar-denominated units that acted as money. (Even after the financial crisis, some $20 trillion in short-term dollar-denominated IOUs, including money market funds, issued by those actors still circulates.) In response to the crisis, the U.S. Federal Reserve effectively shifted much of the wholesale money market onto its own balance sheet, more than doubling its size, first by loans to the financial sector and then by taking permanent holdings of mortgage-backed securities.[5] The Fed's emergency action was both familiar and unparalleled. As the author of the high-powered money at the base of bank-generated liquidity, the Fed could provide the liquidity needed during the crisis. At the same time, the steps it took to support those institutions holding toxic assets were economically untested, legally ambiguous, and confounding to the public at large.

It was neither the first nor the most traumatic of the dramas generated by the way money is made. But with an urgency born of global meltdown, the crisis

---

[4] *The Case of Mixed Money* (1605) in T. B. Howell, *Cobbett's Complete Collection of State Trials and Proceedings for High Treason and Other Crimes and Misdemeanors from the Earliest Period to the Year 1783*, vol. 2 (London: R. Bagshaw, 1809), 114, 118 (*Monetandi jus principum ossibus inhaeret*).

[5] Morgan Ricks, "A Regulatory Design for Monetary Stability," *Harvard John M. Olin Discussion Paper Series* (2011), 8; Perry Mehrling, *The New Lombard Street: How the Fed Became the Dealer of Last Resort* (Princeton, NJ: Princeton University Press, 2011), 2.

demonstrated that how money is made matters. It can—it did—turn the world upside down, shake millions out of work, redistribute wealth, and dominate politics. In the U.S. alone, more than 8 million people lost their jobs in the immediate aftermath of the crisis. Using a narrow definition, the unemployment rate spiked above 10 percent in October 2009; rebalanced to include those who wanted more work or were too discouraged to continue looking, it reached 17.5 percent. Real gross domestic product fell further than at any point since 1946. Households lost $17 trillion of net worth between 2007 and the first quarter of 2009, including $5.6 trillion because of declining home prices.[6] Just as striking, the Fed's monetary policy rather than congressionally designed fiscal stimulus or reform became the instrument most actively invoked to solve the economic recession.[7] Money's modern design in many ways caused the crisis; it then supplied the main strategy to act on that crisis.

The book aims to demonstrate that "making money" has long shaped the English world and that revising the design of money during the early modern period introduced radical change. The argument is historical at its core; at the same time, it makes conceptual claims about money's definition. The narrative runs from the early medieval period in England to the coming of capitalism there during the 17th century. The account ends after considering the way the British developed their new system in the following century and institutionalized their approach in the early architecture of the 19th century Gold Standard. As to the conceptual element, the effort to understand money leads inherently to theories about what it is and how it is operating. The approach taken here draws on standard as well as revisionist economic models, although it diverges from those models in many of its interpretations and conclusions.

"Capitalism" has as many definitions as commentators; I use it as a label that marks the moment when English society institutionalized the orientation towards self-interest as the animating force—the pump—that would produce the country's money. That occurred literally when the English invented a new repertoire of material value, a particular kind of currency. Money, long charged to its users, now issued as a resource underwritten by public funds and endorsed

---

[6] See Center for Budget and Policy Priorities, accessed June 26, 2014, <http://www.cbpp.org/cms/index.cfm?fa=view & id=3252> Simon Johnson and James Kwak, *13 Bankers: The Wall Street Takeover and the Next Financial Meltdown* (New York: Pantheon Books, 2010), 182; Financial Crisis Inquiry Commission, *The Financial Crisis Inquiry Report: Final Report of the National Commission on the Causes of the Financial and Economic Crisis in the United States* (Washington, D.C.: Government Printing Office, 2011), 390–392. Even after prices for both real estate and equities had recovered somewhat and stabilized, household net worth was 16.5 percent less than it had been three years earlier. Commission, *The Financial Crisis Inquiry Report*, 392.

[7] See, e.g., "America's Stalling Recovery Crisis," *Financial Times*, July 8, 2012; "Central Banks: Don't Give Up," *The Economist*, June 28, 2012; Editorial Desk, "Time for Bankers to Intervene," *The New York Times*, June 27, 2012; Christina D. Romer, "It's Time for the Fed to Lead the Fight," *The New York Times*, June 9, 2012.

for expansion by banks operating for profit. The redesign placed a new logic at
the molten center of "capital" itself.

The English experience anchors a more general claim about capitalism because
of the evidence that Britain exported its monetary system with astonishing effect.
In that case, the Eurocentrism of our financial and monetary structures should be
attributed and analyzed. The modern vocabulary of value—one commonly
deployed across the globe today—here gains parochial roots, a historicized
logic, a set of capacities that were unanticipated and escaped evaluation as they
developed. Those characteristics confuse efforts to understand the money that, in
a shape that owes much to its early modern reinvention in England, affects so
many populations in the contemporary world. The effort here is to map money as
an institutionalized practice, deeply connected to the markets it enables and fluid
enough to change dramatically. According to this narrative, a peculiarly English
contrivance eventually presents itself as the abstract medium of an autonomous
market.

The conventions and the counter-theory

The book begins with the conventions that so deeply root our intuitions about
money. A remarkable consensus joins thinkers on both the right and left. It
locates "the market" as a terrain of economic activity and identifies "money" as
mere instrumentality. The market is substance, money is form; the way money is
categorized supports our assumptions that it is a simple commodity, a social
convention, or an abstract "numeraire." A myth that money emerges naturally
from the trades of enterprising individuals or their agreement on a common
symbol of value supplies all the history that is necessary in the modern consensus.
The division of labor between the "market" and "money" in the myth diverts
attention from the institutions that really make and maintain money.

Attending to those practices generates a countervailing theory of money.
Money, whether we look at its origins in a community or its continuous renewal
there, appears as an activity designed to organize a material world. As suggested
by the historical record, money is contrived by a group to measure, collect, and
redistribute resources. The community may be a state, but it can also be a
collective organized along lines of loyalty, religion, or affinity to which people
make recurring contributions of labor or goods. The history in this book considers the way early Anglo-Saxon communities made money and traces their
shifting strategies forward to the sovereigns of the modern world. But "private"
organizations, cities, commercial collaborators, and other entities can undertake
to make money, and many have. As their work organizes their members, they
produce their own politics. Arguably, they build towards a new governing group

and may even be shut down as potential competitors to a higher-level "public."[8] Given how often communities have made money, how constantly they must work to keep up that medium, and how rich is the evidence they leave in their wake, the history of the practice of making money is full. It accords with accounts by participants both old and new, and comports with a number of economic models that map money's creation.

Money appears in groups that draw on the contributions of members to support themselves or their activities. It arises when a stakeholder, acting for the group, uses its singular position to specify and entail value in a way that no individual or bargaining pair of individuals can do. The stakeholder gives a marker to people who contribute resources earlier to the group than they are due and takes the marker back, like a receipt, from those people at a time of reckoning. In an illiquid world—a world bereft of a common measure—the marker used to assess the resources contributed will have extraordinary status: it creates a standard for goods and services that could not previously be compared in a unit shared by everyone. One more twist makes the measure into money. If the stakeholder takes back the units from anyone's hand, those units will convey material value that is useful to anyone who owes a contribution to the center. Unlike other resources in a community without a currency, the stakeholder's units gain the capacity to travel hand to hand as carriers of value recognized by all participants.

As a practice, money allows great capacity to the stakeholder and those assisting that authority. They can govern by taxing and spending: they select the goods or labor they need, marking them with a token, and collect contributions later, taking in the tokens from whoever owes resources. At the same time, individuals within the community can use the standard markers for private exchange. Money provides a novel service as it packages material value in a way that can be immediately recognized and transferred.

In fact, communities that create money for collective purposes can expand their supply of tokens as individuals demand them for their own purposes. The medieval English government sold people money for private use at the mint; its modern successor licenses commercial banks to issue checkable deposits in the sovereign unit of account when they make loans for private use. Both of those methods become essential ways of "making money." They supplement the money made by the fiscal actions of the stakeholder, and they have defining impact on the market that results.

Taken together, the practices that instill money's functions compose the constitutional design of that money. They include political determinations to

---

[8] Thus money is not adequately captured by a "state theory." See Georg Friedrick Knapp, *The State Theory of Money*, trans. H. M. Lucas (London: MacMillan, 1924). The Knappian term, chartalism, is broader and appropriately stresses the structural role of fiscal demand. The approach taken here nevertheless diverges in its emphasis on the singular capacity of the unit of account to allow assessment across items, that unit's foundational dependence on coordinated (as opposed to bilateral) engineering, and the plethora of legal infrastructural elements that enable alienation in money terms, define obligation, and ensure the easy transferability of a medium.

represent value in a particular way—in silver coin, for example, or in paper tax credits; decisions to charge people individually for money or to subsidize it through the general revenue; strategies that give one medium a monopoly or that multiply the credit forms that can circulate. As societies make many choices like these, they configure currencies differently. The moneys that result are highly engineered projects, not the happy by-product of spontaneous and decentralized decision. To be sure, the individuated actions of those using money—a diffuse and rowdy crowd—matter. Those forces become part of the debate over money's design; people's decisions about money create or diminish demand; their agency shapes the flow of money in and out of supply. Money is neither public nor private in a categorical sense; it gains effect through the action of each on the other.

A world of commodity money

By the 11th century, the constitutional career of coin was well underway. Governments in England, as on the Continent, needed a medium that would allow them to move resources; the challenges they faced to collect and distribute value outmatched in many ways the difficulties that individuals faced on that score. As the earliest surviving account of the Exchequer put it at the end of the 12th century, "Money is necessary, not only in time of war, but also in time of peace. For in the former case, revenue is expended on the fortification of towns, the payment of wages to the soldiers, and in many other ways." And when the end to hostilities arrived, "weapons of war are laid aside, churches are built by devout princes, Christ is fed and clothed in the persons of the poor, and the Mammon of this world is distributed in other acts of charity."[9] Currency acted, then, for public ends most and least worldly, each of utmost importance.

Along the way, money also made daily life. The English population began to use pennies in part because they owed their rulers in that coin. But once it worked for that purpose, money also offered a measure and mode of payment that people could circulate between themselves. The "free minting" approach adopted in England traded on the demand by individuals for currency. A common European practice, it charged users for money creation: the mint took silver bullion from individuals and returned them a slightly lesser amount of metal in coined form— units of specified content and carefully decreed count. Those "just pennies" were often worth the sacrifice of raw metal. They alone were accepted and used by authorities, who enforced their flow through the hands of individuals. The English common law action for debt played a unique role in that effort. It defined suits for money differently from other claims, including those for silver, a quirk

---

[9] Richard fitz Nigel, "Dialogus de Scaccario," in *English Historical Documents, 1042–1189*, ed. David C. Douglas and George W. Greenaway (London: Eyre & Spottiswoode, 1953 [circa 1179]), 492.

that protected money's passage by unit count as opposed to weight. In ordinary times, that was unsurprising. But at moments of monetary upheaval, the idiosyncrasy of English law mattered. While Continental jurists developed arguments assimilating coin to metal, English common law debt would preserve monetary "nominalism." Bound within writs later dismissed as archaic was an approach that would come to be adopted across the modern world.

In medieval Europe, moments of monetary upheaval were in fact common. Despite its reputation as a solid anchor for value, commodity money itself caused that instability. The fragility stemmed from coin's nature as a compound of value, one that joined metal content and special status as a liquid form of wealth. Medieval money circulated when content and form netted out to a value, in coin after coin, that people were happy to give and take. But that was a deceptively simple proposition. Coins in use wore down and got clipped, losing silver or gold content. The markets for those metals shifted, changing the value of silver pennies against gold denominations. Sovereigns competed for bullion supplies by raising the prices they offered at their mints. As the commodity value of coins that offered the same count began to differ (old and new pennies, whole and clipped coins, silver and gold cognates), the people holding them began discriminating among them, hoarding or melting some and passing others off by face value. Their actions subverted coin's circulation.

Rescuing money became as essential to a monetary system as establishing it in the first place. Both in England and on the Continent, public authorities managed their coined currencies by constantly recalibrating them. Commonly they depreciated pennies to bring their metal content back into line with their face value. Those initiatives took legal as well as practical shape: they became assertions of political right that configured and redistributed property. Here again, the English set a distinctive course. They took less silver from the penny than other countries, even as they vehemently asserted the sanctity of its count rather than its content. Common law debt reappears as a vehicle of monetary policy, policing the recoveries that creditors could claim at law and sending them to Parliament for relief.

Commodity money, made and remade, became a defining political project, one that absorbed European communities. Their determinations about how to "make money" ordered people and their possessions. Societies soon diverged from each other. The English would keep their money anomalously powerful—across several centuries, the smallest coins bought a half-day labor's worth of goods or more. At the same time, the English maintained the tradition that individuals pay for money at the mint. The combination put an enormous amount of pressure on the penny. That unit and a skeletal array of its fractions were the moneys denominated to capture a huge amount of economic exchange. Yet the coins themselves were scant, as people minimized the amounts they paid for money. Pennies moved quickly hand to hand (or had a high monetary "velocity"), as users forced more exchanges out of the existing currency.

The power of the penny figured in both public and private life. Elites contended over taxes instead of arguing about the when and whether of debasements. That pattern configured high politics, shaped the claims of right made by the wealthy and, perhaps, their habits of mind. Sound money seemed to represent the very character of England, even as sovereigns there asserted the authority to determine absolutely—and at times to alter—the value of each coin. Meanwhile, the strength of the penny stratified the market, inducing exchange at the top that was impossible at the bottom. "The pouere [poor] common retaillours of vitailles, and of o[th]er nedefull thyngs, for defaute of such coigne" often could not make sales, wrote the Commons in 1445, nor could "many of oure seid soveraine lordes pouere liege people . . . bie theyme."[10]

England's approach to making money reached beyond its most immediate carrier, coin: it engendered surprising forms of credit. Medieval authorities would institutionalize a circulating public debt that was among Europe's earliest and most extensive in the picturesque but enormously effective and occasionally coercive form of "tallies," little wooden sticks that marked claims to tax revenue. Tallies could be given to the Crown's creditors, passed between people, and taken back by the government as a kind of currency. Their history has been largely lost. But at a critical moment in the 17th century, England's tally tradition informed its invention of public bonds and, in turn, bank notes.

At the same time, those at the low end of exchange struggled to ameliorate the harsh illiquidity of their awkward currency with an elaborate practice of private consumption credit. That practice bound neighbors together in thick networks of reciprocal relation. But while the interchange enabled economic activity, attempts to understand it as either communal or efficient miss the mark. Money's absence prevented people from deals that were immediately effective, an option the wealthier enjoyed. And litigation over the debt disputes that followed was often oppressive, dividing and dragging down the populations it frequented.

Polities made money very differently on the Continent, where silver coin was commonly diluted until it easily lubricated small transactions, while gold denominations were marked for international trade and maintained constant in metal content. While English money drove many inhabitants to consumption credit, the two-tiered coinage of the Italian city-states more likely invited its users to borrow for investment. In England and in Florence, money conveyed value in the deals, purchases, and payments of daily life, but exactly how it did so—how it related the people holding it to each other, how it connected them to the political

---

[10] W. M. Ormrod (ed.), "Henry VI: Parliament of February 1445, Text and Translation," in *The Parliament Rolls of Medieval England*, ed. C. Given-Wilson et al., item 11. Internet version at <http://www.sd-editions.com/PROME>, accessed June 26, 2014 (Leicester: Scholarly Digital Editions, 2005).

center, how it affected their activities and attitudes to the outside world—depended on a blend of decisions that were political, material, social, and legal. Making money was integral, in other words, to the disparate political economies that Europeans created. Those decisions in turn inflected the area's geopolitics, eventually including the colonizing initiatives that configured European approaches to the south, east, and west.

Money reinvented

The way modern money replaced commodity money has long been a mystery. Most accounts assume that the customs of private banks somehow accreted to create paper money. From the checks issued by goldsmith-bankers to clear accounts, we inherit the bank note as a national money, written on a gold reserve. Even more alchemical is the evaporating importance of metal. Strangely enough, people holding notes were content to let the gold go, trusting to convention that they would be able to pass their paper on to others for value.[11]

In fact, the history does not match the myth. A very different story emerges when we track the processes that remade money in the 1690s—and that make money today. Modern money is pervasively and precisely grounded. It is activated by legal rules, driven by institutions, implemented by practices that change the way people relate, what they owe and to whom they owe it, where they find value and why, all animated by a different theory of human agency. As it emerged at the end of the 17th century, money would be organized on a new principle. Rather than a resource defined by a public's claim on its members, currency was supplied by the government as it recognized and rewarded individual orientation towards profit. That change shook people into a profoundly different relationship, both to the government and to one another.

The narrative here focuses on the basic elements of the drama. The account needs to be peopled and shaded, put into political color, adjusted and improved. But if we select for the exercises that "make money," a structural shift becomes visible, a striking transformation that revolutionized English money and the way it worked. The basics suggest a modern turn that displaced and obscured earlier practices in favor of an approach remarkable on several scores.

First, the change occurred at the center. Government not only made money, it effectively monopolized that power. Money was created "by the authority and commandment of the prince," affirmed the Privy Council sitting as a court at the beginning of the 17th century; the sovereign determined the currencies, both money and credit, that circulated. At the end of the century, the Secretary of the Treasury agreed. Making money is a "right of regality," he wrote. Echoing the

---

[11] For a classic example, see Richard David Richards, *The Early History of Banking in England* (London: P.S. King & Son, 1929), 40–43. For consideration of the convention more generally, see pp. 24–37.

medieval Exchequer manual, he advocated a recoinage to meet the ends of "war," "commerce," and to satisfy "publick, but also ... all private revenues, rents, debts, and other occasions, which concern *the very existence of the great political body*."[12] Cash remained as elemental to conducting war and peace in the early modern world as in the medieval.

What the government made, however, it could remake. The monetary revolution occurred when the government and individuals renegotiated the way they would interact to produce money. Here, much of the action was improvised and erratic. The Stuart monarchs picked up the cost of coin and undermined old traditions like tallies out of desperation, not grand design. They often experimented without anticipating the end results. They began issuing public bonds, for example, without any clear intent to realign the relationship of the monarch with its subjects.

But certain innovations had staying power and structural import—like the role of public debt that circulated and bore interest. Bonds concretely represented the government's promise of future revenues. That promise of future revenues had always been the anchor of money: when a stakeholder pledged to collect contributions in a particular unit, it created demand for that unit. The stakeholder's commitment to take incoming revenues, be it tribute or taxes, in a certain form from many debtors thus effectively defined a society's unit of account. But the innovation of circulating public bonds marked a new era. Bonds signified a fiscal promise to take contributions; that promise would now be mediated by a host of creditors with claims against the public. The change split the public into taxpayers and bondholders, directing benefits previously absorbed by the government from one group of citizens to another. As importantly, the change gave the government a mechanism to secure paper money: notes taken by the authorities to pay down the debt would hold value as cash.

Second, the monetary revolution helped drive the modern era's radical recasting of human agency and its relationship to the public good. If the English entered the Reformation through the side door of Tudor expediency, their decision nevertheless created serious questions about the place of individuals in the larger order. The Civil War that engulfed England in the middle of the 17th century channeled the uncertainty into a contest over "interests": participants debated how public ends and private priorities should be reconciled. Curiously, the Restoration offered the stage on which liberal visions could take concrete shape. It was the Stuart monarchy, re-established, that introduced the English to circulating bonds that paid interest to the government's creditors. When the monarchy did so, it endorsed the theory that individuals could help the public by

---

[12] *The Case of Mixed Money* (1605), 117; William Lowndes, *A Report Containing an Essay for the Amendment of Silver Coins* (London: Charles Bill & the Executrix of Thomas Newcomb, 1695), 109–110 (emphasis in original).

pursuing their own interests. More accurately, it institutionalized that theory. The new approach created a reality in which the quest for profit could bring advantages to the greater group. Investors became patriots, and commercial judgment gained stature. On second look, when the Treasury Secretary invoked public power over money at the end of the century, he paid unprecedented attention to "private revenues, rents, debts, and other occasions." Arguably, liberalism as a construct would draw from that category for its own paradigm of political society.

The ascendance of liberal theory raised enduring questions about the relationship between individual welfare and the larger public good; those questions were acted out in debates over the design of money as the currency of material value. Perhaps most unsettling was how the priority that the new institution of public debt accorded to the interests of investors should be reconciled with authority that the government claimed to manage money.

On the one hand, English law still enshrined nominalism. The doctrine had always protected the sovereign's ability to pronounce the material value of the unit of account. Indeed, it remains good law today. Then (and now), it confirmed money's identity as a sovereign liability: coin was maintained because of the government's ability to establish its value at a level that kept it circulating robustly through society. It followed that, when authorities needed to change the value of money for larger public ends, they could do so despite the fact that their action might injure a narrower set of people who lost because of the change. On the other hand, the government had made long-running contracts that circulated among creditors expecting money with set value. According to the government itself, the industry of public credit depended on protecting their interests for the mutual benefit of all. The highest judicial tribunal soon agreed. In a late 17th century constitutional landmark that came to be known as *The Case of the Bankers*, the House of Lords denied the government's discretion to delay payment to its bondholders.[13]

But that decision only sharpened the constitutional puzzle. The new judgment confirmed that the government was obliged to pay the money promised by its public bonds, although Parliament alone retained the latitude to implement that obligation. At the same time, the older doctrine of nominalism reiterated public authority to adjust the value of money when circumstances so required. The collision between the public's obligation to bondholders and its responsibility to revalue money went to the very core of the developing system: what did an ironclad promise to pay money to an individual mean, when money could be redefined by the government paying it? Conversely, when must a government

[13] *The Case of the Bankers* (1690–1700) in T. B. Howell, *Cobbett's Complete Collection of State Trials and Proceedings for High Treason and Other Crimes and Misdemeanors from the Earliest Period to the Year 1783*, vol. 14 (London: R. Bagshaw, 1812), 1.

redefine money for the common good, despite the ironclad promise in money that it owed to individuals? The quandary would grow more pressing over the next century, as the government expanded the role that investors, pursuing their own interests in profits, played in the system of modern money creation.

That development takes the drama over the invention of modern money, third, to its climax—the transformation that occurred when the English government determined to share its authority over money creation with a bank. Later generations, awash in a world with many forms of liquidity, could remark the "financial revolution" of 18th century Britain without asking about its cash ingredients. But those ingredients were a radical innovation. Longer-term credit, private notes, book accounts, or bills of exchange might hasten the ability of money to circulate, but only money furnished a unit of account that could be spent at face value in all transactions by the government and individuals, and taken in payment the same way. By the 1690s, economic observers understood that as quantities of money dropped, so did prices, all other things equal. But they had no desire to live in a world where prices fell relentlessly, stirring protests as people resisted taxes of rising real value, private debtors lost money, and falling prices pushed exchanges below the monetary floor. More immediately, war increased political ambitions to expand the money supply in the short term.

The Bank of England emerged out of a frenzy of experiments about how the government could borrow immediately by creating cash out of the promise of taxes to come. The story about the way the Bank's notes came to prevail as the England's dominant currency would unfold slowly—but within a decade the attributes that established them as money had taken root. Most extraordinary was the fact that the government now paid instead of charging for the quality of cash. Erecting an architecture that privileged one bank's notes, it ordained them "money" and compensated the investors who issued them. At the same time, the government installed a new theory at the heart of the political economy—the theory that individuals pursuing profits produced money.

The Bank was a consortium of individuals who loaned the Crown money in the form of paper promises-to-pay specie. Sometime after the government began spending Bank of England notes (originally, Bank bills) interchangeably with specie, it started taking them in satisfaction for taxes. The activity effectively equated the paper issues of the Bank with the coin it promised to give if required to redeem them. In conditions of political stability, there was little need for anyone holding a Bank note to cash it in. That included the government—as long as it owed the Bank, it had reason to take Bank notes, some portion of which it could set off against its outstanding debt. It was an advantage no other bank could offer and purely "private" notes could not effectively compete.

In fact, the government could use Bank notes again and again, as long as it taxed enough to maintain the widespread belief that it would soak them all in.

Exchequer bills, one of the alternatives to Bank notes with which the English also experimented, worked exactly the same way. A certain category of paper promises had become money. It offered a unit of account interchangeable with coin. It worked to pay the government or individuals. And insofar as people used it among themselves in the meantime, it moved hand to hand as a medium.

Indeed, the English decision—to create money to borrow now out of the promise of taxes in the future—restated a far older logic about how the incoming revenues of the kingdom could be given current value as money. It turns out that money had been reinvented in much the same circumstances as it was first invented. Confronting the need to collect and distribute resources from those within its authority, the government selected and spent a particular unit of account; it took that unit back in payment for public obligations; and it allowed the measure to act as a medium between individuals in the meantime. That process had given earlier moneys their particular value as the units, whether in coin or tally, that the government would spend first and take back in the future. Now it similarly marked and managed Bank promises-to-pay and Exchequer bills.

That constancy—the foundation of money in the viability of a political community—may be the common aspect that brought contemporaries to recognize a currency. Likewise, it may be the structural attribute that invites later observers to attach the word "money." Incoming revenues are, after all, the material figuring of a political community's basic soundness. The value common to each cash, from coin to Bank notes, lay in a public promise, but rather than a promise of physical treasure, it was the promise to spend and tax in the unit, maintain it as the measure, and enforce it as the medium that marked it as money. That commitment, whether written in a medium with commodity content or on paper, maintained the continuity of money over a millennium of English history.

The continuity of money's character as a public promise is critical precisely because otherwise, the monetary constitution of England had been completely redrafted. Bank-based currency would introduce the political economy of modern capitalism.

A new mechanism now pumped money into circulation. The government minted all of the silver and gold that came to it at public cost. More important, it added Bank notes to the cash stream. When it did so, it endorsed a novel device for delivering units of account—sovereign liabilities still—into circulation. The government borrowed notes, spent them, and collected them to pay off its obligation with interest to the Bank investors. Those notes met the government's fiscal needs, but individuals desired currency as well. The government soon licensed the Bank to lend in the form of notes to individuals. Under the medieval system, people had put up bullion to buy money at the mint. Under the modern system, they put up collateral to the Bank, and borrowed its paper. A flow of notes based on a promise of productivity would replace the flow of coins formed from silver. The new approach to money creation, innovated by public authority and informed by the liberal invocation of individual interests as privileged motivators, would realign the way people understood money, the political and private work that maintained it, and "the market" that resulted.

That claim takes us to the fourth and last aspect of the monetary revolution considered here: its astonishing aftermath. Money's reinvention catalyzed a debate over what money really was that lasted more than a century. Written in the urgencies of the moment, over decades of experimentation with coin and paper, was a fundamental division. For some, the opportunity to think about money as public credit, a promise of value made at the center of a political community, led to proposals that located value—the matter promised—in the internal operations of the nation. According to those theorists, money could be made of out incoming revenues as well as other materials; a sovereign group had potency, the possibility of making money by its own arrangements to establish credit. "Credit theorists" began to articulate money as a constitutional project. Adam Smith, like others, expressed the stakeholder theory of money explicitly.

For others, the answer lay precisely in externalizing value, taking it out of governance altogether. According to this view, money could, indeed should, be understood independent of a political community. As if on cue, John Locke enters the frame at this point. When he defined money as a matter emerging from private exchange beyond (and before) the borders of the state, he was writing liberalism's script. In his hands, money became a finite amount of metal—but it was not a commodity money of the old type. Locke had in mind the silver used by traders across the oceans of the world, an evocative image that would have been unrecognizable to the early English courts. For them, money was a matter irreducibly sovereign, a measure made within the bounds of the state. For Locke, it was an artifact of individuated action explicitly outside of political territory, a medium emanating from decentralized deals. As such, it was a utility naturally occurring—the identity it gained in classical economic theory.

Over the long 18th century, the English brokered a compromise between the two positions, a paradoxical approach that gave capitalism great capacity as well as profound shortcomings. On the one hand, the English adopted Locke's position enthusiastically. The Great Recoinage of 1696 and the architecture of the Gold Standard followed from the position that money was, or should be treated as, a commodity beyond the control of the state—ideally, it was a fixed amount of metal. That position reordered the priorities of governance, sanctifying the claims of creditors and bolstering the legitimacy of credit instruments as the promise of coin with a static content.

The same position effectively destroyed commodity money as a working system. "Commodity money" of the traditional sort had never run according to the Lockean logic and could not be maintained on that theory. As the long history of coin demonstrates, societies using commodity money recalibrated the content of coin regularly to maintain it in circulation. Left without that kind of management, the ladder of silver denominations in place in England since the medieval period fell apart during the 18th century. The gold unit of account became pivotal. More striking still, a set of new moneys began to fill in the rungs of the denominational ladder left vacant. Token moneys, Bank notes, the currencies from country banks, and other credit advanced in the new unit of account—all began operating as supplements to the gold unit of account, now increasingly held on reserve. Shortages of small change would eventually fade as a result, and the denominational barriers that had sorted people relentlessly by the size of the exchange they could make gave way. Unintentionally, but earliest among the Europeans, the English broke away from the strictures of commodity money, even as they claimed to base their system more adamantly on it. The argument that money was or should be a matter outside of political control thus exercised significant influence, some anticipated and some quite unexpected, on the English monetary system.

On the other hand, Parliament constantly exercised its political authority to make money. It may have theorized money as a commodity, but it practiced money according to the prescriptions of those who understood money as a particular kind of credit. The government's decision to tax and spend at a certain rate in the guinea was the event that replaced the silver unit of account with a gold pivot. In turn, public fiscal activity assimilated Bank of England notes to equivalent stature with that gold unit of account. The government's taxing power rose dramatically over the century, creating demand for the money it recognized. During the Napoleonic Wars, Bank notes would function as English money despite being inconvertible into gold coin; that period confirmed their effectiveness as the unit of account independent of gold coin.

During the 18th century, the English constructed the tiered structure of their monetary architecture. Their design related a proliferation of currencies and credit that flowed from country banks, brokers and, eventually, joint-stock banks, to a center that established the potency of those media as money. Most obviously, each of the institutions ranging out from the center issued notes or promised money designated in the public unit of account. Commercial banks reached beyond merchant finance; they created money that laborers, shopkeepers, producers, and others took as payment and passed on in exchange.

English law supplied the engineering that supported the new currencies. Common law debt makes a remarkable reentry here to legitimate fractional reserve lending. Later observers, thoroughly immersed in the institutions of the modern world, often overlook the contrived nature of that operation. But fractional reserve banking allows banks to promise access to the same sovereign units of account to both borrowers and depositors at once. Given the government's interest in policing its own liabilities, who multiplies them, and how they do so, the activity requires sovereign permission. Contemporaries to the early practice denounced it as fraud or even counterfeiting. In the legal debate, common law debt supported the argument that deposits were the bankers' own money, to risk as they wished. As it was interpreted in the early courts, the doctrine thus sanctioned money creation by commercial banks. They lent at a retail level, to individuals as well as businesses, setting England apart from the Continent.

Finally, each banking institution cleared its accounts at the Bank of England: everyone required funds recognized by all as credible in order to settle any cash balances—and only the Bank could ensure that kind of money. The system that Parliament orchestrated thus reached through the unit of account, the courts, and the Bank of England to the plethora of "private" banks and brokers.

The new design was prolific. In effect, the government used its fiscal system to direct money demand to a paper unit of account and then licensed multiple purveyors of cash, allowing them to extend the money supply for private use. The mints once sold money to people in exchange for bullion. Banks and brokers now advanced currency on a promise of future productivity and, if they were careful, good security. They became the experts who determined how money entered circulation and how heavily it flowed. Like the Bank, they issued money according to the profits they anticipated, given the returns they expected from borrowers. Cash based on a promise of productivity was far more accessible than cash based on an advance of bullion. The system thus paired money transparently defined by the government's fiscal authority with the private dispensation of cash.

The cash abundance of the modern world contrasts dramatically with the monetary scarcity of the early world; the system as a whole expanded currency manifold. For centuries, Europeans had improvised modes of transferring credit between trading partners, including banks of transfer and bills of exchange. But when they developed banks of issue, paired with fractional reserve banking and centralized clearing, the English were adding currencies that could travel hand to hand indiscriminately—cash. As Walter Bagehot would note in the late 19th century, "we have entirely lost the idea that any undertaking likely to pay, and seen to be likely, can perish for want of money; yet no idea was more familiar to our ancestors."[14] The very fecundity of the new way of making money must have fed the explosive economic growth that characterizes modernity.

The system that produced such abundant liquidity came with a dark side—the deep fault lines that have rendered modern finance so fragile. The design was disciplined at the center by the need to settle balances in the public unit of account—Bank of England notes or gold coin. But those reserves were tiny

---

[14] Walter Bagehot, *Lombard Street: A Description of the Money Market* (New York: John Wiley, 1873, 1999), 118.

compared to the flow of funds soon carried by the system. They could not provide the cash demanded if everyone holding claims to money wanted to convert them to gold coin or Bank notes all at once. Private bank notes, bills, and demand deposits that held value according to private promises of future productivity, even those that came with collateral, could flourish or fail as currencies depending simply on how immediate and concerted the demand for money was. That contingency in their capacity to provide liquidity rendered them unlike commodity coin with its prepayment of value, acquired and carried in the form of bullion. The booms and busts of modern times began in the late 18th century.[15]

The history here ends with the crisis that forced the English to confront the structure of their system. In 1797, a wartime run on the banks led the government to suspend convertibility: those holding currency from banks could no longer demand that those institutions redeem it for gold coin. That development invited the English to reconsider the trope that money was a commodity produced by private exchange, since it was so obviously a fiction at the time. But rather than embracing the alternative—a money that was public in fact—the architects of the early Gold Standard determined that money should be treated as private in theory and in policy.

Those who engineered the early national version of the Gold Standard were under no illusions. They understood better than many of their heirs that money was, in fact, a mode of mobilizing collective value. They admitted that public authority orchestrated their system, would be required to manage it, and would regularly need to rescue it. For them, however, that reality was a threat rather than an occasion for maintaining the domestic economy. That rich font of activity was, after all, a terrain of cross-cutting claims to public concern that ran all the way from defense to poor relief, with all the dangers of debates about redistribution that attended.

According to these advocates, money should be "made" according to the touchstone of coin's content, gold, as that value was established in international trade. The design posited that the money flow of a society should be organically connected to the value of a commodity set externally to the activity of that society. The effort was to control money production within the polity, a matter still determined by public fiscal practice along with the domestic demand by individuals for cash services, by subjecting that production to a veto that individuals considering their advantage in foreign exchange would exercise. For proponents, a set of prescriptions followed. Regularly, deflation and austerity appropriately corrected money's expansion along with the bad investment and

---

[15] The structure of bank-based credit that extended public money made the Bank's capacity to act as lender of last resort comprehensible as well as necessary. While commercial banks advanced money on the promise of private productivity, the Bank advanced money on the anticipation of future revenues—the expected productivity of the country as a whole. It therefore retained its ability to act by enlisting taxpayers' contributions even when private banks were stymied.

overconsumption it had produced. Responsible banks periodically required rescue, given their structural role as money creators. Public debt imposed obligations on a state like those private debt imposed on individuals; those obligations should not be conditioned on the health of the community, despite the fact that the economy had its source in that domestic space.

Viewed over the long term, the orthodoxy of the early Gold Standard brought the English approach to money to earth far from where it began. Money in the medieval world was an emphatically internal medium. Its making consumed officials who understood the pull of demand for money's commodity content from the outside as a scourge and who struggled to provide money for domestic necessities. By contrast, money for its 19th century engineers was a matter that should be modulated by an external reference point. They sought to discipline their money supply by defining "the market" as the activity that took place outside of states and the political authority they represented.

Ultimately, the insistence institutionalized in the early 19th century that money be understood as private was the strange and selective answer to the constitutional quandary posed when the government determined to make a collective medium—money—according to a method that prioritized individual interests. According to the architects of the Gold Standard, public authority to make money was legitimate only insofar as it furthered the ends of that medium, now understood as commercial. That approach prioritized the agency of entrepreneurs and the business community. If the public purposes of money seemed to disappear, they could be brought back into view by understanding the polity as, itself, a stage for the aggregate of private activity that made the economy. An argument developed as an escape from politics thus returned to colonize the politics at its core.

Within that paradigm, economics came of age as a discipline. In its world, money appeared to be made by the economic exchange of individuals, acting each for their own interest. Their choices claimed sanctity and their activity, rather than the requirements of the political community, indicated the appropriate amount of money in society. "The market" that set the standard was, after all, the market outside the boundaries of political community—the international trade in bullion. Money was infinitely divisible in any case—it could be modeled as an abstraction. That treatment rendered irrelevant the constitutional design that constructed money.

The modern approach to money thus made it unnecessary to attend to the way it was made and maintained in law, politics, and the categories of knowledge that knit society together. The old paradigm of money—a medium charged to individuals by the government but claimed as a public resource—had disappeared. A new amalgam—money publicly financed at a profit to individuals but analyzed as an opaque phenomenon—came to animate the modern political economy.

The combination wrote a peculiar theory of value into place, while universalizing it as the way money operated, without more. In that circumstance, money and the market it helped create would appear the inevitable product of human interest, social convention, and exchange. The new order thus gained a remarkable power to perpetuate itself.

* * *

The drama posed here centers in England—but money enmeshed England from the start in a more complex geography, one that tied Anglo-Saxons to Danes, island inhabitants to populations on the Continent, and Europeans to Africans, those in the Levant, and peoples further east. Indeed, while this history is narrow in its territorial reach, the story is one that extends much further. A desire for the raw materials of money, silver and gold, drove Western Europeans into the extractive ventures of the 16th century. That compulsion reconfigured space and authority across the Atlantic world.

The struggle to make money, in the literal sense, in turn shaped settlement throughout the early modern era. One notable case concerned British North America, where the English by their imperial policy on money induced the colonists to experiment with new ways of making a medium, the early paper currencies of the provinces. Those innovative moneys—and the orientation towards self-governance and local control that they engendered—would help divide the new world from the old.

It was only after the Revolution that Americans became adherents to the English experiment in modern money, but they were soon among the most conspicuous disciples of the new order. To its advocates, the United States needed a government that defined the sovereign money, deployed it through a powerful bank of issue, and preserved the public debt; only that kind of government could unify disparate states and compete internationally. That early instance of contagion suggests the global dynamics that followed.

As its history reveals, medieval money had been a decidedly domestic affair. The traders who moved between worlds used silver or gold, *not* money but a metal that had high value precisely because it could be made *into* money somewhere else. Merchants did not introduce money as the conventional story implies. Rather, they shuttled between economic centers, the translators in a largely disjointed system.

By contrast, modern economic capital flows across borders in monetary form, a matter of contracts that tie together banks, investors, and governments. That commitment integrates the globe into a far more homogeneous monetary territory than has ever existed. In that territory, domestic politics encounters imperatives that are unprecedented. The character of capitalism—its capacities both beneficial and destructive, its modes of migration, the extent to which it penetrates—needs to be analyzed as a network that both defines and diffuses liquidity. Those flows of capital now dominate the economic climate, dispensing abundance and drought.

When the visibility of money as a political project faded, the way it had realigned the societies that authored it also disappeared from view. With that disappearance went compelling questions about the consequences of the transformation—including the role of fiscal action in supporting the value of money, the distributive stakes in the modern arrangement, and the alignment of rights and interests acted out in the ethics of capitalism. That absence, a void of history and theory, undermines the effort so urgent to our present moment to understand the political economy we inhabit.

1

Creation stories

Money has long starred in accounts of modernity and the way it arrived. Many of those accounts converge to a surprising extent. The reigning sources in history, law, and economics, written by those on the left and the right, by social theorists and neoclassical modelers, establish a basic narrative about money and the market it lubricates. According to one of its greatest philosophers, Georg Simmel, money expresses in its complete neutrality "the economic relations between objects...in abstract quantitative terms, without itself entering into those relations." Karl Marx could have deployed the same formulation to capture the way money as a commodity, in fact the "universal equivalent" of all commodities, represents *as* commodities all objects in exchange, veiling the social relations that inhere in their production. Remarkably, the orthodoxy of modern macroeconomics echoes the philosopher and the archcritic of capitalism. "[A]lmost all economists agree," according to one standard textbook, that "the money supply affects nominal variables—variables measured in terms of money—but not real variables" in the long run. The "classical dichotomy" divides the world into real and monetary spheres; money is a signifier, a numeraire, an emphatically empty register of value.[1]

History, however, unsettles the modern imagination about money. According to its practice, money is not a neutral instrument that expresses "the economic relations between objects...in abstract quantitative terms, without itself entering into those relations." Rather, money is a method of representing and moving resources within a collective. When they take the steps that make money, communities intervene intimately into "the economic relations between objects" and the people who hold them. That process lasts as long as money does; it includes the legal dynamics, the conceptual categories, the practical imperatives, the compliance and contestation that create the medium. In short, money makes the market and fully enters into it.

The case for a new approach to money and the market begins with an assessment of the conventions we now take to define that partnership. "Money" and "market," formal and real, play familiar and remarkably constant roles in the dominant narrative about how market-based modernity arrived. According to that story, money arises immediately out of bipolar exchange;

---

[1] See Georg Simmel, *The Philosophy of Money*, 3rd enl. ed. (London: 2004), 125, 133; Karl Marx, *Capital: A Critique of Political Economy*, Pelican Marx Library (Harmondsworth: Penguin, 1976), 162; N. Gregory Mankiw, *Macroeconomics*, 4th ed. (New York: Worth Publishers, 2000), 238.

individuals converge upon that medium to express the material value of objects. Agreement on a "convergence story" is blunt and it falls apart immediately beyond the basic outline—but it is all the more powerful for the points of consensus that it appears to isolate.

Against that consensus, an alternative creation story follows. It draws on the history of money as it appeared in early England and as it unfolds in this book. The new story also attends to economic theories that model the challenge of constructing real value in the form of a measure that many people will recognize. Those sources suggest that money is a particular kind of governance project, one designed for a material world. The process is at once technical and rich in political variation, conceptual diversity, and distributional difference.

"Money" is invented when a community, acting through a stakeholder, denominates in a homogeneous way the disparate contributions received from members, and recognizes them as a medium and mode of payment. To produce money's basic structure, participants advance the time value of resources owed to the center in return for that actor's singular ability to represent those resources in units that are countable and transferable. The units entail the fiscal value of the taxed resources, as it is enhanced by the cash quality they gain as countable, transferable markers. On the basis of money's fiscal infrastructure and in response to people's demand for cash services, societies can expand their money supplies beyond those made for public uses; they can sell money to individuals or license others to sell money to those people. Making money is therefore a material project: it proceeds by intervening into the way people relate to resources and it distributes profits and costs as it does.

Like other modes of governance, money serves both public and private purposes. It can be designed in ways that are democratic or dictatorial, stable or fragile. It selects for certain exchange, entering societies in ways that allocate opportunity. It picks out certain objects as commodities and disallows that identity to others. The practices that make money—the initiatives that create a standard unit from disparate resources, that enforce it as a mode of payment, and that support it as it travels—construct exchange in that medium. "The market" is thus integrally connected to "money."

A. The conventional creation story

The standard narrative paints the coming of capitalism as a process, often long and gradual, that effectively merges with economic modernization. A stain or a tide depending on whether the writer begrudges or approves it, capitalism begins with private property and priced exchange; it arrives when those practices penetrate territory that was formerly outside of "the market."

The basic story articulated by Adam Smith, or attributed to him in some version, springs to mind. It centers on individuals inherently oriented towards truck and barter and the choices they make to improve their circumstances. Those agents are liberated to specialize their labor when society recognizes rights of ownership in work and its results. Then, people can produce for exchange, procure through exchange, and generate increasing profits through exchange. The market—in Smith's day, a physical place that could be imagined free from the cloying restrictions of a mercantilist state—becomes the paradigmatic promise of unfettered interaction in a liberal nation.[2]

Profoundly critical of that emancipatory story, Marx cast capitalism as its desperate underside. Capitalism was located in the immiseration of working man and the estrangement of his labor in its objectified product, in a process emptied of all gratification but the end result, and in the alienation of man and nature. Private property here drove apart man from the creations of his hand and separated workers from owners. Priced exchange operated as the technology that obscured the relations of power that underlay the production of commodities. But tying himself expressly to the classical political economists he savaged, Marx too crafted a narrative that wrote capitalism as a gathering force, or perhaps fate, that was cannibalizing social relations written on other logics.[3]

Between and around these poles, accounts scatter in a hundred directions. Across that profusion, however, several tropes emerge. Pre-capitalist markets are read as bounded areas, fenced off both in ritual and in physical space. Merchants operate as outsiders. They represent a commercial logic at odds with the social bonds that tie communities together. But limited as they are, market actors and practice do not erode customary norms. Rather, they contribute one element to the rich compound of human relation.[4]

That changes over time. Economic production increases where growing populations create regimes of private ownership and move away from subsistence

[2] See Adam Smith, *The Essential Adam Smith* (Oxford: Oxford University Press, 1986), 109–121, 167–190; cf. Emma Rothschild, *Economic Sentiments: Adam Smith, Condorcet, and the Enlightenment* (Cambridge, MA: Harvard University Press, 2001), 8–11, 27–28. For versions of the Smithian story, see, e.g., R. A. Radford, "The Economic Organisation of a P.O.W. Camp," *Economica* 12, no. 48 (1945); Douglass Cecil North, *Structure and Change in Economic History*, 1st ed. (New York: Norton, 1981).

[3] Karl Marx, *Economic and Philosophic Manuscripts of 1844* (New York: International Publishers, 1964); Marx, *Capital*.

[4] For examples of historical and sociological approaches, see Jean-Christophe Agnew, *Worlds Apart: The Market and the Theater in Anglo-American Thought, 1550-1750* (Cambridge: Cambridge University Press, 1986), 1–56; Arjun Appadurai, *The Social Life of Things: Commodities in Cultural Perspective* (Cambridge: Cambridge University Press, 1986), 3–63; Fernand Braudel, *Afterthoughts on Material Civilization and Capitalism*, Johns Hopkins Symposia in Comparative History (Baltimore: Johns Hopkins University Press, 1979); Joyce Oldham Appleby, "Locke, Liberalism and the Natural Law of Money," *Past & Present* no. 71 (1976): 44; Joan Comaroff and John L. Comaroff, "Millennial Capitalism: First Thoughts on a Second Coming," *Public Culture* 12, no. 20 (2000). For a review of the classic approach to medieval towns as economic spaces, see Gerald E. Frug, *City Making: Building Communities without Building Walls* (Princeton, NJ: Princeton University Press, 1999), 26–36. For representations from economics, see Joseph M. Ostroy and Ross M. Starr, "Money and the Decentralization of Exchange," *Econometrica* 42, no. 6 (1974).

towards more extensive trade. Cities replace smaller, more traditional communities. Between and within them, monetized exchange increasingly crowds out
the reciprocal relations anchored in custom. Networks of credit thicken until they
extend beyond the merchant circles that generated them.[5]

At a certain point, markets overflow their bounds, they penetrate everyday life,
they move to the center. As some scholars see it, expanding markets uproot the
early modern English. They are overwhelmed, unmoored, culturally upended in a
world that allows the "fraternization of impossibilities" and an indiscriminate
mix of men and commodities.[6] In the view of other scholars, the triumph of
market organization frees the population from oppression, the conformist pressures that brake progress, and material want. Participants are rational actors who
finally secure protection against expropriation and busily begin building banks,
trading securities, and making capital markets.[7]

In either case, economic exchange appears to have an almost uniform character
and, indeed, authors find developments in similar measure across the Atlantic.
They cast the American 18th century as the story of men and women entering
"the market," assuming new roles as entrepreneurs, leaving independent farms
for waged labor, and increasingly costing out the value of time in loans and
leisure. For some the process is natural, for others tragic, for still others celebratory.[8] Whether sadly or triumphantly, individuals enter the modern age, intimately but now impersonally tied to one another as producers, consumers, debtors,
creditors, wage earners, and employers.

---

[5] See, e.g., Agnew, *Worlds Apart*, 52–56; Comaroff and Comaroff, "Millennial Capitalism," 331–334;
Joyce Oldham Appleby, *Economic Thought and Ideology in Seventeenth-Century England* (Los Angeles:
Figuera Press, 2004), 23–24; James A. Henretta, *The Origins of American Capitalism: Collected Essays*
(Boston: Northeastern University Press, 1991). For reviews of the conventional approach to credit, see
James Steven Rogers, *The Early History of the Law of Bills and Notes: A Study of the Origins of Anglo-
American Commercial Law*, Cambridge Studies in English Legal History Index (Cambridge: Cambridge
University Press, 1995), 1–4, and to modern banking, see Angela Redish, "Anchors Aweigh: The Transition
from Commodity Money to Fiat Money in Western Economies," *Canadian Journal of Economics/Revue
canadienne d'économique* 26, no. 4 (1993): 781–785.
[6] The quote is from Marx, *Economic and Philosophic Manuscripts of 1844*, 169. See, e.g., Karl Polanyi,
The Great Transformation: The Political and Economic Origins of our Time, 2nd ed. (Boston, MA: Beacon
Press, 2001); Agnew, *Worlds Apart*, 17–56; Keith Hart, "On Commoditization," in *From Craft to Industry:
The Ethnography of Proto-Industrial Cloth Production*, ed. Esther N. Goody (Cambridge: Cambridge
University Press, 1982), 38–49; Appleby, "Locke, Liberalism," 44; Craig Muldrew, "Interpreting the Market:
The Ethics of Credit and Community Relations in Early Modern England," *Social History* 18, no. 2 (1993).
[7] See, e.g., Douglass C. North and Barry R. Weingast, "Constitutions and Commitment: The Evolution
of Institutions Governing Public Choice in Seventeenth-Century England," *Journal of Economic History* 49,
no. 4 (1989); Larry Neal, *The Rise of Financial Capitalism: International Capital Markets in the Age of
Reason*, Studies in Monetary and Financial History (Cambridge: Cambridge University Press, 1990); Niall
Ferguson, *The Cash Nexus: Money and Power in the Modern World, 1700–2000* (New York: Basic Books,
2001).
[8] See, respectively, Winifred Barr Rothenberg, *From Market-Places to a Market Economy: The Transformation of Rural Massachusetts, 1750–1850* (Chicago: University of Chicago Press, 1992); Henretta,
Origins of American Capitalism; Allan Kulikoff, *The Agrarian Origins of American Capitalism* (Charlottesville: University Press of Virginia, 1992); Michael Merrill, "The Anticapitalist Origins of the United States,"
Fernand Braudel Review 13 (1990); Gordon S. Wood, *The Radicalism of the American Revolution*, 1st
Vintage Books ed. (New York: Vintage Books, 1993).

The conventional story of economic modernization assigns money an essential role: it is the instrumentality of the market. Contemporary economists emphasize that money provides the liquidity that allows individuals to move beyond barter. Money irrigates exchange by providing a fungible medium, one that obviates the need, if exchange is to occur, for a "double coincidence" of wants—the fortuity that people have commodities they are willing to exchange at a time, quantity, and value that both agree on. A common currency in turn allows goods to be valued over time relative to other goods, establishing prices that convey information about relative worth to buyers and sellers. Finally, money acts as a store of value, an asset that carries purchasing power in liquid form.[9] It is, in fact, the evident functionality of money that renders it so dangerous, according to more critical observers. For them, the ascendance of money effects categorical change because money in its very operation allowed everything to be measured, quantified, and understood as an object for exchange. That representation veils the reality instantiated in every commodity, its foundation in the contingent and increasingly coercive social relations defined by the mode of production.[10]

Whether they consider it a blessing or a curse, commentators agree that money flows from custom or convention. Many narratives stage its start in the wild simplicity of an early world. In that conjured space, exchange was a murky broth of barter. People traded all sorts of objects among themselves—grain, gold, cows and hides, promises, services, cider, and salt. In the fluid mix of exchange, they found silver and gold especially easy to give and take. Metal gradually rose like fat to the surface, becoming a favored medium and marker of value as it passed endlessly from hand to hand. People cut silver and gold into pieces to make the process easier and more regular; disks of the commodity became coin. Its brokers were buyers and sellers converging upon pieces of precious metal to mediate each transaction and, ultimately, to create prices in a common medium.

Content changes and the government assists as society becomes more complicated or bankers become more powerful—but the medium has a constancy across all those details that is clearly sourced in the primal spring of exchange. As Marx

---

[9] James Tobin, "Money," in *The New Palgrave Dictionary of Economics*, ed. Steven N. Durlauf and Lawrence E. Blume, 2nd ed. (London: Palgrave Macmillan, 2008), 3–5; Ross Levine, "Financial Development and Economic Growth: Views and Agenda," *Journal of Economic Literature* 35, no. 2 (1997): 690–703.

[10] For Marx, money thus obscures the social relations that all products of man's labor entail in their very creation. Deceptively coded into exchange value, labor itself can come to appear an object for sale. Labor, a generative force that exceeds the cost of its replenishment, is set against the objective appearance of other values; commodification both submerges and captures its creative capacity. Marx, *Capital*. For rich analyses of money's instrumentalizing aspects by scholars in sociology, history, and literary studies, see, e.g., Keith Hart, "On Commoditization," 1982, and the review by Valenze, Deborah M. Valenze, *The Social Life of Money in the English Past* (Cambridge: Cambridge University Press, 2006), 23–25. For the focus in sociology, see Viviana A. Rotman Zelizer, *The Social Meaning of Money* (Princeton, NJ: Princeton University Press, 1997), 10–12; Geoffrey Ingham, "On the Underdevelopment of the 'Sociology of Money,'" *Acta Sociologica* 41, no. 1 (1998). In cognate fields, see Michel Callon (ed.), *The Laws of the Markets*, Sociological review monograph (Oxford: Blackwell Publishers/*The Sociological Review*, 1998); Marc Shell, *The Economy of Literature* (Baltimore: Johns Hopkins University Press, 1978).

wrote, the "commodity form" into which the value of any other commodity can be translated may be made of any object. Gold prevailed simply because, after serving as an equivalent for other commodities in isolated exchanges, "[g]radually it began to serve as universal equivalent in narrower or wider fields." It became the money form only after it "had won a monopoly of this position in the expression of value for the world of commodities."[11]

Writing only a few years later, Carl Menger agreed on this, if nothing else. An author of the marginalist revolution that came to revitalize classical approaches to economics, Menger understood money as the product of custom: "As economizing individuals in social situations became increasingly aware of their economic interest, they everywhere attained the simple knowledge that surrendering less saleable commodities for others of greater salability brings them substantially closer to the attainment of their specific economic purposes." Continually trading less liquid for more liquid commodities that they would be able to use more easily to buy what they needed, individuals eventually create a medium of exchange: "No one invented it," concludes Menger, "money is a natural product of human economy."[12]

More recent writers reiterate the "convergence" hypothesis to explain money's emergence. Some do so with great sophistication, exploring the conditions under which we might find that Mengerian process without centralized intervention.[13] Many assert the phenomenon much more simply. One account of a World War II prisoner-of-war camp has become iconic. It offers a microcosm of the market or, as the author put it, a case study of a "brand new society" where observers can witness the "growth of economic institutions and customs." And there, in the "living example of a simple economy," individuals naturally converged upon cigarettes—a random commodity that just happened to be commonly available— as a medium of exchange. The basic instrumentality of money occurred, that is,

---

[11] Marx, *Capital*, 163. As Marx put it more generally, "The specific kind of commodity with whose natural form the equivalent form is socially interwoven now becomes the money commodity, or serves as money." Marx, *Capital*, 162.

[12] Carl Menger, *Principles of Economics*, trans. James Dingwall and Berthold Frank Hoselitz, The Institute for Humane Studies Series in Economic Theory (New York: New York University Press, 1981), 263. An ocean away, in politics as well as society, another 19th century historian produced a typical formulation of the phenomenon. "Currency," he explained, "denotes whatever has been adopted, as a medium of exchange, by general consent and practice." Joseph B. Felt, *An Historical Account of Massachusetts Currency Microform* (1839), 10. For classical liberal versions of the story, see David Hume, "Discourse III: Of Money," in *Political Discourses* (London: R. Fleming, 1752), 35–36; John Locke, "Further Considerations Concerning Raising the Value of Money," in *Locke on Money* (Oxford: Clarendon Press, 1991), 410, 423. Some accounts acknowledge this history to be extrapolated as a matter of logic, not fact. See, e.g., Paul Samuelson and William D. Nordhaus, *Economics*, 9th ed. (New York: McGraw-Hill, 1973), 274–276; Kevin Dowd, "The Invisible Hand and the Evolution of the Monetary System," in *What Is Money?*, ed. John Smithin (London: Routledge, 2000).

[13] See, e.g., Robert A. Jones, "The Origin and Development of Media of Exchange," *Journal of Political Economy* 84, no. 4 (1976) (reviewing literature and modeling phenomenon).

out of the decentralized activity of bargaining agents, without politics or collect-ive orchestration.[14]

From its origin as an object chosen spontaneously by people making deals, money matures predictably, along with the market it supports. Contemporary economics textbooks carry the bluntest version of the story. They pick up where Marx and Menger left us, with people passing around gold as a common denominator in exchange. After a while, the government "gets involved" to save people the costs, not to mention the headache, of refining gold, measuring it, and testing it. Coins of a standardized amount and fineness enter circulation as units of account.[15]

"Commodity money"—paradigmatically money made from silver or gold—holds a preeminent place in the teleology of money. If, in fact, individuals naturally converged upon a precious metal as the commodity equivalent of value and if the government steps in simply to facilitate their choice, then coin made of metal does indeed offer the prototype of money produced out of the autonomous acts of individuals, money can be analogized to bullion, and the government plays a distinctly secondary role. In their most notable discussions of money, Hume and Ricardo equated it directly with silver and gold.[16] And in both popular and academic writing today, authors often assume that the "Gold Standard" refers to a time when "gold" circulated outright as money, providing an anchor that stabilized the market.[17] Each formulation evokes money as a representative of value that is real, independent of politics, private, and impervi-ous to tinkering.

Macroeconomists make that identity explicit, modeling an "ideal commodity money" to exemplify the way a medium should work. As they articulate it, an "ideal commodity money" creates a medium with stable value by tying prices for commodities in coin to prices for commodities in metal. Linking the stock of coin to the supply of a metal prevents the quantity of money from fluctuating independently of the market for that metal. The technique should stop the price hikes that would occur if a sovereign anxious to spend more simply issued twice as many coins with half the amount of metal in each. His ploy would

---

[14] Radford, "P.O.W. Camp," 190. The Radford article has become a chestnut of introductory texts in macroeconomics, money, and finance. See, e.g., Mankiw, *Macroeconomics*, 157; Frederic S. Mishkin, *The Economics of Money, Banking, and Financial Markets*, 9th ed., The Addison-Wesley Series in Economics (Boston: Addison-Wesley, 2010), 55, n. 1; Dowd, "The Invisible Hand," 143; Tobin, "Money," 2; see also Donald W. Katzner, "Unity of Subject Matter in the Teaching of Intermediate Microeconomic Theory," *Journal of Economic Education* 22, no. 2 (1991) (advocating use of the article in teaching basic economics).

[15] Mankiw, *Macroeconomics*, 158; see similarly Mishkin, *Economics of Money*, 57–59.

[16] David Ricardo, "On Foreign Trade," *The Works and Correspondence of David Ricardo*, vol. 1 (1817 [2005]), Chapter 7; David Hume, "Of the Balance of Trade," *Political Discourses*, 1752.

[17] See, e.g., Richard Lipsey, *An Introduction to Positive Economics* (London: Weidenfeld and Nicolson, 1975), 683–702; Tobin, "Money," 3. See generally Samuel Knafo, "The Gold Standard and the Origins of the Modern International Monetary System," *Review of International Political Economy* 13, no. 1 (February 2006): 78–102 (reviewing traditional and revisionary approaches to the Gold Standard).

obviously only work until people figured it out and started charging twice as much in the new coins. But in the meantime, the ruler would make off with an undeserved advantage and the arbitrary change in prices would disrupt the market.[18]

According to this view, a government can create an ideal commodity money system by identifying the metal content of each coin (for example, ounces of silver/penny), and converting metal to coin at the demand of users. Coin is easier to use than raw metal, so people will often prefer to take it, selling their goods at a lower price in coined metal than they would demand in silver bullion. Users will choose to have coin rather than silver whenever the value of coin exceeds the value of the silver in the coin—in other words, whenever prices in coin with a particular metal content stay below the level they would be if stated in amounts of metal bullion. When those prices are equal, the holder of coin can buy goods either at the "world price" of goods in silver (ounces of silver/good), or at the price of goods in coin (ounces of silver/good//ounces of silver/penny), which would come to the same thing.[19]

The "commodity money" system projected by the model creates a device that will equilibrate the amount of coin in circulation. People will mint or melt coin depending on how much they value money's services compared to the other things they might do with the metal that is in it, including paying or charging for other commodities. When prices in coin rise above the level at which prices in coin and in metal are equal (i.e., the value of coin falls), users would rather have the silver in the coin, which they can use to buy more goods or for other purposes. Coin will be melted for its silver content. As coin leaves circulation, prices in coin will fall until coin and silver have the same relative value. Conversely, when prices in coin are below the point equal to the value-by-weight of coin, the value of coin will be higher than the metal it contains. People will go to the mint to get coin. That will raise the amount of coin in circulation, in turn raising prices in coin until they reach the point at which the value of coin equals the value-by-weight of coin (in other words, the value of the metal in the coin). Individuals, considering their advantage in matters of exchange, melt or mint in response. They thus tie

---

[18] See, e.g., Redish, "Anchors Away," 785 and n. 13. If, for some reason, the sovereign wanted to have less coin, he could of course double the amount of metal content in each unit and prices would drop. The effect would be the same as when stressed soldiers smoked their cigarette money and so took it out of circulation.

[19] "An ideal commodity money system is designed to equate the price level to a relative price of metal for consumption goods, and by making stocks of coins endogenous, to prevent effects on the price level coming from exogenous fluctuations in the quantities of coins." Thomas J. Sargent and Francois R. Velde, *The Big Problem of Small Change*, The Princeton Economic History of the Western World Indexes (Princeton, NJ: Princeton University Press, 2002), 11; see also Sargent and Velde, *Big Problem of Small Change*, 22 ("An ideal commodity money makes the price level proportional to [the world price in silver (ounces of silver/ consumption good)], where the factor of proportionality is...the number of coins of [a certain type] per ounce of silver"); see also Angela Redish, *Bimetallism: An Economic and Historical Analysis*, Studies in Macroeconomic History Index (Cambridge: Cambridge University Press, 2000), 3.

the total quantity of money and prices to the independent and shared supply of metal.[20]

The ideal commodity money model produced by modern macroeconomic theory is, itself, a kind of genesis story. Its dynamism turns on individuals who can pay for goods in either silver or coin, and choose by comparing the world price of goods in silver with prices in coin. Coin is effectively identified with the commodity; it is distinctive as money only insofar as it imports convenience, measuring and regularizing the commodity. Value is determined by the exchange of real goods, traded according to the natural forces of supply and demand. The decentralized and rational actions of participants produce an equilibrium— including a stock of money—that is ultimately good for everyone. There is no call for politics, as individuals need never collide with a concerted public. Government is a freely available coordinating device, a technical service that costlessly provides the platform for individuated action. The system is self-calibrating, as opposed to centrally defined.

It would be hard to imagine a more inanimate instrumentality than money, as captured by the ideal commodity model. The sheer automaticity of the system, its depersonalized and depersonalizing effects, evokes a barebones agreement from Marx and others. In Simmel's words, it was the "uncompromising objectivity" of money that allowed it, at once solvent and dangerous, "technically perfect," to render everything calculable. Money was "colourless," a matter "free from any quality and exclusively determined by quantity."[21]

If commodity money is the fulcrum of the system, it nonetheless begs revision. Money made of precious metals is heavy and hard to transport. "Imagine the holes you'd wear in your pockets if you had to buy things only with coins!" notes one account.[22] According to the prevailing common sense, banks start issuing paper notes that are claims to gold in reserve. Their practice follows from the long mercantile tradition of private credit. The government, again as a secondary agent, eventually steps in to support a central bank as lender of last resort. As long as people believe that the notes will be converted on demand, they are "just as valuable as the gold itself."[23] The gold reserve is eventually abandoned as unnecessary because "[a]s long as everyone continues to accept the paper bills in exchange, they will have value and serve as money."[24]

---

[20] See, e.g., Sargent and Velde, *Big Problem of Small Change*, 9–12.
[21] Simmel, *The Philosophy of Money*, 127, 281, 367, 441, 444.
[22] Mishkin, *Economics of Money*, 57.
[23] Mankiw, *Macroeconomics*, 158. On banks, see, e.g., Rondo E. Cameron, "England, 1750–1844," in *Banking in the Early Stages of Industrialization*, ed. Rondo E. Cameron (Oxford: Oxford University Press, 1967), 1–2, 20–34; Richard David Richards, *The Early History of Banking in England* (London: P.S. King & Son, 1929), 40–43.
[24] Mankiw, *Macroeconomics*, 158; Samuelson and Nordhaus, *Economics*, 274–276. In most accounts, the government imports not only the capacity to lower transaction costs by making coin, but also the danger that it will abusively skim off a profit by debasing coin.

As our representative textbook concludes, "Thus the system of commodity money evolves into a system of fiat money." The author enjoins people to notice that in the end, "the use of money in exchange is largely a social convention." Everyone values fiat money "simply because they expect everyone else to value it."[25] To some observers, that quality makes money deeply problematic. After all, insofar as money depends simply on "confidence," money seems "one of the supreme fictions," an illusion. The money machine produces paper and fantasy; value is plotted on an axis that runs from "trust" to counterfeiting, and it is not clear that there is much difference between the two except the likelihood that someone will be able to pass on a bill in time to get substance for it.[26] Just as when it was made of gold, money remains an opaque instrument that obscures underlying allocations of power, now in a modern dress of paper.

The point for us is that whether they applaud or condemn it, people agree on the basic trajectory of money's development. Convention has replaced the commodity content of coin while replicating its opacity. Value is carried so intrinsically as a commodity or so diffusely as a social convention that power structures are either non-existent (the neoclassical view) or elusive (the critical view). First a commodity and then a convention suffices. As James Tobin put it, "The moneys chosen by societies have varied tremendously over human history. So have their languages. In each case, what is universal and important is that something is chosen, not what is chosen."[27]

The end to the story is expedient, fashioned for a world that has gone off the Gold Standard. Assuming that money is now "fiat," considering it "chosen" as Tobin does, frees academics and policy makers up to address the other monetary issues that appear pressing. Those issues have overwhelmingly to do with the controls on the government, supports for banks, monetary shocks, and the relationship between the quantity of money and the real economy. That is true both for Keynesians and for those more classical in persuasion. For some, the main issue of monetary policy is to "make fiat money operate as if it were a commodity."[28] For others, the money supply is only one determinant in the complex aggregate that comprises prices in the market for goods and services.[29] For still others, money is a policy tool to be deployed to encourage ideal levels of

[25] Mankiw, *Macroeconomics*, 158.

[26] Patrick Brantlinger, *Fictions of State: Culture and Credit in Britain, 1694–1994* (Ithaca: Cornell University Press, 1996), 24; see also, e.g., Alain Lipietz, *The Enchanted World: Inflation, Credit and the World Crisis*, trans. Ian Patterson (London: Verso, 1985), 78. For the same view, written as farce, see <http://www.theonion.com/articles/us-economy-grinds-to-halt-as-nation-realizes-money,2912/>, accessed June 19, 2014.

[27] Tobin, "Money," 2. Compare Ingham's discussion of Talcott Parsons's approach to money as a language, i.e., another "medium of exchange." Ingham, "Underdevelopment," 5–6.

[28] L. Randall Wray, "Alternative Approaches to Money," *Theoretical Inquiries in Law* 11, no. 1 (2010): 33 (critiquing view). See, e.g., Lipietz, *The Enchanted World*; Milton Friedman, *The Optimum Quantity of Money: and Other Essays* (Chicago: Aldine Publishing Company, 1969).

[29] Tobin, "Money."

savings and investment.[30] With some remarkable exceptions, many of which have an important influence on this work, few scholars, either from economics or otherwise, return to the question of what money is, how it is produced, and how that might matter.[31]

Across its varied retellings, the "convergence" story writes the market into a certain relationship with money. That structure emerges all the more powerfully because it is common to such otherwise disparate accounts. It becomes, in its reiteration, a truism of modern thought. In that status, it evades analysis to a striking extent.

On one hand, the market and money are highly identified with each other. Histories of the market move back and forth between that topic and accounts of money's extension, as if they were proxies for each other, or as if the market were a matter of degree marked by money. Other accounts are more specific. As Karl Polanyi described the epoch of the market economy:

> The transformation implies a change in the motive of action on the part of the members of society: for the motive of subsistence that of gain must be substituted. All transactions are turned into money transactions, and these in turn require that a medium of exchange be introduced into every articulation of industrial life.[32]

On the other hand, the market and money each play a very particular part in the drama they present. Simply put, the market is the end and money is the means; the first is substance, the second is form. Those roles neatly reinforce the larger argument that markets are basically synonymous with modernization. For a great number of scholars, the market is the partner that matters. Here are the "real economy" and the "economic fundamentals" that the discipline of economics seeks, the material advance in quality of life that liberalism claims, and the brutal reality of dispossession and exploitation that Marxist and post-colonial studies locate at the base of capitalism. As Schumpeter described the goal of

---

[30] Charles I. Jones, *Introduction to Economic Growth* (New York: Norton, 1998).

[31] For exceptions, see the economic scholarship that informs the stakeholder approach, cited at pp. 43–50. See also those scholars developing modern monetary theory. For example, L. Randall Wray, "Modern Money," in *What Is Money?*, ed. John Smithin (New York: Routledge, 2000); L. Randall Wray, *Understanding Modern Money: The Key to Full Employment and Price Stability* (Cheltenham: Edward Elgar, 1998); Stephanie Bell, "The Role of the State and the Hierarchy of Money," *Cambridge Journal of Economics* 25, no. 2 (2001): 149. From a very different perspective, see also those working in Neil Wallace's fundamental models of money school, e.g., N. Wallace, "Whither Monetary Economics," *International Economic Review* 42, no. 4 (2001); Angela Redish and Warren E. Weber, "A Model of Commodity Money with Minting and Melting," *Federal Reserve Bank of Minneapolis Research Dept. Staff Report*, No. 460 (2011). Other notable contributions include Farley Grubb, "Specie Scarcity and Efficient Barter: The Problem of Maintaining an Outside Money Supply in British Colonial America," in *Inside Money*, ed. Christine Desan (University of Pennsylvania Press, forthcoming 2015); Steve A. Marglin, *Raising Keynes: A 21st Century General Theory* (manuscript, 2013); Perry Mehrling, *The New Lombard Street: How the Fed Became the Dealer of Last Resort* (Princeton: Princeton University Press, 2011); Morgan Ricks, "Regulating Money Creation after the Crisis," *Harvard Business Law Review* 1 (2011); Roy Kreitner, "The Jurisprudence of Global Money," *Theoretical Inquiries in Law* 11 (2010); Redish, *Bimetallism*.

[32] Polanyi, *Great Transformation*, 44; see also, e.g., Cameron, *Banking in the Early Stages of Industrialization*, 1.

orthodox economics, "Real analysis proceeds from the principle that all the essential phenomena of economic life are capable of being described in terms of good and services, of decisions about them, and of relations between them."[33] Trade in things you can "buy, sell, and drop on your foot" is the productive heart of the economy and the essential object of its discipline, economics.[34]

That view informs other disciplines at a basic level. Consider the prize-winning appeal of Gordon Wood's approach to the American Revolution. It was "radical," argues Wood, in its capacity to find "new democratic adhesives in the actual behavior of plain ordinary people—in the everyday desire for the freedom to make money and pursue happiness in the here and now." This tale of uplift makes material striving the generative force of American politics and culture: Wood describes the development as one located in the "commonplace behavior of ordinary people" that made Americans "almost overnight, the most liberal, the most democratic, the most commercially minded, and the most modern people in the world." Wood adds "capitalistic" in the next paragraph.[35] In less affirmative accounts, real exchange maintains a kind of categorical primacy. Thus "market" exchange does battle with exchange organized around logics that are feudal, communal, traditional, religious, or local. Ideology, culture, psychology, and categories of thought take an increasingly important place in modern scholarship. But they are often deployed to understand a mentality or social practice that is "market" or not, economistic or not.[36]

If the market is "real" economic activity, then money is its "formal" partner. That does not mean that money is unimportant; it is as essential as the function it performs. Only when a medium exists, when value can be measured, and when

---

[33] Joseph Alois Schumpeter, *History of Economic Analysis*, ed. Elizabeth Broody (New York: Oxford University Press, 1994), 277; see also Ingham, "Underdevelopment," 4 (describing the "metatheory" of the real economy to comprise "exchange ratios between commodities in money terms (object–object relations) established as the result of individual acts of utility calculation (individual agent–object relations)").

[34] Mark Blyth, *Great Transformations: Economic Ideas and Institutional Change in the Twentieth Century* (New York: Cambridge University Press, 2002), 127, n. 3 (quoting *The Economist* magazine); for comment, see Marglin, *Raising Keynes*; Perry Mehrling, "Minsky and Modern Finance: The Case of Long Term Capital Management," *Journal of Portfolio Management* 26, no. 2 (2000).

[35] See Wood, *Radicalism*, 7. See also, e.g., Joyce Oldham Appleby, *Inheriting the Revolution: the First Generation of Americans* (Cambridge, MA: Belknap Press of Harvard University Press, 2000); Louis Hartz, *The Liberal Tradition in America: An Interpretation of American Political Thought Since the Revolution*, 1st ed. (New York: Harcourt Brace, 1955); James Willard Hurst, *Law and the Conditions of Freedom in the Nineteenth-century United States* (Madison: University of Wisconsin Press, 1967). For a recent historiography that arguably adds a new chapter, consider the emphasis on consumption. See, e.g., T. H. Breen, *The Marketplace of Revolution: How Consumer Politics Shaped American Independence* (Oxford: Oxford University Press, 2004).

[36] See, e.g., Polanyi, *Great Transformation*; Charles Grier Sellers, *The Market Revolution: Jacksonian America, 1815–1846* (New York: Oxford University Press, 1991); Henretta, *Origins of American Capitalism*; Agnew, *Worlds Apart*. See also those unaligned skeptics of modernity, like Weber, Muldrew, and Sandel: Max Weber, *The Protestant Ethic and the Spirit of Capitalism*, trans. Talcott Parsons (London: Routledge Classics, 2001 [1930]); Craig Muldrew, *The Economy of Obligation: The Culture of Credit and Social Relations in Early Modern England* (New York: Macmillan, 1998); Michael J. Sandel, *What Money Can't Buy: The Moral Limits of Markets* (New York: Farrar, Straus, and Giroux, 2012).

assets can be stored in liquid form can individuals specialize as owners, producers, or workers, set or receive wages, calculate risks and profits; only then can
"the market" penetrate time and space in the way that the standard narrative
identifies as distinctive to modernity. Money's functions—its capacity as a
medium of exchange, unit of account, and store of value—suffice to furnish the
definition of money.[37]

If money is a purely instrumental entity, then it enables but does not affect the
substance of trades. The classical image of the economy follows:

> [The idealized economy is] a frictionless, costless system of multilateral barter, in
> which relative prices and the allocations of labour and capital among various pro-
> ductive activities are determined in competitive markets. [The] proposition is that the
> outcomes of an economy with money are the same as those that would arise from their
> ideal barter model. The corollary is that real economic outcomes are independent of
> the particular nature of the monetary institutions.[38]

If money's character is purely expressive, it amounts to information. Given the
ability to capture value that money represents, agents can make contracts for
future commodity sales and can adjust for contingencies by setting conditional
terms—Arrow-Debreu contracts. That capacity confirms the possibility that
there is a general equilibrium at which the aggregate demand for every good
meets aggregate supply for that good.[39]

Keynes would most famously attack at this point based on the stubborn reality
that, whatever the postulates of classical theory, people attribute substantive value
to having the liquidity provided by money. They insist on holding certain
amounts of it as a store of value, despite the fact that they should be able to
arrange for contingencies without immobilizing an amount of money. That
allocation of resources introduces imperfections into the market for goods and
services. Aggregate demand may fail to meet aggregate supply.[40]

Despite the revolutionary impact of Keynes's theory on economics and its
continued influence at the academic level, in policy making, and in popular

---

[37] See, e.g., Levine, "Financial Development," 690–703; Radford, "P.O.W. Camp," 194; Friedman, *Optimum Quantity*; Ostroy and Starr, "Money and the Decentralization of Exchange."

[38] Tobin, "Money," 10. As Tobin clarifies, this is the sense in which classical economists claimed money was a "veil." They were not claiming that money did not matter or that a society without money would have the same real economy as a society with money. Tobin, "Money," 9–10.

[39] Mark Blaug, *Economic Theory in Retrospect*, 5th ed. (Cambridge: Cambridge University Press, 1996), 553–554. Proponents of the view recognize that the costs of commodity money make it an imperfect choice for money. Adam Smith made the point long ago. See Adam Smith, "Chapter II: On Money Considered as a Particular Branch of the General Stock of the Society, or of the Expense of Maintaining the National Capital," *An Inquiry into the Nature and Causes of the Wealth of Nations* (New York: The Modern Library, 1937).

[40] John Maynard Keynes, *The General Theory of Employment, Interest, and Money* (New York: Harcourt Brace, 1936), 177–207. For a wonderful restatement by Keynes of his argument, recently rediscovered by Steve Marglin, see John Maynard Keynes, "A Self-Adjusting Economic System?," *The New Republic*, February 20, 1935.

thought, belief in the "classical dichotomy" remains dominant. A commitment to the notion that the market is "real" and money is a neutral agent, at least in the long run, controls in the basic economics text and shapes economic decision-making.[41] The strength of that paradigm, or deference to the Keynesian assault, suppresses significant challenge from other disciplines.[42] In unwitting consonance, the obvious recourse for those critical scholars who understand money as a "veil," a con, and chimera is to lift it aside, to get beyond it, and to see through it. Their inclination, in other words, is to find *somewhere else* the actual workings of modernity and the power relations that animate it.[43] We are back to "the market" as the site of the real.

Note how the binary that casts the market-as-real and money-as-information (or alternatively, money-as-illusion) draws from the creation story written for money. Money stems from convention, and convention is immaterial, "costless," or "colourless." It is the result of decentralized activity as opposed to a collective project. While the latter would, by its organization of participants, define value in a way that has materiality, the former defines the terms of value only as knowledge; information (or illusion) is free.

The "market" and "money," defined as they are by the conventional creation story, reinforce each other because of the way they channel our attention; the overall effect is to give the modernization narrative great durability. The formal partner of the money-market dichotomy does not repay analysis because it is a function or a signifier only—merely a means to the market's end. But while it appears empty or technical, "money" packages a controversial view of human nature and society. Money's very existence—if it came about in bipolar exchange between enterprising agents, each calculating his or her own interest—becomes evidence of that activity as the root of economic life and its logic.

[41] See Marglin, *Raising Keynes.* For the absence of liquidity as a consideration in risk assessments, see Mehrling, "Minsky and Modern Finance." The profuse "securitization" of the 1990s and early 2000s was conceived as a way of diversifying risk and so reducing it, thus making an ever more abundant and inexpensive credit available to borrowers. For that view and the response that securitization in fact engendered more risk, see Anastasia Nesvetailova, "The Crisis of Invented Money: Liquidity Illusion and the Global Credit Meltdown," *Theoretical Inquiries in Law* 11, no. 1 (2010): 125–145; Paul Krugman, "The Market Mystique," *The New York Times*, March 26, 2009; Hyman P. Minsky, "The Financial Instability Hypothesis," *Working Paper* No. 74 (1992).

[42] Geoffrey Ingham portrays sociology's aversion to analyzing money as part of a disciplinary settlement between it and economics; William Reddy emphasizes the Whiggish tilt of historians who incorporate the facilitative capacity of money as part of the meta-narrative of Western progress. Ingham, "Underdevelopment"; William M. Reddy, *Money and Liberty in Modern Europe: A Critique of Historical Understanding* (Cambridge: Cambridge University Press, 1987), 34–46. That default is basically complete where the *economic* aspects of money are concerned, although scholars like Viviana Zelizer consider *social* uses and interpretations of money: Ingham, "Underdevelopment," 3; see, e.g., Zelizer, *Social Meaning*; Valenze, *Social Life of Money.*

[43] In striking confirmation that their approaches regard money in a common way, both orthodox neoclassical economists and their critics describe it as a "veil." See Ingham, "Underdevelopment," 4–5, 6–7; compare D. H. Robertson, *Money* (Chicago: Chicago University Press, 1959), 7.

The real partner, the market, relies on that deep coding to gain definition as authentic and undeniable. Once we have agreed on the character of money, the *activity* conducted by money—exchange by enterprising individuals—is confirmed as primal and productive. The message is that the market is at once basic, as basic as its partner, and the site of literal materiality, a materiality that its monetary partner facilitates, transmits, or effectuates, for better or worse.

The money-market dichotomy and its associated intuitions are built into the very vocabulary of the conventional creation story and produced in the practices that story promotes. That is a vocabulary of agency either poured into things or captured in conventions. It is a story of people either liberated or unmoored. It is an approach that understands "the social" as the pattern of their choices or as the fragile space opposed to their atomism. In this world, the political economy pitches between promoting energy and productivity on the one hand, and protecting the public welfare, social meaning, and cultures (popular, indigenous, local, etc.) on the other—as if these were discrete values and it were a matter of striking a balance. The debate turns on whether "the market" may need regulation, and whether the reach of money may need restraint. Indeed, in many ways, the narrative of modernization—as a story of the market and money—operates in terms of innate dichotomies that are entrenched even as they are qualified or resisted. Taken together, these dynamics go a long way towards reifying the contemporary political economy so that it is a found entity, like money itself.

B. Money as a constitutional project

We can imagine conditions that would make the convergence story possible. We assume exchange with enough momentum to generate the medium supposed itself to generate exchange. We assume as well the background terms that would make that initial exchange possible. There must be notions of property that identify objects with individuals, modes of contract or agreement that allow transactions, and enough enforcement to protect those claims of ownership and transfer, all these despite the absence of authorities acting with a medium to pay for such governance work. We assume that, given those hypothesized safeguards, people making a subsistence living in a pre-monetary era set aside an item durable enough to last the amount of time it takes in a barter economy to find a trading partner. (Silver appears again and again as money, although it is expensive, inedible, of little practical use, and unworkable by untrained hands.) In fact, we assume that people safely hold, indeed accumulate, some material like metal in raw form on the prediction that other people will want it, before it has emerged as a medium. We assume that, in an unspecialized world, countable units with enough uniformity, authenticity, and transparency to convey value in countable form appear with enough frequency before money to take office as money.[44] We assume, finally, that once money appears, it stays in circulation by some sort of network effect, insulated from big men who would break the consensus by cornering the medium, marauders who would steal it, and fickle individuals who would renege in their desire for it.

In other words, the area of "assuming" required to make the convergence story work is enormous. As the following chapters argue, the convergence story is also in conflict with the history of money we have. It is even more surely inconsistent with the practice of money today, a matter of paper, balance sheets, and central banks.

Alternatively, we could look for a creation story that explains how money emerges without assuming the exchange it is supposed to enable. Money has arisen again and again, in many places and periods; it must start from a source more robust than a scaffold of assumptions. In fact, a creation story should go beyond money's initial appearance, it should also make sense of money's continued operation. The practice of money daily re-enacts the beginning (and end) of money, as it maintains the flow of money in (and out) of circulation. We need a story that acknowledges, even draws upon, money's constant construction. Finally, a creation story should illuminate the connection between the way money works and the exchange it enables, including the objects labeled commodities by their sale. The relationship between money and the market should be explored, rather than postulated.

Conceptualizing money creation: Money as fiscal value and cash premium

If we consider clues about money's origins and extrapolate from its continuing practice, another story comes into focus. Money appears to be a process that organizes a group and redirects individuals, even as those parties interact to create a way they can assess and transfer value. Rather than emerging from trade, money instead enables trade. Put more accurately, rather than a generic (money) produced by a generic (exchange), money arises as a particular initiative that creates exchanges of particular kinds. Nothing about the phenomenon leads obviously to capitalism, or in any other direction. Rather, as people pioneered different kinds of money, they created different kinds of markets.

If we take the beginning of money seriously, we arrive in a place that is dramatically drier than the broth of barter that modern commentators imagine. There is no "unit of account" or shared means of measuring. There is no universal mode of settling accounts and no common medium. There is no activity that produces price, whether in grain or barley, or the shadow liquidity of silver.

---

[44] A side channel of convergence theorists imagines that people create a unit out of private promises. In order to make that variant work, we assume interpersonal exchange so civilized as to run on an abstract unit of obscure (possibly miraculous) origin and credit alone.

People may exchange items, but "barter" is actually far removed from the triangle of swaps—a cow for ten chickens, ten chickens for the pot desired at the outset— that later commentators often impute to it. However people transfer goods and services between themselves depends not only on how they value those things, but on what practices of claiming, using, giving, and taking goods and other resources exist.[45]

The early English experience offers a setting with some similarities. According to historians of early money, the use of money broke down in Britain after the Roman army left and administrative connections ended. The imperial economy had been highly monetized; spending and taxing in coin spread it throughout the territories, while Roman law supported money's use in private exchange.[46] When the fiscal pump failed and authorities withdrew, the money once pushed into circulation stopped flowing to the island. According to Peter Spufford, "within a generation, by about A.D. 435, coin ceased to be used there as a medium of exchange...although many survived as jewelry, or were used for gifts or for compensation."[47]

More recent accounts, informed by archaeological advances, qualify that conclusion. They suggest that some coins still arrived, although in small numbers, from the Continent, where their use as money continued to some extent. Some communities may also have kept using Roman-era silver coinage for some time to compensate those defending their settlements; samples from 5th century hoards in Britain are clipped in ways that may suggest they were recycled in systematic ways. Hoards have also produced low-value bronze Roman tokens that could have circulated after their issue, if only in some locales. Scholars argue as well that coin found refashioned into ornaments may have played a previous role in exchange.[48]

---

[45] For a review about the way those activities are characterized in economics and anthropology, see Marshall Sahlins, *Stone Age Economics* (New York: Aldine de Gruyter, 1972).

[46] Rory Naismith, *Money and Power in Anglo-Saxon England: The Southern English Kingdoms 757–865* (Cambridge: Cambridge University Press, 2012), 37–39; Gareth Williams, "The Circulation and Function of Coinage in Conversion-Period England, c. AD 580–675," in *Coinage and History in the North Sea World, c. AD 500–1250*, ed. Barrie Cook and Gareth Williams (Leiden: Koninklijki Brill NV, 2006), 149; A. S. Esmonde Cleary, *The Ending of Roman Britain* (London: B. T. Batsford, 1989), 8–12; Peter Spufford, *Money and Its Use in Medieval Europe* (Cambridge: Cambridge University Press, 1988), 9–22. For a discussion of Roman law, see pp. 84–85, 133–134.

[47] Spufford, *Money and its Use*, 9, 14–22; Ian Stewart, "The English and Norman Mints, c. 600–1158," in *A New History of the Royal Mint*, ed. C. E. Challis (Cambridge: Cambridge University Press, 1992), 3–4; Esmonde Cleary, *Ending*, 138–161; J. P. C. Kent, "From Roman Britain to Saxon England," in *Anglo-Saxon Coins*, ed. R. H. M. Dolley (London: Methuen, 1961).

[48] On imported coin and residual Roman coin, see Williams, "Coinage in Conversion-Period England," 151, 153–154, 159–163; Richard Abdy, "After Patching: Imported and Recycled Coinage in Fifth- and Sixth-Century Britain," in *Coinage and History in the North Sea World, c. AD 500–1250*, ed. Barrie Cook and Gareth Williams (Leiden: Koninklijke Brill NV, 2006), 83–88, 91–95. Abdy cautions that the importations appear occasional and "not for any systematic purpose." According to a recent review of the archaeological evidence, light imports circulated through the lowland areas of England in the 6th and 7th centuries, but more significant imports were common only in Kent. Chris Wickham, *Framing the Early Middle Ages: Europe and the Mediterranean, 400–800* (Oxford: Oxford University Press, 2005), 808–809.

But even the revolution in numismatic evidence that has occurred since the 1970s with the advent of metal detecting and the increase in coin finds has not rewritten the bottom line.[49] Gareth Williams, one of the scholars most sensitive to the possibility of monetary continuity, concludes that the evidence "suggests an attempt to prop up a failing system for as long as possible, in the absence of a proper coinage supply from central government." The view that "there was a complete break in the coinage system is hard to challenge."[50] Most recent contributions to the debate agree: from sometime after 410 until about 610, there was little coin circulating as money in England. As Rory Naismith puts it, "minting and coin-use in Britain had to be rebuilt from the ground up."[51]

The vacuum left by coin's demise was not substantially filled, as far as the record reflects, with another medium.[52] In the wake of the imperial retreat, writes Chris Wickham, "exchange structures collapsed everywhere." The material break with the earlier world that occurred in the 5th century was dramatic. The sheer drop in "the sophistication of material culture," Wickham notes, "might seem too total to be credible" but for the very wide base of evidence supporting it. Pottery and other industries disappear. Roman sites are reappropriated for structures so simple as to resemble Iron Age dwellings. Written sources vanish; conversely, Gallic sources rarely mention England.[53] The layer of "dark earth" that covers some Roman towns is especially evocative of collapse. Archaeologists are unsure if the strata represent decayed material of those settlements, a turn to agriculture on the sites, the use of organic building material by later inhabitants, or some combination of causes.[54] Whatever the explanation, the phenomenon is arresting.

On bronze Roman coin, see also Kenneth Dark, *Britain and the End of the Roman Empire* (Stroud: Tempus Publishing, 2000), who argues more strongly for its continued use, and T. S. N. Moorhead, who contests that view. T. S. N. Moorhead, "Roman Bronze Coinage in Sub-Roman and Early Anglo-Saxon England," in *Coinage and History in the North Sea World, c. AD 500–1250*, ed. Barrie Cook and Gareth Williams (Leiden: Koninklijke Brill NV, 2006); see also Esmonde Cleary, *Ending*, 140. On re-used coin, see Williams, "Coinage in Conversion-Period England," 161–169.

[49] Individual coin "finds" offer clues to coin use different from those found in burial sites or hoards. The latter represent coin dedicated to ritual use or laid aside from circulation while coin finds plausibly reflect coin lost in use. Williams, "Coinage in Conversion-Period England," 151–152.

[50] Williams, "Coinage in Conversion-Period England," 158.

[51] See Naismith, *Money and Power*, 15; Anna Gannon, *The Iconography of Early Anglo-Saxon Coinage* (Oxford: Oxford University Press, 2003), 7–8; see also Abdy, "After Patching," 94–95 (arguing that transition to "a bullion-using society where coins (so long as they were of precious metal) were incidental" had occurred by 470 in England).

[52] Cf. Naismith, *Money and Power*, 290; see also p. 39 n. 48 on residual coin use in the 5th and 6th centuries. Christopher Loveluck notes evidence of trade with Continental Europe at Flixborough, England, prior to the late 7th century, but no findings of coin or other media of exchange. Christopher Loveluck, Keith Dobney, and James Barrett, "Trade and Exchange—The Settlement and the Wider World," in *Rural Settlement, Lifestyles and Social Change in the Later First Millenium AD: Anglo-Saxon Flixborough in its Wider Context*. Excavations at Flixborough (Oxford: Oxbow Books, 2007), 112–113.

[53] Wickham, *The Early Middle Ages*, 338, 306, 308–309.

[54] See Esmonde Cleary, *Ending*, 147–148; Richard I. Macphail, Henri Galinie, and Frans Verhaeghe, "A Future for Dark Earth?," *Antiquity* 77, no. 296 (2003): 349–358.

While scholars debate how to interpret the "dramatic material collapse" of 5th century England, they widely agree that it occurred.[55]

The conditions in England after the departure of Roman forces suggest the terrain on which we should look for money's creation. For individuals, the circumstances sharply circumscribed trading. Production of wares moved to the household: ceramics were handmade there; clothing was woven family by family. Households surely dealt with one another but distance and the difficulties of travel, scantiness of communication, and lack of information made barter unwieldy. Commercial demand was virtually non-existent; there is no evidence of exchange networks of any extent until the late 7th century. "All forms of market exchange, beyond the simplest," Wickham concludes, "must have ceased."[56] It is difficult to conceive that a metal, hard to work and impractical for everyday use beyond the aesthetic, would begin to circulate as money because people had incrementally or spontaneously converged on its use.

But individuals were not the only actors in England. Communities operated continuously. As in other worlds, people formed bonds for social life, mutual protection, and shared production. Wickham describes early Anglo-Saxon societies as groups made up of peasants who were self-supporting economically, brought together by ties of "mutual obligation and loyalty," often with family connections. People maintained their stakes in the group with regular contributions. Rulers, often on the order of small chiefs, took tribute in food, labor, and "above all, army service."[57] They obviously offer only one example of authority and varied even across Britain. Groups elsewhere and in other periods could organize around kings or counsels, more structured governing bodies, or representative institutions. We could call those leaders, taken generally, "stakeholders" to capture the variety of ways they anchored groups without implying that "states" engineer every collective activity or act of governing.

Transferring goods between individuals, the agents in the convergence story, is hard enough in a society that is truly illiquid. But individuals can get by in subsistence production, making one-off exchanges, or with idiosyncratic arrangements between reciprocating partners. Mobilizing the material resources and labor of a group is far more difficult. The goal may be defending a territory or taking more of it, clearing and cultivating common space, or policing, educating,

---

[55] Wickham, *The Early Middle Ages*, 308. See, e.g., Naismith, *Money and Power*, 15; Williams, "Coinage in Conversion-Period England," 158–159; Esmonde Cleary, *Ending*, 131; R. Reece, "Models of Continuity," *Oxford Journal of Archaeology* 8, no. 2 (1989). Kenneth Dark reviews the debate and argues for a more developed Romano-Christian culture that survived in Britain until the 7th century. See Dark, *Britain and the End of the Roman Empire*, 10–26.

[56] The number of looms found in England far exceeds those recovered from Gaulish settlements, indicating that each home did its own weaving. Wickham, *The Early Middle Ages*, 809, 307. As Wickham puts it, what was "recession" in Gaul, reversed after AD 500, turned into "catastrophe" in Britain. Wickham, *The Early Middle Ages*, 307.

[57] Wickham, *The Early Middle Ages*, 305, 315, 320–321. Feudal dependencies were a later development.

or caring for people. In early England, the construction of defensive fortifications and bridges was especially common.[58] Whatever the goal and whoever the instigator, a collective enterprise is an enormous challenge in a landscape without liquidity. It requires more than aggregating contributions; it requires collecting and coordinating, evaluating, protecting, preserving, and redistributing them.

Like many other communities, those that emerged in 5th and 6th century England relied heavily on labor drafted from participants and tribute taken in-kind. Charters from the following centuries suggest that kings accepted honey, bread, "ambers" of ale, livestock, cheese, butter, and fish.[59] Those contributions informed their power and the structure of their rule. The early Anglo-Saxon leaders had a practice, for example, of circulating through their territories, a habit that may have been driven by their need to gather support in-kind.[60] That technique must have run into limits given the finite resources of hosting families, and may help explain the small size of many political communities. Larger collective projects would have required a more orchestrated approach. For example, Offa's dyke, a defensive fortification of the 8th century, may have been constructed with labor impressed proportionately across the Mercian territory.[61] Communal undertakings could be organized in other ways—feudal relationships and reciprocal work efforts. But an alternative that appears regularly, across different communities and in very different forms, is making money.

Making money, a phenomenon almost impossible to explain if we limit our field of vision to individuated exchange, becomes easily comprehensible once we enlarge that lens to include the collective activity that links individuals and communities. Stakeholders in the early world, those organizing a group and its resources, had particular need for a medium—but as actors with a unique relationship to those around them, they also had the unmatched capacity to create it. In fact, making money was likely easier than many alternative ways of organizing resources. Money is a way to mark and mobilize material value that can start at the center, work selectively and with limited information, and yet enlist the contributions of a broad group. Contrary to our intuitions, making money requires less political prowess or bureaucratic capacity than orchestrating an initiative by eliciting and redirecting resources, in-kind, from all participants. Conceptualizing money from the clues left behind suggests a process with many variations but a recognizable core.

---

[58] Wickham, *The Early Middle Ages*, 315. The same tasks are emphasized in the later Anglo-Saxon period. See V Aethelred s 1 (1008); Elina Screen, "Anglo-Saxon Law and Numismatics: A Reassessment in the Light of Patrick Wormald's *The Making of English Law*," *British Numismatics Journal* 77 (2007): 169, Appendix.

[59] Wickham, *The Early Middle Ages*, 321.

[60] See D. M. Metcalf, *Thrymsas and Sceattas in the Ashmolean Museum Oxford*, 3 vols., vol. 1 (London: Royal Numismatic Society and Ashmolean Museum Oxford, 1993), 12–13; Naismith, *Money and Power*, 29–30.

[61] David Hill, "The Construction of Offa's Dyke," *The Antiquaries Journal* 65 (1985).

Money is created when a stakeholder uses its singular location at the hub of a community to mark the disparate contributions of individuals in a common way. The moment occurs when the stakeholder takes contributions from people before they are due and gives out uniform receipts in return, each a token intended to document the early contribution. That token, turned in later at a time of reckoning, operates to convert goods and services that were not previously interchangeable or fungible—the variety of contributions due to the center—into matters counted in a standard unit. The initiative requires only one more twist to make money fully operational: if the stakeholder recognizes the receipt and takes it from anyone's hand as an item that exonerates the person holding it from making a contribution otherwise due, the receipt can travel from hand-to-hand and maintain its worth as an item that pays off the center. The result is a token that fixes or entails value in a way that both the stakeholder and individuals can use, a novel accomplishment in a world without an agreed-upon way to measure and transfer resources.

An example makes the strategy more concrete. A small Anglo-Saxon ruler of the early 7th century may have taken goods and labor regularly from a thousand families on rounds of the territory they all inhabited. Facing a threat from another community, however, he might at one point draft extraordinary services and supplies from a hundred of them, rewarding them with tokens to recognize that their contributions had been double that ordinarily due and promising to take back the tokens in the future, each one in lieu of the next quota of tribute. The families could set aside the tokens, satisfied to know that they had fulfilled an obligation in advance. Or, willing to resume giving tribute to their chief on the next round, they could pass their tokens on to another person or family—there may be many takers willing to give value (goods, labor, loyalty, etc.) for a token. Those new families may prefer giving resources now to paying tribute later; they will set their token aside to give the ruler when their quota is due. Or they may make the exchange because they anticipate that they can use the token in another trade. Never before could they depend upon having an item to which virtually everyone else in the community would attribute substantive value. Now, every person has reason to look to the tokens as a meaningful measure, store of (real) value, and mode of payment that can change hands.

Unpacking the example illustrates the way money functions for both the stakeholder and participants. First, the strategy provides the community, acting in the figure of its ruler, an effective way to mobilize goods and services because the token entails real value. Each token awarded by the stakeholder represents actual resources that have been given to the center. Each token has, in that sense, a material referent: the token was given to mark an amount of goods or labor contributed and it will, according to the terms of the system set out above, exonerate someone later from a contribution of the same dimension.[62] A successfully working money thus carries or fixes material value within each token, whether that money is made of silver or paper, whether it takes a commodity or a "fiat" form. In fact, the material referent of a token will be made "real" in physical terms if need be. If those owing contribution to a stakeholder do not pay with a token, they will make their usual contribution in-kind. Later systems may be more completely monetized, so that revenue is expected in cash. But if a debtor to the system does not pay, an authority will confiscate other goods—houses, capital, or earnings—to make good the obligation. The obligations that support a money can take many forms—tribute, rents, fees, tithes, or penalties. But given that taxes most powerfully anchor modern monetary regimes, we can for simplicity call the material referent of a token its "fiscal value."

Entailing value in a token allows a stakeholder to command resources with great effect. The stakeholder can "buy" what it needs when it needs them, paying in receipts that it takes back later. In effect, the stakeholder gains the capacity to spend and tax *in* money *as* it makes money. The stakeholder can spend heavily on one good, labor or military service, while taxing or taking tribute widely. The soldiers or suppliers earning extra tokens in the example above would have reason to trade them to others for goods or services. Those others, owing tribute, tax, fees, or other contributions to the center, could sell the soldiers and suppliers up to the same amount of material they otherwise owe the center. The tokens would enter the community when the stakeholder paid for particular goods, radiate through the group as they circulated, and then return as people offered them to the center instead of other, in-kind contributions. Although it dealt with only a narrow group of suppliers, the stakeholder would thus draw on a broad catchment of contributions.

Depending on how the strategy was managed, it could move the community towards highly monetized dealings: as the stakeholder "spent" heavily at the outset, it would take in more tokens and less tribute of other kinds at the time of reckoning. Eventually, a community could run its public affairs purely by taxing and spending. On the other hand, the strategy could also be a limited initiative, one that reached only certain circles of people. For example, a ruler might pay for certain supplies in tokens, which could come to travel in near proximity to those sellers—merchants, for example, in towns. At the same time, he might continue to require contributions from peasants in goods or labor. Monetary initiatives that were partial or selective in this sense would help produce the dichotomized payment patterns that appear in many societies.[63]

---

[62] For fine-tuning of the contribution's size, which might be lightened in return for its being given in advance, see p. 45 n. 64.

[63] See, e.g., Mark S. Peacock, "Accounting for Money: The Legal Presuppositions of Money and Accounting in Ancient Greece," *Business History* 55, no. 3 (2013): 283–284 (describing specialized exchange between palace and merchants in early Mesopotamia).

The point here is that a stakeholder greatly expands its capacity when it can mobilize resources as it chooses. Money, it will turn out, is an enormously effective mode of governing.

A number of economists have modeled money in ways that confirm its fiscal value. They suggest that money can be conceptualized as an asset or, more precisely, the claim to an asset, that holds value according to the utility people anticipate it will have in extinguishing a future tax obligation. A government can spend by giving people currency that is, basically, a credit good for paying upcoming taxes (or tribute, as in our original example). As long as the government convinces people that it will reliably tax in the notes it has spent— redeeming them, in effect—the notes will hold value equal at least to their future expected value to pay the tax.[64] Comparing money to a financial asset backed by a future revenue stream, the "asset-pricing" approach evokes in its name the importance of money's material referent.[65] Post-Keynesian "functional finance" theories may likewise be read to argue that the government can expand the money supply in real terms by spending and taxing.[66]

But even more classic approaches, those arguing that money is always a medium and not an asset, generate a similar insight. According to these theories, money holds value insofar as demand for it as a medium remains constant relative to its nominal supply, all else equal (an assumption carried forward throughout). When a government adds to the currency in circulation and demand for it does not increase, money will lose value. If, however, the government credibly commits at the same time to contracting the quantity of money in the future, demand for money will rise as people anticipate its approaching scarcity, controlling the effect of the expansion. That is because when individuals,

---

[64] Note that the expected value attributed to money would include a discount, if money is used only as a device to satisfy a future obligation. See pp. 47–48. More generally, see, e.g., Thomas J. Sargent, "The Ends Of Four Big Inflations," in *Conference on Inflation* (Washington, D.C.: National Bureau of Economic Research, 1981); Bruce D. Smith, "American Colonial Monetary Regimes: The Failure of the Quantity Theory and Some Evidence of an Alternate View," *Canadian Journal of Economics* 18, no. 3 (1985); Charles W. Calomiris, "Institutional Failure, Monetary Scarcity, and the Depreciation of the Continental," *Journal of Economic History* 48, no. 1 (1988); Bruce D. Smith, "Money and Inflation in Colonial Massachusetts," in *Quarterly Review (Federal Reserve Bank of Minneapolis)* 26, no. 4 (Fall 2002). A number of asset-pricing models were developed to explain the success of early American bills of credit. Farley Grubb, the scholar with the widest knowledge about and range of data from the colonial era, models paper money as a zero-coupon bond. Although he does not use the terminology of asset-pricing, his instrument holds value contingent on its future redemption. See, e.g., Farley Grubb, "Is Paper Money Just Paper Money? Experimentation and Local Variation in the Fiat Monies Issued by the Colonial Governments of British North America, 1690–1775," *NBER Working Papers*, no. 17997 (2012); Farley Grubb, "Specie Scarcity and Efficient Barter: The Problem of Maintaining an Outside Money Supply in British Colonial America," ed. Christine Desan, in *Inside Money* (Philadelphia: University of Pennsylvania Press, forthcoming 2015).

[65] For this terminology, see Smith, "American Colonial Monetary Regimes," 533; Sargent, "The Ends of Four Big Inflations," 5.

[66] See, e.g., Abba P. Lerner, "Functional Finance and the Federal Debt," *Social Research* 20, no. 1 (1943), reprinted in D. Colander, ed., *Selected Economic Writings of Abba Lerner* (New York: New York University Press, 1983).

confronted with an increase in the money supply, confidently anticipate that the supply will be reduced at a particular point, they will build that assumption into their calculations of monetary value. The increased money supply will be offset by an increase in demand produced as holders, assuming that prices will be dropping as money is withdrawn, decide to hold more money to benefit from the deflation that they predict.[67]

Just as the asset-pricing approach predicted that money would hold its future expected value to pay the tax, classic approaches predict that money will hold value relative to "its expected value as a medium of exchange" given the quantity of money and the demand for it when the money is withdrawn. Theorists in this tradition argue that people are considering the government's "promise regarding the future path of the money stock," along with the expected demand that promise produces, when they calculate future expected value. But the "promise" at issue is the commitment to tax (or take in the money by fees, tithes, or otherwise) made after the act of expansion by way of spending. Consistent with this approach as well then, we could refer to money having a value fixed or entailed by the fiscal system.

Second and distinct from its fiscal value, money holds value because it offers a countable measure that can be transferred to make final payments. Its identity as a token carrying real value is not limited to the person paid. Once authorities at the center have agreed to take the token back from anyone's hand in payment of an in-kind quota, others will recognize it as a standard value cognizable to themselves and to those around them. For the first time in a society without money, there is a unit that represents material value relevant to everyone (or virtually everyone), given their common relationship to the stakeholder. That opens up the possibility of new exchange: people who owe the center regular tribute might rather deal with one of the soldiers or suppliers holding tokens. They could trade goods to him and keep the token to satisfy their future obligation to the center. Or people might trade for a token because they know they can use the token to make another trade; others will take the token if they want to use it to pay the center or for their own productive transactions.

The tokens offer an exclusive quality in this otherwise illiquid world, the quality of cash. They provide a measure of recognized value or unit of account, thus making prices possible. They operate to transfer that value as a medium

---

[67] See Scott Sumner, "Colonial Currency and the Quantity Theory of Money: A Critique of Smith's Interpretation," *Journal of Economic History* 53, no. 1 (1993); see also Peter Bernholz, "Inflation, Monetary Regime and the Financial Asset Theory of Money," *Kyklos* 41, (1988). Note that economy-wide prices may rise initially but only to the level that allows holders of currency to receive the real interest rate (the rate to be gained on a safe investment elsewhere) through deflation of prices (the appreciation of money) to the date on which the currency is expected to contract. If prices rose any higher, people would sell products to get money (thus appreciating its value and lowering prices) because its anticipated increase in value would be greater than returns on other investments elsewhere. Sumner, "Colonial Currency," 142. See p. 47.

when they travel hand-to-hand. And they accomplish payment unconditionally: because they entail value that the stakeholder as a third party recognizes, parties who are strangers can use them to pay others and complete the transaction without further relations. Between the time a token is issued and the time it is retired, then, the token furnishes interim services as cash to individuals.

The premium that people attach to tokens—we might call it a "cash premium" in recognition of the services that cash provides—is just as substantive as the fiscal value of tokens. In order to see the materiality of the cash premium, we need only acknowledge that a person might choose to make a contribution early to the stakeholder in order to acquire a token because of the utility of the token. In effect, the person will be advancing the time value of a contribution for the cash services of the token. Normally, people will decline to provide work or goods before they are due. Working up front for themselves instead of another allows them to make investments—planting seeds, for example—that will be productive later. If, however, money offers services to people that are themselves productive, then some people will work for money before the tribute they owe is due. In our example, making a contribution early for a token might allow a farmer to use the token to buy fertilizer, labor, or a different kind of seed not otherwise available to him. Others might come to the same conclusion—they may sell goods or labor to the farmer before their contribution is due to the center because they want to use the token in the meantime. (This is not to deny that some stakeholders with enough power could force an early contribution. It is just to assert that force is not the only reason people might advance work or goods for money.)

In fact, the cash premium that people attach to money means that they are often willing to buy money directly from a stakeholder, without waiting for that source to spend units into circulation. Free minting, described below, provided one method by which governments sold individuals money for bullion during the medieval period. Later governments arranged other ways to provide money creation on demand, including selling people Exchequer bills or extending them money loans in public bills of credit.[68] Most famously, in the modern era, the government licenses commercial banks to act as agents authorized to multiply the sovereign unit of account. Each method allows people to expand the number of units circulating beyond that produced by the fiscal activity of the stakeholder or government at the center, supplementing the amount of money generated by public spending alone. Each approach has also raised complex questions about how the supplementary money—money created to respond to people's demand for cash services—is tied to the sovereign unit of account established by public fiscal activity and supported by taxpayers. To get far

[68] Exchequer bills are discussed at pp. 339–341. For an example of public lending via bills of credit, see Theodore Thayer, "The Land-Bank System in the American Colonies," *Journal of Economic History* 13, no. 2 (1953).

ahead of our history, that issue is one way to understand the tumultuous history
of commercial banking and, most recently, the financial crisis of 2008.[69]

Again, a number of economic models confirm that cash provides services for
which people will advance the time value of resources. Recall that asset-pricing
models describe the fiscal value of money as its expected future value in extinguishing a tax obligation. That logic explains why a token that offers tax exoneration holds real value. It also predicts, however, that people will discount that
value: a token that works to pay off an obligation due next year or five years from
now is worth something less than the value of that obligation today.[70] That
prediction is qualified by one circumstance: if money is a productive asset—
one that provides significant services—people will hold it without discounting
it.[71] After all, they are getting a return from money in the form of the cash
services it provides. The classic models (those approaching money as a medium,
not an asset) make the same prediction and include the same qualification.[72] In
other words, the discount we would expect if people value money only because
of a future condition is washed out by the premium we would expect if people
recognized as valuable its services as cash in the interim.[73] To the extent that
is true, the value of money—and therefore prices across the economy—remain
stable.

[69] For a sample of approaches that attend to the issue of how governments enable and otherwise relate to
money creation by banks and shadow banks, see Ricks, "Money Creation"; Gary Gorton, *Slapped by the
Invisible Hand: The Panic of 2007*, Financial Management Association Survey and Synthesis Series (New
York: Oxford University Press, 2010).

[70] Again, the time value of resources is at work. Rather than having a token that is non-productive, a
person would rather have the goods or resources that it represents in the year to come. Those goods or
resources could be put to use fruitfully whereas, if the token is only a fiscal asset, it provides no other
services. The asset-pricing models assume, therefore, that people who hold money only as a fiscal asset will
discount its value by the real interest rate—the rate of other productive assets. See, e.g., Grubb, "Paper
Money," 18–27; Calomiris, "Institutional Failure," 65–68. If a stakeholder were operating non-coercively, it
would respect the discount by providing a token that would exonerate someone from a future obligation,
but take a lower in-kind contribution than would be due if the person who owed it provided it at the usual
time.

[71] See, e.g., Calomiris, "Institutional Failure," 51–52, 65–68.

[72] As above, these models assume that there may be inflation on the issue of additional money that is to
be withdrawn in the future. According to this prediction, inflation will be contained because holders of
currency anticipate returns through deflation of prices to the date on which the currency is expected to
contract. Sumner, "Colonial Currency," 142. The qualification follows: If people are getting services from
money (they prefer to take it in exchange), demand for it will negate a loss in money's value. That is, people
will not require a return from it, and prices will not rise when the money supply expands but will remain
stable (or, to the extent that people forgo a return, money will remain more stable). Sumner, "Colonial
Currency," 142.

[73] Both the asset value and the cash premium are time-sensitive, in ways that offset each other.
Discounting an asset against its future value means that an asset is worth the least far out from the time
of use, and becomes progressively more valuable as that time approaches. See, e.g., Grubb, "Paper Money."
Imputing value to an asset because it provides cash services during a certain period implies that the asset
will be worth the most at the beginning of the period, when its capacity to enable trade is at a peak. As the
period draws to a close, the premium fades because the asset is losing capacity to facilitate trades, which take
time to find and arrange.

Recognizing the cash premium attached to money makes sense of the empirical evidence collected on early America, a relatively simple monetary terrain with money made by tax anticipation and limited forms of circulating credit. Legislatures there made stable money in a cash-poor environment when they spent "bills of credit" into circulation as long as they taxed in the bills reliably and settlers used them as money in the meantime.[74]

Mapping the fiscal value of money and its cash premium reveals that they share a structural relationship. Money depends on a basic pact: participants advance the time value of a resource owed to a stakeholder in return for that actor's unique ability to create cash—a way to fix material value in a unit that can be used as a measure, a mode of unconditioned payment, and a medium. There is much more to be explored here: if money is thus engineered, we would expect that its value would change according to how much utility people anticipated it would have for paying taxes and how much value it would hold because of its cash quality.[75] The point for present purposes is that money is a material matter. It entails resources represented by the obligation at stake, enhanced by cash services delivered because of its form. Each of those aspects flows from interventions in the real world—the tribute or taxing regimes put in place by a community and the rules that instill negotiability. The result, money, is far from neutral. "The market" that takes shape is, in turn, a function of a particular money. In many ways, the history that follows is the story of how money and "the market" have changed dramatically over time.

Money's working logic reveals another aspect of its materiality. Producing money involves a deal over matters of real value: people advance the time value of their own goods and labor in return for a stakeholder's peculiar ability to create money. The stakeholder's gains are substantive—creating money "pays" in the ability of that agent to use the resources advanced in exchange for a token. There is no sleight of hand. While the stakeholder is gaining an advance of resources, it is granting in return a capacity, also a matter of substantive value, that no individuals engaged in only bipolar exchange can create. Neither can we categorize money as "neutral" in the sense that it is costless to produce or that its costs

---

[74] Here, see sources cited at p. 45 n. 64 and p. 46 n. 67.

[75] Issues raised by discounting turn on how people gauge the time of taxation relative to spending. Tokens that "expired" at a certain moment would invite discounting towards that moment. Most communities using money roll issue and retirement dates and allow any token to be used for any obligation. Those conditions reduce the discount that people attach to money. See, e.g., Grubb, "Paper Money." The same timing innovations reduce the swings in money's value that would occur as people assessed the amount of time that its cash services would last (although in contrast to the value that flows from its fiscal utility, the value of money that flows from its cash services would diminish, not rise towards the retirement point). The size of the cash premium that people attach to money also depends on how much they value the cash services of money: if there is plenty of cash circulating, people will not attach a cash premium to money if more is issued. In that case, they will take money only at a discount, charging more for goods or services. Put another way, money will hold only its fiscal value and no cash premium. According to the models of money under these conditions, it will gain value (prices will fall) over time as money is retired by being taxed in. For these and other effects, see, e.g., Grubb, "Paper Money"; Calomiris, "Institutional Failure."

are spread without distributive effect. Rather, the process allocates expenses and profits across many parties, including the tax-paying public, those buying money for its cash services, and the stakeholder—who can be a small ruler, a sovereign state, or an agent like a bank licensed to multiply the public unit of account. The point here is that the terms of the deal matter. Money is a medium constructed publicly with costs and profits that are material. "Making money" has been a profoundly important and deeply contested project over English history—and in countless other communities.

That project takes us back to the history. The English experience provided the stage for the alternative creation story; if that story captures the way money works, it should illuminate the drama we find. The story starts with money creation and extends to the market that money makes.

Contextualizing money creation

Conditions in early Britain support the argument that money is fiscally engineered and produces cash services for individuals. Recall that Roman authorities structured their highly monetized economy on a fiscal base. Imperial spending sent Roman coin into circulation across the Empire; tax levies assured every user along the way that imperial units of account would remain in demand. In fact, contracts in Roman law carried only money damages; officials recognized no other medium as a mode of payment. At its height, the Roman code enforced the unit of account in purely "nominal" terms—the amount of silver in a coin mattered not at all relative to that coin's unit value, decreed at the center.[76] That practice did not deter individuals from exchange. According to a number of scholars, the strength of Roman assumptions that money was defined by the official unit and the extent of the imperial economy moved together.[77]

The "catastrophe" that followed Rome's withdrawal from Britain registered in the collapse of material exchange among inhabitants. Indeed, according to Simon Esmonde Cleary, England was more completely devastated than other territories precisely because its economy was so intimately intertwined with the Roman fiscal machinery.[78] For the next two centuries, coin virtually ceased to function as money in Britain.[79] Despite a heritage of moneyed exchange and residual coin, people lived of their own; we might imagine that when money arrived, they would attach a premium to the exchange it made possible. At the same time, the services of cash take more to reproduce, apparently, than the memory and even

---

[76] "Nominalism," as such a rule is traditionally known, implies that the practice is formalistic; to the contrary, the unit decreed is established by the center to pay off the tax obligation. See pp. 84–85, 133–134.

[77] See pp. 84–85, 133–134.   [78] Esmonde Cleary, *Ending*, 138–161.

[79] See p. 39. In fact, the traces of money use that remained may have depended on organized taxing-and-spending. See Abdy, "After Patching," 84–86; cf. Williams, "Coinage in Conversion-Period England," 159–160.

the example of surviving units; as far as we know, no media of exchange came gradually to the fore. According to scholars extrapolating from a scant record, political authority reached a low ebb after the end of the Roman period. The territory was highly fragmented and rulers were weak.[80]

Reviewing the archaeological record, Chris Wickham argues that the initial "turning-point" in the "reconstruction of political power" in Anglo-Saxon lands occurred in the late 6th century. Evidence from that period includes burials designed to show off significant wealth and, in the 7th century, settlements became slightly more structured. Political organization was still simple, but early in the century, small Anglo-Saxon kingdoms doubled in size and became more hierarchically organized. Tribute owed to rulers remained varied and modest, but was well entrenched. It included rent, dues, military service, and other forms of obligation. Chris Loveluck finds evidence of richer economic activity including imported ceramics, tools, glass, and metalware along the coast in the end of the 7th century. Signs of productive exchange and importing increase in the early decades of the 8th century, especially in East Anglia, Kent, and Wessex.[81]

Locally made coins, gold shillings often called thrymsas, appear in the midst of those developments, sometime near the beginning of the 7th century.[82] They may not, of course, have been the money first invented by Anglo-Saxon communities after the earlier collapse. The unit of account used by a community need not be coin. If the material referent of money is an obligation owed and the enhancing attribute of money is its cash quality, paper can function as well as coin to provide money. The Anglo-Saxon kings may have experimented with money made of wood, revitalized old Roman tokens, or tried other ways of recording credits, leaving no permanent record of a contemporary money. Those media could have circulated among selective circles, elites for example, creating cultures that would later be lumped under "gift-exchange" because the "money" made there fits only awkwardly with our more monochromatic expectation about what "money" is. In fact, money's working logic invites many variations that blur the overdrawn dichotomy between "money" and "gift" economies.[83]

---

[80] See, e.g., Wickham, *The Early Middle Ages*, 313–314, 320–325, 332–333; Carlo M. Cipolla, *Money, Prices, and Civilization in the Mediterranean World, Fifth to Seventeenth Century* (New York: Gordian Press, 1967); cf. Naismith, *Money and Power*, 18–19; Metcalf, *Thrymsas and Sceattas*, 12–13. Wales and Ireland have different patterns of development, beyond the reach of this narrative. See, e.g., Wickham, *The Early Middle Ages*, 351–354.

[81] Wickham, *The Early Middle Ages*, 315, 320–323, 340–342; Christopher Loveluck, "A High-status Anglo-Saxon Settlement at Flixborough, Lincolnshire," *Antiquities* 72 (1998): 157–158; see also Williams, "Coinage in Conversion-Period England," 153–154 (noting emergence of Anglo-Saxon kingdoms amidst continuous trading across North Sea).

[82] Williams, "Coinage in Conversion-Period England," 157, 188. "Thrymsas," an Old English variant on the Roman coin tremissis, may be a label mistakenly adopted in the scholarship for the coin that contemporaries would have called shillings. See Metcalf, *Thrymsas and Sceattas*, 29, n. 4.

[83] The idea of a "gift economy" strongly differentiated from a money economy is powerfully articulated by a series of authors. See, e.g., Polanyi, *Great Transformation*; Philip Grierson, *The Origins of Money*

Having said that, coin solves an important problem that bedevils many monetary initiatives. To the extent that money circulates physically—and that property has been essential in many worlds, including our own—the tokens representing the unit of account must be both durable and difficult to imitate. Otherwise, they will be either lost or multiplied without a stakeholder's permission, disturbing the balance between outflow and inflow, supply and demand, tax credit and tax redemption that creates stable value. (While counterfeiting is the far more famous threat, note that the loss of tokens because of their fragility or decay would be just as destructive.) One solution is a token made of material that is rare, imperishable, and takes skill to work. Given such commodity content, a stakeholder need only control the means of producing tokens and the system can function.[84] In fact, a stakeholder with enough authority could impose the costs of production on those obligated to it. The stakeholder need only ask for at least some of its tribute in tokens made from the commodity and available from centralized sources at a fee. The sources will issue commodity tokens in return for commodity supplied by individuals, less the fee taken in tokens.

Coins—tokens made of precious metal—are the obvious example. Objects made of silver or gold hold a place among the wealthy in many communities as ornaments, medallions, or fancy plate. They may be offered in reward or recognition, a role that the stakeholder could institutionalize at the center. Adding the requirement that elite members contribute at least some kinds of tribute in precious metal, refined and standardized by craftsmen directed by the king, would follow comfortably. In the late Roman Empire, gifts of gold from aristocrats to the emperor on his succession had been "regularized" as a tax.[85] The system would then produce the coin required to pay some obligations in money. In addition, the craftsmen could provide additional coin to those willing to buy it for their own purposes with bullion. Made according to this logic, the political character of money is not at odds with its "commercial" use. To the contrary, the money-making practice of the later Anglo-Saxon world looks very like this prototype—money was a royal monopoly that supplied money for both public and private use. Its antecedents in the 7th century are unavoidably speculative— but the evidence is suggestive nonetheless.[86]

(London: Athlone, 1977). For an insightful argument that the polarity has been overdrawn, see Naismith, *Money and Power*, 259–267. Chris Loveluck similarly points out the complexities that "exchange" might entail, although he identifies coin more narrowly with "profit-" or "market-" led transactions. Loveluck, Dobney, and Barrett, "Trade and Exchange—The Settlement and the Wider World," 124–129.

[84] The argument developed here means that the unit of account is not an abstraction. In money systems that employ commodity content, the unit of account takes a material shape; it is not an arithmetic formality. For supporting evidence that the unit of account in early coin systems was identified with certain anchoring coins, see p. 58 n. 116.

[85] See Esmonde Cleary, *Ending*, 8–9.

[86] See pp. 60–61 for discussion of later Anglo-Saxon minting.

Gold shillings appear throughout eastern and southern England early in the 7th century. Initially found mixed with Merovingian imports, they imitated those coins as well as Roman examples in design. Gradually growing in proportion to foreign coin, they turn up across a region so broad as to indicate that they were used for more than external trade. Their numbers, small compared to those on the Continent, were nevertheless significant: using die evidence, Gareth Williams estimates that there may have been tens of thousands extant at their peak.[87]

Gold shillings played a varied set of roles. Pierced, adorned with loops, or mounted, many clearly functioned as jewelry. They may have been used as amulets and turn up in graves regularly. They provided treasure for foreign trade, as well as high-status items for gifts and displays of prestige. On the more utilitarian side, they acted as standard-setting weights.[88] Many coins carry Christian imagery; they appear during England's conversion period and may have been considered important religious symbols. Motifs evocative of Roman authority are even more pervasive. Throughout the medieval period, political officials and aspiring rulers sought to identify their administrations with Rome's power and prestige. Indeed, Christian and Roman heritage were highly fused during this period. Williams argues that the Church promoted notions of "Romanized Christian kingship," including the issue of coins and the introduction of written law as signs of godly rule.[89]

Whether early gold coin circulated as money has been more contested, in part because the finds of this period came to light in hoards or graves; those contexts suggest they had a ritual role or served to display status.[90] Moreover, gold coin would have been far too valuable to change hands in everyday exchange, nor are the surviving coins nearly numerous enough to suggest that reach. On the other hand, more single coins have recently been unearthed along with multiples in productive sites, consistent with their use in exchange. Coins found outside of burial sites are far less likely to have been made into jewelry. Ornamental uses also decline over the 7th century.[91] Many gold coins are highly standardized in content, an oddity if their aesthetics were of overriding importance. After mid-century, "pale gold" debased coin appears and some evidence indicates a drop in

---

[87] Williams, "Coinage in Conversion-Period England," 145–146, 153–154, 169–173, 185, 188; see also Richard Abdy and Gareth Williams, "A Catalogue of Hoards and Single Finds from the British Isles c. AD 410–675," in *Coinage and History in the North Sea World, c. 500–1250* (Leiden: Koninklijke Brill NV, 2006), 11–73; Gannon, *Iconography*, 10–12.

[88] Williams, "Coinage in Conversion-Period England," 161–173, 187–188, 190; Metcalf, *Thrymsas and Sceattas*, 37.

[89] Gannon, *Iconography*, 10–12; Williams, "Coinage in Conversion-Period England," 186–188. On the profound importance of religious and political imagery to early medieval authorities, see also Naismith, *Money and Power*, 39–41, 45–72.

[90] See, e.g., Philip Grierson, "The Purpose of the Sutton Hoo Coins," *Antiquity* 44 (1970); see also Philip Grierson et al., *Medieval European Coinage: With a Catalogue of the Coins in the Fitzwilliam Museum, Cambridge* (Cambridge: Cambridge University Press, 1986), 159–164.

[91] See Abdy and Williams, "Hoards and Single Finds"; Williams, "Coinage in Conversion-Period England," 169, 188–189.

metal content that was sudden and consistent. While scholars disagree about whether gold coin traveled at face value, later communities would debase coin in times of metal scarcity to make it go further as a unit of account.[92]

The circumstances fit the stakeholder story neatly, although some scholars assert that private moneyers established shillings according to a Merovingian example.[93] Anglo-Saxon rulers could have copied Continental coin, perhaps even making the first issues for ceremonial or special use, or for foreign trade. The exchange of coin as a sign of political loyalty or reward would follow easily, especially in cultures where tribute and gift-giving was varied but well established. As in the Roman case, gold coin in England could serve as a mode of tribute within certain circles or for particular purposes, depending on how it was institutionalized. It would thus link kings and elites, and travel between elites to make larger transfers of wealth possible—nothing about the royal production of coin or its basis in a regime of obligation conflicts with its use in private exchange for commercial ends. To the contrary, the public engineering of money structures it sufficiently to create demand by individuals.

Royally directed production would explain the uniformity of the coins.[94] Systemic debasement would fit with the model as well, carried out as rulers struggled to keep up a practice of coin's use. The signals that gold coin was closely associated with political authority—the Roman and Christian iconography characteristic of the coins—make perfect sense under these conditions. Gold coin would be an assertion by increasingly ambitious rulers that had royal uses and symbolic importance, as well as practical value for individuals.[95] Suitably, fines stated in shillings appear in Aethelberht's law code of 600; the usage identifies the king's authority with the unit, whether or not people paid off penalties in other material.[96]

A similar dynamic, writ more broadly, accords with the great surge in silver coinage that followed. "Sceattas," or early silver pennies ("paeningas" or "denarii") appear near the end of the 7th century, just as gold coin fades and signs of richer economic activity increase.[97] These early coins are abundant; Rory

[92] See Metcalf, *Thrymsas and Sceattas*, 39–40, 42–43; Williams, "Coinage in Conversion-Period England," 172–173, 182, 190. Even under regimes enforcing nominal coin values, gold coin was often passed by its commodity content, given its enormous value.

[93] For the argument that coin use in Merovingian Gaul was privately engineered and scholarship skeptical of that conclusion, compare Grierson et al., *Medieval European Coinage*, 158–159, and Naismith, *Money and Power*, 37–41, 142–145, with Metcalf, *Thrymsas and Sceattas*, 24–25, and Williams, "Coinage in Conversion-Period England."

[94] As Michael Metcalf points out, there were large issues of certain coin types. Metcalf, *Thrymsas and Sceattas*, 12.

[95] Wickham argues that such exchange as did occur in early Anglo-Saxon areas was embedded in political relationships. Although he may not have money in mind, that character would comport with the anchor of money in political authority. See Wickham, *The Early Middle Ages*, 808–810.

[96] See Williams, "Coinage in Conversion-Period England," 189; Wickham, *The Early Middle Ages*, 343.

[97] Naismith, *Money and Power*, 264.

Naismith speculates that sceattas may have been "the most plentiful currency" that medieval England produced until the late 12th century.[98] Exchange remained a largely elite activity in 8th century England, one centered on domestic, even subregional, networks; foreign trade did not drive economy activity as much as "the ultimate motor...landed and fiscal demand."[99] Silver coin, still a high value for subsistence populations, would nevertheless reach many more transactions than gold by those somewhat better off and would have been within the reach of more communities to produce.[100] If gold coin traveled in too circumscribed a way to create much monetary currency, sceattas could penetrate further, both as a medium between rulers and those obligated to them and in exchange generally.[101]

In fact, sceattas come with a great variety of imprints, a golden age for iconography on coins. To some scholars, that plethora and the fact that many coins bear moneyers' names seems evidence that making money was a private industry.[102] The same evidence, however, suggests just as easily that many communities had started making coin. As Michael Metcalf puts it, "one kingdom—one coinage," explains the pattern in most of England. Along the coast, he adds that "one wic—one coin" might be a better description, referring to the coast towns where exchange was particularly extensive. But those towns too were within royal authority, as were moneyers. Minting, Metcalf notes, took place in "kingdoms closely governed."[103] The large-scale production of some dies and of sceattas themselves supports that conclusion.[104] Much of the imagery on coins remains royal: there are diademed busts, helmeted figures, and heraldic animals including lions, hawks, and eagles.[105] Religious iconography continues important, a vocabulary essential to kingship in the period (see Fig. 1.1).[106]

---

[98] Naismith, *Money and Power*, 5. As of 2010, more than 2,800 single coins had been found. Naismith, *Money and Power*, 5.

[99] Wickham, *The Early Middle Ages*, 818, 822–823.

[100] For the continued link between elite wealth and exchange, especially domestic trade, see Wickham, *The Early Middle Ages*, 706–707, 822–824.

[101] Rory Naismith contrasts Rome's tax-driven money with the more varied drivers of early Anglo-Saxon coin. A centrally anchored money can be fueled by many types of obligations, including fees, rents, dues, and tolls, as well as taxes. See Naismith, *Money and Power*, 37–39.

[102] Naismith, *Money and Power*, 37–41; Grierson et al., *Medieval European Coinage*, 158–159. The assumption draws on the traditional interpretation of Merovingian coinage in Gaul as privately produced. See p. 54 n. 93.

[103] Metcalf, *Thrymsas and Sceattas*, 3, 12–13, 16–17, 22–24; see also Gannon, *Iconography*, 15–17. For the greater exchange complexity in eastern England, see Wickham, *The Early Middle Ages*, 342, 809–810.

[104] Metcalf, *Thrymsas and Sceattas*, 12.

[105] See Gannon, *Iconography*; Metcalf, *Thrymsas and Sceattas*, 13–14.

[106] See Gannon, *Iconography*, 31–33, 185–191; Naismith, *Money and Power*, 57–62. Ecclesiastical coinage probably also occurred at the sufferance of the king; bishops and other clerics had less political autonomy in England than across the channel. See Wickham, *The Early Middle Ages*, 346; Metcalf, *Thrymsas and Sceattas*, 14. Having said that, the Church like other collectives had the structural position to create a medium by acting as a stakeholder and orchestrating a medium for use within its payment community.

Fig. 1.1 A Northumbrian sceatta, c. 675–750, with eagle and fledgling, perhaps in reference to Deuteronomy 32:11 as prefiguration of Christ as saviour. ©Fitzwilliam Museum, Cambridge; see Gannon, *Iconography*, 114–115.

Fig. 1.2 Light coinage of Offa, King of Mercia, produced under moneyer Ibba at London, c. 780–795. ©Trustees of The British Museum.

In the second half of the 8th century, a series of Anglo-Saxon kings made their authority over coinage unambiguous. They struck their names and titles into coin, successfully set standards for weight and fineness, and supervised moneyers within their kingdoms; some effectively patrolled for foreign coin, requiring it to be reminted (see Fig. 1.2).[107] Dues and required contributions became heavier

---

[107] See Naismith, *Money and Power*, 96–112, 126, 128–140, 168–180, 293–295. The Mercian king, Offa, was particularly effective on that score. See Naismith, *Money and Power*, 206–209; Metcalf, *Thrymsas and Sceattas*, 16–17. Fifty percent of well-preserved coins from the period 757–865 weigh within .10 gram of others from the same phase of minting, as judged by Naismith. Naismith, *Money and Power*, 170. Occasionally, the uniformity of coin did break down; Offa's move to a heavier penny in about 792 or 793 occurred after an era of debasement and imposed a new order that was maintained for most of the 9th century. Naismith, *Money and Power*, 96, 101–106.

throughout the period. There is evidence that in-kind payment of rents began to be converted in part into cash payments during the 8th century, a trend that would continue in later centuries, and the late 8th century Mercian king Offa extended tribute obligations to virtually "everyone" in his territory.[108]

Coin use, first efflorescent when the early silver sceattas began circulating, bloomed again from the late 790s through the 830s, contemporaneous with the strengthening of royal control over the coinage. Single finds of coins minted between 757 and 865 now number more than 1,000.[109] Many such coins have come to light in the country, beyond the towns or sites that would have been home to merchants, clergy, and aristocrats, and are most common to the east and south. Those were areas of more extensive domestic and foreign trade, although not the territories in which the early Anglo-Saxon kings spent most of their time.[110] Assuming coin was a politically orchestrated medium, it was clearly being used for much private exchange. Native coins predominate increasingly over Carolingian imports, but appear promiscuously across local boundaries; Rory Naismith suggests that English kings generally observed a monetary "entente cordiale" among themselves. As he concludes, the patterns and "sheer volume" of coinage reveal "vibrant minting and monetary circulation" across the period, including middle- and long-distance travel.[111] Judging by evidence from the next century, these new pennies probably traveled at face value; coins of slightly different silver content turn up together as if all remained in circulation.[112]

The monetary reforms of these kings coincided with the further consolidation of English territory in the kingdoms of Mercia, East Anglia, Kent, Northumbria, and Wessex; Wickham calls the 8th century an era of "political recomposition," and notes the expanding ability of kings to mobilize resources.[113] The broad thin pennies issued from the end of the century in the southern kingdoms would, with Carolingian pennies that may have been their model, become the norm for European coinage across the medieval era.[114] The moment is a good one to

---

[108] Wickham, *The Early Middle Ages*, 349–351, 378; Naismith, *Money and Power*, 23–30, 36, 277–280.

[109] Naismith, *Money and Power*, 209, 231–232. There are over 1,300 if foreign coins are included, and more than 4,000 if the period is extended to back to pick up the early surge in silver sceattas. Naismith, *Money and Power*, 199–202, 255. Early silver sceattas had faded in use during a period of debasement in the mid-8th century. Naismith, *Money and Power*, 5–6, 96.

[110] Naismith, *Money and Power*, 203–210, 229. Northumbrian use of coin also flourished, although it remained more geographically restricted. It was increasingly debased in the mid-9th century, a pattern that may have allowed it effectively to reach smaller transactions. See Naismith, *Money and Power*, 210, 247–248. For more discussion of such dynamics, see pp. 122–125.

[111] Naismith, *Money and Power*, 209, 218, 252, 258, 278. On agricultural development during the period, see also Loveluck, Dobney, and Barrett, "Trade and Exchange—The Settlement and the Wider World."

[112] Naismith, *Money and Power*, 165–166, 171; see also Naismith, *Money and Power*, 157 (noting difficulty for lay users to judge metallic content).

[113] Wickham, *The Early Middle Ages*, 314, 344; see also Naismith, *Money and Power*, 6–12. Kent would be dominated by Mercia by the third quarter of the 8th century. Naismith, *Money and Power*, 19.

[114] For the mutual influence between England and France, including the surprising evidence that a Northumbrian reform producing thin pennies may have pre-dated all the rest, see Naismith, *Money and Power*, 86–100.

consider exactly how each of money's capacities connected people to political authority and how that connection configured the market.

Making the market

The new narrative explains how each of the capacities associated with money—its function as a unit of account, mode of payment, and medium of exchange—is, at base, a mode of governing. The unit of account, first, arises when a stakeholder takes something that is not fungible—the in-kind service owed by individuals or families—and marks it with a token. Accounts that rely on the "convergence story" of money's creation often simply assume the existence of a unit of account because it is so difficult to understand how people who are engaged only in bipolar exchanges can create a term for value that is shared among them all. But establishing a unit of account is a critical accomplishment that demands an explanation. The capacity of an object to furnish homogeneous comparative terms—a unit of account—to evaluate other objects supplies the terms for "counting" value, i.e., price. That unit is used both as the basis of accounting systems and as the metric into which circulating coin or currency can be converted. Once we admit the agency of a stakeholder common to those engaged in bipolar exchanges, the accomplishment becomes intelligible.

In early medieval England, rulers chose to make the basic unit of account—the penny—out of silver. That choice gave silver a price. For example, a weighed pound of silver of specified fineness might be exchanged for 230 pennies at the mint—the "mint price" received when an individual took that amount of bullion in to be coined. The mint made perhaps 242 pennies out of the bullion, kept 12 for the moneyer and the king, and returned the remainder. The "price" of silver was tied, by definition, to the value of the tribute or tax obligation: pennies made by the mint were the tokens used by the king to pay for resources advanced to him. At the time the tax was due, each penny carried value towards extinguishing the tax obligation.[115] Note that without violence to that reality, observers could assume that coin expressed the value of the silver it contained: at tax time, the arrangement itself identified the value that a penny held for extinguishing the fiscal obligation with the value of silver. In fact, we might say that the silver coin had become a material proxy for the tax obligation. (Money therefore also furnished a "store of value," another function often attributed to money.) It was not, however, the content of coin that gave it a priced value, but the system that made coin into money.[116]

---

[115] If we imagine that a person's annual quota of tribute was marked, when advanced for an early reward, with 230 pennies, then 230 pennies would exonerate him or her from the quota otherwise due at the time of reckoning. (Such an amount would be absurdly high in early medieval England, but in an example it keeps the arithmetic easy.)

[116] The accounting system of a society could use different multiples than the coins in circulation. That system is not a free-floating metric, however. It is instead *anchored* by the unit of account to an existing coinage or money. That is, the unit of account is a term into which all modes of payment can be converted.

Second, tokens clearly acted as a "mode of payment" to the government when they were returned in lieu of tribute or other obligation. As we saw above, the tokens invited use as a mode of payment in private deals as well. Individuals could anticipate that everyone recognized their value, given the demand for them established by the stakeholder. As importantly, exchanges between individuals involving a stakeholder's recognized money merited enforcement by the stakeholder insofar as it approved the exchanges. The stakeholder would support agreements made in its tokens because, in a very real sense, those agreements were its agreements. The agreements opened arteries down which money could flow; the arteries took money out into the community, eventually through smaller and smaller capillaries that carried money to the margins of a community. As the image suggests, money creation is tied tightly to judgments enforcing exchange. Insofar as a government wants to expand its own ability to mobilize resources with money, it opens and maintains those conduits—the more official support for tokens, the greater their capacity to function.

The Roman law's directive that damages be stated in the official unit of account functioned to this end.[117] The earliest records of English law are obscure, but the reach of authorities in courts and church counsels increased during the 8th century, as they became more involved in resolving disputes.[118] When the common law took shape in the 12th century, it adopted the approach taken by Roman law: it required debt obligations to be settled in pennies defined as the unit of account. In fact, the English common law in most instances excluded other modes of payment—including by weights of silver.[119]

Official support for monetary transactions—the judicial enforcement of the mode of payment—is also crucial in another aspect. It is literally the place where a society determines what resources can be bought and sold and, conversely, what resources cannot change hands for money. Those determinations shape exchange and the social world around it. The restrictions on sale of land in feudal orders, the slave-owning structures of the American South, the conditions under which waged labor can be hired are only the most obvious examples; we can add the role that money is allowed in electoral campaigns and consider the debates that attach to selling children, sex, or kidneys. Even black markets take place on terrain defined by their lawful counterparts. Like the "price" provided by the unit of account, determining what constitutes a "commodity" that can be bought and sold for money is essential to the market.

In response, groups in a community may strategize methods of accounting in order to escape from an official unit of account to another anchoring coin that they prefer. For example, creditors in some medieval polities tried to keep accounts linked to a large coin that the government was unlikely to depreciate. For an explanation of the unit of account as an anchor, as well as strategies to evade that anchor, see, e.g., Cipolla, *Money, Prices, and Civilization*, 51; Allen Evans, "Some Coinage Systems of the Fourteenth Century," *Journal of Economic and Business History*, no. 3 (1931).

[117] See pp. 84–85.   [118] Wickham, *The Early Middle Ages*, 344.
[119] See pp. 83–97, 133–138.

Finally, money's engineering informs its activity as a medium, including the way that value comes to be hammered out in exchange. The quality that makes money travel so widely—the stakeholder's commitment to take it back from anyone's hand—does not attach indiscriminately. On their own, IOUs are promises personal to the one who makes them and hold only as far as that person honors them, generally to an immediate acquaintance, with all the caveats and defenses that flow from that relationship.[120] At times, a group might accept the IOUs of each other, but the network extends no further than the relations of trust run between participants. Credit that circulates more broadly depends, like money, on the enforcement power of a governing agent; it proliferated in England only in the early modern period. Until then, coin was the only medium endorsed as fully negotiable between strangers in England.[121] Money was, in other words, the *original* circulating credit. It remains the only currency that travels without any conditionality: insofar as authorities take back tokens from the person to whom they spent the token or anyone else, those officials confirm that the tokens can operate successfully as a "medium of exchange."

That process creates a new interaction over material value within a community; it has an organizing effect on the people who use it. A stakeholder likely spends money only on a certain kind of resources—soldiers and military suppliers, for example. (The word "soldiers" comes, in fact, from the Roman "solidus," the gold coin in which they were paid.) The ability to mobilize resources selectively is, after all, the great advantage that spending narrowly (and taxing more broadly) offers. Entering the community through certain hands, money becomes available in corresponding ways. People who are close enough bid for it with the resources they have and according to what the endowed want; they pass it on in turn as others offer goods to them. Trades occur that could never happen before. But the results trace back to the spending priorities of the government, the way money flowed in, the resources each family held relative to what others wanted, and all the spoken and unspoken rules about who could deal with whom, what could be claimed and what could not be claimed, what could be traded and what was outside of trading.

The process shakes the items traded into particular relationships of value. Eventually, those relationships produce prices for goods and other resources in terms of pennies, the units of account. The pennies, as they are spent, traded, and taxed, ultimately create a set of equivalences: 5 pennies = a sword, 5 pennies = two cows. But there is nothing essential about the sword and the cows and their equivalence. To the contrary, they are interchangeable only in the world created

---

[120] For credit networks as highly embedded matters, see, e.g., Eric Kerridge, *Trade and Banking in Early Modern England* (Manchester: Manchester University Press, 1988), 50–57.

[121] For discussion of public credit's proliferation in the early modern period, see pp. 245–254. For the exclusive powers of coin, see J. K. Horsefield, "The Beginnings of Paper Money in England," *Journal of European Economic History* 117, no. 32 (1977).

by this community's activity with tokens. Only there, with a market that is a function of all the contingencies that contributed to it, is a sword = 5 pennies = two cows. In fact, if the money and the way it is made evaporate, no one will give two cows for a sword, except by happenstance. That is, there is no "real" equivalence between the sword and the cows "revealed" by money. A sword does not equate to the cows in value except through the intervention of the monetary engineering that made the token into a unit, mode of payment, and medium between a set of participants in the particular circumstances of that engineering.

Indeed, once money circulates, it will reshape even the old relations of barter. Trades made without money will take place in the shadow of the moneyed economy; the tokens moving resources towards the center have redefined what each resource is worth between people. Even trades made purely on credit— ongoing relations reciprocal enough to operate indefinitely without a token changing hands—will be rebalanced in the moneyed world.

Money's penetrating quality owes to a last characteristic, one that draws on its capacity as a unit of account, mode of payment, and medium of exchange all together. Once we have a working money, it can be expanded beyond its fiscal core. In fact, English societies from the early medieval period through the modern era have engineered ways to supplement the amount of money created directly by the government's spending and taxing. If the money supply were limited to that publicly injected flow, it would be both scant and erratic. That would be especially true in the early world, where sovereigns spent sparely for civil purposes but mobilized resources suddenly and steeply for military ends, withdrawing money afterwards. The arrangement would leave unsatisfied a huge appetite for money in which to make deals.[122] By contrast, monetary systems can be structured to produce money to answer people's demand for an instrument that provides cash services. Once that engineering is in place, people can expand the money supply by their own action for their own use. That capacity would explain the patterns of money found in 8th century England, where royal authority over money increased but coin pooled with particular depth in areas of private exchange.

The way the English supplemented money produced for the king's use is clear by the 10th century, and scholars have speculated that something similar dates to the beginning of England's silver penny.[123] When English sovereigns established

---

[122] N. J. Mayhew, "Population, Money Supply, and the Velocity of Circulation in England, 1300–1700," *Economic History Review* 48, no. 2 (1995). Another way to understand that "appetite" is as private demand for liquidity that would otherwise affect prices, driving them down. When governments contrived ways to augment the money created by fiscal activity, they were responding to demand for liquidity by expanding the money stock rather than requiring deflation.

[123] Metcalf, *Thrymsas and Sceattas*, 14–16. Naismith appears to agree that the early Anglo-Saxon kings probably controlled the minting of sceattas and early pennies, at least to the extent of charging a flat fee or taking a proportion or moneyers' profits depending on output. See Naismith, *Money and Power*, 42–45.

minting on demand (later called "free minting"), they set up a way to sell coin into circulation. Along the way, minting on demand also allowed the government to distribute to the population the cost of making tokens.

The full story lies ahead, but the basic idea is that people could bring bullion to royal mints and receive coin in return. The government made money by charging for the service. As for individuals, they had to buy as much coin as necessary to cover their taxes.[124] At the same time, individuals could buy more coin when they wanted the cash quality it offered. Their demand was registered in price: when prices fell, coin was worth more and it was increasingly worthwhile to bring bullion to the mint. Despite the fact that authorities took a cut of the silver brought in, the deal was profitable. In the example above, the mint made 242 pennies from a pound of silver and returned 230 to the person who had come to the mint, keeping the remainder as the public charge.[125] Although the individual received back less in terms of silver, he received it back in the form of coin. Coin, as we have seen, was worth more than silver bullion insofar as coin carried cash value. People would buy it as long as that was true.

The technique tied the value of the public obligation (tax or tribute) to the price of the silver commodity set by the center in terms of tokens: the tribute cost a certain amount of raw commodity or a bit less commodity in token form to satisfy. In effect, the tokens furnished the "price" of the larger amount of raw commodity. By identifying the unit of account with content priced in that way, the system created a channel for the expansion of money according to private demand. It allowed individuals who wanted the cash services of money to purchase units of account by putting up the raw material to make money, while protecting the sovereign from any harm, since that limited commodity, once fashioned into money, was identified with money's tax value. People would buy money so long as the resources they could command with that, new, money were worth the cost to them. That was true as long as prices in coin were low enough that those resources were worth more to them than the raw commodity, used for other purposes.

The desire of people for coin in early Anglo-Saxon society did not turn on any comparison they made between prices in coin and a "world price" for silver. As discussed above, models of commodity money usually offer that anachronism as they imagine a reference point for coin's value. They begin with current prices in pennies (penny/good) and assume that people know as well the amount of silver

---

[124] More precisely, in order to get the amount they needed, most people would trade resources with those individuals, generally merchants, who bought coin from the mint with bullion. That group had access to silver bullion and was likely the only group with the capacity to make finer calculation about silver content.

[125] For this proportion and others characteristic of the minting system in place after the 12th century, see p. 72.

in a penny (ounces/penny).[126] That information (pennies/good given a certain number of ounces/penny) produces a hypothetical price in terms of ounces of silver/good. According to that extrapolation, the price offered by a mint to make a coin becomes a matter that can be chosen by people who are comparing the alternative of using silver to buy goods. They will take in their bullion to get coin when prices for goods in coin are less than prices for goods in ounces of silver.[127]

The structure of explanation invites the familiar intuition: just as the world price in a commodity serves as a reference point in the model, it furnished a reference point in the creation of coin. The possibility of comparison assumes, that is, the presence of a commodity already furnishing cash qualities to a community. But that assumption conflicts with the dry conditions that existed by definition before money's creation; it imagines the very capacity that it seeks to explain. Nor does it pass a reality check. As far as the histories of the pre-monetary English world indicate, there was *no market* for goods in terms of silver, "measured in ounces of silver per good."[128] That is, there was no "price" in a medium of ounces of silver—certainly not for consumption goods. The comparison between prices in coin and prices in raw silver for goods on the domestic market is an abstract deduction (given prices for goods in pennies and amount of silver per penny), paired with projection (prices in silver for goods). It does not indicate that the items would actually be traded. It cannot, therefore, do the equilibrating work assigned to it.[129]

---

[126] A user would know the number of ounces of silver/penny if he or she knew the total number of pennies made from a pound of silver bullion. Assuming the 12-ounce pound commonly used in the early medieval period and a constant fineness, a penny would hold 12 oz/242 pennies (the sum of the mint price and the mint charge, also known as the mint equivalent), or about. 05 oz/penny. In fact, it is not clear that the mints shared the mint equivalent with people. See p. 77 n. 29.

[127] See, e.g., Sargent and Velde, *Big Problem of Small Change*, 9–12, and pp. 29–31. To continue the example above, if 1 penny bought more of a good than .05 oz of silver (assumedly because everyone found it easier to use and therefore attributed a cash premium to coin), it would be advantageous to have coin rather than the same amount of silver in uncoined form. More precisely, given that English medieval mints charged for their services, if prices for coin were sufficiently low that 230 pennies bought more than 12 ounces of silver, or one penny bought more than .052 oz of silver/good, people would go to the mint. Once those pennies were minted, they would remain in circulation unless prices rose sufficiently that people would rather have the .05 oz of silver they contained. At that point (leaving aside costs of melting), coin would be melted because despite the sunk costs in producing it, people would rather have the raw silver in it. That is, the charge for minting created a small gap between the minting point (if prices are at or under, people mint) and the melting point (if prices are above, people melt).

[128] Sargent and Velde, *Big Problem of Small Change*, 19. To the contrary, when medieval users concluded that their coin was worth more as silver than as coin, they would melt out (or otherwise find a way to value) the silver in coin and use that metal for purposes other than domestic exchange—most notably, export. Note that the term "world price" has an ironic accuracy. In fact, it was in foreign trade that coin—generally coin of high denomination—would be used at its intrinsic weight, i.e., in ounces of silver/good. In addition, silver was often exported and recoined in countries where it could buy more by count. Once coined, it would, of course, be acting *also as money* in that foreign world. If silver were more highly valued there than in England, however, the exporter could make a profit by coining it and using it abroad. See Redish, *Bimetallism*, 28–34.

[129] For more about how the medieval English government actually induced people to bring bullion to the mint, see pp. 121–122; see also pp. 94–95 (reviewing later limitations on silver sales).

Rather than holding value according to the modern imagination of commodity money, pennies offered a cash premium compared to the indigenous value of silver bullion. Those coming to the mint knew how many coins were given in return for a pound of bullion. If prices were sufficiently low in coin that the quantity of coins received (i.e., the mint price) would be more useful than the raw bullion, people would come to have their bullion converted to coin. That is, as long as coins carried the qualities that gave them purchasing power, people would buy them in preference to holding bullion. Although it is less clear, people may also have known the "mint equivalent," or the sum total of coins made from a pound of silver. As above, that information gave them the silver bullion content of each penny. If prices ever rose so much (i.e., coins lost so much of their value as cash) that people would rather have the silver that was in them to use for other purposes, then people would begin to melt their coins.[130] In this sequence, we can understand why people bought coin in response to the cues that prices give them. Moreover, bullion becomes a marker of value, one that was related to the amount of metal in coin, but not one that previously conducted a shadow world of exchange or produced prices in silver ounces.

Selling people money for their own use benefited both the government and individuals. It allowed the money supply to expand as people demanded more money, avoiding the painful deflation that would otherwise occur if people spread the use of money across more transactions.[131] In addition, when people had the option of buying coin, their decisions tended to maintain prices between a certain range. People went to the mint as long as it was worth their while to get money (as long as coin had so much value because of its cash quality that, even given the charge for minting, it was worth more than silver bullion). They would not continue going to the mint after that point. Indeed, if prices rose beyond the level at which coin held only the asset value of silver, people would melt or export coin, depressing the stock of money and sending prices down again. Along the way, people paid the government its costs for minting, producing the coins that the government would collect when it taxed and spent in turn. Allowing people to supplement the money supply, then, both tended to stabilize prices and paid for coin.

We could put the logic another way, one that returns us to the creation story of money as a constructed medium. Medieval minting tied money creation to a fiscal backbone, while allowing it to expand in response to the demand for cash. When people bought money from the mint, they put up the material value in silver that was identified with the tax obligation. That becomes clear when we

---

[130] The melting point would be a price at which people, given the number of coins required to buy a good, would rather have the silver for some other use. For more, see p. 64 n. 128.

[131] As a mode of redressing demand, deflation assumes a unit of account that is divisible, not a realistic condition in early monetary systems. For the relationship between money stock and demand that would produce deflation, see p. 102 n. 115.

consider that a stakeholder owed 230 pennies would be willing to take, instead, a pound of silver—the material for making the coins due, plus the cost of minting. People who bought extra coin were simply converting their silver into taxable form in order to use it along the way. Their action, like the agency provided by the government, configured the market.

That brings us back in closing to look at money and the market defined by later Anglo-Saxon rulers. We left the story during the late 8th and early 9th century period of political recomposition in England. From the mid-9th century on, that process was refracted through conflict with the Danes; West Saxons from King Alfred's line would eventually consolidate control, expanding their authority over money as they did so.[132] Edgar's monetary reform, taken in 973, established a uniform currency across England; just as coinage on the Continent was fragmenting, the English put in place a system remarkable for its reach and sophistication.[133]

Reconstructing the patterns left behind, historians believe that the "renovatio monetae", whereby old coins were declared invalid and were exchanged for newly issued coins, was a system that very effectively created money and raised revenue. The two were clearly linked. The late Anglo-Saxon monarchs imposed taxes, gelds, and other payments and required that those payments be made in coin acquired from mints they controlled. Periodically, officials changed the type of coin that circulated; those owing public debts apparently had to pay in the new coin.[134] The requirement forced people to the mints on a regular basis. On each occasion, sovereigns imposed a fee for minting. They also reaped revenue, conveniently in coined form, each time.[135]

That system allowed English officials to raise the geld that bought off Viking forces, as well as the revenue that went to more domestic uses. The *Anglo-Saxon Chronicles* may well exaggerate how heavy the toll on English wealth was, but there is no doubt that thousands of coins went north to buy peace, as well as mercenary troops.[136] Extractions continued at a heavy rate under the early

---

[132] Stewart, "English and Norman Mints," 13–14; Naismith, *Money and Power*, 155, 233–234, 295.

[133] J. L. Bolton, *Money in the Medieval English Economy: 973–1489* (Manchester: Manchester University Press, 2012), 88–89.

[134] Bolton, *Money in the Medieval English Economy*, 94; Stewart, "English and Norman Mints," 59. In 1178, the author of an Exchequer treatise, the *Dialogus de Scaccario*, remarked that people from certain counties had at times been allowed to pay their dues with coin of appropriate weight and fineness from any mint, since they had no moneyer of their own. The comment suggests that individuals were usually obliged to pay with the coin of their local moneyer. See generally Stewart, "English and Norman Mints," 55–59.

[135] See generally Bolton, *Money in the Medieval English Economy*, 87–99; Stewart, "English and Norman Mints," 55–56.

[136] The hoard evidence from Scandinavia, Poland, and Russia for the period 979 to 1035, some 60,000–70,000 English pennies, dwarfs the coins recovered from hoards in England from 973 to 1158, only about 52,000. Bolton, *Money in the Medieval English Economy*, 61–62. Early estimates emphasized that heavy taxation drew huge amounts of silver earned from the wool industry into the mints, an accomplishment that in turn brought Vikings as bees to honey. See e.g., P. H. Sawyer, "The Wealth of England in the Eleventh Century," *Transactions of the Royal Historical Society* 15 (1965): 160–164. Bolton argues that taxation and production was lighter; the Vikings came not because England was so wealthy but because its wealth was so conveniently packaged. See Bolton, *Money in the Medieval English Economy*, 91–92; see also

Normans.[137] In rough correspondence, recoinages became more and more frequent over time; more than a decade passed before Edgar (959–975) renewed his money, while only a few years separated the coin types of later rulers.[138] Changing the design of coin made it easy to confirm that people had returned to the mint for new money. Most of the hoards hidden on Anglo-Saxon territory in the late 10th and early 11th centuries contain coins from only one minting; the remaining hoards include only a few pennies from an earlier type. Remintings must generally have wiped out all the coins of a previous series, reaching almost all of the money in circulation.[139] Individuals would have gone to the mints much less often, had they needed only to replace money because it was worn down or damaged.[140] For reasons that are not clear, coins also varied in weight: the earliest coins of each type were heavier and got lighter over time.[141] Despite that difference, most scholars believe that late Anglo-Saxon coin traveled at face value.[142] The fiscal system was more than robust enough to ensure demand for the king's coin and the proliferation of mints that facilitated recoinages would have made money accessible to those who wanted to buy it for their own use.[143] By the time of Edward the Confessor (1042–1066), a system something like the

---

M. K. Lawson, "Danegeld and Heregeld Once More," *Economic History Review* 105 (1990); J. B. Gillingham, "Chronicles and Coins as Evidence for Levels of Tribute and Taxation in the Late 10th and Early 11th-Century England," *Economic History Review* 105 (1990). Either interpretation testifies to the effective operation of the system.

[137] Bolton, *Money in the Medieval English Economy*, 91–92.

[138] Some rulers renewed their money every two or three years, others recoined every six or eight years. The coins are marked by varied designs, including several "Hand of Providence" images, and more than twenty different versions of a cross engraved with the letters *C-R-U-X*. Over 150 years, Anglo-Saxon and early Norman rulers changed the design of their coinage at least fifty-three times. Stewart, "English and Norman Mints", 49–55; Spufford, *Money and Its Use*.

[139] Stewart, "English and Norman Mints," 50–58; Spufford, *Money and Its Use*, 94. Bolton agrees that, at least through 1036, moneyers completely melted down their earlier pieces and produced a new and distinctive coin. Bolton, *Money in the Medieval English Economy*, 94.

[140] Stewart, "English and Norman Mints," 55. In a cache dating to the 15th century when recoining for wear prevailed, a full quarter of the coins were more than a century old. Spufford, *Money and Its Use*, 93, n. 2.

[141] Scholars have long debated whether the weight fluctuations were designed, through their effect depreciating the currency's value, to stimulate English exports. See R. H. M. Dolley and D. M. Metcalf, "The Reform of the English Coinage under Eadgar," in *Anglo-Saxon Coins: Studies Presented to Sir Frank Stenton on the Occasion of his 80th Birthday*, ed. R. H. M. Dolley (London: Methuen, 1961). Recent scholarship considers a different set of rationales for the variation, including the incentives that weight reductions may have posed for people holding coin and discrepancies due to regional differences in production. See Martin Allen, *Mints and Money in Medieval England* (Cambridge: Cambridge University Press, 2012), 136; Bolton, *Money in the Medieval English Economy*, 97; H. Bertil A. Petersson, *Anglo-Saxon Currency, King Edgar's Reform to the Norman Conquest*, Bibliotheca Historica Lundensis 22 (Lund: Gleerup, 1969), 101.

[142] Allen, *Mints and Money*, 136; Stewart, "English and Norman Mints," 50–58; Spufford, *Money and Its Use*, 94; Petersson, *Anglo-Saxon Currency*, 101. Bolton is more agnostic. See Bolton, *Money in the Medieval English Economy*, 92, 94, 97.

[143] Mints proliferated in the last quarter of the 10th century, when they increased almost threefold (from twenty-five to seventy mints) to blanket the English countryside south of York and east of Chester. Their accessibility made the frequent recoinages possible, although larger mints produced the lion's share of the coinage. Bolton, *Money in the Medieval English Economy*, 94–95.

system of minting on demand described above licensed moneyers to produce coin after paying a fee to the sovereign.[144]

As the coin came in, the king levied a charge for minting. Spufford estimates that royal profits amounted to 25 percent of the metal minted on each occasion, a rate suggesting strong centralized authority.[145] In turn, the tax revenue and profits reaped helped finance that rule. Officials supported by indigenous money organized the space they controlled to allow trade, defense, and local order. Mints were concentrated in urban spaces, associated with commercial activity but also administrative and military purposes. Markets grew up there and in the ecclesiastical or political centers sometimes called "productive sites," developing as well if less profusely in the countryside.[146] Their study would take us beyond the bounds of this history; it would, however, be closely connected to money.

The law codes of the 9th and 10th centuries make the ambition of the early Anglo-Saxon kings to control trades in money clear, as well as the responsibility they asserted for those trades. There is a tendency in modern commentary, even commentary on the early medieval period, to draw clear lines between commerce and political activity, and to put money and moneyed exchange on the commercial side.[147] The stakeholder story suggests, however, that public creation and use of money are profoundly important in the constitution of many communities. For the late Anglo-Saxon rulers, a realm justly ordered was an elemental imperative. That imperative included the safeguarding of people and the policing of their relations. Here gather the kings' efforts, including by expenditure of silver coin, to consolidate and defend their realm. Offa's dyke, a military fortification in northwest England, may have been underwritten by royal pennies as well as impressed

---

[144] Bolton, *Money in the Medieval English Economy*, 90–91.

[145] Spufford, *Money and Its Use*, 93–94; Petersson, *Anglo-Saxon Currency*, 100–101; see also generally Pamela Nightingale, "'The King's Profit': Trends in English Mint and Monetary Policy in the Eleventh and Twelfth Centuries," in *Trade, Money, and Power in Medieval England* (Surrey: Ashgate Variorum, 2007). Stewart is less specific about the rate of profit, although he assumes that the Anglo-Saxon system of shifting weights functioned to produce revenues. The royal charge may have been imposed directly on minters at first, and been collected later through a levy placed on boroughs. See Stewart, "English and Norman Mints," 55–56, 58–59. For the strong centralized control of the Anglo-Saxons, see Patrick Wormald, *The Making of English Law: King Alfred to the Twelfth Century*, 2 vols., vol. 1: Legislation and Its Limits (Oxford: Blackwell Publishers Ltd., 2001); Nightingale, "'The King's Profit,'" 61–63, 70–71; Thomas N. Bisson, *Conservation of Coinage: Monetary Exploitation and Its Restraint in France, Catalonia, and Aragon (c.A.D.1000–c.1225)* (Oxford: Clarendon Press, 1979), 6; Spufford, *Money and Its Use*, 92–94; Stewart, "English and Norman Mints," 49, 68–69; see also James Campbell, "Observations on English Government from the Tenth to the Twelfth Century," *Transactions of the Royal Historical Society* 25 (1975) (suggesting roots of Anglo-Saxon centralized control in Carolingian influence).

[146] Naismith, *Money and Power*, 32–36, 131–132, 282; Loveluck, Dobney, and Barrett, "Trade and Exchange"; see also p. 66 n. 143.

[147] A number of histories assume that, e.g., the medieval sovereign's interest in moneyed exchange was driven primarily by interest in the profits that could be extracted from minting, tolls, or other fees. See, e.g., Michael F. Hendy, "From Public to Private: The Western Barbarian Coinages as a Mirror of the Disintegration of Late Roman State Structures," in *Viator 19* (1988); Naismith, *Money and Power*, 32–36, 279.

labor. The military initiatives of later kings, their use of mercenary troops most obviously, surely were.[148]

The imperative of a justly ordered realm extended also to structuring private exchange: the making of markets in money. A provision in the law code of I Edward (c. 900) established that "no one shall buy [and sell] except in market towns." The Grately Code (c. 925–930) made it clear that large deals had to be transacted within the view of authorities, while a series of clauses subjected purchases involving cattle to intricate oversight. Those, notes Elina Screen, were a "flashpoint" for dispute within a society that valued the animals so highly. As she observes, the laws regarding money cohere "within an aspiration toward control both of people and property and the prevention of disputes."[149] The common law would soon articulate the rightful role of money, delineating the categories of its operation and defining its value as the sovereign coin of the realm.[150]

Anglo-Saxon law and its monetary order were, in other words, growing up together. A code of V Aethelred from 1008 suggests the affinity contemporaries saw between law, money, public goods, and the market:

> And the promotion of public security and the improvement of the coinage in every part of the country, and the repairing of fortresses and of bridges throughout the country on every side, and also the duties of military service, shall always be diligently attended to, whenever the need arised, in accordance with the orders given.[151]

Another provision from the same sovereign tied money and the market to law even more simply. "Let us earnestly take thought for the promotion of public security and the improvement of the coinage," it read. "Public security shall be promoted in such a way as shall be best for the householder and worst for the thief."[152] (For one of Aethelred's coins, many of which combined Christian and royal iconography, see Fig. 1.3.)

That commitment promoted money as a means of exchange more broadly among lay people. It prompted landowners who owed gelds to privilege the money that could pay them; by the 9th century, rent was probably a significant use for coin in rural areas.[153] The landlords' demand made money more valuable to tenants; peasants as well as wealthier English began to hold pennies. Larger mints in regular production along with smaller mints more sporadically active spread money across the countryside. While liquidity remained low by modern standards, it seeped into the deals made by many more people in England and, for

---

[148] Spufford, *Money and Its Use*, 90–91; Bolton, *Money in the Medieval English Economy*, 91.
[149] Screen, "Anglo-Saxon Law", 157.
[150] See pp. 83–97, 125–138, 267–274.
[151] V Aethelred s 1 (1008), as reprinted in Screen, "Anglo-Saxon Law," Appendix.
[152] VI Aethelred c 31–32 (1008), as reprinted in Screen, "Anglo-Saxon Law," Appendix.
[153] Naismith, *Money and Power*, 278.

Fig. 1.3 Coin of Aethelred II (c. 1008) produced under moneyer Blacaman, including steed, cross, and bird. © Trustees of The British Museum.

that matter, in Scandinavia. Even when it was not present, it furnished the terms of value and the measure for credit. The Domesday Book, William I's survey of England's population and resources, "presents a picture of a society full of money, and money payments."[154]

Reconsidering its creation story suggests that "making money" is a constitutional project. In medieval England, silver and gold were only the beginning, not the end, of the story. They furnished the material upon which the medieval world would act out a debate over how to package, pay, and circulate value. That effort distributed resources. It shaped nation building. It brought England into competition with other sovereigns. It configured new ways to represent counted value—public debt, circulating credit, and elaborate hierarchies of credit are all part of the story, as are markets, banks, securities, and financial crises. The way the English made money shaped and reshaped the way people conceptualized it and the way they conducted monetary policy. As a matter engineered on a fiscal frame, enhanced by the unique cash quality it offered, and expanded for a charge, money has never been neutral. The story continues in the next chapter.

---

[154] N. J. Mayhew, *Sterling: The History of a Currency* (New York: Wiley, 2000), 3; Spufford, *Money and Its Use*, 86–90; Christopher Dyer, *Making a Living in the Middle Ages*, New Economic History of Britain (New Haven: Yale University Press, 2002), 98.

2

From metal to money

Producing the "just penny"

"[B]efore there is any money, there must be a statute," pronounced the earliest surviving treatise on money written in England.[1] By the time the observation was put on paper sometime in the 1280s, the English had inaugurated the system of making money they would use throughout the Middle Ages. That system replaced the tradition of the renovatio monetae, while pulling ingredients of practice from it. The conflict between Henry I's daughter, Matilda, and her competitor for the throne, Stephen (reign, 1135–1154), had decimated the earlier monetary system, along with strong centralized authority itself. When Matilda's son, Henry II and the first of the Plantagenets, took the throne in 1154, he did not attempt to resurrect coin renewals with their heavy material costs and intricate logistics. Instead, he moved to a system that produced coin by minting it on demand. Money was available at a price to inhabitants, who bought it according to the amount they needed to meet public and private requirements.

The history here follows the English into the high Middle Ages as they created the system that came, rather incongruously, to be called "free minting." The design of "free minting" was written in the proclamations, rules, customs, and laws that configured the way silver and gold became a unit of account, mode of payment, and medium of exchange. Under the new approach, the English government set a price for bullion in coins and offered to buy as much raw metal as people brought to it. Minting was thus "free" in the sense that it was unlimited; it was clearly *not* free for the asking. In exchange for silver bullion, the mint returned a certain number of silver coins—effectively, it offered a price for silver in money. The price included a charge that covered minting and other costs; from the total number of coins made out of a bullion brought in, authorities deducted and kept their fee.[2] In return, the government sold people a money that would work in both private and public worlds.

Free minting, like the renovatio monetae, traded on the fact that public authority both supplied a specific money and inaugurated demand for it in

---

[1] *The Red Book* contains the "Treatise on the New Money." Johnson attributes the manuscript to William de Turnemire, about 1280, but a somewhat later author and date (about 1286–1287) comport better with the rates for recoining it quotes. Compare, Charles Johnson, trans./ed., *The De Moneta of Nicholas Oresme and English Mint Documents* (London: Thomas Nelson, 1956; repr., Ludwig von Mises Institute, 2009), xxxiv with N. J. Mayhew, "From Regional to Central Minting, 1158–1464," in *A New History of the Royal Mint*, ed. C. E. Challis (Cambridge: Cambridge University Press, 1992), 120–123.

[2] See pp. 78–79.

particular. Deliberately consolidating his realm, Henry increasingly centralized control over the mints. Fewer, highly supervised establishments now served the kingdom instead of the plethora of mints needed in the era when money was frequently demonetized. (Henry and his successors declared recoinages only when the coin had become seriously worn, or when they wanted to introduce new denominations.[3]) People came to the mint when taxes and fees imposed by public authorities, along with the uses for money they had in daily life, made the cost of money worth paying. Demand for money would develop significantly over the next century.[4] To the extent that it drove the value of money to be higher than the value of raw metal, people paid the mints to produce coin.

The critical quality was liquidity. That began with the ability to measure material value in a unit. Consistent with earlier Anglo-Saxon and Anglo-Norman practice, Henry II used silver coin to represent material value in a way that could be "told" or counted. Second, coin came with a virtual guarantee that it would be the item most widely offered and demanded for payment of debts. The minting process itself deployed the unit of account to that effect: the government both paid and charged for coin in its own measure. Officials would reinforce that pattern when they spent and taxed more generally, all in coin. Predictable supply and demand for money as a mode of payment also induced people to treat money as a store of value. Third, the government endorsed the exchange of coin from the time the mint issued it until the time authorities taxed the coin back. That privilege was embedded in the very vocabulary of the common law. The ancient writ of debt selected the count of coin, not the weight of coin in silver, as the essence that constituted or effectuated payment. That practice promoted coin as the measure of private exchange as well as public obligation. Indeed, the common law and a bevy of supporting prohibitions entrenched coin as the exclusive money of early England. That status was deliberately engineered, an arrangement that had to be maintained and defended as conditions changed and people tested the limits of the system.

---

[3] At those moments, 1158, 1180, 1247, 1279, 1344–1351, 1411, and 1464, the lay population brought in its money, just as it had under the renovatio monetae. See Mayhew, "From Regional to Central Minting," 83–84 and n. 3, 89–90. The reduction in renewals correlated with a new practice at the Exchequer: It began to "blanch" coin brought in or require additional payment if the coin did not meet minimum quality standards. Mayhew, "From Regional to Central Minting," 90; S. Harvey, "Royal Revenue and Domesday Terminology," *Economic History Review*, 20, no. 2 (1967): 221–228. That practice would, indirectly, pressure people to take coin in to be reminted when it had reached a point of obvious wear. Insofar as the renovatio monetae system went without such a practice, it reinforces the assumption that the earlier method included a requirement that taxes be paid in new coin, which would not require an assay of value.

[4] For accounts that explore the rising demand for money in circumstances where people perceived it as increasingly useful to pay public and private obligations, see, e.g., N. J. Mayhew, "Population, Money Supply, and the Velocity of Circulation in England, 1300–1700," *Economic History Review* 48, no. 2 (1995); Peter H. Lindert, "English Population, Wages, and Prices: 1541–1913," *Journal of Interdisciplinary History* 15, no. 4 (1985); Charles W. Calomiris, "Institutional Failure, Monetary Scarcity, and the Depreciation of the Continental," *Journal of Economic History* 48, no. 1 (1988).

Mapping the design of the free minting system suggests, finally, the peculiar kind of liquidity it produced. The English created a currency that circulated quickly (or moved at a fast monetary "velocity") and carried a remarkably high purchasing power. Those qualities would shape both politics and exchange.

A. The unit of account, or "good and lawful sterlings"

The "Treatise on the New Money" is both a meditation and a practice manual on the unit of account. There are atmospherics of alchemy in the Treatise. It does, after all, concern the instructions for transmuting silver into money, more than metal. As the author puts it, he wrote for those who "through their love of justice, desire to know the reasons for and manner of making coined money, and the trial of the assay," a subject that is regarded as "difficult and intricate." But if this is alchemy, it is alchemy of a very worldly sort. It includes setting the specifications of coin's content and count, minting coin, testing it, proclaiming it, and policing it. Constituting value as a measure was not an abstract or loosely social matter—it was written into rules and practices about who defined the unit that mattered and how that related to material value required by public authorities or desired by individuals. Those directives captured tangible value in particular ways that would become part of governance.[5]

The statute inaugurated the process by "clearly and distinctly" determining the metal content of coins and their number.[6] Throughout the medieval period, the Crown controlled the amount of metal, in terms of weight and fineness, relative to the count of money. The first specifications appear in the *Dialogus de Scaccario*, the Exchequer treatise written under Henry II at the start of the free minting system, although precise stipulations survive only from the next century and Edward I's reform of the coinage. Silver bullion was first refined, then weighed and apportioned into amounts of (alloyed) silver that would be cut into the specified number of coins. According to the practice instituted in 1279, a Tower pound of silver produced 243 pennies each about 1.44 grams (22.2 grains) heavy at a fineness close to 93 percent.[7]

Over the next century, official documents reiterate coin's fineness, weight, and count. The Treatise on the New Money modifies the specifications in 1286 or

---

[5] Johnson, trans./ed., *De Moneta/English Mint Documents*, 65.

[6] Johnson, trans./ed., *De Moneta/English Mint Documents*, 66.

[7] Martin Allen, *Mints and Money in Medieval England* (Cambridge: Cambridge University Press, 2012), 147, 159–162. The number of pennies cut from the pound would remain almost constant until the mid-14th century. Allen comprehensively reviews evidence of the changes in the penny's weight and fineness from Edgar's reform (973) to 1544. Allen, *Mints and Money*, 134–169. The "Tower pound" used to purchase silver was lighter at 5,400 grains than the English troy pound at 5,760 grains, a measure used in testing fineness at least insofar as it followed the practice established by the Treatise on the New Money sometime after 1280. See Johnson, trans./ed., *De Moneta/English Mint Documents*, xxxiv–xxxv and 70, n. 1 and, for theory as to the reasons for that arrangement, Mayhew, "Central Minting," 89–90. Use of the Tower pound was ended in 1526. Allen, *Mints and Money*, 153.

1287; later documents again readjust them. (Like those on the Continent, the English gradually reduced the amount of silver in the penny. Unlike their counterparts, however, the English overwhelmingly lessened the weight of the penny, instead of adulterating its fineness. That choice was deliberate; like many apparently technical matters, it was actually part of the intense drama over who controlled the medium of value and how. When they secured the king's agreement to reduce weight instead of fineness, elites rendered changes in the commodity content of coin relatively conspicuous—and thus more contestable.[8]) In 1335 and regularly from 1343, coin's specifications appear in the indentures, the contracts made between mint masters and the Crown.[9] That money—a counted value based on a certain amount of metal in coined form—took its central place as the unit that defined price.

Along the way, the unit of account also acted as an anchor for fractional and multiplied value. Thus, the penny could be counted in dozens (shillings) and shillings could be counted in scores (pounds). While neither shilling nor pound coins existed, they had arithmetic reality in accounts.[10] Physical denominations also entered into use with reference to the penny's value—the farthing as a quarter-penny and the groat as 4 pence, for example. Just as determinations about fineness and weight mattered, so too did denominational decisions: they would ease certain levels of exchange and leave others dry, distributing economic advantage as they did.[11]

Once public authorities had determined the content and count of coin, it had "then [to] be put in hand and finished by the order or special licence of the prince." Minting was an authority at the center of sovereignty. The Treatise makes the embodiment of metal in the specialized style of coin intrinsic to

---

[8] See p. 121 n. 33 *cf.*, p. 161.

[9] See Duties of the Officers of the Mint (1248), in Johnson, trans./ed., *De Moneta/English Mint Documents*, 51–52; Assay of the New Money (1248), in Johnson, trans./ed., *De Moneta/English Mint Documents*, 53–55; The Form of the New Money (1279), in Johnson, trans./ed., *De Moneta/English Mint Documents*, 56–58; A Treatise on the New Money (1280), in Johnson, trans./ed., *De Moneta/English Mint Documents*, 67–77; The St. Edmundsbury Trial Place, in Johnson, trans./ed., *De Moneta/English Mint Documents*, 86–87. For the indentures, see C. E. Challis, *A New History of the Royal Mint* (Cambridge: Cambridge University Press, 1992), 700–758. The penny was depreciated over time by lightening it in weight but, aside from a few aberrational periods, not fineness. That is, more pennies were cut from the pound (in terms of the Tower pound, there were 270d. in 1346; 360d. in 1413, and 450d. in 1464). Allen, *Mints and Money*, 149, 151–152. The weight of the penny thus lost touch with the weight of (alloyed) silver, as the price of silver rose.

[10] See Allen Evans, "Some Coinage Systems of the Fourteenth Century," *Journal of Economics and Business History*, no. 3 (1931): 487–490, 494–495; Peter Spufford, *Money and Its Use in Medieval Europe* (Cambridge: Cambridge University Press, 1988), 33–34. As these accounts emphasize, the fact that accounts could be kept in arithmetic terms that did not match actual coins in circulation does not mean that those accounts were independent of actual coins. Rather, "the value of any given system of account" was stable "only in proportion to the stability of the basic coin". Evans, "Some Coinage Systems of the Fourteenth Century," 495.

[11] See pp. 192–205. In principle, fractions and multiples of the penny carried amounts of silver proportioned to their value. Martin Allen traces the deviations in practice. (See Allen, *Mints and Money*, 148–150.)

Fig. 2.1 Medieval mint workshop, woodcut from Ralph Holinshed's *Chronicles of England, Scotland, and Ireland* (1577).

money's definition. As it continues, "you must know that all money consists of two things, matter and form":

> Its matter is obtained by working in gold, silver and copper, and its form by coining, as by engraving a die which imprints a recognisable and distinguishable form on the coin, without which it can never be a coin any more than wax can be a seal until it has received the impression of its device.[12]

In English medieval mints, silver was hammered thin, sheared into coin-size pieces, and then struck to impress a design onto each coin (see Fig. 2.1).[13] As common to each mint was the claim that they performed a public prerogative. The early documents convey that claim, as does the behavior of royal officials. The dies for coin were treated "as though they were the king's seal," and the Warden of the Mint was charged with protecting it as "his supreme duty."[14] Edward I's officials scrupulously guarded both dies and the standards used to verify the fineness of silver. They would delay and deny, for example, a plea by the Abbot of St. Edmunds to take custody of a standard. They ultimately sent only dies and detailed information about count, weight, and fineness. In short, they huffed, "he should be told to make his money just as the king does."[15]

The officials' behavior followed the lead of Henry II, who had retired the *renovatio monetae* in part because free minting could be managed at fewer, more closely held mints. Whenever possible, Henry II narrowed minting privileges by reassuming them at the death of ecclesiastical claimants or nobles, by legal inquest challenging their legal basis, or by undermining the profits of local

---

[12] Treatise on the New Money, in Johnson, trans./ed., *De Moneta/English Mint Documents*, 66.

[13] See Angela Redish, *Bimetallism: An Economic and Historical Analysis*, Studies in Macroeconomic History Index (Cambridge: Cambridge University Press, 2000), 54; Mayhew, "Central Minting," 159–163.

[14] Treatise on the New Money, in Johnson, trans./ed., *De Moneta/English Mint Documents*, 77.

[15] Against the Abbot of St. Edmunds (1280), and The St. Edmundsbury Trial Plate, Johnson, trans./ed., *De Moneta/English Mint Documents*, 85–87.

mints. He aggressively swept away the hereditary rights of moneyers and prosecuted them fiercely for any misconduct, real or imputed. His descendants
maintained that course. The author of the Treatise likely refined the process for
purifying silver because, as a newly appointed mintmaster, he was well aware that
one of his predecessors, Philip de Cambio, had been hanged in 1279 for coin that
contained too high a level of alloy. (Modern tests suggest that the fatal coin
actually met the sterling standard which was, in those years, somewhat more
approximate.)[16]

Any shortfall in coin's fineness, weight, or count was caught by an elaborate set
of checks. Although moneyers originally performed their own tests, the process
was gradually improved and standardized: it protected a sovereign medium and
disciplined behavior deep into the realm. As the author of the *Dialogus* described
the assay for fineness, it operated to "protect the *public* interest," because each
sheriff, anticipating that he might personally lose if the coin he brought in failed
to meet the sterling standard would take "good care … that the moneyers placed
under him do not exceed the limits of the appointed standard" or stretch the
bullion further by adding more alloy.[17] The Treatise and accompanying documents gravely treat the assay, done at the king's mints, and the "trial of the pyx,"
performed more occasionally at the Exchequer.[18] The "pyx" referred to a box that
held money to be tested, a namesake to none other than the vessel that held the
consecrated Eucharist. The process itself takes on the tone of an adjudication, a
"trial of the money" and its makers. Those men—the warden who kept the dies,
the master of the mint, and the official who bought bullion at the exchange—held
one key each to the three locks on the pyx. It was so secured "because it involves
danger, and judgment of life and limb."[19]

---

[16] For the care taken of dies and standards, see, e.g., Assay of the New Money (1248), in Johnson, trans./
ed., *De Moneta/English Mint Documents*, 53; The Form of the New Money (1279), in Johnson, trans./ed., *De
Moneta/English Mint Documents*, 56; Treatise on the New Money (Revised Version), in Johnson, trans./ed.,
De Moneta/English Mint Documents, 89–90. For the centralization of mint control and harsh treatment of
moneyers, see Mayhew, "Central Minting," 84–92; Johnson, trans./ed., *De Moneta/English Mint Documents*, xx–xxi. For the sad story of Philip de Cambio, see Mayhew and Walker, "Crockards and Pollards,"
133–135.

[17] Richard fitz Nigel, "Dialogus de Scaccario," in *English Historical Documents, 1042-1189*, ed. David
C. Douglas and George W. Greenaway (London: Eyre & Spottiswoode, 1953 [circa 1179]), 497, 513–517,
542, 567–568 (emphasis in the original). The method used by the Exchequer to police the specifications of
coin's metal content depended on the era and source of the incoming funds. Coin taken "ad scalam" was
assessed a general 6d. charge for lightness; coin taken "ad pensum" was weighed and assessed more
particularly for any shortfall in weight; "blanched" coin was tested, by sampling, for fineness. See fitz
Nigel, "Dialogus de Scaccario," 515–517; Mayhew and Walker, "Crockards and Pollards," 132.

[18] See Duties of the Officers, in Johnson, trans./ed., *De Moneta/English Mint Documents*, 52; Form of the
New Money, in Johnson, trans./ed., *De Moneta/English Mint Documents*, 56–57; Treatise on the New
Money, in Johnson, trans./ed., *De Moneta/English Mint Documents*, 78–81; see generally Allen, *Mints and
Money*, 164–169; see also Johnson, trans./ed., *De Moneta/English Mint Documents*, xxxv; Mayhew, "Central
Minting," 120–127.

[19] Treatise of the New Money (Revised Version) in Johnson, trans./ed., *De Moneta/English Mint
Documents*, 91, 93; see also Treatise on the New Money in Johnson, trans./ed., *De Moneta/English
Mint Documents*, 80–81.

As the account continues, "When the Master of the Mint has brought the pence, coined, blanched [assayed], and made ready, to the place of the trial," it took its central place on a counter "covered with canvas."[20] The examination commenced, acted out on the body of coin by the men who stood to be exonerated or implicated by the ritual:

> Then, when the pence have been well turned over and thoroughly mixed by the hands of the Master of the Mint and the Changer, let the Changer take a handful in the middle of the heap, moving round nine or ten times in one direction or the other, until he has taken six pounds. He must then distribute these two or three times into four heaps, so that they are well mixed. Then he must weigh out, from these well mixed pence, three pounds, well and exactly, by a standard pound of 20s which is correct to a grain. And so, having weighed out each pound by itself as correctly as possible, he must hand one pound to the Warden to count, another to the Master of the Mint, the third to any of the company or to himself, and they shall count diligently.[21]

At sterling fineness, coin should count out to the proper number per pound. The margins were thin—only coin "a penny in the pound heavier or lighter" than the stipulated 243 pence was "fit for delivery."[22] Coin that deviated more radically was "bad and unfit," disqualified for use as the king's money. The consequences for the king's men could be grave as well.[23]

The "just penny" took its rightful place and its full meaning at the end of the process. Specified and refined, weighed and counted, guarded, tested, and judged, it was now proclaimed. As the Treatise on the New Money ordained, such coin "must be made generally known by public proclamation in the accustomed way by the prince's crier." It was then "ready for use and may not be refused by any of the public without penalty."[24] Earlier sources suggest the same sanctity—the

---

[20] Treatise on the New Money (Revised Version) in Johnson, trans./ed., *De Moneta/English Mint Documents*, 91, 93.

[21] Treatise on the New Money (Revised Version) in Johnson, trans./ed., *De Moneta/English Mint Documents*, 91.

[22] Moreover, a very limited number of pennies could be over or under the required standard of content by grain. Treatise on the New Money (Revised Version) in Johnson, trans./ed., *De Moneta/English Mint Documents*, 92; see also Treatise on the New Money in Johnson trans./ed., *De Moneta/English Mint Documents*, 76; Allen, *Mints and Money*, 147–148. Pennies over 240 count went to the buyer during this time, on the theory that it was "just that every merchant have for his profit on every pound 3d." Treatise on the New Money (Revised Version) in Johnson, trans./ed., *De Moneta/English Mint Documents*, 91; see Mayhew, "Central Minting," 104–105.

[23] Treatise on the New Money (Revised Version) in Johnson, trans./ed., *De Moneta/English Mint Documents*, 91. For example, a master whose coin was unfit to be delivered "will be at the prince's mercy or will in life and members". Treatise of the New Money (1280), in Johnson, trans./ed., *De Moneta/English Mint Documents*, 80, 81. For prosecutions of moneyers, see, e.g., Allen, *Mints and Money*, 164–169; Mavis Mate, "Monetary Policies in England, 1272–1307," *British Numismatic Journal* 41 (1972): 37–44.

[24] Treatise on the New Money (1280), in Johnson, trans./ed., *De Moneta/English Mint Documents*, 66. For an example of the emphasis put on proclamation of the legality of the coin of the realm (or illegality of foreign coin), see "Parliament of 28 Edward I, 1300," in PROME, Appendix (The Parliament Rolls of Medieval England (PROME), accessed June 19, 2014 <http://www.sd-editions.com/PROME/home.html>). ("Order to sheriffs to proclaim ordinance that after the eve of Easter next no money except sterlings to be current in realm since, although king had lately caused it to be proclaimed that each penny of pollards,

sense that money, once adjudicated to have merit, was then publicly empowered. For example, a report on a public assay of money in 1248 declared the money "good and lawful and approved by all," according to the "custom of the realm."[25] Framed by the creative process that actually produced coin, the legalism of the monetary vocabulary regains its vitality: this is value tried, verified, and decreed by the highest authority in the land.

Once money was decreed, its official status trumped competing claims by content. "Forbidden money," the Treatise called bullion or "money not current," even if it was bullion of a very high grade.[26] Likewise, when the Crown instituted the recoinage in 1248, the money judged "not good nor lawful" was taxed at the mint—despite the fact that it actually held an amount of silver sufficient to meet the sterling standard and that the mint already charged customers for any loss in silver weight by wear.[27] Lawful pennies, meanwhile, kept that status regardless of some slippage—there could be pennies very slightly heavy or light, as long as the money overall met the standard when tested in the usual ways.[28]

The just penny was an object set apart, then, from bullion or any other commodity. It had been altered by its royal treatment. That was not formalism but an endorsement written in the precision of the measurements made, the intricacy of the bureaucracy elaborated to produce it, and the gravity of the stakes for the men involved. By the time the just penny was proclaimed, it was literally more than its weight and its fineness—the added value of the just penny, captured in the count, made money worth its price.

Indeed, royal proclamations did not publish the statistics about metal content.[29] Those proclamations instead declared pennies "current" or dubbed them

crockards and like to be current for a halfpenny and no-one to refuse it, king has now caused pollards, crockards and like to be wholly condemned by the counsel of his magnates because he has learned their currency not to advantage of realm," dated 26 March.)

[25] Assay of the New Money (1248), in Johnson, trans./ed., *De Moneta/English Mint Documents*, 54; see also Duties of the Officers of the Mint (1248), in Johnson, trans./ed., *De Moneta/English Mint Documents*, 52 (commenting that money at an assay "must be judged before the clerks and the Changer ... of lawful weight and of good silver," and "good, lawful, and right," after which, "the Changer must give these pence in exchange"). For the "just penny" and "just pence terminology," see Form of the New Money, in Johnson, trans./ed., *De Moneta/English Mint Documents*, 57; Treatise on the New Money, in Johnson, trans./ed., *De Moneta/English Mint Documents*, 78 (noting that "just pence ... is fit for delivery, and then its delivery must not be prevented because the pence are decreed to be fit for use").

[26] Treatise on the New Money (1280), in Johnson, trans./ed., *De Moneta/English Mint Documents*, 71.

[27] Assay of the New Money (1248), in Johnson, trans./ed., *De Moneta/English Mint Documents*, 54; Mayhew, "Central Minting," 107–108. Those bringing old money to the mint could ask that it be "tried in the fire," although it is unclear whether many did. As Nicholas Mayhew points out, few people even had scales to contest the government's conclusions on weighed coin. Mayhew and Walker, "Crockards and Pollards," 131.

[28] See Form of the New Money (1279), in Johnson, trans./ed., *De Moneta/English Mint Documents*, 57; Treatise on the New Money (1280), in Johnson, trans./ed., *De Moneta/English Mint Documents*, 80; Treatise on the New Money (Revised Version) (1290), in Johnson, trans./ed., *De Moneta/English Mint Documents*, 91–93.

[29] Redish, *Bimetallism*, 27–28 (noting public posting of mint price but *not* mint equivalent in units of account).

the "good and lawful sterlings" required for exchange.[30] Parliamentary references to "current" money were common.[31] Those labels recapitulate the peculiar status that attached to a unit that could itself be used as a measure. But they also invite us to consider money in its other dimensions, as a means that would be offered and taken in exchange around the kingdom.

B. The mode of payment, or why sheriffs privileged the penny

After producing the just penny, the government immediately endorsed it as a mode of payment. Its policy did more than put an imprimatur on the money. It made lawful coin a necessary part of ordinary life. "Nothing pertaining to the king ... is so much handled by men as the coin," wrote Bartholomew of Lucca.[32] Coin was the vehicle that carried value from government to individual and back. That movement was constant as the king hired suppliers, paid soldiers, and in turn demanded money from subjects. Secured by its role as the public means of payment, money assumed pride of place as the means people used to mark value or make transfers in everyday exchange with each other. Although it was not always available, it was the most acceptable way to pay others in English society.

The first time the government used its just pennies was when it paid people buying coin at the mint. After coin had been declared "good and lawful sterling," "the Changer must give these pence in exchange" declared a document about the duties of mint officials in 1248. Money newly issued within the permissible range by weight was "accepted for the Master to pay to the merchants" who supplied most of the bullion, confirmed a mint directive about the 1279 recoinage.[33] The

---

[30] Stat de Falsa Moneta 1299 (27 Edw 1); see also Stat de Moneta, likely 1284 (12 Edw I); Stat de Moneta Parvum, likely 1291 (20 Edw I). The Statuta de Moneta appears to reproduce material originally attached to a writ from 12 Edward I, according to the editors of *The Statutes of the Realm*. The Statuta de Moneta Parvum appears to reproduce the text of a writ dated, according to a postscript reprinted in *The Statutes of the Realm* text, to 20 Edw II. See Great Britain, Parliament, I *The Statutes of the Realm*, 219–220 (London: G. Eyre and A. Strahan, 1810–1828), available online at HeinOnline English Reports (Buffalo, NY: W. S. Hein, 1993). The dating used here accords with that used by Allen, *Mints and Money*, 355. Enacted as Edward I moved toward devaluing the imitation pennies, the Statuta de Falsa Moneta did not prohibit their use in minor exchange, but required sterling for significant commercial exchange. See generally, pp. 138–149. For other examples, see pp. 93–94.

[31] Parliamentary references to and provisions for "current" money include the answer made by the Crown in 1343 to the Commons' prayer that only money at sterling standard circulates: "Good money should be current as it has been before this time, until it is ordained otherwise." "Parliament of 17 Edward III, 1343," in PROME, item 57. For other references, see "Parliament of 13 Edward III, 1339," in PROME, item 14; "Parliament of 17 Edward III, 1343," in PROME, item 14 and 15; "Parliament of 20 Edward III, 1346," in PROME, item 11; 25 Edw 3 stat 5 c 13 (1351–1352); "Parliament of 25 Edward III, 1352," in PROME, item 32; "Parliament of 19 Henry VII, 1504," in PROME, item 12; 19 Hen 7 c 5 (1503–1504).

[32] Bartholomew (Ptolemy) of Lucca, as quoted by Thomas N. Bisson, *Conservation of Coinage: Monetary Exploitation and Its Restraint in France, Catalonia, and Aragon (c.A.D.1000–c.1225)* (Oxford: Clarendon Press, 1979), 1.

[33] See Duties of the Officers of the Mint, in Johnson, trans./ed., *De Moneta/English Mint Documents*, 52; Form of the New Money, in Johnson, trans./ed., *De Moneta/English Mint Documents*, 57. When exchange

amount paid out included a deduction for minting and other costs, as well as a fee to the Crown. The charge, sometimes called gross seignorage, may have been standardized by Henry II as early as 1158 at one shilling in the pound.[34] Seignorage rates would be periodically adjusted; a significant reform took place in 1262.[35]

The requirement that government officials give out only current coin had a long pedigree. The renovatio monetae had renewed the coinage every several years through that very practice: "the Cambiatores, or Keepers of the exchanges, received instructions when the type was changed, and it would be their business to see that the money circulated by them was of the current type."[36] The Crown policed the performance of its agents carefully, checking records against each other and sending commissions into action to investigate suspicions that old or improper money was being distributed.[37]

More generally, the government used the money it minted to pay its creditors. Recall that the renovatio monetae acted as the engine producing pennies that were used to pay tribute to the Danish invaders. The early Anglo-Saxon rule that "there is to be one coinage over all the king's dominion" suggests that the government used that coin as well for domestic obligations.[38] A century after the Norman Conquest, the author of the *Dialogus* expressed the perennial concern of sovereigns: he connected Henry I's determination to make more coin to his need to pay the expenses incurred "in suppressing rebellion overseas and in distant parts of his dominions."[39] The Edwardian proclamations ordaining the money

of silver for coin was immediate, a merchant was paid by number (e.g., 240d. per pound at this time). When the mint took bullion and returned coin later, the merchant was generally paid coins by weight according to the quantity brought in (e.g., up to 243d per pound). Apparently, individuals then paid up minting and seignorage charges. Mayhew, "Central Minting," 105, compare 107–108, 118–119, 126. Edward I experimented with taking the extra profit by weight at a certain point. See Mayhew, "Central Minting," 105, 119; Mate, "Monetary Policies," 50.

[34] See Mayhew, "Central Minting," 89–90, for the intriguing suggestion that the charge, along with an increase in the penny's weight, allowed Henry II to align a troy pound of silver handed in at the mint with a Tower pound of coin handed back. (The troy pound was the standard used in Henry's Continental territories.) Before that point, royal charges for minting under Henry II may have depended on whether mints were "farmed," generating revenue for moneyers who paid the king an annual fee, were "privileged," paying no fee to the Crown, or were worked directly by the Crown. In line with the work of Pamela Nightingale, Mayhew suggests that Henry II's move to consolidate the mints was, in fact, a means of regaining the profits captured by moneyers under the more disjointed system. Mayhew, "Central Minting," 85–87.

[35] See, e.g., Mayhew, "Central Minting," 118–119, 132–134; Redish, *Bimetallism*, 27–28, 50–52, 89–92 (Appendix). For the most comprehensive review of mint profits, see Allen, *Mints and Money*, 170–213.

[36] George C. Brooke, "Quando Moneta Vertebatur: The Change of Coin-Types in the Eleventh Century; Its Bearing on Mules and Overstrikes," *British Numismatic Journal* 20 (2d ser., vol. X) (1929–30): 114.

[37] See, e.g., the measures taken in 1180, 1251, and 1279, described by Johnson, trans./ed., *De Moneta/ English Mint Documents*, xxii, xxviii–xxix, xxxii–xxxiii. For bureaucratic developments to police coin, see Mayhew, "Central Minting," 99–107.

[38] Dorothy Whitelock (ed.), *English Historical Documents*, 2nd ed., vol. 1 (London: Eyre Methuen: 1979), 420 (Athelstan's Laws). Although existing scholarship does not address the possibility, the law may have applied to the new coins produced at each renovatio monetae.

[39] fitz Nigel, "Dialogus de Scaccario," 516.

to be called "current" and "lawful" applied on their face to public officials and it appears that those officials complied; when documents record the kind of coin used by the Exchequer, it was current if not always newly minted coin. As the episode of the imitation pennies reveals, the Crown occasionally recognized a foreign coin as legitimate tender. By contrast, officials fought, destabilized, and eventually stamped out competitor coinages that they disapproved.[40]

The government demanded payment by the same token, literally. Again, the renovatio monetae provides an early example. Obligated to pay taxes in a particular coin, people turned to the mints, delivering old money and bullion in exchange for the renewed money they owed their rulers. Early Anglo-Saxon laws are full of fines and fees levied in pence and "shillings," a monetary multiple rather than a weight of silver.[41] By the time of the Domesday Book, the king took rents and other payments in pennies; lords and thegns also took coin from those who owed them, even as many in-kind levies continued.[42] As Sir Matthew Hale noted in his early modern commentary, *History of the Pleas of the Crown*, "Anciently, all money was paid in number...and this was the common reservation and account of all farms, and estimating of accounts."[43]

In the century after Domesday (the 12th), the records of Exchequer practice begin. They document revenue paid into the Lower Exchequer (the Exchequer of Receipt) in money that was "counted over, put down in writing and notched on tallies."[44] As they did where government payments were concerned, official references to "current" coin, "good and lawful sterling" and the like applied on their face to tax obligations, except those levied in-kind. The king's tax farmers and receivers had a conspicuous incentive to protect themselves by accepting only the king's coin: if the revenue they collected was not accepted by the Exchequer, they were on the hook for the shortfall. In fact, the sheriffs in office during the episode of the imitation pennies at the end of the 13th century selected for current coin so assiduously that it got in the Crown's way. When it was legal to use the foreign pennies, they had accepted them. But when the king devalued that coin, the sheriffs switched back, refusing to accept anything but sterlings.

---

[40] See p. 78 nn. 30–31, pp. 138–149. For use of current coin, e.g., Mate, "Monetary Policies," 50–51 and n. 1, 64 and n. 8. For an example of the campaign against foreign coin, see Mate, "Monetary Policies," 68–69, and the episode of the imitation pennies, see pp. 138–149.

[41] See p. 65; Whitelock, *English Historical Documents*, 407–423; see also Oresme, *De Moneta*, xxi.

[42] Christopher Dyer, *Making a Living in the Middle Ages*, New Economic History of Britain (New Haven: Yale University Press, 2002), 26–42; Spufford, *Money and Its Use*, 87–90.

[43] Sir Matthew Hale, *Historia Placitorum Coronae [The History of the Pleas of the Crown]*, 2 vols., vol. 1 (London: E. Rider, Little Britain, 1800 [1672]), 205. Hale appears to be quoting the Domesday manuscript, referring to a directive to sheriffs ("vicecomes") who are directed to make payment to the treasury ("thesauro") by number: "vicecomes A. Reddit compotum de 100 l. numero," or "in thesauro 100 l. numero." He may also be quoting the *Dialogus*. Hale, *Historia Placitorum Coronae [The History of the Pleas of the Crown]*, 205. As discussed below, Crown officials regularly checked money paid by count for weight and fineness.

[44] See fitz Nigel, "Dialogus de Scaccario," 494.

Fig. 2.2 Receiving and weighing coin at the Exchequer, in Eadwine Psalter c. 1160, as reproduced in J. G. Green, *A Short History of the English People*, ed. A. S. Green and K. Norgate (New York: Harper, 1893), 184.

They had to be ordered by the Crown to receive pollards and crockards, although at the new, lower value.[45] In the next century, parliamentary reference occasionally confirms the understanding that tax payments "should be made in money current in the land."[46] By then, it seems to be a background rule no longer necessary to state explicitly except at moments like 1504, when the bad condition of the coinage drove Parliament and the Crown to emphasize that even cracked pennies would be accepted for all public payments.[47]

The procedures used to test newly minted coin for weight and fineness appear again in the Exchequer, now put to work to protect the king against underpayment in coins that have been worn down, "clipped," or counterfeited. The timing makes sense: problems with weight and clipping would increase after the frequent recoinages of the renovatio monetae ended. In the *Dialogus*, the task of taking in and testing coined money organizes the officers—there are "tellers" to count, a "silverer" to supervise the assay, knights who weigh and lock up the pennies. A government bureaucracy is born and grows in the very effort to receive money revenue (see Fig. 2.2).[48]

---

[45] See Mate, "Monetary Policies," 67 n. 4.

[46] "Parliament of 20 Edward III, 1346," in PROME, item 11.

[47] "And moreover, that all kinds of pennies, being silver and having the stamp of the king's coin, shall be allowed and be current for payment both to him in all his receipts and to all his receivers, and to all other lords spiritual and temporal and their receivers, and to all others within this his realm, without being refused or rejected in any way, with the sole exception of pennies bearing spurs or the mullet ... to be allowed as halfpennies only, and not more". "Parliament of 19 Henry VII, 1504," in PROME, item 12. See 19 Hen 7 c 5 (1503–1504).

[48] See fitz Nigel, "Dialogus de Scaccario," 494–496; see generally Mayhew and Walker, "Crockards and Pollards," 130–133; Johnson, trans./ed., *De Moneta/English Mint Documents*, xxi. In the early 1290s when

The Exchequer's care in scrutinizing the silver (and later gold) content of coin underscores the importance it attributed to current and counted coin. It reminds us that the official determination to identify money with a count does not mean that the content of coin did not matter. To the contrary, supporting the count of coin required policing coin's quantity and source, action that in turn policed the monetary system. Note that when the Exchequer assessed the silver content of coin, it was not accepting bullion or silver plate. Rather, it was maintaining coin by insisting that it meet the minimum standard. That imperative would keep people coming to the mint for new money as the old wore away. As Stephanie Bell points out, policing coin also disallowed taxpayers from diluting the material value of the tax obligation. Ultimately, that obligation represented a real investment of work—the effort necessary to acquire money for the levy. If taxpayers could evade that effort by lightening coin or counterfeiting it, they undermined the ability of the sovereign to direct their work and diminished the extent to which the sovereign could acquire it.[49]

Finally, keeping coin constant in its ratio of content to count maintained it for people to use in ordinary exchange. From the time public authorities had started using coin to pay them and demanding coin in taxes, it had offered people a store of value. By concerting the production and flow of money among people, the government created a predictable supply and demand for its pennies, allowing people to estimate their worth and transfer them to one another in payment. As they did so, people's desire for an item with currency to use in their own exchange fed into the demand undergirded by the public's requirements.

When they accepted pennies, people wanted "good and lawful sterlings" rather than money that was clipped or underweight, let alone counterfeited. Most individuals probably insisted on this far less often than the Exchequer—many had little leverage over those paying them and, as we will see, limited opportunity to get coin. But people disfavored coin that fell below the minimum standard, fearing their own inability to pass it along. In that way, they also policed coin's metal content, although they could not lawfully demand that it meet a higher-than-official standard as they could have if coin actually offered its commodity value.[50]

In fact, when the public began to attend to the weight of coin too closely, it signaled trouble in the circulatory system of money. The Count of Flanders, Gui de Dampierre, had gone so far as to prohibit his subjects from weighing coin

---

clipped or counterfeit coin was especially rampant, the Crown ordered all coin taken into the Exchequer to be tested. Mate, "Monetary Policies," 58–59. It is not clear how comprehensive the check was otherwise.

[49] Stephanie Bell, "The Role of the State and the Hierarchy of Money," *Cambridge Journal of Economics* 25, no. 2 (2001): 155.

[50] See, e.g., Stat de Moneta likely 1284 (12 Edw I) (allowing weighing of clipped coin); "Parliament of 19 Henry VII, 1504," in PROME, item 12 (providing that clipped coin could be "utterly refused and renounced in payment"); 19 Hen 7 c 5 (1503–1504) (similar).

at all, except at the mint or exchange. It was an extreme and idiosyncratic policy, one probably doomed to fail.[51] But it highlights the dangers that stalked when people began discriminating between the metal content of coin and its count— the dramas that occurred in that event fill the next chapter. By contrast, when money was circulating successfully, it was traveling "by tale," or by count. That, after all, was the goal of creating a "unit of account" and a standard mode of payment. English authorities extensively enforced coin as a currency that traveled on its own terms between individuals, an effort that takes us to money as the medium of exchange.

C. The medium of exchange and the importance of the count

According to most historians of the medieval economy, people making ordinary trades in silver money generally made them by count. (High-value coin, especially gold, was in a different category. Those transacting large trades, especially at the international level, had the wherewithal and the motivation to test and weigh coin of such high metallic value.[52]) Scales were too few to weigh the money used in ordinary exchange and too rough to weigh coin to the grain.[53] Yet more obviously, there was no way that laypeople could check the fineness of metal.[54] The best that most people could have done was second-guess the circulating coin for wear and damage, a scrutiny derivative of the look and heft of the government's offer.

Far from encouraging people to orient themselves to metal content, the government enforced coin's face value. With a consistency that was striking compared to other Europeans, the English institutionalized money as a matter that moved by count. They embedded that practice in the common law of exchange, publicized it in rules on currency, and policed it as the exclusive medium. Between its issue and its demand by the government in taxes, coin thus circulated between private individuals with the blessing of the sovereign.

Legal histories commonly trace the "foundation of the common law" to the rule of Henry II (1154–1189).[55] The same era brought the free minting system, along with an upsurge of written records. None of those developments was a stark break from earlier practices; each built instead on Anglo-Norman and earlier

---

[51] While the narrative focuses on the affirmative measures taken by the Crown to promote money's circulation by count, there are some indications that English authorities also actively disfavored action by individuals to weigh coin. See, e.g., Mayhew and Walker, "Crockards and Pollards," 131.

[52] See, e.g., Mayhew and Walker, "Crockards and Pollards," 131 and n. 37; cf. Carlo M. Cipolla, *Money, Prices, and Civilization in the Mediterranean World, Fifth to Seventeenth Century* (New York: Gordian Press, 1967), 13–26.

[53] See, e.g., Mayhew and Walker, "Crockards and Pollards," 131.

[54] See, e.g., Treatise on the New Money (1280), in Johnson, trans./ed., *De Moneta/English Mint Documents*, 67 ("this can only be known by experts who have learned by practice. But hardly anyone can be found so fully expert as not often to be mistaken in this"); Treatise on the New Money (Revised Version) (1290) ("scarcely anyone is found so perfectly skilled that he is not frequently deceived"). For the process of assaying by touchstone and its complexities, see Redish, *Bimetallism*, 21–24.

[55] John H. Baker, *An Introduction to English Legal History*, 3rd ed. (London: Butterworths, 1990), 15.

Anglo-Saxon traditions. But Henry II's reign offers a good entry point for examining the way the English supported monetary exchange during the medieval period.

Recall that the Anglo-Saxon kings had engineered a system, the renovatio monetae, in which money was periodically recoined and probably circulated by count. By the time Henry began his own monetary reforms, the practice of taking money by count was reinforced by another wave of influence. During the 12th century, Europeans rediscovered Roman law in the codified form produced under Justinian, six centuries before. Justinian's *Corpus*, including a Code of laws, along with the Institutes containing instructive material on the law and a Digest containing interpretive comment, encapsulated the Roman law of antiquity. That law had been written for a stable and highly monetized society; if monetary upheavals occurred or disputes over the way to count money existed, they were not reflected in Justinian's text. Indeed, that work ignored the controversies over money's value that occurred during and after the Roman Republic. It assumed a money that circulated by count (i.e., by tale) and represented value in a unit of account. Authorities taxed and spent in that currency, and enforced it as the medium of private exchange. As later generations would learn, the only remedy enforced under Roman law was compensation in the form of money damages. *Materia forma publica percussa*—a substance struck in public form, coin was used to value all resources even as it was held by people as personal property.[56]

References to money as a counted form appear throughout the *Corpus*; the law on loans would become particularly important to the English and Europeans more generally. Roman law structured loan contracts consistently with its emphasis on money's count and commercial capacity. The law categorized a loan of money or other fungible things (*res fungibilia*) as a consumption or *mutuum* loan, a bargain that effectively transferred ownership of an item from one person to another. (As a 13th century English commentator would put it, "*meum* becomes *tuum*.") The transfer accomplished the purpose of the loan: it conveyed a resource to the borrower that he or she would spend, plant, invest, or otherwise "consume." When the time came to pay off the loan, the borrower need not return the same items borrowed, but only items of the same kind. To put the idea in commercial terms, a party had borrowed a resource to employ productively; it had produced wealth of some kind; he or she should now return the value of that loan. By

---

[56] See Wolfgang Ernst, "The Glossators' Monetary Law," in *The Creation of the Ius Commune: From Casus to Regula*, ed. J. W. Caims and Paul J. du Plessis (Edinburgh: Edinburgh University Press, 2010), 220–221; W. V. Harris, "A Revisionist View of Roman Money," *Journal of Roman Studies* 96 (2006): 22–24; Thomas Rufner, "Money in the Roman Law Texts," in *Money in the Western Legal Tradition*, ed. Wolfgang Ernst and David Fox (Oxford: Oxford University Press, forthcoming, 2015). Before the rediscovery of Justinian's *Corpus*, Roman law survived in much of Europe in a variety of customary forms; Theodosius's code and abridgements, written about a century before the *Corpus*, were the principal written sources of Roman law. The *Corpus* later included the Novels, laws issued by Justinian after the Code had been completed.

contrast, parties might arrange the loan of an asset for use (*commodatio*), as opposed to consumption. In that case, the specific good—a house, a horse, or a tool, for example—had to be returned when the loan was settled.[57]

As the Digest formulated it, the *mutuum* loan concerned "those things that are dealt in by weight, number, or measure." As the Institutes continued, things like money (*pecunia numerata*), wine or oil, silver or gold "we deliver by counting, measure or weight, with the understanding that they shall belong to the parties receiving them, and that not the identical articles but others of the same nature and quality shall be returned to us."[58] Consistent with this prescription and its label as wealth *numerata*, money moved "by counting" and was considered separately from silver or gold, which were weighed (assuming a given fineness).[59] Buyers and sellers, debtors and creditors would assume the circulation of money by tale, each coin taken in terms of the unit of account.

The rediscovery of Justinian's *Corpus* redirected European legal development. Scholars across the region, most notably in Italy, labored to understand and apply Roman law to their own circumstances, adding marginal commentary to the original text. Those "glosses" became a medium of debate about the meaning of the *Corpus*. Spawned in a monetary environment that was much more fragmented and less stable than the Roman Empire at its zenith, many of the glosses contested the rule that the count of money should be used exclusively to settle obligations. To varying extents, the civilian lawyers of the Continent argued that, when money's silver or gold content had been changed, legal obligations were due in coin valued by its intrinsic metal worth. That is, the count of money should not control; money must travel by weight (assuming constant fineness) instead. An authoritative compilation of glosses largely conveying that view was published in 1260, displacing the earlier, layered accretion of marginal commentary. Like civilian lawyers, canon lawyers struggled to understand and use the *Corpus*. To a somewhat lesser extent, their interpretations also denied the emphasis that early Roman law put on valuing money by count.[60]

[57] Ernst, "The Glossators' Monetary Law," 220–222; Thomas J. Sargent and Francois R. Velde, *The Big Problem of Small Change*, The Princeton Economic History of the Western World Indexes (Princeton, NJ: Princeton University Press, 2002), 74–75. The quote is from Henry de Bracton, *Bracton on the Laws and Customs of England*, trans. Samuel E. Thorne, vol. 1 (Buffalo, NY: William S. Hein, 1997), 284. Roman law also recognized other arrangements, like an agreement that one party would safe-keep another's goods (*depositum*); the *depositum* appears close in its logic to the English bailment. D. J. Ibbetson, *A Historical Introduction to the Law of Obligations* (Oxford: Oxford University Press, 1999), 9.

[58] Digest 12.1.2.1, in Theodor Mommsen and Alan Watson (eds.), *The Digest of Justinian* (Philadelphia: University of Pennsylvania Press, 1985); Institutes 3.14, in S. P. Scott (ed.), *The Civil Law, including... The Enactments of Justinian* (Cincinatti: Central Trust Company, 1932).

[59] See Ernst, "The Glossators' Monetary Law," 220; Sargent and Velde, *Big Problem of Small Change*, 74–75.

[60] Accursius compiled the influential gloss that came to be known as the *Glossa Ordinaria*. See Ernst, "The Glossators' Monetary Law"; Theodore F. T. Plucknett, *A Concise History of the Common Law*, 5th ed. (Boston: Little Brown, 1956), 294–296; Sargent and Velde, *Big Problem of Small Change*, 69–99.

As they shaped their own law on exchange, English jurists had the inheritance of earlier Anglo practice, the newly recovered Roman texts, and some amount of scholarly work on those texts before them. In a remarkable divergence from Continental practice, the English early and consistently institutionalized an approach according to which money moved by count. Exactly why they did so—why they charted a course that other Europeans would only adopt after centuries of debate—is not clear. Surely it followed in part from the strong precedent of Anglo-Saxon and Anglo-Norman practice. That practice, prevailing over a consolidated realm, escaped at least some of the challenges posed to Continental sovereigns from foreign coin traveling across their borders. In turn, those early English jurists who read Roman law appear to have picked up Roman practice on this point. They wrote before the *glossateurs* had coalesced around a position that criticized the emphasis on money's count. Perhaps most importantly, the English approach to money loans was entrenched in legal doctrine early on. According to the common law action of debt, the amount of money owed in a dispute was a matter of count, not weight. Value denominated in a unit of account rather than value represented by an amount of silver controlled.

The "earliest writ of a contractual nature to be regularly issued," common law debt emerged in the 12th century. At first, it appears as an executive command, a "royal intervention in matters of money debts." Granted by Henry I to individual grievants, particularly Jews who had no other recourse, the writ ordered delinquent debtors to pay. Eventually, the writ was extended to offer debtors the opportunity to contest that charge in front of royal judges. In that rather backwards fashion, the writ became a vehicle more widely available to parties contesting money debts and came to encompass disputes that local authorities had previously resolved. The writ of debt would become the most commonly used contractual action, providing a robust indicator of English law on payment.[61]

The English legal scholarship of the period articulated the writ of debt in ways consonant with early Roman law, not later medievalist commentary on it. The jurists who produced that literature were administrative officers, men equipped to read Justinian's Code. The earliest treatise, Glanvill's *Treatise on the Laws and Customs of England*, was produced about 1180, before the influential compilation that brought together the civilian glosses on the *Corpus*. The *Treatise*'s text makes clear that the action had first taken shape to resolve disputes over money, not disputes over other fungibles, including silver, or over other chattels:

[61] A. W. B. Simpson, *A History of the Common Law of Contract* (Oxford: Clarendon Press, 1975), 53–55; R. C. van Caenegem, *Royal Writs in England from the Conquest to Glanvill*, Publications of the Selden Society, vol. 77 (London: Quaritch, 1959), 254–257; S. F. C. Milsom, *Historical Foundations of the Common Law*, 2nd ed. (London: Butterworth, 1981), 243–245.

The king to the sheriff, greeting. Command N to render to R, justly and without delay, one hundred marks [*marcas*], which he [R] alleges that he [N] owes him [*debet*] and which, he complains, he is unjustly withholding [*deforciat*] from him. And if he does not do so, summon him by good summoners to be before me or my justices at Westminster on the third Sunday after Easter to show why he has not done so. And have there the summoners and this writ.[62]

The writ of debt would be expanded widely enough to include claims for fungible goods other than money, like silver, wheat, and wine, and for personal property, as Glanvill's commentary made clear. But money awards, articulated as such, took pride of place as paradigmatic, as they had been in Roman law.[63]

The vocabulary of the money form was arguably ambiguous at first, but soon indicated that money as a unit of account controlled in debt actions. At the time Glanvill's *Treatise* was written, the term it used as an example of a value claimed—the mark—was both a weight-standard and monetary unit of account. Early Anglo-Saxon material had, more clearly, used moneys of account. And by the 13th century, examples of "debt" used in legal writing employed terms that clearly signified the same. The *solidus* or shilling, and the *libre* or pound, were arithmetic matters; they were multiples of pennies, not real coins. The vocabulary thus identified the substantive obligation of debt with an abstract monetary value, not a weight.[64]

As a conceptual matter, early English jurists clearly connected the action for debt to the Roman law of obligations. Glanvill's *Treatise* picked up the division between loans for consumption, "when anyone lends another something which can be counted, weighted or measured," and loans for use, "as when I gratuitously loan you some thing of mine to make use of in your service."[65] Scholars have debated how completely Glanvill assimilated Roman theories of obligation;

---

[62] G. D. G. Hall, ed., *The Treatise on the Laws and Customs of the Realm of England Commonly Called Glanvill*, Oxford Medieval Texts (Oxford: Clarendon Press, 1993), BkX[2], 116–117. The language also reflects the movement of the writ from an executive order (the first substantive sentence) to a judicial summons (the second sentence). Glanvill's *Treatise* was likely written sometime in the late 1180s. Simpson, *A History of the Common Law of Contract*, 54, n. 2.

[63] Simpson, *A History of the Common Law of Contract*, 53–54; Ibbetson, *A Historical Introduction*, 18. A similar indication of money's basic priority is that claims for goods generally had to be given a monetary value. See, e.g., Stat of Wales 1284 (12 Edw 1 c 6).

[64] For Anglo-Saxon practice, see pp. 65–69. For later English practice, see, e.g., Stat of Wales 1284 (12 Edw 1) (*solidus*); Fleta, Vol. II, in *Publications of the Selden Society*, vol. 72, ed. H. G. Richardson and G. O. Sayles (London: Quaritch, 1953), 206 (*libras, marcas*). Fleta uses the term "pecunia" elsewhere, see Fleta, 187, 190, 210, 213; see also (1310) YB 3 Edw II, 22 SS 21, David J. Seipp, ed., *Medieval English Legal History: An Index and Paraphrase of Printed Year Book Reports, 1268–1535* (Boston: Boston University, 2013) no. 1310.131ss (*livres*) (hereafter Seipp's Abridgement). As the English added denominations to their system (significantly from 1279 on), the monetary value indicated by the multiples of the unit of account could be filled by different coins. The "sum certain," required by the writ according to those enforcing it, did not then refer to specific coins. See Simpson, *A History of the Common Law of Contract*, 61. Similarly, Glanvill's *Treatise* describes a sale as the exchange of a good for a certain "price" (*precium*), rather than amount of silver. Again, the term implies a monetary unit of account. Hall, *Glanvill*, BkX[14], 129.

[65] Hall, *Glanvill*, BkX[3] and [13], 117 and 128.

Germanic influences on his work were arguably more profound.[66] Critical for our purposes is the narrower point that he followed Roman legal practice that put money-as-a-counted-medium in a separate category from other goods, even fungible goods. Several decades later, the most ambitious medieval work to be produced on the common law emphasized the distinction. The manuscript on the *Laws and Customs of England*, written or compiled over the first half of the 13th century and attributed to Henry de Bracton, identified the *mutuum* loan for consumption as that consisting of "things reckoned by weight, number or measure." It then defined the categories expressly, noting that metals like "copper, silver, and gold" went by weight and "wine, oil, or grain" went by measure. "Coined money," by contrast, went by number. In other words, people borrowed coined money by count, and repaid it the same way. As Bracton explained, "[s]uch things, [ascertained] by weighing, counting, or measuring, are given so that they at once become the property of those who take them...[and] not the very things but others of the same kind are returned to the creditor."[67]

The scholarly tradition represented by the work attributed to Glanvill and Bracton coexisted in England with a legal practice that was much less learned and more directly applied. That work neglected many aspects of early treatises; arguably, it developed without sustained engagement with the Roman texts or their civilian interpretation. But some of the formulations captured by the Glanvill and Bracton treatises had entered lay-legal circulation by the late 13th century. A commentary aimed at those administering estates reproduced Bracton's analysis of loans, and appeared to treat money differently from all other goods.[68] Bracton's work also influenced the practices of those adjudicating cases. It was copied and recopied by "men connected with courts, judges and lawyers and those hoping to become such," over the course of the century. It thus had some impact as the ancient practice of "counting"—orally stating a claim or defense—as that practice gave way to a more professionalized pleading. As S. F. C. Milsom relates, the counts were assimilated to writs, captured in writing, and collected in registers.[69] The king's "original writs" came from his Chancery, an office that did much of its administrative work in Latin; its staff would be

---

[66] See, e.g., Ibbetson, *A Historical Introduction*, 17–18. As Ibbetson notes, Glanvill's approach to debt may owe more to Roman law than his work on other topics. Ibbetson, *A Historical Introduction*, 17. Having said that, Glanvill emphasized "entitlement" as the basis of a plaintiff's claim, rather than following the Roman focus on the act of contract itself. Glanvill's approach comports with the common law's emphasis on evidence of a loan, such as a pledge. Ibbetson, *A Historical Introduction*, 19.

[67] Bracton, *Bracton*, 284. Assumedly, a creditor like anyone else receiving money could demand that it be whole—unclipped, and of official weight. But according to a nominalist approach, the creditor could not demand *more than* a coin of official current weight, no matter what the official weight of the coin originally conveyed.

[68] Plucknett, *Common Law*, 264–268. Fleta distinguished loans for consumption (*mutuum*) and use, treated money as distinct from silver, and aligned it with items that were counted. Fleta, 186–187, 197, 200. On Fleta, see Theodore F. T. Plucknett, *Studies in English Legal History* (London: Hambledon Press, 1983), 1.

[69] Samuel Thorne, Translator's Introduction, in Bracton, *Bracton*, xv; Milsom, *Historical Foundations*, 37–44; see also Baker, *English Legal History*, 200–203.

literate in the early commentaries and well aware of the classical division between loans for consumption and loans for use.[70] Another manual, meant to convey the common law in the vernacular Law French, followed Bracton's analysis of obligation and used money as the exemplar of debt, while confusing many of Bracton's finer distinctions.[71]

By that time, the structure of the common law likely subdivided the writ of debt in a way that distinguished money claims from all others. Registers of writs from the 1220s contain only simple forms for debt, although those forms clearly follow Glanvill insofar as they assume a money debt as the paradigmatic kind of debt.[72] By the 1260s, the registers publish different writs for debt (*debet et iniuste detinet*) and for other chattels (*iniuste detinet*), adding a money equivalence for the latter.[73] That formulation for debt had been in place for at least a decade, as a case that went to judgment in 1250 demonstrates.[74] According to 1284 legislation that published the king's "original writs" for use in Wales, the writ for debt when money was at stake was proper when it stipulated that the defendant "owes and unjustly detains" (*debet & injuste detinet*) the money. By contrast, debt actions for other goods, whether "sacks of wool" or chattels more generally, were supposed to stipulate only that the defendant "unjustly detains" (*injuste detinet*) the good and state a money equivalence for the item.[75]

The 1284 language suggests that money was treated particularly from very early on, consistent with inherited tradition and the writ's original form as a "royal intervention" into the payment obligations of subjects. Specifically, the formula used in debt actions for money appears to have been different from the start from all other debt actions, those for fungible items other than money as well as for chattels.[76] That reading makes sense of the Statute's language, which

---

[70] Baker, *English Legal History*, 114–116; Elsa de Haas, "General Introduction," in *Early Registers of Writs*, ed. Elsa de Haas and G. D. G. Hall (London: Selden Society, 1970), xii–xvi.

[71] *Britton*, trans. Morgan Francis Nichols (London: Clarendon Press, 1865), 155–159; compare *Britton*, 173; Milsom, *Historical Foundations*, 264–265. The manual attributed to Britton (or le Breton) in turn influenced later registers of writs, including the *Brevia Placitata*. See G. J. Turner, *Brevia Placitata*, The Publications of the Selden Society, vol. 66 (London: Quaritch, 1951).

[72] See Elsa de Haas and G. D. G. Hall (eds.), *Early Registers of Writs*, vol. 87 (London: 1970), 13, reproducing a *justicies* writ for debt, no. 38, from a register from Canterbury known as the Irish Register. The writ used monetary terminology (*solidi* or shillings). It was followed by a directive that writs issue for a deed, shield, horse, or other chattels "[i]n the same manner." See also de Haas and Hall, *Early Registers*, 25, reproducing a *justicies* writ, no. 27, using monetary terminology (*solidi* or shillings). For dating, see G. D. G. Hall, "Commentary," in *Early Registers of Writs*, ed. Elsa de Haas and G. D. G. Hall (London: Selden Society, 1970), xxxiii, xl, xli.

[73] Compare de Haas and Hall, *Early Registers*, 76–77 (nos. 143, 143a) with de Haas and Hall, *Early Registers*, 77 (nos. 146, 146a, 147, 147a). The monetary language continues. In addition to the examples cited, see de Haas and Hall, *Early Registers*, 77 (no. 144, *peccunie* or money, and no. 145, *solidi* or shilling). For dating, see Hall, "Commentary," lv.

[74] See *Maud de Pavely v Basset* (1250) David Crook, ed., *Curia Regis Rolls* (Woodbridge: Boydell Press, 2002) no. 1502, 242–243. My thanks to Paul Brand for this reference.

[75] Stat of Wales 1284 (12 Edw 1 c 6). The language of the writ for money debt was "...*centu solidos quos ei debet & injuste detinet*..." That for chattels or sacks of wool was "...*que ei injuste detinet*..."

[76] Milsom, *Historical Foundations*, 262–263.

differentiated money from either "sacks of wool" or chattels; two examples would only be necessary if the aim was to distinguish money from fungible goods, exemplified by sacks of wool, as well as personal goods. That is also the way that contemporary pleaders and lawyers behaved. As a range of early cases indicates, they treated claims for fungible goods—including quarters of wheat, sacks of wool, and quarters of barley or oats—as matters that merited the non-monetary language of "unjustly detains."[77] The distinction also comports with the consumption/use categories (*mutuum* and *commodatio*), while subdividing the consumption category more finely.

If so, the distinctive quality of money debts was evident much earlier than historians have assumed. In an influential history, Brian Simpson reads the logic of actions for "unspecified" and "specified" goods as basic to the action of common law debt. He finds a blunt division between the treatment of all fungibles and the treatment of chattels, a distinction that would be institutionalized at the end of the medieval period in different actions for debt and detinue.[78]

---

[77] A claimant in 1292 pled that quarters of wheat (a fungible good) were "detained," not "owed and detained." The defendant in the case contested the propriety of debt, arguing a writ of annuity or covenant should lie, but did not contest the writ's formulation. *Anon* (1292), J. H. Baker and S. F. C. Milsom, *Sources of English Legal History: Private Law to 1750* (Butterworths, 1986), 225 (hereinafter B&M); Seipp's Abridgement no. 1292.145rs. Case notes on 1310 pleadings specified that fungibles other than money took a plea of "he detains" and not "he owes." As the text put it, "All things that consist in number (except money), weight or measure, should be demanded by way of debt, thus: 'Command that he render so many quarters of wheat' or 'so many sacks of wool, of such a price,' and not 'chattels to the value of etc.' And in the count one shall say 'wrongfully he detains from him so many quarters of wheat, of such a price, and wrongfully because,' and not 'and the [sic] which he owes, etc.'" Divers Notes (1310) YB 3 Edw II, SS vol. 22, 26, Seipp's Abridgement no. 1310.137ss. (The Notes also indicate that "sacks of wool" are considered fungible goods; they are not treated in this period like sealed bags of money, which would be considered particular chattels. Later authorities would sometimes use "sacks" in the sense of sealed bags of money. See, e.g., Anthony Fitz-Herbert, *The New Natura Brevium* (London: Eliz. Nutt and R. Gosling, 1743 [1534]), 306. In any case, the early cases employing the non-monetary formulation also involve other fungibles.) The pleading in a 1320 case involving quarters of barley and oats also used the "he detains" formulation *Warren v Poyle* (1320) YB Mich 14 Edw II, SS vol. 104, 59; see also S. J. Stoljar and L. J. Downer (eds.), Introduction, SS vol. 104, xx–xxi (1988) (noting use of "he detains"). Defendant challenged the propriety of claiming those goods when a penalty had been set, but not the formation. (The case was disposed on another matter (the existence of an acquittance).) In (1321) YB 14 Edw II, SS vol. 86, 345, Seipp's Abridgement no. 1321.300ss, a party brought a writ of debt using the language "he wrongfully detains" for two acres of wheat—as if he thought two acres of wheat was a non-monetary fungible good. The plaint was abated (rejected), not because of the language, but because the party should have sued in "detinue of chattels." Two acres of wheat apparently did not qualify for debt, which according to the case note lay only for "things which can be numbered, such as money, or weighed, such as wool; or measured, such as a quarter of wheat and such like." I leave aside here the uncertain development of actions by executors. See F. W. Maitland, Introduction, SS vol. 20, lxxxvii (1905) and cases cited.

[78] As he indicates, several early claimants used the action for debt to recover "unspecified" matters that went only by measure, like quarters of wheat. *Anon* (1292) B&M 225, Seipp's Abridgement no. 1292.145rs (writ of debt used for quarters of wheat). *Anon* (1306), A. J. Horwood, *Year Books of the Reign of King Edward the First, Michaelmas Term, Year 33, and Years 34 and 35* (London: Longman, 1879), 150, Seipp's Abridgement no. 1306.034rs (endorsing plea of 1292 case); *Orwell v Mortoft* (1504x1505) B&M 406, 408; Seipp's Abridgement no. 1504.018, B&M 406, 408, in Seipp's Abridgement no. 1540.018 (plea of debt appropriate for quarters of malt, language unidentified), all cited in Simpson, *A History of the Common Law of Contract*, 58, n. 1. (Another case cited by Simpson, (1467) YB Hil 6 Edw IV, Seipp's Abridgement no. 1467.006, does not appear to support Simpson's point as the case is allowed to go to law despite a plea of "he detains" for loose barley.) And several claimants used the non-monetary

In his view, a finer split within the fungible category—the split between money and other fungibles—was a subordinate development that occurred during the 14th century.[79] In fact, a second look at Simpson's cases shows that they are not at odds with debt as an action that more immediately distinguished money from all else. His cases involving fungibles other than money categorized those goods as appropriately brought by writ of debt—but that was appropriate because the writ of debt was an umbrella writ for all fungibles in this period.[80] Even as they used the writ of debt for fungibles other than money, the parties in those cases either employed the non-monetary language ("unjustly detains"), or did not make explicit the language they used.[81] In other words, the parties in his cases may well have been treating claims for fungibles differently from those for money. It bears adding, however, that a register from the early 14th century does identify both money and wheat as matters "owed," if specifically in the context of a recognizance or acknowledgement of debt.[82]

In any case, Simpson agrees that, by sometime in the 14th century, money claims had parted ways from all the others. When a man in 1376 claimed non-monetary things—wheat and an annual rent of hens, he used the writ of debt and the non-monetary "unjustly detains" formulation. Arguments about how to capture his rent arrangement aside, the plaintiff put the common ground color-fully: "although the writ is *detinet* only without *debet*, it is good enough, for a dead chattel or a living chattel it is otherwise than for coins." In fact, the formulation was a command of that very office which issued the writs and had every reason to know the Roman tradition from the start. As the record concluded, "For a man can have no other writ in the Chancery, which was agreed by all."[83]

---

formulation "he detains," as opposed to the monetary language "he owes" when they sued for a "specified" good like a sealed bag of money or gold. (1309) YB 2 Edw II, SS vol. 19, 194, Seipp's Abridgement no. 1309.210ss; *Luffenham v Abbot of Westminster* (1313) YB Hil 6 Edw II, SS vol. 43, 65, Seipp's Abridgement no. 1313.029ss; *Anon* (1339), B&M 267, Seipp's Abridgement no. 1339.086rs; *Anon* (1439), B&M 267, Seipp's Abridgement no. 1439.005, cited in Simpson, *A History of the Common Law of Contract*, 57, nn. 7, 8.

[79] Simpson, *A History of the Common Law of Contract*, 57–58; see also Baker, *English Legal History*, 365–366. Simpson and other legal scholars agree that these distinctions occurred in the language of the writ; debt for money and detinue formulations remained formally within the action for debt until the late Middle Ages. Simpson, *A History of the Common Law of Contract*, 57–58.

[80] See, e.g., Stat of Wales 1284 (12 Edw 1 c 6); Baker, *English Legal History*, 433–434; Milsom, *Historical Foundations*, 263.

[81] See p. 90 n. 78. Thus the 1292 claimant had used the writ of debt, but had also employed the language "unjustly detains," and the 1306 case adverted to the 1292 case as correct. The cases Simpson cites to show that money in a sealed bag merits the formulation "he detains" are not to the contrary; they distinguish chattel claims (money in a sealed bag here constituting a particular chattel) and money claims, but say nothing about claims for other fungibles and their possible difference from money claims.

[82] See de Haas and Hall, *Early Registers*, 224, reproducing a recognizance of debt for money or wheat, no. 492, from a Bodleian register of about 1318–1320. See Hall, "Commentary," lvi. For the clear distinction between money "owed" and chattels "unjustly detained" in other examples, see de Haas and Hall, *Early Registers*, 221–223, 225–226, 229–230 (nos. 478–480, 482, 485, 487, 498–499, 515–517, including no. 480, using "unjustly detains" for "certain silver or a silver cup" (*quendam argentum vel supam argenteam*)). An example of the contrasting formula for executors is at de Haas and Hall, *Early Registers*, 222 (no. 483).

[83] (1376) YB Trin 50 Edw III, Seipp's Abridgement no. 1376.031. I have used Simpson's translation, Simpson, *A History of the Common Law of Contract*, 58, n. 5. See also *Shipton* (1442), B&M 391, 394; Seipp's

From early on then, the common law treated money in a way that highlighted its particularity. The terms of the writ separated "money" from other goods, including silver and gold. Those metals were claimed in the language of *injuste detinet*, while money required *debet et injuste detinue.*[84] According to the logic of that division, if a pleader wanted a loan made in coin to be repaid in silver or gold as a weight rather than a coin, the very formulation of his pleading should have differed.

Having isolated money as distinctive, the common law records confirm that it was a matter that was reckoned by number. A set of pleading notes made in 1310 thus put money into the counted category when it distinguished it from *other* numbered fungibles, "All things *that consist in number (except money)*, weight or measure, should be demanded... [using the language 'he detains']." More straightforwardly, the record on a case in 1321 included the observation, "that plaint of debt only lies *for things which can be numbered, such as money,* or weighed, such as wool; or measured, such as a quarter of wheat and such like."[85] The special "moneyness" of coin popped up elsewhere here or there, perhaps most memorably in an odd 1490 trespass dispute between a tanner and a shoemaker. The quarrel was over the tanner's right to repossess leather, given that the shoemaker had already transformed it into slippers, shoes, and boots. Yes, the court determined, because the original leather was still recognizable as the underlying material. The same reasoning would collide, however, against the character of coin, "if it had been pennies or groats (4 pence coins), and a piece (of worked silver) is made from them, this cannot be taken (back), because of the pennies (*deniers*), one cannot be known from another." Coin was thus the fungible item, not the silver within it.[86]

The English action for debt thus enforced money as a medium that moved by number between individuals. In the legal records more generally, money appears

Abridgement no. 1442.056, B&M 391, 394 (Fortescue); (1455) YB Mich 34 Hen VI, Seipp's Abridgement no. 1455.089; Fitz-Herbert, *Natura Brevium*, 262–263.

[84] See, e.g., (1309) YB 2 Edw II, SS vol. 19, 194, Seipp's Abridgement no. 1309.210ss.

[85] See respectively, Divers Notes, (1310) YB 3 Edw II, SS vol. 22, 26, Seipp's Abridgement no. 1310.137ss (emphasis added); (1321) YB 14 Edw II, SS vol. 86, 345, Seipp's Abridgement no. 1321.300ss (using law French *argent* for money). See also (1483) YB Hil 22 Edw IV, Seipp's Abridgement no. 1483.017 (noting that money could not be distrained "because one penny (*denier*) cannot be known from another").

[86] The same rule on inconvertibility would stop an attempt to take back malt in place of wheat; the fungible item was wheat. See *Vannellesbury* (1490) YB Hil 5 Hen VII, Seipp's Abridgement no. 1490.006. A similar rule applied in criminal pleas. Judge Fincham observed the interchangeability of coins in terms that treated them as such, rather than as ounces of metal: "you cannot prove ownership of any particular grain, no more than of particular coins [*deniers*], because all grain of the same kinds and *all coins of the same kind are so alike that no one can distinguish his own from another's*": (1329) YB 3 Edw III, SS vol. 97, 194, Seipp's Abridgement no. 1330.373ss. It would be possible to argue that "of the same kind" qualified "coin" to limit it to coin of a certain recoinage—except that no one ever did. See p. 93 n. 87. It is more likely that the qualification protected the right of creditors, like every person, to demand coin that was up to snuff in terms of current weight, i.e., not clipped, marred, or overly eroded.

to be moving non-controversially by count.[87] In fact, the common law was so tailored to the counted character of coin that it would repel claims to the weight of silver within coin when money was depreciated. That story lies ahead, but it underscores the sanctity of the count in English law: even under stress, the rule would prevail that money traveled in the units denominated by the sovereign. The penny's status as a unit of account was no accident, and it was suitably policed by the courts in disputes over payment.

The value of the penny as a measure, mode of payment, and medium enforced in transactions would have induced people to use it even without legal tender rules, as economists have pointed out.[88] If legal tender rules are not necessary, however, they effectively identify and publicize the money that a political regime has selected to issue and support. They also leave a trail for later observers like ourselves, one that reveals the practice of the earlier community according to its authorities. By that light, the English directed individuals to coin as the exclusive currency that would travel between them as the unit of account.

The Anglo-Saxon rule that "there shall run one coinage throughout the realm" dated to the reign of Athelstan in 930 and was "frequently reiterated," according to Peter Spufford.[89] The proclamation first stipulated uniformity in its insistence on a single kind of coin. Second, it confirmed the currency of coin in its assertion that money would "run" through the kingdom, as opposed to providing a medium for public obligations alone. In the mid-12th century, a provision from Hovenden's Chronicle remarks, at the moment of a recoinage, on a similar imperative. As George Brooke translates it, "a new coinage was made which was the sole currency in the kingdom."[90] The injunction mandates the royal coin as the going medium, a monopoly that would include the unit of measure.

The same command emanates from the mint documents that multiply by the mid-13th century. According to orders associated with the recoinage of 1247, old coin "should be current with the new money and be in no wise refused," as long as it was unclipped.[91] Several decades later, the New Treatise directs that money,

---

[87] Cases challenging tale payment simply do not crop up as an area of dispute, while scholars of common law contract appear to assume money moving by count without controversy. Simpson, *A History of the Common Law of Contract*, 53–54, 80; see also *Midelton v Anon* (1346) YB Trin 20 Edw III, Seipp's Abridgement no. 1346.131rs (defendant claiming to have paid "by tale" and to have tallies as receipts).

[88] See, e.g., Adam Smith, "Chapter II: On Money Considered as a Particular Branch of the General Stock of the Society, or of the Expense of Maintaining the National Capital," *An Inquiry into the Nature and Causes of The Wealth of Nations* (1937 [1776]), 311, accessed June 19, 2014, <http://www.marxists.org/reference/archive/smith-adam/works/wealth-of-nations/book02/ch02-2.htm>; Farley Grubb, "Is Paper Money Just Paper Money? Experimentation and Local Variation in the Fiat Monies Issued by the Colonial Governments of British North America, 1690–1775," *NBER Working Papers*, no. 17997 (2012), 46–48.

[89] Spufford, *Money and Its Use*, 87.

[90] Brooke, "Quando Moneta Vertebatur," 115. The chronicle reads "novam fecit monetam quae sola recepta erat et accepta in regno." It may indicate a requirement that coin be taken at face value even more directly insofar as it identifies coin as that "which alone was received and accepted in the kingdom."

[91] See, e.g., Johnson, trans./ed., *De Moneta/English Mint Documents*, xxvi (noting 1247 order to sheriffs to disallow certain money from currency); Calendar of Patent Rolls 1247–1258, 22, 22 July 1248 (Westminster), as translated in Mayhew, "Central Minting," 107, n. 70; see also Calendar of Close Rolls, vol. 10,

once proclaimed, is "ready for use and may not be refused by any of the public without penalty." A statute of a few years later makes an exception in a period of rampant clipping, permitting people to weigh coin to make sure it was up to the sterling standard. At the end of the century, the norm of the face count is reasserted: an ordinance condemns those who refuse current money (there, foreign pennies at a rate of two to the sterling penny) as an act of "great contempt" and "in great disobedience" of the king. Nor can individuals act out their dismay by charging more in a coin they distrust. They must offer goods "at reasonable prices" and "for such money as is current," receiving it "according to the ordinance aforesaid."[92] At the end of the Middle Ages, another crisis of poor quality coin pushed Henry VII and his Parliament to be explicit once again: all higher denomination coin that had been declared current and are "not clipped, shrunk or otherwise impaired," should "pass and be current throughout the said realm at their face value," even if they were cracked. The same act required pennies to be accepted in all payments.[93] Throughout the era then, coin declared lawful by the Crown was the medium it supported for use in private exchange, to be offered and taken at face value.

At the same time, the government prohibited competition to its currency. One form of control followed from its success in defining the unit of account. The price the government gave for silver at the mint (in pennies/ounce of silver) constrained the domestic price for silver. Individuals had no reason to sell silver for less in domestic coin than the amount the government was willing to pay. That price, adjusted upwards by the charge for minting, normally also provided a ceiling. Buyers would not give more in pennies for silver bullion than the difference, valued in pennies, between the content of silver they purchased and the content they gave in coined form. That difference was, of course, the cost of pennies at the mint (all assuming full-weight coin). Although they could disregard the cost of coining money as already paid and presumably paid by another person, buyers would gain nothing by using any more coins than the mint price plus the minting fee to buy silver. Prices for bullion thus could rise to the point at

---

1256–1259, ed. A. E. Stamp (London, 1932), 88 (gold coin to be current ("currat") for buying and selling at a fixed exchange rate to silver coin, and silver coin to be current as used ("currat similiter sicut currere consuevit")).

[92] For the Treatise on the New Money (1280), see Johnson, trans./ed., *De Moneta/English Mint Documents*, 66. For the permission to weigh coin, see Stat de Moneta, likely 1284 (12 Edw I), I *The Statutes of the Realm*, 219–219 [sic], and for the exigent circumstances of the crisis, Mate, "Monetary Policies." The ordinance requiring use of current coin at reasonable prices referred to the imitation pennies. See pp. 144–146. In that case, merchants were actually neglecting the relatively high metal content of the foreign pennies and charging higher prices than that content or the official count warranted because they feared the imminent demonetization of the foreign pennies. For the ordinance, see Jan. 28, 1288–1300, in Lib. Cut. II, 563–564.

[93] The injunction included gold coin and multiples of pennies (four- and two-penny pieces) and extended to foreign coin that had been declared current in England: "Parliament of 19 Henry VII, 1504," in PROME, item 12; see 19 Hen 7 c 5 (1503–1504).

which the silver content of the pennies equaled the silver content of bullion. Beyond that point, if people wanted silver, they would melt pennies and retrieve it from pennies rather than increase the price they would pay for bullion.[94]

For domestic purposes, the only detour around prices set in the pennies was to pay for silver, by definition illiquid, in commodities. That market had little chance of overcoming the commensurability problems that stalked it, the very problems that coined silver resolved. But even if it had, the government intervened against the possibility. At least in the late 13th century, individuals could not "change silver" (presumably buy or sell) of any kind "except at the king's exchange," nor could goldsmiths buy any silver except old plate anywhere "but at the exchange." All silver (and implicitly, gold) work had to be done "in the main streets in public view, under heavy forfeiture at the king's will."[95] Almost unremarked in the economic history, the government's action would have handicapped the market in silver for other than monetary uses. If the limit on transactions was enforced to any significant extent, it would route all such transactions to the exchanges where, under existing rules, trades would be made in money.[96]

Contrary to the logic of the commodity money model, then, there was no robust alternative use of metal as a commodity medium. The disciplining effect imputed to that competition—the notion that people were constantly calculating the worth of the monetary commodity against its non-monetary commodity value in order to price the cash quality of coin—would also fail. People were, rather, engaged in a calculation of value that was highly embedded, affected by their own needs to pay others and the government in silver coin. Their evaluation could, as we will see, compare silver's value in domestic money against its value in transborder exchange. But that evaluation was also driven by the monetary use of silver in neighboring countries. In short, the alternative uses of silver as a commodity were pervasively informed by its public and official use as money, in England and by other regional authorities.

Public officials also refused to sanction transfers of private credit on the same conditions as money. Neither bills of exchange nor promissory notes were effective to satisfy public obligations. Moreover, they were not payable on sight, and they moved between holders by endorsement, binding those who signed as guarantors of payment. Thus, unlike coin, they did not offer value indiscriminately to parties interested in exchange. Rather, bills of exchange allowed people with offsetting needs for cash in different locations to trade it between

---

[94] To be precise, it would cost those wanting uncoined silver something to retrieve silver from coin; they would be willing to pay a bit more than mint equivalent (the mint price plus the charge for the pennies in pennies) to avoid that cost. For the many problems introduced by less than full-weight coin, see pp. 110–120.

[95] Form of the New Money, in Johnson, trans./ed., *De Moneta/English Mint Documents*, 57–58.

[96] For a contemporary example of a sovereign's decision to prohibit the market in a monetary metal, in a case in the U.S., see *Perry v United States*, 294 U.S. 330(1935).

themselves. More generally, credit instruments memorialized and provided security for the reciprocal commitments of merchants, suppliers, and consumers who could economize on the use of money by swapping goods—finished cloth for the raw materials to make it, for example. In that case, only the money necessary to settle up the balance changed hands. But because credit depended on the existence of reciprocal demands between parties, it facilitated certain exchanges and left others unassisted.[97]

Henry II and his successors also fenced out foreign competitors to domestic money, continuing the traditional bar on foreign coin that the early Anglo-Saxon rulers had put into place. England's relative isolation made it more possible than it was on the Continent to enforce such a prohibition. Despite some memorable lapses, like the episode of the imitation pennies and an informal exception for Scottish coin, "for the most part English commerce was conducted in English coin." Finally, English authorities mobilized against counterfeiters, if not always successfully. The guerrilla warfare consumed officials, pushing them to experiment with new technology, to adopt it and occasionally to resist it, on the ground that it could hinder, or help, those trying to pass off cheap duplicates.[98]

Whatever their failures on the margin, English authorities succeeded by all these means in entrenching money as a medium of exchange that was virtually exclusive. That fact that medieval prices happened in pennies, not grains or pennyweights of silver, is itself evidence of money's dominance. That monopoly returns us to the operation of free minting.

Where money—so exclusively defined—was scant, bullion could be expected to flow to the mint. Many transactions would benefit from the cash quality that coin as a counted medium offered; those involved would take that currency when they could get it, keeping prices in coin low. Prices would thus regularly reach the "minting point" and those with silver (mainly merchants) would bring their metal in, creating money for their own use as well as the expenses of the

---

[97] On the limits to private credit's negotiability, see, e.g., J. K. Horsefield, "The Beginnings of Paper Money in England," *Journal of European Economic History* 117, no. 32 (1977); James Steven Rogers, *The Early History of the Law of Bills and Notes: A Study of the Origins of Anglo-American Commercial Law,* Cambridge Studies in English Legal History Index (Cambridge: Cambridge University Press, 1995), 97–100; Jongchul Kim, "How Modern Banking Originated: The London Goldsmith-bankers' Institutionalisation of Trust," *Business History* 53, no. 6 (2011): 942–945; L. S. Pressnell, *Country Banking in the Industrial Revolution* (Oxford: Oxford University Press, 1956), 89–90, 170–171. For the traditional function of the bill of exchange as a legal instrument, see Rogers, *Law of Bills and Notes,* 94–100, 114–115. For an example of the way credit's availability distorted the trades of merchants in the late 13th and early 14th century, see Pamela Nightingale, "Monetary Contraction and Mercantile Credit in Later Medieval England," *Economic History Review* 43, no. 4 (November 1990): 560–575. Nightingale tells the story of credit by following the trail of debt defaults, evidenced in certificates of debt sent to Chancery for enforcement.

[98] For the prohibition of "forbidden money" as coin not current, see p. 77, see also pp. 78–82, and for an example of the enforcement of requirement that only English coin be used and an exception to it, see Mate, "Monetary Policies," 68–69; see also pp. 138–149. The evaluation of the amount of foreign coin circulating is from Mayhew, "Central Minting," 131–132. On the importance of counterfeiting as a concern that affected the shape of monetary policy, see Redish, *Bimetallism,* 21–26, 54–61.

government. That is, even if people had been able to weigh coin, indeed, insofar as they could, the monetary enterprise depended on producing a unit that would circulate on its own integrity. It was precisely the difference between the value of bullion—a value that was real and recognized—and the value of coin that brought people to the mint. That marginal advantage of money over silver depended on the penny's identity as a unit publicly acclaimed, used and accepted for payment, and circulating by face value.[99]

Hypothesizing money as a commodity, scholars have at times asserted that people must have valued coin by weight. They are met by the argument from others that certain phenomena in the medieval world would not be comprehensible if coin moved by weight. Government authorities could not have gained revenue by debasement, for example, if people had known and adjusted their use of coin according to its content. Nor would events follow "Gresham's Law"—the truism that "bad money drives out good" because weak and debased coin that bore the same face value as stronger money induced people to hoard or melt the better coin. Those effects did indeed depend on the counted circulation of coin. But another answer is simpler yet: if money amounted to a commodity, free minting would not have functioned to produce it.

D. The fast-moving and high-powered pennies of medieval England

Engineering a supply of "just pennies" against the demand created for them, the English produced a flow of money. That flow was peculiar, a function of its engineering. Specifically, public and private actors required coin of a certain content and form; free minting provided that coin as individuals paid, penny-by-penny, for an item with cash quality. Those forces interacted to generate currency with a distinctive quality: money that traveled quickly from hand to hand and carried a very high purchasing power. Both officials and ordinary people expressed and acted on their sense that money was difficult to hold on to and very valuable. Their reactions suggest the issues of governance and exchange that lay ahead.

We have seen the start of demand for money already under the Anglo-Saxons and its spread by the time of the Domesday Book. P. H. Sawyer argues that England held more of its wealth in coin during the 11th century than France or Normandy, given the supply of silver produced by her wool exports. While that wealth was unevenly distributed, the use of money was broadly dispersed. Royal

---

[99] It is worth exploring whether the point here goes further still. Money held a virtual monopoly in the early world where people picked up the costs of minting. As the chapters ahead document, the government eventually picked up the costs of minting. At the same time, it allowed a significant expansion of negotiable forms. Restricting them may no longer have been necessary, once individual incentives to pick up the cost of creating money were not important.

taxes had reached the peasant population, while estate surveys from the 11th century document the amounts due from that group to manorial lords. The Church added another layer of charges to the load carried by those working the land. Scholars agree that, by the 12th century, money rents were widely displacing rents due in-kind, and landlords were sufficiently sensitive to price changes that they would responsively restructure the way they used peasant labor, switching between money rents and demands of service as one or the other offered better value.[100]

Medieval towns catered relatively early to complex commercial interactions that took place in money: laborers, artisans, petty traders, and larger merchants exchanged their specialized products in those venues. But between 1200 and 1350, weekly markets spread throughout rural England; the number licensed by the Crown ran "into thousands," according to R. H. Britnell. That number may overstate the change because many licenses simply recognized long-standing markets, reflecting the Crown's growing power to denominate such spaces. Villagers and farm workers had been trading informally for centuries—Sundays offered an especially common time and church an especially common place to meet. But the boom was real nonetheless: the country's tradespeople, laborers, and farm families were turning increasingly to more organized markets to sell and buy. During the 13th century, the weights and measures used in licensed markets were standardized, forestalling and regrating were prohibited, and price and quality were regulated.[101]

The burgeoning number of markets ran to a significant extent on money. Trade continued to deliver silver to England during the 12th and 13th centuries, and mint output rose. Estimates of currency supply are notoriously difficult, especially for the period before the mid-13th century; Martin Allen's recent work details the current set of estimates and emphasizes their limitations. The relative growth of currency appears, however, quite clearly across the studies. The English silver currency in 1158 may have amounted to £15,000 to £30,000. By 1180, it had

---

[100] Although the indications in the Domesday Book are debated, P. H. Sawyer parses the overlaps and omissions to argue that it actually understated the money-paying population, and suggests relatively high levels of money use in Germany as well. P. H. Sawyer, "The Wealth of England in the Eleventh Century," *Transactions of the Royal Historical Society* 15 (1965): 153–163; P. H. Sawyer, *The Wealth of Anglo-Saxon England: Based on the Ford Lectures delivered in the University of Oxford in Hilary Term 1993*, 1st ed. (Oxford: Oxford University Press, 2013); see also Dyer, *Making a Living in the Middle Ages*, 39–40, 101–105, 138–143; P. D. A. Harvey, "The English Inflation of 1180–1220," *Past & Present* 61 (1973): 4; Spufford, *Money and Its Use*, 87–90. For the 12th century and the move from leasing to direct farming catalyzed by price inflation, see Harvey, "The English Inflation of 1180–1220," 4–5, 20; Clyde G. Reed and Terry L. Anderson, "An Economic Explanation of English Agricultural Organization in the Twelfth and Thirteenth Centuries," *Economic History Review* 26, no. 1 (1973): 134–137; Edward Miller, "Farming of Manors and Direct Management: Rejoinder," *The Economic History Review* 26, no. 1 (1973): 138. For the rising use of money in Europe more generally, see Spufford, *Money and Its Use*, 241–243, 378 (noting "bulk of peasant rent" to be in coin by the end of the 12th century).

[101] Dyer, *Making a Living in the Middle Ages*, 187–191; R. H. Britnell, "The Proliferation of Markets in England, 1200–1349," *Economic History Review*, 2d ser. 34 (1981): 209–212; Maryanne Kowaleski, *Local Markets and Regional Trade in Medieval Exeter* (New York: Cambridge University Press, 1995), 180–191.

increased significantly, approaching £100,000. By 1210, estimates put it between £100,000 and £300,000, and in 1247, a recoinage produced some £417,000 to £440,000. By 1279, silver coin amounted to something between £500,000 and £800,000. By 1299, total silver currency exceeds £1,100,000 and may be as high as £1,400,000.[102]

Markets had first flourished next to mints, where coined money entered exchange. But during the 13th century, markets were springing up along the roads and riverways of the countryside, even as mints were becoming more centralized. Britnell argues that widespread demand for cash by craftspeople and other specialized workers and by those benefitting from increased agricultural productivity drove much of that development. Other explanations cannot account for the scatter of new markets across the land. Trade in exports invigorated rural commerce, especially in the wool producing areas, but the mushrooming markets of the 13th century were not conduits for the large transfers of wool and grain that moved out of the country, nor did they appear in areas closely associated with regional specialization. The pattern of markets does not indicate, either, that they were dedicated to supporting the life of towns, although some of them served as gathering points for products destined for urban markets. Nor would the demand from baronial households or monasteries suffice to sustain local markets.[103]

Rather, markets appear to have served the craftsmen, laborers, and others who "depended on selling commodities or services to buy their food and raw materials." Centers for trading made it easier for them both to offer their services and to buy what they needed; settlements of families who made a living in the newly established markets spread out around them. Landless workers hired by the agricultural job (threshing or thatching, for example) bought at the markets, while small holders who needed to supplement their incomes sold produce, prepared foods (bread or ale), or rural products like cloth. Small traders brought wares like coal or salt from a greater distance. Markets grew, then, because of the demands of the laboring population and "an increase in local purchases by small households," made possible as agricultural productivity increased.[104]

That exchange in turn depended on a demand for money generated by both public and private authorities. "For most small farmers the need to sell produce in

---

[102] Allen, *Mints and Money*, 322–326, 328, 330. Growth in the silver money supply continues through the second decade of the 14th century and then begins to drop. Allen, *Mints and Money*, 330. The gold coinage remained only a fraction of the money supply in the mid-13th century, but became more significant later in the century. The English added gold coin consistently to their money supply from 1344 on. Allen, *Mints and Money*, 326–327, 331.

[103] See Britnell, "Market Proliferation," 212–218.

[104] Britnell, "Market Proliferation," 215–217, 218; see also Kowaleski, *Local Markets*, 180 (considering benefits brought by urban markets). Farm servants paid annually and domestic servants paid in kind had less need of money. Markets did not continue to multiply in the 14th century, as some accounts of modernization might imagine. Britnell, "Market Proliferation," 219–221.

order to pay rents, fines and taxes was a sharper spur to marketing activity than the need for manufactures or services."[105] Britnell's conclusion follows from the organization of the lay world into one where rents were increasingly asked in money rather than in-kind or in labor, competition for employment on land had increased, and annual contracts for service had become less common. Lords took additional rents for newly cleared and cultivated land, subdivided land in some regions to add tenants, and institutionalized heavier cash demands on villeins. Those demands could be met in exchange for a fee—charges for the right to marry, move, or take over new land (entry fees). Other charges by the manor included tallage, aids, heriots (death duties), and recognition fees that marked the beginning of a new lord's tenure. Justice administered by manorial courts also imposed fees for settling disputes and charges for minor infractions.

According to Christopher Dyer, the total money annually due from a typical tenant in a church estate of the early 13th century amounted to 2s. 6d. rent, 14d. "lardsilver" or help in stocking the larder, and 1d. "hurtpenny" for the pope (or more commonly, the lord), aside from labor due still unconverted into cash. M. M. Postan concludes that money dues generally consumed up to 50 percent of a villein's gross output in the same century. The artisans, small traders and producers, laborers, and service people who lived in towns were yet more dependent on the cash economy, as were the landlords, merchants, and officials who congregated there, generating a demand for services, produce, and eventually luxuries from overseas trade.[106]

As for the public side of demand, that driver came from the political strategy that assessed and imposed taxes and other fines in coin. Those obligations lay heavily on the rural population by the early 14th century if not before.[107] Charges for market violations, fees, and urban tolls (disproportionately paid by rural participants coming to town markets) were common to towns as well as countryside. Maryanne Kowaleski's research on late 13th and 14th century Exeter conveys a world of many small monetary payments, including urban tolls that could amount to one to two pennies per market trip. "The Song of the Husbandman" captured the way public demand cut during the period, and put it into a peasant's mouth. "To seek silver for the king I sold my seed," he cried, stating as well the misery that sometimes followed, "wherefore my land lies fallow and

[105] Britnell, "Market Proliferation," 217; see also Dyer, *Making a Living in the Middle Ages*, 33, 39–40.
[106] Dyer, *Making a Living in the Middle Ages*, 138–143; M. M. Postan, ed., *The Cambridge Economic History*, vol. 1., *The Agrarian Life of the Middle Ages* (Cambridge: Cambridge University Press, 1966), 603–604; John Robert Maddicott, "The English Peasantry and the Demands of the Crown 1294–1341," *Past & Present*, Supplement 1 (1975), 11–12; Spufford, *Money and Its Use*, 249–252, 382–387. Pamela Nightingale notes that, since up to half the peasant population had not enough land to support themselves, they would have been obliged to earn wages in cash or kind to buy food. See Pamela Nightingale, "Money and Credit in the Economy of Late Medieval England," in *Medieval Money Matters*, ed. Diane Wood (Oxford: Oxbow Books, 2007), 54.
[107] See pp. 155–158, 165–167.

learneth to sleep."[108] The Crown's use of money, taken up and extended by the lay world, had made it a necessary part of English life.

That imperative brings us to the issue of supply. The husbandman of "The Song" complained more than metaphorically about the search for silver. As the English operated it, the free minting system required a high-value item—silver—to be dedicated to use as money and produced a supply of coin that failed to satisfy people. The problem lay in part in the fact that the system imposed the cost of producing money directly on individuals. That charge meant that coins issued from the mint only when it was cost-effective for one user as opposed to beneficial for a group.[109] Moreover, people were apparently very sensitive to the cost of money. From her review of mint data, Angela Redish argues that the demand for coin was highly elastic—the price charged for it greatly affected people's decision whether to go to the mint. Officials consequently kept the charge for coin relatively low; it was almost always less than 10 percent, and generally less than 5 percent. But that charge was enough to keep people away. Nicholas Mayhew, teasing apart the sources of bullion for the late 13th and early 14th century, confirms that only the merchants, required to change their foreign money into English coin, brought bullion to the mint in ordinary times. As they pointed out unhappily, the transition from the renovatio monetae to free minting had shifted the virtual tax imposed by the government's charge to them.[110] Their problem had, of course, a more generalized effect: tying minting to personal determinations to convert metal into coin put a drag on the system relative to other methods for producing money. The strategy constrained the amount of coin produced, independent of other problems that bedeviled medieval coin because of its commodity content.[111]

---

[108] Kowaleski, *Local Markets*; Peter Coss (ed.), *Thomas Wright's Political Songs of England: From the Reign of John to that of Edward II* (Cambridge: Cambridge University Press, 1996), 152. For the dating of "The Song," see Coss, *Political Songs*, lii.

[109] Farley Grubb's work on the invention of efficient barter techniques to mitigate the costs of procuring liquidity is relevant here, although it is based on the early American invention of paper money. Farley Grubb, "Specie Scarcity and Efficient Barter: The Problem of Maintaining an Outside Money Supply in British Colonial America," in *Inside Money*, ed. Christine Desan (Philadelphia: University of Pennsylvania Press, forthcoming 2015). It suggests a kind of money scarcity that turns on the fact that individual incentives to pay for money may result in an equilibrium that is not optimal for a group. Charles Calomiris, by comparison, identifies situations in which collective engineering might mitigate problems caused by the way that price changes impose costs on individuals holding money. See Calomiris, "Institutional Failure."

[110] On seignorage rates, see Redish, *Bimetallism*, 34, 51–53; see also Albert Edgar Feavearyear, *The Pound Sterling: A History of English Money*, 2nd ed. (Oxford: Clarendon Press, 1963), 3, 435 (Appendix i). On the merchants' burden, see Mayhew, "Central Minting," 83–84 and n. 3, 90, 108, 153, 167–169; Pamela Nightingale, "'The King's Profit': Trends in English Mint and Monetary Policy in the Eleventh and Twelfth Centuries," in *Trade, Money, and Power in Medieval England* (Surrey: Ashgate Variorum, 2007), 61–75.

[111] The destruction of coined money was also a matter of individualized calculation: it would occur when prices rose enough that any holder would melt his or her coin. Since that occurred, at least theoretically, only when users had factored in and recouped the government's charge for money (they would not melt coin until its value had fallen so far that it was worth only the amount of metal it contained), it would not pose the same problem as the drag on creating liquidity. Taken together, however, the drag on creating liquidity and the freedom to destroy it would both work to limit liquidity. (Note that there would be some

The demand generated by public and private actors and the supply furnished through free minting met to cover English exchange only thinly, according to several indicators. Drawing evidence from mint accounts, hoards, and the number of surviving dies (the means for striking coin), Martin Allen estimates how much money was available per person in early England. His estimates start at 4–7 shillings in 1300, drop to about 2.8–6.6 shillings around 1340, and rise to 5–9 shillings after the plague in 1351. The bullion famine that took hold in the later 14th century quickly reduced that slight increase. By the early 15th century, only about 1–2 shillings per capita were available in silver, with the rest held in gold. By the 1470s, the supply increased slightly to about 3–5 shillings in silver.[112]

Those estimates average holding across people regardless of wealth; the levels of money held by people of modest means would have been much less. That group carried the heavy loads we saw earlier in both taxes and rent. If the amounts of money spent on those obligations in the 13th century carried over roughly into the next, half or more of a peasant's money would easily be consumed by those burdens.[113] That would leave people of modest or poor means with very little currency. Finally, that dearth would have been exacerbated by the seasonal tides to money's flow. The agricultural calendar brought boom times at harvest followed by periods when taxes and money rents depleted the currency. Those who had little wealth were particularly vulnerable.[114]

In the face of those numbers or, perhaps more accurately, behind those numbers were English pennies that moved quickly between holders, working very hard to service exchange. Considering information on coin supply, price, and national income, Mayhew estimates money's velocity—the rate at which the existing supply of coin must have circulated in order to service the transactions that occurred.[115] His work suggests that coin traveled at a significantly higher

qualification on destroying liquidity because people would have to pay for melting it and retrieving the silver it contained.) Cf. Sargent and Velde, *Big Problem of Small Change*, 23–24 (explaining irreversibility of making and melting coin in terms of arbitrage profits to individuals).

[112] Martin Allen, "The Volume of the English Currency, 1158–1470," *Economic History Review* 54, no. 4 (2001): 606–607. Allen's figures are modified slightly by the adjustment of his estimates in Allen, *Mints and Money*, 317–376. For his estimates on the drop in silver bullion, see Allen, *Mints and Money*, 334–339.

[113] See p. 100.

[114] Europeans across the Continent were turning to money in the early Middle Ages along with the English, as they also developed systems of taxation. Thus sales, wages, and rent had become predominantly monetary transactions by the end of the 13th century in France. See Spufford, *Money and Its Use*, 241. The parallel raises interesting issues of comparison: the English may have taxed more heavily relative to mint production or distributed the burdens of taxation more widely, for example. The difference would have contracted money in the lower reaches of English society more sharply than taxation did elsewhere.

[115] Macroeconomic approaches to money use an identity, the "equation of exchange," to express the relationship between a given aggregate of money, velocity, price, and output (or national income). As the equation, $MV = PT$ indicates, the interaction of supply and demand for money will, by definition, produce a price level. The left side of the equation identifies the money supply (M) or number of units circulating (100 tokens, for example) and the "velocity" or rate at which the units change hands (V). That side of the equation thus expresses how rapidly an amount of money must move to accomplish a number of transactions. The right side of the quantity equation identifies the number of transactions (T) that occur

velocity in 1300 and for much of the 15th century than it did in the late 15th century or the early modern and modern periods. (Coin velocities during much of the 16th century were also very high, as people passed on debased coin and then adjusted to stronger coin.)[116] The numbers, while uncertain and blunt to many variables, suggest that people in much of the Middle Ages did not keep pennies on hand.[117] As money supplies increased in the early modern era, people kept much larger amounts; they seem to have been building up a margin for daily use.

It may be that people in the earlier period passed on coin quickly because they wanted little of it for the exchange they planned to make. Much economic activity, after all, remained unmonetized. But people may also have been economizing on coin, given pressing priorities for its use; they would have been unable, given those exigencies, to use money for exchanges they might otherwise have lubricated with it. If so, then they lived uncomfortably close to the edge in much of the Middle Ages, strategizing the ways to get coin in order to pay the charges that were made in that currency.

According to standard monetary theory, money cannot be "scarce" over the long term. Rather, prices in money will fall so that the monetary aggregate covers the number of transactions made in it. That reasoning helps explain the low level of prices during the medieval period. In the late 13th century, unskilled laborers earned about one penny a day; sheep sold for a little more than a shilling (12 pence), and a cow cost about eight shillings.[118] Moreover, prices rose only

in an economy and the price value of each (P). (Economists often substitute Y, the total outcome of the economy, for T, on the ground that transactions and output are closely related; the more productive the economy, the more transactions occur.) As an identity then, the equation of exchange non-controversially specifies that the flow of money payments matches the exchange of goods and services for which it is used. Perhaps more accurately, the equation specifies that the amount of money used in payment (the number of units actually deployed) matches the price expressed across the number of exchanges. The identity reveals that changes in money's supply (M, the number of units) or changes in money's velocity will change price, assuming constant output. This is the standard textbook version: N. Gregory Mankiw, *Macroeconomics*, 5th ed. (New York: Worth Publishers, 2003), 161–175, 272 n. 6, 274–279. The equation of exchange is sometimes used along with the assumption that velocity, the rate at which money is changing hands, is a constant. Another way to put the assertion is that the amount of real balances (M/P) or money with purchasing power that people want to hold for every dollar of income, or k (the inverse of V), is constant. Mankiw, *Macroeconomics*, 162–163. If the assumption holds true and if output is also steady or at least cannot quickly change, then expansions to the money stock will immediately affect price. The hypothesis, known as the quantity theory of money, is controversial, unlike the identity itself.

[116] The high velocity at which coin traveled during the Great Debasement and associated turmoil during the Tudor era temporarily interrupted a more consistent trend down through the rest of the early modern and modern period. See generally Mayhew, "Population," especially 244, Table 1. Mayhew's data could not capture velocity between 1300 and 1470, by which point it had fallen significantly. The 1470 figure was, however, taken right after a recoinage and did not distinguish silver and gold coin use. The figure was probably higher for most of the century. A figure that selected for low-denomination silver coin use would likely be much higher yet. See Mayhew, "Population," 250; see pp. 104–105, 192–205. People would continue to hold more money as the money economy expanded; money demand has thus tended to increase in the modern era and velocity of money to fall. See Mayhew, "Population," 239–240.

[117] Cf. Lindert, "English Population, Wages, and Prices: 1541–1913."

[118] Mayhew, *Sterling*, 19–20; Sargent and Velde, *Big Problem of Small Change*, 48. Between 1301 and 1351, wages for an Oxford laborer remained virtually flat at approximately 1 & ½ pennies/day. Wages then

slowly in medieval England, and remained virtually flat in much of the 15th century. The pattern makes sense in a world where silver coins were limited, especially because the increasing monetization of exchange could mop up any expansion of coin.[119]

Standard monetary theory is, however, built on the assumption of a unit of account that is infinitely divisible. That assumption follows from the circumstances in the modern world, with its high prices, decimal units, and developed institutions of credit. Given that assumption, fractional money is available to reach very small deals and as many deals as necessary. Insofar as the unit of account can be parsed so finely, there is no supply "scarcity."

By contrast, the medieval English made a money that was astonishingly blunt. Until the late 13th century, only the penny circulated. After that point, it was supplemented by a skeletal array of fractional change—farthings and halfpennies. The daily experience of a worker drives home the difference with the modern day. While the 13th century worker earned a penny or four farthings per day, an unskilled worker who made $100 per day in the 21st century would take home 10,000 pennies.

The medieval circumstances inform Mayhew's findings on the velocity of the early penny. They suggest that the penny as a coin carried the burden of an enormous amount of economic activity. Insofar as people priced exchange—and there is significant evidence that they priced a large part of it by the 13th century—only the coined penny, halfpenny, and farthing could be transferred to capture or clear payment balances for all the transactions. In order to use it in that way, the medieval English would have passed around existing coin very

rose slightly: Edward III had depreciated the penny a small amount at the same time that the Black Death cut the English population roughly in half, increasing the amount of coin in circulation per capita. Wages moved up 14 percent to almost 2 pennies/day, where they remained until 1371. In 1372, wages rose to 2 & ¾ pennies/day, where they remained until 1403. That increase of 50 percent over the 1351 wage brought the pay rate for laborers in Oxford *over the century* up only 70 percent, despite the drastic demographic drop after the Black Death. In the early 15th century, wages rose to about 3 & ¼ pennies/day. After about a decade, they rose to almost 3 & ¾ pennies, where they stayed until the 16th century. *Over the entire 15th century*, then, wages in Oxford rose only a bit more than 14 percent; wages for other locales and labor tracked that dimension of change. For wage rates, see R. Allen's data on pay in silver grams/day, converted to pennies using Redish's figures on the mint equivalent to get wages in pennies/day. Robert C. Allen, "The Great Divergence in European Wages and Prices in the Middle Ages to the First World War," *Explorations in Economic History* 38 (2001); Redish, *Bimetallism*, 89–91; conversion data on file with author.

[119] After a long period of price stability in place by the 11th century and possibly earlier, prices began to rise around 1170. That upward movement continued into the early 14th century, when prices began to fall, dipping significantly in the 1330s and '40s, rising somewhat through the third quarter of the century, and then falling again from the late 1370s to a "plateau" where they remained for much of the 15th century. See N. J. Mayhew, "Prices in England, 1170–1750," *Past & Present* (2013): 4–5 (including both Phelps Brown-Hopkins and Allen indices). The purchasing power of laborers, at least *as abstracted* from scale-of-exchange problems, rose as prices for goods declined. (Robert Allen's consumer price index, which measures the value of a basket of goods in grams of silver, fell by about 40 percent between 1350 and 1540. See Redish, *Bimetallism*, 113 (citing Allen's unpublished work).) Hard as it is for a modern observer to accept, the story of the time was not inflation; price changes were not drastic and pale compared to modern trends. The real monetary drama was instead one that existed in times of relative price stability at least in the order of magnitude that mattered.

quickly. Their strategy was supported, as we will see, by informal institutions of local credit that became entrenched.[120] At higher velocities, a smaller money supply could produce prices that were as low as those in a world in which people had more money but held onto more of it.[121]

That phenomenon makes sense of contemporary reaction. Overwhelmingly, officials and lay people alike complained that money was scarce, that the currency was too dear, and that crisis lurked. From the time Edward I reorganized the mint through the next two centuries, the parliamentary record overflows with consternation over the meager condition of the currency. Crown, barons, and Commons debated constantly over ways to reduce the export of coin and bullion, the melting of silver coin, the diversion of silver for jewelry or plate, clippings and counterfeiting, and the use of "black money" or base foreign coin. A statute passed in 1335, for example, required that searches be carried out so that "no man of what[ever] estate or condition he be" could carry "sterling money" or silver out of the realm. Indeed "the hostelers, in every port where there any passage is, should be sworn to search their guests," in the same manner as the official searchers would and for a suitable reward. Gold or silver discovered was forfeit to the king, the better to increase "good money" within the realm.[122] Henry VI came up with a particularly ingenious solution towards that end a century later. According to Roger Ruding, the king turned to alchemy "for the supply of his mints with bullion." In a patent which he granted "for practising that art," the

[120] See pp. 205–228. The increasing monetization of a society is sometimes modeled as a condition that makes money more desirable for an increasing number of transactions, or shifts out the demand curve for money (the demand for money understood as a function of income and interest). In that case, the introduction of credit allows a constant supply of money to work harder; the velocity of money increases to meet demand that users would otherwise seek to fill by holding more money. The expansion of credit is limited, however, by the cost of extending it, and so remains tied to the amount of money in circulation.

[121] As the equation of exchange ($MV = PY$) indicates, if the money supply M diminishes, but velocity V increases, price and national income can remain constant. Note also that if increasing monetization is raising the output or number of transactions in a community, an expansion in credit (reflected as rising velocity) could allow the increase in economic activity without a change in prices (the fall that would otherwise occur if more transactions were being serviced with the same amount of money). The expansion of credit would then mitigate deflation due to an expanding economy. On the other hand, monetization might not have proceeded if credit had not been available because it would have driven down prices, and that deflation could have put a brake on economic activity.

[122] 9 Edw 3 stat 2 (1335). The statute provided an "Oath of the Searchers," to render a "true indenture" and account "and that you shall not dispense with any one, for love or for favour, to get private gain, whereby the King may be a loser: So help you God and his Saints." The same Parliament instructed the warden of the mint to make a certain amount of halfpennies and farthings, specifying a diminution in fineness that lasted until 1343 or 1344; the higher mint price offered for bullion induced people to bring more of it in. See Rogers Ruding, *Annals of the Coinage of Great Britain and its Dependencies: From the Earliest Period of Authentic History to the Reign of Victoria*, 3rd ed. (London: printed for J. Hearne, 1840), 210–211; Mayhew, "From Regional to Central Minting," 144–145; Appendix I, Mint Output, in Challis, *A New History of the Royal Mint*, 679. Despite those measures, the scarcity continued through the decade, driving prices down so that a quarter of wheat sold in London for two shillings, "and a fat ox for six shillings and eightpence" in 1336. A later measure provided for increasing the salaries of the men working at the mint "on account of the additional expense which was incurred in making those small monies." Ruding, *Annals of the Coinage*, 212.

king apparently drew with "utmost confidence" the obvious conclusion: he would be "able soon to pay all his debts with real gold and silver produced by the STONE."[123]

The officials' agitation fits with popular complaints and contemporary or scholarly observations about the dearth of coin. The earliest comes from a historian of Richard I (1189–1199), who noted the "great scarcity of money at home, and small coinages during all the time of his reign." Less stress registers during the 13th century, when silver flowed into England; a sense of monetary difficulties returns as the 14th century opens. For the next 200 years, the Commons regularly transmitted petitions about "the very great scarcity of sterling money," the need for small money "to pay for smaller measures," and the need for "the augmentation and increase of coin."[124] As the next chapter suggests, however, at times it was all the king could do to keep the high-powered and fast-moving penny in circulation.

* * *

From its inception in the early Middle Ages, money in England figures as a project that was constitutionally engineered: it was made by the legal and political practices of the land. It appeared when the community organized—or was organized—to produce it, often at the initiative of a military ruler. The project was intimately related to raising and distributing resources, most easily done in the form of a money revenue. That goal was entirely compatible with creating a

---

[123] The debate is almost constant; for some examples, see Ruding, *Annals of the Coinage*, 210–217, 239–240, 259–263, and the responses to the complaints about money's scarcity, p. 106 n. 124. Henry VI's spectacular solution is in Ruding, *Annals of the Coinage*, 278.

[124] Ruding, *Annals of the Coinage*, 175, quoting Martin Folkes, the author of Table of English Coins (1745). Fourteenth and 15th century complaints are at "Parliament of 13 Edward III, 1339," in PROME, item 4 (complaint about scarcity of money); "Parliament of 20 Edward III, 1346," in PROME, item 16 (petition concerning "a very great scarcity of sterling money in this land"); "Parliament of 36 Edward III, 1362," in PROME, item 27 (petitions for "an abundance of gold and silver; and to make other small denominations of gold to the value of twelve or ten pence"); "Parliament of 37 Edward III, 1363," in PROME, item 14 (request for small change); "Parliament of 2 Richard II, 1379," in PROME, item 44 (requests to Commons for money "to pay for small measures"); "Parliament of 5 Richard II, 1381," in PROME, item 26 (complaints about "the great poverty in the kingdom at present, which is empty of riches and of all other wealth because of... the removal and withdrawal of gold and silver money from the kingdom"); "Parliament of 9 Richard II, 1385," in PROME, item 4 (Parliament called because money loss from England had led "to the manifest impoverishment of all the kingdom"); "Parliament of 4 Henry IV, 1402," in PROME, item 46 (noting "great hardship among the poor people" given scarcity of small denominations); "Parliament of 7 Henry V, 1419," in PROME, item 11 (exporting of money had led to "to such injury and impoverishment of the whole realm that if a remedy is not provided at present it is probable that all the minted coin still remaining in the realm will shortly be removed from it"); "Parliament of 9 Henry V, 1421," in PROME, item 18 (officials "should be obliged and compelled to bring all the gold and silver they receive by way of exchange, ... to the Tower of London, to be melted down and made into coin; for the augmentation and increase of coin, for the advantage of the realm, and for the benefit of the people; without it being sold, alienated, or put to any other use"). For other complaints chronicled by Ruding, see, Ruding, *Annals of the Coinage*, 207 (1307, problems occasioned by demonetarizing of pollards); Ruding, *Annals of the Coinage*, 215–216 (1343) (testimony about "great want" of money in kingdom); Ruding, *Annals of the Coinage*, 245 (1393) (petitions concerning lack of small change); and Ruding, *Annals of the Coinage*, 274 (1431), 275 (1445), 277 (1454–55), 277–278 (1456), 281–282 (1462), 282 (1464), 284–285 (1467), 288 (1477), 292 (1483), 294 (1487).

medium for private use, indeed it was promoted by that complementarity; a community full of active exchange made more substantial public levies and spending possible.

As the records in the later Middle Ages reveal, making money was an enormously complicated task. Identifying a unit of account, establishing it as the mode of payment, and supporting it as a medium of exchange—each office of money marshaled people and material wealth in new and particular ways. The results were likewise distinctive—the high velocity and great purchasing power of English coin made it a difficult medium, one that created both political controversy and social hardship.

Coin, then, carried the attributes of its making. A product contrived by humans with the resources they had at hand, coin was subject to all the conditions—the finite and deteriorating quality of metal, the uncertainties of political judgment, and limits of collective organization—that gave real objects their value. The fragility of commodity money only increased as it moved.

3

Commodity money as an extreme sport

Flows, famines, debasements, and imitation pennies

On Christmas Day, 1299, sheriffs from Exeter to Oxford received the word they had been dreading. The king had proclaimed that the foreign coin they frequently took from taxpayers in lieu of English pennies was now worth exactly half as much as it had been before. Most of the foreign coin carried silver of the same fineness and slightly lower weight as sterling pennies. Many bore a portrait of a king who looked remarkably like an informal Edward I, bareheaded and beardless, while others gave him a crown of roses. Given their similarity to English pennies, the imitations had been current in England for several years, lawfully taken and paid at the same value as sterling pennies, one for one.[1]

At the beginning, the imitation pennies seemed harmless, even helpful; Edward I had allowed them to circulate legally in order to supplement England's scant coin. But the situation carried a hidden danger. When they issued imitation pennies, European rulers were actually trading on England's good name with a coin that was cheaper to make and had a marginally lesser metal value. Continental mints could use those savings to offer a slightly better price for silver: insofar as the coins traveled at the same value as English pennies, people got more for their money by bringing silver to Continental rather than English mints. Those holding bullion or sterling coin sent it out of England, converted it into copycat pennies, and brought the imitations back home to use. By 1299, the silver supply of England appeared to be emptying into Europe. At the same time, English mints sat idle, old English coin was wearing ever thinner or leaving the realm altogether, prices were rising, and coining revenues had dropped, all to the profit of foreign mints and traders.[2]

Aimed to discourage the use of imitation pennies, the Halfpenny Proclamation devalued them against sterling. In that moment, the money that the sheriffs held

---

[1] The proclamation was announced in the previous month; it took effect as scheduled. Writ of King Edward (November 25, 1299), in Henry Thomas Riley, ed., *Liber Custumarum*, vol. II (London: Longman, Green, Longman, and Roberts, 1860), 562–563. For more detailed histories of the episode, see N. J. Mayhew, *Sterling Imitations of Edwardian Type* (London: The Royal Numismatic Society, 1983); N. J. Mayhew and D. R. Walker, "Crockards and Pollards: Imitation and the Problem of Fineness in a Silver Coinage," in *Edwardian Monetary Affairs (1279–1344)*, vol. 36, ed. N. J. Mayhew (Oxford: British Archaeological Reports, 1977), 125–132; Mavis Mate, "Monetary Policies in England, 1272–1307," *British Numismatic Journal* 41 (1972): 34, 61–64.

[2] See Mate, "Monetary Policies," 60–61; Michael Prestwich, "Edward I's Monetary Policies and Their Consequences," *Economic History Review* 22, no. 3 (1969): 408–409; Mayhew, "Crockards and Pollards," 127–132.

as revenue was suddenly reduced. Every imitation penny they had collected at face value would be worth a halfpenny when they turned it in to the Exchequer. The sheriffs understood that they had been trapped. The legal machinery that made and enforced money, indeed the machinery that they helped operate, was poised in this case to grind their livelihood down. The sheriffs responded furiously, launching a volley of protesting petitions to the king.

The sheriffs were not the only ones dismayed. Vendors began refusing the copycat coin for fear it would soon be demonetized and they would be left with a money not current. Borrowers who had planned to pay off their debts with the copycats now needed twice as many. Creditors often refused the pennies altogether, wary that they would not be able to pass them on. Those who brought the foreign money into the royal mints found the price given for them there was scandalously low, yet the king had prohibited melting them for silver.[3] The controversy swirled, provoking the king and his officials to respond. They cajoled, insisted, punished, and exempted, both promoting and revising their policy into existence.

The episode of the imitation pennies was one crisis among many in the long and chaotic career of commodity money. Making a metal coin that actually succeeded—one that acted as a currency moving throughout society to measure and pay off exchanges both by public agents and ordinary people—was a daunting project. The very dynamics that made commodity money operate also created difficulties that threatened circulation itself. Coin, after all, was something like a promise: the body of each token claimed a count that was interchangeable across all its counterparts. That promise was destabilized by many ordinary events that changed the content or count of coin.

Communities adopted a variety of strategies to keep coin circulating. It turned out that in order to re-stabilize commodity money, authorities regularly had to recalibrate its content relative to its count—an operation that effectively changed the value of money in people's pockets. And for reasons that turned on the engineering of coin, authorities almost always reset money's value by diminishing the amount of silver in coin with greater metal to match that in coin with less metal. Despite the apparent solidity of coin, contrary to its repute as an anchor of value, and independent even of abusive debasements, officials regularly *reduced* the metal content of money in order to keep it operating, a dilution that continued over many regimes and across centuries.

When authorities leveled coin down, they raised a question that would become notorious. Should people, like the sheriffs who held imitation pennies, pay what

---

[3] Mate, "Monetary Policies," 66–67. The odd nature of the episode, mapped in more detail below, injured both debtors *and* creditors. Pollards were technically "appreciated" in value, an increase in metal value per count that hurt debtors and benefited creditors. But because they feared that the foreign coins would soon be demonetized and were unsure about their silver content, creditors attributed little value to the coins and treated them as if they had been depreciated.

they owed according to the new face value of coin? Or, should they calculate the amount of metal that was in the coin they had originally owed and offer that or its equivalent instead? Here, the English mapped a course through the common law that belies modern projections. They did not move from "metal" to "nominal" value in some evolutionary arc. Rather, they insisted from the start that money was not metal but a counted creation: the dusty vocabulary of common law debt—suddenly vivid—confirms their early nominalism.

As the nominalism/metallism conflict exemplifies, managing commodity money caused as much contention as concert. Far from a self-equilibrating medium, coin was instead an unstable compound, one that threatened constantly to evaporate, or slide out of the country, or pool only in certain circuits of exchange. Restoring its flow required decisions that revised the way people related to each other and their larger community. As the burdens and benefits of holding money changed, people in all locations, public and private, pressed claims, carried or lost them. The process of maintaining money configured the lay of the market. The next sections map the patterns produced by medieval money—the difficulties that destabilized it, the strategies that people used to re-establish circulation, and the settlements they negotiated to resolve conflicts over its value.

A. The instability of commodity money

As engineered by European societies, commodity money brought enormous advantages to the communities that used it. At the same time, it imported chronic vulnerabilities. Indeed, the power and the fragility of commodity money were two sides of the same coin.

On the one hand, silver and gold gave substance and authority to coin. Metal represented value in a tangible form; the security and durability thus conveyed may have been particularly important in a time when sovereignty was frail and contested. Moreover, silver and gold served as a common point of reference across regimes. Supply was both finite and conspicuously matched by wide-spread, inter-regional demand. As Nicholas Oresme put it, coin must be made of a "precious and rare material," one not easily multiplied. "That may be the reason Providence has ordained that man should not easily obtain gold and silver," he concluded, "and that they cannot well be made by alchemy, as some try to do." It was as if they were "justly prevented by nature, whose works they vainly try to outdo."[4]

On the other hand, the same qualities—a precious metal base, commonly used across neighboring countries, finite in kind and amount—opened coin to

---

[4] Charles Johnson, trans./ed., *The De Moneta of Nicholas Oresme and English Mint Documents* (London: Thomas Nelson, 1956; repr., Ludwig von Mises Institute, 2009), 5, 6.

constant destabilization. At first encounter, the fragility of commodity money is less obvious than its power, but it was just as inherent to the constitutional alchemy of the "just penny" and its Continental counterparts. Communities only began with silver as the basic ingredient for money. Silver did not "run current" until communities converted it into coin that would satisfy the tax obligation (a value they identified with an amount of commodity) and allowed it to circulate in the meantime (adding a premium over commodity value due to the cash services now provided). Communities in turn instilled and exploited the cash premium that distinguished money from metal, using it to stimulate minting and cover its costs. As the very design of "free minting" documents, the method attracted people to the mint by offering the faculty of cash for sale. The coin they received then circulated with that extra capacity; we can imagine liquidity like a lubricating layer of value around the commodity base of coin.[5]

The layers of value that made up a coin—its commodity value enhanced by its advantage as cash—composed the compound value of a coin. The coin's count corresponded or was supposed to correspond to that compound value. For example, a one-penny piece had a standard compound value, the same as every other one-penny piece. Coins passed interchangeably, one for another, when each penny's count correctly captured its metal value as enhanced by the cash premium it carried because of its monetary capacity. Considering that total (commodity and cash values) as its compound value, we can say that commodity money worked when each penny shared the same count-to-compound value as every other penny.[6]

But that is a strikingly narrow condition, one very difficult to accomplish. Money in the medieval world was made up of a large universe of pennies, thousands upon thousands of circulating objects. The penny was soon joined by coins of other denominations and metals. Granted that people used various coins interchangeably when each coin's count-to-compound value was the same.

---

[5] Similarly, money was not actually interchangeable with bullion but converted from it. Convertibility depended on the whole enterprise of minting coin and privileging it into money (or destroying coin and disabling it as money). It aimed to produce a unit of account that carried value and paid off debts, rather than to provide a substitute on order for silver.

[6] This approach to coin's value draws from a number of accounts, including the economic models that support the stakeholder approach developed in Chapter 1, see pp. 43–49 and the work of Thomas Sargent and Francois Velde, who break the value of commodity money into commodity and liquidity components. See Thomas J. Sargent and Francois R. Velde, *The Big Problem of Small Change*, The Princeton Economic History of the Western World Indexes (Princeton, NJ: Princeton University Press, 2002), 18–27, 103. Also important is Angela Redish's work, which compares coin's count to its metal content (as opposed to its compound value). As Redish defines it, the "mint equivalent" is the unit of account value that a coin carried per its metal content: shillings per ounce of silver, for example. See Angela Redish, *Bimetallism: An Economic and Historical Analysis*, Studies in Macroeconomic History Index (Cambridge: Cambridge University Press, 2000), 27–30. If circulating coins offered the same face value but one had a lower mint equivalent, it carried more metal than its peer and that metal was relatively "undervalued." Redish, *Bimetallism*, 28. Comparing mint equivalents as Redish defines them captures many destabilizing events, although it does not reveal shifts in the cash premium of coin, such as that which occurred when people feared the demonetization of the imitation pennies.

But if the ratios across allegedly identical coins and, as scaled up or down, across larger or smaller coins in the same system, did not correspond, problems occurred. They appeared both in the production of money at the mint and in its circulation. A brief tour of the demands placed on commodity money reveals how difficult the medium was to engineer.

Medieval Europe boomed in the 13th century—cities grew, economic exchange expanded, local minting flourished on the basis of newly discovered silver mines. The penny was too large to capture the plethora of small deals that people now conceived, and it was too small for the larger transactions, military and mercantile, that governments and laypeople began to attempt more commonly. The solution seemed clear: like other Europeans, the English created both smaller and larger coins. Silver farthings and halfpennies came first, appearing in significant numbers near the end of the 13th century, along with the groat worth 4 pence. Officials assumed that every coin should be made of metal and that the amount it contained should correspond exactly to its relative value as a currency. English groats, for example, contained four times as much silver as the penny.[7] In a system with commodity gradations of coined value, the count-to-compound value offered by each coin (the face value it offered relative to its commodity value as enhanced by its cash premium) had to correspond to the count-to-compound value offered by other coins, proportionate to each coin's place in the monetary hierarchy.

The difficulties were increased when the English added bimetallism to their approach. As Angela Redish recounts, silver was hard-pressed to answer the burgeoning demand to spend on different scales. When it was fine, the metal was so precious that it had to be minted to a very small size to provide small change— a 13th century silver penny was less than two-thirds the weight of an American dime. Farthings and halfpennies could easily become too tiny for safekeeping and too brittle to stamp. In a world where wages amounted to two to three pennies a day, the problem was critical. On the other extreme, coins larger than 31 grams, or worth 22 pennies, were big enough to invite counterfeiting—cheap fillings were hard to detect in a larger package.[8] Adding metals of lesser or greater quality offered a way to increase the currency's range. The English declined for centuries to alloy their small silver coin, a refusal that would have harsh consequences for everyday exchange. But they began minting gold nobles in the mid-14th century, at a moment when European silver mines had begun to run dry. The noble was worth 80 pennies and was designed to have a mint equivalent that, at the proper ratio of gold to silver prices on the commodity market, matched the mint

---

[7] Albert Edgar Feavearyear, *The Pound Sterling: A History of English Money*, 2nd ed. (Oxford: Clarendon Press, 1963), 439; Thomas J. Sargent and Francois R. Velde, *The Big Problem of Small Change*, The Princeton Economic History of the Western World Indexes (Princeton, NJ: Princeton University Press, 2002), 4–5, 132.

[8] See Redish, *Bimetallism*, 18–24, 48; Sargent and Velde, *Big Problem of Small Change*, 48.

equivalent of 80 silver pennies. Given money's intrinsic value (a certain amount of precious metal) and assuming a cash premium across coins, coin now had to be scaled both across different metals and across a hierarchy of denominations, each object a package of commodity and services proportionate to its counted value.[9]

The advent of new denominations and bimetallism would complicate the task of maintaining money in circulation, but the basic challenge remained the same. If the count-to-compound value of coins was constant, proportionate to each coin's intended place in the monetary hierarchy, people used them interchangeably and money circulated smoothly. Problems occurred if the ratios did not correspond, however. That was because coin's count and compound values drew from different sources. Its count or face value stated its worth in units of account while its compound value included the intrinsic worth of the silver or gold it contained along with its cash premium. Insofar as one or the other value controlled in a transaction, the difference between them mattered: it invited people to discriminate between coins by dedicating them to different uses. Generally, people preferred to hold the coin that was higher in compound value. That was usually—although not always—the coin of greater silver or gold content. People spent or passed on the coins that were relatively light, taking advantage of the face value of that money in many ordinary exchanges. As people began distinguishing coins, they disrupted the way money flowed in their communities.[10]

The unstable tectonics of medieval money—these shifts of count against compound value—were basic to its engineering. The very qualities that attached to a commodity—its susceptibility to wear and clipping, its appeal as an international resource, the fact that markets for different metals changed over time—made it likely that the close correspondence between relative values across many coins that was necessary to preserve a working system of commodity money would fail time and again. Another problem was just as inherent to commodity money's engineering. Coin offered a cash premium because it was easier to use than silver bullion, but that premium could vary across coins if certain kinds or denominations were easier to use than others. Both variation in coin's commodity

---

[9] On the turn to gold, including experiments with a gold penny in 1257, and a gold florin in 1344, see Martin Allen, *Mints and Money in Medieval England* (Cambridge: Cambridge University Press, 2012), 350–351, 358–360, and for an example of the way gold and silver mint equivalents were supposed to equate, see Redish, *Bimetallism*, 18–20, 27–32. The medieval English left the size of the cash premium untheorized, focusing their attention on the scaling of intrinsic value.

[10] When they circulated at the face value of one penny, the imitation pennies posed the classic case of "poor money driving out good." See Mate, "Monetary Policies," 56. When the pennies were devalued, however, they posed a different kind of "poor money" problem, one involving the cash premium of money. After the devaluation, their intrinsic value measured by commodity content was above that of English halfpennies. But the imitations lost such legitimacy when devalued that people began to avoid them, passing them off for counted value rather than holding them for their metal content. See pp. 144–148.

content and in the size of its cash premium disrupted the conditions that allowed money to circulate. The characteristic difficulties appeared again and again.

Metal loss was perhaps the most intractable problem. Wear still makes its familiar mark today, especially on softer coin. Throughout the second half of the 20th century, a handful of American coins chanced to contain a beautiful holdover from an earlier decade—the Liberty dime was 90 percent silver and carried Liberty as a youth in profile, wearing a winged cap. A patina was part of the dime's grace, along with the way the edges of its images were softly fading away. The coin of the Middle Ages, made with an earlier technology, wore even more relentlessly and surely less romantically as it passed from hand to hand. According to Nicholas Mayhew, coin lost about 2 percent of its content per decade. Clippers and shavers, stealing little bits of the coins' edge to sell as bullion, added significantly to the toll.[11]

Under those circumstances, new coin was routinely undervalued: it contained more metal than its older counterpart although it shared the same face value. (Put another way, new coin had a lower "mint equivalent" than old coin—fewer coins of its silver content could be struck from a certain amount of silver.)[12] The move to more denominations added to the problem. Coin of different size changed hands at different rates. Small change would move more quickly and would be especially vulnerable to wear. Testing their coin in 1798, the English found that crowns in circulation were 3.3 percent lighter than at issue, while shillings were a full 25 percent lighter. According to that pattern, new issues of smaller coin would more often have dramatically different mint equivalents from those of older issues, disrupting the critical supplies of small change. In addition, the mint equivalent of smaller denominations, shillings in the example from the later period, would fall out of sync with those of larger coin. Larger coin would become relatively undervalued.[13]

Long before it became known as "Gresham's Law" after a 16th century commentator, the slogan that "bad money drives out good" had categorically located the effects of undervaluation. Anyone holding undervalued coin could be expected to save it for those transactions where money would be valued by metal content, not count—predominantly international exchange. "Bad money," the light coin worn down by use, would drive out "good money," the heavier undervalued coin that people exported. The more severe the undervaluation, the faster the hemorrhage of money. Gresham's Law may draw the picture too

---

[11] See N. J. Mayhew, "Numismatic Evidence and Falling Prices in the Fourteenth Century," *Economic History Review* 27, no. 1 (1974): 2, 3. Compare the estimates in Peter Spufford, *Money and Its Use in Medieval Europe* (Cambridge: Cambridge University Press, 1988), 317, n. 1 (3.6 percent per decade); Allen, *Mints and Money*, 318, 333, 335–336 (suggesting 1–4 percent wastage per year for silver coin, but including loss to hoarding, conversion, and loss). Redish, *Bimetallism*, 54–61, reviews the long delay before the English adopted minting technologies that significantly reduced clipping in the late 17th century.

[12] See pp. 63–64.

[13] Redish, *Bimetallism*, 28–29.

starkly. Some studies suggest that communities tended to keep higher denomination undervalued coin circulating at a premium (that is, circulating it by weight, not by count) while melting or exporting low denomination undervalued coin; others find more ambiguous patterns.[14] But whether people reacted uniformly, predictably within categories of coin, or in their own erratic fashion, undervaluation chronically bedeviled the attempts of medieval communities to create a regular flow of currency.

When the English innovated a gold currency, they multiplied the sources of instability. Their bimetallic system, like others, was designed to circulate coins in silver and gold that had a common unit of account: both a silver groat and gold "unite," for example, were convertible into sterling pennies or shillings. The trick was to set the silver and gold content of coins that had the same counted value so that the ratio tracked the ratio of silver to gold prices on the world commodity market. At that ratio, the domestic counted value of gold and silver accurately reflected their relative value internationally.[15] Users would mint, melt, and use both silver and gold coins according to the same calculations. Their river of coin would run smoothly, while benefitting from a whole new reservoir of metal.

The catch was that setting a silver-to-gold ratio for coin's content that was accurate in the long term was basically impossible. Mint officials might call the ratio according to the commodity market for metal exactly right on the day that coin was issued—but changes in the market would soon moot their judgment. If gold rose in value, for example, gold coin that had been worth the same as a silver coin by count would become undervalued. The discrepancy would disrupt domestic patterns of spending, just as it did when people melted heavier pennies and dumped old ones. But bimetallic discrepancies triggered flows of silver and gold across the border even more readily. Merchants aware of gold and silver prices abroad would pay for foreign transactions in whichever coin held the greatest value there. In the meantime, their partners would send back the other metal, which had a relatively greater value in England. That dynamic could empty a country of silver or gold, whichever was undervalued. Predictably, the movement would be more radical when the undervaluation was more severe. At a certain point, it became profitable for arbitrageurs to export a coin containing undervalued metal, use the value it brought abroad to buy the metal overvalued at home, and import that metal for minting.[16]

---

[14] Redish, *Bimetallism*, 30–33, reviewing the debate.

[15] See Redish, *Bimetallism*, 28–30. As Redish points out, this assumes a unified foreign buying and selling price for bullion and abstracts from foreign mint prices and equivalents. Redish, *Bimetallism*, 29, n. 14.

[16] Redish, *Bimetallism*, 29–32. Arbitrageurs would export gold and import silver when the mint equivalent of gold (the number of units made from an amount of gold) was less than the mint price of the silver (the number of units sold by the mint for a given amount of silver), adjusted by the price ratio of gold to silver on the world market. At that point, they could pay for the minting costs of silver and still come out ahead. As Redish points out, their calculus would also have been affected by other costs left out here, like the cost of moving money and melting it. Redish, *Bimetallism*, 31–32.

Undervaluing one metal for a long time—and silver was the metal most often undervalued in the 14th and 15th centuries—desiccated the supply of that bullion to the mint. From the 1350s to the 1420s, and then again for most of the 15th century, gold poured in for coining at a much higher rate than silver. The coin brought in during a 1460s recoinage, for example, was two-thirds gold coin to silver. The dominance of gold made the currency "extremely top-heavy" for everyday use. Gold coin lubricated only the largest exchanges—three gold coins might make up a pound, the equivalent of 240 silver pennies.[17] People at the bottom of the economic ladder were at the greatest dearth for an accessible medium.

Medieval money's engineering produced a third source of instability. When European communities selected silver and gold as the common touchstones for money, they created competition over those metals between themselves. The scramble usually started when one sovereign raised the mint price it offered to those bringing in coin. While it could reduce the amount it charged customers and leave the mint equivalent undisturbed, more often the government slightly lightened the new coin. Until the difference came to light, the strategy would attract bullion from neighboring countries. And insofar as coins like pennies and deniers passed interchangeably across the borders of countries that were neighbors or near-neighbors, a small debasement might work indefinitely.[18] The technique could be used across an entire coinage, and across both metals. Even after the changes came to light, diluting the coin supply often had tonic effects. It increased the absolute supply of metal to the mint. And it recycled domestic supplies, replacing fewer units of a more valuable currency with more units of a less valuable one. As discussed below, that trade-off created coin well suited to nourish smaller exchange.[19]

By contrast, neighboring countries found their money supplies diminishing. Faced with money that was undervalued compared to the competor's coin, people avoided taking bullion to the mint, hoarded heavier coin, or exported it.[20] As the money supply fell and the value of money increased, prices dropped. That might have restored equilibrium in a world with a highly divisible money

---

[17] Allen, *Mints and Money*, 359–368; Mayhew, *Sterling*, 32–33; see also Redish, *Bimetallism*, 30–33, 107–135. Over the 16th century, and certain parts of the 17th, gold was more chronically undervalued. Redish, *Bimetallism*, 43–44.

[18] See Johnson, trans./ed., *De Moneta/English Mint Documents*, xxxvii; Mayhew and Walker, "Crockards and Pollards," 127–128, 131–132.

[19] See Spufford, *Money and its Use*, 289; Carlo M. Cipolla, "Currency Depreciation in Medieval Europe," *Economic History Review* 15, no. 3 (1963); see pp. 122–125, 202–203.

[20] Redish, *Bimetallism*, 47–48; see also Charles Johnson, trans./ed., *The De Moneta of Nicholas Oresme and English Mint Documents* (London: Thomas Nelson, 1956; repr., Ludwig von Mises Institute, 2009), xxxvii–xxxviii (discussing circulation of foreign pennies in late 13th century England). For occasions on which English sovereigns debated or actually reduced their gross seignorage take without disturbing the mint equivalent, see N. J. Mayhew, "From Regional to Central Minting, 1158–1464," in *A New History of the Royal Mint*, ed. C. E. Challis (Cambridge: Cambridge University Press, 1992), 176; Glyn Davies, *A History of Money: From Ancient Times to the Present Day*, 3rd ed. (Cardiff: University of Wales Press, 2002), 192–193.

(less money would cover all transactions at lower prices). But in a world with little fractional coin, deflation simply left more small deals without a money low value enough to accommodate them. The drop also triggered popular discontent and slowed economic activities, as borrowers drew back, fearing that loans would be harder to repay as money gained in value. That ordeal could occur again and again, when a competitor debased repeatedly.

Communities thirsty for more liquidity had every reason to depreciate their own coinage in response. Their incentive would only increase as more economic activity fed the demand for money or as supplies of bullion fell for other reasons.[21] Competitive debasements were especially common on the Continent, where small price inducements at the mint and slightly higher mint equivalents for coins that passed at the same counted value as others could easily draw metal across borders. But the English took part as well when they felt their currency threatened, depreciating the unit of account in terms of its silver content.[22]

Wear and tear, changes in bimetallic value, and competitive debasement—each changed the value represented by the commodity content of some coins, making it diverge from the commodity content of other coins with the same count. A last source of instability concerned that other component of coin's value, the cash premium, and the manner in which it too could vary to disturb the congruence between coins' compound values and their counts.

The pioneering work here is done by Thomas Sargent and Francois Velde, who frame the problem by considering the conditions under which a commodity money system would succeed in producing multiple coins of different denominations. As their approach clarifies, the terms of production for each size coin mattered. Setting those terms was, however, a tricky business.[23]

Recall that under free minting, the government defined coin as a particular amount of metal (for example, a certain number of pennies/ounce of silver) and set a certain price for it, offering to convert bullion for a fee. Users brought bullion to the mint when they preferred to have those coins rather than the larger amount of bullion they held before paying the fee. That occurred when prices for goods (pennies/good) were low enough for the deal offered by the mint to be worthwhile for them—that is, when prices were at the "minting point" or below. If prices for goods rose above the minting point, people would stay away from the mint. And if prices for goods rose so far that people would rather have the bullion in the coin than the coin—Sargent and Velde call this price level the "melting point"—they would melt coin to retrieve its silver content.[24]

---

[21] See p. 119.

[22] See, e.g., the episodes from 1344 to 1351 described by Mayhew, "Central Minting," 143–149, 163–171, and in Mate, "Monetary Policies," 61, 63.

[23] Sargent and Velde, *The Big Problem of Small Change*, 7–30.

[24] People would hold coin, in other words, if it were worth more than silver, but not if it were worth less. The enhanced value of coin came from the liquidity services it offered: that cash premium compensated users for the fee they were charged in silver. The fact that people only bought coin when it was worth paying the minting fee accounts for the fact that a gap separated the minting and melting points. Coin, purchased

As Sargent and Velde point out, the coin supply in a particular coin would only be stable so long as prices in that coin were between the minting and melting points. For each denomination then, prices stated in the denomination needed to be within the minting and melting points. The size of the interval depended on the fee imposed by the government. In order to run a multidenominational system, the government thus needed to set fees for each denomination so the relevant intervals intersected and all denominations existed.

We can imagine the difficulties that attended that task without more. Authorities might charge more for smaller coin given the extra costs to produce it. They might set particular quantity limits or quotas that interfered with the supply of some denomination. Or those users buying coin might fail to represent accurately the demand for a denomination. Sargent and Velde point out a more fundamental problem, however. It turned on the fact that the cash services provided by different denominations could vary.

In the medieval world as now, people needed money to service small as well as large transactions. In fact, the prices that prevailed in medieval England defined everyday wages and living expenses at a level that required many low denomination coins. The capacity of small change—and only small change—to facilitate those exchanges set it apart from other denominations. Put another way, it gave small change a higher liquidity value relative to its metal content than larger coins.[25]

That difference may not have mattered where plenty of small change circulated. In that case, those holding coin would have no reason to conserve small change. But in times of shortage, the higher cash premium of small coin relative to its count would become evident to people or, perhaps more accurately, activated for them. Given their additional need for small coin, people would hoard it relative to larger coin. Larger denominations would appreciate in value; that rise in purchasing power made them worth holding. Small change, by contrast, depreciated in value. Ultimately, the price intervals within which different denominations remained in circulation became misaligned. Ironically, people would melt small change given its depreciation, exacerbating the small change shortage.[26] Minting policies themselves worsened the situation: authorities produced relatively fewer small coins than larger ones, given their higher relative cost per unit produced.[27]

when it was worth that amount more than silver, had to fall in value to be worth its silver value alone. Only when it fell a bit further (prices rose a bit further) would people consider melting it.

[25] Sargent and Velde, *Big Problem of Small Change*. Observers have pointed out that large denominations held greater liquidity value for large transactions, given how inconvenient it was to effectuate them with low-value coin. The point may be correct, and yet incompletely wash out the liquidity advantages of small change, given the higher frequency of small transactions and the more absolute bar (as opposed to inconvenience) that an absence of small change presented to those transactions.

[26] Sargent and Velde, *Big Problem of Small Change*, 18–30.

[27] At times, the Crown corrected for the higher price of small change, either granting additional compensation for its minting or charging more when moneyers made large denominations. See Form of

If Sargent and Velde are correct, the problems created by the particular liquidity of small coin may have been especially severe in England. Authorities there prioritized maintaining the proportional commodity content of different denominations. While they tried at times to compensate moneyers or holders for the higher cost of making small change, they did not further diminish the commodity content of those coins—a strategy that would have produced coins across the denominational hierarchy with compound values that matched their counts.[28] Continental jurisdictions more frequently issued small coins that had low commodity contents but high liquidity premia, creating essential currency for the little deals of everyday life. In any case, shortages of small change were common across medieval Europe. While they had many causes—including the disproportionate charge attached to making smaller coins, the extreme wear and tear on small change, and bimetallic flows that favored gold—they may have been aggravated by the fact that medieval monetary practices inadequately recognized the cash advantages of small coins.

The many dangers that stalked commodity money were heightened by other circumstances, including shortfalls in the supply of the commodity metals selected to produce coin, technological difficulties in minting, and limits on expertise. The "bullion famine" that likely gripped England and the Continent in the late Middle Ages offers an example. By the late 14th century, Europeans had exhausted local mines and a chronic balance of trade problem drained silver and gold to the East. Flows of metal to the mints across Europe slowed and were stubbornly difficult to reinvigorate.[29] While some scholars dispute the length and tenacity of a famine, they do not dispute that shocks to the material infrastructure of medieval money would readily complicate the delicate enterprise of inducing money to circulate well and evenly in society.[30]

---

the New Money, in Johnson, trans./ed., *De Moneta/English Mint Documents*, 56; William's Indenture, in Johnson, trans./ed., *De Moneta/English Mint Documents*, 61; Allen, *Mints and Money*, 148–150.

[28] Allen, *Mints and Money*, 148–150; Mayhew, "Central Minting," 130. In order to fully analyze the "small change" effect, it would be necessary to factor in the policy of the English mints to issue coin in a standard and predetermined distribution of denominations.

[29] Allen, *Mints and Money*, 271–272, 337–338; Mate, "Monetary Policies"; see also Andrew M. Watson, "Back to Gold—and Silver," *Economic History Review* 20, no. 1 (1967).

[30] Skeptics argue that a bullion famine could not have lasted indefinitely because a drop in bullion should have driven up the value of metal and coin minted from it. Insofar as the country was operating as a closed economy, that movement would lead to a permanent drop in prices; the problems that haunted the English should have been soluble with the invention of new and lower denominations. Insofar as the country was linked into global networks, low prices would eventually have induced a flow of bullion towards England in return for the goods available at the newly deflated prices. In either case, or to the extent that the economy so responded, the bullion famine would have eased. For the narrative of bullion famine, see, e.g., Spufford, *Money and Its Use*, 339–362. For the response, see Sargent and Velde, *Big Problem of Small Change*, 124–135; N. Sussman, "The Late Medieval Bullion Famine Reconsidered," *Journal of Economic History* 58, no. 1 (1998): 126–154. According to O'Rourke and Williamson, however, price convergence in goods did not occur until the 19th century. Kevin H. O'Rourke and Jeffrey G. Williamson, "When Did Globalization Begin?," *European Review of Economic History* 6, no. 1 (2002). Shortages in bullion could, then, have remained a local phenomenon. Moreover, prices, particularly for wages, are notoriously sticky.

Throughout the 13th century, one ill effect after another plagued England's commodity coinage.[31] Judging by the official records, the most trying was the instability introduced as old coin lost metal content, either to clippers or to wear and tear. At other times, a coin would become suddenly less cash-like, as did the imitation pennies when the government devalued them. So ordinary people culled and hoarded, they overcharged by count in some coins and undercharged in others, they melted coins or sent them abroad. As those decisions aligned with each other, their effects were amplified. The discrepancies grew, uncorrected by the commensurability that commentators might imagine, as if each coin carried an explicit exchange rate against each other. In short, the way people treated coin threatened always to spin it out of circulation.

B. Leveling down: resetting the standard in an unstable world

No government could ignore ground-level shifts in the circulation of commodity money. Confronted by money's unstable tectonics, those engineering the system had to recalibrate the relationship between money's count and its compound value. A peculiar pattern soon emerged. Again and again, medieval officials reset their commodity moneys by depreciating coin: they leveled down coin stronger in metal content to bring it into congruence with lower-strength coin. The strategy did not correct all the problems that came with commodity money; Sargent and Velde argue that governments only resolved the difficulties created by the variation in coin's cash premium in the 19th century.[32] But leveling down did remedy other difficulties created by changes in coin's commodity content. As it became standard, the practice of depreciating coin runs counter to modern assumptions that commodity money provided a static anchor against loss. Decisions about depreciating money merged into monetary policy, as the variety of approaches taken by European governments shows.

When medieval money's circulation faltered, authorities struggled to rebalance it. They focused on two methods, each of which corrected disparities between the commodity contents of coins worth the same face value. Undervalued coin could be diluted—debased in fineness or lightened in weight—so that it no longer carried more metal than its count relative to other coin warranted. Or overvalued coin could be appreciated—increased in metal content—so that it reached the same level as other, generally heavier coin with the same face value. Each alternative interfered with the property values of those holding coin. Assuming

Note that governments would again be faced with the reasons to debase their coinage, rather than incur the pain of deflation.

[31] See pp. 138–149.

[32] The modern solution is to control the aggregate amount of currency in circulation while allowing individuals to determine its denominational composition; they can do that if different denominations are convertible on demand by the governemnt. See Sargent and Velde, *Big Problem of Small Change*.

that the government continued to impose the costs of recoining on individuals, it could burden either those holding the undervalued, mostly new coin or those holding its old and worn counterpart. Yet as Angela Redish documented in her study of English and French monetary interventions, "in virtually all instances, it was the former that occurred." Medieval communities chose to act on under-valued coin, leveling it down to the same commodity content as older, weaker coin.[33]

Their reasoning becomes clear when we look at the practicalities, using the problem caused by worn coin as an example. By the time coin was sufficiently degraded to require recalibrating, prices had likely assimilated the erosion, rising some amount for that reason. If the costs of recoinage were imposed on those holding inferior coin, they would find the money they held reduced in their hands when they went to the mint. A recoinage in the mid-13th century appears to have taken that course; it provoked furious protest from commentators that "twenty shillings could scarcely be obtained from the money-changer's table for thirty." English authorities afterwards avoided strengthening their own circulating coin for more than four centuries, until the Great Recoinage of 1696.[34] As that event demonstrated, contracting the coin supply drove prices down as a monetary matter and thus raised the value of the new money. But that fall in value was not immediate, leaving those with new coin short in terms of existing obligations. It thus distributed losses as it occurred, particularly harming those who owed debts in money now worth much more than it was when the debts were incurred.[35]

By contrast, the costs of recoinage could be imposed on those holding the coin with higher commodity content. Diluting slightly the amount of metal in new coin allowed the mint to cut more coins from each pound of silver, raising the mint price it could offer. That enticement would reach those with bullion; they would bring more raw silver to the mint immediately. And while those holding coin minted just before the dilution could complain that their money was now heavier than required, they had a remedy. Because the mint took coin by weight, those holding heavy coin could bring it in for recoining, pay some minting costs, and come away without a loss in terms of the unit of account. (The loss in silver

---

[33] Redish, *Bimetallism*, 33. Aside from a brief experiment in the mid-14th century and the "Great Debasement" of Henry VIII, the English physically depreciated coin by reducing its weight, rather than reducing its fineness. Either succeeded in diminishing the commodity content of a unit of account and thus "depreciated" the coin. But diminutions in fineness (debasements) were much harder for users to identify than reductions in weight and drew more political objections for their lack of transparency. Mayhew, "Central Minting," 144–148. Cf. (1369) YB 43 Edw III, David J. Seipp, ed., *Medieval English Legal History: An Index and Paraphrase of Printed Year Book Reports, 1268–1535* (Boston: Boston University, 2013) no. 1369.168ass (hereafter Seipp's Abridgement) (rumors of debasement punishable). See pp. 160–171.

[34] Matthew Paris, quoted by D. W. Dykes, "The Coinage of Richard Olof," *British Numismatic Journal* 33 (1964): 78; Assay of the New Money, in Johnson, trans./ed., *De Moneta/English Mint Documents*, 53–55; Redish, *Bimetallism*, 33, n. 17. The episode of the imitation pennies, discussed below, strengthened foreign coin before demonetizing it.

[35] For the effects of the Great Recoinage, see pp. 364–367.

that they might claim was another matter, one that would come to the courts.)[36] By the mid-14th century, the English had settled on the strategy. In 1344–1351, 1412, and 1464, the government managed to recalibrate the money supply "by incentive rather than by decree." After those depreciations, individuals holding coin with high commodity value reminted it at a profit even after paying the minting costs and seignorage.[37]

Diluting the commodity content of coin had other attractions as well. Perhaps most importantly, it slowly expanded money's reach to smaller price points. When a government depreciated coin, it traded fewer coins with higher metal content for more coins with the same count but less metal per coin—a higher mint equivalent.[38] All things equal, prices would rise as more coin of less value entered circulation. (Even if prices did not rise because, say, the number of money transactions was increasing, more coin would enter circulation.[39]) As prices rose, the unit of account would be able to capture smaller deals; fractional change would be worth even less, reaching yet more deals. Diluting money thus eased the blunt denominational barriers that had defined and boxed off monetary value since commodity money began in Europe.

Recoinages addressed the problems of worn or clipped coin, bringing discrepant units like old and new pennies back into equivalence with each other. Governments could also act by decree. "Crying up" or "crying down" the count of a denomination raised or lowered its face value without reminting. That strategy allowed authorities to resolve discrepancies between classes of coin, silver denominations against gold ones, for example, or small change against larger denominations. Like depreciating coin at the mint, "crying up" a coin diminished its commodity content relative to its count.[40] And like depreciating

---

[36] Mayhew, "Central Minting," 103–105. Depreciation of coin did not necessarily cause price inflation— that would depend on other circumstances, including the degree to which an increase in money supply was sopped up by an increase in monetization.

[37] Mayhew, "Central Minting," 148. Crying coin up (depreciating its metal content relative to face value) or down (appreciating its metal content relative to face value) distributed the losses or gains associated with a change in value in similar ways. It avoided the burden of minting costs but could not operate effectively where equivalency needed to be restored to similar-appearing coins.

[38] Insofar as the government was raising the price for silver or gold given a shortfall at the mint, it could be seen as simply accommodating its rising value. Put another way, the government participated in raising the price of silver or gold. See, e.g., Mayhew, "Central Minting," 144.

[39] Prices in England did not increase in a sustained way from the mid-14th until the early 16th century. The stability of medieval prices occurred despite the fact that the value of silver and gold rose, as Angela Redish puts it, "systematically." Redish, *Bimetallism*, 43–44. For the price index, see N. J. Mayhew, "Prices in England, 1170–1750," *Past & Present* (2013), 5 (Phelps Brown-Hopkins and Allen indices).

[40] If, e.g., a penny token was decreed to be worth two pence, it would have been effectively depreciated, as a penny now carried only half as much silver as it had previously. To the same end, officials would occasionally insert a new coin into the hierarchy of denominations, one with a higher mint equivalent for its counted value. Alternatively, when coin was "cried down" or decreed to be worth less face value, it would be effectively appreciated: if a penny was declared equal to a halfpence in value, the halfpenny would carry a metal value that was twice as high as it had been previously. When a ruler wanted to displace debased money from circulation, he could reduce its face value disproportionately, as the French king did in 1420. Those with that coin could mitigate their loss slightly by taking it to the mint for recoining into new, now strengthened coin. See Spufford, *Money and Its Use*, 289–290, 309; Redish, *Bimetallism*, 33, 61–62.

coins at the mint, "crying up" coin was less oppressive to those holding it than "crying down." It left holders with more units of account in hand and, if properly gauged, restored an undervalued coin to use.[41] By contrast, "crying down" coin left holders with fewer units of account in hand during the correction.

Given the options, medieval authorities chose to bring the commodity value of strong coin down relative to its counted value, so it was no longer more attractive to hold than other, more highly valued denominations or issues. Pennies in England lost weight between the late 13th and mid-14th centuries (1.4 to 1.2 grams), the start of a trend that continued through the 17th century.[42] Between 1343 and 1666, the amount of silver in English coin fell by more than 60 percent, the amount of gold in coin fell by slightly more.[43] As monetary historians agree, these were interventions designed to remedy the loss of metal over the years, interspersed with occasional depreciations to respond to competitive debasements in Europe.[44]

The English trend, remarkable in its consistency and ultimate direction, was mild compared to the patterns on the Continent. The Italian city-states began depreciating their silver coinage in the 10th century. By 1252, the grams of silver corresponding to 240 pennies had dropped 82 percent from their original value (390 grams to 70 grams) in Milan, and 95 percent (390 grams to 20 grams) in Venice. Depreciation in France was similar, about 79 percent (390 grams to 80 grams). By contrast, the drop in England was less than 2 percent (330 grams to 324 grams).[45] The tendency of the Italian cities to diminish the silver content of their pennies went far beyond the regular recalibrations that wear and tear would make necessary. In Carlo Cipolla's view, authorities were responding instead to the high demand that their growing populations and expanding economies made on the limited silver supply: decreasing the amount of silver in each coin diluted the money supply sufficiently to contain deflation as exchange increased. In addition, the merchant classes that controlled those centers found their export businesses benefitted by depreciation; they could reasonably prefer it to taxation as a mode of contributing revenue for public needs. Moreover, each polity would readily turn to debasement in the competition with its sisters for bullion. That was particularly true insofar as the pennies of the region were used across borders interchangeably.[46]

---

[41] See, e.g., Redish, *Bimetallism*, 68 (reviewing English attempts to align gold and silver coin values in the early 17th century).

[42] See Redish, *Bimetallism*, 47 and n. 2; Mayhew, "Central Minting," 134 (Table 3).

[43] Redish, *Bimetallism*, 89–90. According to Redish's figures, the sterling £ (the mint equivalent) contained .769 troy lbs pure silver in 1343, and .299 troy lbs pure silver in 1666, a 61.1 percent drop. The sterling £ (the mint equivalent) contained .06 troy lbs pure gold in 1343 and .022 troy lbs pure gold in 1666, a 63 percent drop.

[44] See Allen, *Mints and Money*, 153; Davies, *History of Money*, 170; Redish, *Bimetallism*, 89–92; Mayhew, *Sterling*, 44; Spufford, *Money and Its Use*, 316–318.

[45] Cipolla, "Currency Depreciation in Medieval Europe," 422 (Table 1).

[46] See Cipolla, "Currency Depreciation in Medieval Europe," 418–421. Cipolla also describes a cycling pattern in the supply of small change: after a debasement, private mint masters would produce large

After a lull in the first half of the 13th century, the trend towards depreciation in Continental Europe picked up again. With the caveat that exchange rates can be extremely misleading, Peter Spufford uses those figures to establish an overall trajectory of change. By 1500, coin in Flanders passed at about one-sixth of its 1300 value, as mapped against the relatively stable gold Florentine florin. In Austria, coin passed at one-fifth its earlier value, in France about one-fourth. In England, by contrast, the penny remained remarkably stable and circulated in 1500 at a value diminished by less than one half.[47]

War partly explains late medieval Continental practice.[48] In France, Flanders, Italy, and most radically Castile, ruling powers faced with military demands depreciated coin, effectively seizing silver revenue from those holding money. The abrupt appreciations of the coin that followed in France brought riots and protests from the poor.[49] But independent of those desperate wartime measures, the basic monetary problems catalogued above drove the long-term trend. Across the Continent of fragmented and fractious sovereignties, mint officials consistently turned to competitive debasements in order to keep bullion coming in.[50] They acted periodically to depreciate new issues given wear and tear on the old.[51] They intervened as necessary to rebalance gold and silver values.[52] And, as silver supplies dwindled during the 14th century, diminishing the content of coin served as it had for centuries to parlay the existing bullion into more liquidity. In the Italian cities after the mid-13th century, the adoption of gold coinage actually permitted merchants the best of both worlds: they would hold stable their gold coinage, using it for international trade, while allowing silver coin to depreciate in metal content at the domestic level. Prices did not fall, despite the rising value of both gold and silver as their supply tightened.[53] Without theorizing the effects of

---

supplies of coins that they could sell at a profit until prices rose sufficiently in money to reach its metal value, at which point, people would stop coming to the mint. Carlo M. Cipolla, *Money, Prices, and Civilization in the Mediterranean World, Fifth to Seventeenth Century* (New York: Gordian Press, 1967), 32–33. Sargent and Velde's theory on the liquidity value of small change may shed light on whether the cycling effect described by Cipolla also fed cumulative debasement.

[47] Neither sampling nor averaging exchange rates is sure to reflect economic phenomena accurately given daily and seasonal variation in the rates, the rapidity with which currency could be depreciated and strengthened, and the ambiguity of the causes of change in rates. See Spufford, *Money and Its Use*, 290–295; Cipolla, "Currency Depreciation in Medieval Europe," 422 (Table 1).

[48] Cf. Spufford, *Money and Its Use*, 289–290.

[49] Spufford, *Money and Its Use*, 304–310 (France), 306–307, 310–314 (Low Countries), 314–315 (Castile); Cipolla, "Currency Depreciation in Medieval Europe," 418–419 (Italy). Castilian rulers did not succeed in restoring their unit of account, ending the 15th century with the worst debasement on the Continent, a "maravedis" that had lost 95 percent of its value against the Florentine florin.

[50] See, e.g., Spufford, *Money and Its Use*, 311 (Flanders). The pattern extended to mints competing within a polity where control of mints was decentralized. See Cipolla, "Currency Depreciation in Medieval Europe," 421.

[51] Spufford, *Money and Its Use*, 312–313 (Low Countries), 316–317 (Aragon).

[52] See, e.g., Redish, *Bimetallism*, 50–51, 62–63, 68.

[53] Cipolla, "Currency Depreciation in Medieval Europe," 418–419 (Italy); Cipolla, *Money, Prices, and Civilization*, 33–34. Flemish merchants may also have cooperated politically to support depreciation. See Spufford, *Money and Its Use*, 306–307, 310–312.

leveling down coin, European polities improvised that strategy as they struggled to maintain their circulating currencies.[54]

As Europeans plotted their monetary courses, they shaped their political economies. The two-track Italian strategy imposed the cost of declining metal content on the less wealthy, who used silver coin and generally took their wages fixed in that currency. The pattern pushed down real wage rates and triggered political protests; city politics in Florence were upended when workers gained power on a monetary platform in 1378. At the same time, the depreciation of small coin kept liquidity circulating at lower levels.[55] The cross-cutting benefits of the strategy may have informed the compromise that held at least briefly after the workers' victory and the class relations that existed longer term.

The decisions the English made to minimize the leveling down of coin were just as important. As the next chapters explore, elites in England preferred using taxation to depreciation for raising revenue. That politics eventually settled constitutional authority for money's valuation with the Crown and responsibility for fiscal matters with Parliament. In the realm of monetary policy, English commitment to the "sound penny" during the Middle Ages would stratify its exchange and inform ideologies of the market, ultimately influencing English arguments about individual right.[56] Along the way, decisions about how to recalibrate coin regularly created contention between those affected by the change. English law here played an important but counter-intuitive role, entrenching the count of money in ways that influenced the monetary policies that creditors would support.

C. Making it stick: current exchange, past deals, and the early English attachment to "nominalism"

Recoinages were acts of political self-assertion. The sovereigns who declared them aimed to rescue and restabilize a circulating medium. The people who bore them determined by their behaviors whether the money would be redeemed and, at times, whether sovereigns would survive. The drama was, from the start, acted out through and against law. Both monarchs and individuals acted through provisions, rules, judicial cases, and protests that implemented the change or challenged it. The institutions made and revised in that interchange became part of the architecture, the infrastructure that made a political community. That design also defined economic life—opening trade up with money, regulating the value of money, and determining who would bear the costs of reform.

---

[54] On the probable disjuncture of theory and practice, see Cipolla, *Money, Prices, and Civilization*, 27–30.

[55] See Cipolla, Money, Prices, and Civilization, 34–36, 42–51; compare Sargent and Velde, *Big Problem of Small Change*, 142–146 (detailing problems with circulation of low value coin).

[56] See pp. 160–171, 266–294, 414–421.

The first steps were straightforward. When they recalibrated their money supplies, officials invoked the very institutional apparatus they used to make the "just penny." Inheriting a medium from the century before, authorities regularly revitalized it, rebalancing it to replace the one that no longer answered. They readjusted content and count, sold the new coin, used it when they spent public funds, required it when they taxed, and proclaimed the current money of the realm. Maintaining money, like inventing it, required (re)institutionalizing value.

But moments of transition kicked up some additional problems, as people registered and sometimes resisted the changes dictated at the center. Officials found they had to patrol the reforms they intended. That was true both as people undertook new exchanges in a revised currency, like sales in the market, and as they sought to complete exchanges that were mid-stream when the monetary change occurred, like debts previously incurred and still outstanding.

As for prospective exchange, the problem perhaps most common was that people would disfavor a coin they distrusted. At times, that was old coin and at times it was new. Henry III apparently intended, for example, that the Long Cross pennies he issued in 1247 would circulate alongside older Short Cross coins of adequate weight, at least for a transitional period. But anticipating their demonetization, his subjects began rejecting the older pennies or raising prices in them. Bailiffs soon took the king's order to the streets that "all great and good pennies and halfpennies of the old money, not clipped should be current with the new money and be in no wise refused." The order required officials to scrutinize deals made daily at prices that could change for many reasons, a difficult task that officials soon mooted. After sampling the older coinage with a formal assay, they asserted that it was all lighter in content and assessed the shortfall against anyone holding it. The older pennies vanished from circulation.[57] Half a century later, Edward I's decision to change the face value of the imitation pennies touched off a storm of similar problems. As we will see, the king reacted just as quickly, moving to channel public behavior with methods that ranged from administrative and penal injunctions to moral exhortation.

As for exchange that was underway and incomplete when monetary change occurred, authorities had more leeway. These were transactions built on money as it *had* been circulating. Cleaning up the problems created among parties to those deals was a finite and backwards-looking task compared to introducing a recalibrated coin and establishing it in future exchange.[58] Nevertheless, managing interference with existing relationships was politically volatile and, as monetary

---

[57] Johnson, trans./ed., *De Moneta/English Mint Documents*, xxviii; Duties of the Officers of the Mint, and Assay of the New Money, in Johnson, trans./ed., *De Moneta/English Mint Documents*, 51, 54–55; Mayhew, "Central Minting," 107, n. 70.

[58] Ongoing obligations like rent or feudal dues were not so discrete, a fact that may have pushed the English to the path they chose. See p. 131.

exchange became more extensive, the disruption caused by changes in money's value reached further into everyday transactions.[59]

A sample deal presents the issue. One party may have borrowed money from another at a time when the unit of account, the penny in England, carried 24 grains of silver, agreeing to repay it in a year. Controversy arose if officials in the meantime diminished the silver content of the penny to 20 grains: should the debtor repay his or her creditor in the old pennies (or their equivalent by weight) or in new pennies at face value? The first course preserved the constancy of *silver* owed: if the debtor had borrowed five pennies each of 24 grains, he now owed the same amount of silver in return (120 grains)—even though that would require overpayment in terms of the pennies' current count (six pennies at 20 grains each). The second course preserved the constancy of the *unit of account* owed: if the debtor had borrowed five pennies, he now owed the same number of pennies—even though that would constitute underpayment in terms of weight originally received (five pennies at 20 grains each producing 100 grains).[60]

In theorizing about money, the alternatives of "metallism" and "nominalism" have an iconic status. Part of that status flows from the misconception that the terms suggest something larger than they do. First, the fact that a system may be "nominalist" because of its emphasis on money's count does not mean that the commodity content of money does not have value or does not matter to people. To the contrary, the bullion content of coin mattered profoundly to the early English. Indeed, it was the discrepancy between the bullion content of coin and its face value as a unit of account that created the destabilizing patterns described above. When people raided coin for its metal content, however, they acted because they wanted to use the bullion for a use *other than* as domestic money—including sending it abroad to be reminted into another sovereign's currency or even to conduct arbitrage activities that would eventually net them a profit in domestic coin. That activity did not make them or their system "metallist" in daily practice, a label that would apply only if they made everyday domestic exchange according to the bullion content of their coin rather than its unit of account value.[61] Second, "nominalist" and "metallist" arguments arose, by and large, when the government had changed the bullion content of money. But repayment policy to creditors after a monetary change was, in many ways, the tail

---

[59] See, e.g., Spufford, *Money and Its Use*, 290.

[60] See Sargent and Velde, *Big Problem of Small Change*, 103–105. Arguably, bargains in which money had changed hands for products not received were also affected by a monetary change. A creditor of goods could claim that old coin effectively "bought" a different quantity of goods than those now passing for the same price. Perhaps such cases exist on the Continent but, to get ahead of the story somewhat, they appear to be obviated by England's resilient nominalism.

[61] Again, very high-value coin, generally gold, was often excepted from nominalist practice precisely because it was so precious. It was also used for transborder trade, a territory beyond the control of domestic monetary authority. See p. 54 n. 92; see also C. E. Challis, "Lord Hastings to the Great Silver Recoinage, 1464–1699," in *A New History of the Royal Mint*, ed. C. E. Challis (Cambridge: Cambridge University Press, 1992), 234–236, and pp. 124–125, 347; see also pp. 409–414.

on the dog of daily exchange. The substantive legal enterprise—the body of the beast—was making money that traveled by count in the vast majority of everyday circumstances. Metallism and nominalism generally refer to alternative ways of returning to that norm after a sovereign intervention changing money's value.

That said, for those who assume that money acts out a teleology of modernization, the answer is evident. Money, according to this view, moved from a commodity into an increasingly fictitious form like paper money and bank notes. If so, societies must have treated it accordingly. They must have hewed to the metallist option at the outset and moved towards nominalism in the modern day. Acknowledging that metallism created problems for people left to measure the commodity content of coin, this account casts it as a means that disciplined borrowers and secured lenders against the abuses of sovereigns and states. Against that baseline, nominalism appears to take hold logically as money lost its tangible touchstone: when money came to hold value only as a numeraire, or matter of convention, public authorities gained the ability to reset it. As the narrative continues, fiduciary and fiat moneys are tremendously enabling despite their dangers, as is the proliferation of credit that acts as liquidity in many modern venues. Modern societies thus tolerate nominalism as a sorry corollary to the new developments.[62] The teleological story makes sense of the fact that by the mid-17th century, European polities had settled—converged, as it were—on the "nominalist" answer. Modern economies do the same, excepting contracts tied to an outside currency.[63]

Told as a progression, the account of metallism and nominalism also locates the place of "law" in modern conceptions of money. Law sorts out the relationship between debtors and creditors after sovereigns intervene—generally to dilute the metal in money. Rather than comprising the rules and provisions that first made and defined money, law enters when that medium is abusively altered. Instead of a constitutive element of the medium of exchange, law is a remedial use of political power to resolve private disputes catalyzed by a troublemaking monarch. Law thus polices pre-existing exchange rather than enabling that exchange with a medium.

Against these stories, the English history—and perhaps European history more generally—stands in sharp contrast. Our point of departure has already changed. From an operational angle, making money circulate was a legal project, indeed, the underlying legal project. Commodity money was not a piece of metal, but a

---

[62] See, e.g., Eliyahu Hirschberg, *The Nominalistic Principle* (Ramat-Gan, Israel: Bar-Ilan University, 1971); F. A. Mann, *The Legal Aspect of Money*, 2nd ed. (Oxford: Clarendon Press, 1953), 66, 71–75. Mann assumes medieval metallism on the Continent, but asserts at least some English divergence in the late Middle Ages. Sargent and Velde suggest a sophisticated evolutionary process, articulating the movement from metallism to nominalism as a technical progression towards modern economic understanding of fiat money. Sargent and Velde, *Big Problem of Small Change*, 102–106 (identifying the French jurist, Charles Dumoulin (1500–1556) as introducing nominalism to France and England).
[63] Mann, *Legal Aspect*, 64–74, 119–131.

compound of value with a certain count. When a government recalibrated money, it enforced that change uniformly on money holders. That is, the government practiced a kind of "background nominalism" in public payments and collections. Money holders could, however, complain about the burdens they carried during the transition and how those burdens should be distributed. Here, both creditors and debtors tried at times to escape complying with the new count (nominalism) by claiming wealth in metal (metallism). Metallism and nominalism were not alternatives that played differently across time—metallism giving way to nominalism. They were alternatives that played (and play) differently across sovereign space—nominalism occasionally giving way to a negotiated and exceptional metallism.

We can look first at the way that nominalism and metallism operated in a commodity money system. That sketch suggests the power that each approach held in the medieval landscape. We can then map the English strategy—a steadfast nominalism occasionally sweetened with metallist compromises. Along the way, the law as private dispute resolution does figure, but it figures in an unexpected way: the common law action for debt acted as a vehicle that identified and reinforced nominalism.

Nominalism and metallism

When they recalibrated commodity money, governments reset the relationship between its compound value and its count. We have seen that they could do that by adjusting the physical content of coin, reminting coin to bring the commodity value of all coin into conformity with its count. Or governments could recalibrate by adjusting the count of coin, "crying up" or "crying down" denominations of coin to bring their count into conformity with their commodity value. In either case, nominalism committed a government to recognizing the count of money as the value that controlled obligations oustanding during the transition.

As an operating principle, nominalism gained force from the fact that money establishes relative value across all items that are priced in that medium within a particular community. Because wealth in money exists as relative value, it can be held constant across changes to the unit of account since those changes equally affect all items priced in that unit of account (that is, all items valued in money), within the community. If the creditor in the example above lived in a nominalist system, he or she would receive only 5 pennies, now each a bit lighter. But the domestic price of silver would also have also increased, by definition, so that all people held the same amount of penny-priced silver wealth in their 5-grain silver pennies. All of the creditor's silver would have gained in value; the prices the creditor had to pay and the taxes he or she owed are the same as everyone else's prices and taxes. A recalibration, in other words, changed the value of all units of account evenly. In terms of the domestic system (epitomized by the closed

conditions hypothesized by models of the ideal commodity money) and in terms
of the unit of account, the creditor lost nothing. Even if prices rose, they rose for
all at the same pace; a long-term contract did not immunize a creditor from
inflation.

That lockstep effect granted, those with more wealth held (or due) in money
were more exposed when money's value was reset than those with less wealth
held (or due) in money. The impact on them depended on the way money was
recalibrated. As the reform changed the amount of commodity content and count
they held, those holding money might gain or lose relative to the government and
to their peers. An example involving leveling down conveys the range of possible
impacts. First, the government might design a confiscatory recoinage. It could
reduce the silver content of coin drastically, harvesting bullion at the mint,
enriching itself in terms of the number of new monetary units produced, and
reducing the wealth of those holding coin (or bullion). By contrast, a government
could design a recoinage that left those holding money with the surplus of silver
at the mint, perhaps to encourage people to bring in more silver. Such a recoinage
would be redistributive among private parties, not confiscatory. "Crying up" coin
had the same effect; it increased the number of monetary units that individuals
held, without enriching the government.[64] The beneficiaries of a recoinage or
enhancement that increased the count of their money would have more buying
power than their peers until prices adjusted. Finally, a recoinage could have fairly
neutral results. A government aiming to make uniform a coinage that had
partially eroded could level down to institutionalize the lower level content. It
could use the silver in heavier coin to pay for the costs of its recoining without
producing substantial profits to those holding the coin. The English approach
may have approximated that result.[65]

It is no wonder that recalibrating money was politically controversial, given the
range of effects it could have. Against the kind of dispute, nominalism had
enormous benefits. It disallowed parties owed or owing money to second-guess
a change by opting for metal rather than counted value in ongoing contracts.

At the public level, nominalism was virtually necessary, a background assumption that played a structural role in maintaining the constancy of the terms of
exchange. In any society using money, public transactions, just like private ones,
are interrupted by a monetary change. Many debts are outstanding to the
government, including all the taxes that have been levied. And many debts are
owed by the government, including salaries and other spending. A new unit of
account is, as we have seen, defined by public demand and issue. In effect, central

---

[64] Indeed, the government might lose commodity content as it took in taxes in coin that had a higher
unit of account value with a lower commodity content. See, e.g., Redish, *Bimetallism*, 70.

[65] A similar set of examples could be constructed for cases when the government strengthened coin,
either in a recoinage or by "crying down" the face value of coin. The Great Recoinage of 1696 and the
episode of the imitation pennies play out those alternatives as a matter of history.

authorities opt for nominalism in public exchange to effectuate "money" itself. They cannot adopt metallism—or make myriad exceptions to the new unit of account—without undermining their ability to rescue coin or, for that matter, raid it.[66]

A modern court captured that basic logic in 1934, after the U.S. Congress had devalued the American dollar in terms of gold.[67] The depreciation changed what the government owed, as much as what it collected. The U.S. Supreme Court found itself compelled to reject the claim by a creditor holding a public Liberty bond that the U.S. owed him the amount of gold contained in the earlier dollars. The court's reasoning in a sister case concerning state and city obligations applied as well to the case involving federal commitments. When states and municipalities took in their taxes, just as when railroads took in their fares and public utilities took in their charges for services, they took in money at the new standard. Given that limit on their income, they must be able to pay off existing obligation in the same standard. As the court put it in the case involving the U.S., it could not deny Congress the authority to operate "a single monetary system with an established parity of all currency and coins," even if it meant that those holding the government's bonds—like the government awaiting its tax receipts—would collect less in gold.[68]

English governments carried depreciations into effect by using a new unit of account. They did not demand more silver from taxpayers nor pay more silver to creditors, from soldiers to suppliers. Indeed, in the medieval world, the "background nominalism" constituted by payments to and from the government likely penetrated further than it would in the modern day. Given the shifting lines of obligation and dependency that traced from peasants to lords, lords to monarch, it was not completely clear where the radius of central authority dissolved. The payments due to a lord by his inferiors like the payments due from him to the king could be conceptualized as part of sovereign exchange that would be transacted only in the current unit of account.[69] "Money" as a medium that circulated by count was, in a literal sense, a vector along which sovereignty traveled, one that defined a political community.

---

[66] See Charles Dumoulin on the "miserable entanglements of lawsuits on these matters," quoted by Sargent and Velde, *Big Problem of Small Change*, 104.

[67] The devaluation, legislated in January 1934, diminished the gold content of the dollar from 25 & 8/10 grains nine-tenths fine to 15 & 5/21 grains, nine-tenths fine. See generally Christine A. Desan, "Beyond Commodification: Contract and the Credit-Based World of Modern Capitalism," in *Transformations in American Legal History—Law, Ideology, and Method*, ed. Daniel W. Hamilton and Alfred L. Brophy (Cambridge: Harvard Law School, 2010), 125–126.

[68] See *Norman v Baltimore and Ohio R.R. Co.*, 294 U.S. 240, 315 (1935); *Perry v United States*, 294 U.S. 330 (1935), 355–357. The court did specifically condemn the federal government's action, holding that it was more blameworthy as the sovereign author of the money that was devalued. Nevertheless, the court left claimants without a remedy for the breach.

[69] See pp. 148–149.

Nominalism in private exchange extended that relationship, tying the fate of money holders to the determinations of the public stakeholder. The American cases on devaluation made the advantages of that strategy clear. A monetized world is a world full of debtors and creditors; they are often the same parties. A nominalist rule enforced parity in the monetary system and kept exchange moving.

Against that baseline, metallism figured as a kind of protest. The claim to share in the gains or be free of any losses produced by a depreciation contested the legitimacy of that depreciation or its impact on a particular group. Appropriately, metallism operated by prioritizing a non-monetary value—the commodity content of pre-depreciated coin. Preserving non-monetary value allowed those who could claim it to opt out of the monetary system when it injured them.

In the case of depreciation, long-term creditors paid back in new money missed the opportunity to benefit from any gain in count that came from a recoinage or an enhancement. At the same time, they lost commodity content they might have wanted to sell in a foreign market. The higher value of silver in terms of a domestic unit of account—the guarantee that nominalism offered within a community—made no difference to the market for silver abroad. In such circumstances, creditors mounted the metallist claim to be repaid according to the amount of silver they had originally lent.[70]

Metallist arguments were strongest when monetary change created particularly heavy losses or gains for a group. English recoinages that leveled coin down to correct undervaluation did not produce silver harvests for those holding coin. Debtors, borrowing for immediate use, did not look like gainers. They depended on networks of current exchange to acquire coin and pass it on. By contrast, creditors on the Continent made a more sympathetic case. Those claimants were especially exposed to the loss of metal content if their contracts only ambiguously specified the unit of account that sufficed to repay. In early medieval Europe, pennies of different sovereigns were often used interchangeably. In that case, nominalism brought no benefits at all. As a system that controlled units of account across a domestic community, it could not protect people paid in a foreign coin. At times, foreign coin could be greatly debased to the abrupt loss of creditors. And where inter-regional trade flourished, the loss of bullion mattered more because many people were consuming foreign goods. In those circumstances, metallism—the demand that value owed by a debtor be measured by the amount of metal originally transferred—appealed more strongly.

---

[70] For a similar set of reasons, debtors had reason to make a metallist claim when money had been strengthened in their hands, either through a recoinage or by being cried down (diminished in count relative to silver content). They carried the costs of a reduction in count and owed more in terms of commodity content that had value abroad. Debtors made a metallist claim by tendering pre-reform coin and waiting to be challenged in court.

Medieval realities moved nominalism and metallism from insular logics to political strategies that conflicted and, at times, coexisted. In the English system, nominalism dominated throughout the period: private creditors generally received the money they claimed according to its current and official face value. That result arguably followed from the whole point of the monetary enterprise— money was a counted medium, the government maintained that count in its own exchange, and sought to perpetuate that count in exchange more generally. But principle aside, the English also directly institutionalized nominalism, along with occasional exceptions to it.

Nominalism in the English common law

As we have seen, the English inherited Anglo-Saxon and Roman traditions that identified money as a medium that moved by count. The history suggests that both traditions were also nominalist—that is, they enforced the "counted" nature of money across changes to that money's metal value. As to the Anglo-Saxons, the conclusion must be speculative, but given how frequently the content of coin changed in some periods, tying repayment to metal value would have required constant reassessment. That burden could be avoided insofar as sovereigns succeeded, as they appear to have done, in maintaining exchange by face value despite such changes to coin's content.[71]

Roman law likely adopted the same approach in theory, if not always in practice. As we have seen, the Roman commitment to count was clear in principle. That commitment made substantive sense in a commercial culture with a centralized and relatively stable monetary system, where wealth could be valued by a standard unit of account. The *mutuum* contract provided a way for individuals to transfer capital enumerated in that unit, use it productively, and return capital enumerated in the same way. That approach did not reify metal content as a representative of value; it emphasized instead the functional purpose of money to measure wealth.[72]

---

[71] For the early Anglo-Saxon period, see Rory Naismith, *Money and Power in Anglo-Saxon England: The Southern English Kingdoms 757–865* (Cambridge: Cambridge University Press, 2012), 165–166, 171; see also Naismith, *Money and Power*, 157 (noting difficulty for lay users to judge metallic content). Most scholars believe that coin circulated at face value under the later Anglo-Saxon kings. See p. 66 n. 142.

[72] For sources supporting nominalism in Roman law, see Wolfgang Ernst, "The Glossators' Monetary Law," in *The Creation of the Ius Commune: From Casus to Regula*, ed. J. W. Caims and Paul J. du Plessis (Edinburgh: Edinburgh University Press, 2010), 1–4; W. V. Harris, "A Revisionist View of Roman Money," *Journal of Roman Studies* 96 (2006), 19–20; Sargent and Velde, *Big Problem of Small Change*, 70, 74–75; Marcello de Cecco, "Monetary Theory and Roman History," *Journal of Economic History* 45, no. 4. The degree to which Roman practice was nominalist is contested, although the debate turns in part on the mistaken proposition that nominalism is incompatible with a population's recognition that coined money had a bullion value. To the references above, compare Mann, *Legal Aspect*, 71 (Roman nominalism uncertain); Walter Scheidel, "Coin Quality, Coin Quantity, and Coin Value in Early China and the Roman World," *Princeton/Stanford Working Papers in Classics* (2010) (identifying metallism as an approach attending to the intrinsic value of coin).

Justinian's *Corpus* did not address the issue whether the count or metal content of coin controlled to pay off a debt when money had been altered between the time a deal was made and the time it was settled. That silence would invite Continental jurists during the high Middle Ages to read Roman law's injunctions as metallist. Many modern scholars think it more likely that nominalist practice was assumed by those writing the Code; it simply went without saying.[73]

The English, as we have seen, wrapped the practice of those traditions into its common law. Here, the story takes a unique turn. It appears that English writ system, built around money as a counted medium, rigidly protected that character: tied to the frame of the writ, money would remain a matter that moved by count across changes to its metal value. It was an ironic result, given that the English were notoriously less receptive to Roman law than their Continental counterparts. The common law blended local concerns with centralized authority to produce a domestic system that was sui generis.[74] But while the relative insularity of the English common law had a limiting effect on outside influences, it also had an enabling quality, a capacity to protect and even reinforce those elements that it incorporated. The writs, those royal prescriptions that ordered resolution of a dispute, were instruments of sovereign command. There was a corresponding investment in their uniformity. They would become highly stylized written forms, used by all parties, that stated and categorized a conflict. Responses to the writs developed through litigation to comprise a repertoire of acceptable answers. The writs and responsive pleadings would eventually become too rigid to serve in a changing world. In the meantime, however, they powerfully perpetuated those aspects that they captured. Likewise, they shut out certain elements of challenge.[75]

Incorporating earlier practices, English common law clearly treated money as a particular entity, one that moved by number.[76] Insofar as the courts held that principle constant when they enforced debt actions, they wrote nominalism into the law. The earliest evidence flows from a case, *Maud de Pavely v Richard Basset* (1250), in which money had been strengthened, so that new coins carried more silver than their predecessors.[77] If metallism controlled, Pavely's debtor owed her only the amount of silver carried in the old coin: that was the quantity of metal that would have conveyed according to the original contract. Indeed, the debtor Basset proffered that older coin at Christmas 1248, about a year into Henry III's

---

[73] For medieval Continental objection to nominalism in Roman law, see p. 85.

[74] See, e.g., John H. Baker, *An Introduction to English Legal History*, 3rd ed. (London: Butterworths, 1990), 14–35.

[75] See Baker, *English Legal History*, 14–35, 63–111.

[76] See pp. 83–97.

[77] *Maud de Pavely v Basset* (1250) David Crook, ed., *Curia Regis Rolls* (Woodbridge: Boydell Press, 2002) no. 1502, 242–243.

recoinage of Short Cross into Long Cross pennies. By that time, an official assay had declared that the old Short Cross pennies were significantly lower in silver content than their predecessors.[78] Despite the fact that she had contracted for the older pennies, Pavely demanded the new coins. The case went to judgment and the Curia Regis itself—the king's council which pre-dated the common law courts—confirmed in 1250 that Pavely was within her rights.[79] Basset had borrowed money that held less silver; he owed back in new coins and the greater amount of silver they carried.

Fifty years later, officials under Edward I assumed that nominalism controlled the obligation to pay in both private exchange and public obligations. As for private exchange, Edward's officials treated nominalism as the default rule when they changed the value of the imitation pennies. The Halfpenny Proclamation expressly allowed a party who had a debt outstanding to claim repayment in the coin specified in the original contract; the proviso indicated that nominalism usually applied.[80] As to public exchange, Edward's officials were a bit more strict. As the section below relates, the sheriffs would have to petition repeatedly for relief from their obligation to pay twice as many pennies, now worth half as much by count as they had been when collected, despite the overpayment in silver that would result.

Consistent with nominalist practice, a plaintiff in 1470 appears well aware that an action in debt would get her only the current face value of the money she lent, despite a specialty (or sealed agreement in writing) that stipulated repayment in coins of a particular type. Suing in debt after those coins were depreciated,[81] she asked only for the total owed by count (£40), rather than total owed as it was identified in the specialty (£40 in groats and nobles "of the same metal to the value as they were in 1462–1463").[82] Despite the limit to the request (repayment in coins with lesser metal per count than those bargained for), the defendant's advocate argued that the writ should be dismissed on the ground that it did not accord with the written specialty; it was analogous, he asserted, to asking for "bushels" of wheat when an agreement specified repayment in "heaped" bushels. Small gratitude perhaps for the plaintiff's restraint, but the defendant may have thought his creditor was stymied: if the writ of debt did not allow more than a

---

[78] See pp. 139–140.
[79] *Maud de Pavely v Basset* (1250) *Curia Regis Rolls* no. 1502, 242–243.
[80] Writ of King Edward (November 25, 1299), in Henry Thomas Riley, ed., *Liber Custumarum*, 562–563.
[81] The noble had been "enhanced" to be worth 100 pennies rather than 80; the gold bullion value it carried was effectively diminished by being spread across a greater number of units of account. Silver coinage was also diminished by weight. See Redish, *Bimetallism*, 89, 91.
[82] *Copley v Danvers* (1470) YB Hil 9 Edw IV, Seipp's Abridgement no. 1470.006. The formulation of the specialty itself implies nominalism as a standing practice—otherwise, it would have been unnecessary to attempt locking in the metallist alternative. As restated by the defendant's advocate, the plaintiff only demanded the debt in "the same coin (cune) that now circulates (curt)" (*Copley v Danvers* (1470) YB Hil 9 Edw IV, Seipp's Abridgement no. 1470.006).

simple demand by unit of account and if the demand had to accord with the written specialty, she might not be able to enforce the debt. The debtor's strategy itself implies a world organized around nominalism: in it, bargains that glossed monetary value failed in court because they did not accord with the writ.

The court's response did not reach quite so far, but, on balance, it too suggests nominalism as the norm. According to the chief justice in the Court of Common Pleas, no writ of debt according "heaped" bushels was available in Chancery.[83] The inference that no writ of debt according money specified by metal content follows, although the justice did not clarify his thinking; he may have intended only to reject an analogy between money and other fungibles. In any case, his junior colleagues were willing to entertain the notion that an action in debt had the latitude asserted by the defendant. They suggested that the plaintiff might have introduced the text of the specialty by counting specially—that is, by identifying it in her opening plea. Here, however, the chief justice put a stop to the speculation, denying that the pleader could demand "more than is in the writ, this will be without warrant."[84] We are back to a common law formula that channeled debt claims for money owed into a writ that identified value in terms of the official unit of account. In turn, the court disapproved the debtor's attempt to box his creditor out of court. It refused to dismiss the writ, a determination that would allow the creditor—appropriately chastened—to sue for the face value or the debt (here, a lesser amount than stipulated in the specialty).[85]

Creditors like the one in 1470 may have strategized ways around the writ of debt—the judges in her case discuss whether she might have used covenant or another kind of special count. Each writ, however, imposed particular conditions and disabilities on pleaders that made them unattractive to pleaders like the one left claiming fewer coins here. Covenant, for example, required documentation under seal.[86] Given those limits, no other common law category appears to offer an easy metallist detour around debt. To the contrary, royal authorities were imperialistic about the action of debt, providing for its use locally and facilitating suits by merchants.[87] That makes even more striking the absence of metallist claims in that universe of cases. Depreciations were relatively few in medieval

---

[83] The justice suggested, by contrast, that the argument may have been possible in an action of covenant.

[84] *Copley v Danvers* (1470) YB Hil 9 Edw IV, Seipp's Abridgement no. 1470.006. The chief justice here invoked a 1455 precedent in which a creditor owed Flemish money was disallowed from stating its English equivalent in the count. See (1455) YB Mich 34 Henry VI, Seipp's Abridgement no. 1455.089.

[85] As the judge admonished the debtor, "it is for your advantage that [the plaintiff] does not demand this, because a noble is worth more now than it was" (*Copley v Danvers* (1470) YB Hil 9 Edw IV, Seipp's Abridgement no. 1470.006).

[86] S. F. C. Milsom, *Historical Foundations of the Common Law*, 2nd ed. (London: Butterworth, 1981), 248. In any case, Fleta treats writs for annual rents and services as a subcategory of debt. See Fleta, "Vol. II," in *Publications of the Selden Society* (London: Quaritch, 1953), 209.

[87] See Fleta, 210, 206–209; Stat of Wales (1284) 12 Edw 1 c 6; Baker, *English Legal History*, 27–28, 31–33, 372–373; Statute of Merchants; see also G. D. G. Hall, ed., *The Treatise on the Laws and Customs of the Realm of England Commonly Called Glanvill*, Oxford Medieval Texts (Oxford: Clarendon Press, 1993), BkX [1] and [12], 116, 126 (noting royal interest in controlling debt rather than ecclesiastical courts).

England before Henry VIII's Great Debasement, and were relatively modest. Nevertheless, large creditors existed and lost silver value at times—and yet they did not ask for redress.[88]

In his comprehensive history of contract, Brian Simpson described debt as fundamentally monetary in nature. The observation has particular power since it filtered up from his general reading of the cases; Simpson was not panning for the nominalism/metallism distinction when he made it. As he wrote,

> Of course it was realized that a debt was only a thing in a somewhat abstract sense; the creditor could not lay claims to any particular coins and say that they, and they alone, were the coins to which he was entitled. But this obvious fact cannot have seemed to be particularly important, and understandably so, for the whole point of having coined money is to make the specific identity of coins immaterial to their value as a medium of exchange.[89]

So it was that nominalism, clad in the armor of the common law debt, prevailed as part of the way money worked in England. Parties to exchange anticipated the repayment they could expect after a devaluation, which was repayment at current value of coin. Their expectations fed into the high politics of the realm, the governing bargains that developed, and the flow of money that resulted.[90] More occasionally, participants protested the standing tradition and, like the sheriffs under Edward I, tried to carve out exceptions. Ultimately, the English arrived in the early modern period with their commitment to nominalism intact. According to the practice books, legislation, and proclamations traced by David Fox, that commitment would survive even the provocation of Henry VIII's debasement.[91] The most famous statement of English nominalism, *The Case of the Mixed Money*, came in 1605, when the Privy Council sitting as a judicial body endorsed Elizabeth I's debasement of coin in Ireland.[92]

England's tradition set it apart from the debates occurring on the Continent, where civilian and canon law scholars found more reasons to recommend metallism. The conditions that made the sanctity of the "count" harder to maintain—multiple sovereigns, porous borders, erratic and sometimes severe debasement—also made it hard to enforce nominalism. Both coined money and bullion circulated, offering different modes of value.[93] The circumstances undermined the advantages that a nominalist approach offered, premised as it

---

[88] See p. 93 n. 87.

[89] A. W. B. Simpson, *A History of the Common Law of Contract* (Oxford: Clarendon Press, 1975), 53–54.

[90] See pp. 151–171, 190.

[91] David Fox, "Money and Monetary Obligations in Early Modern Common Law," in *Money in the Western Legal Tradition*, ed. Wolfgang Ernst and David Fox (Oxford: Oxford University Press, forthcoming 2015).

[92] *The Case of Mixed Money* (1605) in T. B. Howell, *Cobbett's Complete Collection of State Trials and Proceedings for High Treason and Other Crimes and Misdemeanors from the Earliest Period to the Year 1783*, vol. 2 (London: R. Bagshaw, 1809), 114; see generally pp. 267–274.

[93] Ernst, "The Glossators' Monetary Law," 223–225; Spufford, *Money and Its Use*, 131, 142.

was on the notion that people all held the same kind of coin, experienced the same sovereign demand for it, and had limited and similar exposure to regional markets for silver. Metallist arguments about money's value developed.[94]

Metallism for creditors was part of a much broader effort to theorize a way that money could hold value impervious to abuse by officials—Nicholas Oresme's famous work, *De Moneta*, is representative here.[95] But even where metallism took hold, it operated against a baseline of money (setting aside high value gold coin) that circulated by count the great majority of the time. As we have seen, that condition is what made free minting possible and what made debasement profitable. The controversies around money were not, then, indications that it moved or could move like a simple commodity, although some participants might have wished it would. They were instead evidence of the tremendous complexity and unstable nature of the compound that made up commodity money.

D. The episode of the imitation pennies

Over the course of the 13th century, the English experienced all the challenges that commodity money posed: the instabilities that the ordinary use of money introduced, the strategies that officials attempted in response, the disputes it created in turn. One of the oddest monetary dramas of all occurred at the end of the century, when Edward I realized that sterling pennies were being displaced in their own country by foreign copycat coins.

The century started out more calmly. It had been a good time for English exports, and silver flowed to the mints over the first several decades. The clippers were in action as well, their job facilitated by the simple state of minting technology. Throughout the medieval period, coins were struck on "blanks" inserted between two dies. The lower die was a stationary piece anchored in a workbench and engraved with the image, generally the king's portrait, which would become the obverse of the coin. The upper die was a cylinder held by hand and engraved with the reverse image at one end. It was placed on top of the blank and hammered down to make its imprint. Ideally, the reverse design appeared dead center and filled the entire face of the coin. Where it slipped to the side, however, people might easily shave off the bits of metal left bare. Without rim or raised edge, the coin was especially vulnerable. As it lost metal to clippers, it fell out of sync with coin that was undamaged. By mid-century, officials began to fear

---

[94] See, e.g., Ernst, "The Glossators' Monetary Law"; Sargent and Velde, *Big Problem of Small Change*, 73–114. It is not clear that the metallist jurists succeeded in convincing judicial and administrative officials, who had many reasons to prefer nominalist enforcement of sovereign coin. See, e.g., the attempt by Italian merchants to use a large and stable coin as unit of account, instead of the small and depreciating one preferred by debtors. Cipolla, *Money, Prices, and Civilization*, 48–50.

[95] See Johnson, trans./ed., *De Moneta/English Mint Documents*.

(a)

Fig. 3.1a Short Cross coin of Henry II, produced under moneyer Walter, c. 1180–1194. © Trustees of the British Museum.

(b)

Fig. 3.1b Long Cross coin of Henry III, produced under moneyer Ricard after 1247. © Trustees of the British Museum.

that clipping was crippling the currency as people raised prices in bad money, culled out the good, and minimized trips to the mint. Under Henry III, authorities redesigned the pattern on the reverse of the coin to make stealing silver harder, extending a "long cross" across its entire diameter, in place of a smaller "short cross" on earlier pennies (see Fig. 3.1a and Fig. 3.1b).[96]

After the Long Cross reform, Henry then turned to the perennial issue posed by the fact that commodity money, passed hand to hand, wore down relentlessly.

---

[96] Johnson, trans./ed., *De Moneta/English Mint Documents*, xx; Stewart, "English and Norman Mints," 76; Mayhew, "Central Minting," 106–109; Mate, "Monetary Policies," 36.

Calling together representatives of London along with the City's goldsmiths, he ordered an official assay to compare the silver content of the old and new coins. The public performance was not a formality: receiving the verdict that the old money "was not good nor lawful," Henry then used it to justify the recoinage. That was savvy political practice, but Henry went one step further. He applied the London results certifying the lesser silver content of one batch of Short Cross coins to raise the public charge attached to recoining all of them. His action placed the charge for the recoinage on those holding weak coin. It was one of the few times when a sovereign chose to substantiate rather than level down existing coin and, judging by Matthew Paris's charge that the mint was robbing people by returning a third fewer new coins for the old ones brought in, it triggered vehement protest.[97] But Henry apparently succeeded, protecting his money supply and returning the extra profits to his moneyers. His "effrontery," as one scholar puts it, takes us from money's difficulties to the politics and distributive effects they evoked, but rightly so—the dramas created by coin traveled as far as it circulated.[98]

The recoinage that began 1247 produced some 138 million pennies (£550,000 to £575,000) in three years. New silver coin continued to issue during the remaining years of Henry III's reign at the highest rates it would reach during the century. But even that good fortune had its own darker side. As English trade flourished and silver poured into England, demand for a larger coin rose.[99] In 1257, Henry III issued England's first high denomination coin, a "gold penny" worth 20 silver pennies. But the gold penny failed miserably, perhaps because it was too valuable to capture much demand. More likely disastrous, however, was that the mint had priced gold too low relative to silver in the mint prices it offered for each kind of penny. Effectively undervalued, gold pennies were cannibalized for the precious metal they contained and ceased to circulate almost as fast as they were minted.[100]

If Henry mourned the loss of his gold penny, his problems paled beside those of his son, Edward I. The 1270s were years of monetary crisis. Almost three decades after Henry III's recoinage, coin was heavily worn and increasingly threatened by clipping, judging by the rise in prosecutions for that offense. People

---

[97] See Assay of the New Money (1248), in Johnson, trans./ed., *De Moneta/English Mint Documents*, 54; Matthew Paris, quoted by Dykes, "The Coinage of Richard Olof," 78. The 1247 public assay found old coin to be lower in silver fineness, at a rate that was then applied to all Short Cross pennies. Modern tests have not confirmed that shortfall. If the old coin's inadequacy was purely a matter of wear, the generalized use of the assay results inappropriately justified the higher public charge for the recoinage. See Mayhew, "Central Minting," 107–109.

[98] Mayhew, "Central Minting," 107, n. 72.

[99] Long Cross coins issued from the London and Canterbury mints at the rate of £52,000 per year. Under Edward I and II, they issued at an average of £40,000 per year. Mayhew, "Central Minting," 113, 130.

[100] Mate, "Monetary Policies," 35. Johnson assumes that gold was overvalued; in this account it also left circulation quickly, by the government's decision to withdraw it: Johnson, trans./ed., *De Moneta/English Mint Documents*, xxix–xxxi.

had long broken pennies into halves and quarters to make smaller change. That practice continued apace during the decade, leaving coin even more vulnerable to clipping. The trademark indications that money was failing occurred. Inflation set in, more likely due to the prevalence of light and worn coin than other factors like supply shocks, shifts in the balance of trade, or an influx of silver. Merchants, both foreign and domestic, complained about the bad quality of the coin. The flow of bullion to the mints slowed—no one wanted to pay silver for new coins that were worth a diminishing amount and would be measured against older coins that bought as much by count.[101]

Mavis Mate recounts the dilemma faced by Edward I, indebted to pay for his recent crusade and at war in Wales. Like his father, he began by making the case for a recoinage. Moneyers and suspected clippers were indicted, prosecuted, and heavily fined. Jews, who had been prohibited a few years earlier from money-lending and found other alternatives practically inaccessible, were both particularly vulnerable and especially targeted. Many were imprisoned and perhaps fifty, along with a smaller group of Christians, were eventually hanged. According to Mate, Edward I would use the fines he collected from those dubbed monetary offenders to finance part of the recoinage, its necessity now documented by the extent of their crimes.[102] The politics of recoinage thus reached into the relations between religious traditions.

To attract a flow of silver to the mint, Edward I lessened the content of the coinage slightly. In 1279, his mints cut 243 pennies from the pound, up a bit from previous practice, and in 1280, the count temporarily reached 245 pennies to produce a bit of extra revenue for the king. Edward changed the portrait on the coin, replacing the heavily bearded portrait of his father with his younger, clean-shaven face. As in 1247, the redesign was integral to engineering a new money: it compelled people to bring in their old money by setting the new coin apart as distinctive. The incoming master of the mint, a skilled moneyer from Marseilles where the purest silver was made, also improved English minting techniques. Other changes, including the innovation of round halfpennies and farthings, strengthened the coinage still further. The recoinage rolled to a successful end by sometime in 1282.[103]

But money also had a geopolitics, one that sometimes changed the meaning of success. Given its soundness, merchants and travelers were happy to take English sterling with them when they went abroad, where others accepted that coin by count for many transactions. All good and well to have a reputation for sound money—in this case, however, money's name drew it out of the country. To make

---

[101] Mate, "Monetary Policies," 37–44; Allen, *Mints and Money*, 351–353; Mayhew, "Central Minting," 127–138.
[102] Mate, "Monetary Policies," 37–44.
[103] Allen, *Mints and Money*, 147–148; Mate, "Monetary Policies," 44–53.

matters worse, the penny soon attracted imitations. Those coins rode on the good reputation of English coin; many of the early imitations had a lower silver content than English pennies, but people took them at face value. As heavy English pennies left England, lighter imitations entered. Within a few years, the phenomenon threatened to "bring the money of England to nothing."[104]

Aiming in 1284 to arrest "the subversion of all our money," Edward commanded his officials to take the problems in hand. His orders restricted imports of foreign coin to certain uses and ports, forbade the entry of clipped English coin, ordered the confiscation of underweight foreign coin, and authorized the Warden of the Exchange to weigh clipped money to adjust its value in exchange since "many of the poor and rich people cannot know the light and clipped money."[105] An order of the same period prohibited the export of English money. Officials checked traffic at the ports, searching incoming boats and confiscating coins. It was a tricky business—the goal was to police the coinage without obstructing commerce. Officials often worked at cross-purposes, merchants complained of unwarranted arrests, money was confiscated and, at times, returned when its owners so demanded or European sovereigns intervened on their behalf.[106]

The flow of silver to English mints began to drop in the late 1280s, and became dramatic by the late 1290s. The London mint had received £61,000 of foreign silver in 1286; it took in only £1,246 ten years later, including silver painfully extracted from domestic mines.[107] By that time, officials in the Low Countries had inaugurated a whole new crop of imitation pennies, and they probably aggravated the problem. These were "pollards" and "crockards" that bore a king's portrait, at times happily bedecked with roses. The princes producing them became Edward's allies in 1294, when war with France began. As taxes on English customs rose to pay the costs of war, trade fell off along with the supply of silver it brought. French merchants and their supporters stayed away altogether. At the same time, the king's spending on the Continent rose—troops and allies all took English pennies. Finally, the French debased their money supply, driving up the price they paid for silver and attracting a flow of bullion to their mints.[108] The supply of English sterling shrank relentlessly.

Focusing on the war, his allies, and rebels in Wales and Scotland, Edward accepted the imitations that seeped into the country. Pollards and crockards were

---

[104] Stat de Moneta, likely 1284 (12 Edw I); see Great Britain, Parliament, I *The Statutes of the Realm*, 219–220 (London: G. Eyre and A. Strahan, 1810–1828), available online at HeinOnline English Reports (Buffalo, NY: W.S. Hein, 1993). For dating, p. 78 n. 30.

[105] Stat de Moneta, likely 1284 (12 Edw I).

[106] Mate, "Monetary Policies," 56–63; Mayhew and Walker, "Crockards and Pollards," 130–131.

[107] Mate, "Monetary Policies," 62; see also Prestwich, "Edward I's Monetary Policies and Their Consequences," 409.

[108] Mate, "Monetary Policies," 61–63; Prestwich, "Edward I's Monetary Policies and Their Consequences," 409–412.

allowed to pass for popular exchange and even the king's Wardrobe used them in payment.[109] As later tests have shown, some of the coins were actually quite high caliber. Imitating mints typically produced pennies that were very close in weight and fineness to English pennies, although many mints succumbed to the temptation to debase their coins over time. According to one record, the exchange rate between imitation pennies and the real thing was 22 pollard shillings to 20 sterling shillings, reflecting close if not identical commodity content. English coins themselves were increasingly worn and people picked out and put aside the heavy new pieces. That action left the sterling still circulating closer in silver content to the imitation pennies.[110]

The war's end brought a moment of truth. As men returned from the Flanders fields, they brought with them more and more pollards and crockards. At the same time, traders took English silver abroad; the mint prices there were often better for money that passed at the same face value at home.[111] In August 1299, Edward appointed agents to investigate the complaint "that native and foreign merchants take out of the realm sterlings, and vessels and jewels of silver and gold, and exchange them beyond seas for pollards, crockards, and other bad money which they bring back to England and re-exchange for fresh sterlings."[112]

What had started as a trickle of English silver out and foreign coin in had become a tide. The Canterbury mint closed altogether. By that point, the copycats were an essential part of the British money supply. Something like £250,000 in pollards and crockards circulated, almost 25 percent of the coin available, assuming the total output of the English mints between 1278 and 1299.[113] Corrected for the export of English coin during the 1290s—some £350,000 by Michael Prestwich's estimate, the actual proportion of foreign pennies was far higher. Relative to her own coin, England in the last decade of the century was

---

[109] Writ of King Edward, in Riley, *Liber Custumarum*, 562–563 (prohibiting circulation of pollards and crockards to "pass current in our said realm, in such manner as has been done heretofore."); Stat de Falsa Moneta 1299 (27 Edw 1) (noting "now We have understood that wools and other merchandize aforesaid are commonly bartered and sold for pollards and crockards, and other like money..."); see, e.g., Order to cause restitution, August 2, 1299, in Deputy Keeper of the Records U.K. (ed.), *Calendar of the Close Rolls*, vol. 4, 1296–1302 (London: 1906), 264 (restoring pollards to foreigners who had them in legitimate domestic exchange); Acknowledgement of the receipt [of loans] in such foreign coins, October 22, 1299, in *Patent Rolls*, vol. 3 (1292–1301), *Patent Rolls* (1895), 447; Payment of loans by Wardrobe at: E 101/354/24 (undated, approximately 1300, identifying use of pollards for [*pro*] sterling as payment); Wardrobe Transaction (1299) in *Liber Quotidianus, 1299–1300*, 52–53 (noting that pollards had been received at sterling value before the Proclamation and would be paid out afterwards at 2:1 value); see also Mate, "Monetary Policies," 63–66 and n. 5; *Anon YB 3 Edw I* (RS), pl. 92, 208–210 (Cornwall Eyre, 1302), in Seipp's Abridgement no. 1302.137rs (pollards given in place of pennies).
[110] Mayhew, *Sterling Imitations*, 3–6; Mayhew and Walker, "Crockards and Pollards," 128–130. The exchange rate is from Prestwich, "Edward I's Monetary Policies and Their Consequences," 412 (citing the Account of Elias Russel and Gilbert Chesterton, in P.R.O. E372/166).
[111] Mayhew and Walker, "Crockards and Pollards," 127–132; Mate, "Monetary Policies," 56, 66 and n. 8; Johnson, trans./ed., *De Moneta/English Mint Documents*, xxxvii, xxxviii.
[112] Appointment of John de Cobeham and William de Carleton (August 23, 1299) *Patent Rolls*, 435.
[113] English mint output during that time was about £800,000. Mate, "Monetary Policies," 70 nn. 1–2.

indeed "filled with divers bad monies, known by the names of pollards and crockards."[114]

The last two years of the century were consumed by Edward's attempts to displace the imitation pennies and re-establish sterling. The episode exposes the way authorities intervened to reset monetary values in defense of domestic commodity money. It also reveals the critical and at times unpredictable part that ordinary people played as they responded and at times obstructed reform. Both officials and ordinary English negotiated in turn, compromising on nominalism among other principles. In that way, they improvised their way through the crisis.

Edward began by devaluing the copycats to reduce their appeal. "No penny of such manner of money," ran the Proclamation that took effect on Christmas Day, 1299, "shall pass current, except for one halfpenny, that is to say, two for one sterling."[115] If the copycats were "cried down" or demoted in value compared to the English penny, merchants could no longer prosper by taking sterling out of the kingdom and recoining it at a profit in foreign form. To the contrary, the decree motivated those holding foreign coin to recoin it: it now held only half its value if used by count in ordinary exchange, but it was worth almost as much as sterling at the mint.[116] Finally, the reform preserved the English penny untouched by depreciation.

If that was Edward's logic, it was lost on most of the population. People began refusing to take foreign pennies altogether, even at the halfpenny rate, or raised their prices more than two to one. The Halfpenny Proclamation had so successfully disparaged the foreign coins that many expected them soon to be demonetized. At the same time, they lost faith that the pennies had high silver content, or were unable to test them. In late 13th century England, it would fall to the large Italian banking houses to gather up the heavy foreign pennies and cash them in at a nice premium.[117]

Analytically, the episode was one of those occasions on which the compound value of coin, that composite of commodity plus cash value, became decoupled

---

[114] Stat de Falsa Moneta 1299 (27 Edw 1); Prestwich, "Edward I's Monetary Policies and Their Consequences," 411; Mayhew, "Central Minting," 137 (noting appearing of foreign pennies "in manorial accounts all over England").

[115] Writ of King Edward (November 25, 1299), in Riley, *Liber Custumarum*, 562–563.

[116] This assumes that the mint took pollards and crockards by weight, as per its usual practice. Mayhew and Walker, "Crockards and Pollards," 135–137.

[117] See, e.g., Treatise on the New Money (1280), in Johnson, trans./ed., *De Moneta/English Mint Documents*, 67 (explaining limits on lay knowledge of coin's content). The government prohibited the melting down of foreign pennies, making it harder for people to assay them. See Writ to Officials of London (January 29, 1299), in Riley, *Liber Custumarum*, 565–566. Such regulation of the market for silver was fairly standard. See pp. 94–95. There is also significant evidence that the mints fraudulently underrepresented the amount of silver in the copycat coins, further damaging their reputation. See Mayhew and Walker, "Crockards and Pollards," 136–137. For the licensing of the Italian families to take pollards and crockards, see April 12, 1300, *Patent Rolls*, 505; Mayhew and Walker, "Crockards and Pollards," 137.

from its count. Uncertain about the foreign coin's silver content, most people marked it down. And anticipating its impending demonetization, they began to attribute less cash quality to it, stalling its ability to circulate. Those reactions drove down its value as a medium, a striking result given its relatively high commodity value. While the government's intervention had *appreciated* the copycat pennies in terms of its silver content, popular response converted it into a de facto *depreciation*, the copycats at less than the English halfpenny. The change hurt both those holding the coin, which all thought less valuable, and those who were disinclined but required to receive it at its new count.

The results in everyday life were less abstract. Ordinary buyers and sellers balked, sending the markets into disarray throughout the spring of 1299–1300. The king responded with a battery of measures. Within a week of the Halfpenny Proclamation, his officials were in the streets, reinforcing that decree in order "that the peace of our Lord the King be kept," along with the assizes of bread, ale, and wine. Finding that those selling victuals had "exorbitantly enhanced their wares, by reason of the prohibition of the money, to the great detriment of the people," the king set price ceilings on meat, game, eggs, and fish. "Eight larks for a penny" and "a cod for six pence, the best," were maximums that, if broken, could send a man to prison. Each trade was to appoint overseers to enforce the ordinance, nor could they allow any man to withdraw from the craft on pain of losing his franchise.[118] A month later, the king commanded officials in London to seize violators and their goods, broadcast the regulations once again, and force "wares [to] be exposed and be sold at reasonable prices, and for such money as is current in our realm ... and that money be received according to the ordinance." The disregard by "many persons of the city of London and elsewhere" had greatly damaged "the good folks the people of our realm, and all those who buy such things or ought to buy the same." Disobedience was punishable as contempt of the king.[119]

Throughout the spring, the Mayor's Court in London brought up vendors to answer for raising prices in foreign coin or rejecting it altogether. Ten named men and "other chandlers" were attached for "selling the pound of tallow candles dearer after Christmas, in contempt of the King's Proclamation." Fishmongers, cornmongers, coppersmiths, leather-sellers, and butchers—all faced similar charges. Curriers, cordwainers, tanners, and "kissers" also appeared, their turmoil as interconnected as their practices. "If prices were higher in [my] trade," claimed one cordwainer in front of the jury, it was due to the tanners, curriers, and kissers raising their rates.[120] As craftsmen clashed, neighbors informed on other

---

[118] See Proclamation made in the City of London (Christmas week, 1299), in Riley, *Liber Custumarum*, 567–568.

[119] See Writ of the same King (January 28, 1299), in Riley, *Liber Custumarum*, 563–565; Letter of King Edward ... as to the Rejection of Money, in Riley, *Liber Custumarum*, 566–567.

[120] February 26, 1299–1300, A. H. Thomas, ed., *Calendar of Early Mayor's Court Rolls Preserved Among the Archives of the Corporation of the City of London at Guildhall AD 1298–1307* (Cambridge: Cambridge

neighbors. Two collectors disagreed on whether a member of their ward had paid the right amount in pollards; the case ended in a contempt charge when one insulted both his colleague and his boss, "*Jeo ay chie a vous & au Ray ausi*" or, in more modern English, "I shit on you and the King too."[121]

The disputes were widespread, appearing in courts outside London. Brewers were accused of selling "one gallon of beer for sterling and another for pollards," and bakers "one loaf for sterling and another for pollards." An Oxford man was required to accept pollards for his horse, in what appear to be twice the quantity that would suffice in sterling. And in Yorkshire, a man went to prison for rejecting pollards and grabbing a pledge from the person who offered them.[122] Throughout the spring and across the land, the king's officials struggled to persuade people making fresh transactions that the imitation pennies should be current at their new halfpenny value.

Another set of cases concerned those deals made when the copycats had been worth a penny. Here, authorities apparently anticipated difficulties and tried to negotiate them. If the king had followed normal English practice, outstanding obligations should have been settled according to a nominal principle: the foreign pennies would be good tender at a halfpenny value. Debtors would owe twice the number of foreign coins if they chose to use them, while creditors would receive a surplus in silver over what they had loaned. The outcome apparently boded ill to officials, and they wrote an exemption from nominalism into the Proclamation. The exemption reached both written contracts and more informal agreements or, in common law terms, all obligations that could be claimed by actions of covenant and actions of debt. After providing that all copycat pennies should pass as "one halfpenny," the Proclamation read:

University Press, 1924), 61, accessed June 19, 2014, <http://www.british-history.ac.uk/report.aspx?compid=31969#s43>. Curriers cured and prepared raw leather acquired from butchers; cordwainers made it into shoes; kissers sold or worked leather. John Blair and Nigel Ramsay, *English Medieval Industries: Craftsmen, Techniques, Products* (London: Hambledon Press, 1991), 298, 308; Caroline M. Barron and Anne F. Sutton, eds., *Medieval London Widows, 1300–1500* (London: Hambledon Press, 1994), 11.

[121] See cases from January 11, 1299, and February 23, 1299, to March 18, 1300, Thomas, *Cal. Early Mayor's Court*, 53, 59–66, accessed June 19, 2014, <http://www.british-history.ac.uk/report.aspx?compid=31969#s23.> For the informers, see February 11, 1299, in Thomas, *Cal. Early Mayor's Court*, 58. For the contempt case, see February 13, 1299, in Thomas, *Cal. Early Mayor's Court*, 58–59, all accessed June 19, 2014, <http://www.british-history.ac.uk/report.aspx?compid=31969>.

[122] See Leet Roll of 28 Edward I for Conesford, Nedham, Manecroft, Wymer, and Westwick (1299–1300), 5 Selden Society 50 (1981). (The leets occurred in the spring, 1299–1300, and would thus presumably pick up conduct occurring after Christmas Day, 1299.) For the Oxford case, see also E159/74 (002, 2) [1299–1300], and compare D. Farmer, "Prices and Wages," in *The Agrarian History of England and Wales*, ed. H. E. Hallam (Cambridge: Cambridge University Press, 1988), 745–755, 799–806. For the Yorkshire case, see Hilary Jenkinson and Beryl E. R. Formoy (eds.), *Select Cases in the Exchequer of Pleas*, Publications of the Selden Society, Main Series 48 (London: Bernard Quaritch, 1932), 187–188. There were variations on the theme. For example, in Lincolnshire, a sheriff was fined when he collected sterling for a party on November 25, 1299, but paid him the same amount in pollards, evidently after the proclamation date. See Jenkinson and Formoy, *Select Cases in the Exchequer of Pleas*, 187–189.

So, nevertheless, that debts which are due by contract and covenant, made before the said day of Christmas, shall be paid in such money and in as large a number of pennies as the covenant, and the contract, and the bargain was before made for. And so be it to all manner of wares valued or bought within the same time.

According to the text, parties should settle existing obligations in the coin that had been agreed upon despite the crying down of the copycats.[123]

The proviso protected some debtors, allowing them to pay off contracts with copycats, and some creditors, supporting their right to sterling. But given popular reaction against imitation pennies of any kind, it was creditors who objected the loudest. The exemption set off a flurry of litigation as people argued about the terms of the "covenant," or "contract," or "bargain" they had made. One debtor claimed he could pay at least a portion of his debt in "common money," probably pollards or crockards, while his creditor produced a deed that specified payment in "good and lawful sterling." In another case, a seller initially demanded sterling "by virtue of the contract between them," but settled for copycats at the Proclamation rate of two to one.[124] And another case went to the jury to determine whether a buyer who paid crockards for cloth on Christmas Eve had agreed to swap that payment for sterling pennies the following Monday if the seller "could not make convenient use of the said money" by that time. The jury backed the seller and ordered the buyer to come up with the extra funds, noting that an extra round of payment in crockards would amount to a payment equal to the domestic money owed.[125]

In all of the cases, the desire of people to pass off the imitation pennies is palpable—as is the stance of the courts. They would enforce contracts for sterling but allow two foreign pennies to be paid for each sterling. It was an interesting nod towards nominalism, even as their hands were tied by the proviso in the Proclamation. As the courts interpreted it, creditors could insist on sterling, thus carving out a higher value, but debtors could satisfy the sterling claim with foreign pennies at the new exchange rate of 2:1. A last case, *Pong v Lindsay*, comes to us only in garbled form, but appears to reiterate that position. A creditor sued on a bond made—and possibly due—before imitation pennies were cried down. He acknowledged that he had rejected partial payment when it was offered in imitation pennies and that the pennies would have taken the place of sterling one for one if, as the case seems to suggest, the offer occurred before Christmas, 1299. The debtors maintained that they had offered and could offer the imitations at a two for one value, and the judges resolved the case with that settlement. Quite

---

[123] Writ of King Edward (November 25, 1299), in Riley, *Liber Custumarum*, 563. It is not clear whether the proviso reached people with long-term unwritten contracts, as for rent.

[124] *Danesty v Botonner* (1299–1300) Thomas, *Cal. Early Mayor's Court*, 55–56, accessed June 19, 2014, <http://www.british-history.ac.uk/report.aspx?compid=31969#s29>.

[125] *May v Stanground* (1300) SS vol. 23, 80.

likely it was a compromise, "rough justice" in uncertain times when the point was
to reconcile parties to a monetary reform.[126]

The *Pong* case comes down to us only through the lens of later monetary
troubles. John Dyer, publishing a digest of reports in 1585, used the case to assert
nominalism. As Dyer squibbed the case, any sum of money due in a case "ought
of necessity to be referred to the day; for if twenty pounds are to be paid, they
cannot be paid but as they are at the time, for money is its own measure;
otherwise it is of corn."[127] Dyer's insistence suggests debates over nominalism
during the 16th century: Tudor debasement under Henry VIII, followed by
monetary uncertainty and strengthening under his descendants, would have
made nominalism more controversial then than at any earlier moment. But if
the case does indeed date to Edward and his officials, their point was less dogmatic
and more practical. They wanted most to navigate their way to the end of the crisis
and were willing to bend nominalism somewhat to get them there.

That conclusion returns us to the sheriffs who opened the chapter. As tax
receivers for the king, they held pollards and crockards that they had collected
when the money was taken at par with sterling. As of Christmas, 1299, however,
the revenues they held in imitation pennies were only worth half as much while
the amount they owed the king remained at full strength. We could call the
sheriffs' obligation to pay public revenue in current value "nominalism" or we
could consider it a straightforward manifestation of the principle that money
moved by count. As monetary authority, the government anchored the definition
of "money" by demanding and paying it at its current face value. The conflation
of the sovereign roles exposed the way "money" was defined: the unit of account
was, at bottom, what the government demanded from those who owed it.

But here, the sheriffs seemed as deserving as participants in private deals and
more perhaps, given the amount of money they held. The sheriffs, however, fell
outside the Proclamation's proviso: they could not sue for a covenant, contract,
or bargain with the king, nor had they made a deal about "wares valued or
bought" before Christmas. And the government had a point. The case was a
tricky one; after all, it would never be clear how much the sheriffs had collected in
imitation pennies before the Proclamation, which could be submitted later in
place of sterling taken from inhabitants.[128]

---

[126] *Pong v Lindsay* (1553) 1 Dyer 82b; 73 ER 178. I have been unable to find the original case, although it
may be same as one identified as *Elias Pouger v John Lindsey* by Paul Brand.

[127] *Pong v Lindsay* (1553) 1 Dyer 82b; 73 ER 178. The *Pong* case is modified in abridgement to stand
more clearly for a nominalist result. See Dyer, *An Abridgment of the Reports*, no. 82 (215) and no. 83 (218);
see also Charles Viner, *A General Abridgment of Law and Equity*, 2nd ed., vol. 20 (Cornhill: George Stahan,
1793).

[128] The sheriffs hypothetically could have protected themselves to some extent by taking imitation
pennies to the mint and capturing their silver value, and perhaps some did. The concern of others testifies to
their ignorance of metallic value and/or their distrust (perhaps warranted) of the prices offered by the mint.
See p. 144 n. 117.

In the end, Edward's officials negotiated once again. They established a process for the sheriffs, along with bailiffs, farmers of dues to manors, and some of the king's ministers in the same predicament. The treasurer and barons of the Exchequer would investigate the claims—including all the evidence they could find of who had been taxed, what kind of coin they had paid, and how much the Exchequer had credited to each sheriff's account—and grant relief when appropriate. The cases ran on through the first decade, as the parties to the monetary reform slowly mopped up the mess they had made in defending England's coinage.[129]

That goal was accomplished despite all the difficulties. Resistance continued and prices rose throughout the spring 1299–1300. Contemporaries blamed the king's policy on the imitation pennies for the inflation, and several later scholars agree. According to J. Titow, the good to moderate harvests of the previous years would not otherwise suggest an increase in agricultural costs.[130] By April 1300, the king had concluded that the copycat currency was not worth maintaining, and he declared it demonetized. But in important respects, his policy had succeeded. The foreign pennies had been displaced, silver flowed to the mint, and, within a few years, prices fell.[131]

* * *

Commodity money presents a stable face to the world. Once created, it appears like the commodity it contains, circulating in patterns that are removed from political will or social preferences. In that image, it advertises the common sense of exchange that runs on its own logic, a hardwired or underlying dynamic as old as individuals making a deal. But in fact, commodity money was very different from bullion simply converted into money when it was cut into even pieces. Making commodity money created a compound that was notoriously unstable. The relative undervaluation of certain coins, international competition for metal, the big problem of small change—all routinely drove the compound value of commodity money apart from its count. As they did, they disrupted money's circulation, including the flow of metal to the mint and the stability of prices.

Public recalibrations were part of the process of rescuing coin and restoring its currency. Invisible to later observers assuming a natural circulatory system, legal engineering operated constantly. Proclamations, royal orders, legal decrees, and institutional practices both mundane and dramatic provided the pumps and dredges, the channels and shunts that kept money moving across time and space. As predictably as they occurred, recalibrations took the form of depreciating

---

[129] See May 12, 1301, in U.K., *Calendar of the Close Rolls*, 447; see also Mate, "Monetary Policies," 71.

[130] See, e.g., Mate, "Monetary Policies," 67, 70 (citing contemporary witnesses); J. Titow, "Evidence of Weather in the Account Rolls of the Bishopric of Winchester 1209–1350," *Economic History Review* 12, no. 3 (1960): 381, n. 1.

[131] See March 26, 1300, in U.K., *Calendar of the Close Rolls*, 385; see also Mate, "Monetary Policies," 70–74.

money, an "inherent tendency," as one scholar calls it, that changed the commodity value of coin that people held.[132] Controversies were endemic, independent even of those more traumatic times when sovereigns raided their coin's content abusively or during wartime. Resolving those controversies became part of medieval law: the choice between nominalism and metallism was just one of the ways that communities defined obligation and distributed the cost of a monetary economy.

Exchange in 13th century England cannot be understood independent of commodity money—and that is saying more than we usually imagine. The history takes us from high politics to each layer of the social structure. The next chapters pick up that story.

---

[132] Redish, *Bimetallism*, 4.

4

The high politics of medieval money

Strong coin, heavy taxes, and the English invention of public credit

In 1363, a revealing exchange occurred between the Commons and Edward III. It began when the Commons requested that "the money of England that now exists shall be safely regulated and protected, by the advice of the lords and those who have a knowledge of money, in order that the profit of the land remains in the kingdom."[1] The occasion was one of six parliaments called in the 1360s. It was the decade in which the Crown would for the first time succeed in obtaining a tax that was effectively permanent during peacetime as opposed to war. The Commons would, in the same period, gain increasing importance as a body able to leverage concessions from the Crown in return for such grants.[2]

The Commons' petition, which seems so understated now, would not have been cryptic to contemporaries: it responded to the enormity of problems that had haunted the currency for the better part of the century. Those problems were, in fact, the classic set of difficulties that a money made of metal according to the English method invited.

First, Europe had exhausted the supplies of silver it could mine locally; the physical amount of silver available for minting began to fall around 1300. Wear added to the loss, second. If it ate away at metal at a rate of somewhat more than 2 percent every ten years, then on a currency supply of about one million pounds—approximately the amount that circulated in England at the beginning of the century—"about seven tons of silver vanished into thin air through wear every decade."[3] Third, European sovereigns began competing for silver bullion, both to increase their money supplies and to pay for war. Between 1336 and 1342, Philip VI of France raised the price he offered for a mark of silver at the mint from 60 gros tournois to 240 "new" (and much debased) gros tournois. Silver rose in price and flowed toward France. Finally, small change virtually disappeared from circulation in England just as it became more essential. Prices had fallen precipitously from 1310 through 1350 as the value of silver had risen and taken the

---

[1] "Parliament of 37 Edward III, 1363," in PROME, item 12.

[2] See G. L. Harriss, *King, Parliament, and Public Finance in Medieval England to 1369* (Oxford: Clarendon Press, 1975), 466–467, 503; W. M. Ormrod, "Edward III and the Recovery of Royal Authority in England," *History* 72, no. 234 (1987): 18–20.

[3] See N. J. Mayhew, "Numismatic Evidence and Falling Prices in the Fourteenth Century," *Economic History Review* 27, no. 1 (1974): 2, 3.

purchasing power of English coin with it. As prices fell, people tried in vain to find smaller denominations to make everyday transactions. Their complaints arrived in Parliament like a refrain across the century.[4] Altogether, the currency supply in England between 1319 and 1351 probably dropped from approximately £1,800,000 to £2,300,000 to about less than half or as little as a third of that amount.[5]

Under the circumstances, the Commons petition to the king is worth a second look. Most remarkable may be what the petition did *not* say. The Commons was asking for "bullionist" interventions: early medieval states tried all sorts of measures to keep metal within their borders and get it to their mints, including prohibiting the export of domestic coin, requiring the conversion of plate into coin, and policing against "invasions" of foreign coin. But while it desperately wanted a remedy for its money problems, the Commons conspicuously avoided asking for the obvious solution: depreciation of coin's content was the easiest way to cure wear, compete with foreign mints, or multiply the number of coins in circulation especially given a radical shortfall in metal supply.

The king confirmed what was left unsaid. On the issue he identified as "par la sutivete q'chiet en la Monoie," Edward III pledged that he would "do whatever should be for the advantage and ease of the Commons, without changing the money or reducing it in value." The obscure bit of Anglo-Norman likely identified the problem with coin as the "underhandedness" (or secrecy) that diminished the money—probably either a reference to the foreign debasements or the domestic coin clipping that were exacerbating the currency problems.[6] In neither case, nor presumably any other assault on English coin, would the Crown depreciate it.

The action captured by the Commons' petition and the king's response exposes a tradition that was constitutional in character: when king and Commons negotiated an approach to value, they were creating a particular political relation between the sovereign and his subjects. The fundamentals at issue included how value should be measured, collected for the public, and maintained as currency

[4] On rates of wear, see p. 114. On Philip's debasement, see Peter Spufford, *Money and Its Use in Medieval Europe* (Cambridge: Cambridge University Press, 1988), 305. Debasements from the late 12th century to the late 13th century were periodically reversed and the money would be "strengthened" for a period. The reversals never fully corrected for the degree of debasement, however, so that the price of silver gradually rose over the century. See Mayhew, "Numismatic Evidence," 13–14. On falling prices and small coin shortages, see respectively the Phelps Brown-Hopkins and Allen indices reprinted in N. J. Mayhew, "Prices in England, 1170–1750," *Past & Present* (2013), 5 and the plethora of petitions to Parliament, at p. 106.

[5] Martin Allen, *Mints and Money in Medieval England* (Cambridge: Cambridge University Press, 2012), 329–331.

[6] I am grateful to Karl Shoemaker for translating the phrase. PROME puts the language somewhat more blandly as "the complexities relating to money." "Parliament of 37 Edward III, 1363," in PROME, item 12. Rogers Ruding admitted to being baffled by the phrase. See Rogers Ruding, *Annals of the Coinage of Great Britain and its Dependencies: From the Earliest Period of Authentic History to the Reign of Victoria*, 3rd ed. (London: printed for J. Hearne, 1840), 230, n. 7.

for private purposes. The English answered that debate over time by working out an approach that paired strong money with regular and significant taxation. The combination allowed the Crown to meet its fiscal needs while keeping the metal content of coin high. As a constitutional practice, the English tradition was unusual in Europe.

The cooperation between the Commons and the king on display in 1363 highlights a second point. The English approach—the pattern of pairing strong money with high taxes—reflected an alliance between landholders and the Crown and an allocation of authorities between them. The practice favored elites compared with those at the bottom of English society, who would have benefitted from policies that brought more metal to the mint and spread it further in the form of weaker money. Instead, the English kept the value of money high while arguing about the targets of taxation. Magnates and Commons would come to identify issues of taxation as appropriate territory for legislative action, while leaving issues of monetary value to the Crown. That allocation could be validated in theory while remaining non-threatening in practice as long as the Crown maintained a strong money. And in the meantime, landowning elites sanctioned levies that lay heavily on those working the land.

Behind the scenes of the parliamentary episode that occurred in 1363 was a third element in the governance strategy that it represented. The approach brokered by the Crown and lay elites made them accidental pioneers in inventing a circulating public debt. The English tally started life as a device that smoothed the harsh conditions created at the conjuncture of strong money and reliable taxation. Making money strong meant that fewer coins with higher purchasing power circulated; that practice limited the flow of currency, especially to certain groups and in certain seasons. Taxes were hard to collect under the circumstances. Yet taxing people regularly meant that people knew taxes would be imposed and eventually obtained. Faced with an immediate shortfall of cash but a predictable course of taxation to come, the Crown began to anticipate incoming levies for current use; given the broad and predictable reach of taxes, it could do so credibly and in an institutionalized way. By the 1360s, the Crown was using tallies to "spend" revenues that had not yet arrived at the Exchequer and people holding tallies had begun to pass them from hand to hand, creating a medium out of public debt. Three centuries later, the English tally would serve as the prototype for paper public debt—bonds.

Just as people paid for coin, they paid for tallies. Instead of a price for minting money, the Crown effectively charged people by distributing tallies because those tokens acted as IOUs but did not include interest. In effect, people holding tallies made the Crown a free loan until they cashed their tallies for public funds. Coins and tallies thus shared a striking characteristic: they were moneys for which people individually paid the state. That feature determined the amount of money in circulation and affected the way people regarded it.

A. The English approach to value: strong money and heavy taxes

Money was a prime object of negotiation between early sovereigns and those they ruled. That character flowed from the double face of coin—its character as a vehicle for political authorities who needed to collect and distribute resources and, at the same time, for laypeople who wanted to exchange work and goods. The issue was how money would figure as the medium that allowed officials to meet public needs while serving the demands of individuals in daily life and business. In medieval Europe, several alternatives emerged.

The repertoire began with approaches like the renovatio monetae. That system worked by coercing money and metal frequently to the mint. Communities or their members had to make payments to the center in a certain, oft-revised type; they brought in their bullion or regularly recoined their money into the newly dictated style to meet that obligation. Political authorities harvested significant amounts of metal from those who held silver or old coin; they presumably took it in the new coin, directly at the mint. Taxes due in the revised medium contributed another amount. In between recoinages, coin could circulate at stable values, at least as far as monetary forces were concerned.[7]

Rulers could also raise revenue by combining taxes and straightforward seignorage charges with more surreptitious raids on money. With or without official recoinages, they could raise the price they offered for bullion (the mint price), and thus attract silver or gold to the mint. If they increased the number of coins they made from a given amount of metal (the mint equivalent) at the same time, they could take the same or an even greater profit from the larger amount of metal now flowing to the mint. In addition, if they kept the dilution of coin's content secret, they could spend new coin at the same prices as old, at least until the change in the coin's content was detected and prices rose in response. Debasement thus offered a tempting way for authorities to raise revenue while producing money.

Finally, political leaders could mint coin for advertised prices as needed by their populations. Demand for money to pay taxes and to have a liquid medium for private exchanges would bring a certain amount of metal to the mint. Officials could charge to cover the cost of coining but rely on taxes to raise revenue, instead of harvesting as much metal directly from those holding old coin and bullion or debasing coin.

Each approach to raising revenue in monetary form existed somewhere in Europe, and each installed money as a medium essential to a society. But while each strategy succeeded at raising revenue and at establishing a medium, each

---

[7] See pp. 65–69.

created a very different relationship between political authorities and laypeople. The alternatives thus amounted to different practices of governance, worked out through the currency of value.[8] Out of the European repertoire, the English chose a clear approach that they maintained with almost unbroken consistency. They opted to coin strong money and collect revenue through heavy taxes, at first on money itself and then on other sources; the practice configured their domestic politics.

In retrospect, the English course emerged early in the efflorescence of metal money. During the 10th century, Saxony silver washed across Europe from new sources in the Harz mountains. According to a number of historians, silver crossed the channel in return for English wool.[9] Others contend that the influx of new silver has been exaggerated.[10] But virtually all agree that, by the end of the century, the Anglo-Saxon rulers had monopolized the public medium of coin. Recall that the Anglo-Saxon kingdoms had perfected the renovatio monetae in a way that set them apart. While scholars of early money debate the details, they widely agree that the Anglo-Saxon approach exhibited a "degree of royal control" that was "impressive," one that allowed political authorities to extract a large amount of royal profit, up to 25 percent, from each coining process. At the same time and while shifting the weight of the coinage in complex ways, the Anglo-Saxon method maintained money at a stable value.[11]

Even as they took great profits at the mint, Anglo-Saxon leaders extracted additional taxes from their subjects. The danegeld, designed to raise the revenue necessary to buy off Danish attacks late in the 10th century, imposed the first national land tax in Western Europe since the end of the Roman Empire. We have seen how much silver in the form of coin that measure and others gathered for export from England.[12] From the second decade of the century, a "heregeld"

---

[8] For an analysis that frames related issues of depreciation and stability as governance issues, see Carlo M. Cipolla, "Currency Depreciation in Medieval Europe," *The Economic History Review* 15, no. 3 (1963), 414–415.

[9] Spufford, *Money and Its Use*, 74–75, 87; see generally S. R. H. Jones, "Devaluation and the Balance of Payments," *Economic History Review* 44, no. 4 (1991); P. H. Sawyer, *The Wealth of Anglo-Saxon England: Based on the Ford Lectures delivered in the University of Oxford in Hilary Term 1993*, 1st ed. (Oxford: Oxford University Press, 2013); P. H. Sawyer, "The Wealth of England in the Eleventh Century," *Trans-actions of the Royal Historical Society* 15 (1965), 160–163; H. R. Loyn, "Boroughs and Mints, A.D. 900–1066," in *Anglo-Saxon Coins; Studies Presented to F.M. Stenton on the Occasion of His 80th Birthday, 17 May, 1960*, ed. R. H. M. Dolley (London: Methuen, 1961), 122–135. P. H. Sawyer contrasts the practice in other countries to use foreign or low quality coin; Sawyer, "The Wealth of England in the Eleventh Century," 149, 160; Sawyer, *The Wealth of Anglo-Saxon England: Based on the Ford Lectures delivered in the University of Oxford in Hilary Term 1993*, 112–114.

[10] See, e.g., J. L. Bolton, *Money in the Medieval English Economy: 973-1489* (Manchester: Manchester University Press, 2012), 93–100 (reviewing debate).

[11] See Bolton, *Money in the Medieval English Economy*, 100; pp. 65–67.

[12] See Bolton, *Money in the Medieval English Economy*, 61–62. Bolton cautions that traditional estimates based on the *Anglo-Saxon Chronicle* are likely inflated, but agrees that the disciplined production of coin for payment north was impressive. Bolton, *Money in the Medieval English Economy*, 99–100. See also

imposed a 5,000 pounds tax on the population annually to pay Scandinavian mercenaries for defense. Between tribute and compensation, up to 1,000,000 pennies may have gone north.[13]

Inheriting (forcibly) the effective Anglo-Saxon combination of strong money and significant taxation, William I and his sons maintained it.[14] As Pamela Nightingale reconstructs the evidence, William retained the practice of demanding taxes in new coin, although he no longer demonetized the old. He standardized the penny weight and kept it constant, a change that allowed the English penny to be integrated with his possessions across the channel. He probably replaced the complex system of harvesting metal used by the Anglo-Saxons with a standardized charge for minting, began reducing the number of local mints, and added new methods to police the quality of the coin. No longer a system for taking as much metal directly from the flow of silver to the mint, the recoinages nevertheless remained a way to ensure the production of good coin.[15]

William's demand for coin was high. As conqueror, he took heavy tribute from the English and passed on both land and revenues to his supporters. In later years, he relied greatly on mercenaries, men who valued the standardized English coin.[16] His sons continued paying large amounts for military services—knights, fortifications, ransoms, pensions to allies, and the costs of the officials to administer it all. As a contemporary would describe William II, he was "that wealthy man, a pourer out of English treasures and a wonderful merchant and paymaster of knights."[17] The Anglo-Normans financed their spending by taxing heavily, as had their predecessors. The danegeld remained vital through the reign of Henry I,

---

J. A. Green, "The Last Century of the Danegeld," *English Historical Review* 96, no. 374 (1981): 1; but see James Campbell, "Observations on English Government from the Tenth to the Twelfth Century," *Transactions of the Royal Historical Society* 25 (1975), 43 (noting possible precedents for national systems of taxation in Francia). For the expenditures of coin, see Sawyer, "The Wealth of England in the Eleventh Century," 145–149; C. E. Challis, *A New History of the Royal Mint* (Cambridge: Cambridge University Press, 1992), 58; Spufford, *Money and Its Use*, 74, 91.

[13] Spufford, *Money and Its Use*, 91.

[14] In fact, there is evidence that they even exported the monetary expertise, keeping English moneyers in their posts, but making monetary reforms in Normandy. See Thomas N. Bisson, *Conservation of Coinage: Monetary Exploitation and Its Restraint in France, Catalonia, and Aragon (c.A.D.1000–c.1225)* (Oxford: Clarendon Press, 1979), 18.

[15] Methods of "assay" and "blanching" allowed William to test pennies. For this account of William's changes, which remain debated, see Pamela Nightingale, "'The King's Profit': Trends in English Mint and Monetary Policy in the Eleventh and Twelfth Centuries," in *Trade, Money, and Power in Medieval England* (Surrey: Ashgate Variorum, 2007). As Nightingale indicates, the amount of profit taken from minting itself may be obscured by William's conversion of local minters into royal employees. See Nightingale, "'The King's Profit'"; see also N. J. Mayhew, "From Regional to Central Minting, 1158–1464," in *A New History of the Royal Mint*, ed. C. E. Challis (Cambridge: Cambridge University Press, 1992), 86–87. The evidence that coin was no longer demonetized, perhaps even before William's reign, is supported by the fact that hoards after 1040 begin to contain coins from more than one recoinage. See, e.g., Spufford, *Money and Its Use*, 93, n. 4; Challis, *A New History of the Royal Mint*, 59.

[16] According to a contemporary, the necessity of maintaining credibility with mercenaries motivated the savage reprisals that Henry I took against the moneyers found guilty of debasing coin in 1124. See J. O. Prestwich, "War and Finance in the Anglo-Norman State," *Transactions of the Royal Historical Society* 4 (1954): 33–34.

[17] Suger, *Vie de Louis VI le Gors*, ed. H. Wawuet, 8, as cited by Prestwich, "War and Finance," 67.

imposed more regularly in the face of threatened invasion; other exactions, fines and payments contributed more revenue to the Crown.[18]

When Henry II (1154–1189) re-established royal authority after the civil war of the mid-12th century, he marked it with the traditional strategy. Although he left behind the renovatio monetae, he continued the rationalization (or perhaps bureaucratization) of minting begun by William I. He strengthened the penny again, aligning the English weight standards with the troy pounds used in Normandy, and increased minting charges. Eventually, royal officials would assume control over the "exchange" operation, taking in silver and trading it for newly minted coin.[19]

Henry II developed taxation in the same bureaucratic direction, now to a degree that changed the system qualitatively. The impositions of the earlier Anglo-Norman kings, significant though they were, had been rooted in feudal obligations (the extraction of dues from supporters bound to the king by his political and juridical authority over them) and supplemented by irregular levies for emergency defense of the kingdom (the danegeld and the heregeld). The latter levies became increasingly incongruous and fell out of favor; Henry pushed his feudal rights to revenue all the harder, as did his sons. Their efforts to maximize royal revenue after a period of inflation eroded the Crown's finances at the end of the 12th century and arguably triggered the barons' revolt, memorialized in the Magna Carta. But Henry and his successors also maneuvered to expand their claims to revenue beyond the vassal class, creating obligations that fell on the wider population. The Assize of Arms, for example, assessed the incomes of all free men including mercenaries, as well as feudal tenants, and obliged them to equip themselves with arms. Although only imposed occasionally at first, tithes on incomes and movables had the same broad reach.[20]

Over the next century, taxes that were imposed on a national basis rose in England. The Crown innovated levies on parties over whom it did not have feudal rights—subjects rather than tenants. It justified those impositions by pointing to the great needs of the kingdom, often for military expeditions abroad. Early in the 13th century, it pitched its arguments to the "widest possible circle of the King's

---

[18] Sawyer, "The Wealth of England in the Eleventh Century," 146, 153; Prestwich, "War and Finance in the Anglo-Norman State"; Harriss, *King, Parliament, and Public Finance*, 5; Green, "The Last Century of the Danegeld."

[19] See p. 95; see also Nightingale, "'The King's Profit,'" 62, 64–70; Allen, *Mints and Money*, 143.

[20] See Harriss, *King, Parliament, and Public Finance*, 1–15; P. D. A. Harvey, "The English Inflation of 1180–1220," *Past & Present* 61 (1973): 14. Feudal obligations developed by Henry II included scutage and components of the tallage, although each was limited by custom and practice. They stemmed from the authority of the Crown over his vassals and knights (some could be passed down to tenants), while the imposition of fines and payments followed from his ability to administer justice. Harriss, *King, Parliament, and Public Finance*, 5, 10–14, 27. As the danegeld fell out of use, a land tax called the carucate took its place temporarily. National in scope, it was justified by exceptional need, as had been the danegeld. Harriss, *King, Parliament, and Public Finance*, 14–15. For the causes of the late 12th century inflation in England, which were not due to a depreciation of coin's metal content, see Harvey, "The English Inflation of 1180–1220," 15–29.

immediate vassals," those tenants in chief who had composed the counsel of the realm identified in the earliest versions of Magna Carta. As G. L. Harrris notes, the claim of the magnates to represent other classes had no legal definition, but clearly "there was a notion that the great council could lawfully oblige other classes to pay taxation in virtue of its and their consent." In the second half of the century, the practice of summoning representatives of the country to meet in parliament on questions of national taxation developed. If at first their role was merely to confirm the judgment of the magnates, it would evolve under the pressure of increasing requests to become a necessary expression of national concord.[21]

As Edward I escalated spending on war at the end of the 13th century, sovereign demand for levies, as well as military obligations, bore more heavily on the population. Taxes sanctioned by the Parliament cut deeply into the peasant world. The frequency of imposing the tax on movables almost doubled, for example, while rates rose.[22] From the second decade of the 14th century, prices fell towards the time of the Black Death. The beginning of the Hundred Years War in 1337 drove expenses up again.

It was in those circumstances that Edward III experimented with lessening the metal content of small coins and lightening the penny in a series of small increments. As the next pages show, the strategy went some way towards easing the problems that gripped the English poor. A more dire solution intervened, however. As the plague took its grievous toll on the population, the relative supply of money increased. Through the end of the century, England's governing groups kept the metal content of coin constant. Meanwhile, the king won ten years of direct lay taxes from 1344 to 1355, gained a series of wool subsidies during wartime from 1342 onwards, and succeeded in converting those subsidies into the permanent peacetime levy we saw at the beginning of the chapter. In the following century, English rulers and elites would hold the course they had improvised over the earlier centuries: the tax burden carried by the population continued to be heavy, while money remained strong.[23]

---

[21] Harriss, *King, Parliament, and Public Finance*, 25–26, 27, 30–31, 41–48; see also John Robert Maddicott, "The English Peasantry and the Demands of the Crown 1294–1341," *Past & Present*, Supplement 1 (1975): 1–2; Bertram Percy Wolffe, *The Royal Demense in English History* (London: George Allen & Unwin, 1971), 10. The magnates displaced the familiar council and came to condition grants of aid on their effective use to benefit the community. Harriss, *King, Parliament, and Public Finance*, 32–33, 36–37. The barons did however distinguish sovereign requests for aid from feudal duties, sometimes acceding to the latter while denying the former. Harriss, *King, Parliament, and Public Finance*, 35–37.
[22] Harriss, *King, Parliament, and Public Finance*, 43–48; Maddicott, "English Peasantry," 1, 6–10. Maddicott speculates that landlords began leasing out their demesnes instead of farming them directly to escape the tax. He also emphasizes the hidden costs of the tax, such as unauthorized exactions and inflations by tax takers. Maddicott, "English Peasantry," 7–10. For the difficulties that taxation caused to the lower income English, see pp. 164–166.
[23] See Ormrod, "Royal Authority," 10; P. K. O'Brien and P. A. Hunt, "The Rise of a Fiscal State in England, 1485–1815," *Historical Research* LXVI (1993); see also Maddicott, "English Peasantry," 5 (noting continued heavy taxation but alleviation of crisis after 1341 as war profits reached England and the

As a politics, the English tradition contrasted dramatically with the riot of experiments that occurred on the European Continent. Although much of what happened to coin remains obscure, political authority fractured in French, Spanish, northern and central Italian territories. A plethora of minor powers, often those with market and toll rights, minted their own coin locally; no standard approach controlled the issue of how to meet fiscal demands in the form of money.[24] But depreciating coin—so much more common a Continental strategy—generally played a larger role in revenue raising. It could also be flexibly adopted: authorities diminished metal content by different degrees, depending on their circumstances.[25] As Thomas Bisson points out, they contrived "successive petty debasements" at times and declared more drastic recoinages at others. Sometimes, they let old money trickle in; sometimes, they demonetized it and forced it to the mint. As Cipolla adds, officials were acting for different reasons or in response to different problems: while some rulers diluted coin to skim revenue off for their own use, others used debasement to finance government expend-itures, to answer the demand for more coin, or to appease merchants who wanted a weakening home currency to make their exports cheaper to foreigners.[26] In any case, the cumulative and sometimes steep depreciations contributed far more to rulers there than in England. The constancy of the English alternative of strong money and heavy taxes flowed from a particular alliance, one that made monet-ary governance in the shape of a strongly centralized state with paired monetary and fiscal regimes.

---

population decline after the Black Death brought some benefits to survivors); Harriss, *King, Parliament, and Public Finance*, 466–517; Spufford, *Money and Its Use*, 316–317 (considering the English system, including frequent parliamentary grants and customs revenue, as "far more sophisticated and efficient" than Continental versions).

[24] As Thomas Bisson notes, the devolution of powers was not complete; many lords held their rights to coin money as concessions from a higher sovereign. Despite that link, however, in those regions, "most coinages ceased to be fully public institutions in the eleventh and twelfth centuries" (Bisson, *Conservation of Coinage*, 3–5; Cipolla, "Currency Depreciation in Medieval Europe," 416–417). Germany and eastern Europe followed the same course according to Philip Grierson (Philip Grierson, "Sterling," in *Anglo-Saxon Coins*, ed. R. H. M. Dolley (London: Methuen, 1961), 273), and as implied by Spufford (Spufford, *Money and Its Use*, 95, 302).

[25] See pp. 123–125. Coin could be depreciated relatively easily and, if authorities wished, at immediate profit to themselves. A greater number of coins could be struck from every pound of metal, allowing the mint to offer a higher mint price for silver. The increase, if significant enough, made it profitable for people to bring both bullion and old coin into the mint to be recoined. They would get more back in counted tokens than they brought in and, where the diminution in metal went unannounced, they would spend them at old prices; the loss that occurred when prices rose in the new and less-silver coin would, by contrast, be borne by users more generally. Finally, the mint gained from the operation insofar as the increase in mint price was less than the increase in the mint equivalent, increasing seignorage. That take was additional to the fact that the process would bring more silver to the mint overall and thus push up seignorage across the board. Incentives would be affected by the cost of melting, an aspect especially relevant to those holding old coin.

[26] See Bisson, *Conservation of Coinage*, 7–12; Cipolla, "Currency Depreciation in Medieval Europe," 414–415, 418–419.

B. The alliance and its allocation of authority

Recall the claim, put forward by the magnates and assumed by other classes early in the 13th century, that the great counsel of the landed could speak for the country in consenting to taxes. As Harriss put it, their claim to that voice could be traced to the end of Henry II's reign, and "was a response to the growing political and administrative unity under the vigorous policies of the Angevin kings." But if we focus on money as a governance project, the relationship between English rulers and elites was even longer rooted and more synergistic. Those with wealth in land were not only responding to the "growing political and administrative unity" that had developed in England—they were part of it, as demonstrated by the successful arrangement they brokered. They had prospered under the trad-itional English approach to coin and taxation, had supported that fiscal-monetary pact repeatedly, and would become instrumental in enforcing its rules. When the group that the Crown needed to consult regularly expanded—Parliament took recognizable shape by the late 13th century—the traditions worked out by the Crown with the magnates continued to satisfy the larger elite.[27] The alliance strengthened and shaped centralized authority in England.

The mutuality built on an interest shared by medieval elites across Europe. As a 14th century financial officer in Navarre put it, there were everywhere "three sorts of men," each of which wished the currency to be to "their advantage":

> The first sort of men are those who have rents … especially those who have their rents in money of account. This sort of men clearly wish one sort of money, that is, money of strong alloy.

> The second sort of men are those who engage in commerce, who wish for another sort of money. That is the middle sort of money … Trade is always poor except when money is in a middle state …

> The third sort of men are those who live from the work of their bodies. These would wish to have weak money … When money is current which is not strong, everything always becomes cheap, and there is always enough currency, [and all the feeble money draws the strong money to itself.][28]

The officer's first category captured the situation of the landed classes in England. While many forces could create price inflation, such as bad harvests, balance of trade surpluses, or the influx of metal from newly discovered mines like those of the 13th century, depreciation of the currency commonly contrib-uted. As Nicholas Oresme would object on behalf of French landowners com-plaining about the peasantry, "the devalued state of the currency has effectively

---

[27] See Harriss, *King, Parliament, and Public Finance,* 30–31, 35–36.

[28] Guillaume le Soterel, as quoted by Beatrice Leroy, "Theorie monetaire et extraction miniere en Navarre vers 1340," *Revue Numismatique,* 6th ser., 14 (1972): 110, as cited in Spufford, *Money and Its Use,* 305–306.

cut down for *them* the amount they have to pay *us* in dues and rents amongst other things."[29] Insofar as well-endowed English could stabilize the value of money, they could shield themselves from such losses.

English elites benefited from their strong money in a more indirect way as well, one that not only protected the value of their money, but also promoted their political power. Excluding depreciation of coin from the arsenal of royal weapons or minimizing its deployment helped elites control Crown attempts to raise revenue. Minting remained a sovereign prerogative in England as throughout Europe in the early Middle Ages.[30] At the practical level, it was difficult for lay subjects to oversee or police operations at the mints, although they would at times demand inquiries. When rulers used depreciation of coin to raise revenue, or to skim personal profits for that matter, they acted outside of elite view and reach. By contrast, magnates in England asserted a supervisory role over taxation and, by the 12th century, had begun to develop the notion that it required their consent. Insofar as the Crown had to satisfy fiscal demands by using taxation instead of depreciation of coin, English landowners gained more opportunity to demand a role in governance.[31] Of course, they could also determine how the burdens of taxation would fall.

Those with money and voice in early England consistently supported the decisions of sovereigns to keep the English penny strong. The 1363 petition to Edward III asking that coin "be safely kept and ordered" was part of that pattern. It followed far earlier indications that the Crown was consulting a constituency on money matters. In 1100, Henry I published a charter of liberties declaring that "the common *monetagium* which was collected through the cities and through the counties," was abolished. The *monetagium* would refer in Normandy's later history to a tax on money, usually granted by representatives to the king in return for the guarantee of a stable coinage. The reference in Henry's charter is more mysterious—the debate about its implications is convoluted—but the agreement not to impose the tax may suggest that Henry was acknowledging a tradition of strong coin that was less open to negotiation in England.[32] Two decades later,

---

[29] Spufford, *Money and Its Use*, 310. Spufford's source is not specified; for the sentiment without express class overtones, see Nicholas Oresme in Charles Johnson, trans./ed., *The De Moneta of Nicholas Oresme and English Mint Documents* (London: Thomas Nelson, 1956; repr., Ludwig von Mises Institute, 2009), 18. On the advantages of the English landlord, see Cipolla, "Currency Depreciation in Medieval Europe," 420–421; Spufford, *Money and Its Use*, 318.

[30] See generally Bisson, *Conservation of Coinage; The Case of Mixed Money* (1605) in T. B. Howell, *Cobbett's Complete Collection of State Trials and Proceedings for High Treason and Other Crimes and Misdemeanors from the Earliest Period to the Year 1783*, vol. 2 (London: R. Bagshaw, 1809), 114.

[31] See, e.g., Spufford, *Money and Its Use*, 307; Bisson, *Conservation of Coinage*. For the evolving role of English elites to consent to taxation, see Harriss, *King, Parliament, and Public Finance*.

[32] See Ian Stewart, "The English and Norman Mints, c. 600–1158," in *A New History of the Royal Mint*, ed. C. E. Challis (Cambridge: Cambridge University Press, 1992), 56. Bisson argues that the charge was a money tax imposed by William I when he encountered England's stable currency, noting that the English would have resented the charge as a break with their tradition of strong money, although he does not address the fact that the population would have been used to paying the heavy charges of the renovatio

Henry would take savage action against moneyers accused of debasing money illegally as if to demonstrate his own adamancy against acts that deteriorated the coinage.[33]

The abundance of metal flowing to England, as to the rest of Europe, eased pressures to depreciate coin during the 13th century. Sovereigns across the region largely preserved the metal contents of their money.[34] As Europe slid towards war at the end of century, however, Philip IV began an immensely profitable series of debasements; the provincial nobility in France objected, while those in England feared the example and anticipated that the English king might follow it. Petitions presented in Parliament lobbied against any depreciation of coin and did so with great success. In his ordinances of 1311, Edward II agreed not to alter the value of the money without consulting the barons. Nor did he dilute the currency, despite rising military expenses.[35]

Forty years later, another generation repeated the drama. Philip VI of France began debasing his currency, again to increase revenues for war expenditures against England, led now by Edward III. The provocation came at a difficult time: a recession gripped England even as the Crown tried to mobilize for war.

At first glance, the crisis would seem natural, a product of falling metal supplies and bountiful harvests. Early in the 14th century, Europeans exploited the last large silver deposits that men could reach with available technology. At the same time, war and trade tensions disrupted the wool trade and the flow of bullion to England that it usually produced. By the 1320s, England's moneyers had begun to run dry, and the mint at Canterbury closed. The amount of metal coming to the mint continued to fall through the 1330s and 1340s. Prices fell from 1310 on, and the abundant harvests of the 1330s pushed the profits on grain down even further.[36] An observer complained that "There is a desperate shortage of cash among the people. At market the buyers are so few that a man can do no business, although he may have cloth or corn, pig or sheep to sell, because so many are destitute."[37]

---

monetae. See Bisson, *Conservation of Coinage*, 20–23. Another possibility is that the *monetagium* referred to a charge placed on boroughs in lieu of earlier ways of harvesting metal at the mint. See Bolton, *Money in the Medieval English Economy*, 101. That charge may have seemed obsolete insofar as the Anglo-Saxon method of harvesting metal had been abandoned and gratuitous if a standard charge for minting had been added. In Stewart's view, the borough tax (a charge referred to as *de moneta*, not the *monetagium*) was too significant to have been waived by the king. Stewart, "English and Norman Mints," 56.

[33] Nightingale, "'The King's Profit,'" 64. Nightingale argues that Henry may have been scapegoating the moneyers for some deterioration of the money due to shortages in the metal supply. His act might also have been used to justify an additional tax (the *ad scalem* tax) as if it were necessary to address the monetary crisis. The possibility would perform very neatly the pairing of strong money and high taxes under the Angevins.

[34] Many of the European sovereigns were bound by agreements not to depreciate coin in return for grants of taxation. See generally Bisson, *Conservation of Coinage*.

[35] Spufford, *Money and its Use*, 302.

[36] Mayhew, "Central Minting," 143–144; Maddicott, "English Peasantry," 48. For the decreasing amount of metal coming to the mint, see Mayhew, "Numismatic Evidence," 7.

[37] Anglo-Norman Political Songs 111, as quoted in Maddicott, "English Peasantry," 49.

To categorize the recession that gripped the countryside as a function of silver and grain would be a mistake, however. It was instead how people made money and markets out of them that mattered. "Closing mints was only one response to the scarcity of silver," as Nicholas Mayhew has observed. More commonly, Continental rulers raised the price the mint would pay for it. When the metal supply in their country began to drop, the English could likewise have diluted the metal content of their coin, attracting more bullion to their mints and increasing the number of coins in circulation. Absent that intervention, the diminishing money supply would push prices down—and indeed, prices fell across the board and in years unaffected by the good harvests. The strong penny of England had always packed a high purchasing power; now it rose even higher. People sought small change in vain—after all, a halfpenny bought twice what it normally did and a whole ox would go for 6s. 8d.[38]

In those circumstances, the "desperate shortage of cash" identified at the time takes on new meaning. England was caught in a terrifying currency shortfall, one exacerbated by the heavy money taxes laid by the king. Men sold plow animals and essential equipment to meet the levies; others went into debt or lost possessions to government suit; still others left their land and holdings to evade taxation. As the coin squeezed from a hard-pressed population came in, it was sent out of the country to pay for military expenses abroad.[39] By the 1340s, the stress laid on the lay world of modest means was enormous—rumors of peasant unrest circulated, along with complaints that purveyance had swallowed the last food stocks and men had sold their seed corn to make tax payments.[40]

From 1335 to 1344, the Crown experimented with raising the price for small change, halfpennies and farthings, at the mint. Moneyers lowered the fineness of the silver and put the difference towards a higher price they paid for bullion. The measure could be defended in economic terms as a response that reflected the rising value of silver. Alternatively, it could be justified as a strategy that, whether it followed rising prices for silver or helped produce them, recognized the value of multiplying liquidity in times of scarcity. The initiative succeeded immediately as those holding silver responded to the new mint prices: the flow of silver to the mint jumped from about £336 in 1333–1334 to £1,132 in 1335–1336, and to £1,619 in 1336–1337. In the last full year of the debasement, 1342–1343, output reached £14,753. Even that amount, however, falls to Martin Allen's observation that the silver currency was diminishing so sharply over the period as to dwarf the increases in flow.[41]

---

[38] Mayhew, "Central Minting," 144; Maddicott, "English Peasantry," 48. According to the Phelps Brown-Hopkins index, prices dropped more than 35 percent between 1310 and 1340; according to the Allen index, they fell almost 30 percent. See Mayhew, "Prices in England," 5.

[39] Maddicott, "English Peasantry," 52–53, 58.

[40] See generally Maddicott, "English Peasantry," 4, 23–24, 30–31, 64–65, 69.

[41] Allen, *Mints and Money*, 283–284. Allen notes that the silver currency was estimated at £1.5 to £1.9 million in 1331, and fell to about £0.5 million to £0.8 million by 1351.

Prices continued to drop and hardship in the countryside intensified. Criticism of the king's decision to go to war circulated and popular discontent mounted. Parliamentary scholars of the period point out the mediate place of the land-holders in the Commons at the time. On the one hand, their role in consenting to taxation gave them opportunity and, in a literal sense, "office" to comment, to present grievances, and even to voice opposition. In some ways, the crisis in the countryside empowered the Commons as representatives of the realm. The members' local connections also motivated their concerns; not only were they aware of local hardship, they were also exposed to local wrath. Occasionally, they were even treated to local support. A protest song of the times, one harshly critical of the king's taxes, advocated:

> A king ought not to go out of his kingdom to make war, unless the commons of his land will consent:—by treason we often see very many perish;—no one can tell in whom to trust with certainty.—Let not the king go out of his kingdom without counsel.[42]

On other hand, the landed elites in the Commons identified with the magnates above them, who shared their concerns and position as landowners. The long tradition of leaving money unaltered instilled an expectation that such a course would continue; that tradition also promoted their interests as a group receiving fixed rents. Edward's debasement of small change violated such touchstones. The experiments seemed especially suspect insofar as the Crown had lessened the fineness of metal, a way of diminishing metal content that was more difficult for holders to detect than changes in a coin's weight. Faced with rising criticism, the mint backed away from its attempts to multiply small change; it would not try lessening the fineness of metal as a remedy again during the Middle Ages.[43]

As wealthier English mobilized, they moved away from that "third sort of men," those the observer in Navarre said lived from the work of their bodies and wanted to have "weak money." Rising prices would have helped tenants, artisans, and others who owed fixed rents, taxes, and other debts. While the amounts of those obligations had been set earlier, they could be paid off by money that had lost value. If the same group could sell their goods and labor on a rising market, they would increase the face value of their earnings relative to their fixed obligations. The inflation of the late 12th century had advantaged tenants who owed rents fixed by contract or similar commitment. The recession at mid-14th century brought, of course, precisely the opposite problems. In taxes, rents, and

---

[42] *The Song Against the King's Taxes*, in Peter Coss, ed., *Thomas Wright's Political Songs of England: From the Reign of John to that of Edward II* (Cambridge: Cambridge University Press, 1996), 182. For dating of the *Song*, see Coss, *Political Songs*, liii–liv. For discussion of the Commons' consent to war, see Harriss, *King, Parliament, and Public Finance*, 233–234.

[43] Mint indentures specifying coin weights and finenesses are published in Appendix 2, Challis, *A New History of the Royal Mint*, 699–758. The character of changes in the penny (weight, legal value, or fineness) between 1343 and 1542 are listed at Redish, *Bimetallism*, 89–90 (Table 3A.1).

debts, men owed fixed amounts that loomed ever larger as prices for everyday produce dropped.[44]

To make matters worse, the peasantry bore a heavy load of public obligations, including the tax on movables and the purveyance, which was taken in coin for some items. The customs taxes introduced by Edward I added to their difficulties and, in the 1330s, Edward III's efforts to exploit wool revenues harmed producers who were paid less by exporters; a commentator predicted it "thus to destroy the poor people by a bitter burthen."[45] In a move that could be claimed to alleviate that burden or to epitomize it, the Parliament in 1340 granted the king a tax in-kind: rural dwellers owed the ninth sheaf, the ninth lamb, and the ninth fleece to the king for government sale and profit. The tax avoided the problem haunting the rural population—the shortage of small change. But "designed to leave untouched the peasant's small reserves of cash," it operated "by taking his produce instead." At the same time, it exempted corn from its levy, protecting the lords' profit on that crop.[46]

The decisions epitomized the distance that separated the Commons from the poorer population. While *The Song Against the King's Taxes* protested the foreign war, the corruption of tax collectors, and the scarcity of money, its recurring theme was the turpitude of those wealthy men who granted taxes to the Crown out of the poverty of the people. The king's great need for money could be satisfied "among the rich," the poet wrote; it would have been better to "have taken a part from the great, and to have spared the little." Still it was not the king, "a young bachelor and not of an age to compass any malice," who had sinned by taking money from the poor; it was instead his Parliament. As the poet charged:

It is no trouble to the great thus to grant to the king a tax; the simple must pay it all, which is contrary to God's will.—This counsel is not at all good, but polluted with vice; it is ill ordained, that those who grant should pay nothing.—For those who make the grant give nothing to the king, it is the needy only who give.

How will they perform good deeds out of the sweat of the poor,—whom the rich ought to spare, by gift or favour?—they ought to tax the great, for the fear of God;—and

[44] See Harvey, "The English Inflation of 1180–1220," 19, 24; Maddicott, "English Peasantry." For the more complex effects of inflation on those subject to being forced into paying with labor services instead of money rent, see Harvey, "The English Inflation of 1180–1220," 20–23. For the harsh effects on Jewish money-lenders, see Harvey, "The English Inflation of 1180–1220," 24. Episodes of popular protest in England and on the Continent greeted attempts to "strengthen" money. For the former, see pp. 139–140, 366–367; for the latter, see, e.g., Spufford, *Money and Its Use*, 289–290, 309.

[45] *The Song Against the King's Taxes*, in Coss, *Political Songs*, 183; Maddicott, "English Peasantry," 2, 16, 19–22, 25, 27–28, 30, 58; Harriss, *King, Parliament, and Public Finance*, 240; see also Maddicott, "English Peasantry," 30 (noting that sheriffs required to pay prises could collect from royal debtors to do so). For the rise in conscription and the local taxes required to supplement it, see Maddicott, "English Peasantry," 34–45. Maddicott identifies the peak years of oppressiveness because of government levies as 1336–1341. Maddicott, "English Peasantry," 45–67.

[46] Spufford, *Money and Its Use*, 305; Maddicott, "English Peasantry," 46–47, 50. For an account of Edward III's relationship with his ministers, the barons and great lords, and the Commons, see Ormrod, "Royal Authority."

spare more the people, who live in pain.—Thou who art rich enough, live not thus upon the poor.

and again:

O God, who wast crowned with the sharp thorn,—have pity with divine grace upon thy people!—may the world be comforted of such ruin!—To tell unvarnished truth, it is mere robbery.—The property of the poor taken without their will, is as it were stolen.[47]

A theology that identified riches with communal responsibility to the less fortunate animated the poet's screed. "I do not know how they can save their souls," he wrote of those "who would live upon other people's goods, and save their own." But wrapped into the forecast of perdition, the *Song* also made a more immediate challenge to the kingdom: "Out of emptiness who can give"? As it entered the Hundred Years' War, England's insistence on strong money and taxes that were widely perceived as inequitable contributed to fiscal disarray; Edward III scrambled to find revenue for his early campaigns.[48]

Philip VI's decision to raise a major amount of revenue by debasing his own coinage took place in the midst of the English recession. By 1349, he had reduced his coin to 20 percent silver and 80 percent alloy; the technique provided 522,000 livres of revenue out of a total receipt of 782,000 livres. The rising price of silver meant that Edward III could not compete with European mints except by decreasing the amount of metal in the penny. Wary of the rage against debasing any coin, he would lighten the penny slightly in weight rather than fineness in 1344, 1345, and 1346, and more significantly in 1351.[49]

Over the same decade, Edward III famously engaged the growing ambition of his barons and Commons. But the very terms of that struggle incorporated the alliance that bound those parties together. Despite the grave need to bring silver to the mint, elites reacted against Edward's decision to alter the penny. According to Rogers Ruding's reading, the depreciation of metal "appears to have occasioned dissatisfaction," while the treasurer who had advised it "became extremely unpopular, or . . . was evil spoken of among the people." By that time, the anxiety of landholders in the Commons had mounted sufficiently to move them to act in more unity with the barons. In response to their shared objection, Edward agreed to dilute the coinage no further. More striking, he agreed to consult Parliament before altering it in the future.[50]

---

[47] *The Song Against the King's Taxes*, in Coss, *Political Songs*, 184–185.

[48] *The Song Against the King's Taxes*, in Coss, *Political Songs*, 185; Harriss, *King, Parliament, and Public Finance*, 232–252.

[49] See mint contracts in Challis, *A New History of the Royal Mint*, 701, 703; Redish, *Bimetallism*, 89 (Table 3A.1). In terms of penny count per pound of fine silver, the mint struck 240 to 243 coins from a Tower pound from 1279 with few aberrations until 1346, when it struck 270. In 1351, it increased that number to 300. See Allen, *Mints and Money*, 149; Mayhew, "Central Minting," 134.

[50] Ruding, *Annals*, 226–227; Spufford, *Money and Its Use*, 318. On the alliance created by Edward and his fiscal success, see Ormrod, "Royal Authority."

As for small change, the king let lapse another experiment he had tried to make it more abundant. During the recession, he had started to pay moneyers more to mint small denominations, a bonus necessary to cover the extra labor that came with striking many low value coins. The Crown would underpay moneyers to make halfpennies and farthings from 1351 for the next century. Parliament's ability to tolerate the searing change shortages that followed confirmed the priority it accorded to strong money at the top.[51] As we will see, that decision would stratify England's social space, as it had in the past: strong money nurtured larger transactions while drawing those at the bottom into economic dependency on those with more liquidity.

During the decades at mid-century, the Crown and Commons also worked out between themselves the authority to raise taxes. Harriss argues that the balance they struck lasted for the next two centuries. According to it, the Crown retained the initiative over the shape and character of levies. But the Crown accepted the obligation, now regular and increasingly institutionalized, to consult the Parliament on matters of revenue and to justify its requests according to criteria of "the common profit" of the realm and its "common need." The Black Death played its tragic role in cementing the arrangement: taking almost half of the English population at the end of the 1340s, it left more coin circulating among survivors. Prices rose, helping those living from wages and sales of produce. To the landowners in the Commons, the rise in labor's value was sudden and mystifying. It was also threatening, a development that increased the power of those who had already demonstrated such discontent in the countryside. As its scholars portray it, the experience confirmed the solidarity assumed by members of the Commons with greater landowners and the Crown. That unity influenced the political programs they supported.[52]

Englishmen with wealth did not, of course, always succeed in avoiding inflation (or in avoiding taxes for that matter). During the 13th century in particular, prices had risen in England, as silver flowed out of new mines in Germany. But as a relative matter, landowners in England were happily positioned. The Crown did not dilute the metal content of coin to any significant extent before the 1340s. Until that period, the depreciation of coin added virtually no fuel to any price increases.[53] After that period, the metal content of England's penny fell gradually:

---

[51] See generally Allen, *Mints and Money*, 360–368; Mayhew, "Central Minting," 149 and n. 206. The mint contracts are in Challis, *A New History of the Royal Mint*, 701–703.

[52] Ormrod, "Royal Authority," 10–13; Harriss, *King, Parliament, and Public Finance*, 356–375. For the distribution of mortality from the Black Death and estimated total, see Michael Prestwich, *Plantagenet England: 1225–1360* (Oxford: Oxford University Press, 2005), 542–546.

[53] For a contemporary and highly theorized complaint on behalf of the Continental landed, see Johnson, trans./ed., *De Moneta/English Mint Documents*,1–48. Spufford analyzes Oresme's sympathies in the context of the complaints by landholding elites in Europe at Spufford, *Money and Its Use*, 300–314A; see also Oresme Lapidus, "Metal, Money, and the Prince: John Buridan and Nicholas Oresme after Thomas Aquinas," *History of Political Economy* 29, no. 22 (1997). On the inflation of the late 12th and early 13th centuries and its impact on the economic relations of landowners, tenants, villeins, and sovereign, see

between 1344 and 1492, the penny lost about 41 percent of its metal content. Prices, however, remained remarkably stable; after a temporary spike following the Black Death, they were virtually flat through the 15th century.[54] As approximated by each coin's exchange value against the Florentine florin, which stayed constant in weight and fineness, currencies on the Continent lost much more value.[55] As Peter Spufford indicates, landowning elites on the Continent advocated for many of the same measures as their English colleagues, but did so with much less success.

The unique program that bound the governing classes together in England influenced the way they conceptualized their constitutional roles. In particular, taxation came to figure as the paradigmatic arena for legislative engagement and participation. At the same time, the management of money's value came to appear the natural prerogative of the Crown.

Debate about taxation and monetary policy on the Continent furnishes a useful comparison. Within that debate, one influential argument held that royal authority to extract levies in defense of the realm was effectively absolute. Sovereigns on the Continent faced a more fractured political terrain; they defended national boundaries that were more fluid, and they made or feared more frequent military threats. The circumstances justified the claim that taxes were always necessary, a doctrine of "perpetua necessitas." That doctrine diminished the ability of elites to protest levies. By contrast, English rulers continued to work within the custom that taxes would be asked and due only when exigencies demanded them. English elites retained a role in evaluating and accepting claims of necessity even though once they accepted those claims, their consent to levies was virtually required. As king and Parliament kept to the course of consultation and consent, the procedures they developed and the regularity of their interaction contributed its own momentum. Over time, a culture of legislation developed. It located the Crown as the authority that guided and protected the kingdom, identified armed and other dangers, and coordinated commercial and military initiatives. But the division of responsibility established a role for Parliament that included assessing the needs claimed by the Crown and evaluating the demands it made. In that process, the

Harvey, "The English Inflation of 1180–1220"; see also Spufford, *Money and Its Use*, 243–244, 290A. Harvey also notes that increases in taxation during the period may have represented royal attempts to capture gains otherwise lost through inflation. Harvey, "The English Inflation of 1180–1220," 13.

[54] See Redish, *Bimetallism*, 89 (Table 3A.1). The penny dropped from 20.30 to 12 grains of silver, .925 pure. See Mayhew, "Prices in England," 5 (Phelps Brown-Hopkins and Allen price indices).

[55] The number of English pennies trading against the florin increased from 36.5d. to 55d. The penny thus dropped 33 percent in value against the florin between 1350 and 1500; the Flemish groot dropped about 80 percent in value between 1348 and 1500; the florin of Barcelona dropped about 48 percent in value between 1350 and 1480, and the Austrian pfenning dropped 72 percent between 1354 and 1498. (After its remarkably unstable career earlier in the medieval period, French coin eroded gently, at approximately the English rate.) Note that not all exchange rate differences would be due to changes in metal value, although exchange rates were set on bullion bases. For those figures and the change in other countries, see Spufford, *Money and Its Use*, 292–293A (comparing silver currencies).

Commons claimed a protective charge over the property of subjects. That assertion would turn out to be protean.[56]

The emphasis in Continental and English debate was almost exactly the opposite on the issue of monetary policy. Diluting their coinages frequently and at times desperately, European rulers engendered a raging debate over depreciation of coin by the 14th century. The bishops and great French barons had objected at the beginning of the century, when Philip IV diluted coin to raise money for war; at one point (1298–1299), he had reaped the lion's share of royal revenue from debasing coin. In the following years, nobility in Brabant and Aragon protested efforts by their own rulers to extract profits the same way, and the treasurer general of Navarre advised his king how landowners, merchants, and working men divided over that controversial strategy.

In the midst of Philip VI's radical debasements, Nicholas Oresme developed an elaborate critique of actions that depreciated coin. Oresme wrote as an advocate for landed wealth. His book, *De Moneta*, emphasized that weakening the metal content of coin raised prices on imported luxuries, minimized the problems that strong money created for those exporting goods, and neglected the hardships it visited on those owing fixed rents and working for fixed wages. A party political tract, it would succeed in capturing the concerns of the most powerful magnates of the times. *De Moneta* soon became the French orthodoxy, displacing the Thomistic defense of sovereign authority over value that had previously prevailed.[57]

Oresme's argument turned on the proposition that money belonged to the community, not to the king. Depreciation of coin was, after all, a means of taking property: it was "in effect a tax." Moreover, it was a tax that could be levied easily and collected rapidly. It fell on resources that took a money form, hitting the wealthy part of the population that took its profits that way. As such, no depreciation of coin should occur without the consent of representatives (a suitably elite portion of the national community) in political assembly. Oresme went on to underscore the substantive harms caused by lightening coin. Making central the view of his constituency, his analysis stressed the sanctity of money's metal value. Only in emergencies should a society ever lessen the strength of its coin. Oresme's approach could later be claimed for those understanding money as a commodity. But as a matter of governance, he had actually removed monetary value from the sovereign prerogative and located it as a matter for communal policing and consent.[58]

---

[56] See generally Harriss, *King, Parliament, and Public Finance*, 311–355, 509–517 and passim.

[57] This paragraph follows Spufford's analysis. Spufford, *Money and Its Use*, 300–306. For the earlier approach, see Arthur Eli Monroe, *Monetary Theory Before Adam Smith* (Cambridge, MA: Harvard University Press, 1923), 25–41.

[58] Oresme, *De Moneta*, 10–11; Spufford, *Money and Its Use*, 300, 307. For discussion of Oresme's "metallist" or "commodity" approach to money, see Lapidus, "Metal, Money, and the Prince: John Buridan and Nicholas Oresme after Thomas Aquinas"; Thomas J. Sargent and Francois R. Velde, *The Big Problem of Small Change*, The Princeton Economic History of the Western World Indexes (Princeton, NJ: Princeton University Press, 2002), 97–99.

By contrast, English agreement on the way to govern value made protracted debate over the depreciation of coin virtually unnecessary. Likewise, it left English elites unaccustomed to considering money as an element of their political power. Ironically, their posture would leave Parliament slow to react when Henry VIII violently debased the currency during the 16th century. Henry's assault on money would come in turn to seem more a matter of royal betrayal, more aberrational, and more anomalous than an occasion that invited political engagement. In the circumstances, Parliament would depend largely on Henry VIII's successors to repair the damage he had done.[59]

Consistent with that approach to governing value, the English judiciary confirmed the power of royal prerogative at the end of the reign of Elizabeth I. *The Case of Mixed Money* concerned the Queen's effort to pay for military maneuvers in Ireland by debasing Irish coin. Legitimating that act, authorities handed down a lengthy disquisition on money, one that linked England's particular history with the power of its sovereign. The argument used that connection between past practice and royal authority to banish any doubt that managing money and establishing its value was a matter for the Crown.[60] That story lies ahead, but as an intervention arguably cumulative of earlier jurisprudence, *The Case of Mixed Money* captured the principle hammered out across medieval practice. The right to mint "inheres in the bones of princes," wrote the Privy Council, arguing that both common and civil law "included [it] among the rights belonging to the prince" that could not be disinherited from royal power.[61] While Parliament had participated in legislating on some monetary matters like prohibiting coin's exportation, the king acted alone in determining monetary value.[62] As for the theoretical tradition that claimed more authority for the community, *The Case of Mixed Money* emphasized England's distinctive history and record on money to reject that proposition. "[S]ome doctors [of the civil law] are of opinion that the prince cannot change money without the consent of the people," wrote the Council quoting an earlier commentator. That view may have force elsewhere, but it failed in the face of England's long-standing practice. "If the prince were accustomed to changing money on his own authority, without

---

[59] C. E. Challis, "Lord Hastings to the Great Silver Recoinage, 1464-1699," in *A New History of the Royal Mint*, ed. C. E. Challis (Cambridge: Cambridge University Press, 1992), 228–251; Albert Edgar Feavearyear, *The Pound Sterling: A History of English Money*, 2nd ed. (Oxford: Clarendon Press, 1963), 48–86; David Fox, "The Structures of Monetary Nominalism in the Pre-Modern Common Law," in *Money in the Western Legal Tradition*, ed. Wolfgang Ernst and David Fox (Oxford: Oxford University Press, forthcoming, 2015) (noting constancy of traditionally nominalist principles during Tudor debasements).

[60] *The Case of Mixed Money* (1605) in T. B. Howell, *Cobbett's Complete Collection of State Trials and Proceedings for High Treason and Other Crimes and Misdemeanors from the Earliest Period to the Year 1783*, vol. 7 (London: R. Bagshaw, 1811) 114. For a longer discussion, see pp. 267–274. The case was decided by the Privy Council, acting as the highest judicial authority for cases arising in Ireland.

[61] *The Case of Mixed Money* (1605), 118 (*Monetandi jus principum ossibus inhaeret, Jus monetae comprehenditur in regalibus, quae nunquam a regio sceptro abdicantur*).

[62] *The Case of Mixed Money* (1605), 119. Henry VIII's debasements furnished the court with precedents for that proposition.

consent of the people—and there exists no memory even for the origins of this custom in time—then he can do such a thing freely."[63] In England, power to determine the metal content of money remained with the prince.

C. The lost history of public tallies

The silver and gold coin of the early English world, meeting so perfectly the monetary imagination of later centuries, overshadows other, less expected moneys. The next section tells the story of English tallies, a dramatic monetary innovation of the medieval period. Tallies were a form of public debt: they were wooden tokens given out by the government as IOUs, claims that entitled the holder to a portion of the revenue coming into public coffers. When they started to circulate, they began to act as money.

Ironically, it was the archetype of money—the silver and gold coin of England—that invited the strange new form—the tally. When the English insisted that coin contain a constant metal content, they limited how far and fast money flowed. The penny was simply too valuable to lubricate many transactions; it left much small urban exchange dry and traveled through the peasant world only during certain seasons and for certain uses. But even though money might not wash easily across the land, taxes were pervasive. As the main option for raising revenue, the Crown had developed its sophisticated and extensive system of levies. The combination meant that the government might be faced with delays as it collected revenues—but it could also write credible IOUs on the incoming funds. Tallies became a mode of public borrowing, effectively extracting advances of revenue, generally interest-free, from participants. They also functioned as a way to increase the money supply. The two were, of course, related: just as in the case of more conventional money, government need for revenues dovetailed with the production of circulating credit.

Long after the heyday of tallies, events conspired to hide their history. Early modern writers, especially those with experience in an older world, registered and explored the phenomenon.[64] But their classical successors, defining money as a commodity that arose only from the exchange of independent individuals, did not recognize tallies as a medium. As they would with other public credit currencies, they simply left the odd wooden markers off the map.[65] As if

---

[63] *The Case of Mixed Money* (1605), 121. (The Latin, as loosely quoted from Reinier Budelius: "*principem sine assensu 'populi monetam mutare non posse,'* yet he concludes, '*si princeps consuevisset mutare monetam auctoritate propria, sine consensu populi, a tempore cuius initii memoria non existit, tunc libere imposterum eum hoc facere posse.*'")

[64] See, e.g., Charles Davenant, *Discourses on the Publick Revenues and on Trade* (1698).

[65] The token coins of the same period—copper, tin, and cheap alloys—also fall out of most models of early money. For exceptions in recent scholarship, see Sargent and Velde, *Big Problem of Small Change*; Philip L. Mossman, *Money of the American Colonies and Confederation: A Numismatic, Economic and Historical Correlation*, Numismatic studies, no. 20 index (New York: American Numismatic Society, 1993).

ritualistically to confirm that disappearance, Parliament in 1834 ordered centuries of old Exchequer tallies to be burned. Dumped into basement furnaces, the tallies stoked a fire so fierce that it escaped control and destroyed the Houses of Parliament.[66] With that material erasure, tallies virtually vanished from significant discussion. Only institutional histories of the Exchequer and its accounts memorialized them.

But before they were rendered intellectually incongruous, burned, and forgotten, tallies had furnished the English state with an essential medium. During some years of the medieval period, a majority of public revenues paid to public creditors took the form of tallies. The tokens also circulated, most clearly in certain networks of people in and around London, as a kind of auxiliary money. And as they used tallies, the English gained experience with an expressly fiat currency, one based on the credit of incoming revenues. By the colonizing period, that practice was at least 400 years old. It offered the most obvious model for early American paper money—another currency based on public credit and one that became enormously important to the communities in which it traveled.[67] Tallies also provided a reservoir of knowledge upon which those designing both public bonds and bank money—the radical instruments of the monetary revolution of Restoration England—drew. And when tallies went into decline, as they did in the 17th century, they invited those developments into the void they left. The lost history of public tallies thus illuminates the character of early money, its role as an aspect of governance, and its transformation.

The English story of public credit begins only a few centuries after metal currency had become well established in the realm. We can hear the demand for money that drove the innovation in Henry III's commands to his sheriffs: one received notice that he should "pay forthwith into the Exchequer the moneys therin mentioned" and "warn all fermers [tax farmers] within his baily-wick, to pay-in the areres of their ferms at the same time, as they tendred the holding of their ferms and their own safety." Another was cautioned yet more ominously to turn in his revenues "if he would eschew corporal punishment, loss of his goods, and the King's displeasure; . . . [for] if he failed therein, he should be so severely chastised, that others should learn by his example how dangerous it was to disobey the King's Precepts."[68] The words exuded urgency and, even, a sense of futility. At times, royal expenses simply came in faster than the revenue. That perennial problem was compounded by the unwieldiness of the free minting

---

[66] James F. Willard, "An Early Exchequer Tally," *Bulletin of the John Rylands Library* 7, no. 2 (1923): 278.

[67] See, e.g., Leslie V. Brock, *The Currency of the American Colonies, 1700–1764, A Study in Colonial Finance and Imperial Relations*, Dissertations in American Economic History (New York: Arno Press, 1975); Christine A. Desan, "From Blood to Profit: Making Money in the Practice and Imagery of Early America," *Journal of Policy History* 20, no. 1 (2008).

[68] Thomas Madox, *History and Antiquities of the Exchequer of the Kings of England*, 2nd ed. (London: 1769; repr., 1969), 356.

Fig. 4.1 The top tally shows two £20 notches; the second shows seven one shilling jagged cuts, and eight one shilling cuts on the upper side. The bottom stick carries eight narrow penny lines on its upper side. The tallies were issued to Robert of Glamorgan, Sheriff of Surrey and Sussex in 1293–1294. From M. T. Clanchy, *From Memory to Written Record*, 371.

system, the risks and delays of carrying coin across long distances, and the inefficiencies of local administration throughout the period.[69]

Crown administrators developed a solution. "English medieval finance," writes a historian of the Exchequer, "was built upon the tally and the assignment."[70] "Tallies" reflected their early origins in picturesque detail: they were sticks cut from wood, "usually of hazel," notched to reflect a certain amount of money by cuts of different sizes.[71] See Fig. 4.1. The classic source on the early Exchequer, *Dialogus de Scaccario* or *The Dialogue concerning the Exchequer*, a treatise completed in approximately 1179, describes the denominations represented by each kind of notch. It begins:

> At the top of the tally a cut is made, the thickness of the palm of the hand, to represent a thousand pounds; then a hundred pounds by a cut the breadth of the thumb; twenty pounds, the breadth of the little finger; a single pound, the width of a swollen barleycorn; a shilling rather narrower, yet so that converging cuts remove some of the wood and leave there a little furrow; a penny is marked by a single cut without removing any wood.[72]

[69] Hilary Jenkinson, "Medieval Tallies, Public and Private," *Archaeologia* 74 (1925): 306.

[70] Anthony Bedford Steel, *The Receipt of the Exchequer, 1377–1485* (Cambridge: Cambridge University Press, 1954), xxix; see also Glyn Davies, *A History of Money: From Ancient Times to the Present Day*, 3rd ed. (Cardiff: University of Wales Press, 2002), 146–152. Willard, "Exchequer Tally"; Anthony Steel, "The Negotiation of Wardrobe Debentures in the Fourteenth Century," *English Historical Review* 44, no. 175 (1929).

[71] Reginald Lane Poole, *The Exchequer in the Twelfth Century* (Oxford: Clarendon Press, 1912), 86.

[72] Richard fitz Nigel, "Dialogus de Scaccario," in *English Historical Documents, 1042–1189*, ed. David C. Douglas and George W. Greenaway (London: Eyre & Spottiswoode, 1953 [c. 1179]), 490, 504. See also

Issued as early as the 12th century, tallies served initially as receipts, "acquit-tances upon record" proving a payment into the English Exchequer.[73] When a tax farmer or other depositor brought money into the Exchequer, the amount would be recorded on the tally. The stick would then be split down the middle; one half (the "stock") would be held by the depositor, while the other half (the "foil") would be kept at the Exchequer.[74] Later, most commonly when a tax farmer or other official came in to account for the revenues he owed the Crown, he would present the stock of the tally as his receipt. Exchequer officials would fit it with the other half to verify that he had already delivered the money.[75]

According to the *Dialogus*, tallies were small, "the distince between the tip of the forefinger and the thumb when fully extended" or about eight inches.[76] Apparently almost indestructible except by flame—the fate that would eventually claim them so completely—they were also light, adaptable, and effective in a world where few were literate. At the same time, the matching stock and foil system made them resistant to fraud. Well suited for their role, privately pro-duced tallies were used by individuals and by sheriffs acting more informally for the reign.[77] Only those issued at the Exchequer, however, became "system-atized ... into an official instrument cut according to certain rules" including a standardized material, notches, cutting angles, and inscriptions.[78] The method and uniformity clearly distinguished public tallies, making them highly recog-nizable and easily used.[79]

Refined and increasingly stylized as a receipt, tallies soon took on another function, one that connects them to that other staple of medieval finance, "the assignment." An assignment was an act or instrument that drafted revenue before

Jenkinson, "Medieval Tallies," 294–296; Hilary Jenkinson, "Exchequer Tallies," *Archaeologia* 62 (1911): 373.

[73] Crooke Report 1670, as quoted in Hilary Jenkinson, "Note Supplementary to 'Exchequer Tallies,'" *Proceedings of the Society of Antiquaries* 25 (1913): 32. See fitz Nigel, "Dialogus de Scaccario," 495 (identifying the tally as "a receipt of the money" given by Exchequer officials).

[74] Poole, *The Exchequer in the Twelfth Century*, 89; see also Jenkinson, "Medieval Tallies," 297. According to some accounts, the term "stock" later gave its name to the "Bank stock" held by those lending money to the Bank of England. Poole, *The Exchequer in the Twelfth Century*, 89.

[75] fitz Nigel, "Dialogus de Scaccario," 503–504; C. D. Chandaman, *The English Public Revenue, 1660-1688* (Oxford: Clarendon Press, 1975), 286; Feavearyear, *The Pound Sterling*, 110. The foils were kept in a chest "where Domesday is kept," until stored by the Deputy Chamberlains in their office. Those officials would retrieve them to be "'joyned on occasion with the Accountant's stock," notes Hilary Jenkinson quoting a 17th century report on early Exchequer practice, "to the true performance of which duty they are sworn at their appointment." Jenkinson, "Exchequer Tallies, Note," 34.

[76] fitz Nigel, "Dialogus de Scaccario," 504. Hall's and Jenkinson's histories imply that tallies grew much longer especially when used to record larger amounts in the early modern period, peaking during the 19th century. Hubert Hall, *The Antiquities and Curiosities of the Exchequer* (London: E. Stock, 1891), 123; Jenkinson, "Exchequer Tallies," 378; Hilary Jenkinson, "An Original Exchequer Account of 1304," *Proceedings of the Society of Antiquaries* 26 (1913): 36.

[77] Hilary Jenkinson describes tallies as "rapidly popularized" throughout Europe as financial instru-ments Jenkinson, "Exchequer Tallies," 367–368.

[78] Jenkinson, "Exchequer Tallies," 368. The *Dialogus* specifies notch sizes and cutting angles quite particularly. See p. 173.

[79] Jenkinson, "Medieval Tallies," 291, 297, 319–321; Jenkinson, "Exchequer Tallies," 373, 379–380.

its time; it was a mode of creating credit on the anticipation of income. Anticipating revenue may have started informally. Beginning in the 12th century, the
Crown had repaid lenders by directing them to draw on those holding royal
funds—tax collectors, sheriffs, or other royal debtors—in the provinces.[80] That
strategy developed into a routinized practice. Faced with creditors at the Exchequer while collectors in the countryside were still taking in revenues, the Crown
began sending claimants directly to the collectors. Writs issued to those officials
confirmed the arrangement, and they paid creditors in the field. When time came
for them to account to the Crown for the revenues they had received, the
collectors submitted the writs that had ordered payment to creditors, receiving
a tally as a receipt.

By the early 14th century, the Exchequer often simply issued the tally, originally given to the collector at his final audit, directly to the creditor.[81] The creditor
took the tally to the collector or other Crown debtor, traded it for payment, and
the collector held the receipt, now in the shape of a tally, demonstrating that he
had appropriately dispensed the revenue. Tallies clearly anticipated revenue: they
represented a promise of revenues from the Crown, revenue that was held
elsewhere or was still being collected. "The writ and the tally," writes one scholar
of the period, "were therefore used in much the same fashion as a modern
cheque."[82]

As the practice grew, the Exchequer tended "to become more and more of a
clearing-house for writs and tallies of assignment and less and less the scene of
cash transactions."[83] By 1376, tallies operated to anticipate £51,155 of the

---

[80] Jenkinson, "Medieval Tallies," 304; Hilary Jenkinson and Charles H. Haskins, "William Cade," *The
English Historical Review* 28, no. 112 (1913).

[81] Willard, using the tax returns in early 14th century Surrey, traces the evolution of the system. The
Crown began by using writs of libertate or privy seal directing collectors to pay creditors in return for letters
patent of receipt. According to a slightly latter practice, collectors accepted the writs, paid as directed, and
received a tally as receipt. Finally, the Crown issued tallies directly to creditors, who cashed them for funds
from collectors in the field. The collectors then accounted to the Exchequer for money paid out to creditors
by turning in the tallies. See James F. Willard, *Surrey Tax Returns* (London: Roworth, 1922), xv; see also
Willard, "Exchequer Tally," 270, 272–275 (reviewing evidence of establishment of new procedure in the
early decades of the 14th century). S. B. Chrimes identifies a yet-earlier model for tally use, arguing that
Exchequer tallies of anticipation were given to Wardrobe officials for military finance and obviated much of
the cash business of the Exchequer by the end of the 13th century. See S. B. Chrimes, *An Introduction to
the Administrative History of Mediaeval England*, 3rd ed. (Oxford: Basil Blackwell, 1959), 141–142;
see also Jenkinson, "Exchequer Tallies, Note," 34–35 (arguing for similarly early use of tallies as "checque
or assignment").

[82] Willard, *Surrey Tax Returns*, xvi. For evidence of anticipation by tally, see Willard, "Exchequer Tally,"
275–276. The writ and tally existed alongside a variety of similar instruments, notably the debentures issued
by officials of the Wardrobe to pay for many of the Crown's expenses during wartime. See Steel, "The
Negotiation of Wardrobe Debentures in the Fourteenth Century"; see also Willard, *Surrey Tax Returns*,
xv–xvi (noting use of the privy seal, bills of the wardrobe, and letters under the great seal); Willard,
"Exchequer Tally," 270, 272; Steel, *The Receipt of the Exchequer, 1377–1485*, xxix–xxx (similar).

[83] Steel, *The Receipt of the Exchequer, 1377–1485*, xxx. For similar assessment of the importance of
tallies, see Jenkinson, "Medieval Tallies," 290 (referring to tallies as conditioning all financial developments
of the time, including "the system of Public Accounts, of Exchequer Bills and their discounting, of Public
Loans and Public Credit"); Willard, "Exchequer Tally," 272; Jenkinson, "Exchequer Tallies," 369–370.

£165,845 total revenue "received" at the Exchequer that year, or a bit more than 30 percent. (During this period, the great majority of revenue did pass through the Exchequer, the main exception being local tax income.)[84] They never dipped below that proportion of the revenue for the balance of the period tracked by Steel. Indeed, for most years they comprised more than 45 percent of the revenue, peaking in the mid-15th century at numbers around 60 percent. See Table 4.1 (Total receipts at Exchequer by cash and by tally, 1377–1485).[85]

At that rate of issue, tallies were an enormously important vehicle for conveying value. As explained below, they likely also furnished a kind of currency among certain circles. Insofar as that is right, their production might be compared with mint output, at least to check orders of magnitude. For six of the ten decades between 1377 and 1477, tallies issued at higher rates than coin, both silver and gold (all mints). For all decades, tally output exceeded silver coin output, generally by a huge margin. Although coins obviously stayed in circulation longer, the number of pounds annually spent by way of Exchequer tally would have had a significant impact on English monetary practice.[86]

Steel's monumental study of the Exchequer of the Receipt documents the assignment practice for the period 1377–1485 using Receipt and Issue Rolls, which reflect assignments in line-by-line entries. See generally Steel, *The Receipt of the Exchequer, 1377–1485*. For an explanation of the records and rolls, see Willard, *Surrey Tax Returns*, xxv–xvi; J. L. Kirby, "The Issues of the Lancastrian Exchequer and Lord Cromwell's Estimates of 1433," *Bulletin of the Institute of Historical Research* 24, no. 121–151 (1951): 122–125, 129; and Steel, *The Receipt of the Exchequer, 1377–1485*, 1–12.

[84] See Kirby, "Lancastrian Exchequer," 143–145; see also Steel, *The Receipt of the Exchequer, 1377–1485*, xxv (suggesting loss of local revenues from ordinary revenue).

[85] For a study focused on the first half of the Lancastrian period (1399–1433) that confirms the dimension of anticipation recorded by Steel, *The Receipt of the Exchequer, 1377–1485*, see Kirby, "Lancastrian Exchequer." Kirby concurs that the "greater part" of both issues and (nominal) receipts were made up of assignment. Kirby, "Lancastrian Exchequer," 138–141. One scholar, studying the early years of the 14th century, found that assignment, at that point largely by writ, was used more pervasively during peacetime. James F. Willard, "The Crown and Its Creditors, 1327–1333," *English Historical Review* 42, no. 165 (1927). By contrast, the demand of soldiers for tangible money produced a reduction in the assignment in some war years. Steel, reviewing the later practice of the Exchequer, describes a change to greater use of tallies during wartime and periods of exigency when existing revenues failed to meet present needs, leading sovereigns to anticipate taxes by tally. Steel, *The Receipt of the Exchequer, 1377–1485*, xxxiii. Steel's study begins in 1377 because Exchequer records at that point begin to distinguish explicitly tallies of receipt from tallies of assignment. Steel, *The Receipt of the Exchequer, 1377–1485*, xxxi.

[86] The comparison in the text is rough, but should capture blunt dimensions of output. It compares Total Receipts by Tally, from Table 4.1, with total mint output from Allen, *Mints and Money*, Table C.3. Because mint outputs are not available with the same starting and ending dates by decade, I have included output figures from all mints with an ending date within the decades that follow. "Total" represents gold and silver output; "silver" is output in that coin alone. 1377–September 1387 (£114,815 total, £12,346 silver), September 1387–October 1397 (£314,789 total, £6,548 silver), October 1397–September 1407 (£109,942 total, £4,641 silver), September 1407–September 1417 (£641,111 total, £36,744 silver), September 1417–September 1427 (£799,423 total, £37,832 silver), September 1427–September 1437 (£546,812 total, £416,699 silver), September (gold)/February (silver)1437–June 1447 (£77,783 total, £32,158 silver), June 1447–September 1457 (£85,278 total, £56,467 silver), September 1457–September 1467 (£429,713 total, 142,423 silver), September 1467–September 1477 (£443,942 total, 116,487 silver). (Accounts from a number of years are missing, and period dates are adjusted to existing end-of-period dates given by Allen.) While there is some slippage of mint output across the decade borders, there is no double-counting.

Table 4.1. Total receipts at Exchequer by cash and by tally, 1377–1485

Decade[d]	Total Receipts[a] (£1,000)	Receipt by Cash[b] (£1,000)	%	Receipt by Tally of Assignment[c] (£1,000)	%
1377–1387	1426.18	780.74	54.74	649.63	45.55
1387–1397	1194.94	613.33	51.33	569.15	47.63
1397–1407	968.31	390.02	40.28	580.10	59.91
1407–1417	1065.99	672.36	63.07	365.04	34.24
1417–1427	1025.39	502.69	49.02	493.34	48.11
1427–1437	1124.97	462.68	41.13	668.26	59.40
1437–1447	1086.00	393.86	36.27	696.06	64.09
1447–1457	615.81	227.71	36.98	389.64	63.27
1457–1467	361.87	136.41	37.70	227.76	62.94
1467–1477	399.00	201.52	50.51	198.77	49.82
1477–1485	263.00	122.77	46.68	137.87	52.42

Author's calculations based on data from Anthony Steel, *The Receipt of the Exchequer 1377–1485* (Cambridge: Cambridge University Press, 1954), Appendix D, Tables C–D. For the data's limitations and methodological challenges, see Steel, *The Receipt of the Exchequer 1377–1485*, xvi–xx.

Total Receipts reflect all revenues that Exchequer officials recorded as available for public spending either (1) in cash from tax revenues or genuine loans received at the Exchequer (Receipt by Cash) or (2) by assignment of tax revenues available in the hands of tax officials in the field (Receipt by Tally of Assignment). The latter resources were represented by *pro* tallies—receipts issued to creditors that they were to submit to an apppropriate tax official in return for cash or an exoneration of tax owed to the same amount.

The calculations are based on the assumption that Steel's "Nominal receipts" column in Appendix, Table C equals the sum of the "Real receipts" (cash received at the Exchequer) and "Book-keeping" columns in the same table. This assumption was tested using the data in Table C and with very few exceptions the inconsistencies between the terms were negligible. In turn, the "Book-keeping" column in Table C breaks down into the three quantities tracked in Table D: "Genuine loans," "Fictitious loans," and "*Prestita restituta*," allowing those types of resources to be allocated to Receipt by Cash or Receipt by Tally of Assignment, or neither, as appropriate.

[a] The Total Receipts sum represents Steel's numbers for "Nominal receipts" (Table C data defined as "Real receipts" and "Book-keeping") less the "*Prestita restituta*" component of "Book-keeping" (Table D). *Prestita restituta* were bookkeeping entries made when an advance (*prestita*) had been made to a royal official to dispense money for a particular purpose. The *prestita restituta* entry marks the discharging of the official's obligation (Steel, *The Receipt of the Exchequer 1377–1485*, xxxviii–xxxix). According to Steel, *prestita restituta* "…at least when legitimately used, represent book-keeping entries pure and simple…" (Steel, 391). They are therefore neither resources received as cash or assumed available for spending by *pro* tally in the field.

[b] The Receipt by Cash column is equal to the sum of the "Cash" column in Steel's Table C and "Genuine loans" column in Table D. "Cash" in Table C represents the amount of cash received at the Exchequer. For such amounts, the Exchequer of Receipt issued *sol* tallies (*sol* from *solutum* or "paid") for the accountant to present during his audit at the Upper Exchequer. During the period covered in the table, *sol* tallies were not assignable: they could only be used by the original accountant and did not circulate.

The "Genuine loans" figure typically represents loans in which cash was delivered to the Exchequer by lenders. According to Steel, the Exchequer did not issue tallies for genuine loans but letters patent under the royal seal (Steel, *The Receipt of the Exchequer 1377–1485*, 16–17; also see xxxi, n. 4 and accompanying text). Steel's figures for "Genuine loans" might be overestimated, and to that extent, the relative role played by the Receipt by Tally of Assignment column is proportionately underestimated. According to Steel, in order to conceal interest payments forbidden by the prohibition of usury, the Exchequer might have recorded greater sums than were actually lent to it (for example, a one-year loan for £75 would be recorded as a loan for £100, implying a 25 percent interest rate). See K. B. McFarlane, "Loans to the Lancastrian Kings: The Problem of Inducement," *Cambridge Historical Journal* 9, no. 1 (1947); Steel, 18–20.

[c] The Receipt by Tally of Assignment column is equal to the sum of the "Assigned" column in Steel's Table C and "Fictitious loans" column in Table D. The "Assigned" column refers to the issuance of *pro* tallies, the main category of tallies discussed throughout the chapter.

"Fictitious loans" (*mutua per talliam*) are discussed in greater detail in pp. 180–181 n. 100. In brief, they were generally *pro* tallies dishonored by the tax collectors on whom they had been drawn by the Exchequer. If returned to the Exchequer, they could be crossed out and reclassified as a "loan" from the royal creditor. The Exchequer would simultaneously reissue a new *pro* tally to the creditor. According to Steel, the reclassification took place to maintain the totals calculated in the receipt rolls (Steel, *The Receipt of the Exchequer 1377–1485*, xxxii–xxxii, Appendix B). To the extent reclassification took place to preserve the totals, it appears that the reissued *pro* tally would *not* be recorded separately in the Exchequer of Receipt. For the purposes of Table 4.1, the "Fictitious loans" figures therefore belong in the Receipt by Tally of Assignment column because they substitute a fresh assignment of revenue for an earlier (and here canceled) assignment of revenue.

[d] The Exchequer year was divided into two terms, Easter and Michaelmas. Table C data provides an aggregate figure for both terms, while Table D maintains separate figures. Steel uses double notation (e.g., "1384–5") for the Michaelmas rolls, and a single notation to mark the Easter rolls (Steel, 3).

Data available from the beginning of the 16th century fits the same pattern, although the use of tallies to anticipate funds dropped in the following decades, reaching a low point late in the reign of Henry VIII.[87] That drop might reflect parliamentary attempts to contain Crown spending,[88] the disarray of Exchequer practice or its attempted reform in 1540[89], the effects of the Great Debasement in the late 1540s when light coin would swamp other outputs,[90] or Tudor attempts throughout the century to increase specie sources of liquidity[91]—the history of tallies remains to be written. Tallies would return in the early modern world to invite the revolution of public credit.[92]

The credit created by the government flows directly into the story of early money, unremarked even as it changes that very currency. Surprising as it may seem, the hallmarks of money attach to the little wooden sticks by sometime in the 14th century. Tallies issued in the existing unit of account, they operated on a fiscal infrastructure, and they apparently circulated among certain groups.

First, sovereigns clearly issued highly distinctive tallies in existing units of account, and made them convertible for coin. In that way, they flagged tallies as an instrument with the capacity to act as money. The stylized character of tallies made them relatively impervious to counterfeit and their quality kept them from deteriorating.

Second, tallies resembled coin insofar as the Crown used them as payment and accepted them for payment. Tallies represented a claim against tax authorities good for money or good for the role that money played—exoneration from a

---

[87] In 1505, tallies anticipated funds of £35,774, out of a total ordinary revenue of £122,287, or about 29 percent. Frederick Schnabel, data for 1505 (unpublished 2006 draft on file with author). Schnabel's figures include ordinary revenue from *all* the central treasuries, thus stating a more comprehensive total as denominator than would the total from Steel, who focused on revenue taken in at the Receipt of the Exchequer only. More generally, see O'Brien and Hunt, "The Rise of a Fiscal State in England, 1485–1815," 141–142; G. R. Elton, *The Tudor Revolution in Government: Administrative Changes in the Reign of Henry VIII* (Cambridge: Cambridge University Press, 1953), 398–413; J. D. Alsop, "The Exchequer of Receipt in the Reign of Edward VI" (Thesis, Cambridge University, 1978), 211.

[88] Parliament had put a ceiling on the amount that the Treasury could pay by tallies charged on the tax receivers for the King's Household in 1482, thus capping the Crown's spending on household purchases by anticipating revenues. See Chrimes, *Administrative History*, 265. Parliament's effort to control this outflow of funds led to the establishment of the Civil List. Chrimes, *Administrative History*. It is unclear that the cap would have resulted in a decrease in tally use, unless Parliament's allowance cut back existing spending by tally.

[89] At about this period, the practice diminished and complaints about it rose; it became increasingly difficult to cash tallies, and the practice may have been reduced as part of the Exchequer reform of 1540. Elton, *Tudor Revolution*, 398–413. I am grateful to Fred Schnabel for this insight.

[90] Mint output during the Great Debasement was fourteen times its amount earlier in the century, and the need to assign revenue may have been anomalously low: in 1545 and 1551, the Crown assigned only 2 percent to 3 percent of its total ordinary revenue. Schnabel, data for 1545 and 1551 (unpublished 2006 draft on file with author).

[91] The royal commitment to expanding revenue reached land rents and feudal dues under Henry VII, the capital of the monasteries dissolved under Henry VIII, and the Customs, which were reformed by Elizabeth I. See M. J. Braddick, *The Nerves of State: Taxation and the Financing of the English State, 1558–1714*, New Frontiers in History (Manchester: St. Martin's Press, 1996), 61–62, 73–74; Frederick C. Dietz, *English Public Finance, 1558–1641*, 2nd ed., vol. 2 (New York: Barnes & Noble, 1964), 21, 44.

[92] See pp. 235, 239–245.

public obligation. (As elsewhere, taxes were the most common such obligation, thus the shorthand reference to tallies as built upon a "fiscal infrastructure.") That character is evident in the way that tallies functioned. According to their design, Exchequer records matched tallies issued with liabilities owed by tax farmers. When they issued tallies designed to anticipate specific revenues, officials thus paired the supply of tallies with a device that provided for their predictable withdrawal.[93]

The history of money showcases many similar instruments. Economists have modeled the way that American colonial paper money held purchasing power effectively, or "added" real balances to the money supply. There, when notes were denominated in terms of specie and the tax obligation, which could be satisfied in either medium, was large enough to absorb the aggregate amounts of specie and paper available, bills of credit added to the stock of money for public or private use.[94] Put more intuitively, the issue of paper money allowed a government to pay off a creditor and then cancel its IOU by imposing an additional tax obligation worth a certain specie amount without taking specie out of circulation. Tallies in early modern England would have held value in the same way. In effect, the English administration controlled supply and ensured demand for the tokens, assimilating them to coin. The quantity of the tokens using a given unit of account could thus affect the price level, stated in that unit. And as in the American colonies, the government issued tallies to supplement a limited specie money stock.

Tallies' fiscal engineering calls for more research: the models of paper money suggest that impact of tallies on price would depend on the quantity of tallies issued relative to the amount of coin circulating, the tax obligation receivable in those media, and people's expectations about how tallies and coin would be withdrawn.[95] The structural effect of tallies is, however, already evident. At a minimum, tallies provided a kind of money substitute. Public creditors holding tallies likely used them as a kind of transferable credit—as we will see below, tallies probably circulated. Eventually, those holding tallies could go to those tax collectors and trade their tallies for coins.[96] But more remarkably, tallies also likely expanded the money supply directly. A public creditor who owed taxes could turn the tally in for that obligation, without claiming any cash at all.

---

[93] See pp. 174–176, 181.

[94] See Scott Sumner, "Colonial Currency and the Quantity Theory of Money: A Critique of Smith's Interpretation," *Journal of Economic History* 53, no. 1 (1993); Charles Calomiris, "Institutional Failure, Monetary Scarcity, and the Depreciation of the Continental," *Journal of Economic History* 48, no. 1 (1988); Bruce D. Smith, "Money and Inflation in the American Colonies: Further Evidence on the Failure of the Quantity Theory" (Ontario: Centre for the Study of International Economic Relations, 1987).

[95] The discount at which tallies traveled could reflect, in part, failures by imperial officials adequately to control the issue of tallies relative to their withdrawal.

[96] A circulating credit instrument would lower demand for money (raise velocity), thus also affecting price in a unit of account. See N. J. Mayhew, "Population, Money Supply, and the Velocity of Circulation in England, 1300–1700," *Economic History Review* 48, no. 2 (1995).

Similarly, the public creditor could circulate the tally to someone who could use it in that way.[97] In those cases, the tally added to the coined money supply.

Finally, the administrations using tallies improvised the feature that allowed tallies to travel. Virtually all of the institutional historians of the Exchequer agree on an aspect of the anticipation tally that otherwise goes unrecognized—that it circulated. The practice likely began informally, an arrangement among public creditors, tax collectors, and Exchequer officials that benefited each. By the 14th century if not earlier, individuals holding tallies apparently transferred them at times to others, who cashed them with the collectors in the field, either for coin or for credit on a tax obligation. They did so without formal legal sanction; instead, they had the compliance, and perhaps profit, of the officials who mattered—those in the Exchequer in charge of certifying the course of public payments. Those clerks needed only to allow tallies to be paid off by local officials without proof that the person cashing them was indeed the creditor to whom they were originally issued.[98] Assumedly, tax collectors could also participate in the opportunity for profit by facilitating the transfer, or benefit by acquiring a receipt of tax payment and reducing the friction between the government and its creditors. Creditors gained as well: insofar as they transferred a tally, they had an instrument that they could use to pay a debt, make a purchase, or trade for readier money.[99] Creditors apparently generally sold off tallies at a discount (about which more later in this chapter), but sell them off they did: tallies often traveled or could travel, changing hands between their issue and the time they were cashed or used to pay off a public obligation.[100]

---

[97] For suggestions of that use, see Steel, *The Receipt of the Exchequer, 1377–1485*, xxxvi, 404; Harriss, "Fictitious Loans," 191 (noting that creditor's tallies issued to him on his own levy as collector of customs at London); cf. Davies, *History of Money*, 151. In such a system, the money supply could assumedly be further expanded (and the government could get the present value of issues immediately) insofar as the government "anticipated" taxes further into the future. As we will see, the Crown exploited that latitude in the 17th century. See pp. 239–245.

[98] See Steel, *The Receipt of the Exchequer, 1377–1485*, xxxvi.

[99] See generally Steel, *The Receipt of the Exchequer, 1377–1485*, xxxv–xxxvi; G. L. Harriss, "Fictitious Loans," *Economic History Review* 8, no. 2 (1955): 189.

[100] See generally Harriss, "Fictitious Loans," 198–199; Jenkinson, "Medieval Tallies," 290, 304 (referring to discounting of public loans and credit more generally); Steel, *The Receipt of the Exchequer, 1377–1485*, xxxi–xxxii (reviewing circumstance of cashing tallies in the field, possibility of overdrafts); Kirby, "Lancastrian Exchequer," 123–125 (similar); Steel, *The Receipt of the Exchequer, 1377–1485*, xxxvi n. 2 (citing Chrimes suggesting discounting); Willard, "Exchequer Tally," 275–276 (noting occurrence of overdrafts); K. B. McFarlane, "Loans to the Lancastrian Kings: The Problem of Inducement," *Cambridge Historical Journal* 9, no. 1 (1947): 63 and n. 67. The rate at which tallies were dishonored is difficult to ascertain. Steel believed that tallies were dishonored when revenues failed to meet the amounts assigned on them, either because tallies had been overissued or tax collection had been inadequate. Defaulted tallies would be identified as fictitious loans to the sovereign (i.e., as uncashed claims against it) in the Exchequer records and paid with newly issued tallies. See Steel, *The Receipt of the Exchequer, 1377–1485*, xxxv–xxxvi, 20–23, 391–392, 455–474. He argued that the viability of tallies reflected the fiscal reliability of sovereigns, and estimated the number of tallies dishonored under Edward III at about one in forty, and those dishonored under Richard II at about one in twenty-eight. Steel, *The Receipt of the Exchequer, 1377–1485*, 364–368, 405. (Assumedly, tallies uncashed but not returned to the Exchequer would escape Steel's records. Steel, *The Receipt of the Exchequer, 1377–1485*, 192–194.) According to G. L. Harriss, however, Exchequer records

The clues to the fact that tallies circulated is laced throughout the Exchequer's arcana—the gaps, marginalia, and implied transactions of accounting books or, more precisely and less accessibly, the "pells," rolls, and scripts of the early records (see Fig. 4.2). It is suggested in the elegant and illegible hand of medieval scribes, coded in Latin and law French, and recorded most regularly on hazel-wood sticks long ago burned. It has, in other words, remained largely the property of those skilled few who excavated it and argued among themselves about its details, all the while leaving it isolated from the history of money. But the evidence that tallies had currency is cumulatively persuasive.

Throughout the medieval period, anticipation tallies were inscribed with an amount, the name and office of revenue collector who would cash them, the revenues on which they were levied, and the date. By contrast, they did not bear the name of the creditor *to whom* they were assigned—"hence tallies could be passed from hand to hand as negotiable instruments, or bequeathed to one's executors or heirs."[101] Although important creditors often took home tallies made out in large amounts, many others including household and Exchequer officials went away with smaller tallies.[102] A study of the Lancastrian Exchequer

were not so transparent. Tallies regularly went unpaid because of defects in form: levied upon a person, not a revenue, they were rendered invalid by the death or replacement of a monarch or his tax collector. Harriss, "Fictitious Loans," 188–189. Defective tallies were canceled until the later years of Henry V, with payment available by a reissued tally. From the end of Henry V's reign, defaulted tallies were recategorized as "fictitious loans" and reissued, but that recourse required petition to the Crown and was generally limited to influential creditors; it was not a matter of right. Smaller creditors were presumably left without remedy; tallies that appeared "good" on Exchequer records might then actually have been defaulted. Other categories of creditors, such as household creditors, at times procured relief as a class from the monarch's executors. Harriss, "Fictitious Loans," 189–194. Tallies, when sufficiently large, could also be secured in various ways. Harriss, "Fictitious Loans," 191–198. Harriss's argument suggests that rates of default on tallies do not reliably indicate fiscal problems in a monarchy, but also indicate that gauging rates of default is very difficult.

[101] Harriss, "Fictitious Loans," 189; see also Steel, *The Receipt of the Exchequer, 1377–1485*, xxxvi ("the *pro* tally never bore the name of the payee, which was always theoretically the crown [but practically, the creditor], but that of the prospective payer [the tax collector], so that it could easily change hands"); Willard, "Exchequer Tally," 272–273 (tally made out in name of collector); Jenkinson, "Medieval Tallies," 369–370, 373 (explaining tally face as effectively "a cheque payable to bearer" and quoting the receipt roll entry as an "invariable" form of working on public tallies); Jenkinson, "An Original Exchequer Account of 1304," 40–41, n. 2 (contrasting use of payee's name on private tallies with use of payor's name on public tallies). (Note that the former practice, common at the private level, would make those tallies difficult to transfer.) Date of year and term were apparently added to the inscription on tallies in 1281; the day and month were added somewhat later. Jenkinson, "Medieval Tallies," 375; Kirby, "Lancastrian Exchequer," 127, n. 1.

When the tally was issued, witnessing to the (anticipated) payment of money into the Exchequer by the collector, it was entered into the receipt rolls. The amount of payment and identity of recipient (i.e., the creditor) supposed to be paid by the collector on behalf of the Crown was entered into the issue rolls. Willard, "Exchequer Tally," 273–274; see also Willard, *Surrey Tax Returns*, xli–xliii (reprinting writs ordering Surrey officials to pay creditors in exchange for tallies); Jenkinson, "Medieval Tallies," 370–371 (quoting representative receipt roll entry; adding that "pro" notation identifying creditor also appeared as marginalia in the receipt roll). It would be possible, then to compare the creditors identified in the issue rolls with the identities of those cashing in tallies in the field, logged in the records of local collectors, to trace the number of tallies transferred (assuming that collectors accurately recorded the identities of those cashing tallies).

[102] Kirby, "Lancastrian Exchequer," 138; Steel, *The Receipt of the Exchequer, 1377–1485*, 404.

Fig. 4.2 Section of Treasurer's Receipt Roll, November 1457, Michaelmas Term, 36 Henry VI, P.R.O. E401/858. Public Records Office

over a period of a dozen years gives numbers that may be representative. It found that the anticipation tally most commonly issued, in the hundreds every year, was one for "small payment," and identified 50 shillings as illustrative and 10 pounds as a maximum.[103] Another scholar identifies tallies "varying from a halfpenny upwards," including tallies for 11 pennies, 17 shillings, and 13 shillings 4 pence.[104] A 50-shilling tally would far exceed the amounts handled by most people, but would be appropriate for large purchases or payments.[105] Tallies not only issued in small (as well as larger denominations), they also remained unreturned to the Exchequer for relatively long periods. Collectors commonly brought them to account sometime beyond the year in which they were issued; a stretch of time existed, in other words, during which they could have been discounted once or several times.[106]

Erratically, the rolls or other evidence explicitly document the currency of tallies—including their transfer between parties or their accumulation by large creditors—although not in ways that confirm how chronic it was.[107] Less directly, but more consistently, the sources suggest the negotiability of debt through the very issue of the tally: a particular notation that appears hundreds of times in the rolls (*pro [A] per manus [B]*) appears to indicate that Exchequer officials would issue a tally to one party as the financial representative—or creditor—of a royal creditor.[108] If so, the Exchequer offered a financial service to those creditors,

---

[103] Kirby, "Lancastrian Exchequer," 138. Kirby notes that payments to certain categories of larger creditors were broken down into a number of different tallies to aid their cashing. Kirby, "Lancastrian Exchequer," 39. That strategy could also make them more easily transferable.

[104] Jenkinson, "Medieval Tallies," 295, 303; Jenkinson, "Exchequer Tallies," 376–377; see also Jenkinson, "Medieval Tallies," 299, n. 5 (tally of 11s. 8d.); Hall, *The Exchequer*, 121 (tally of 4s. 4d.). Exchequer tallies in the hundreds and even thousands of pounds also issued to large creditors. See Kirby, "Lancastrian Exchequer," 138–139; Jenkinson, "Exchequer Tallies," 376–377.

[105] At a wage rate of 5 pence/day for unskilled labor in 1467, 50 shillings would be amount to 120 days work. See Sargent and Velde, *Big Problem of Small Change*, 48.

[106] Kirby, "Lancastrian Exchequer," 137 (1422–1434). Harriss, tracking those occasions on which a collector's return of a tally to the Exchequer for an accounting was clear during the period from 1439 to 1461, found that fifteen tallies were returned within three terms of being struck (two terms per year), fifteen within the following year; seven in the next two and a half years; and another seven between five and ten years after issue. Harriss, "Fictitious Loans," 196, n. 4; see also Steel, *The Receipt of the Exchequer, 1377–1485*, xxxvi (noting Chrimes's hypothesis that tallies sometimes changed hands several times over and there were "long delays" before payment). A creditor in 1447 identified two years as the amount of time it would take him to cash a tally for 10 marks. Harriss, "Fictitious Loans," 196, n. 4.

[107] A mid-15th century settlement agreement openly stipulates several transfers of public tallies between parties, for example. See Steel, *The Receipt of the Exchequer, 1377–1485*, 280 and n. 3; see also Steel, *The Receipt of the Exchequer, 1377–1485*, 29 (describing another occasion of explicit transfer). McFarlane describes a similar episode as unremarkable. See McFarlane, "Loans to the Lancastrian Kings," 63, n. 67. And, a study that traces the "reissue" of tallies rendered invalid by a monarch's death reveals that the invalidated tallies, although issued to a wide variety of departments for their expenses, had ended up in the hands of only a few creditors, assumedly because they had acquired them at a discounted value. Those creditors then petitioned a new monarch for the "reissue" of the tallies to them directly. See Harriss, "Fictitious Loans," 191 (tallies issued in the 1390s during Richard II's reign, reissued in 1403–1404, under Henry IV).

[108] Steel suggests that the practice evolved from that allowing public officials from the Wardrobe to arrange for payment of government contractors. Steel, *The Receipt of the Exchequer, 1377–1485*, 379–381, 404. Steel's interpretation is apparently endorsed by G. L. Harriss. See Harriss, "Fictitious Loans," 197, n. 5.

allowing a private individual who had established a claim against the government to give, sell, or discount that claim to another, who would receive a tally in payment.[109]

More broadly, transferring tallies would be consistent with the practice of transferring certain other evidences of public debt (Wardrobe debentures, letters patent, and letters obligatory) effectively treated as legal, and arguably even mundane, by the early 14th century.[110] Those issued *pro* tallies could sue the collectors on whom they were assigned, certainly when those collectors had accepted them and perhaps as soon as they had adequate revenues. The remedy was cumbersome, and many unsatisfied creditors negotiated with collectors or worked out other modes of obtaining the payments.[111] Nevertheless, their right set those holding tallies apart from other creditors to the Crown, who were haunted by the king's sovereign immunity from suit.[112] Whether those receiving tallies by transfer from the initial holders could sue as well is not clear; if they could, their rights would be more secure.[113] Insofar as legal or informal remedies increased the reliability of tallies, they would function more effectively as currency.

Some of the evidence that tallies moved from hand to hand is inferential, atmospheric, or anecdotal. According to a statute of 1286, tallies lost could be renewed, a directive that would make circulation to any extent impossible: no government could offer a replacement for lost cash. But by 1297, the practice had been limited to those cases specifically authorized by the Treasurer and, by the middle of the next century, had become rare.[114] Several executive ordinances of the 15th century prohibited certain kinds of traffic in tallies: an ordinance of 1445

[109] Steel, *The Receipt of the Exchequer, 1377–1485*, 380. The party receiving the tally would presumably be required to prove the claim's transfer in some way.

[110] Steel, "The Negotiation of Wardrobe Debentures in the Fourteenth Century" (Wardrobe debentures, letters patent); E. B. Fryde, "Materials for the Study of Edward III's Credit Operations, 1327–48," *Bulletin of the Institute of Historical Research* 22 (1949): 116–117. Fryde portrays the negotiation of letters obligatory as significantly more qualified than Steel.

[111] See Harriss, "Fictitious Loans," 188–189.

[112] The fact that tallies formally represented claims upon an official, as opposed to the Crown, removed the obstacle of sovereign immunity from suits for enforcement. See Harriss, "Fictitious Loans," 188–189; see also William Searle Holdsworth, *A History of English Law*, 17 vols., vol. 7 (London: Sweet & Maxwell, 1982), 7–45; Louis L. Jaffe, "Suits Against Governments and Officers: Sovereign Immunity," *Harvard Law Review* 77, no. 1 (1963). Those who would receive *sol'* tallies in the Stuart period sometimes took measures to secure them, such as requiring a bond for repayment from the collector on whom they were assigned. See Robert Ashton, *The Crown and The Money Market, 1603–1640* (Oxford: Clarendon Press, 1960), 50–51. For the reluctance of lenders to supply Crown needs in the money market where immunity prevented legal recourse, see Ashton, *The Crown and The Money Market, 1603–1640*, 10. By the late 17th century, that *pro* tally had become a highly formal legal claim. See Chandaman, *The English Public Revenue, 1660–1688*, 288–289, 294–295.

[113] By the mid-17th century, assignees may have been suing on notes. See W. Percy Harper, "The Significance of the Farmers of the Customs in Public Finance in the Middle of the Seventeenth Century," *Economica* 25 (1929): 68.

[114] See Kirby, "Lancastrian Exchequer," 148–150, Appendix. At the beginning of the 14th century, the number of renewals sometimes was as high as forty, although most of those tallies came from only one or two collectors. By the middle of the 14th century, the time at which both the practice of anticipation and

threatened to dismiss any officer who bought "any taille, obligacioun, or assignement of any creditour," and another of 1478 had a similar aim.[115] The prohibition suggests that the practice was so well entrenched or so significant that the Crown felt it had to restrain obvious official speculation, or perhaps that government officials had an unfair advantage in the trade. In fact, several Exchequer scholars point to the success of laymen surrounding the Crown bureaucracy at making profits as independently indicative of a thriving discounting business. Helping creditors with neither the time nor the tolerance to cash tallies by offering a market for those sticks could make small men rich, suggests Anthony Steel, and "richer men . . . fortunes."[116]

Finally, scattered references in medieval literature indicate the common use of tallies to pay ordinary men for the king's expenses and purveyance. In one extract from a London chronicle about a 1359 feast hosting a French king, a visitor scornfully observed "that he never saw so royal a feast and so costly *made with tallies of tree, without paying of gold and silver.*"[117] Indeed, the frequency with which officials paid with tallies instead of coin provoked vehement objection at certain periods. As one Englishman complained in the late 13th or early 14th century, "it would be better to eat from wooden platters and pay in coin for food than to serve the body with silver and give pledges of wood."[118] If tallies were a fact of life both frequent and familiar, their currency would be more likely.[119]

Taken together, the traces left by the tallies suggest that they circulated most commonly within a particular sector and geography of the English world. Those who moved within the court's radius, including the sovereign's administrative apparatus, surely encountered and possibly passed on tallies—government officials, royal lenders,[120] soldiers, and others performing services to the Crown,

currency might be established, many terms saw only one renewal, which otherwise "rarely rose above six" (Kirby, "Lancastrian Exchequer," 150).

[115] Household ordinance of 1445, from A. R. Myers, "Some Household Ordinances of Henry VI," *Bulletin of the John Rylands Library* 26 (1954): 459. The ordinance of 1478 is described by J. R. Lander, "The Administration of the Yorkist Kings," M.Litt. thesis, Cambridge University Library, as cited by Steel, *The Receipt of the Exchequer, 1377–1485*, xxxv, n. 2; see also evidence of a prosecution against two men for discounting tallies cited by Steel, *The Receipt of the Exchequer, 1377–1485*, xxxv, and the 1304 ordinance that prohibited selling Wardrobe debentures at a profit. Steel, "The Negotiation of Wardrobe Debentures in the Fourteenth Century," 439.

[116] Steel, *The Receipt of the Exchequer, 1377–1485*, xxxvi; see also Jenkinson, as cited in Steel, *The Receipt of the Exchequer, 1377–1485*, xxxv. The practice could not, of course, be explicit, for danger of violating contemporary prohibitions on usury. See McFarlane, "Loans to the Lancastrian Kings," 61–62; Steel, *The Receipt of the Exchequer, 1377–1485*, xxxvi.

[117] See Steel, *The Receipt of the Exchequer, 1377–1485*, xxxiv-xxxv (quoting Coulton's *Chaucer and his England*).

[118] The quote is from *The Song Against the King's Taxes*, in Peter Coss, ed., *Thomas Wright's Political Songs of England: From the Reign of John to that of Edward II* (Cambridge: Cambridge University Press, 1996), 186, but I use here Maddicott's translation. See Maddicott, "English Peasantry," 26.

[119] Jenkinson, "Medieval Tallies," 304 (noting likelihood of private discounting given frequency of tally use for assignment).

[120] The Crown had no reason to limit the use of tallies to public creditors supplying goods and services. It could also build in an effective interest payment to those lending it money by recording a price paid in

public creditors from large suppliers to small vendors. And despite the image conveyed by institutional historians of the Exchequer of men with tallies traveling far afield to claim money from distant revenue farmers, most tallies were apparently "cashed" in London on revenue agents and tax farmers when they came into account at the Exchequer.[121] If so, it makes all the more sense that those holding tallies would find a market for them there with others willing to hold the tokens for that event. Specie itself, the conventional coin of the realm, was concentrated in the same area and among the same population. In fact, that population would disproportionately include larger taxpayers, a set of people for whom tallies carried immediate and obvious value: they would be the most likely to use tallies instead of money to meet those obligations, thus leaving coin in circulation and effectively augmenting its supply.[122]

Tallies had a last important feature, one that they shared with coin. Most likely, they effectively imposed a charge on those using them. Merchants and others bringing bullion to the mint had to pay for coin. Similarly, public creditors accepted tallies without acquiring interest expressly, although an interest charge could have been added surreptitiously. Insofar as creditors took tallies at face value, they made a virtual loan interest-free to the government. Writ larger, currency in that case gains a striking characteristic: before the modern period, people paid the government for both coin and tallies. American paper money would share the same feature. That charge mattered in ways we can ask about only once we see the pattern, revealed by comparing the early currencies—all of which appear to come at government charge to users.

First, then, the evidence that tallies did not carry interest. Tallies made no express grants of interest until 1660, when it was authorized by statute.[123] It is difficult to know how often before that point tallies carried a more implicit

tallies, but receiving a lesser payment from the lender. According to McFarlane, that strategy became a likely way around usury laws. See McFarlane, "Loans to the Lancastrian Kings," 63–68. The possibility that the Crown used a similar device to build in interest payments to suppliers or those providing services is considered at pp. 186–189.

[121] Harriss, "Fictitious Loans," 188–189. For the earlier image, see, e.g., Steel, *The Receipt of the Exchequer, 1377–1485*, xxi–xxxii. By waiting for revenue agents to arrive in London, creditors holding tallies avoided the risk that their trips into the countryside would be met by a collector who had not yet collected his revenues, had been over obligated, had prioritized others, or was otherwise unable to pay the holder. Creditors' ability to demand payment also became most clearly enforceable under existing law once a collector had "accepted" a tally; collectors were more likely to "accept" tallies when they had their revenues ready for accounting at the Exchequer. Harriss was able to identify the location at which tallies were cashed with collectors from the case records of debt actions against those collectors in the Exchequer plea rolls. See Harriss, "Fictitious Loans," 188–189 and n. 6. For the fact that speculation in the market for tallies had developed by the mid-17th century, see Harper, "The Significance of the Farmers of the Customs in Public Finance in the Middle of the Seventeenth Century," 68–70.

[122] See McFarlane, "Loans to the Lancastrian Kings," 56 (noting that creditors taking tallies against their own tax obligation were secure from loss due to collector default); Kirby, "Lancastrian Exchequer," 145–146 (noting that collectors always paid by assignment on revenues they were themselves obligated to produce); Jenkinson, "Exchequer Tallies," 371 (suggesting use of tallies to cancel public obligation).

[123] Richard David Richards, *The Early History of Banking in England* (London: P. S. King, 1929), 59; 12 Car 2 c 9 (1660).

reward at certain times or to certain takers. Government officials could obviously have built in compensation for the delay in getting cash that came with a tally by paying more for goods in tallies than other buyers would pay for the same goods in coin. Their overpayment would add compensation for the delay-in-coin-payment to the purchase price of goods. Having said that, the Exchequer histories do not suggest that tallies were used, until the time of the Stuarts, to borrow copiously on revenues not yet due, as opposed to revenue not yet received at the Exchequer. Insofar as tallies were an instrument that saved the Crown transport as opposed to extending the time before cash payment was due, holders would be less likely to engage a nuanced calculation of their tallies' present value and demand it from the sovereign.

The willingness of holders to take tallies at face value would also depend on how valuable—or coercive—the Crown was as a buyer, and how easily tallies could be transferred as currency in the interim before they were cashed. During much of the medieval period, those aspects would be related, given the burdens imposed by money's scarcity. The more dependent a community was on public sources of liquidity, the more willing its members would be to "pay for" currency by forgoing interest in return for an instrument that was easily transferable.[124] Regardless of that advantage, the king's market power or use of force could also operate to dictate price.[125] As J. R. Maddicott documents for the late 13th and early 14th centuries, purveyance could easily be taken at prices below market rate, and compensation made in tallies—the practice brought grievances by waves into the officials.[126] Finally, it is unclear how far royal officials themselves understood the payment of interest to be legally or morally prohibited.

Tallies did often travel at a discount during the medieval and early modern periods, but the existence of the discount does not indicate, in and of itself, that users were charging for the reduced present value of future payment. More obviously, the discount would reflect the partial, rather metropolitan, nature of tallies' circulation and doubts about their redeemability. Assuming that tallies traveled at a discount because of these factors, the question then becomes whether the government paid for goods at an inflated rate when it used tallies;

[124] Early Americans appear for that reason to have circulated paper money without demanding interest. In the colonies, bills furnished virtually sole currency for paying public creditors. The prices paid by the government in newly issued tax anticipation notes were not expressly higher than the market price in those notes. Cf. Farley Grubb, "Is Paper Money Just Paper Money? Experimentation and Local Variation in the Fiat Monies Issued by the Colonial Governments of British North America, 1690–1775," *NBER Working Papers*, no. 17997 (2012).
[125] For exploration of the complexities mediating forms of public payment, see, e.g., McFarlane, "Loans to the Lancastrian Kings"; Harriss, "Fictitious Loans", see also Maddicott, "English Peasantry," 15, 34, 50–67 (describing oppressiveness of purveyance and the prises in mid-14th century).
[126] Maddicott, "English Peasantry," 25–27. For contemporary complaints about the use of tallies in purveyance, see *The Song Against the King's Taxes*, in Coss, *Political Songs*, 186 ("It is a sign of vice, to pay for food with wood"); see also *The Simonie [Poem on the Evil Times of Edward II]*, in Coss, *Political Songs*, 338, 399 ("They use the king's silver for their own pleasures, and produce wood, or tallies, instead of contributing to the prosperity of the people").

in effect, officials would assume a kind of exchange rate between tallies and specie that took into account the discounted face value in specie units of account at which tallies traveled. Independent of any interest charge, the officials could in that way pay for the costs of the credit risk they had created. If the government had used tallies at less than their nominal value when it issued them, it would swallow that loss when it cashed them (or set off a holder's tax obligation) at nominal value.

As for whether officials did, in fact, pick up either interest charges, costs for credit risks, or both, for that matter[127]—the question makes the turgid historical record on issues like circulation look transparent. One scholar describes tradesmen in early Stuart England as usually including "an element of effective interest" in their prices by selling goods to royal buyers at higher prices than to private buyers; often that difference could be "very considerable."[128] It is not clear, however, that the tradesmen were referring to purchases made in tallies, as opposed to purchases made on a promise of payment.[129] Whether to attribute higher prices paid by the Crown to the currency in which the Crown paid remains a mystery.[130]

By contrast, there is no suggestion in the Exchequer histories on earlier periods that the Crown paid higher prices than individuals did when it used tallies, although it is not clear those histories had either the inclination to ask the question or the materials to answer it. As in the Stuart years, the practice would have reduced the advantage of the tax anticipation strategy, making it a more expensive way to pay for goods. It would also have cheapened the value that

---

[127] A government could pay creditors at the nominal interest rate, building in compensation for the expected discounted (depreciated) rate at which tallies traveled and the real interest rate.

[128] Ashton, *The Crown and the Money Market, 1603–1640*, 34–35 and n. 7.

[129] According to the account, while vendors often built an element of interest into the cost of an item, the Crown could and apparently did sometimes postpone paying its bills beyond the expected delay—and so recouped some of the calculated costs. Ashton, *The Crown and the Money Market, 1603–1640*, 34–35 and n. 7. If the Crown was paying in tallies, it seems to have left its bills unpaid by failing to issue tallies at all. In that case, tradesmen may have acted to compensate themselves for the delay before payment in tallies, just as they might have for a delay before payment in money. It also seems possible that they could "charge" for another expected delay once they got tallies, but it is hard to know whether to read the description this aggressively. Another possibility turns on the fact that *sol'* tallies began, at about this period, to displace the more secure *pro* and formal tallies; tradesmen may have exacted higher prices if they expected to receive the newer tallies. There is also much evidence that, in the later 17th century, creditors exacted higher prices from the government when receiving tallies in payment. See P. G. M. Dickson, *The Financial Revolution in England: A Study in the Development of Public Credit, 1688–1756*, Modern Revivals in History (Aldershot: Greg Revivals, 1993): 341–364. That practice occurs, however, after a critical shift in the structure of the monetary system and a turn towards the public grants of interest on circulating media. See pp. 231–232, 245–254.

[130] Another tidbit of evidence from the same period implies that the Crown failed to pay interest on tradesmen's debts, but leaves it unclear whether that was by virtue of postponing their payment, or by paying in a non-interest-bearing currency. Lord Coke apparently divided the public debts into three categories: the "eating debts, such as were taken up at interest; the second crying debts, due to soldiers, mariners, tradesmen and such as live on labour, the third pressing debts." It is tempting to hazard that the "eating debts" endangered the Crown while the "crying debts" evoked that response from those they may have impoverished. Coke's description was, however, opaque even to contemporaries. The quote and Bacon's reference to it is in Ashton, *The Crown and the Money Market, 1603–1640*, 34.

attached to easy transferability, granting that closely held quality to creditors without exacting a contribution in return.[131]

Granted that recognizing public credit as currency reveals new uncertainties in the histories we have, it also extends them in new directions. It appears likely that tallies functioned in the English world for almost four centuries, allowing monarchs and their polities to anticipate the value of revenues without paying, or without paying fully, for the advance. At the same time, those holding the public debt had improvised a currency with the wooden tokens they held, recapturing the present value of the promise or some portion of it by transferring it among themselves.

Indeed, once we recognize that cash services are a quality constructed by the interaction of public and individual participants, the nature of public debt currencies as a deal they drove with one another becomes clear. Insofar as the English made tallies into a medium, the government got the use of the creditor's resource while postponing payment with an instrument that could only be cashed when tax revenues came in or when the tax obligation came due.[132] Tallies carried an advantage for creditors as well, one that set them apart from private notes. Insofar as they tied currencies to the official unit of account, issuing and withdrawing the tokens in a predictable way, and allowing them to circulate, Anglo-American sovereigns ordained them as money.

The way early modern governments in England made money out of public debt instruments thus resembled the way they made money out of metal: they leveraged their sovereign authority to exact a contribution from users in return for the construction of a common resource that supplied currency. In both cases, holders contributed to the state, paying production and seignorage fees when they brought money to the mint or forgoing interest (or some portion of interest) on the public IOUs they received as tax anticipation instruments. In return, members received a circulating medium, one that represented fiscally anchored value enhanced by its cash quality.

[131] By contrast, there is some evidence that monarchs may have discounted tallies as they issued them in order to provide a security for those who lent *money* as opposed to goods and services. In return for an advance of money, tallies could be issued for a greater amount, effectively paying interest for the loan. McFarlane, "Loans to the Lancastrian Kings"; Steel, *The Receipt of the Exchequer, 1377–1485*, 18–20. That strategy would be consistent with the Crown's behavior elsewhere. It had, during the medieval period, borrowed money at interest but without providing for easy transferability of its debt instruments (unlike the case of tallies) and would, during the Restoration, expressly distinguish between borrowing money at interest and taking advances of property and services without interest. In the latter case, the Crown paid a lower money price, but made the payment in the form of easily transferable debt instruments that provided cash services to the user. The point here is that a loan in money to the Crown would bring interest, although the tally might be passed on. For the approach to royal lenders, see pp. 240–241; Ashton, *The Crown and The Money Market, 1603–1640*. For the practice during the Restoration, see also p. 260.

[132] American paper money was, in fact, rarely redeemable for silver or gold coin, a resource that colonial governments could not easily accumulate. See Grubb, "Paper Money."

That charge for money marked it conceptually and practically. At the most abstract level, paying for money located it as a medium that came at common cost, authored by a public process. At a more grounded level, fees at the mint determined how much coin was made and configured, more generally, the geopolitics of Europe. As we have seen, imposing a cost on individuals tied the production of coin to the point at which that money was sufficiently valuable to be worth the fee for minting it. That baseline kept the money supply low compared to modern levels. And insofar as the charge for money produced the complex minting and melting intervals of medieval coin, it engendered the difficult monetary dynamics that haunted Europe throughout the medieval period. War was fought as much at its mints as on its fields and oceans.

The high politics of money in England minimized the losses that diluting coin visited on money holders. Instead, those governing English society kept coin strong and supported the Crown by developing a robust system of taxation. The approach habituated the English to a world of relatively stable and remarkably high-powered money, conditions that came to seem natural and necessary. It located taxation, by contrast, as an essential area of policy making. The settlement provided for the fiscal needs of the Crown and protected the growing power of landowners. Less conspicuously but just as reliably, the kind of money produced by the English facilitated certain exchanges and left others dry. As liquidity reached people to different degrees, it sorted them into a layered political economy. That story takes up the next chapter.

As for tallies, they helped the English sovereign anticipate revenues and thus put "the wealth of his kingdom at his immediate disposal," compared with other rulers.[133] They also operated as a vector that tied the Crown to its public creditors. Insofar as those holding tallies were not getting interest on them, they were more likely to resist tallies that were not promptly and credibly withdrawn by a specific levy. The device thus reiterated the commitment of public creditors to a system of reliable and regular taxation. Tallies in that way reinforced the fiscal-monetary pact that was the linchpin of England's political economy of governance.

[133] Harriss, *King, Parliament, and Public Finance*, 511.

5

The social stratigraphy of coin and credit in late medieval England

Drawing near the mid-14th century, a poet lamented "the fifteenth," a tax that took a significant portion of each household's income. As he put it in *The Song Against the King's Taxes*:

> Now goes in England from year to year—the fifteenth penny, to do thus a common harm. And it makes them go down, who used to sit upon a bench; and it obliges the common people to sell both cows, vessels, and clothes. It does not please thus to pay the fifteenth to the last penny.[1]

To modern eyes, the complaint suggests a monarch who taxed down to the last crumb, the end of a peasant's scant worth. But on second look, the *Song* is making a slightly different point. Along with the burden that taxes brought, the *Song* identifies the power of the penny. "The fifteenth penny" was not a tiny morsel. It was a significant cut of a person's wealth. To pay might require selling essentials, including livestock and household utensils. The *Song's* condemnation was literal: it captured the blunt dimension of the units in which the tax fell.

When the Crown and its allies designed English money as an array of coins with a high determinate metal content that they defended over time, they created a medium that stratified exchange. The purchasing power of England's penny was high: it facilitated exchange that was large compared with the deals common in daily life. Fractional change was in short supply; finely divisible currencies were a phenomenon of the future. Over several centuries, the English unwittingly took steps that worsened the problem. Given its high purchasing power and the skeletal array of lesser denominations, the penny serviced a great number of transactions in medieval England, including most of those made by people of modest means. But neither pennies nor fractional change left the mint in the proportion that would have allowed them to circulate at the same pace as larger denominations. The predicament sorted people's access to the market according to the size of the exchange they made and left them to improvise alternatives.

The predicament posed by England's penny shaped exchange in a second way. Credit for modest exchange was pervasive, common to villagers and urban-dwellers at every level of wealth. Across users, it was overwhelmingly oriented

---

[1] *The Song Against the King's Taxes*, in Peter Coss, ed., *Thomas Wright's Political Songs of England: From the Reign of John to that of Edward II* (Cambridge: Cambridge University Press, 1996), 183.

towards consumption rather than the pooling of money for investment. It arose from lateral relations: neighbors lent between themselves rather than depending on specialists or intermediaries. And it involved small sums: people were accounting for resources in money but settling balances less often. The way the medieval English used credit set them apart from Continental populations, an anomaly remarked in the scholarship. Apparently, inhabitants were using credit to compensate for the overly high-powered and fast-moving money they held. To that extent, the character of English credit flowed from the character of English money.

Credit, configured as selectively as it was, did not neutrally counteract money's rigidity. Rather, it revised both economic activity and the social relations that took place around it. Credit expanded the kinds of exchange that occurred, creating new opportunities. At the same time, it brought hidden costs, as the practices of debt litigation that are left behind reveal. The very power of England's money, reaching in scant and awkward fashion to the low-value economy, pushed the people who used it into new and disempowering dependencies.

Together then, English money and home-grown credit helped to stratify the social world, layering it according to how easily the coin of the realm serviced it and what forms of credit that coin induced. Circuits of exchange stacked and connected to one another, composing a hierarchy of opportunity and dependence. Money, throughout the Middle Ages, was no mere means of measure; it was defining the exchange that was available and all that depended on it.

A. A coin too discriminating to meet the demand

The problem of scale

Strong money and heavy taxes were familiar parts of English governance by the 14th century. They formed what was becoming a foundational pact over the way authority over resources should be distributed between the king and his constituents. But the deal was also constitutional in a less familiar way. It brokered the high-powered penny, and that peculiar currency represented a politics that becomes visible when we add money to the category of governance. The issue produced by the high-powered penny was one of scale: denominations of English coin carried purchasing power that was very high relative to the size of much daily exchange. The relationship between the value of the available denominations and the price level of transactions determined the zone of transactions that came within money's reach. That zone could shift up or down depending on the unit's value. An approach that kept a unit strong and prices low pitched the zone of transactions easily serviced by money at a formidable level. In that sense, the kind of money created by English policy was very discriminating: it lubricated large transactions but was not dilute enough to service small transactions or to facilitate many middling deals with change.

Attuned to inflation and its more proportionate impact, later scholars overlook the phenomenon, one that occurred in stable times and affected only certain transactions.[2] A commitment to strong money, even as it avoided price changes because of drops in commodity content, left some transactions parched of liquidity all of the time. Recall that our observer in Navarre, when sorting men according to the strength of money they preferred, commented that men living on the work of their bodies wanted a weak currency. Weak money ensured not only that "everything becomes cheap" (the effect that inflation had on fixed rents), but also that "there is always enough currency."[3] The Navarrian meant it in real terms: higher prices across the board meant that coin had less value. That allowed small exchange to be parsed more finely; coin could service buying and selling at a more modest level. By contrast, insofar as deflation occurred, it escalated the pressure on the penny and its subdivisions by raising the purchasing power of each unit; every small denomination remained critically important as a step in the hierarchy of value.

A few examples expose the extent of the problem. The 13th century laborer who made one or two pennies per day found them far too valuable to buy bread by the loaf or ale by the cup. In fact, even one farthing bought four cups of ale, and farthings never left the mint in enough quantity to be common. A halfpenny would fetch a thirsty worker much more than he could drink. Alternatively, it bought between two and four pounds of the best white bread, or a pound of cheese. Rather than buy food daily with money, the laborer would use credit, run an account, trade labor or goods in-kind, or make his own food and drink from grain he bought in bulk. In the second half of the 13th century, when the wages for unskilled labor were 1 penny/day and the penny was the only denomination that existed, that denomination was 100 percent of the daily wage; even broken in

---

[2] Inflation or deflation affects those holding money evenly or proportionately, although it can have arbitrary effects insofar as some people hold more wealth in money. Price hikes take the same amount of value from every piece of currency, although they "tax" more heavily those with higher stores of money or fixed incomes—the landowning elites of the last chapter for example. Those who have low stores of money lose the same percentage of value, although they may suffer less insofar as they are holding less wealth susceptible to the loss in value. The medieval English recognized that dynamic just as readily as modern observers. The argument of the last chapter suggests a consensus about inflation and its distributive effect: insofar as an alliance over keeping money strong existed, it drew on the advantages that elites perceived from staving off depreciation in the medium that held their wealth. (They may not have been right in the long term. Some inflation might have boosted wool exports, invited more daring uses of credit, or increased the productivity of peasants that landlords might have captured. For examples of the way that landlords and their tenants reacted to inflation by struggling over modes of pay in the 13th century, see P. D. A. Harvey, "The English Inflation of 1180–1220," *Past & Present* 61 (1973): 19–23; Pamela Nightingale, "Money and Credit in the Economy of Late Medieval England," in *Medieval Money Matters*, ed. Diane Wood (Oxford: Oxbow Books, 2007), 54; compare continental examples, Peter Spufford, *Money and Its Use in Medieval Europe* (Cambridge: Cambridge University Press, 1988), 243–245.) In any case, insofar as prices rose or fell because of the way governments managed their coinage (i.e., rose or fell for monetary reasons), the changes that inflation or deflation brought to social interactions, to law and custom, or to simple economic exchange—they too were functions of the kind of money that England made.

[3] See Guillaume le Soterel, quoted at p. 160 n. 28.

two, it was half a day's earnings. By the middle of the next century (14th), daily wages for unskilled labor had risen to 1½ to 2 pennies or slightly more. If farthings (quarter-pennies) were available, they would represent 11 percent of the daily wage, halfpennies 23 percent of that wage, and pennies 45 percent.[4]

The depreciation of the penny could change all that because, as each penny lost purchasing power and prices rose, the greater number of cheap units reached smaller deals. Imagine a radical depreciation of coin that raised wages from one to 20 pennies a day (or 80 farthings) and affected other prices proportionately. After the transition, the relative value of work and food would be the same as it had been before: four cups of ale would cost a quarter of the daily wage or 20 farthings. But the laborer could purchase just one cup with five of the farthings he had earned that day. The shift to lower value money moved the zone of transactions easily made by money down to allow small exchanges. (Of course, in a one denomination world, large transactions could become unwieldy by virtue of all the pennies they now required.)

The cumulative depreciations that took place on the Continent had moved the zone of money transactions in just such a way. In mid-14th century Florence, for example, the smallest denomination (a silver-base metal alloy) was 3 percent of the daily wage. In the Flanders, the smallest denomination (also an alloy) was 1 percent of the daily wage.[5] Across the medieval world, the meaning of purchasing power and its packaging was no doubt different from later periods: in particular, money would be much less necessary if many transactions were not monetized. The opposite is also true, however, and is just as relevant: many transactions would not be monetized because they could not be serviced by the packages of value that were available. The fact that England was so different from the Continent flags its monetary situation as a political choice. The elite alliance over strong money and heavy taxes had engineered England's peculiar problem— it located people in a monetarized economy, but gave them an ill-scaled medium to work with.

---

[4] For wage estimates, see Thomas J. Sargent and Francois R. Velde, *The Big Problem of Small Change*, The Princeton Economic History of the Western World Indexes (Princeton, NJ: Princeton University Press, 2002), 48 (wage estimated at 2.2d.); E. H. Phelps Brown and Sheila V. Hopkins, "Seven Centuries of Building Wages," *Economica* 22, no. 87 (1955): 205 (wage between 1½ and 2d.). (Wage estimates using Robert Allen's silver wage data, converted into English pence are very close to the Phelps Brown and Hopkins estimates for the 14th century. See pp. 103–104 n. 118.) Farthings and halfpennies could also be broken in two, although that practice become uncommon after the late 13th century. See Martin Allen, *Mints and Money in Medieval England* (Cambridge: Cambridge University Press, 2012), 354.

[5] All from Sargent and Velde, *Big Problem of Small Change*, 48 (Table 4). These numbers are indicative only, given discrepancies that must be assumed across wage scales. But continental monetary values sometimes diminished so much in value that it was no longer worth maintaining all denominations. That had been the fate of the Venetian denarius, initially analogous to an English penny, which was so debased over time that the Venetians eventually invented the "grosso"—at approximately the weight of the original English penny—to travel at 24 times the worth of the denarius. See pp. 123–124; see also Spufford, *Money and Its Use*, 329.

The problem was even worse than meets the eye. In the abstract, the relationship between the value of the penny and the price level pitched high the zone of easy money exchange. But as the English actually made money, they under-issued the very coins that operated at the bottom of that zone. Considering how many people lived and exchanged at the "penny level" and how many coins they had reveals the problem.

In Maryanne Kowaleski's portrait of medieval Exeter, about 80 percent of the population were artisans, laborers, or servants. Households with barely more than a seventh of the wealth of the propertied elite, their employed members earned wages comparable to those of the Oxford laborer in our example.[6] If that 80 percent majority made or should have been able to make as many deals—deals limited with the level of a daily wage or less—as the 20 percent at the top, then it needed a currency in rough proportion to its size relative to the size of the wealthier group. While the example is highly speculative, it may even understate the problem. The "penny level" population was probably more numerous compared to upper income English in rural areas than in a town like Exeter. Moreover, even if the wealthy actually made more deals than the poorer (as opposed to a similar number of deals with larger volumes and values), those bigger players also had the upper array of gold coin to use for their exchanges. In addition, the wealthier portion of the population still had small transactions to make; they did not limit themselves to large transactions and bulk purchases. While only pennies and smaller change could facilitate petty exchange, they could also service larger trades although with less convenience. Very approximately then, we might assume that at least 80 percent of coins circulating should have been in pennies or smaller denominations. (The *value* of that coinage would obviously be far less, since it would have such trivial worth compared with the larger denominations.)[7]

---

[6] See Maryanne Kowaleski, *Local Markets and Regional Trade in Medieval Exeter* (New York: Cambridge University Press, 1995), 101–104, 108a.

[7] In terms of the quantity equation for each denomination, the example holds V, velocity, constant as the goal of the exercise. P, price, remains constant because it is an aggregate across all transactions (although the price of large denomination transactions will be higher). The example suggests that economic activity takes place roughly in proportion to the size of the population and assigns each portion of the population a coin. Assuming the silver penny and the silver groat, worth 4 pence, we would assume that four times as many people used the penny for daily life as the groat. For ease of calculation, we can stipulate that T, number of transactions, for the penny's quantity identity is four times the size of the T, number of transactions for the groat. The money supply needed, given all the other assumptions, would be four times as high for the penny as for the groat. (For example, for the penny, if there were 80 transactions that cost one penny, 4d. x V = 1d. x 80; for the groat, if there were 20 more expensive (i.e., one groat) transactions: 1g. x V = 1g. x 20.) That would allow the penny, the only denomination that could service many transactions, to fill that function with the same kind of availability (V = 20) as money brought to larger transactions. (Both the penny and the groat might also service more expensive transactions; the example here would remain useful if they did so in roughly proportionate measure.)

By contrast, the quantity equation illustrates what would happen if the government coined an equal amount of pennies and groats (M in each equation), and the other assumptions stay the same. For pennies making 80 transactions happen, 4d. x V = 1d./item x 80 items/yr, V = 20. For groats, 4g. x V = 1g./item x 20

Martin Allen has gathered evidence about the coin denominations available after the middle of the 14th century. The Black Death (1348–1350), carrying off up to half of the English population, left their survivors with a somewhat more abundant medium per person. But at almost the same time, silver coming to the mint began to decrease, limiting the output of new pennies and leaving their purchasing power relatively high. The English also began minting larger denominations in both silver and gold. If anything, those changes diminished the supply of pennies more significantly than they diminished the need for those pennies.

As for gold, it facilitated only large transactions. The noble, first minted in 1344, carried a value of 6 shillings and 8 pence (80d.). Assuming a daily wage of 1 & ½d. for our Oxford laborer, the noble represented more than 53 days labor; even if wages doubled after the Black Death, a noble took about a month to earn. Nobles also came in half-noble and quarter-noble size; even the latter carried a fairly hefty value at 20 pennies.[8] And while gold made exchange easier at the top, the beginning of bimetallic minting interfered with the flow of silver to England: whenever mint prices favored gold (or undervalued silver), as they did for most of the late 14th century in England, merchants made deals that brought gold there and sent silver abroad. Over the last half of the 14th century, England lost an astonishing amount of silver. Edward I had recoined 100 tons of silver in 1278–1280; Henry IV could recoin only 2 tons of silver—along with another 70 tons of gold—in 1412–1414. Prices remained stated in the basic unit of account, the silver penny, even as that coin became less and less available.[9]

As for the new silver denominations, they created convenience for transactions that were significant if not extravagant. Half-groats and groats were worth two and four times as much as the penny; those values were close to or above the daily wage of the Oxford laborer in the later 14th century.[10] At the same time, the new coinage funneled metal away from use for the penny and its inferiors. Forty pence of economic activity might occur via ten transfers of a groat—or forty transfers of a penny. If a large amount of silver went into making groats, then the remaining pennies would have to work even harder to service the exchanges that the groats could not reach.[11]

---

items, $V = 5$. Velocity is much lower for the groats because only 1 groat in the example is needed to buy each item.

[8] Quarter- and half-nobles were also minted in smaller proportions than nobles. See Martin Allen, "The Proportions of the Denominations in English Mint Outputs, 1351–1485," *British Numismatic Journal* 2007, no. 77 (2007): 191. For wage rates, see pp. 103–104 n.118.

[9] Spufford, *Money and Its Use*, 340–341; Martin Allen, "The Volume of the English Currency, 1158–1470," *Economic History Review* 54, no. 4 (2001): 606–608.

[10] The silver groat was first introduced, unsuccessfully, during Edward I's recoinage of 1279–1281. The groat and the half-groat were successfully reintroduced in 1351. Allen, *Mints and Money*, 352, 360.

[11] While models using the quantity identity of money generally demarcate V in basic units of account, V is actually a composite of the rate at which smaller denominations are moving to lubricate smaller transactions (representing a number of transactions in those denominations) and larger denominations are moving to lubricate larger deals (representing a number of transactions in the larger denominations). (The

The shortfall we would anticipate is borne out in the evidence about the denominations that circulated after 1351.[12] Martin Allen has recovered the clues from a variety of sources, including the contracts between the Crown and its minters, physical equipment still surviving or described in the records, results of a ritualized pyx trial, and coin hoards.[13] Each suggests a relative dearth of small denominations.

First are the contracts or "indentures" made between the king and mint officials. They specify denomination proportions in many if not all cases before 1434, although it is not clear that officials complied with those directives. Pennies and smaller change were to make up 56.4 percent up to 68.6 percent of silver coins during the 14th century. Between 1422 and 1445, when silver coming to the mint was almost non-existent, the indentures specify a 10 percent higher portion to be used for small denominations, up to 78.6 percent.[14] At those rates, smaller coin would have been somewhat scant, even during the 14th century; it would have been grievously short during much of the 15th century as silver coming to the mint dropped.

But formal agreements appear to overstate the supply of low denominations, perhaps by a wide margin. Small coin cost proportionately more to make than larger coin; as a later scholar put it, "twelve times as much labor was involved in making 12 pennies as in making one shilling."[15] With some exceptions, minters did not get reimbursed for their trouble, and they often took the easy way out.[16] Recall the profusion of petitions to the Crown and Commons about the unmet

distinction is not important in modern models because modern currencies build on units of account by making every other denomination convertible into that unit on demand to the government; that was not true of medieval coin.) If the velocity at which each denomination moved is to stay roughly constant, then the money supplied in each denomination should match the level of transactions requiring that denomination. Thomas Sargent and Francois Velde conceptualize the problem by suggesting that the quantity identity of money broke into two when the medieval denominations required for certain transactions were in short supply. Sargent and Velde, *Big Problem of Small Change*, 25–26. See also N. J. Mayhew, "Population, Money Supply, and the Velocity of Circulation in England, 1300–1700," *Economic History Review* 48, no. 2 (1995): 253.

Note that the modern tendency to use *Y* or income as a proxy for *T*, the number of transactions, further obscures the composite nature of *V*. The proxy aggregates total economic activity into a volume of value, rendering invisible which part of that volume was composed of activities at each denominational level.

[12] For Allen's discussion of small change shortage before 1351, see Allen, *Mints and Money*, 352–358.

[13] Hoard evidence is assumed to be biased towards larger coins, as those would be more worthwhile stashing. Allen therefore uses hoard evidence mainly to track relative trends in coin production, rather than offering it as an indication of the proportion of denominations existing in circulation. See Allen, "English Mint Outputs," 202.

[14] The indenture made in 1363 also required that the mint master annually infuse another £100 of farthings into circulation—perhaps the result of the fuss made in 1363 that began the chapter. Allen, "English Mint Outputs," 191–192; see also Allen, *Mints and Money*, 360–361 (Table 11.3).

[15] Philip Grierson, quoted in John Munro, "Deflation and the Petty Coin Problem in the Late-Medieval Economy: The Case of Flanders, 1334–1484," in *Bullion Flows and Monetary Policies in England and the Low Countries, 1350–1500*, ed. John Munro (Farnham: Variorum, Ashgate Publishing Ltd., 1992), 402–403.

[16] Early 15th century indentures provided for the additional cost of minting small coins by allowing more to be struck from each pound of silver, as did a short-lived mid-century statute. Allen, "English Mint Outputs," 193–194, 202. The debasement of small change in the 1330s also provided more profit to minters.

demand for currency; a great many of them specified the problem as a lack of small change and may suggest that cause.[17] After one complaint by the Commons in 1423, Henry VI directed the master of the mint to produce more low denomination coin since "little or no such small coins are made, but only nobles and groats to the great harm of the people, and to the master [of the mint's] own profit."[18]

When Allen looked, second, at the dies used to make coin, he found that they survived or were authorized in proportions that bear out the protests. At York (1353–1355), London (1355–1361, 1369–1377), and Calais (1427–1431, 1435, and 1441), the equipment used to make larger denominations (groats and half-groats) is disproportionately abundant to the amount of coin the indentures stipulate, while the equipment used to make small denominations is dispropor-tionately limited. At Calais, the discrepancy goes all the way down: halfpenny dies dropped from 13 percent to 2 percent of the total in 1430–1431 and farthing dies completely disappeared—although those fractional coins should have made up 28.6 percent of the mint's production of silver coins, according to indentures.[19] Dies for larger coins wore out more quickly than the dies for smaller coin and would need to be replaced more often. But even controlling for that problem, the die supplies suggest that minters routinely diverged from their orders: the London evidence on pennies indicates that two to more than seven times as many dies would have been needed as probably existed to make the output allocated in the indentures.[20] A study of the later 13th century found more than four times as many dies existed for groats as for pennies, although the Crown seemed to be minting more halfpennies and farthings.[21]

---

[17] See p. 106 n. 124.

[18] "Parliament of 2 Henry VI, 1423," in PROME, item 55. The complaint also elaborately charged the master of the mint with paying too little for bullion received at the mint and minting only "a little blanched money" to the "great distress and harm of the poor people of this realm." See also petition evidence reviewed in Allen, *Mints and Money*, 360–362.

[19] At Calais in the decades after the Commons complained, groat dies made up two-thirds of the total although groats should have comprised only 7.1 percent of the mint's coins. According to the same evidence, half-groat dies were twice as common as penny dies. Allen, "English Mint Outputs," 191, 198 (citing studies based on dies supplied at Calais in 1427–1431, and dies authorized in 1435 and 1441). The divergence for the York mint, while significant, was not quite as wide. See Allen, "English Mint Outputs," 197, 199 (1355 indenture specified 13.5 percent groat production while groat dies supplied in 1353 were 41 percent of total).

[20] See Allen, "English Mint Outputs," 200 (Table 11). The study estimated from surviving evidence the total number of dies that were in use and calculated total pennies produced given the productive capacity of each die. It compared that with projections of the total number of dies that would have to have existed to produce the number of pennies dictated by the indentures. The multiple comes from the die estimate needed for allocated output divided by the die estimate for actually existing dies. Penny production may have been up from 1361–1369. See Allen, "English Mint Outputs," 207.

[21] See Allen, "English Mint Outputs," 200, 207. The number of dies estimated to have existed were 32 (groats), 7 (pennies), and 14 (farthings). Halfpenny numbers are not yet estimated but are high. See Allen, "English Mint Outputs." Testimony at a parliamentary inquest on the coinage in 1381–1382 had witnessed, yet again, to the shortage of small change. For the parliamentary inquest, see Rogers Ruding, *Annals of the Coinage of Great Britain and its Dependencies: From the Earliest Period of Authentic History to the Reign of Victoria*, 3rd ed. (London: printed for J. Hearne, 1840), 239–243. For other assessment to the effect that

By the early 15th century, the amount of silver coming to the mint was tiny compared with gold. A rare surviving record from a pyx trial in 1414, Allen's third source, indicates that only 38.4 to 46.3 percent of the coins made from that silver stream went to small denominations (pennies, halfpennies, and farthings).[22]

Finally, while pennies had predominated in the silver coin hoarded from the mid-14th century (74.5 percent of 1350s hoards), they fell through the rest of century (59.2 percent, 1351–1412, excluding 1350s hoards). As the 15th century took off, groats and half-groats make up the lion's share of the hoards. From 1412 to 1464–1465, groats account for 60.4 percent, half-groats another 16.4 percent, pennies 22 percent. After about 1430, the fortunes of the penny fell part-icularly low. While hoards vary in size and probably over-represent large denominations—the coins that people may have felt were worth stashing—they might more reliably suggest trends in coin holding.[23]

The Crown made some efforts to add halfpennies and farthings to the currency after the 1380s.[24] There were, in addition to the coins produced by the royal mints, some pennies made in ecclesiastical facilities.[25] Each of those responses may have alleviated somewhat the difficulties posed by the government's basic approach to money. More conspicuous throughout the commentary left behind, there were the self-help remedies, including the turn by many English to foreign coin.

But that shifts the story from the government and its mints to the people in search of coin. The monetary stress sketched above confirms the reason to follow along: it is overwhelmingly clear that the government posed people a serious predicament because of the kind of money it made. The Crown minted a money that was unwieldy for many uses and it underproduced the penny along with small change for much of the 14th and 15th centuries. People operated in a world where money came in packages larger than much of daily life and all too often unavailable anyway.[26] The drama is how the quality of money they held

small change was very scarce, see C. E. Challis, *A New History of the Royal Mint* (Cambridge: Cambridge University Press, 1992), 701–705; N. J. Mayhew, "From Regional to Central Minting, 1158–1464," in *A New History of the Royal Mint*, ed. C. E. Challis (Cambridge: Cambridge University Press, 1992), 149, 166–168.

[22] Gold output was some £133,919 compared with silver output at £4,983. Allen, "English Mint Outputs," 194–195.

[23] Allen, "English Mint Outputs," 202–208. Martin Allen extrapolates from the hoard evidence more nuanced possibilities about the ebb and flow of smaller coinage, including concerted efforts to increase halfpenny and farthing supplies from 1377 to 1412, a "brief boost" to the halfpenny after 1446, and the shifting career of the groat and half-groat. The mint's silver output was, however, very limited from 1399 to 1408, averaging only £148. Allen, "English Mint Outputs," 207 and n. 98.

[24] See, e.g., Allen, *Mints and Money*, 361, 362.

[25] Martin Allen, "Ecclesiastical Mints in Thirteenth-Century England," in *Thirteenth Century England VIII: Proceedings of the Durham Conference, Durham Conference 1999*, ed. M. Prestwich, R. Britnell, and R. Frame (Woodbridge, 2001).

[26] The phenomena identified by Sargent and Velde, left aside here, would worsen the situation. As discussed in Chapter 3, if smaller denominations had a higher liquidity value than larger denominations in times of shortage, they would depreciate in value. Prices in small coin would be disproportionately high, a pattern that would induce people to melt small coins.

influenced exchange and the relations that took place around it—how people prospered or came to grief, adapted or took advantage, evaded the constraints of the coinage or lost out because of them.

Improvising exchange under the monetary floor

"When Mac Murrough, an Irish chief, met the earl of Gloucester, Richard's commander-in-chief, he was mounted on a horse which cost him, as it was said, four hundred cows." A later observer offered the tidbit as an exoticism that cast the Irish as a backward people, pre-monetary even at the end of the 14th century. Barter's disadvantages had been recognized since the time of Aristotle. In circumstances bereft of a unit of account, barter left people without a standard measure and unable to generate the collective conclusions about value represented by price. Even when a shadow unit existed, trade in-kind required that two parties have commensurable goods at the same time and place. Otherwise, resources perished; middlemen flourished; and people declined to specialize for an unpredictable market.[27]

Despite those disadvantages, Mac Murrough's deal captured a practice that was common not only in Ireland, but also in contemporary England. It happened, however, more often at the bottom than at the top of English society. Apparently, where people had little choice, they traded what they had for what they needed. Where they had more choice, they moved away from barter and the disadvantages that came with it. The discrepancy meant that the well-off operated at an advantage not only in their absolute amount of wealth but in their access to liquidity.

Between themselves, peasants and urban-dwellers alike exchanged work for produce, livestock, or other items. In his study of credit in 14th century midland villages, Chris Briggs found a large number of debts due in grain, animals, or other goods. In the first half of the century, such cases made up 40 percent of debt disputes resolved in one village court; over the second half, such cases still comprised almost a quarter of the court's business. While the details that gave rise to in-kind obligations are lost, surely some judgments adjudicated what remained of barter swaps that went sour.[28]

Perhaps more typical in a world that money penetrated but taunted with low liquidity, people of limited means made exchanges that mixed barter and cash. The Oxford worker might thatch a roof in town in return for a number of chickens—with only one balance owed in coin, say a penny and a half. The hybrid arrangement would allow a transaction valued in money. At the same

---

[27] Ledwich, *Antiquities of Ireland*, as quoted in Ruding, *Annals of the Coinage*, 248; Nightingale, "Money and Credit," 54.

[28] For the breakdown of debts in-kind, see Chris Briggs, *Credit and Village Society in Fourteenth-Century England*, British Academy Postdoctoral Fellowship Monograph (2009), 32, 34–35.

time, it would save the need to make change more than once. Those with long-running relations even more easily institutionalized a pattern of exchange: a laborer carried loads, unpacked goods, or repaired premises while a retailer reciprocated with food, salt, and pottery. Trading partners could run a tab indefinitely, do so in amounts that included fractional change, and settle up only occasionally.[29]

Barter operated elsewhere, but increasingly as a fallback. Rents paid in-kind or in labor—a kind of barter of goods or service for land—were fading by the end of the 12th century. Landlords in some areas reverted to it in later years, but they apparently did so for strategic reasons; when money was depreciating, payments in-kind or in labor conveyed more value to the creditor. In the future, elites would succeed in constraining inflation so closely that they could move more wholeheartedly into the monetary world.[30]

With that assurance, those who made bigger deals and could use cash—larger merchants for example—turned to trade in-kind only when it was convenient. One such circumstance occurred when partners to exchange mutually and predictably depended on each other. For example, the rural cloth industry paired merchants who could deliver wool, dyes, and alum with weavers and dyers who put those raw materials to use and returned finished cloth. In fact, the capacity of the cloth industry to function with less recourse to coined money during the 14th century may have given it a competitive advantage. It was insulated from the shortfalls in bullion and coin that occurred during the Hundred Years War and interrupted the ability of wool exporters, in contrast to those in the cloth industry, to pay their producers. But outside of those convenient conditions (or the times when one party or another, like the landlords above, were trying to escape changes in the value of money), barter was a less preferred alternative. According to Pamela Nightingale, the account books of a London iron merchant reveal that he bartered only with his own servants and with close trading partners with whom he had reciprocal relations. Barter accounted for less than 5 percent

---

[29] Examples are at Marjorie Keniston McIntosh, *Autonomy and Community: The Royal Manor Of Havering, 1200–1500*, Cambridge Studies in Medieval Life and Thought; 4th ser., 5 (Cambridge: Cambridge University Press, 1986), 169–170; Elaine Gravelle Clark, "Debt Litigation in a Late Medieval Vill," in *Pathways to Medieval Peasants*, ed. J. A. Raftis (Toronto: Pontifical Institute of Mediaeval Studies, 1981), 265. Chris Briggs finds few express examples of disputes based on long-running tabs, but that may be because those disputes did not make the earlier and assumedly settled part of a long-running trade explicit. See Briggs, *Credit and Village Society in Fourteenth-Century England*, 30–31. For the ubiquity of such arrangements in early America, where liquidity was scant and small change may at times have been especially rare, see Bruce H. Mann, *Neighbors and Strangers: Law and Community in Early Connecticut*, Studies in Legal History (Chapel Hill: University of North Carolina Press, 1987), 11–27.

[30] See p. 98. The example reveals that barter could be safer than monetary exchange for people, including small villeins or free tenants, who were chronic debtors in a deflationary world, the condition of the English for several stretches in the late medieval period. When landlords could demand cash, money remained mildly deflationary, and circulated in a coin that selectively suited elite exchange because of its high purchasing power, the difficulties for small actors with many debts to pay would be at their height.

of his transactions as a whole and did not extend to his retail or distributive trade. The contrast with Briggs's suggestive numbers underscores Nightingale's conclusion that "use of barter outside the village was therefore limited."[31]

Given the problems posed by barter, Englishmen improvised other ways to compensate for the difficult money they encountered. A petition presented by the Commons in the early 15th century spelled out a widely used alternative: the use of small foreign money, the base coin of other realms that was cheap enough to fill in the space under England's higher monetary floor. At the time, that space had been rendered even larger because the government's minting policies had exacerbated the drop in silver bullion that was coming into Europe; England was coining very little silver money at all. The Commons began by asking the king whether he would ordain a remedy "for the great hardship among the poor people on account of the scarcity of silver halfpennies and farthings, which used to be, and still should be, the most useful form of money for the said people, and are now so scarce, because none is fashioned or made these days." The Commons then continued:

> [O]ut of great necessity, people in various places are using coin from foreign lands, such as Scottish halfpennies, and others called galley-halfpennies, and clipped half-pennies from other places, to the great ruin and debasement of the coinage, and in several other places badges of lead.[32]

"Galley-halfpennies" were Venetian *soldini*, tiny coin so-called because they arrived in England on the merchant galleys that came each trading season. According to a contemporary doge of Venice, England received 10 million of them each year in the early 15th century. Soldini were worth 12 Venetian denari *piccoli* or about half an English penny; they were made of a half-silver alloy or "white silver," and had a bullion value significantly less than their English counterparts.[33] As for the denari piccoli themselves—they had long since become "black money," coins that combined a small bit of silver with a much greater amount of base metal, like copper. Black money (or "billon") supplied low-value money to virtually all the cities of Europe. The coin allowed urban populations to make the everyday exchanges so difficult to arrange by barter or even book account: the more specialized tradesmen and artisans became, the more multilateral arrangements they would have required to translate their products into the range of everyday objects they needed. In Venice, for example, *quattrini* worth 4

---

[31] Nightingale, "Money and Credit," 54; Pamela Nightingale, "Monetary Contraction and Mercantile Credit in Later Medieval England," *Economic History Review* 43, no. 4 (November 1990).

[32] "Parliament of 4 Henry IV, 1402," in PROME, item 46. Little is known about the use of lead tokens, which are mentioned only rarely in the parliamentary record. For a discussion of their possible import, see Spufford, *Money and Its Use*, 331–332; Allen, *Mints and Money*, 362–363; see also William J. Courtenay, "Token Coinage and the Administration of Poor Relief during the Late Middle Ages," *Journal of Interdisciplinary History* 3, no. 2 (1972).

[33] Spufford, *Money and Its Use*, 328; Allen, *Mints and Money*, 363–364.

denari paid for a loaf of bread. In Pistoia, a city that used Florentine denari, 4 quattrini bought a pound of mutton, and 18 denari bought a pound of pork.[34]

Alone among the major European cities, London went without official billon—the English coined neither white nor black money.[35] While the problems for its population became especially dire during the late 14th and 15th centuries, the parliamentary record indicates that Englishmen had been hijacking foreign coin to use as small coin for centuries. Ruding's *Annals of the Coinage* records Crown and legislative concern from the last decades of Henry III's reign (1216–1272), when "immense quantities ... of foreign base coins were brought into the realm." The annalist understood the phenomenon as one that operated to "the impoverishment of [the King's] people" by driving more valuable English coin into hoards and out of circulation. Officials agreed again and again: petitions against the practice, prohibitions against importing foreign coin, penalties, and enforcement measures occur in virtually every decade of the next two centuries.[36] Several merchants convicted of facilitating an influx were apparently executed in one particularly extreme case.[37] At a minimum, people using foreign coin could not depend on the sovereign to police its transfer or enforce agreements made in it. As the episode of the imitation pennies demonstrates, however, at times even the sovereign allowed the practice. Sargent and Velde argue that when the English lay population insisted on using foreign coin, they were engineering a spontaneous and necessary debasement of their own coin supply. The English were, in other words, filling the space below their own, more problematic, monetary floor.[38]

Substituting foreign coin was a shadowy solution, one that put the people using it at risk. Lacking coin, people sometimes simply held back on buying goods at all or overpaid for want of change. As the author of *The Song Against the King's Taxes* put it:

There is so much scarcity of money among people,
that people can in the market, there are so few buyers,
although they may have cloth or coin, swine or sheep,

---

[34] Spufford, *Money and Its Use*, 330.

[35] See pp. 123–125.

[36] Ruding, *Annals of the Coinage*, 190. For references in the late decades of Henry III, and in 1299, 1310, 1319–1320, 1328, 1337, 1341, 1343, 1346, 1348, 1351, 1367, 1371, 1377, 1400, 1401, 1404, 1409, 1411, 1414, 1415, 1423, 1431, 1456 (Ireland), 1462 (Ireland), 1476, and 1487, see Ruding, *Annals of the Coinage*, 190, 199, 201, 207–209, 212–213, 215, 222–223, 225, 227, 232–233, 236, 249, 250, 253, 254, 256–258, 270, 274, 277–278 and n. 3, 281, 287, 294.

[37] See Ruding, *Annals of the Coinage*, 223–224.

[38] Sargent and Velde, *Big Problem of Small Change*, 30–31. For an example of such borrowing, see Ruding, *Annals of the Coinage*, 294 (Henry VII, 1487). The petition referring to galley-halfpennies (see n. 33) itself responded to an early 15th century measure prohibiting foreign coin, according to Ruding, who noted that "the provisions of this statute could not ... be carried into effect, on account of the great want of small money" (Ruding, *Annals of the Coinage*, 250). The Crown responded by assuring the Commons that he would have the mints dedicate a third of all silver bullion to halfpennies and farthings: "Parliament of 4 Henry IV, 1402," in PROME, item 46.

make nothing of them, in truth there are so many needy people,
The people is not joyful, when money is so scarce.[39]

The Commons identified the same obstacle to exchange four decades later. "They the said Commons had no small money to pay for the smaller measures," their petition noted, as well as "other little purchases," religious donations, and works of charity. Parliamentary complaints about the scarcity of money in the 14th and 15th centuries commonly connected that dearth with the "great poverty of the realm" and the "manifest impoverishing of the whole kingdom."[40]

The scarcity of small change was especially scathing. As the Commons continued in a later petition, it left the poor "often badly served; for that when a poor man buys his victuals and other good necessary to him, and has nothing but a penny which he wishes to change for a halfpenny, he often loses his penny through lack of a halfpenny."[41] A half century later, the Commons spoke in its own tongue; perhaps for that reason, its message conveys the problem with particular power. The exacerbating circumstance was a scarcity of small change, so dire in that instance that:

> men travailling over contrees, for part of their expenses of necessite most departe oure soveraigne lordes coigne, that is to wete, a peny in two peces, or elles forgo all the same peny, for the paiement of an half peny; and also the pouere common retaillours of vitailles, and of o[th]er nedefull things, for defaute of such coigne ... oftentymes mowe not sell their seid vitailles and things, and many of oure seid soveraine lordes pouere liege peple, which wold bye such vitailles and other smale thinges necessarie, mowe not bie theyme, for defaute of half penyes and ferthings not hadde, nouther on the parte bier, nor on the partie seller ...[42]

A last complaint brings us back to where we started, with the Irish. If they used little money at the end of the 14th century, they shamed the Crown for making an inadequate amount available to them at the end of the next. According to Ruding, the shortfall of coin in Ireland meant that "the common people could not have small coins for buying and selling or paying small sums to servants, labourers, and artificers, by which many of the inhabitants had departed, and were about to depart the land, and leave their habitations desolate and waste."[43]

[39] Coss, *Political Songs*, 186. As the poet continues, "If the king would take my advice, I would praise him then, to take the vessels of silver, and make money of them ..."
[40] Ruding, *Annals of the Coinage*, 237, 239 and n. 2, 243 (Petition of 1378); see also Ruding, *Annals of the Coinage*, 252, 259.
[41] "Parliament of 17 Richard II, 1394," in PROME, item 38. Ruding's translation of "il perdra son denier" as "spoiling" the penny may have referred to breaking it, or to losing it in overpayment. Ruding, *Annals of the Coinage*, 245, n. 5. He interpreted the double cross design of coinage at the end of the 13th century as a design that allowed people more easily to break pennies, "by which shift onelie the people came by small Monies," see Ruding, *Annals of the Coinage*, 194, n. 10. Allen notes, however, that the cutting of pence declined after 1279 and could not compensate for the undersupply of fractional denominations. Allen, *Mints and Money*, 354.
[42] "Parliament of 23 Henry VI, 1445," in PROME, item 11.
[43] Ruding, *Annals of the Coinage*, 292.

Ruding's comment recaptures the gravity of a problem that left no records. It haunted people who had no conception that money might work another way. In their world, gold pooled in the wealthier strata of society where people could make purchases for larger households and longer terms.[44] Silver coin was scant, and got even scanter at the lowest end. At the bottom of society, money's awkward operation regularly relegated people to barter, the quasi-legality of base foreign coin, or the simplest option of all, forgoing exchange altogether.

Price, as information based on a unit of account shared proportionately across all denominations, could not properly process activity occurring under the monetary floor.[45] That register of preference thus obscured people's exclusion from the market for want of small denominations. The circumstances made pathological the disparities routinely at work in a system that integrates bids made by people with very different reaches and resources. Money in medieval England packaged liquidity so bluntly that it literally sorted access to exchange. In that elusive but chronic fashion, the selectivity of money also sorted people. Those able to use larger denominations enjoyed the benefits of cash services. Their advantages were subtly increased by the handicap on exchange endured by those who lacked the lesser denominations they needed for daily life.

B. The peculiar credit of the English

Compared with medieval and early modern credit on the Continent, the English approach to credit stands out as strange. While middlemen were common in Europe, they were not in England. While the majority of debt on the Continent took the shape of cash loans, such loans were much less frequent in England. While the wealthy generally lent to the less wealthy and strangers to strangers in France, familiars within the same socio-economic echelon borrowed and lent to each other promiscuously in England. The oddities of England's credit have puzzled scholars for years.[46] Those oddities also make it difficult to answer some apparently basic questions. Was English credit exploitative even if no middlemen orchestrated it? Did people borrow and lend out of exigency or for investment? Did credit add to productive economic exchange or simply endanger those who used it?[47]

---

[44] See R. H. Britnell, *The Commercialisation of English Society, 1000–1500*, 2nd ed., Manchester Medieval Studies (New York: Manchester University Press, 1996), 161. On the classification of "nobles and groats" as coin too large for common use, see "Parliament of 2 Henry VI, 1423," in PROME, item 55.

[45] Credit, as we will see, was not a one-to-one substitution for money.

[46] For a map of the debate, see, e.g., Briggs, *Credit and Village Society*, 1–18, 214–223.

[47] On the presence of middlemen in early modern Europe, see Philip T. Hoffman, Gilles Postel-Vinay, and Jean-Laurent Rosenthal, *Priceless Markets: The Political Economy of Credit in Paris, 1660–1870* (Chicago: University of Chicago Press, 2000), and to a more controverted extent in medieval Europe, see Spufford, *Money and Its Use*, 336–337; Briggs, *Credit and Village Society*, 67, 216. On the dominance of cash loans compared with deferred sales or other arrangements in Europe, see Briggs, *Credit and Village Society*,

Considering the predicament created by England's money makes many of the mysteries of English credit disappear. Like everyone else, the English sometimes borrowed and lent because of a sudden shortfall in resources or a desire to invest, and nothing in the next pages is meant to minimize those motivations. But the English had an additional set of reasons: credit became a last and enormously creative way they responded to their overloaded silver coin and the unwieldy units of account they had been given.

While credit answered many of the ends participants sought, it was not a simple extension of currency, let alone one that neutralized the politics of England's money. As a medium, credit created liquidity through a bipolar agreement that depended on communal enforcement: the promises that underlay credit could be asserted and contested in courts. Many credit arrangements obviously never reached that point; they depended on everyday relations and disappeared with them. But at times litigation tracked into the world of familiars, pervading their interaction along with the credit they offered each other. The contrast between money and personal credit exposes the importance of the difference. Unlike personal credit, money operates by allowing immediate exchange. Its value has been previously arbitered, as it were, in the orchestration that creates cash. Insofar as the English denominational structure boxed people out of using coin, it prevented them from making discrete transfers of value and relegated them to the more costly remedies (both informal and judicial) that policed personal promises to pay.

At the same time, credit remained tied to the terms of money—it would thus echo, indeed amplify, the pattern of advantage distributed by money's politics. Far from an accordion-like entity that moved inversely to money and easily compensated for its dearth or excess, credit appears by many indicators to exist in rough consonance with the money supply. In medieval England, that money supply poorly nourished low-level exchange and was susceptible to periodic crises. People using credit thus became all-the-more vulnerable: whether they borrowed from neighbors at the same wealth level or larger lenders, their creditors could hold them to the very money terms that credit taken to enhance liquidity had been designed to avoid. And when amounts of coin in circulation dropped, credit contracted as well, devastating those who depended on it.

The story of credit starts below by considering how England's money oriented much of its population towards a particular kind of credit. Using that monetary lens exposes the success of English credit in creating liquidity. But the approach also reveals credit's dangers, the burdens that attended when credit was called in. Recognizing those dynamics suggests that English credit organized social relations, operating to exacerbate the stratified delivery of liquidity to the population.

41–42. On the specialized lending that brought strangers across wealth levels together in Europe, see Spufford, *Money and Its Use*, 336–337; Briggs, *Credit and Village Society*, 67, 216–217.

The shape of English credit

England's money came in large packages and was difficult to hold on to given the need for it. The credit that people created at mundane levels of exchange responded to each dilemma. First, credit lessened denominational demands by allowing all sorts of trades that used money's terms but minimized the number of times that small amounts of value had to change hands discretely. Second, credit allowed people to use the existing units of account, assuming their presence by advance. It thus helped speed the circulation of the scant penny and its associates, spreading their utility across more exchanges.[48]

Often, credit could meet both ends at once. For example, the Oxford laborer could easily find a way *around* buying ale or bread in distinct exchanges that demanded small change on hand. Instead, he would make a standing arrangement to have ale from a brewer each day of the workweek, say six days excluding Sunday. Ale, at a farthing for four cups, came to three farthings after a cup a day for two weeks, or to a penny and a half after a month. Local law may well have encompassed the arrangement as one deal, much as the common law later treated installment contracts. The running accounts kept by those who dealt with each other repeatedly were another kind of credit that obviated the need for ready cash and for settling up often. Similarly, sales credits allowed unilateral exchanges of goods for cash. The Oxford man might buy an item in the market outright, but ask to pay later—not because he needed the advance given his resources but because he had insufficient amounts of that wealth in cash form or had the wrong denominations available. The deal would be especially easy as long as money's value was not likely to change, the advance was small, and the amount could be paid off or demanded at the behest of either party. A default in any such case—an installment arrangement, a running account, or a sales advance—could easily amount to several shillings.

Credit was prevalent in English medieval life, and much of it appears to be just such a type. The pattern holds across both town and rural areas and across many different periods. The simple ubiquity of credit—a testament to the prevalence of credit used in everyday exchange—is perhaps most conspicuous. Based on a fine-grained study of debt cases in Exeter's borough courts, Maryanne Kowaleski found credit so widespread at "all levels of urban society" that "most people appeared in debt court at some point, whether as a creditor or debtor." Over a decade, significantly more than 54 percent of the town's adult population brought or defended such a suit. A full 80 percent of householders listed on the murage

---

[48] In terms of the quantity equation, credit is conceptualized as raising the velocity (V) of money. See, e.g., Mayhew, "Population," 254. Note that unlike money, which is conceptualized as affecting the money supply (M), credit is not receivable for taxes, does not provide final payment, and is not negotiable between strangers, except as those qualities are provided by law.

tax rolls appeared at least once in that decade as debt litigants; most of those absent were either poor or women. Debt litigation in turn comprised 65 percent of the pleas before the Exeter borough courts. As Kowaleski concluded, exposure to suit basically reflected the "degree of [a person's] participation in local commerce."[49]

While urban populations were exceptionally involved in trade, rural inhabitants from many communities also appear in debt disputes remarkably often. Chris Briggs's study of "middling" peasant households, those holding 10–18 acres, in the midland region of England found 46.2 percent were involved as debtors between 1339 and 1349. At least a third of smaller peasant households also appeared as debtors. Briggs's analysis of a set of villages in the same area and over the previous decades found that 35–60 percent of tenants were litigants in debt disputes, depending on the community. (Records from some communities for other years reflected both higher and lower rates.) As in town, a striking amount of village litigation concerned debt—50 percent, according to Phillip Schofield's study of a county court in 1332 to 1333.[50]

Litigation obviously represented only those credit relations that were contested. Much more borrowing and lending happened successfully enough that it left no written record; one medievalist estimates that debt disputes represent only about 20 percent of the credit extended every day. If that is even roughly right, we can conclude with Chris Briggs that "almost everyone was involved" in rural credit networks. Credit remained significant through the 14th century and the first three decades of the next; after that point, debt litigation dropped at least in the manor courts as money supplies contracted.[51]

Credit's prevalence in England is just what we would expect if it were highly demanded for its ability to speed the transfer of coin and diminish denominational problems. Credit was common, however, on the Continent as well. The unique shape of the English version comes clear by looking at the way much credit functioned and the people who participated in it.

---

[49] Kowaleski, *Local Markets*, 202, 349. The population figure used as the denominator includes children; excluding them would push the percentage of adult litigants higher than 54 percent. The murage tax was applied to all heads of household. Kowaleski, *Local Markets*, 102, 349.

[50] Chris Briggs, "Credit and the Peasant Household Economy in England Before the Black Death: Evidence from a Cambridgeshire Manor," in *The Medieval Household in Christian Europe, c.850–c.1550: Managing Power, Wealth, and the Body*, ed. C. Beattie, A. Maslakovic, and S. Rees Jones (Brepols: Turnhout, 2003), 238; Briggs, *Credit and Village Society*, 108–111 (the percentages given here are drawn from Table 4.2, which compared tenants against manorial tenant lists); Phillipp R. Schofield, "Access to Credit in the Medieval English Countryside," in *Credit and Debt in Medieval England c.1180–c.1350*, ed. N. J. Mayhew and Phillipp R. Schofield (Oxford: Oxbow Books, 2002), 108. For the prevalence of medieval rural credit more generally, see Phillipp R. Schofield, "Dearth, Debt and the Local Land Market in a Late Thirteenth-Century Village Community," *Agricultural History Review* 1997, no. 45 (1997): 12, 16; Clark, "Medieval Vill."

[51] N. J. Mayhew, *Sterling: The History of a Currency* (New York: Wiley, 2000), 37; Chris Briggs, "The Availability of Credit in the English Countryside, 1400–1480," *Agricultural History Review* 56 (2008): 1, 5, 8–10, 20–23; Clark, "Medieval Vill," 250–251. Briggs's assessment is from Briggs, *Credit and Village Society*, 111. For the relative contraction of credit in times of monetary shortage, see pp. 224–225, 228.

Peter Spufford calls it "day-to-day credit," the petty and constant extensions of credit between tradesmen and their customers or between neighbors with milk and cheese, cloth, or tools that another neighbor wanted to buy. Day-to-day or consumption credit was "absolutely necessary," Spufford continues, "when black money was scarce, or when the smallest denominations were larger than the payments involved in the purchase of ordinary requirements of bread or meat, beer or wine." While supplies of billon might wax and wane on the Continent, England lived in the dilemma created by overpowerful denominations—one where even small change had high value—all the time. Moreover, even that small change was working too hard to be easily available. As a consequence, English credit at the everyday level was overwhelmingly oriented towards facilitating consumption as opposed to investment.[52]

Most consumption credit would leave no trail: "we know and can know next to nothing" about it, notes Spufford. It did its work informally, on a handshake and an agreement, and vanished just as easily. Even when it did not work, when a customer never returned with the farthing or halfpenny she owed, it often would not have been worth suing. In those circumstances, the pattern that debts left on record is even more striking.

In urban Exeter, 50 percent of debt litigation involved sales made on credit, instances in which sellers gave buyers credit for the price (or part of the price) of their purchases. These were small advances: about 60 percent of them were for amounts less than 5 shillings, like the 6 pennies that a party named Henry Wynd apparently owed for apples he had purchased. In the case of credit sales, a slight majority of both creditors and debtors were outsiders to Exeter and their deals disproportionately involved farm goods. The numbers reveal a market town, pulling people in from surrounding lands to trade as much with one another as with anyone in Exeter.[53]

The credit story was much the same when country people stayed home. In the midland communities studied by Chris Briggs, sales credits constituted the single largest category of debt cases for money in four of six manor courts, out of the debt cases where the substance of the debt can be identified. In his more detailed study of one manor court in the half century before the Black Death, credit sales outnumbered cash loans at a rate of about 2.3 to 1. As at Exeter, these were small advances—in one midland village, as many disputed debts were for amounts smaller than 15 pennies as were for amounts larger and if the median for amounts on *sales* credit disputes had been broken out, it would likely be even lower, perhaps by a significant stretch. In each village, roughly a quarter to almost a half of all money debts were for less than one shilling and some 10 percent of all money debts were for sums of 5d. or less.[54] As Briggs points out, the size of these debts was small even in comparison to peasants' income and expenses.[55] When we recapture the denominational problems that people faced, it becomes clear that many of them borrowed neither to gather resources for investment nor out of exigency, given the larger absolute size of their resources. Rather, they were trading around the monetary obstacles that impeded everyday life.

Clark's study of debt litigation in late 14th and early 15th century Essex and Norfolk tells a similar story. Peasants most commonly extended credit for sales to each other; according to the manor court roll at Writtle, they often made deals for animals, as well as "manufactured goods" (shoes, leggings, boots, cloth, hemp-halters and saddles, knives, spurs, and other things made of wood or iron), grain and legumes, and malt. They advanced each other goods and waited for payment or, at times, paid the purchase price and waited for goods, a delivery that their upfront payment alone may have made possible. The amounts, again, were modest.[56] The interactions they facilitated, on the other hand, could be complex. "Villagers," Clark writes, "both bought and sold on credit." They were trading constantly, "one man selling casks made of poplar, buying wood and repairing a house, another roofing cottages and selling straw, still another tailoring tunics, selling wheat but also buying wool":

> Customers supplied the materials and craftsmen provided the tools and techniques necessary to produce a finished product. Tailors received cloth and on occasion an old tunic to copy; weavers were furnished with wool already spun and oftentimes dyed. Customers at this stage held craftsmen in their debt but once materials had been processed, craftsmen expected payment.[57]

[54] For the substance of disputes, see Briggs, *Credit and Village Society*, 34; Briggs, "Credit and the Peasant Household Economy," 242. The manor records used by Briggs contain a high level of cases in which the substance of the debt was not expressed. For the size of debts, see Briggs, *Credit and Village Society*, 58–60; see also Schofield, "Access to Credit," 115 (finding most debts involved substantially less than 5 shillings). The highest median debt in Briggs's midland villages was 3 shillings. The range in the percentage of debts for sums less than one shilling began at 23.5 percent in Willingham and topped out at 41.6 percent at Balsham. Briggs, *Credit and Village Society*, 59. For the size of debts in Briggs's more detailed study, see Briggs, "Credit and the Peasant Household Economy," 241–242, finding a median at 48d. for peasants of a middling income, and 12d. for peasants with smaller income. The range of debts ran from 1.75d. to 52 shillings. The larger numbers probably represent loans rather than consumption credit.

[55] Briggs, *Credit and Village Society*, 58, 60. In Briggs's assessment, there is not enough data on European rural credit to get clear comparisons on size of debts. See Briggs, *Credit and Village Society*, 57, n. 71.

[56] Sales credit composed 46.6 percent of all debt disputes. Clark, "Medieval Vill," 253–261. Neither Kowaleski nor Briggs found many cases expressly involving advances of purchase price, and other scholars consider it uncommon. Compare Kowaleski, *Local Markets*, 203, 208 (distinguishing cases for detinue, which Clark may be considering with debt cases); Briggs, *Credit and Village Society*, 38–40 (also considering possible purchase price advances within unidentified debts). As for the size of debts, Briggs helpfully reproduces Clark's numbers, which show almost 50 percent of all pleas (including loans, which would drive amounts up) to fall in the lowest size category she computed (in Norfolk, 3d.–4s. 11d; in Essex, 1d.–5s.). Briggs, *Credit and Village Society*, 59–61.

[57] Clark, "Medieval Vill," 256.

As Clark's narrative reveals, this was a world of exchange not autarky. Moreover, it was a world assessed and ultimately payable in units of account; Clark, after all, is portraying the network of credit that appeared in suits for money. Medieval English were massaging liquidity out of their limited system by using credit.

In that effort, people improvised far beyond sales credit. The deals they made to get around the awkwardness or overload of money could easily include deferred payments for services or wages. Both at 15th century Writtle in Essex and in the 14th century midland villages studied by Briggs, those categories made up the most common categories of dispute after sales credits. Town-dwellers operated similarly, routinely extending credit to renters and to those paying for services.[58] While some advances undoubtedly went to cover a debtor's outright need, others surely went to facilitate the flow of silver.

By contrast, cash loans made up a much smaller proportion of debt disputes in local courts. Rural folk landed in court over such disputes at a low rate in the 14th century (4.5 percent in one study of the midland villages), and only slightly more often in 15th century Writtle (8.8 percent).[59] In town, cash loans were also less common (7 percent of cases), although other cases that correspond with borrowing in larger amounts—suits on bonds and against those who pledged to back another's debt—show up there as well; Exeter was clearly a commercial hub compared with the villages. The total even with those disputes, however, made up less than a fifth of the litigation in town. They did tend to involve bigger amounts, a pattern suggesting that they represented borrowing and lending for investment rather than consumption. Other investment loans were being litigated at the common law level, where cases over the 40-shilling jurisdictional threshold went. Those cases occupied the wealthier mercantile class.[60]

The daily life of most people, in comparison, was concerned with claims over sales and leases, labor and rents. The kind of credit they were using set them apart from their European counterparts, who made loans in cash or kind much more

[58] Clark, "Medieval Vill," 254 (23 percent of debt litigation involved service and labor). For the midland story, see Briggs, *Credit and Village Society*, 30–40 (finding same category as "next most significant" after disputes about deferred payments for sales, rates varying from 5.5 to 14.2 percent). For the urban scene, see Kowaleski, *Local Markets*, 203. Rent and service credit were the next largest categories in the Exeter courts after sales credits (12 percent and 10 percent respectively of all debt litigation), and most such disputes were over small amounts (71 percent and 60 percent respectively concerned less than 5 shillings). Kowaleski, *Local Markets*, 203.

[59] The percentage of Briggs's midland villages captures the average of those cases involving expressly identifiable cash loans. As Briggs points out, other deals could have been structured to produce cash advances. See Briggs, *Credit and Village Society*, 34, 38–40. Loans contributed 8.8 percent of the debt disputes at Writtle. They were not for larger amounts, as least not as Clark broke out her evidence, but actually occur over lower amounts in somewhat greater numbers than all pleas generally. Clark, "Medieval Vill," 254; see also Briggs, *Credit and Village Society*, 59 (Table 2.5).

[60] In Exeter, only 35 percent of cash loans (themselves only 7 percent of all disputes) were for less than 5 shillings. For this and the breakdown on cases made with pledges or on bond, see Kowaleski, *Local Markets*, 203. For common law litigation, see, e.g., Kowaleski, *Local Markets*, 213–214, 281.

commonly and relied less heavily on the "day-to-day" credit that lessened denominational demands and speeded the circulation of silver in England.[61]

English credit below the mercantile level was distinctive in a second way. While middlemen and specialists acted as lenders in Europe, "most credit received in English villages flowed from one villager to another." "This was, overwhelmingly, peasant credit," Chris Briggs writes about the credit relations captured in the manor courts. He states more generally the consensus among scholars of medieval credit in England. As Clark described the practice in the late medieval vill of Writtle, "[a] man simultaneously could be the creditor to one neighbor for a loan, the debtor of a second for the use of a plow, and to a third send his son or daughter as a servant." In Exeter likewise, neighbors lent to neighbors: even the poorest echelon of Exeter householders appeared frequently as both creditors and debtors. Neither gilds nor churches played a significant part in lending, nor do landlords appear to have been important creditors, at least among those living on their manors.[62] What Briggs calls "peasant credit" met perfectly the end of extending liquidity and making change. This was lending between those who were involved in everyday exchange, a relation that linked neighbors, not tenants with manor lords or peasants with gilds.

Scholars on English credit have diverged somewhat more about whether local credit was hierarchically organized as opposed to traveling between equals.[63] But the problems created by money's limits suggest that both forms of credit would most likely be present, one operating to allow people to make deals with those richer than they were, another operating to allow them to make deals with those similarly situated. "Commercial ties ran horizontally, and they ran vertically, throughout the vill's debt structure," writes Clark of her networked creditors and debtors. "Each transaction aligned [a man] differently with his fellows. Each transaction involved him in a credit relationship capable of facilitating additional exchanges." It was credit that worked across the differences to "expedite the material flow," and people participated with various levels of power and resources.[64]

In Exeter, for example, the wealthy were disproportionately likely, for their numbers, to be creditors and disproportionately unlikely to be debtors. As householders declined in rank and affluence, those numbers reversed; the bottom 81 percent of householders were more likely to be debtors than more powerful players by a margin of 24 percent. Having said that, 54 percent of those less

[61] See Briggs, *Credit and Village Society*, 41–42; Spufford, *Money and Its Use*, 336–337.

[62] Briggs, *Credit and Village Society*, 40, 105–106; Clark, "Medieval Vill," 270; Kowaleski, *Local Markets*, 108, 204–205 (Table 3.5); see also Briggs, "Credit and the Peasant Household Economy," 232, 244.

[63] Compare, e.g., Briggs, "Credit and the Peasant Household Economy," with Schofield, "Dearth, Debt and the Local Land Market in a Late Thirteenth-Century Village Community," and Phillipp R. Schofield, "The Social Economy of the Medieval Village in the Early Fourteenth Century," *Economic History Review* 61, no. 1 (2008).

[64] Clark, "Medieval Vill," 270.

endowed householders were, nonetheless, creditors. They were, in other words, commonly making (as well as taking) advances from each other. Likewise, "oligarchic" creditors were slightly overrepresented as creditors in sales cases and quite a bit less likely to be debtors in such transactions. After all, they had more goods to sell and the wherewithal to make advances, while needing fewer outlays themselves. But again, sales credits were passing back and forth at a high rate both at the bottom and the top of society: half of less affluent householders (those in the lower 88 percent of town by income and influence) were debtors, but so were *a full quarter* of householders at the top (those in the upper 6 percent of town by income and influence). The English were endlessly lending to each other, within wealth strata as well as between them.[65]

In the rural areas, lending occurred both vertically—richer to poorer—and horizontally—between neighbors of approximately equal resources. In the medieval countryside, richer landowners and peasants provided the larger loans to their neighbors. In locales like late 13th century Hinterclay, people acted as creditors or debtors but not both, nor did the poorest villagers claim enough credit to appear in the court roll at all. In the records of another manor during the first half of the 14th century, substantial peasants lent to middling peasants the majority of the time, even for fairly small amounts. A similar pattern held in the next century, when larger cultivators acted as creditors in almost a third of Writtle's debt transactions. Regularly, vertical credit reached beyond the village: richer peasants took credit from outsiders. Those relationships went beyond borrowing around the limits on liquidity and offered them access to money for investment.[66]

At the same time, credit relations for smaller sums thickly filled the space between even modest neighbors, a kind of horizontal hatching that distinguished England's tradition of local lending. Phillipp Schofield describes the practice around Downham manor in the early 14th century. While larger peasants borrowed from beyond the village, a middling group of inhabitants regularly extended smaller amounts of credit to each other. They also made advances to a less wealthy group, peasants who appear less often and at the smallest level of pleas, answering to their somewhat larger creditors from the middling group. At Oakington at mid-century, many middling households that appeared as debtors in one dispute show up as creditors in another: "a substantial proportion of credit ties involving middle peasants linked them with other households, of roughly equal economic status, resident in their own villages." At Writtle manor in the

---

[65] Kowaleski, *Local Markets*, 102–103, 108, 112. For examples of the credit relations between peer professionals, see Kowaleski, *Local Markets*, 204–205.

[66] Schofield, "Access to Credit," 110–119; Briggs, "Credit and the Peasant Household Economy," 245; Clark, "Medieval Vill," 262. Kowaleski also finds that wealthier townspeople borrowed at times from lenders from far beyond Exeter for larger sums. Kowaleski, *Local Markets*, 287 (Table 7.3), 288–293.

next century, Clark found that 12 percent of disputes over outright loans involved partners at the same level of wealth, who loaned back and forth reciprocally to each other, mixing goods and cash. Several strata of lending occurred at the village level, then, with credit frequently moving between peers as well as up and down between the layers.[67]

In England, as on the Continent, credit was an important part of medieval life. English patterns of lending and borrowing diverged in distinctive ways, however, from those in Europe. First, people made many deals on credit to allow consumption, even at higher reaches of society. Second, those deals did not involve middlemen or specialists; this was lending that occurred in mid-stream, as it were, at the local level as buying and selling were underway. Credit often extended from wealthier member of communities to less advantaged people. But third and also particular to English credit patterns, everyday lending linked people horizontally as well as vertically. When they borrowed from neighbors who held similar amounts of wealth, people were not importing resources into the community to invest. Often, they were working across barriers posed by coins that were both awkward and unavailable.

Reconsidering the claims of English credit

Much of the literature on credit assumes that it arises from a pair of possibilities. Borrowers may seek credit to compensate for a shortfall in resources. That shortfall may be severe, forcing an individual to borrow wealth to survive. Alternatively, borrowers may seek credit because of an opportunity for greater productivity that cash would make possible. As Briggs draws the dichotomy, it runs from "exigency credit," the kind of credit taken on when a household "needed to borrow simply to maintain their basic production or consumption" to "investment credit," the kind of credit taken to expand resources and "motivated by a drive to maximize income or consumption."[68]

Assuming that dichotomy, one scholarly school approaches credit as a desperate measure when used by modest or poor households. M. M. Postan's work on pre-plague England informs this interpretative trend; his focus arguably casts credit in neo-Malthusian terms. Progressive and Marxist social histories reinforce a background skepticism about the likelihood that a device like credit, so capable of extracting resources, will operate to positive ends. Read in this light, the frequency of consumption loans suggests that people used credit in times of dearth; the lack of specialized lenders implies weak institutions that would fail in

---

[67] Schofield, "Access to Credit," 114, 117–118; Briggs, "Credit and the Peasant Household Economy," 143; Clark, "Medieval Vill," 265; see also Briggs, "The Availability of Credit in the English Countryside, 1400–1480," 7.

[68] Briggs, *Credit and Village Society*, 43.

crisis; and the dependence of poorer peasants on advances bodes their doom when harvests are poor.[69]

Another group rejects the earlier view as unduly pessimistic. Influenced by a surge of recent studies on credit in early modern Europe and England, this newer approach is informed by institutional economics and its emphasis on the potential of market mechanisms to reduce costs for many actors; it draws as well on social history and its appreciation for the power of communal networks. Read in this revisionist light, the prevalence of credit at all levels of English society and in normal times suggests that it was a productive device rather than a hedge against exigency; the breadth and non-specialized character of lenders indicates that credit practice was resilient and, insofar as it occurred horizontally, not extractive; and the involvement of poorer peasants signals their access to channels of economic development. If the older paradigm was skeptical about the beneficence of credit, the revisionist approach gives it a more affirmative role, offering social networks that reduce transaction costs and, in that moment, reconciling social historians to economists.[70]

Recognizing that credit in England took its peculiar shape to answer daily money problems reframes the existing debate. Insofar as the English improvised credit to get more mileage out of an ill-designed medium, they were seeking liquidity rather than an advance for its own sake. In other words, credit may not map onto the spectrum scholars assume, from a means of obtaining an essential resource to a way to "maximize income." If that is right, then the potential it held as well as the dangers it entailed look rather different.[71]

Reconnecting the kind of credit people used to the character of the money they had reveals that credit "worked," as many revisionist authors claim. Credit operated to ameliorate difficult conditions, in particular, the inadequacy of the medieval English medium. At the same time, the new approach throws credit's success into light as a rescue. Credit compensated to a significant extent for impotencies in the design of cash, especially at the bottom of English society. Insofar as those impotencies could have been cured, what we might call "liquidity credit" remedied a gratuitous hardship. And as with any remedy, there were side effects. Credit was not a simple trade for money, one medium for another. When they used liquidity credit instead of money, the early English entered a world of promises that had to be arbitered and made commitments that were ultimately tied to money. Those circumstances brought significant dangers.

---

[69] M. M. Postan, *Medieval Trade and Finance* (Cambridge: Cambridge University Press, 1973); Briggs, *Credit and Village Society*, 7–9 (reviewing historiography).

[70] See generally Briggs, *Credit and Village Society*, 3–7. For the influence of institutional economics, see North and Thomas, as cited in Kowaleski, *Local Markets*, 179. Compare the European studies, Hoffman, Postel-Vinay, and Rosenthal, *Priceless Markets: The Political Economy of Credit in Paris, 1660–1870*; Thomas Brennan, "Peasants and Debt in Eighteenth-Century Champagne," *Journal of Interdisciplinary History* 37, no. 2 (2006).

[71] Briggs, *Credit and Village Society*, 43.

To take the achievements of liquidity credit first, they were in fact significant. As Elaine Clark wrote about the evidence she gathered at Writtle, it indicated "the diversity of the commercial exchanges that were facilitated by the use of credit... the range and complexity of the economic arrangements that enabled villagers with limited amounts of cash at their disposal to engage in trade." From the manor court rolls, Clark pulled a tapestry of trade—the villagers she caught selling casks on credit, buying wood and roofing cottages on contract, receiving cloth in return for a garment and getting perhaps a little small change from the deal. There were butchers conveying pelts to glovers and meat to customers "already in their debt for loans of cash and the purchase of animals." Butter and cheese, Clark noted, "regularly changed hands on a credit basis among herdsmen, poulterers and dairymen."[72]

In an effort to convey how thickly credit passed back and forth at Writtle, Clark diagrammed the outstanding obligations of a subset of villagers, those who appeared as both creditors and debtors during a single year. See Fig. 5.1. The diagram is a small patch of the interaction she drew narratively, striking in the diversity and overlap of its weave. It captures transactions involving sales, unless expressly noted to the contrary, and underscores the richness of the village exchange that credit made possible.

Briggs, finding similar depth in the midland villages, suggests that the system may have obviated somewhat the demand for cash loans: "There would have been relatively little need for loans if without them villagers could still acquire on credit the commodities they wished to buy."[73] The line between consumption credit and larger loans was not so clear after all; borrowers surely crossed it at times and benefitted from the resources they could claim. Briggs also scrutinized the extension of credit in five villages in order to determine whether it was withdrawn during times of dearth, high mortality (particularly the plague years), or monetary contraction. While his results varied significantly by locale, credit was remarkably resilient in many years.[74]

As Maryanne Kowaleski points out, the credit extended in Exeter promoted "the flow of trade by spreading risk and reducing the cost of using the market." The availability of credit lowered negotiation costs in particular—the obstacles that buyers and sellers would otherwise encounter when they had to agree about "quality, amount, and price of good, as well as time and place of exchange and of payment." As Kowaleski argues, the resilience of credit might have protected

---

[72] Clark, "Medieval Vill," 256, 258. As the debt studies reveal, the very poorest English did not participate in the day-to-day credit that makes its way onto the court rolls. Rather, that credit correlates with economic activity. See, e.g., Clark, "Medieval Vill," 267.

[73] Briggs, *Credit and Village Society*, 63.

[74] Briggs, *Credit and Village Society*, 176–213. As Briggs notes, it is difficult to distinguish robust court activity due to creditors calling in credit from robust court activity due to their confident supply or expansion of credit. His method differentiated the two by tracking cases that should have reflected loan transactions initiated (not just called in) during hard times. See Briggs, *Credit and Village Society*, 178–187.

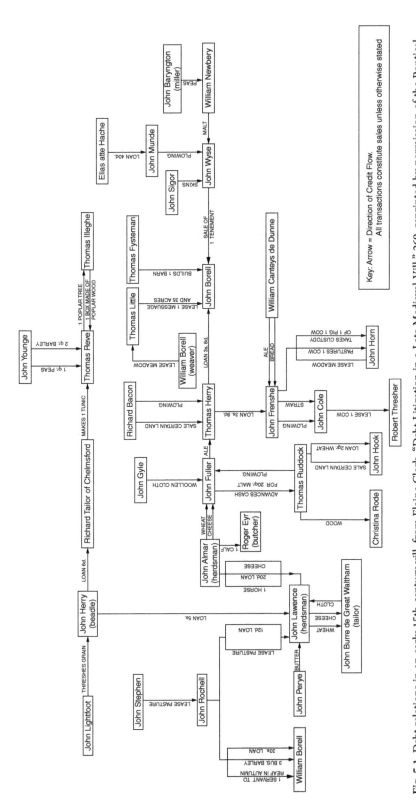

Fig. 5.1 Debt relations in an early 15th century vill, from Elaine Clark, "Debt Litigation in a Late Medieval Vill," 269, reprinted by permission of the Pontical Institute of Medieval Studies.

economic activity in Exeter, although high litigation rates could also indicate the beginning of the bullion famine there.[75]

Granted the accomplishments of liquidity credit, its ingenuity aimed at a problem created by the design of English money. The remedy brought profound costs and risks that cursed most severely those with low incomes, those who were most dependent on silver denominations and least able to hold onto the penny. In the end, and across horizontal relations as well as vertical advances, the need for credit operated systematically to their detriment.

First, credit could not replicate the cash qualities of money. As a currency, money was (and is) effectively "pre-approved." Community demand for money guaranteed that it had value, independent of the relationship of the two immediate participants to an exchange. The collective orchestration of value in money, in other words, secured a transfer of value. Parties with money could make a deal, pay, and call themselves quit of obligation as far as the fact of payment was concerned. By contrast, liquidity credit relied on a bilateral commitment to the effect that value in the form of cash (or, occasionally, goods) would change hands in the future. While that agreement could be enforced communally, that very enforcement method was immensely burdensome. The English courts may have been good[76]—but they weren't *that* good: while those with money could make discrete and effective transfers of value instantly, those using private credit could not. Instead, they opened themselves to the lawsuits that often enforced the transfers of value initially made by personal agreement.

The politics of the point is worth emphasizing: neither money nor bipolar credit operated outside of the collective constitution of medieval society. When people could not use a society's money because of its awkwardness or unavailability, they were knocked out of the form, cash, that had been established and certified by the community as a mode of final payment. As a result, they were more dependent on the liquidity offered by a personal credit relationship, and more likely to take it. That personal credit relationship could also be adjudicated by the community—but its vetting occurred in ways that lay heavier on the immediate parties involved.

Most conspicuously, parties to personal credit litigated when they had disputes. The litigation rates used above to document how many people used credit day to day return in full force here. That 80 percent of taxpayers in Exeter would go to court during a ten-year period, or that 33–60 percent of peasants in a

---

[75] Kowaleski, *Local Markets*, 202, 179. Prices were dropping rapidly across much of England during the decade of Kowaleski's study (1377–1388). Mayhew, "Prices in England," 5. As deflation increased the value of money, creditors had more reason to call in their debts. If they did so in Exeter, the rising rate of debt litigation may have occurred because outstanding credit was being brought in, rather than because new credit was being extended. For the argument and historical evidence that creditors may sue at higher rates when prices are dropping, see Claire Priest, "Currency Policies and Legal Development in Colonial New England," *Yale Law Journal* 110, no. 8 (2001).

[76] See Briggs, "Credit and the Peasant Household Economy," 247–248.

midland village would make the same trip over similar time spans during the century, or that 46.2 percent of rural inhabitants would appear as defendant debtors in the decade before the plague—these are arresting figures. Likewise, Clark's tapestry of exchange in Writtle seems less romantic when we remember that it was drawn from the record of debt *disputes*. As she put it just after describing the long-running reciprocal pattern of loans, "Both parties balanced contributions and receipts but if these, for any reason, ceased to be mutually beneficial, then people resorted to court action, to suits and to counter suits."[77]

It is difficult to compare the impact of litigation across different contexts. The expenses of suit, accessibility to the courts, and cultural valences of litigation all can make for very different experiences.[78] But litigation is rarely positive, pleasant, or communally constructive.[79] The high rates of medieval litigation suggest that liquidity credit had deeply destructive side effects.

In terms of cost alone, litigation over debt disputes cut into the small budgets of many city and country folk. Plaintiffs did not pay local courts when they initiated a suit, but officials levied amercements—fines—on losing parties. In local courts, those charges would be 2 to 3 pennies. Authorities also responded to pleas by coercing defendants to appear, either through drafting "pledges" (individuals who would be liable for an absconding party) or by seizing a defendant's goods. The courts' processes spun out other costs as well. For example, pleas acknowledging a debt amounted to 2 pence in urban and rural courts.[80]

Other costs came in time and trouble; a defendant would have to round up and produce compurgators to support an oath that money was not owed. As Edward Purcell has shown for a very different era, distance from court alone could sort parties into winners or losers, harshly disadvantaging parties who had to travel and driving them to drop claims or defenses. A fair number of litigants (37 percent) in the Exeter courts came from beyond "walking distance," or about six miles. But the journey would have mattered even for many locals; in Devon, a later observer put it, "even five miles seems tantamount to a pilgrimage." Finally, local courts assimilated the biases of their members. Those in Exeter systematically favored the "oligarchy," whether as creditors or debtors. Manor courts may have leaned the same way, or transmitted more random animosities that were

---

[77] Clark, "Medieval Vill," 265.

[78] When litigation escalated in the early modern world, it reflected a population in deep distress and a countryside in crisis—western Massachusetts, for example, at the time of Shays' Rebellion, or the struggle over tax policies in 1780s Pennsylvania. See Claire Priest, "Colonial Courts and Secured Credit: Early American Commercial Litigation and Shays' Rebellion," *Yale Law Journal* 108, no. 8 (1999); Priest, "Currency Policies"; Terry Bouton, *Taming Democracy: "The People," The Founders, and the Troubled Ending of the American Revolution* (Oxford: Oxford University Press, 2007), 145–167.

[79] As Dickens famously put it, "Suffer any wrong that can be done you rather than come [to the courts of Chancery]." Charles Dickens, *Bleak House*, 7 (New York: Norton ed., 1977).

[80] See Briggs, *Credit and Village Society*, 13–14; Kowaleski, *Local Markets*, 216–218; Clark, "Medieval Vill," 253.

just as damaging.[81] If, as Kowaleski points out, litigants regularly settled in order to avoid suit, they were more likely assessing the burdens that litigation brought than embracing a happy resolution.[82]

The strife and bitterness that came along with lawsuits are only part of the story. Those day-to-day arrangements, the "very simple credit" that "would never have found its way into the court rolls at all", brought its own insidious bite.[83] As Phillipp Schofield points out, collisions over everyday debts, small loans, and informal advances regularly soured the relations between kin, neighbors, and acquaintances. If their debts did not bring them into court directly, they sometimes ended up there anyway, answering to the illegal seizures, housebreakings, and petty assaults that sully the records and ruin any chance of a more romantic (or neoclassical) interpretation.

Schofield recounts an example, one that did show up on the court records, of the feud-like relations he found endemic to village life. In it, two families harassed each other across a series of encounters. It started with a suit for debt by a Bernard against a Passelewe. Another Passelewe—perhaps a brother—burned down the house of a different Bernard. That newcomer Bernard succeeded in having the lord seize the arsonist's goods and later sued the first brother for defamation. That brother, himself the original Passelewe defendant, then sued two different members of the Bernard family for debt. These final suits came in 1321, a time of "real hardship in the countryside." This was feud and litigation, feud as litigation, in all its destructive force.[84]

The last twist in the Bernard–Passelewe story suggests a third characteristic of liquidity credit made it dangerous, beyond the costs and strife that came with conflict. Unlike other kinds of credit, liquidity credit was brokered on an internal contradiction. It was extended specifically to compensate for a shortfall in liquidity, but it remained tied to money's terms. The tension structured vulnerability into the relationship of creditor and debtor. For example, a creditor could call in any debts that were due at moments when money might be scant. The final Passelewe suits came in 1321, a harvest year so poor that prices for wheat rose higher than they had been in the previous half-century. The timing of the suits was itself part of the feud that tore at the villagers' well-being.[85]

The irony of liquidity credit—the fact that a device designed to cover for liquidity's weakness remained tied to the very resource that was inadequate—extended as far as creditors required cash payments. If creditors were willing to

---

[81] See Edward A. Purcell, *Litigation and Inequality: Federal Diversity Jurisdiction in Industrial America, 1870–1958* (New York: Oxford University Press, 1992), 28–48; Kowaleski, *Local Markets*, 113–114, 286 (Table 7.2). The quote is from a 19th century man, in Kowaleski, *Local Markets*, 285.

[82] Kowaleski, *Local Markets*, 218.

[83] Schofield, "Access to Credit," 114.

[84] Schofield, "Access to Credit," 116. For examples involving very petty debts, including one halfpenny, see Schofield, "Access to Credit," 118.

[85] For grain prices in 1321, see Schofield, "The Medieval Village," 44 (Figure 1).

settle for payment in some other way, their advances could lubricate exchange without exploiting the deficiencies of medieval money. How harshly the backlash of liquidity credit cut, then, depended on how many debt disputes demanded money payments. Rates at which litigated credit disputes required money settlements were fairly high in the early 14th century and rose over its course. In the midland villages that Chris Briggs studied, money was due from about 60 percent of the time at the low end (Oakington, 1291–1350) to 86 percent of the time at the high end (Willingham, 1377–1400). Across the century, they were due an average of almost 73 percent of the time. That rate apparently increased in the 15th century: in the midland village of Oakingham, about 83 percent of disputes were adjudicated for money, and suits in Clark's vill were overwhelmingly denominated in money. According to Chris Briggs, "as far as one can determine, the debts expressed in money were expected to have been discharged with actual coin."[86]

This third danger—the vulnerability of debtors who lacked liquidity to demands for money repayment—could arise in any number of everyday circumstances. There was the danger that payment would be called in at times particularly parched of currency. The scholars on medieval debts split on the question whether most debts had specific due dates. It seems likely that many of the informal and ongoing relations that backed most sales and service credits engendered a kind of open-ended credit.[87] If so, debtors would have little protection if credit were called in when coins were low; court costs alone could be disabling at such times. Even if debts had fixed due dates, uncollected debts remained available to be called in at later times on demand of a creditor. That would expose a debtor to a vindictive demand for payment, as the Bernard–Passelewe example suggests, at times when taxes lay especially heavy, crops had not come in yet, or the harvest had been poor.

But a demand for repayment could be just as damaging and perhaps just as embittering, if it were made by a creditor him- or herself in need of funds. As Clark described much of credit-based trade, "[a] man sold a quarter of wheat, extended a loan, or let a croft of land to one of his neighbors, then demanded

---

[86] Briggs, *Credit and Village Society*, 32; Clark, "Medieval Vill," 254 (separately identifying 2.3 percent chattel loans); Briggs, "The Availability of Credit in the English Countryside, 1400–1480," 5–6.

[87] Both Clark and Marjorie Keniston McIntosh adopt this view, which comports with their sense that much litigation arose out of ongoing credit relations, including running tabs. Clark, "Medieval Vill," 270–271; Briggs, *Credit and Village Society*, 69 (reviewing their argument). Clark finds that about 20 percent of cases (195 cases of 948 prosecutions) were explicitly due "when requested." It appears that about 11 percent of cases specified a due date for debts (101, assuming total of 948). Chris Briggs, by contrast, argues that most credit was fixed term. About 6 percent (71 cases of 1,206 cases studied) of his cases specify due dates as compared with one case that notes payment due "when [the plaintiff] shall request it" (Briggs, *Credit and Village Society*, 69). That interpretation fits with his assumption that debt disputes represented discrete and "self-contained" entities. Briggs, *Credit and Village Society*, 30–31, 70. Much depends, in the latter interpretation, on the assumption that the small number of cases indicating either practice correctly reflects the dominant pattern. The length of time between the extension of credit and the initiation of court action is unknown for most village debt litigation. See Briggs, *Credit and Village Society*, 178. For some hypotheses, see Clark, "Medieval Vill," 251; Briggs, *Credit and Village Society*, 180, 187.

payment only when he himself needed ready money." The death of her husband prompted a woman called Amicia to call in debts from seven villagers. The debts were worth a grand total of 2s. 1d., or about 3½ pennies per person, but she may have needed the money as she tried to rebalance the household without her husband.[88]

Those times were often periods of hardship or crisis more generally. For example, in the last decade of the 13th century, heavy lay subsidies coincided with bad harvests. Whether they sued vindictively or out of need, creditors came to court at rates that far exceeded earlier periods. At the manor studied by Phillipp Schofield, the number of private pleas brought in the six years from 1293 to 1299 more than doubled compared with an earlier period of similar length (1277–1284), and the cases taken to conclusion more than tripled.[89] Chris Briggs has also identified rates of litigation in a set of manor courts with dearth years between 1290 and 1331, and between 1349 and 1399. Although they varied considerably by locale, they were significant for several hard years.[90] While it is impossible to know how much of the credit caught in the Schofield and Briggs studies was extended because of liquidity problems rather than other reasons, surely some of it was; debtors were to that extent exposed to suit at a time of great dearth, simply because of England's difficult medium.

Here, an observation about the success rates of plaintiffs and defendants may be relevant. Plaintiffs in debt cases won an overwhelming percentage of the time; defendants often acknowledged their obligation instead of contesting it, and paid a fine to the court for its trouble.[91] The pattern makes sense if credit was routinely extended to cover for money's shortfall. Just as much, it suggests a world in which people found it as difficult to pay their debts as it was impossible to deny them.

---

[88] Clark, "Medieval Vill," 271; Schofield, "Access to Credit," 118; John Robert Maddicott, "The English Peasantry and the Demands of the Crown 1294–1341," *Past & Present*, Supplement 1 (1975), 58, 62–64. For an example of a creditor owed a significant sum but likely suing only as he needed portions of it, see Clark, "Medieval Vill," 278, n. 84.

[89] Private pleas increased to 35 from 16; cases taken to conclusion increased to 31 from 9. Schofield, "Dearth, Debt and the Local Land Market in a Late Thirteenth-Century Village Community," 13. Schofield also notes that recoveries of debt (including outright plaintiff victories and "licencia concordandi") spiked, rather than "recognizances" or acknowledgements of debt obligation. The former probably reflect old credit that was being called in, the latter reflect new credit being extended. In other words, the increase in litigation suggests that credit was contracting, not expanding.

[90] Briggs, *Credit and Village Society*, 188–193, 205–207. Briggs's goal was to track the provision of credit during hard times; the presence of debt plaints thus bespoke a resiliency of credit supply.

[91] Plaintiffs prevailed unambiguously in the 15th century 60 percent of the time, including 17 percent acknowledgement of debt by the defendant ("licencia concordandi"). Clark, "Medieval Vill," 252. In another 20 percent of cases, the plaintiff declined to prosecute; Clark believes that many of those cases lapsed because a defendant had agreed to pay. Clark, "Medieval Vill," 253. Plaintiffs did, however, have a fine to pay in that instance, so some cases may represent times that plaintiffs anticipated losing. The analogous numbers in Exeter during the 14th century were plaintiff victories 55.3 percent, including 17.8 "licence of concord," and 36.7 percent failure to prosecute. Kowaleski, *Local Markets*, 218. In the half-century before the plague, an astonishing 26.2 percent of defendants simply acknowledged rather than contested their debt, and that undercounts by leaving aside cases on ambiguous subjects: Briggs, "Credit and the Peasant Household Economy," 247.

Perhaps most frequently in the hard scrabble world of much medieval life, the line between extraction and justified demand was not so clear. Credit sales, Clark concluded elsewhere, allowed a neighbor to help another in need. But while subsequent transactions "could work to the advantage of any debtor, [that] did not preclude a creditor from exploiting a customer's need by turning a profit from the bargain."[92] The English countryside, like much of Europe, filled up with coin after harvest time, as peasants sold produce. It emptied of money a few weeks later: many debts were due in September, as were major rent payments.[93] (A disproportionate number of debts were also incurred in September, perhaps with the seasonal surge in economic activity.) The pattern meant that many English paid their obligations when they were most flush with coin. By the same token, "the city sucked the countryside dry again of the cash that it had sent out."[94] Rural folk went without much coin from harvest to harvest. That long annual ebb would have given sellers an advantage over buyers short of cash funds for much of the year.

In these circumstances, creditors could strategize according to the availability of currency in addition to and independent of the need a potential debtor might have for resources (a factor which also would have fluctuated with the seasons). Those selling on credit or paying in advance at moments when coin was scant— the summer, for example—could drive a bargain better by that margin. At times, that benefit surely rewarded hard work and sacrifice; at the other times, it simply reflected the leverage that superior resources made out of the grinding inadequacy of coin. Clark describes long-running relationships of debt—the way peasants without plow animals took an advance of help preparing the land, and then came back again and again for other kinds of credit. Easy credit was useful, but also operated "like a decoy." "It pulled these villagers into debt and it kept them dependent."[95] In other words, the unwieldy medium of the English effectively added a burden to those most handicapped by it, whether by increasing their vulnerability to the timing of suit or affecting bargaining power over prices because they had credit not coin.

The non-productive nature of much English credit—the fact that people used credit, made in terms of money, because of currency problems as opposed to calculations about wealth more generally—also would have exacerbated the dangers that conventionally came along with credit. Much everyday credit between neighbors likely passed back and forth without interest added. In fact, the prevalence of consumption credit in early Europe may have motivated the

---

[92] Clark, "Medieval Vill," 261, 271.
[93] See Clark, "Medieval Vill," 267–268, 278, n. 76; Spufford, *Money and Its Use*, 382–385.
[94] Spufford, *Money and Its Use*, 385.
[95] Clark, "Medieval Vill," 257, 260–262, 266–268, 270–271. For example, 21 out of 32 debts for animal care involved debtors who had already established a relationship with the creditor, and charges for the service were significant. Clark, "Medieval Vill," 262.

condemnation of interest as usury. But despite that prohibition, some deals surely included hidden interest charges—setting the very trap that animated usury prohibitions. Sellers could raise their prices for deferred payment, while buyers could lower their offers when they paid for a good in a cash advance.[96] But interest charges would, of course, increase the ultimate demand for cash per se, placed on a borrower when time for repayment came due. The fix for a cash handicap, in other words, sometimes came with an additional charge (interest), payable in the very medium that was scant.

Compounding the dangers of credit used to expand liquidity in everyday life was its very accessibility. Insofar as monetary problems engendered a practice of credit that was truly day to day, they habituated people to living on prospect. For the many English who were creditors and debtors, active spinners in the thick web of reciprocal exchange, the experience of giving credit may have countered the temptation of taking it. But for others, especially those living through times of great dearth, sickness, and poverty, the ubiquity of credit must have added to the danger that they would take on too many obligations to repay, in precisely the medium that was so scarce.

Oppressive litigation, strife, and the paradox that liquidity credit would make people all the more vulnerable to currency's shortfall—these dangers attended English credit in normal times. But a last danger attached in the periods when the money supply contracted. In those periods, liquidity credit injected unnecessary risk into the medieval English world with particular brutality. When the amount of money that circulated per capita dropped, credit could also be suddenly withdrawn. That volatility worsened the distress brought by monetary crises.

The problem reiterates the connection of credit to the money on which it depends. Just as the quality of England's money affected the character of its credit, the *quantity* of money in circulation likely affected the *amount* of credit available. As a 16th century commentator put it, "credit is always most, when there is most Money to satisfy the same." It is no accident that the bloom of credit for the wealthy in the Middle Ages started in Italy, where liquidity was particularly abundant. As for the short periods, an early modern observer had an aphorism for that too, "Where there was but little money, the Credit was also very little." And indeed, mercantile creditors in 14th century England appear to have withdrawn credit when they anticipated that coin supplies would shrink. Likewise as the bullion famines of the late 14th and early 15th century took hold across Europe, large Florentine banking houses failed and the elaborate networks of merchant credit that had quickened medieval trade began to erode.[97] As modeled

---

[96] Spufford notes that usury prohibitions were relaxed in Europe as commercial credit spread in the 14th century: Spufford, *Money and Its Use*, 259–260. For hidden interest charges, see Briggs, *Credit and Village Society*, 74–79; Clark, "Medieval Vill," 256–257; Spufford, *Money and Its Use*, 338.

[97] See Nightingale, "Monetary Contraction"; Briggs, *Credit and Village Society*, 201–202; Spufford, *Money and Its Use*, 347–348, 360; cf. Raymond De Roover, *Early Banking before 1500 and the Development*

by later theorists, credit does not expand the money supply indefinitely because credit comes at a cost. Lenders require payment in money, and the interest charged for their forbearance increases as the money supply shrinks (unless they anticipate a cross-cutting profit from deflation) and as the risk that they will not be repaid rises.[98]

The same dynamic would have endangered small medieval debtors, pressing them to pay in times of falling prices and ever scanter liquidity. The social histories of credit that we have do not always map credit outlays against monetary contractions, but the patterns captured by studies of the decade before the Black Death, the third quarter of the 14th century, and much of the 15th century suggest just the kind of harm that a creditor cutback would bring.[99]

During the decade before the Black Death, silver coin per capita dropped steeply in England. European silver mines had not produced much for decades, nor were merchants able to remedy the worsening situation with new silver, given their poor trade balance with the East. England had just entered war with France; taxes wrung the peasant population of coin; as it was levied, silver was sent out of the country for military expenses. At the same time, England's adversary reverted to radically debasing its currency; France made itself a magnet for silver bullion, diverting it from English mints. According to Martin Allen's calculations, silver currency circulating in England fell precipitously, dropping approximately 55 percent between 1331 and 1351. Prices had been falling since the second decade of the century; after 1330, they slide approximately another 10 percent.[100]

Evidence about credit disputes looks rather different in this context. According to a study at one manor court during the decade, debt litigation rose steeply: creditors brought 39 cases between 1337 and 1349, as compared with 38 cases over the previous 47 years. At first glance, the litigation spike might seem to suggest a great expansion of credit. In fact, the surge probably reflects a concerted demand by creditors to *recover* outstanding debts. There is no data on when the credit in dispute was first extended. However, as money became scant in England, creditors as well as debtors would have needed cash. Moreover, the period's deflation effectively invited creditors to act: as prices fell, the currency owed by debtors was worth more. Research on early America shows that, under such circumstances, creditors called in their debts. Finally, as money supplies fell, creditors had more

of Capitalism (Geneva: Librairie Droz, 1971), 12–13 (emphasizing chronic balance of payments problems in failure of banks). The early modern quotes are from Mayhew, *Sterling*, 38.

[98] N. Gregory Mankiw, *Macroeconomics*, 5th ed. (New York: Worth Publishers, 2003), 271–274.

[99] Chris Briggs's work is a notable exception here. For his careful attempts to identify the contraction of village credit at times of monetary contraction, see Briggs, *Credit and Village Society*, 200–205, 207–210.

[100] See p. 104 n. 119. The decline was from £1.5 to £2.0 million in 1331 to £0.7–£0.9 million in 1351. Allen, "The Volume of the English Currency, 1158–1470," 603. According to the Phelps Brown-Hopkins index, prices dropped 36.7 percent between 1310 and 1340, and 10.1 percent after 1330. The Allen index identifies a price drop of 19.2 percent after 1320, and 9.1 percent after 1330. See Table 1 in N. J. Mayhew, "Prices in England, 1170–1750," *Past & Present* (2013), 5.

reason to fear the risk that debtors would default; especially if usury prohibitions, legal, moral, or cultural, made it difficult to raise interest rates, lenders would tend to retrieve outlays instead.[101]

In a later study, Chris Briggs found more mixed results. Tracking cases that should reflect credit extended within the previous year, he finds a drop-off in litigation from 1325 to 1337 in three towns, followed by continued quiet in some towns into the late 1330s and others where debt litigation continued or increased.[102] For Briggs, the activity was a sign that credit may have continued resilient during scant years. Granted that credit in short times could be extremely valuable, the point here is that credit extended to mitigate monetary shortfall would have become even more difficult to repay over times of monetary crisis.

Studies on both rural manors and Exeter's courts record rising amounts of debt litigation several decades later, during another period of deflation; prices declined from 15 percent to 25 percent between the 1360s and the 1380s. At the same time, England's silver supply was sliding to grievously small amounts of silver coin per capita.[103] Scholars have assumed that both country and town lenders were likely to gauge the state of the coin by gathering information on mint output; the flow of silver from the mints fell radically in the 1360s. While it undulated somewhat over the following decades, it remained at or below 5 percent silver (95 percent gold) until the 1420s, compared with an output of about 30 percent silver at mid-14th century.[104]

The circumstances suggest that creditors, far from expanding credit in the late 14th century, may have increased litigation to draw in outstanding debts. In Exeter, which remained relatively prosperous, the effort may have been mild—litigation rates rose only 10 percent or so.[105] Those increases were more marked, however, in several manor courts. In those pastoral locales, debt litigation increased, then fell off, and remained low even during the second and third decades of the 15th century, when the outflow of silver coin picked up some-what.[106] It seems quite likely that, perhaps after extending credit initially into the

---

[101] See Briggs, "Credit and the Peasant Household Economy," 241, 247; Priest, "Currency Policies." Briggs's study also reveals that the spike in debt litigation concerned suits that were all of somewhat larger value (mean = 47.3d., median = 38.0d.), compared with a half-century of litigation that included a limited number of much larger suits, but many small ones (mean = 92.3d., median = 28.0d.). See Briggs, "Credit and the Peasant Household Economy," 241, 247. That pattern would make sense if creditors were moving selectively to cash in obligations that were worth more. By contrast, it is not clear why hard economic conditions would trigger new credit outlays all lumped at a high end of borrowing.
[102] Briggs, *Credit and Village Society*, 181–182, 202–203.
[103] After the Black Death in 1351, England's money supply stood at approximately 5s.–7s./per capita; it declined to about 1s.–2s. per capita in 1422. See Allen, "The Volume of the English Currency, 1158–1470," 607; Nightingale, "Monetary Contraction," 561–562. For prices, see Table 1 in Mayhew, "Prices in England," 5.
[104] Briggs, "The Availability of Credit in the English Countryside, 1400–1480," 8 (Table 1).
[105] Kowaleski, *Local Markets*, 202 and n. 25.
[106] Briggs, "The Availability of Credit in the English Countryside, 1400–1480," 8 (Table 1), 9; Briggs, *Credit and Village Society*, 209–210. As Briggs notes, the litigation peaks in several towns between 1379 and 1384 could reflect an attempt to extend credit as the coin shortage began to bite. Increased litigation could also, however, have been motivated by the favorable circumstances for recovery that dropping prices

void left by silver coin, lenders drew it in and kept it in, disregarding even the monetary improvement that came in the 15th century. They may have feared that debtors would not repay coin, or that the money supply was still straitened; their aversion would have prolonged the credit constriction.[107]

Given all these circumstances, day-to-day credit in medieval England was a dangerous medium. From its dependence on post hoc enforcement to the exposure it created for debtors left with an ill-suited liquidity, credit differed from money. Moreover, insofar as people borrowed to ease monetary barriers, monetary contractions exposed them to particular hardship. The debt litigation patterns we have reflect the upper level of village credit relations; many smaller disputes never made it so far. But they too would have left those owing liquidity debts vulnerable to the exactions of their creditors. Insofar as England's approach to money pressed people towards credit they would not otherwise have needed, it undermined their daily struggle towards economic stability.

The problems presented by liquidity credit ultimately revise the question about how extractive was England's credit. That elaborate system of local advance clearly aided those using it, allowing them to build rich networks of exchange. But it also taxed them relative to English who could escape the handicaps brought by awkward denominations and overworked small money. Independent of whether wealthier creditors were acting exploitatively, the system appears to have redistributed resources by bluntly burdening those with less cash income.

That group bore the costs of adjudication; fees came from the losers in litigation and went to the state or manor authorities. More elusively, the tensions caused by constant elaborations of credit and debt periodically disrupted village life; the fragility of mutual dependence even when times were good generated enough hardship to qualify the assumption that credit comprised a beneficent communal reciprocity. Those with less access to coin assumed the risk that credit owed (or for that matter, advanced) would destabilize them when it was called in. There are also the indications that the system had a kind of constant, low-level, regressivity: poorer peasants did tend to borrow more from those with more money than vice versa; creditors won most of the time and debtors lost; and in deflationary times, debtors paid in a money that was more valuable than they had borrowed. Finally, constrictions in coin would particularly disadvantage and

---

presented to debtors. At Writtle, the manor studied by Elaine Clark, litigation rates were higher in the late 14th century than they would be after 1425, but they peaked in the first two decades of the 15th century, then declined through the rest of the century. The study does not have a long 14th century baseline; it may be that creditors in that prosperous region were reacting more slowly to monetary contraction, as at Exeter, or that the area was only belatedly affected by them.

[107] As Briggs points out, lenders might also have worried that judicial enforcement of debt obligations was failing; he finds evidence that it was less efficient over the course of the century. Briggs, "The Availability of Credit in the English Countryside, 1400–1480," 13–24.

destabilize populations heavily dependent on credit. People could retreat to barter, but that was a world without the currencies that irrigated exchange.

By contrast, credit operated at the top of English society in a very different way. Its efflorescence occurred in the commercial revolution of the 13th century, a time when the plentiful money supply and escalating scale of demand allowed merchants to build up relations of mutual confidence. During the next century, for example, middlemen in the London Grocers' Company used credit from wool exporters to extend loans to shearers, dyers, and drapers in the countryside, financing their production, which went in turn to the exporters. Grocers took significant profits from the arrangement, sinking them into land and houses.[108] The strategy worked as long as their payments balanced over time; when one party accumulated too large a debt, he would have to settle up in coin. Similarly, royal merchants created arrangements to supply the Crown, advancing resources in return for commitments of revenue. Like extensions of private credit, that business also depended on settlement by clearing debts, sometimes by elaborate means. In those enterprises, English businessmen were not handicapped by their national currency.[109] Its denominations captured effectively the values that they wanted to buy and sell.

When money supplies fell across Europe, contractions of credit put some large merchants out of business; Pamela Nightingale documents the way lending networks disintegrated among the grocers just as they did further down. But if mercantile credit were not immune to disturbances in money, that currency had long operated for investment rather than as a remedy for monetary deficiencies.[110]

In fact, credit relations at higher strata in the English world and in much of Europe operated with great effect at international levels. The middlemen in the London Grocers' Company who procured wool for export fed exchange across borders. Traders there used mutual extensions of credit to reduce the need to move cash. When they needed to settle balances, they drew bills of exchange to transfer value from one location to another. As James Rogers describes it, the bill was also a kind of credit arrangement, one made between parties with offsetting monetary balances. A London wool exporter might build up profits in Antwerp while a Flemish exporter of lace had a surplus in London. To repatriate his funds, the Englishmen need only commit funds to the Flemish party in return for an appropriate amount in England.[111] The exchange could easily come to include

---

[108] Nightingale, "Monetary Contraction," 568–569; Spufford, *Money and Its Use*, 252–260.

[109] See Nadav Orion Peer, "Medieval Clearing: The Royal Court, Merchants, and the Great International Fairs" (draft 2014, on file with author).

[110] Nightingale, "Monetary Contraction."

[111] James Steven Rogers, *The Early History of the Law of Bills and Notes: A Study of the Origins of Anglo-American Commercial Law*, Cambridge Studies in English Legal History Index (Cambridge: Cambridge University Press, 1995), 32–43; see also Raymond De Roover, *Money, Banking and Credit in Medieval*

lending for profit, if the London merchant lent funds to the Flemish exporter to buy lace, export it to London and sell it there. The Flemish exporter would then repay the London merchant in English money.[112] The rich world of mercantile credit thus supported extensive international trade, one that involved both private and public actors.[113]

The point for present purposes is just how effective mercantile credit was. Coin, exchanged at rates determined by bullion content in domestic units of account and adjusted by local demand and supply, remained essential to the deal. England's strong money was not always so propitious for the price of English goods. But it was an accessible and reputable currency for traders, who could use credit to move money rather than compensate for its disadvantages.[114]

* * *

As the English engineered them from the 13th to the 15th centuries, money and credit delivered different opportunities and burdens to people. As for coin, it came in denominations that sorted exchange, leaving those at the bottom without a medium sufficiently fine to reach all exchange easily. As for credit, it developed in response to money's inadequacies; much day-to-day credit in England enabled many deals that would have failed for lack of liquidity, if not wealth. But like money, credit calculated to supply liquidity also sorted exchange. Particularly common on the low end of exchange, that kind of credit concentrated its dangers there, including costs, strife, and the great vulnerability that came when the money supply dropped.

Bruges: Italian Merchant-Bankers, Lombards, and Money-Changers—A Study in the Origins of Banking, The Rise of International Business (London; New York: Routledge/Thoemmes Press, 1999), 49–75.

[112] Medieval bills, fertile in their capacity, were nevertheless not negotiable. See De Roover, *Money, Banking and Credit in Medieval Bruges*, 54.

[113] The medieval mercantile world has a vast literature. See, e.g., De Roover, *Money, Banking and Credit in Medieval Bruges*; Richard K. Marshall, *The Local Merchants of Prato: Small Entrepreneurs in the Late Medieval Economy* (Baltimore: Johns Hopkins University, 1999); Pamela Nightingale, *A Medieval Mercantile Community: The Grocers' Company and the Politics and Trade of London, 1000–1485* (New Haven: Yale University Press, 1995); Marie-Therese Boyer-Xambeu, Ghislain Deleplace, and Lucien Fillard, *Private Money and Public Currencies: The 16th Century Challenge*, trans. Azizeh Azodi (Armonk, NY: M. E. Sharpe, 1994); Abbott Payson Usher, *The Early History of Deposit Banking in Mediterranean Europe* (Cambridge, MA: Harvard University Press, 1967). Although it is beyond the bounds of this book, that complex of trade relations constantly informed the way countries engineered money at home. To take only one example, European sovereigns influenced each other in choosing to make domestic currencies with the same commodity content, and their actions affected the value of silver and gold and the behavior of those holding it. Those metals became the material used to clear complex credit networks, tying those networks to domestic monetary dynamics.

[114] De Roover, *Money, Banking and Credit in Medieval Bruges*, 61–64. Current accounts banking appeared at the same time as international credit and began, like those inventions, in northern Italy where money was most plentiful. As money-changers began taking deposits for safekeeping, they gained the capacity to act as clearinghouses for local merchants, transferring funds between accounts at the order of one party or another. That service eased exchange, although checks were not negotiable. When they lent more than they held, which happened by the 14th century, local banks also expanded the money supply, although the English lagged in developing banking. Spufford, *Money and Its Use*, 256–259; De Roover, *Money Banking and Credit in Medieval Bruges*.

The currencies of the medieval world, both money and credit, were technologies deeply tied to the transactions they undertook. All the more obviously, the history of modernization cannot be cast as if the main action was movement from a bartering to a moneyed world, or even from a world with less money to a world with more. Rather, the medieval experience presented a drama of power, opportunity, and dependence acted out in the forms of money and credit that people made.

6

Priming the pump

The sovereign path towards paying for coin and circulating credit

In English history, the 17th century is famed for constitutional turmoil. It produced the rise of Parliament, a duel between the courts of common law and prerogative, the beheading of one king and the ouster of another, intense religious division and a civil war, the restoration of monarchy, and the Glorious Revolution. With those transformations went another, one thoroughly intertwined with the arrival of what we have come to identify as modernity. The 17th century opened with the money that the English had used since the Middle Ages. People carried metal coin that had been purchased at the mint and they accepted tallies that anticipated revenues due to the government, passing them on or cashing them in. By the end of the century, the English exchanged new forms of currency. Their cash included coin minted free of charge and Bank notes. Their public debt took novel shape in interest-bearing instruments that could be traded easily and impersonally.

The departure that engendered such consequences was the decision by the government to pay monetarily to create liquidity, both by picking up the costs of minting money and by assuming the charge for interest-bearing public bonds circulating for the first time in England. The baseline for the change was the monopoly power the government held to create money. As an early modern court rehearsed the medieval record, only the sovereign could establish "the standard of money coined by his authority within his own dominions." But while "no other person" could make money "without special license or commandment of the king," the sovereign could dispense new licenses, and new latitude, to make money.[1]

Through the medieval period, the sovereign traded the attributes it alone could grant—the definitive identification of a unit of account, control of the money path, the quality of negotiability—in return for popular contribution to the cost of making money—the fee people paid for coin or the interest they forswore when they carried tallies. Under the new approach, the government deployed its power very differently. First, it subsidized the cost of coin from general revenues.

---

[1] *The Case of Mixed Money* (1605) in T. B. Howell, *Cobbett's Complete Collection of State Trials and Proceedings for High Treason and Other Crimes and Misdemeanors from the Earliest Period to the Year 1783*, vol. 2 (London: R. Bagshaw, 1809), 114, 117, 116.

A seemingly small and pragmatic change, it would have large ideological consequences. The quality of liquidity, once subsidized by the government, afterwards
seemed to come for "free." Second, the government added negotiability to
interest-bearing instruments of borrowing that had previously operated only to
represent a debt. After the shift, the instruments themselves contributed a stream
of credit-based currency; circulating bonds could be passed on to new holders.
Credit currency thus allowed money to travel more quickly between people.[2]
That decision, like the earlier one to pick up the cost of coin, promoted the
production of liquidity to a new extent, supporting it with the expenditure of
general revenues instead of exacting individuated contributions in exchange for
each addition to cash or credit.

The story begins on the early side of the century, with the intensification of the
constitutional tumult that would redefine so much. That starting point is expedient, to be sure. To an unfortunate degree, it performs Christopher Hill's
assertion that, in finance, "the Middle Ages ended in 1643." The high monetary
drama that engulfed the late Lancastrian and Tudor monarchies appears here
only as prelude, a trio of stepping stones to reach the early modern stage.[3]

Most famously, the Tudors left their descendants a monument that, by its
ostentatious violation of England's sound money tradition, illuminated that
sound money course as the norm. From 1542 to 1551, Henry VIII and his son
Edward VI radically debased both silver and gold coin. The tactic allowed them to
expand the quantity of coin circulating by skimming off progressively greater
amounts of metal at the mint, coining that, and spending it as if it were money
unchanged in content or quantity. As the weaker money circulated and depreciation began, the mint repeatedly raised its price to attract more metal. At its most
dilute, silver coin was 25 percent fine, down from the traditional sterling standard
(96.5 percent fine). Effected by deception and brute force, the Great Debasement
was transparently a ploy to raise revenues, unlike the gentle depreciations taken
previously in England that aimed to restabilize the money supply.[4] Prices had
begun to rise before 1542, perhaps because more silver was coming to the mints
from the monasteries expropriated of their treasure and because of the war's
inflationary effects. By 1547, prices had risen by 20 percent to 25 percent; with

---

[2] Public bonds offered "near cash" vehicles; in that sense they were another form of liquidity. They can
alternatively be understood as accelerating the rate at which the existing money supply—the unit of
account—circulates. See p. 179 n. 96.

[3] Christopher Hill, as quoted in P. K. O'Brien and P. A. Hunt, "The Rise of a Fiscal State in England,
1485–1815," *Historical Research* LXVI (1993): 151.

[4] C. E. Challis, "Lord Hastings to the Great Silver Recoinage, 1464–1699," in *A New History of the Royal
Mint*, ed. C. E. Challis (Cambridge: Cambridge University Press, 1992), 228–244; Albert Edgar Feavearyear,
The Pound Sterling: A History of English Money, 2nd ed. (Oxford: Clarendon Press, 1963), 46–75. For the
dimension of extra income gained through debasement, see O'Brien and Hunt, "The Rise of a Fiscal State in
England, 1485–1815," 153–154. See also Glyn Davies, *A History of Money: From Ancient Times to the
Present Day*, 3rd ed. (Cardiff: University of Wales Press, 2002), 198–203.

further debasements under Edward VI, prices climbed about 100 percent above their pre-debasement level, roughly doubling at their high point.[5] Elizabeth I would reform the coinage,[6] but the Great Debasement long informed English debates on monetary policy.

Henry VIII raided English coin to raise revenue—his motive directs attention to the relative weakness of Britain's fiscal machinery in the 16th century. That state of affairs is a second important part of the prelude to the early modern era, given the role that fiscal engineering plays in structuring money. According to a number of indicators, Britain's revenue-raising machinery had developed little since the late 14th century. While Henry VII increased revenues over the meager collections of the 15th century, he did so without structural reform.[7] In fact, the Tudor strategy of devolving responsibility for revenue collection and accounting to separate offices of state arguably hampered effective administration. For their largest sources of revenue, the Tudors exploited anomalous and one-time expedients—the dissolution of the monasteries and debasement.[8] Otherwise, the Tudors and the early Stuarts depended on the prerogative powers of the Crown, including taxes levied directly on the wealth of subjects, hereditary revenues like the customs, Crown income from land, feudal rights, and other sources, along with claims to additional income that one scholar calls "bastard revenues"—ship money, monopolies, and other expedients.[9]

The Tudor and early Stuart monarchies could claim to master the game—they controlled up to three-quarters of both indirect and direct taxes, and even those portions granted by Parliament were not effectively policed by it. Ultimately, however, the game was a losing one. According to projections that capture at least orders of magnitude, government revenue as a portion of national income dropped after the 1550s, and remained low in the following decades. As a relative matter, the decrease may have left the Tudor and early Stuart monarchs, except during the 1540s, with less fiscal capacity than their 14th and early 15th century counterparts. Stagnation at best, their lack of capacity was particularly dangerous

---

[5] Feavearyear, *The Pound Sterling*, 50, 61–69, 76. Slightly lower price rises between 1530 and 1550 are reflected in the Phelps Brown-Hopkins and Allen indices. See Nicholas Mayhew, "Prices in England, 1170–1750," *Past & Present* (2013), 5.

[6] See Feavearyear, *The Pound Sterling*, 80–84.

[7] The failure of the Lancastrian rulers to bring in revenue is captured graphically in O'Brien and Hunt, "The Rise of a Fiscal State in England, 1485–1815," 148–151.

[8] O'Brien and Hunt, "The Rise of a Fiscal State in England, 1485–1815," 151–154. Revenue held virtually constant from 1490 to 1640, at magnitudes similar to that of the mid-14th century, aside from a decrease during the 15th century and temporary increases in the 1540s. See M. J. Braddick, *The Nerves of State: Taxation and the Financing of the English State, 1558–1714*, New Frontiers in History (Manchester: St. Martin's Press, 1996), 8–9; O'Brien and Hunt, "The Rise of a Fiscal State in England, 1485–1815," 149–151.

[9] See O'Brien and Hunt, "The Rise of a Fiscal State in England, 1485–1815," 138–144; Braddick, *Nerves of State*, 15. On the problems of late Tudor finance and early Stuart finance, see Conrad Russell, *The Crisis of Parliaments: English History, 1509–1660*, The Short Oxford History of the Modern World, Reprinted (with corrections) ed. (Oxford: Oxford University Press, 1974), 31–38, 271–277, 304–307, 317–322.

to the continued survival of the English state given the rising cost of warfare over the period.[10]

As Michael Braddick tells the story, the fiscal capacity of the English government reached a nadir and then began a strong ascent in the 17th century. Civil War demolished most of the prerogative as a source of income and left control over taxation in parliamentary hands. By the end of the century, the rising ability of the British state to borrow long term ushered in a government with such fiscal muscle that it was qualitatively different from its punier predecessors. Over comparable peacetime periods, Charles I took in an amount of revenue of the same scale as the medieval sovereigns. His son Charles II would expand that revenue by 2.7 times. By the 1720s, the Hanoverian state had multiplied that revenue by a factor of 11, and after the Napoleonic Wars, the administration commanded 36 times the purchasing power of Charles I.[11]

Last in the triad of monetary phenomena that stand out in the period from the late 15th to early 17th centuries is the heavy flow of metal, especially silver, that came to English mints, in sharp contrast to the low figures of the late Middle Ages. The change had many possible causes. England's overseas trade netted a balance in some periods, and war payments, diplomatic victories, piracy, and profiteering brought in more metal.[12] The Great Debasement had disproportionately affected silver, overvaluing that metal relative to gold.[13] Most famously, the tumultuous struggle for silver and gold that drove exploratory and colonizing efforts in Africa and the New World sent huge amounts of bullion to the mints. Silver flowed from Spain to England and continental Europe through much of Elizabeth I's reign.[14] According to a recent estimate, coin in circulation between 1546 and 1600 increased by a factor of 2.41.[15]

Money remained at the center of governance as the medieval period ended and the early modern world emerged. Each of the episodes sketched here affected that process in ways that invite more exploration. The Great Debasement, for example, violated the elite alliance that traded strong money for heavy taxes;

---

[10] See Braddick, *Nerves of State*, 9–11; O'Brien and Hunt, "The Rise of a Fiscal State in England, 1485–1815," 156–163. For the declining ability of the Tudor and Stuart monarchs to levy direct taxes on the wealth of their subjects, see O'Brien and Hunt, "The Rise of a Fiscal State in England, 1485–1815," 167–168.

[11] The numbers are at O'Brien and Hunt, "The Rise of a Fiscal State in England, 1485–1815," 155. More generally, see Braddick, *Nerves of State*, 12–19, 189–192; O'Brien and Hunt, "The Rise of a Fiscal State in England, 1485–1815," 133–134; John Brewer, *The Sinews of Power: War, Money, and the English State, 1688–1783* (New York: Knopf, 1988).

[12] C. E. Challis, *The Tudor Coinage* (Manchester, U.K.: Manchester University Press, 1978), 183–190.

[13] C. E. Challis, *Currency and the Economy in Tudor and Early Stuart England*, vol. 4, New Appreciations in History, ed. Gareth Elwyn Jones (London: Historical Association, 1989), 10–12; Feavearyear, *The Pound Sterling*, 56, 70.

[14] Challis, *The Tudor Coinage*, 190–198; C. E. Challis, "Spanish Bullion and Monetary Inflation in England in the Later Sixteenth Century," *Journal of European Economic History* 4, no. 2 (1975).

[15] Mayhew, "Prices in England," 29. For proportions of gold and silver coin, see Mayhew, "Prices in England," 28.

the trauma it caused arguably entrenched that pact for subsequent generations. The Tudor period also exposes the close connection between the strength of the fiscal state and the reach of its monetary system. Tudor problems raising revenue informed the attempts by the early Stuart monarchs, James I and Charles I, to find new ways to finance the kingdom—a monetary story we pick up below. Finally, the great influx of silver and gold from Africa and the New World likely lifted European expectations about their money supply in ways that drove their experiments in making money; that experimentation was the main event in the coming century.

We enter the early 17th century with a bare sense of the intervening years, to be sure. But if it is sudden, the leap from the medieval to the early modern world focuses the narrative on the contrast between commodity money, as it circulated for centuries, and bank-issued money, as the form that dominates the next epoch. It was that transformation that broke apart the English experience in matters of money.

Money's design was open to radical change during the constitutional upheaval that occurred under the Stuart monarchs. The next sections recount how the monetary revolution began incrementally, continued over a set of experiments, and culminated when the government assumed a new posture as the sponsor of liquidity. They describe how the old methods that had created both coin and tallies for centuries died.

As to coin, the government began paying for its production at the mint out of tax revenues. Exchanged ounce for ounce for silver, money would come to seem costless. And refracted through the new and oddly narrowing lens of liberalism, coin looked more like a commodity, pure and private, than it ever had before. As to tallies, their demise generated the conditions for a new kind of circulating credit: government bonds that traveled hand to hand as had the older tallies but that bore interest from the beginning and operated to borrow money instead of compensating people for illiquid resources like services and supplies. Bonds offered the unprecedented opportunity to reach a large pool of popular lenders. The change would make investors out of a broad swath of citizenry for the first time. Bonds also furnished the English with a new kind of liquidity: circulating credit that the government paid individuals to hold.

For all the potential that bonds held to usher in a new era, they failed to resolve the ongoing money crunch—the need for a "running cash" appropriate for everyday use. The chapter ends with a look at that money crunch. It would catalyze the move that established private orientation towards profit—the investment calculus of the Bank of England, its members, and its borrowers—as the pump used to produce money in the modern world.

A. Making money free

Charles II is most renowned in the history of finance for the Stop of the Exchequer, an infamous default on the servicing of the royal debt.[16] But ironically, it was during Charles II's reign that the English government first moved concertedly towards paying investors to produce money. It happened improvisationally, indeed probably unintentionally. Participants solved one problem and created others; they reacted as often as they acted affirmatively; they moved by experience and intuition, without an overarching theory; and the whole affair took decades, involved many different actors, and coheres largely in retrospect. From that angle, however, the drama grew from the demise of the traditional media and the conditions it created.

The traditional minting system collapsed cleanly, divesting the state of its seignorage, but clearing the space to reconceive the structure of coinage at the same time. Minting prices and melting points, competition between sovereigns for silver, ebbs and flows of bullion across borders—such phenomena had long influenced the supply of metal to the mint, confounding official attempts to make money and maintain it smoothly in circulation.[17] The 17th century was beset by such problems. "I heard a wise man compare the hammers of the Mint in the state unto the pulses in a natural body," wrote an Englishman in 1621, "For as if these beat strongly, it argues health, but if faintly, weakness in the body is natural." Following the metaphor, C. E. Challis evaluated England in the first half of the 17th century as "as source of some anxiety to its physician."[18] The Elizabethan era left behind monetary troubles, despite the rich flow of metals to England. Population growth, increased urbanization, rising prices, and more extensive monetization—all pushed up demand for coin during the Queen's reign. As far as scholars of the period have been able to establish, the expanding currency had not kept pace.[19] Shortly after James I took the throne, the government exacerbated the problem by overvaluing gold relative to silver. Gold coin made up 60 to 90 percent of mint output every year between 1609 and 1631.[20]

---

[16] For further discussion of the Stop, see pp. 281–287. The actual effect of the Stop—a delay in payment that became a default for some lenders and a postponement for others—has been controverted. See, e.g., J. Keith Horsefield, *British Monetary Experiments, 1650-1710* (Cambridge, MA: Harvard University Press, 1960); James Milnes Holden, *The History of Negotiable Instruments in English Law* (Holmes Beach, FL.: Gaunt, 1955), 211–212; C. D. Chandaman, *The English Public Revenue, 1660-1688* (Oxford: Clarendon Press, 1975), 297–300.

[17] See pp. 110–120.

[18] Challis, "Lord Hastings to the Great Silver Recoinage, 1464–1699," 307–308 (quoting debate in 1621 Commons).

[19] For a sample of the efforts to map the era, see, e.g., J. R. Wordie, "Deflationary Factors in the Tudor Price Rise," *Past & Present* 154 (1997); Challis, *Currency and the Economy in Tudor and Early Stuart England.*

[20] Challis, "Lord Hastings to the Great Silver Recoinage, 1464–1699," 313 (Table 35). The overvaluation of gold allowed the Crown to claim more seignorage, a matter it prioritized during the period despite the damage to the domestic economy. Challis, "Lord Hastings to the Great Silver Recoinage, 1464–1699," 316.

In Shakespeare's world, silver was that "pale and common drudge 'tween man and man," the workhorse of the monetary system. Gold, by contrast, was a luxury, gratuitous to everyday life, that "gaudy" metal, "hard food for Midas."[21] Pending adjustment of the mint prices, silver pooled in the domestic market for plate or left the country in the hands of merchants. At the lowest levels of exchange, private tokens, often made of lead, circulated from Elizabethan times on. The early Stuarts commissioned copper farthings, which functioned until banned by Parliament in 1644. After 1632, a series of idiosyncratic deals, hostile seizures, and the falling price of silver on the Continent brought significant amounts of silver to the mint from Spanish and French sources.[22] After a decade and half, however, the flow dwindled; it remained low during the Commonwealth and Protectorate.[23] Although they vary considerably, many probate inventories from the first half of the century include very little coin. Even assuming that heirs and others helped money disappear before officials arrived, Craig Muldrew estimates that the majority of non-wealthy decedents in one sample probably left less than 5 shillings.[24] From mid-century, mint output of silver was extremely erratic; demands for a better money supply rose each time the coin supply dropped off.[25]

In 1663, Charles mechanized the minting process. Rolling mills flattened the bullion and presses cut out blanks and stamped them. The technology improved consistency across coins and, by leaving a grooved imprint around the circumference of each, made clipping or shaving easy to detect. Insofar as mechanization rendered pennies and other denominations more obviously standardized and made stealing small pieces of silver or gold more difficult, it increased coin's durability.[26] But the metal sent to the mints by the government did not meet demands for more coin, which rose with expanding economic activity.[27] Full-weight milled coin was also more liable to be exported, while the older, hammered coins that still circulated continued to erode.

---

[21] W. Shakespeare, *The Merchant of Venice* (1750), 44. Thanks to Craig Muldrew for the lovely reference.

[22] By agreement, the Spanish shipped silver they needed in Flanders by way of England for safety reasons. The English retained a portion of the silver in return for payment in Antwerp in Flemish coin. After that arrangement broke down at mid-century, the English took a series of Spanish ships with silver cargoes. And at the Restoration, Charles II would sell Dunkirk to the French for silver payment. Challis, "Lord Hastings to the Great Silver Recoinage, 1464–1699," 307–324; Feavearyear, *The Pound Sterling*, 87–95.

[23] Challis, "Lord Hastings to the Great Silver Recoinage, 1464–1699," 320, 327.

[24] Craig Muldrew, "'Hard Food for Midas': Cash and Its Social Value in Early Modern England," *Past & Present* 170 (2001): 91–92, 101; see also Mayhew, "Population," 244, 246–247; Peter H. Lindert, "English Population, Wages, and Prices: 1541–1913," *Journal of Interdisciplinary History* 15, no. 4 (1985): 624 (Table 3). The situation was, however, far better than the late 16th century, when the money shortage was extreme. For figures, see Mayhew, "Population," 244, 247. For a review of the circumstances that haunted the late 16th century and for more inventory studies, some indicating more coin on hand, see Muldrew, "'Hard Food for Midas': Cash and Its Social Value in Early Modern England," 88–89, 95–96, 100–101.

[25] Horsefield, *Monetary Experiments*, Gold, money, inflation, and deflation, 5–6 (including Chart II).

[26] See Angela Redish, *Bimetallism: An Economic and Historical Analysis*, Studies in Macroeconomic History Index (Cambridge: Cambridge University Press, 2000), 54–61.

[27] For the thriving English activity, see pp. 256–257.

Under those circumstances, the fee imposed on individuals for minting seemed an ill-advised limit on the absolute amount of bullion available for coin. Facing a chorus of complaints from merchants and tradesmen, Charles II agreed to subsidize the cost of coining in 1666. The Act for Encouraging of Coynage directed the government to pay all expenses for assaying, melting, and minting coins. Those bringing bullion to the mint received the full weight of the metal they brought back in coin; holders no longer waited for coin to gain enough value to make the production and seignorage fees worthwhile. Effectively, the government had raised the price it paid for the money metals, and it levied taxes elsewhere to meet the additional costs. The arrangement, initially experimental, remained in effect until revised along with the Gold Standard in 1925.[28]

The Act for Encouraging of Coynage had an immediate effect. The flow of both silver and gold to the mint increased. In 1666, £37,000 in silver had been minted. In 1667, that number jumped to £53,000, and in 1668 to £124,000. Over the next decade and a half, mint output per year averaged over £138,000.[29]

The Restoration shift to paying for coin had a more long-lasting consequence as well. When Charles II subsidized the cost of minting, he submerged the difference between coin and bullion in the common perception. Full-bodied coin had previously traveled at a premium over the same quantity of raw silver or gold: its value as a more liquid form of value increased its worth an average of 5 percent to 10 percent over bullion.[30] But after the change, coin appeared to be silver or gold without more, a natural product rather than an artifact of sovereign power.

The equation was more than imaginary; it was experienced. When the government began paying for coin, it induced those with bullion to bring silver or gold to the mint as long as they desired—given relative mint prices—to put that metal in money form.[31] They would do so until the cash premium on an additional unit was worth no more to them than the utility of the same content

---

[28] 18 & 19 Car 2 c 5 (1666). The Cavalier Parliament imposed import duties on wine, beer, cider, vinegar, and spirits. For background, see Feavearyear, *The Pound Sterling*, 95–96. For the practice through the 18th century, see Charles, Earl of Liverpool, *A Treatise on the Coins of the Realm in a Letter to the King* (London: Oxford University Press, 1805), 6.

[29] Challis, "Lord Hastings to the Great Silver Recoinage, 1464–1699," 340 (Table 42). Flow to the mint was not steady; rather, it was affected by episodic acquisitions like the capture of Spanish silver.

[30] N. J. Mayhew, *Sterling: The History of a Currency* (New York: Wiley, 2000), 97–98; Ming-Hsun Li, *The Great Recoinage of 1696 to 1699* (London: Weidenfeld and Nicolson, 1963), 15 (noting significant cash premium on Dutch money); Thomas J. Sargent and Francois R. Velde, *The Big Problem of Small Change*, The Princeton Economic History of the Western World Indexes (Princeton, NJ: Princeton University Press, 2002), 9–10, 16–21 (modeling value of commodity money as including "fiat component"). The continued circulation of worn coin at face value or close to it depends on the premium it carries as coin rather than bullion, creating the opportunity for arbitrage explored in Chapter 3. For another example, although one lacking information about currency at face value, see, e.g., Redish, *Bimetallism*, 28 (noting that worn coin circulating in 1798 averaged from 3.3 to 25 percent lighter than new, full-weight coin).

[31] As in earlier centuries, those with bullion were generally merchants. That reality is underscored periodically by official directives to that community, limiting their ability to hold or export bullion. Those proscriptions had bite when the mint price was too low to induce minting. See, e.g., the measures

of bullion. In other words, the government's policy made the cash quality of money free, dispensing it without charge until demand for it at the mint price had been met. The medieval gap between minting point and the melting point vanished: a coin would never be worth more than its counterpart in bullion— because if it were, people would simply bring bullion to the mint and get it coined. Coin looked to be silver (or gold), formally packaged, even though that equivalence assumed the costs borne by the public to produce coin up to the level of monetary liquidity demanded by those holding bullion. Indeed, while coin would never be worth more than bullion, as it traditionally had been, it would often be worth *less* than bullion. While coin now came free from bullion, bullion did not come free from coin: if a person needed bullion, he or she would have to pay to melt coin.

The shift had ideological impact. Money came to seem costless, simply a stylized form of silver or gold. The essential role of government in defining the unit of account, determining the supply and demand for money, and supporting its negotiability, lost salience. Indeed, insofar as it cost money to melt coin and recover bullion, the government's role in packaging that resource could be conceived as an interference with the free activity of enterprising men.[32]

B. The decline of tallies as currency that came at a charge

The government moved at about the same time towards paying for circulating credit. That development is only visible against the background we regained above—the old practice of using tallies as a virtual currency made out of public debt. English monarchs had long enlarged the money available for public use by anticipating revenues: it gave tallies as tax credits to public creditors for goods or services. For centuries, the government had sweetened the reward for the interest-free advance made to it by tally holders. It allowed tallies to circulate, creating a currency out of them insofar as it gave a present value to the tokens that people held.[33]

In the 17th century, tallies weakened and failed, taking with them the avenue they represented for sovereign borrowing. Their decline left behind a vacuum; when tallies finally died, the need for another mode of borrowing increased. But tallies had also modeled an instrument of public credit that could circulate; they were an indigenous and national form of public borrowing, one overlooked by

---

ordered by James I to redress the silver shortage, in Challis, "Lord Hastings to the Great Silver Recoinage, 1464–1699," 315.

[32] See pp. 180–189.

[33] The trade stated simply here is worked out with qualifications in Chapter 4, which reviews the evidence on interest and circulation. See pp. 180–189. Tallies also had analogues—other devices for borrowing that should be added to the history. See, e.g., Richard David Richards, *The Early History of Banking in England* (London: P. S. King, 1929), 29–30, 53–64.

later writers excavating precedents further afield, like the medieval municipal bonds of Venice and Florence. As tallies declined, officials would recreate instruments of circulating public debt, now interest-bearing. Buried with the story of tallies and their demise, then, are clues to the way those engineering the Restoration invented new forms of borrowing from the public and began to pay for them.

It was the constitutional warfare of the 17th century, a struggle famously inflected through finance, that destroyed tallies. Inheriting fiscal machinery with limited capacity, the early Stuarts responded by pressing their prerogative power—they reached for revenue from militia rates and ship money, seizures and sales of lands, monopolies, and licenses, colonization, forced loans, and impositions.[34] Their strategy collided with the ambitions and commitments of elites within Parliament and beyond; the conflicts over revenue helped catalyze the crisis at mid-century.[35]

The Stuarts' efforts to borrow using tallies fit within that struggle. Theoretically, sovereigns could anticipate taxes further and further in advance, by giving tallies for resources and emphasizing the taxes to follow.[36] The more they stretched the strategy, however, the more officials exposed the vulnerabilities of a system based so transparently on the extraction of funds. The credibility and therefore viability of tallies depended on the certainty that taxes would be imposed so that the tallies could be cashed. But the argument that people could rely on heavy levies to come was never a winning one politically.

Early English governments also borrowed money voluntarily loaned for interest. Before the late 16th century, many of those loans came from abroad; they dried up with the rise of international hostilities between England, the Netherlands, and Spain at the end of the Tudor period. The Stuarts therefore turned increasingly to the domestic market for loans; they raised money primarily from large financiers, syndicates of lenders, and the Corporation of London.[37] Whoever the lender, the sovereign paid for the use of a medium already

[34] See, e.g., Braddick, *Nerves of State*, 68–90; Frederick C. Dietz, *English Public Finance, 1558–1641*, 2nd ed., vol. 2 (New York: Barnes & Noble, 1964), 144–288, 362–379.

[35] See, e.g., Russell, *Crisis of Parliaments*; O'Brien and Hunt, "The Rise of a Fiscal State in England, 1485–1815," 154. The constitutional crisis under the early Stuarts has generated a rich literature. See, e.g., J. P. Sommerville, *Royalists and Patriots: Politics and Ideology in England, 1603–1640*, 2nd ed. (London: Addison Wesley Longman, 1999); Glenn Burgess, *The Politics of the Ancient Constitution* (University Park, PA: Pennsylvania State University Press, 1992); Richard Cust and Ann Hughes, *Conflict in Early Stuart England: Studies in Religion and Politics, 1603–1642* (London: Longman, 1989); Conrad Russell, *Parliaments and English Politics, 1621–1629* (Oxford: Clarendon Press, 1979); Mark Kishlansky, "The Emergence of Adversary Politics in the Long Parliament," *Journal of Modern History* 49 (1977); Christopher Hill, *The World Turned Upside Down; Radical Ideas During the English Revolution* (London: Temple Smith, 1972).

[36] Americans long after would anticipate taxes far into the future with paper money during desperate moments, most famously the American Revolution. For the American strategy, see E. James Ferguson, "Currency Finance: An Interpretation of Colonial Monetary Practices," *Willam and Mary Quarterly* 10, no. 2 (1953).

[37] Robert Ashton, *The Crown and the Money Market, 1603–1640* (Oxford: Clarendon Press, 1960), 50–51, 1–30; Richards, *The Early History of Banking in England*, 5–7.

"liquid," as it were, when it borrowed money at interest. There was no imperative to bestow easy transferability on the loan instruments, and their negotiability was not an attribute that lenders demanded or, at least, demanded successfully. Loans were represented in notes or bills that did not circulate, or in demand notes issued to particular lenders.[38]

That kind of public borrowing did not compete with tax anticipation by tally or undermine the logic of a system that treated public creditors according to the kind of advance they made (whether those creditors liked it or not). Some IOUs from the government certified that money had been lent (a note of loan), other IOUs constituted a claim of revenues that could be passed along and eventually used to pay taxes, thus creating money anew (a tally). George Downing identified the alternatives, noting in 1666 that loans to the king for money were interest-bearing, while anticipations of credit were "such of them as are not for money lent, but goods sold, or by the King's direction, have no interest payable upon them."[39] Each debt to a holder was rewarded de facto—the first type with interest, the second type with the capacity to circulate. The difference depended, as always, on the underlying capacity of the government to dispense liquidity more effect-ively than other agents or collaboratives.

Different as they were, the methods used to borrow money and to anticipate revenues were not airtight. For one, those holding tallies before the 17th century may have extracted interest from the sovereign to some extent. For another, those who lent the Crown money may sometimes have been repaid with tallies that they then had to use or pass on.[40] A more significant blurring of forms occurred during Charles I's reign, when royal strategies used to raise loans bumped up against the practice of anticipating resources, dislodging them to some extent. The displacement may have been completely unintentional; it could still have drastic effects.

The process began in the gray space between borrowing money and anticipat-ing revenues when spending on goods and services. As alternative sources of support slipped away, the early Stuarts relied more heavily on tax anticipation; they became particularly dependent on customs farmers to advance revenue to

---

[38] Elizabethan demand notes could be assigned by endorsement. The development of successive assignments is a separate and later event. For the earlier practice, see Richards, *The Early History of Banking in England*, 5–7. For standard practice on promissory notes and the law of monetary obligations, see James Steven Rogers, *The Early History of the Law of Bills and Notes: A Study of the Origins of Anglo-American Commercial Law*, Cambridge Studies in English Legal History Index (Cambridge: Cambridge University Press, 1995), 177–186; Theodore F. T. Plucknett, *A Concise History of the Common Law*, 5th ed., (Boston: Little, Brown and Co., 1956), 669–670.

[39] See *A State of the Case, between Furnishing His Majesty with Money by Way of Loan, or by Way of Advance of the Tax of Any Particular Place, Upon the Act for the £1250000* (1666), 5.

[40] On the extent to which interest attached to tallies, see pp. 186–189. On the use of tallies to pay lenders, see K. B. McFarlane, "Loans to the Lancastrian Kings: The Problem of Inducement," *Cambridge Historical Journal* 9, no. 1 (1947): 56, 66–67. But see Anthony Bedford Steel, *The Receipt of the Exchequer, 1377–1485* (Cambridge: Cambridge University Press, 1954), 16–20, whose mapping of the Exchequer record suggests that few *pro* tallies would be issued for genuine loans.

them by tally. But while royal collectors had long cashed tallies when they received the revenues to pay them, customs farmers began a new practice that eventually undermined the traditional one. The farmers apparently started cashing tallies upon request. That is, they advanced the rents they owed the Crown to its creditors, accepting tallies written on those rents as overdrafts and giving out money of their own rather than postponing creditors.[41] Their practice effectively terminated the non-interest-bearing advances made by a diffuse group of creditors who had held tallies and replaced them with money loans to the Crown from a more concentrated group of lenders. In effect, those lenders assumed the burden of loaning to the Crown, taking it from a group that had previously borne it in the more decentralized form of the delayed payments they received as public creditors.

The traditional role of tallies as circulating tokens had also been affected: the tallies that customs agents held would no longer travel as currency—they were "dead" in the sense that they had already been accepted by tax collectors, and had value only to those agents as evidence of the amounts they had paid out. In turn, the customs farmers would demand, and eventually receive, interest on the money they advanced; the Stuarts began paying interest for loans from the farmers sometime between 1625 and 1632.[42] After all, the farmers were lending a resource already liquid to the Crown (their own money) and could appropriately expect compensation for that grant.

The old practice may have broken down for a number of reasons. The Crown itself might have pushed the change. The Stuarts had great leverage over their customs farmers, having defended them again and again from reform proposals to abolish the farms in favor of more efficient ways to collect taxes.[43] The turn towards borrowing from the customs agents was also part of the guerrilla warfare that raged between the Stuarts and their legislative opponents: the customs flowed from a complex set of rights, a number of which were successfully claimed as part of the royal prerogative until 1640.[44] Insofar as the arrangement enabled

---

[41] The descriptions by Ashton and Harper, who wrote without the baseline of earlier tally practice, make it clear that the customs farmers were actually advancing money, as opposed to postponing the moment when they would "accept" a tally. See Ashton, *The Crown and the Money Market, 1603–1640*, 52; Robert Ashton, "Revenue Farming under the Early Stuarts," *Economic History Review* 8, no. 3 (1956): 312. Robert Ashton, "Deficit Finance in the Reign of James I," *Economic History Review* 10, no. 1 (1957). For the earlier practice, according to which a revenue farmer waited until revenues were available before accepting a tally, see G. L. Harriss, "Fictitious Loans," *Economic History Review* 8, no. 2 (1955).

[42] See Ashton, "Revenue Farming under the Early Stuarts," 312–313 (reviewing provision of interest to advances from current rent, overdrafts of rent, and advances of future rents).

[43] See, e.g., Ashton, "Revenue Farming under the Early Stuarts," 311, 313–318. On the Customs generally, see M. J. Braddick, *The Nerves of State: Taxation and the Financing of the English State, 1558–1714*, New Frontiers in History (Manchester: St. Martin's Press, 1996), 61–64; Dietz, *English Public Finance*, 330–337. The Crown made other privileges available to the customs farmers as well, such as restricting the amount of rent due relative to the amount of Customs revenue collected. Ashton, "Revenue Farming under the Early Stuarts," 318.

[44] See Braddick, *Nerves of State*, 49–55.

the Crown to anticipate existing levies, it allowed the Crown to borrow and spend without recourse to Parliament.

The customs farmers had reason to enjoy the change as well. They had leveraged their position, gaining interest on their advances. The stream of customs revenue also offered farmers some security for the overdrafts. In fact, the customs farmers soon tapped others as sources of funds. They began to form syndicates of lenders to the Crown, suggesting that the arrangement was profitable.[45]

The altered tradition was not quite a new order. As a form of public borrowing, it was consonant with the existing practice on loans. The Crown here was paying interest on a liquid medium evidenced by instruments (the dead tallies) that did not circulate. At the same time, the strange twist on the old practice both raised the profile of domestic borrowing and weakened tallies. As for domestic borrowing, the new arrangement made local lenders of money more important to Charles than they had been to his immediate predecessors.[46] The Crown had long had trouble competing in the conventional market for loans, where the protections provided by sovereign immunity combined with the possibility of default made the monarch a bad risk.[47] The virtual market constructed by the customs farmers, secured by the revenues they claimed, offered an alternative.

At the same time, the bargain that Charles I negotiated with his customs farmers weakened tallies because it diminished the advantages to the Crown of using tallies in the customary way. Tallies now were quickly converted by the farmers into a liquid advance; they acted as a request or channel for a money loan rather than as a method of creating a non-interest-bearing public credit currency. Given that fact, the Stuarts appropriately paid interest on them, as the Crown traditionally had for other money loans. As in that case, the customs farmers kept the instruments that evidenced the advance, here the tallies that had been accepted from creditors. The Crown had effectively started to pay for a broader group of money loans than it ever had before. As a fiscal legacy, Charles I left tallies as a major mode of Crown borrowing, one that brought in money loans but sacrificed the advantages of acquiring goods in anticipation of taxes *and* cost the Crown in interest. The revision neither killed tallies nor transcended them, but it marked them for eventual obsolescence.

---

[45] See Ashton, "Revenue Farming under the Early Stuarts," 319–322. For later history on the efforts of the farmers to maintain their hold, see Chandaman, *The English Public Revenue, 1660–1688*, 22–31. Financial elites in the City parted ways with Charles I, and threw their support behind Parliament. Those elites had many reasons to abandon Charles, but to them might be added the fact that Charles had stronger bonds with the customs agents than City investors, if they were not among the syndicate members gathered by the agents.

[46] For the concerted borrowing by Lancastrian kings from domestic sources, see, e.g., McFarlane, "Loans to the Lancastrian Kings: The Problem of Inducement."

[47] For the significant interest rates that may have attached to sovereign borrowing from domestic sources in the Lancastrian period, see, e.g., McFarlane, "Loans to the Lancastrian Kings: The Problem of Inducement," 67–68; Steel, *The Receipt of the Exchequer, 1377–1485*, 16–20. For the difficulties experienced by the Stuarts, see Ashton, *The Crown and the Money Market, 1603–1640*, 9–15.

The English Civil War produced another burst of experimentation, this time among private individuals. It accustomed an English elite to the notion of leaving money in deposit, where it could serve as credit for others. Partners in domestic commerce had long been using credit to facilitate reciprocal relations.[48] By the early 17th century, those left with funds on hand—factors holding money for merchants, goldsmiths with coined stock, or money scriveners who brokered loans—sometimes lent out money on their own account. Their activity rose during the Civil War, perhaps because many people wanted to leave their money somewhere safe amidst the political turmoil. By the 1660s, a group of bankers in London paid relatively high rates of interest to attract depositors. Samuel Pepys, for example, considered leaving money with Edward Blackwell for 6 percent.[49]

Once deposited, money could be transferred between parties using "orders to pay" that took a variety of shapes. According to Eric Kerridge, notes, letters, or instruments carried varying degrees of formality. Most, as he parses the practice, were inland bills of exchange, the means by which domestic merchants had long moved coin and ordered payment of obligations.[50] As James Rogers reconstructs the practice of transferring inland bills by endorsement and assignment, it probably became established in England in the early 17th century.[51] The system had clear limits. It served those with commercial trading relations and remained dependent on coin to clear. It faltered when seasonal abundance reduced the number of bills available, or other fluctuations mismatched demand and supply for bills; certain areas were continually under or over served. By the mid-17th century, however, inland bills and other bills written to a party or his order likely functioned to allow funds to be assigned by endorsement to a series of parties.[52] (By contrast, promissory notes made to a party "or bearer" did not transfer the

---

[48] Promises to pay or bills obligatory passed among circles of merchants in 16th century England, payable after transfer with the consent of the debtor. Eric Kerridge, *Trade and Banking in Early Modern England* (Manchester: Manchester University Press, 1988), 40–42. Creditors also accepted more informal, unsealed bills when they were written by debtors considered reliable; the instruments were unenforceable at law until 1704,: Kerridge, *Trade and Banking*, 41–42. Similarly, orders to pay, or bills of exchange, in use from medieval times, allowed parties with a surplus of funds in a location like London to use them to fund activity there. Those bills were assignable with certain limitations. See pp. 228–229; see also Kerridge, *Trade and Banking*, 45–46, 71–75.

[49] See Rogers, *Law of Bills and Notes*, 116–124; Kerridge, *Trade and Banking*, 46–54, 66–71; Richards, *The Early History of Banking in England*, 92–131; Feavearyear, *The Pound Sterling*, 102–104. For the fairly high interest rates that such bankers paid depositors, see Mayhew, *Sterling*, 88–90, who notes that the high rates suggest the limited and network-dependent character of circulating paper.

[50] See Kerridge, *Trade and Banking*, 47–66; see also J. H. Clapham, *The Bank of England: A History* (Cambridge: Cambridge University Press, 1970), 5–10.

[51] Rogers, *Law of Bills and Notes*, 170–173.

[52] Kerridge finds English practice distinctive in the occurrence of successive assignment by the mid-17th century. Kerridge, *Trade and Banking*, 61–62, 67–68; see also J. K. Horsefield, "The Beginnings of Paper Money in England," *Journal of European Economic History* 117, no. 32 (1977): 119–120; Horsefield, *Monetary Experiments*, xii–xiii, 237. The legality of transferring inland bills was implicitly endorsed by the courts in the late 1660s, although they were only confirmed negotiable in 1697. Kerridge, *Trade and Banking*, 74.

party's right to sue to a bearer until Parliament's intervention in 1704.[53]) The precedent furnished by inland bills and their commercial cognates would acculturate those familiar with them to the notion that credit could circulate.

C. A new form of public debt: circulating promises to pay

When Charles II took the throne after the Civil War, he inherited the residue of the old tally practice at a time when investors were exploring the advantages of credit that was transferable. The circumstances invited innovation and furnished the ingredients for it. If the government could borrow from a small group of people with a credit instrument that carried interest, why not borrow from a wider group in a form that catered to their desire for a credit instrument that could be transferred?[54] Breaking out beyond the finite universe of customs farmers and big lenders, the Crown could popularize public debt. That development would lower the interest rate at which the government now paid for borrowing money, even as it institutionalized that payment. It would also create a new kind of public credit that circulated.

The determination to pay for circulating credit occurred immediately after Charles had decided to pay for coin. Parliament had granted the king a generous amount for annual expenses at the beginning of his reign, but that money alone could not finance the series of wars with the Dutch that Charles II entered.[55] From the mid-1660s on, the king's efforts to accommodate Catholicism and to explore an alliance with France worsened relations with Parliament and diminished its willingness to grant additional funds.[56] Loans from the commercial community ran thin, as the plague threw London and its business community into turmoil.[57]

---

[53] See An Act for giving like Remedy upon Promissory Notes as is now used upon Bills of Exchange, and for the better Payment of Inland Bills of Exchange (3 & 4 Anne c 9 (1704)). As Rogers reconstructs the difference, "bearer" notes may have threatened to undermine the procedural protections generally accorded debtors contracting to pay under the common law. Those considerations were not implicated by inland bills, insofar as those instruments functioned to allow commercial parties to assign funds they had accumulated to another business party. See Rogers, *Law of Bills and Notes*, 170–193. Although the line between inland bills and promissory notes is obscure, Rogers and Horsefield treat goldsmith-bankers' notes as generally falling into the latter category. See Rogers, *Law of Bills and Notes*, 170–193; Horsefield, "The Beginnings of Paper Money in England," 121–125; see also Richards, *The Early History of Banking in England*, 40–49 (arguing that types often conflated).

[54] It would be worth exploring whether the increasing prevalence of negotiability may effectively have eroded the government's monopoly and thus its ability to trade that control for an interest-free loan.

[55] Bruce G. Carruthers, *City of Capital: Politics and Markets in the English Financial Revolution* (Princeton, NJ: Princeton University Press, 1996), 32. The start of Third Dutch War in 1672 drove total public spending up to more than twice the annual grant (£1.2 million): it reached £2.5 million. Carruthers, *City of Capital*, 32, 54. Additionally, the revenues actually gathered under Parliament's annual grant often failed to reach the amount authorized. Carruthers, *City of Capital*, 56.

[56] Carruthers, *City of Capital*, 32–34.

[57] See Henry Roseveare, *The Treasury, 1660–1870: The Foundations of Control*, Historical Problems, Studies and Documents, no. 22 (London: Allen and Unwin, 1973), 31–32; Chandaman, *The English Public Revenue, 1660–1688*, 295.

Charles II began reforming the tax system, improving collection and increasing administrative efficiency.[58] But many of those measures were long in coming, and the revenues they produced were never immediate enough to meet the exigencies of war. Tallies, traditionally used to bridge the gap, had been transformed in the crises that marked his father's reign, when they had effectively operated as requests for money loans from the customs farmers. The stability of Charles II's regime was still provisional. In a move apparently calculated to improve the legitimacy of tallies, the king in 1660 authorized officials in certain circumstances to attach interest to them even when they were first issued.[59] Charles II in that moment went further than his father, who had attached interest only after tallies had been accepted by tax farmers in return for funds advanced. But the circumstances pushed royal officials to look for still more ways to borrow; their experiment undid the existing approach to public credit.

The lead designer for the project was George Downing. Born in Dublin, Downing was a worldly and eclectic policy maker by the time of the Restoration. The nephew of John Winthrop, he had grown up in New England, studied in the first class at Harvard, and thrown in his lot with Cromwell during the English Civil War. It tested all of his diplomatic skills to navigate the political transition to the monarchy, but they met the challenge wonderfully. Downing parlayed his experience abroad in Holland into a continuing post under Charles II after Cromwell's fall.[60]

Authorities across Europe were experimenting with different forms of public credit as Downing came into office, as he surely knew. Officials in Burgundy, Florence, and Germany, as well as England, had tried lotteries since the medieval period. Holland attempted in the 16th century to raise money by interest-bearing annuities, although it had not succeeded in making much money from them. Administrators offered a tontine to investors in mid-17th century France, adopting the idea of an Italian.[61] And in England, a flurry of proposals appeared, suggesting various schemes to make credit current or to innovate new ways of anticipating public revenues. As tallies demonstrated, the ability of sovereigns, city-states, and ultimately nations to draft resources from their members supported their strategies of borrowing. As long as public authorities could credibly promise future revenues, they could engineer different instruments of public credit and try to get them established.[62]

---

[58] Brewer, *The Sinews of Power*, 92–95.

[59] 12 Car 2 c 9 (1660).

[60] "Downing, Sir George," in *Encyclopaedia Britannica*, ed. Hugh Chisholm (Cambridge: Cambridge University Press, 1911).

[61] Anne L. Murphy, *The Origins of English Financial Markets: Investment and Speculation before the South Sea Bubble*, Cambridge Studies in Economic History (Cambridge: Cambridge University Press, 2009), 46–49.

[62] See pp. 296–301, 311–320, 331–341.

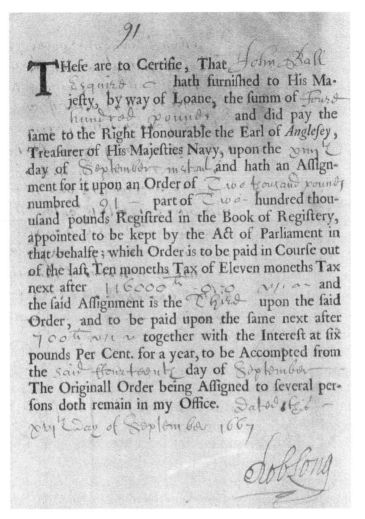

Fig. 6.1 One of the first printed public bonds, an Order for Repayment issued by the English government in 1667, P.R.O. E407/119.

Downing's plan was to open up the public debt—to make lending to the government an attractive opportunity to an array of investors if not (yet) the man or woman on the street. He worked with the domestic ingredients he had and the European models before him. The first English bonds took the form of "Tallyes of Loan" accompanied by "Orders for Repayment" that determined their priority claim to public revenues. Packaged in customary wrapping, these were fresh instruments of public borrowing—interest-bearing promises-to-repay.[63] See Fig. 6.1.

---

[63] See the Additional Aid Act 1665 (17 Car 2 c 1 s 7). For an early attempt by Charles II to induce smaller lenders to loan money to the Crown for interest, see 12 Car 2 c 9 ss 10–11 (1660).

The new instruments had features intended to attract a broad audience: they were designed to be both safe and liquid. As for safety, Tallyes of Loan were funded by an identifiable revenue stream. Each early borrowing initiative was linked to a statutory levy; as taxes came in, the promise took effect to pay lenders as their claims were registered.[64] As Downing emphasized in a pamphlet he published to introduce the new program, the investment was thus secured on the whole of a dedicated revenue.[65] Like anticipation by tally, borrowing by bond generated promises of value by the government. In the case of borrowing, however, the national revenue backed the promise, as opposed to the tax collected at a "particular parish or place."[66]

In turn, loans were numbered, publicly registered, and paid off "in course" as they came due. The Act expressly disallowed officials from giving preference to any "one before another" whose claim was prior by date. Any public servants who demanded money in return for maintaining the "in course" guarantee or who gave anyone "undue preference" were liable to suit and loss of office.[67] The popular name for Tallyes of Loan conveys that guarantee. "Treasury Orders," as they came to be called, expressed the statutory command that loans to the king would be honored; settling them was not discretionary.[68]

As for the liquidity of Treasury Orders, Downing calculated that attaching currency to them would make lending to the Crown attractive to a larger number of investors. They could pass on Treasury Orders when they needed to and so lend without locking up resources. More would invest without demanding as much in return. In fact, the strategy anticipated the structure of much later finance: it would allow the government to borrow long term, while lenders made only short-term commitments. As participation rose, the government would be able to reduce the interest on its securities. Dutch annuities paid 8.3 percent in the 1590s, but only 4 percent in the middle of the 17th century.[69]

[64] See, e.g., the first public borrowing effort in the Additional Aid Act 1665 (17 Car 2 c 1 s 7). See generally, Roseveare, *The Treasury*, 23–24; Chandaman, *The English Public Revenue, 1660–1688*, 295. In 1667, the "in course" promise of repayment was extended to apply to payment orders issued on the king's ordinary revenue. PRO Printed Proclamations, Charles II, SPDom 45/12 no. 244a, cited in Roseveare, *The Treasury*, 32, n. 48. The orders issued on this promise were the ones on which the Crown defaulted in the Stop. See Chandaman, *The English Public Revenue, 1660–1688*, 297–298.

[65] *A State of the Case, between Furnishing His Majesty with Money*, 2; see also Roseveare, *The Treasury*, 24; Carruthers, *City of Capital*, 60–61.

[66] *A State of the Case, between Furnishing His Majesty with Money*, 2. The first Additional Aid Act also guaranteed payment for goods or services advances. Consistent with traditional practice, however, these claims were not interest-bearing. See the Additional Aid Act 1665 (17 Car 2 c 1 s 7).

[67] The Act specified that the "partie offending shall be lyeable by action of debt or on the case" (Additional Aid Act 1665 (17 Car 2 c 1 s 7)). The Treasury Order system did not end the tax farming system directly. However, it was dismantled over the next two decades. See Brewer, *Sinews of Power*, 92–95.

[68] Additional Aid Act 1665 (17 Car 2 c 1 s 7); Roseveare, *The Treasury*, 23–25; Horsefield, *British Monetary Experiments*, xii. Compare the discretionary tradition of sovereign repayment described in Christine A. Desan, "Remaking Constitutional Tradition at the Margin of the Empire: The Creation of Legislative Adjudication in Colonial New York," *Law and History Review* 16, no. 2 (1998): 267–274.

[69] Chandaman, *The English Public Revenue, 1660–1688*, 295, n. 2; Carruthers, *City of Capital*, 81–82.

Under Downing's direction, the authorizing legislation extended to government bonds an attribute—the generalized capacity to circulate—that had previously attached only to coin and tax anticipation tallies. The instruments held by public creditors could be transferred by written endorsement. In his pamphlet advertising the bonds, Downing promoted the advantage of transferability. As he argued, "by this means men do daily accommodate their occasion by buying or selling of them." That allowed men to "convert the same into money." By contrast, while tallies had long traveled hand to hand, those instruments carried no statutory guarantee of transferability. Although an informal market for them existed, it had no legal security. Dismissing as inferior the currency that traditional tallies offered, Downing noted that a holder might be unable to convert them, "be his occasions never so pressing." He also took steps to make the Treasury Orders convenient to lenders outside of London, who could purchase Orders and collect interest on them at locations country-wide. Traditional tallies circulated instead on customary practice and tended to change hands near London.[70]

When it blessed Treasury Orders with currency, the government changed the way it dispensed public enforcement of that quality. The interest-bearing bond became a vehicle of liquidity in its own right, one which the sovereign endowed with transferability in order to borrow money at a lower rate. The new instruments carried interest at 6 percent, a nice profit but far better for the Crown than the 10 to 12 percent it had been paying its traditional lenders. More remarkable than the reduction in its interest rate was the way the Crown had accomplished that deal. Rather than maintaining coin and tallies as the exclusive media it recognized, it granted the quality of currency to a new form of credit. In effect, the Crown traded the capacity to circulate for a better deal in the domestic market for money loans.

The public bonds themselves were not quite money, despite some contemporary and later scholarly claims.[71] They could not be cashed on demand, a feature that would have violated the "payment in course" guarantee. Nor did they come in denominations that facilitated small exchanges. Public bonds were, instead, the thin edge of a paper credit wedge. Even as they left the demand for money per se unsatisfied, they invited extension towards a new form that would act as money. The government would borrow again, this time in bank notes that were, in effect,

---

[70] For Downing's argument that borrowing from the general public would reduce interest rates, see *A State of the Case, between Furnishing His Majesty with Money*, 4. For transferability by endorsement, see the Additional Aid Act 1665 (17 Car 2 c 1 ss 7, 10); see also 19 & 20 Car 2 c 4 (1667) (extending transferability to Orders issued on the ordinary revenue). By contrast, Downing emphasized that anticipations of tax were not "assigneable by endorsement, Registered without power of revocation" (*A State of the Case, between Furnishing His Majesty with Money*, 3). For the circulation of the new instruments outside of London, see *A State of the Case, between Furnishing His Majesty with Money*, 2–3, and compare the exchange of tallies, pp. 178–186.

[71] For the assumption by historians of the Exchequer that its orders could be called "money," see Chandaman, *The English Public Revenue, 1660–1688*, 297; William A. Shaw, "The 'Treasury Order Book,'" *Economic Journal* 16, no. 61 (1906): 40.

private bonds or "promises to pay." (Like conventional bonds, early Bank notes even graced their holders with an interest dividend.) That development built upon Downing's innovation—the government's new willingness to grant currency to a fiduciary instrument.[72]

In order to drive home the virtues of the new regime, Downing advertised the system. In 1666, he published *A State of the Case*, a brief on behalf of the new loan program. The pamphlet compared the new method of "furnishing his Majesty with money by way of loan" with the old method of anticipating taxes by conventional tallies. "The King's letter is to invite to the former," wrote Downing, "as better both for the lender and for the King." Downing detailed the advantages it carried for investors first. They could lend on the security of a national revenue stream, could make loans and collect interest at convenient locations, and could assign their Orders. The king also gained. He could raise money quickly, receive the confidence of his subject-investors, pay a lower interest rate, and obtain funds independent of incoming revenue that could be used "arbitrarily" or flexibly according to the exigencies. The mutuality of advantage would soon come to characterize liberal notions of the market. The idea that the common good could be obtained as people pursued their private interests turned upside down traditional notions of public ordering.[73]

As if to invoke witnesses for that proposition, Downing appended a list of investors from one county. They included notable royalists (Lord Horatio Townshend, Sir Robert Paston), past and present Members of Parliament (Townshend, Paston, Phillip Woodhouse, Sir John Holland, Sir Ralph Hare), and representatives from families of note (the Knevet family, for example, had long roots in Norfolk). Finally, Downing included a copy of "an Order of Repayment." Its language compelled confidence: it was an "order . . . taken" to Exchequer officials "that you deliver and pay of such His Majesties Treasure." The revenue committed to repay the loans was specified ("the sum of 1250000 l. lately granted to His Majesty by Act of Parliament") as was the precise moment when the Order was to be paid ("in course next after 702907 l. 15s. 11d.").[74]

Next, Downing used the press to publicize government bonds as a guaranteed instrument. He posted the "in course" order of payment to investors and published notices of government obligation and redemption dates when they came due in the *London Gazette*. See Fig. 6.2.[75] The gesture established the reliability of the system, the profits to be made from it, and the patriotism involved in becoming a lender to the public. It was the first time a public investment

---

[72] See pp. 296–301, 311–320, 322–327.

[73] See *A State of the Case, between Furnishing His Majesty with Money*. For discussion of developing liberal theory, see pp. 266–267, 274–281.

[74] *A State of the Case, between Furnishing His Majesty with Money*.

[75] For additional notices, see specimens from the *London Gazette*, transcribed in Roseveare, *The Treasury*, 125–126.

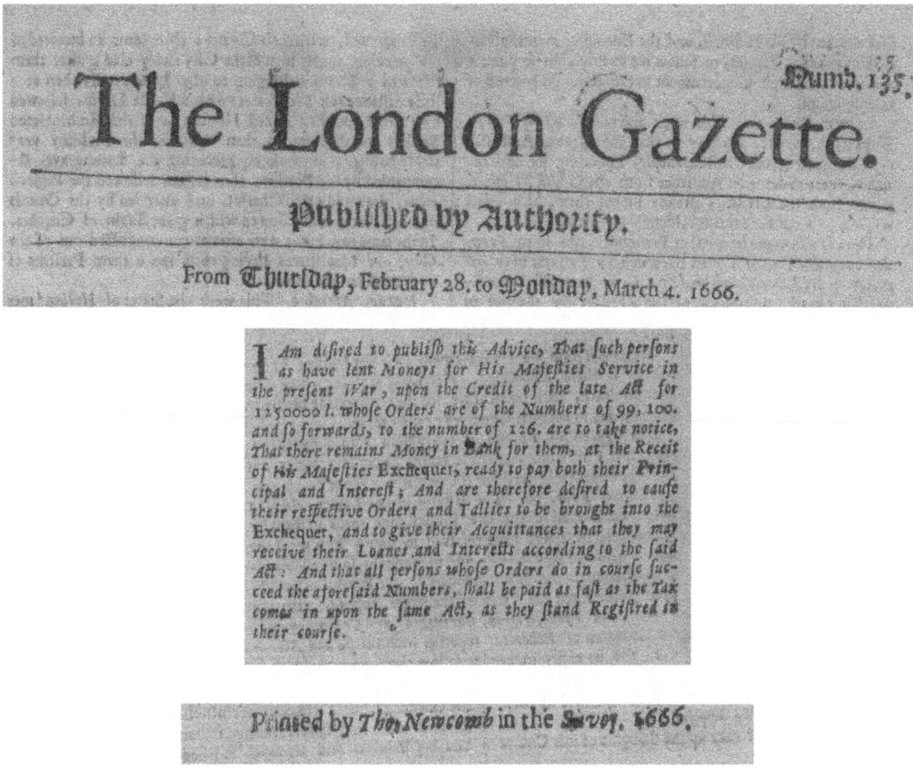

Numb. 135.

The London Gazette.

Publiſhed by Authority.

From Thurſday, February 28. to Monday, March 4. 1666.

I Am deſired to publiſh this Advice, That ſuch perſons as have lent Moneys for His Majeſties Service in the preſent War, upon the Credit of the late Act for 1250000 l. whoſe Orders are of the Numbers of 99, 100. and ſo forwards, to the number of 126. are to take notice, That there remains Money in Bank for them, at the Receit of His Majeſties Exchequer, ready to pay both their Principal and Intereſt; And are therefore deſired to cauſe their reſpective Orders and Tallies to be brought into the Exchequer, and to give their Acquittances that they may receive their Loanes and Intereſts according to the ſaid Act: And that all perſons whoſe Orders do in courſe ſucceed the aforeſaid Numbers, ſhall be paid as faſt as the Tax comes in upon the ſame Act, as they ſtand Regiſtred in their courſe.

Printed by Tho. Newcomb in the Savoy. 1666.

Fig. 6.2 Notice to holders of Treasury Orders, *London Gazette*, No. 135 (February 28–March 4, 1666). Compare the modern appeals made by the British government during World War I, in Fig. 6.3.

opportunity was so broadcast.[76] In 1667, the king publicly reiterated that message, stressing the contribution of the creditors and the assurance of their repayment. They had acted for "the public service" and "the public safety," and had "been so useful to us." Despite hostilities with the Dutch, "their respective interests [were] in no danger at all." The king held his pledge to them "firm and sacred," and would not "on any occasion whatsoever" allow an interruption in payments.[77]

The practice of public lending would penetrate English society. Downing's system grew over the course of the Restoration; a partial default known as the Stop of the Exchequer affected only one group of Treasury Orders.[78] Treasury

[76] Roseveare, *The Treasury*, 24.

[77] Charles II, *His Majesties Declaration to All His Loving Subjects to Preserve Inviolable the Securities by Him Given for Moneys: And the Due Course of Payments Thereupon in the Receipt of the Exchequer* (John Bill & Christopher Barker, 1667).

[78] Although later scholars often assumed that the payment order system was discontinued after the Stop (see, e.g., Horsefield, *British Monetary Experiments*, xii), that default affected only those fiduciary orders issued on the ordinary revenue. Those orders, unconstrained by being tied to a specific revenue measure, were in fact overissued. See Chandaman, *The English Public Revenue, 1660–1688*, 297. The rest of the payment order program was retooled and extended by 1677. It applied to "most of the remaining parliamentary supplies" during the remainder of Stuart reign. Chandaman, *The English Public Revenue, 1660–1688*, 298.

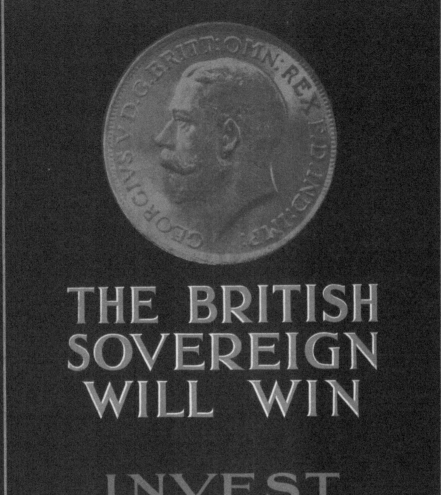

Fig. 6.3 World War I posters promoting lending to the government. The second poster includes in the background an interest-bearing bond or "scrip voucher." The Royal Mint Museum.

Orders were only the first of a long line of vehicles designed to facilitate loans to the government. Annuities, lotteries, tontines, Exchequer bills, and loans from joint-stock companies added to the public funds over the next century.[79] The Additional Aid Act that pioneered Tallyes of Loan aimed to raise £1.25 million. By 1694, the public debt grew to £6.1 million and by 1750, to £78 million.[80] Citizen participation rose with the size of the public debt. In its early years, a limited number of English took up Downing's invitation to lend to the government. Twenty-five goldsmith bankers held the great majority of government Treasury Orders in 1672. If their depositors—mainly guild members and merchants from the London area—are considered indirect investors, the number swells to about 1,600.[81] But by 1750, 60,000 individuals held government bonds. Their investment attached them ever more firmly to the administration that borrowed from them. As Bruce Carruthers has demonstrated, party politics developed along lines that often if not always ranged those interested in government investment and commerce (Whig), against those committed to older, land-based forms of wealth (the Tories).[82] In ways that historians of the Financial Revolution have explored, the institutional innovation emphasized here became a staple of English political debate.

D. The cash bottleneck

Public credit would reshape English finance. But that story cannot be told, as it often is, without the story of money.[83] Bonds depended on money for their measure: they promised payment in a unit of account that had meaning as an immediate amount of value. As that distinction suggests, credit and money were not interchangeable: money may have been a form of credit, but not all credit was money. The English in the 1660s created instruments that could move

---

[79] P. G. M. Dickson's work has long set the standard in the literature on the financial revolution. P. G. M. Dickson, *The Financial Revolution in England: A Study in the Development of Public Credit, 1688–1756*, Modern Revivals in History (Aldershot: Greg Revivals, 1993). For the deep roots of the early modern developments, see Roseveare, *The Treasury*. More generally, see, e.g., Brewer, *Sinews of Power*; Neal, *Financial Capitalism*; Carruthers, *City of Capital*, 71–83; Murphy, *English Financial Markets*.

[80] Carruthers, *City of Capital*, 10.

[81] Carruthers, *City of Capital*, 64–67. Carruthers, developing research begun by Roseveare, uses data collected after the Stop of the Exchequer to create a fascinating picture of the social and professional character of lending to the government.

[82] See generally Carruthers, *City of Capital*, 7–8, 22, 69–70, 83–85; Steve Pincus, "Addison's Empire: Whig Conceptions of Empire in the Early 18th Century," *Parliamentary History* (2012). For the influential, although somewhat less focused argument, that the interest of moneyed men in secure public investment resulted in increased protection to their property rights after the Glorious Revolution, see Douglass C. North and Barry R. Weingast, "Constitutions and Commitment: The Evolution of Institutions Governing Public Choice in Seventeenth-Century England," *Journal of Economic History* 49, no. 4 (1989). See pp. 287–294.

[83] Keith Horsefield, by contrast, focuses on the currency shortage of the late 17th century as a matter not cured by the development in public borrowing. Horsefield, *Monetary Experiments*, 237–244.

money more quickly from hand to hand, but they had not added to their fragile money supply.

In practical terms, the circulating credit created after 1667 injected liquidity into a cash-strapped society, especially as secondary markets for the sale and purchase of government bonds developed.[84] The trade in securities moved capital from those who wanted investments to those who needed resources, facilitated exchange more generally, and brought interest rates down or at least into convergence.[85] It was a revolutionary change, one that induced a new flow of funds to the state and unsettled doctrines of contract, which would shift to strengthen the novel institution.[86] But while the innovation of public borrowing by bonds had enormous power, it ran into limits.[87] The Crown was paying the public to circulate money to it, rather than adding to the amount of cash in society. And cash was in very short supply.

According to some macroeconomic approaches, there cannot be true monetary scarcity. By definition, whatever amount of money is available serves the number of exchanges made in an economy; prices adjust to allow all transactions to occur. Thus, if a money supply decreases relative to the amount of economic activity that people want to conduct, prices will drop. Because each transaction will "cost" less, there will be enough money to cover them all. The same logic applies to a society with a stable money supply where economic activity is expanding, effectively shrinking the money supply. In the early modern world, for example, increasing monetization could raise the demand for money at a faster pace than rising bullion supplies could service. Once prices adjusted, however, all transactions would still have a price and could be settled in money.

The theory fails to capture a variety of ways in which the money supply may be inadequate, either over the long term or because of difficulties created by changing prices. First, the notion that prices can change so that the money available is adequate to cover all exchanges assumes an infinitely divisible money supply. As in the medieval world, denominations were limited in early modern England, especially at the low end. Erratic circulation and seasonal swings of money's flow could also hamper the process and uniformity of adjustment.[88]

The theory also sets aside the disruptions that the process of price adjustment causes. Price information can feed into decisions about investments and spending

---

[84] See Murphy, *English Financial Markets*, 37–38, 58–64; cf. Dickson, *The Financial Revolution*, 355–356.

[85] See Murphy, *English Financial Markets*, 43, 194–196; Carruthers, *City of Capital*, 80–83; Horsefield, *Monetary Experiments*, xii; Cameron et al., *Banking in the Early Stages of Industrialization: A Study in Comparative Economic History* (New York: Oxford University Press, 1967), 9.

[86] See pp. 281–294.

[87] Recall Downing's argument to investors holding Orders under the Additional Aid Act that they could "convert the same into money"—investors did *not* hold money itself in the figure of Treasury Orders. His position fits with the definition of money used here as a medium denominated in the unit of account that could be used in final settlement of public and private debts.

[88] For the denominations in the mid-17th century, see Horsefield, *British Monetary Experiments*, xi. For such problems in the early modern world, see Muldrew, "'Hard Food for Midas': Cash and Its Social Value in Early Modern England."

to depress or destabilize the economy. Debtors facing an unexpected deflation may decrease borrowing, for example, given concerns about the payments they owe, and thus drag down economic activity despite expanded spending by creditors. Even price drops that debtors and creditors anticipate can produce damaging effects, as people lag in adjustments, including the interest rates they pay and charge on money.[89] Price "stickiness" in wages in particular adds to the problem, inviting turmoil as participants divide over the way transitional harms will fall. Political stability is, in this sense an economic issue, and it poses challenges independent of popular unrest. As early modern commentators emphasized, when money supplies were very low, tax collection was extremely difficult. For nations at war, the difficulties escalate because fiscal demands increase at just the time that families lose manpower and find their livelihoods undermined.[90]

Conditions in the 17th century suggest that money in England was effectively scarce in the sense that caused a variety of such problems. Recent histories identify that time as one of expanding economic activity. Labor moved off the land by enclosures and fen drainage provided the manpower for an increasing variety of manufacturing, from textiles to knives and metalware to glass. Mining of coal, lead, and iron rose: by the end of the 17th century, coal production was twelve times what it had been in the mid-16th century, while lead and tin production doubled between the 1660s and 1680s. Shipbuilding flourished in the late 17th century, as trade increased and the later Stuarts strengthened the navy.[91]

The image of England's boom is not uniform. According to a number of indicators, the wool industry struggled, as smugglers took raw wool to France for fashioning and competing states obstructed the legal export of woolen goods. The East India Company and the Navigation Acts hampered some commercial exchange, although accurate figures on the balance of trade are lacking. Despite those impediments, lighter cloth began to reach larger markets in Spain, Portugal, and the Mediterranean; merchants also opened more routes to India and Asia as the century passed. The British colonies in North America and the West Indies drove up demand for both agricultural exports and finished goods. At the same time, they began to provide raw materials for finished products. Sugar refining and processing grew in England, for example, because of the colonial connection, and goods from the New World flowed to the rest of Europe. But courtesy of the Navigation Acts, they did so in British ships and after passing through British

---

[89] See, e.g., N. Gregory Mankiw, *Macroeconomics*, 5th ed. (New York: Worth Publishers, 2003), 299–301. Conversely, deflation can cause a rise in the purchasing power of money and/or a perception of that rise that will make people feel wealthier.

[90] See Muldrew, "'Hard Food for Midas': Cash and Its Social Value in Early Modern England," 78–79.

[91] Steven Pincus, *1688 The First Modern Revolution* (New Haven: Yale University Press, 2009), 51–59; Murphy, *English Financial Markets*, 10–38.

harbors. The first marine insurance schemes appeared alongside that development, as did fire insurance. Applications for patents rose in the 1680s and as economic activity increased, investors began to experiment with the joint-stock form.[92]

According to a variety of indicators, England experienced falling prices across much of the Restoration period. Tracking forty-four commodities, Ming-Hsun Li finds that a majority declined in price between 1662 and 1693. J. Keith Horsefield, selecting for non-agricultural indices, documents falling prices from 1667 to 1683, aside from an upturn during the Third Dutch War. Both scholars conclude that the low volume of silver coin was a significant, perhaps the most significant, cause of the price drops. That trend is consistent with the hypothesis that existing cash failed to keep up with the demand for it to service economic activity at stable prices.[93] The declining prices are all the more remarkable given that they should otherwise have risen, all things equal: wear and tear, clipping, shaving, and counterfeiting were driving down the value of the silver coin at the same time.

Another sign of low liquidity—substitutes for silver coin—appeared. They did not reverse the trend in prices, although they presumably mitigated it. Towns and private businesses—inns, brewers, bakers, and other tradesmen—had issued tokens since the Elizabethan period. The tokens may have been important at the local level, although they never circulated nationally. In 1672, Charles II prohibited them and, following earlier Stuart examples, issued copper farthings and half pennies instead.[94]

Even as commercial activity increased in England, the problems that bedeviled England earlier in the century reappeared. In the 1680s, gold became overvalued. The mint issued almost four times as much gold as silver coin, depriving people of that everyday currency.[95] Access to cash continued to vary enormously. The poor and people of lower income maintained most of their exchange on credit,

---

[92] Compare the accounts given by Pincus, *1688*, 51–59; Murphy, *English Financial Markets*, 10–38; and Eugen Von Philippovich, *History of the Bank of England and its Financial Services to the State*, trans. Christabel Meredeth, vol. 41, Senate Documents (1911), Book reprinted as congressional document, 49, with that of Ming-Hsun Li, who portrays England as transitioning in a more halting fashion from its agricultural economy. Li, focusing on monetary phenomena including deflation, finds evidence of economic depression during the period. See Li, *The Great Recoinage of 1696 to 1699*, 6–7, 15–25.

[93] Horsefield, *Monetary Experiments*, 3–5; Li, *The Great Recoinage of 1696 to 1699*, 4–7. After almost two decades of deflation, Horsefield finds prices beginning to rise in the mid-1680s. Presumably, the deteriorating quality of the coin finally prompted people to raise their prices, and thus registered as an inflationary force. By 1689, prices began rising steeply, pushed up by government spending as England entered the war against France. See Horsefield, *Monetary Experiments*, 5; see pp. 341–342.

[94] Up to 12 million private tokens may have been produced between 1649 and 1672. The copper coin issues lasted from 1672 to 1676, but were widely counterfeited and disfavored by employers. Muldrew, "'Hard Food for Midas': Cash and Its Social Value in Early Modern England," 101–104. Tin issues followed copper from about 1684 to 1694, when they were replaced again by publicly commissioned copper coin. See C. E. Challis, *A New History of the Royal Mint* (Cambridge: Cambridge University Press, 1992), 370–379. For an overview, including the earlier 17th century Stuart issues, see J. Keith Horsefield, "Copper v. Tin Coins in Seventeenth-Century England," *British Numismatics Journal* 52 (1982).

[95] Challis, "Lord Hastings to the Great Silver Recoinage, 1464–1699," 379–381 (including Table 53).

saving coin for taxes and settling balances. By contrast, the business elite in London held up to £2 million in cash, or up to one-fifth of the circulating coin.[96] According to Li, interest rates were high, around 8 percent as measured by corresponding land values.[97]

Ironically, the reforms attempted by Charles II, including milled money and subsidized minting, exacerbated the situation. Milled money resisted clipping and shaving, but that made its full-weight silver content all the more discrepant from the old, worn, and abused hammered money. People began hoarding and exporting milled money. According to Adam Smith, merchants at times delayed settling large deals so that they could weigh the coins they received. And because the mint no longer charged people for money, the premium on coin dropped compared with silver bullion. People melted coin without concern about the cost of reminting it. Although the government produced more than £3 million in new milled silver between 1670 and 1690, virtually none of it still circulated in the 1690s. Worse yet, the hammered money that remained had lost up to half its value by weight.[98]

Something like £10 to £14.5 million in coin, half to two-thirds of it in silver, circulated at the time of the Glorious Revolution.[99] That amount of coin provided between £2 to £3 per individual. Money moved between people at a pace similar or almost as high as it had earlier in the century.[100] Compared to modern figures, it traveled quickly between users; from the 18th century on, individuals would increase their demand for money, holding significantly more rather than passing it on as fast.[101]

[96] See Muldrew, "'Hard Food for Midas': Cash and Its Social Value in Early Modern England," 93, 96–108. Muldrew puts the concentration higher, at one-quarter to one-third, but one-fifth accords better with Lindert's estimate of £10 million in circulating coin. Lindert, "English Population, Wages, and Prices: 1541–1913," 633–634.

[97] See Li, *The Great Recoinage of 1696 to 1699*, 7–8.

[98] William Lowndes, *A Report Containing an Essay for the Amendment of Silver Coins* (London: Charles Bill & the Executrix of Thomas Newcomb, 1695), 106–107; Challis, "Lord Hastings to the Great Silver Recoinage, 1464–1699," 379–382 (including Tables 53 and 54); Muldrew, "'Hard Food for Midas': Cash and Its Social Value in Early Modern England," 89–91.

[99] Estimates for the total money supply are rough. See Lindert, "English Population, Wages, and Prices: 1541–1913," 633–634 (1688); N. J. Mayhew, "Population, Money Supply, and the Velocity of Circulation in England, 1300–1700," *Economic History Review* 48, no. 2 (1995): 247 (1690). If private bank notes and tallies are included as money, the estimate rises to about £20 million. See Mayhew, "Population," 247. See also p. 624.

[100] Estimates on money's velocity are also rough, and do not correct for the proportion of gold coin, masking the additional strain on the lower value coin supply to service smaller exchange. Lindert's estimates for both early and late 17th centuries are somewhat higher than Mayhew's. Both authors assume that tallies and some private bank notes added several million pounds to the circulating currency, an assumption that would reduce velocity estimates as it raised figures on the money stock. See Lindert, "English Population, Wages, and Prices: 1541–1913," 624, 632–634 (including Table 3); Mayhew, "Population," (including Table 1). Mayhew's recent work finds somewhat lower velocity rates in 1688 than in 1643. See Mayhew, "Prices in England," 37 (Table 8).

[101] Commentators agree that the money supply expanded in the 18th, 19th, and 20th centuries at a rate that significantly exceeded the rise in prices and national income. The increase in money with purchasing power suggests that people in the modern age were holding a much greater amount of money than their

Even correcting for a much more monetized world, the effectively inexhaustible money demand of the English after 1688 suggests that England on the cusp of
the Glorious Revolution was chronically short of money, defined as tokens that
people wanted on hand to settle their public and private obligations. That
conclusion comports with evidence of the high credit:coin ratios used by the
London business elite. Even though this group concentrated a hugely disproportionate amount of coin in its hands, the ratio ranged from 14:1 to 28:1, according
to several probate inventory samples.[102]

Traditional tallies continued to supplement money at higher levels, but Treasury Orders partially crowded out the old practice and the potential for expanding
the money supply that it carried.[103] As part of the effort to guarantee funds to
repay the loans, Downing's reform dictated that the revenues dedicated to that
task should come straight to the Exchequer without diversion. No other tallies—
the usual instrument of anticipation—could be issued on the revenue that was
used for Treasury Orders.[104] In fact, Downing policed the system, stamping out
the conflicting issue of unnumbered anticipation tallies.[105] At certain periods, he
claimed additional revenues for his program; when he dedicated them to the
repayment of Treasury Orders, they became unavailable to fund traditional

ancestors. See Lindert, "English Population, Wages, and Prices: 1541–1913," 624, 632–634 (including
Table 3); Mayhew, "Prices in England," 12–13; James C. Riley and John J. McCusker, "Money Supply,
Economic Growth, and the Quantity Theory of Money: France, 1650–1788," *Exploration in Economic
History* 20 (1983); Michael Bordo and Lars Jonung, *The Long Run Behavior of the Velocity of Circulation:
The International Evidence* (Cambridge: Cambridge University Press, 1987), 4–12 (velocity falling until the
mid-20th century).

[102] See Muldrew, "'Hard Food for Midas': Cash and Its Social Value in Early Modern England," 93.

[103] Other public credit instruments—debentures, etc.—formed part of the tradition represented by
tallies, and invite exploration in their own right. As noted above, "Tallyes of Loan" continued to be issued
with Treasury Orders, perhaps because they were so well established as the tokens that evidenced
government debt. These new tallies did not, however, function the way that traditional tallies had, as
immediate claims upon a revenue agent in the field. By the same token, traditional talllies were not
guaranteed "in course" repayment. Having said that, traditional tallies by the late 17th century had changed
in legal form from their medieval counterparts. The *pro* tally that dominated in an earlier period had been
largely displaced by the "*sol*" (for *solutum*, or "paid") tally. The *sol* form, used only as a receipt in the
medieval period, now circulated as an instrument of anticipation. See Chandaman, *The English Public
Revenue, 1660–1688,* 287–289, 291–295; Dickson, *The Financial Revolution,* 350–351.

[104] Chandaman, *The English Public Revenue, 1660–1688,* 295.

[105] Affronted by Downing's reform and chilled by the possibility that the "in course" guarantee would
destructively limit Exchequer discretion to repay tallies, the Treasurer, the Earl of Southampton, responded
with an effort to raise money on the credit of the Additional Aid Act by anticipation tally, offering 6 percent
interest on the advances. According to the terms of the statute, however, the revenues that came in had to be
repaid to lenders who had advanced money to the government. In effect, Southampton's offer meant that,
as money advanced in return for tallies came in, it had to be used to repay lenders who held Treasury
Orders. The potential for long-term loans that Downing sought to develop was being converted back into a
system of erratic advances by tallies. This time, however, the tallies bore interest and so carried all of the cost
of borrowing and none of the Treasury Orders' promise of pacing and legitimating the king's credit. The
predicament took a "country-wide campaign" to clear; Downing and the Treasury Commission used letters
and published a pamphlet explaining the system publicly. Roseveare, *The Treasury,* 25; see *A State of the
Case, between Furnishing His Majesty with Money.* When the system was extended to the ordinary revenue,
officials worked to cut the use of tallies there as well, and to clear the ordinary revenue of prior claims:
Chandaman, *The English Public Revenue, 1660–1688,* 297–298.

tallies.[106] By the 1690s, creditors discounted traditional tallies sometimes steeply according to what revenues and what order of payment attached to them, matters not always clear.[107]

In any case, it appears that virtually all tallies bore interest during this period, making them a costlier strategy for the government. The practice may have carried over in part from the early 17th century, when customs officials had cashed tallies on request.[108] The example of interest-bearing Treasury Orders also appears to have been contagious. At first, only those Treasury Orders that rewarded people for advancing cash offered interest. Another class of Treasury Orders that went to pay creditors for supplies and goods or to spending departments for future spending or immediate discounting, called by C. E. Chandaman "fiduciary orders," did not bear interest.[109] That difference echoed the older logic in which non-interest-bearing tallies were given for goods and services while interest-bearing notes were issued for cash loans. [110] But if attaching interest was not compelled logically insofar as tallies still operated in the old way, the practice soon spread to them.[111] It may be that as the currency of instruments became a more common property, it also became a cheaper one, undermining the government's ability to trade it for value.

[106] The ordinary revenues (customs, excise, and hearth tax) were generally unrestricted, but were allocated to the payment of Treasury Orders between 1667 and 1671 and 1679 and 1688. Chandaman, *The English Public Revenue, 1660–1688*, 287–295, 300–302. For the system of Treasury Orders, compare Chandaman, *The English Public Revenue, 1660–1688*, 295–300.

[107] Dickson, *The Financial Revolution*, 346–346, 351–352. The proportions of tallies issued with and without a commitment to repay "in course" are not clear from Dickson's account. On the discounting of tax anticipation tallies, see Dickson, *The Financial Revolution*, 343–357. For contemporary witness, see, e.g., *A Letter to a Friend, Concerning the Credit of the Nation: and with Relation to the Present Bank of England* (printed for E. Whitlock, 1697), 13–14.

[108] Recall that Charles II had also ordered payment of interest on some tallies. 12 Car 2 c 9 ss 10–11 (1660). The practice, which probably appeared informally and inconsistently at earlier moments, was apparently familiar to officials in the following years. Roseveare, *The Treasury*, 25; *A State of the Case, between Furnishing His Majesty with Money*.

[109] In other words, these, administratively useful, payment orders were deployed to anticipate revenue within the "in course" system. They joined those representing actual cash loans made to the government. Chandaman, *The English Public Revenue, 1660–1688*, 295–300. Fiduciary Orders issued to the spending departments were modified by the addition of the language "or his assigns" to the name of the public payee. For the provisions regarding those orders issued on the ordinary revenue, see 19 & 20 Car 2 c 4 (1667); Chandaman, *The English Public Revenue, 1660–1688*, 297 and n. 4, 298; Roseveare, *The Treasury*, 31–34. For contemporary reaction, see Samuel Pepys, Mynors Bright, and Henry Benjamin Wheatley, *The Diary of Samuel Pepys* (London: G. Bell, 1924), November 6, 1667. The statutory language concerning these Treasury Orders does not specify, as it does for Treasury Orders issued in return for cash loans, that payment on the Orders would occur only when taxes had been collected, but Chandaman verifies that practice in his study of the period's revenue. Chandaman, *The English Public Revenue, 1660–1688*, 286–287, 295–302.

[110] Roseveare, *The Treasury*, 24; *A State of the Case, between Furnishing His Majesty with Money*, 5. Administrative tallies may have been acceptable for taxes, i.e., cashable immediately—if so, they would represent an attempt to conserve the function of old tallies.

[111] See Chandaman, *The English Public Revenue, 1660–1688*, 296–297 (assuming all orders were interest-bearing; this presumably refers to later practice). Compare Roseveare, *The Treasury*, 33–34 (noting success of discounters to claim interest on advances, although Orders were not explicitly interest-bearing).

The growing importance of Treasury Orders returns us to credit and a last question: could Treasury Orders and other forms of credit themselves resolve the cash bottleneck that hampered economic exchange, public and private, in late 17th century England?

Unlike traditional tallies, Treasury Orders could not be used in lieu of cash for taxes, a quality that would have given them immediate value, nor could that practice evolve informally (as it had for tallies) because it would have violated the "in course" guarantee made to others.[112] The capacity of Treasury Orders to speed the currency of money was itself rudimentary. Although they circulated to some degree, that practice never became easy, as Downing had claimed; their transfer had to occur at a central location and after formalities observed there.[113] The extent to which a significant secondary market for Treasury Orders existed in the late 17th century is debated.[114] Scholars also divide over how quickly markets developed for other forms of public debt that the English innovated during the period, including annuities, tontines, lottery loans.[115] As we will see, the transferability of all such instruments mattered greatly, as the government calculated when it began attaching that incentive to Treasury Orders.[116] But even as they began to change hands, bonds and other public instruments were too limited in reach, high in denomination, and rigid in structure to act as cash. Shares in the joint-stock companies functioned primarily as investments;

[112] See Additional Aid Act 1665 (17 Car 2 c 1) (failing to make Treasury Orders current for paying public obligations). By contrast, currency "even unto the Exchequer" had been suggested by at least one pamphleteer; the suggestion was apparently rejected. See Sir William Killigrew, *An Humble Proposal Shewing How This Nation May Be Vast Gainers by All Sums of Mony, Given to the Crown, without Lessening the Prerogative* (1663, republished 1690, 1696).

[113] For the circulation of Treasury Orders, see Chandaman, *The English Public Revenue, 1660–1688*, 297, 298–99; *A State of the Case, between Furnishing His Majesty with Money*, 2–4. For its limited nature, see Carruthers, *City of Capital*, 62. Dickson implies a more robust market of illegal transfers in tallies. See Dickson, *The Financial Revolution*, 355–356.

[114] Compare Carruthers, *City of Capital*, 62 with Davies, *History of Money* (arguing that a larger secondary market for Treasury Orders existed). The concentrated ownership demonstrated by Carruthers makes his claim that Treasury Orders did not function with anything like the circulation required of a "money" more likely. See Carruthers, *City of Capital*, 62–67 (tracing concentrated ownership of Treasury Orders). Carruthers reviews contemporary moral and political objections that also hampered the currency of debt instruments. Many Englishmen, especially Tories, refused to deal in what they considered stock jobbing and speculation, disapproved of the political influence that they assumed traveled with the new investment opportunities, and disliked the new men of wealth who took advantage of both. See Carruthers, *City of Capital*, 85–86.

[115] Compare Carruthers, *City of Capital*, 75–76 (annuities), 76–77 (lottery loans), with Murphy, who argues that the secondary market in Million Adventure tickets and to a lesser extent, life annuities, was much more substantial, although the extent of the market is difficult to gauge. See Murphy, *English Financial Markets*, 37–38, 58–64 (finding secondary market of uncertain size for Million Adventure tickets, lesser market for life annuities, and small but liquid market for transfers, conducted at the Bank, of Bank stock). Compare Horsefield, "The Beginnings of Paper Money in England" (rejecting annuities, bills of exchange, goldsmith-banker notes, country bank notes as paper money); see also Horsefield, "The Beginnings of Paper Money in England," 74–75 (noting failure of tontine to appeal to investors).

[116] See pp. 290–294.

secondary markets in them did not develop, in any case, until the second decade of the 18th century.[117]

Private credit instruments also failed to fill contemporary demands for cash, although the great need for currency surely stimulated the development of notes and inland bills in the second half of the century.[118] For traders with reciprocal patterns of exchange, those instruments were indispensable. They could not, however, function easily to pay workers or make one-off exchange. The notes issued by the goldsmith-bankers arguably came closer than other alternatives to functioning as money within London. Their use fell, however, after the Stop of the Exchequer, which discredited not only the government, but also a number of goldsmith-bankers who were ruined as the government's creditors.[119] Two decades later, goldsmith-banker notes were again in use. R. D. Richards emphasizes the rich business activity accomplished with them, although others argue that both public and private creditors took them cautiously.[120] Legally rendered negotiable only by statute in 1704, the notes required cashing within a limited amount of time, which varied from one to three days, according to different courts.[121] The circumstances led one monetary historian, Keith Horsefield, to dub goldsmith-banker notes more like "musical parcels" rather than money: the point was to get rid of them quickly.[122]

Although informal institutions of credit played an enormous role in England through the early modern era, the history suggests that significant hardships attached to the system, given its reliance on relations of debt—including high litigation rates, dependency, exploitation, and insolvency.[123] That experience also

---

[117] See Carruthers, *City of Capital*, 76, 82; Horsefield, *Monetary Experiments*, 237.

[118] See pp. 244–245.

[119] Davies, *History of Money*, 252, 254; Horsefield, "The Beginnings of Paper Money in England," 121–122 (noting also effect of the Great Fire in London, 1665, and Dutch wars).

[120] Richards, *The Early History of Banking in England*, 39–50. The Exchequer apparently accepted the notes of a limited number of reputable bankers. Individuals were on their own to gauge the notes' credibility and currency before it became official in 1704. See Horsefield, "The Beginnings of Paper Money in England," 122–124. For a contemporary description that lauds goldsmith-banker notes as money until a decline with the War of the Spanish Succession, see *A Letter to a Friend Concerning Credit and How It May Be Restor'd to the Bank of England* (Printed for Andr Bell, 1697), 1–2, 6–7.

[121] Horsefield, "The Beginnings of Paper Money in England," 124; see also Clapham, *Bank of England*, 32 (describing the policy of the Bank of England to cash notes immediately and to decline identifying them as cash); Richards, *The Early History of Banking in England*, 154 (similar). See pp. 317–318.

[122] Horsefield, "The Beginnings of Paper Money in England," 124–125; see also A. D. Mackenzie, *The Bank of England Note; A History of its Printing* (Cambridge: Cambridge University Press, 1953), 1 (identifying circulation of goldsmith-banker notes as very limited compared with "the purpose of a general issue note"). Davies identifies the notes, by contrast, as a "significant supplement" of the money supply, although it is not clear if he is assuming it functioned to extend credit or to act as cash. Davies, *History of Money*, 252–253. The notes did not function to transfer cash around the country, according to Horsefield, who identifies bills of exchange as doing more of that work. Horsefield, *Monetary Experiments*, 237–239.

[123] For the role of credit in the medieval world, see pp. 191–192, 205–230; and in the early modern period, Muldrew, *Economy of Obligation*; Muldrew, "'Hard Food for Midas': Cash and Its Social Value in Early Modern England," 83–85.

suggests the limits on the capacity of credit to facilitate exchange. As in the medieval period, credit expanded and contracted with the money supply, although factors like the way accounts were settled and the character of credit instruments would affect the pace of the change. Thus, early modern monetary crises appear to have caused credit crunches in the 1590s and the 1620s.[124] And as Eric Kerridge notes in later periods, the availability of credit lessened when much credit was already outstanding.[125]

The English complained bitterly about the inadequacy of the money supply from mid-century on. Ralph Josselin called 1652 "a sad dear time for poor people, only their work cheap; money almost out of the country." A decade later, Samuel Pepys wrote in his diary that workers in the naval dockyard were "going away for lack of money to get work of hay-making or anything else to earn themselves bread.... we have not enough [money] to stop the mouths of the poor people."[126] In his "Brief Memoires relating to the Silver and Gold Coins of England," mint official Hopton Haynes declared that the deterioration of coin was "discernable" in 1672, so that coins smaller than groats (4 pence) slowly disappeared and groats themselves were so counterfeited that "the whole species sunk in 2 or 3 years" after 1676. Worn and clipped, the stuff still circulating was "as flat and as smooth as the blanks at the Mint are before they have been in the press."[127] In a 1671 speech before the House of Lords, a peer condemned Charles II and his reign for having failed in terms that skewered its imperial aspirations:

> [O]f his new majesty's coin there appears but very little; so that in effect, we have none left for common use, but a little lean-coined money of the late three former princes; untill it be of copper farthings; and this is the metal that is to vindicate, according to the inscription on it, the dominion of the four seas.[128]

As the peer suggested, monetary scarcity affected the entire economy.

John Locke, writing in 1691, mapped that reality, tying scarcity at the bottom to the economic illness at higher levels. Farmers and manufacturers, failing money, paid their laborers in corn or commodities, which those workmen took or "sit still and starve." The trade in commodities for pay in turn destroyed markets for the farmers and landholders, who were forced to sell their "butter, cheese, bacon, and corn etc." to the manufacturers. That slowed the ability of those owing rents to pay landlords "and 'tis no wonder to hear everyday of

---

[124] Muldrew, "'Hard Food for Midas': Cash and Its Social Value in Early Modern England," 94–96; see also Mayhew, "Population," 253–254 (including analysis in quantity identity terms); Mayhew, "Prices," 9–14 (similar).

[125] See Kerridge, *Trade and Banking*, 50.

[126] *Diary of Ralph Josselin*, ed. Macfarlane, and *Diary of Samuel Pepys*, ed. Latham and Matthews, as quoted in Muldrew, "'Hard Food for Midas': Cash and Its Social Value in Early Modern England," 106.

[127] Hopton Haynes, *Brief Memoires relating to the Silver and Gold Coins of England* (1700), as quoted in Challis, "Lord Hastings to the Great Silver Recoinage, 1464–1699," 380.

[128] House of Lords Parliament, "The History and Proceedings of the House of Lords," ed. House of Lords (London: Timberlake, Ebenezer, 1742), 107.

farmers breaking, and running away." "For if the tenant fail the landlord," Locke concluded after tracing the attempt of each person to save up enough money to make his payments, "he must fail his creditor, and he his, and so on, till somebody break, and so trade decay for want of money." The "great contentions" that resulted from bad money amounted "to the disturbance of the public peace," concluded William Lowndes, Secretary of the Treasury after the Revolution.[129]

The problem came to a pitch at the public level, a particular concern to Secretary Lowndes. "The receipt and collection of the publick taxes, revenues and debts (as well as of private mens incomes) are extremely retarded," he noted, "to the damage of His Majesty, and to the prejudice of a vigours prosecution of the war." As revenues fell short, they left the government unable to support, let alone expand, its workforce. The laborers that Pepys saw as so tenuously committed to public employment in the 1660s were joined by soldiers, sailors, and suppliers; all had to be paid consistently to render them reliable. And yet, collecting sufficient revenue was virtually impossible. According to Keith Horsefield's figures, the annual tax levy between 1691 and 1699 amounted to £4.56 million. We have seen that estimates put the circulating coin before the Recoinage at between £10 and £14.5 million.[130] As William Petty, Charles Davenant, and others emphasized, the government could not maximize its own collection without decimating domestic trade.[131] As the 17th century closed, then, the English confronted a chronic shortage of currency.

It was an ironic end, given the breadth of their monetary innovation. The government had moved from charging people for liquidity to subsidizing the cost of coin and paying for circulating credit. The new strategy underwrote the production of cash and credit currencies rather than exacting a price for each use of its authority to orchestrate a money. The changes went deeper still, affecting the way people thought about money and the state. When the public grant of transferability had been highly limited, money's origins in public authorship were conspicuous. By contrast, when that grant was diffused, the creation of liquidity could seem a matter arranged by the parties involved.[132]

---

[129] Locke, "Some Considerations of the Consequences of the Lowering of Interest, and Raising the Value of Money," in ed. Patrick Hyde Kelly, *Locke on Money*, 2 vols., vol. 1 (Oxford: Clarendon Press, 1991), 236–239; see also Lowndes, *Amendment of Silver Coins*, 114–115.

[130] For the annual tax levy, see Horsefield, *Monetary Experiments*, 9 (average drawn from Table 1). For the money supply, see p. 258. Horsefield's older calculations put the amount somewhat higher. See Horsefield, *Monetary Experiments*, 14 (Table 2). See also Craig Muldrew's estimate of a slightly lower annual tax levy, but smaller money supply, for the suggestion like that which follows from Lindert and Mayhew's numbers that almost one half of the circulating coin supply would be cycled through the Exchequer if collected in coin. Muldrew, *Economy of Obligation*, 93.

[131] See, e.g., William Petty, *Verbum sapienti*. Keith Horsefield's work on the British monetary experiments of the 17th century suggests the dimension of the debate. Horsefield, *Monetary Experiments*; Horsefield, "The Beginnings of Paper Money in England," 121.

[132] Likewise, the value of money would be assimilated in a new way to the value of other resources. It could now be "borrowed" in similar forms and interest on money would come to seem analogous to rent, or profit on capital. The same kind of process, one that denuded property and capital from the sovereign

Perhaps the most far-reaching of the 17th century's revolutions was the one that located the private orientation towards profit as the force that seemed to make money. That story, including the rise of interests, rights, and a liberal world view, warrants its own chapter.

structures that underpinned them—property and contract rights, and the regulatory rule of law more generally—may similarly have changed the status of land and capital.

7

Interests, rights, and the currency
of public debt

In 1658, Samuel Lambe described as common sense the belief that pursuing public ends was the best way for individuals to achieve their own well-being:

> if all people under one government did seek the generall good, every single person would then receive a particular benefit thereby.[1]

A few years later, pamphleteers had flipped the logic entirely. They argued that if each person followed his own interests, it would enhance the productivity of the whole. As one of the Bank of England's promoters put it, there was an identity between the public and the private interest because pursuing individual ends resulted in benefits to the Nation, investors "being under this happy circumstance, *That they cannot do good to themselves but by doing good to others.*"[2]

The reversal was radical. It reached from political theory into law and jurisprudence to reorganize the English constitution along recognizably liberal lines. At the same time, the new approach became essential to the way the English conceptualized their exchange. Indeed, the shift aligned "interests" as a category that explained agency in matters both political and material with "rights" that merited legal recognition in law.

Despite its importance, the instalment of "interests" as a linchpin of modern analysis and constitutional architecture happened in subtle, somewhat elusive ways. The timing is easier to map. Sometime after the mid-17th century, the opprobrium traditionally attached to the drive for profit and material self-promotion broke down. According to Albert Hirschman, it was after the Civil War that the English began to understand individuals' concern for their own interests—particularly their attention to money profit—as a force that could operate affirmatively for the greater good.[3] The change was mysterious to Hirschman, although he found it manifest in the pamphlet literature.

While the larger philosophical shift drew from many sources, the English innovation in public finance explains key elements of the transition. When investors lent to the nation, they furthered their own interests while contributing

---

[1] Samuel Lambe, *Seasonable Observations Humbly Offered to His Highness the Lord Protector* (1657), A2.
[2] Michael Godfrey, *A Short Account of the Bank of England* (1695), 3–4 (italics in original).
[3] Albert O. Hirschman, *The Passions and the Interests: Political Arguments for Capitalism Before its Triumph*, Twentieth anniversary ed. (Princeton, NJ: Princeton University Press, 1997), 31–42; see also J. A. W. Gunn, *Politics and the Public Interest in the Seventeenth Century*, Studies in Political History (London: Routledge & Kegan Paul, 1969), 1–2, 11.

to the greater community. Public borrowing literally reconciled profit-seeking to the public good. Downing's bond scheme traded on that equation: the practice of public debt both pioneered a new application for "interest" and popularized it.

The practice of public debt also catalyzed legal debate, as people struggled over its character. The 17th century opened with a case affirming sovereign authority over money and closed with one limiting sovereign authority over its own bonds. The high constitutional cases of their day, they are long-neglected dramas about the structure of government. But together, they generated another controversy about the place of interest, particularly interest in profit, in that architecture. While the first case defined public capacity to adjust money's value, the second denied public capacity to modify the amounts due to creditors; public contract for the first time signified a static commitment. The issue, of course, was how the cases fit together.

Working out an answer amounted to organizing the dynamics of money and credit. The ingredients of that drama lie ahead, including the invention of a new money. But the tension between the constitutional cases of the 17th century highlights the importance that public debt held in shaping the new order. The chapter ends by suggesting that a circulating public debt drove the definition of private rights, rather than depending on those rights to develop as so often argued. As that revised sequence suggests, the categories of "the market" and "the law" suggest a misleading separation. The market in public debt had been created by the government when it attached currency to its bonds; that initiative in turn moved authorities to revise the legalities that attached to credit. The Glorious Revolution did not divide the government from the market; rather, it changed the way the government made the market.

A. The legalities for liquidity I: nominalism as political theory

As the English moved conceptually and practically into a new order, they struggled over its legal architecture. That reconstruction project became part of the monetary experiment. Like bookends, legal dramas over money opened and closed the 17th century. We can begin where the century did, with a case that powerfully affirmed the Crown's prerogative to change the value of money. That decision has never been displaced, despite the ascendance of rhetoric and law that emphasizes individual interests and rights against the government on monetary matters. Indeed, the interplay of the early case's logic and later jurisprudence created a profound tension within the legalities that support money in the modern world. Taming that conflict would produce the categories that eventually located money as a private matter, thus immune from public intervention, except when it required rescue by that very authority. Understood in that way, money became neutral and real exchange became independent of the means that made it

Fig. 7.1 Coin like the shilling in this figure was proffered by a private debtor to pay his creditor after Elizabeth I declared the coinage, debased in silver content, to be "lawful and current" in 1601. Used with permission of John Strafford-Langdon.

possible—the dichotomy that founds much economic thought. To get there, we pick up the story as we find it with the last Tudor.

In 1601, Elizabeth I created the issue that reached the courts a few years later; it was one familiar in the long career of commodity money. Facing unrest in Ireland, the Queen had reduced the amount of silver in the coin she used there; she minted the excess into new pennies to pay the troops who put down the rebellion. See Fig. 7.1. By her order, the new coinage became "the lawful and current money of this kingdom in Ireland," while the "pure coin" that had been circulating in the area was demonetized. The Queen's action affected all those with deals still to settle, like Brett, a merchant from the east coast of Ireland who had contracted to pay a London supplier for wares. Brett presented the £100 he owed at the appointed time and place. For a reason that escapes history but would make for good theater, the pay-off was at "the tomb of earl Strongbow in Christ-church, Dublin." See Fig. 7.2. Brett offered Elizabeth's lighter coins in payment on the ground that they were now the "sterling, current and lawful money of England" that was due in the Irish deal.[4] When his creditor rejected the tender, the dispute went to the courts. The issue was clear: in the event that the monarch diminished the silver content of coin, was a debt due in the unit of account as it was currently defined or in the old money that contained a larger amount of metal?[5]

---

[4] *The Case of Mixed Money* (1605) in T. B. Howell, *Cobbett's Complete Collection of State Trials and Proceedings for High Treason and Other Crimes and Misdemeanors from the Earliest Period to the Year 1783*, vol. 2 (London: R. Bagshaw, 1809), 114, 115.

[5] *The Case of Mixed Money* (1605) in T. B. Howell, *Cobbett's Complete Collection of State Trials and Proceedings for High Treason and Other Crimes and Misdemeanors from the Earliest Period to the Year 1783*, vol. 2 (London: R. Bagshaw, 1809) 114.

Fig. 7.2 The 12th century tomb of Strongbow (the earl of Pembroke) was rebuilt during Elizabeth's reign, which may have made it a notable place. The smaller effigy is thought to be Strongbow's son, who died as a child.

Judicial authorities confirmed England's traditional practice in resounding terms.[6] This was nominalism, restated for a new generation: the unit of account decreed by the sovereign controlled as the measure and mode of payment in domestic exchange, regardless of changes to the commodity content of that unit. Perhaps the judges thought that the primer was necessary, given the notorious events of the 16th century.[7] Elizabeth had restored the coinage to the sterling standard, but her maneuver in Ireland was controversial. She took it to raise exigent funds rather than to maintain the money supply. The circumstances were enough to create questions about the basic authority of the sovereign to set the terms of money's value. Those questions were particularly troublesome to the new Stuart monarchy in the face of a Parliament that was already expressing resistance.

The Privy Council, acting as the judicial authority over appeals from Ireland, put any uncertainty to rest. *The Case of Mixed Money* became the landmark statement of English nominalism for the next four centuries (and counting[8]), an emphatic assertion of the monetary canon along at least three dimensions. *The Case of Mixed Money* was, first, a celebration of the executive prerogative over money. Indeed, in the Council's opinion, money amounted to an attribute of

---

[6] For the medieval law on nominalism, see pp. 83–93, 133–138.

[7] See pp. 232–233.

[8] See *Auckland City Council v Alliance Assurance Co.* [1937] AC 587; *Broken Hill Proprietary Co. v Latham* [1933] Ch 373; F. A. Mann, *The Legal Aspect of Money*, 2nd ed. (Oxford: Clarendon Press, 1953, 75–80).

sovereignty. "It appertaineth only to the king of England, to make or coin money within his dominions," declared the Council, setting out on a review of authorities that ranged from early parliamentary legislation to the 12th century treatise writers, "Glanvil, Britton, and Bracton," to more recent common law. "The authority of the Prince" was at the center of the narrative: metal of a certain weight and fineness was not money without a denomination and an impression "as wax is not a seal without a stamp." "And all this ought to be by authority and commandment of the prince," for that made the money lawful, just as his proclamation made it current.[9]

The king's authority was exclusive: "His proclamation only" established the standard of money; he alone changed that standard. "So no other person can do it," the opinion continued, "without special licence or command of the king." The image of monopoly actually understated the relationship between money and sovereignty, the one was integral to the other. It "inheres in the bones of princes," wrote the Council quoting European civil law about the right to mint, it "is included among the rights belonging to the prince" and could not be disinherited (*abdicantur*) from the royal power. The equation went back to biblical roots. "Money has meaning because it advises us, through the impression, to whom it belongs," wrote the judges. The image on money was Caesar's, "give to Caesar what is Caesar's."[10]

Elizabeth's proclamation warned that those who refused her new unit of account, shilling for shilling and sixpenny piece for sixpenny piece, became "contemnors of her royal prerogative and commandment."[11] The condemnation rang true to medieval formulations. Just as it was when Edward I intervened to revalue the pollards and crockards, rejecting the official money was a personal affront to the king. Through the Tudor period, proclamations on the coinage listed the criminal penalties that attached to disobedience, including arrest and imprisonment. It is less clear how effectively 16th century officials enforced the prohibition, but contemporary accounts in the Irish episode told of soldiers forcing people to circulate the debased coin "by cannon."[12] The invocation of contempt confirmed that money was a matter highly identified with sovereignty.

---

[9] *The Case of Mixed Money* (1605), 117.

[10] *The Case of Mixed Money* (1605), 118 (*Monetandi jus principum ossibus inhaeret, Jus monetae comprehenditur in regalibus, quae nunquam a regio sceptro abdicantur*); *The Case of Mixed Money* (1605), 117 (*Et moneta dicitur a monendo, quia impressione nos moneat, cujus sit moneta. Cujus imago est haec? Caesaris: Date Caesari quae sunt Caesaris*); see also *The Case of Mixed Money* (1605), 121 (reiterating prerogative of English monarchs to coin, enhance, and "abase" money, as allowed both by common law "but also by the rules of the imperial law"). The Council took care to emphasize that, in early English government, acts by the sovereign were due to Crown authority alone, even if they were confirmed by Parliament: *The Case of Mixed Money* (1605), 119. I gratefully acknowledge translations from *The Case of Mixed Money* provided throughout by Stephen Cha-Kim and Rowan Dorin.

[11] *The Case of Mixed Money* (1605), 118, 115.

[12] For medieval sources, see pp. 145–146. For the Tudor period, see David Fox, "The Structures of Monetary Nominalism in the Pre-Modern Common Law," in *Money in the Western Legal Tradition*, ed. Wolfgang Ernst and David Fox (Oxford: Oxford University Press, forthcoming 2015).

The second notable aspect of *The Case of Mixed Money* was its discussion of money's purpose. Like its author, that purpose was public, an emphasis that resonated with earlier tradition. As Joel Kaye has written, both Aristotelian and scholastic theory identified "not profit and the desire for gain but the establishment of equality [as] the proper motive and end of exchange." Aristotle had discussed money most extensively in the *Nichomachean Ethics*, locating it within the topic of justice. That chapter, which became part of the medieval curriculum at Oxford, approached money as an entity with the potential to introduce order across the chaos of human relation. The capacity to measure all things allowed value to be quantified and compared, enabling people to make deals that were commensurable and therefore fair.[13]

Aristotelian understandings had changed over centuries of academic debate, rising monetization, and social experience to produce more dynamic ideas of money's role and more sophisticated analyses of risk, interest, and value.[14] But basic elements remained, anchoring a conception of money as a *mensura publica*—Jean Bodin's formulation, quoted by the judges. Every commonwealth needed to have "a certain standard of money," they wrote at the outset of their opinion. Their formulation tracked Aristotle's discussion in the *Nichomachean Ethics*:

> For no Commonwealth can subsist without contracts, and no contracts without equality, and no equality in contracts without money.[15]

The Council invoked the 16th century Flemish lawyer Budelius (Rene Budel) for the same sentiment, one that cast money as alone able to create moral exchange through its ability to price all things in just terms.[16] Attention to the difficulties of barter, a state of affairs rendering both transportation and the "division of things"

---

[13] Aristotle, *Nichomachean Ethics*, written 350 B.C.E., trans. W. D. Ross, Book V, Internet Classics Archive, accessed March 10, 2014, <http://classics.mit.edu/Aristotle/nicomachaen.html>; Joel Kaye, *Economy and Nature in the Fourteenth Century: Money, Market Exchange, and the Emergence of Scientific Thought*, Cambridge Studies in Medieval Life and Thought, 4th ser., 35 (New York: Cambridge University Press, 1998), 45, and 37–55. For the complexities of Aristotelian theory on money, see in addition to Kaye, Barry J. Gordon, *Economic Analysis before Adam Smith: Hesiod to Lessius* (London: Macmillan, 1975), 42–52; Odd Inge Langholm, *Wealth and Money in the Aristotelian Tradition: A Study in Scholastic Economic Sources* (New York: Columbia University Press, 1983).

[14] See, e.g., on the medieval scholastics, Kaye, *Economy and Nature*, and sources cited in n. 13. On later scholastics, see, e.g., Raymond De Roover, "Scholastic Economics: Survival and Lasting Influence from the Sixteenth Century to Adam Smith," *Quarterly Journal of Economics* 69, no. 2 (1955); Marjorie Grice-Hutchinson, *The School of Salamanca: Readings in Spanish Monetary Theory, 1544–1605* (Oxford: Clarendon Press, 1952).

[15] *The Case of Mixed Money* (1605), 116. For the Aristotelian text, see Aristotle, *Nichomachean Ethics*, Book V, sec. 5.

[16] *The Case of Mixed Money* (1605), 116 (*moneta est justum medium et mensura rerum commutabilium, nam per medium monetae fit omnium rerum, quae in mundo sunt, conveniens et justa aestimatio*, or "money is the just medium and measure of all exchangeable things, for it is through the medium of money that a just and fitting price for all the things that exist in the world may come about").

impossible, reinforced the "great utility" of money.[17] Money had been "invented" as well for "the facility of commerce, as to reduce contracts to an equality." "Let there be one faith, weight, and measure," concluded the jurists reverting to Budelius, "and let there be one money, and the order [*status*] of the entire globe will be inviolate."[18]

Money's tonic quality, its affirmative purpose, justified the sovereign's authority to make it and to remake it. *The Case of Mixed Money* considered the long history of change in the commodity content of English coin, including the episode of the imitation pennies, the Great Debasement, and a myriad of rebalancing exercises in both England and Ireland. *Publicae utilitatis*, the public utility, supported those actions.[19] Elizabeth's own decision was like that taken by the state of Rome; it had enhanced its money to defend itself against Hannibal's assaults. The Council found Rome's self-defense appropriate—"the justice of that state was then famous throughout the world." In the end, the judges rested with an adage that conflated money and its management. *Nihil est magis justum quam quod necessarium*—nothing is more just than what is necessary.[20]

That principle also captured a third aspect of *The Case of Mixed Money*. Money was a domestic political matter, as its genesis in sovereign authority and its public purpose indicated. Nominalism, at bottom, plainly asserted the reality that political decisions made money, as it had for centuries. The Council's formulation was aggressive:

> the king by his prerogative may make money of what matter and form he pleaseth, and establish the standard of it, so may he change his money in substance and impression, and enhance or debase the value of it, or entirely decry and annul it, so that it shall be but bullion at his pleasure.[21]

The political identity of money was tied to the reach of the English Crown, one that the Council read to be consonant with Stuart ambitions. It rejected the

---

[17] *The Case of Mixed Money* (1605), 116.

[18] *The Case of Mixed Money* (1605), 116 (*Una fides, pondus, mensura, moneta sit una, Et status illaesus totius orbis erit*).

[19] *The Case of Mixed Money* (1605), 121 (*princeps potest mutare monetem ratione publicae utilitatis*, viz *tempore belli, vel si alias utile populo sit futurum, ita etiam, ut ex corio fieri possit*, or "the prince may alter money for the sake of public utility, for instance in a time of war, but if at any time it should prove useful to the people, he could even have it made of leather").

[20] *The Case of Mixed Money* (1605), 121.

[21] *The Case of Mixed Money* (1605), 118; see also *The Case of Mixed Money* (1605), 128. The Council cited a series of common law precedents. It also recounted Lyndwood's early 15th century commentary on a c.1332 constitution of Archbishop Simon Mepham arguing that when, after a man's death, an outstanding deal had to be completed either in "the money now flowing, or in the value of the sterling which was flowing at the time of the making [of the deal]," current money should control because "the money having changed, the deal [*statutum*] must be seen as having changed, so that certainly it should be understood according to the new terms/circumstances, and not according to the old." See *The Case of Mixed Money* (1605), 129 (*in moneta jam currente, vel valor sterlingorum que currebant tempore statuti . . . Nam mutata moneta, mutari videtur statutum, ut scilicet intelligatur de nova, et non de veteri*).

contention that English kings had ever waited on popular consent when they revalued coin, dismissing Continental proposals to that effect. Long accustomed to making monetary changes, the prince "can do such a thing freely."[22]

The point was larger than a matter of governance's form, even the form of absolutism. The principle at issue reached the character of money itself. Confronted with the question whether the Irish coin at issue was "sterling" for purposes of the contract, the Council embarked on a remarkable foray near the end of its opinion. It traced the genealogy of the English unit of account or, as the judges put it, "the name and the nature of sterling money were enquired and discovered." The journey began with a debate over what money was first associated with the political territory that was England. It continued through a discussion of the silver penny as the measure of "every other coin or piece of silver"—that is, as the unit of account. The opinion then reviewed the course of the penny's commodity content, noting its diminution over the centuries. That exercise left them to consider whether Elizabeth's Irish coin could count as sterling since it was underweight even as against the current standard.[23]

The Council's genealogy took it to the ultimate issue: whether the value of money was natural or political, intrinsic or extrinsic, "the preciousness and weight of the substance" or "its valuation or metonymy...its shape and stamp." It was the "extrinsic good" (*bonitas extrinseca*), the Council concluded, that "is the form and essence of money (*formalis et essentialis monetae*)...for without such form, the most precious and pure metal that can be is not money." It is not the "natural material of the body of money," they reasoned, quoting the 16th century French jurist Molinaeus (Charles Dumoulin), "but its imposed value that is the form and substance of money, which is not of a physical body, but rather a contrived one."[24]

The logic dismissed the importance of the commodity content of money in favor of its public definition. In rapid fire, the Council returned to Molinaeus ("By law it matters not whether more or less silver is contained within it, so long as it is official (*publica*), genuine, and legitimate"), invoked the 14th century Italian jurist Baldus ("With coinage, one should pay more attention to its use and circulation than to its substance"), and reached all the way back to Seneca ("Both the man who owes gold coins and the man who owes leather imprinted with an official stamp is said to be in debt"). It was, in other words, money's political

---

[22] *The Case of Mixed Money* (1605), 121 (*si princeps consuevisset mutare monetam auctoritate propria, sine consensu populi, a tempore cujus initii memoria non existit, tunc libere imposterum eum hoc facere posse*, or "if the prince were accustomed to changing money on his own authority, without consent of the people—and there exists no memory of the origins of this custom in time—then he can do such a thing freely").

[23] *The Case of Mixed Money* (1605), 123.

[24] *The Case of Mixed Money* (1605), 125 (*non materia naturalis corporis monetae, sed valor imposititius* [sic] *est forma est substantia monetae, quae non est corpus physicum sed artificiale*).

identity—indeed, its identity as a matter *owed to the sovereign*—that made it money.[25]

The Case of Mixed Money captured and presented, in rich detail, the jurisprudence that supported English money as a nominalist entity through the medieval period. But the monetary experiments that followed also drew deeply on *The Case of Mixed Money*. From George Downing's effort to create a circulating public debt to the invention of Bank notes (as we will see), each deployed the authority that the government held over its own debt in order to create new currencies. *The Case of Mixed Money* could never, then, be superseded. But although it remained authoritative, *The Case of Mixed Money* could be rendered inconspicuous, eclipsed by reasoning that seemed incompatible with it.

B. The ascendance of interest

"Interest" is basic to theories of human action in Western modernity; arguably, it is the lens that makes agency itself visible. Identified by philosophers Thomas Hobbes and James Harrington as a register that explained human experience, individual interest served in the hands of writers like David Hume and Adam Smith to explain essential patterns of human behavior. It became a moral vocabulary to Jeremy Bentham and his colleagues, subsequently appearing as the compass of welfare economics. The discipline of economics more generally developed around the assumption that individual decision-makers acted consistently to maximize their own interests, paradigmatically material profit. In political science, rational choice approaches take that orientation as primary, and much behavioral theory aims to qualify rather than to displace the explanatory power of that motivator.[26]

But for all its contemporary resonance, individual interest was far from an organizing tenet in medieval Europe. Human agency itself fit oddly in an order understood as divine, except perhaps insofar as free will was a puzzle in the

---

[25] *The Case of Mixed Money* (1605), 125 (Molinaeus: *de jure non refert sive plus sive minus argenti insit, modo publica, proba, et legitima moneta sit*; Baldus: *in pecunia potius attenditur usus et cursus quam materia*; Seneca: *Aes alienum habere dicitur, et qui aureos debet, et qui corium forma publica percussum*). (The printed version of the case misprints Baldus, Baldo degli Ubaldi, as Balaus.)

[26] Thomas Hobbes, *Leviathan, or the Matter, Forme, and Power of a Common-wealth, Ecclesiasticall and Civil* (London: Andrew Crooke, 1651); online at Project Gutenburg Ebook, accessed June 25, 2014, <http://www.gutenberg.org/files/3207/3207-h/3207-h.htm>; James Harrington, ed., *The Commonwealth of Oceana; and, A System of Politics*, Cambridge Texts in the History of Political Thought (Cambridge: Cambridge University Press, 1992); David Hume, "Discourse V: Of the Balance of Trade," in *Political Discourses* (London: R. Fleming, 1752); Adam Smith, *The Theory of Moral Sentiments*, 250th anniversary ed. (New York: Penguin Books, 2009); Jeremy Bentham, *An Introduction to the Principles of Morals and Legislation* (Oxford: Clarendon Press, 1907). For the development of interest in liberalism, see, e.g., Appleby, *Economic Thought and Ideology in Seventeenth-Century England* (Los Angeles: Figueroa Press, 2004); Poovey, *A History of the Modern Fact: Problems of Knowledge in the Sciences of Wealth and Society* (Chicago: Chicago University Press, 1998); Michel Callon, ed., *The Laws of the Market*, Sociological Review Monograph (Oxford: Blackwell Publishers/*The Sociological Review*, 1998); C. B. Macpherson, *The Political Theory of Possessive Individualism: Hobbes to Locke* (Oxford: Clarendon Press, 1969).

drama of redemption. Self-interest, greed, the drive for material well-being and profit—all were condemned as vices for centuries. According to their medieval genealogy, they were human proclivities that divided peaceable communities and obstructed a person's path towards salvation.[27]

The Reformation opened new avenues of thought about individual experience and feeling. Protestant theologians dismissed the need for authoritative inter-mediation between God and humanity, attacking ecclesiastical hierarchy and, in many cases, advocating direct religious engagement. Their emphasis located faith as an intensely personal commitment and diffused liturgical practice to popular levels. The connection to human agency was not direct—Max Weber would most famously assert the cruelty of Calvin's insistence that people lacked any impact on their predestination to be saved or damned. But religious ferment undermined traditional hierarchies and turned attention to the individual's recognition of God.[28]

The insistence on inner or perhaps innate religiosity extruded the worldly. At the same time, it shaped that material level, like the sacred, as a more atomized matter. Earthly existence became a contested arena, one related by religious thinkers to the spiritual in different ways. According to Weber's reading of the reformed sects, work became a manifestation of individual piety. Insofar as adherents competed to assuage anxiety about their own godliness, they dedicated themselves to productive activity. Each moment was to be sanctified by the use of God's creation. That discipline arguably reframed commercial efforts, locating profit as an acceptable artifact of effort.

On a narrower point that had peculiar momentum, John Calvin connected reformed thought to material incentive yet more directly than Weber had suggested. When he considered material activity, Calvin argued that interest on loaned money legitimately rewarded its use. Catholic scholastics had, by the 16th century, diluted prohibitions that barred charging for money. Compensation for risk and for the gain that money would have generated had a person kept it justified payment for it, as did other rationales like the costs incurred in trans-porting it or in having repayment delayed.[29] Nevertheless, Catholic doctrine discouraged lending at interest, and clergy until the mid-18th century could

---

[27] See Morton W. Bloomfield, *The Seven Deadly Sins: An Introduction to the History of a Religious Concept* (East Lansing: Michigan State College Press, 1952), 74–75 and passim (avarice); Arthur Eli Monroe, *Monetary Theory Before Adam Smith* (Cambridge, MA: Harvard University Prees, 1923), 170–173, 248–271.

[28] See Christopher Hill, *The World Turned Upside Down; Radical Ideas During the English Revolution* (London: Temple Smith, 1972); Max Weber, *The Protestant Ethic and the Spirit of Capitalism*, trans. Talcott Parsons (London: Routledge Classics, 2001).

[29] John Thomas Noonan, *The Scholastic Analysis of Usury* (Cambridge: Harvard University Press, 1957), 105–132; Gordon, *Economic Analysis*, 187–217, 244–272; Eric Kerridge, *Trade and Banking in Early Modern England* (Manchester: Manchester University Press, 1988), 34–35.

deter lending at interest in the locales they controlled.[30] By contrast, Calvin's position cleanly accommodated efforts to structure greater economic incentives into public arrangements (or to allow them in private arrangements), although it did not approximate the modern approach to agency as an interest-driven matter.[31]

Local governments in the Dutch republic began developing public debt with the promise of interest to compensate lenders. That strategy functioned critically during the late 16th century, when the provinces faced overwhelming military expenses in resisting Spanish occupation. Authorities could defer revenue demands into the future while using borrowed funds. In turn, public creditors gained a stake in the successful levy of taxes. No longer would all citizens share an identity as taxpayers; some now gained monetarily from the compliance of their peers.[32]

At the same time, the public face of "interest" was undergoing reconstruction. In medieval Europe, the "common good" or *salus populi* had operated to justify political rule that guaranteed civil order and military defense. But by early in the 16th century, Machiavelli challenged the assumption that the common good comprised a harmonious set of prescriptions by emphasizing the worldly course that sovereigns followed when defending their polities; Hirschman begins his intellectual history of "interest" with the Italian statesman. That term, understood as the purpose of princes and kings, apparently entered English parlance from the Continent about a century later.[33] As J. A. W. Gunn reconstructs its genealogy in England, "interest" was popularized by the writing of a Protestant, the Huguenot Duke of Rohan, rather than writing of Machiavelli. It referred to the end of statecraft, as in "the interest of England," and gained legitimacy in that guise.[34]

It may be that interest became so fertile a concept in England because of what happened next. The Civil War divided Parliament and the Crown, and the Protectorate fractured political agreement further; the circumstances put "the interest of England" into direct contention. Commentators of every stripe

[30] See David Dickson, "Catholics and Trade in Eighteenth-Century Ireland: An Old Debate Revisited," in *Endurance and Emergence, Catholics in Ireland in the Eighteenth Century*, ed. T. P. Power and K. Whelan (Dublin: Irish Academic Press, 1990), 89–93. See, e.g., R. Arcedeckne, *A Short View of the Practice of Giving Money at Interest* (1734); Dickson, "Catholics and Trade," 89–93; see also Jeremiah O'Callaghan, *Usury or Interest Proved to Be Repugnant to the Divine and Ecclesiastical Laws, and Destructive to Civil Society* (London: C. Clement, 1825), 136–137. I am grateful to James Hartley's insight for the argument here and to Patrick Walsh's scholarly guidance.

[31] See André Biéler, *Calvin's Economic and Social Thought*, trans. [from the French 1961] James Greig, ed. Edward Dommen (Geneva: World Alliance of Reformed Churches, 2005), 145–148.

[32] See Margolein 'T Hart, Joost Johker, and Jan Luiten Van Zanden, eds., *A Financial History of the Netherlands* (Cambridge: Cambridge University Press, 1997), 11–34. For material suggesting that the Dutch allowed higher interest rates than did officials in other countries, see, e.g., Arcedeckne, *A Short View of the Practice of Giving Money at Interest*, 72, 82.

[33] Hirschman identified Machiavelli as a peddler of the concept who was generally influential, while Gunn considers the English adoption of the term more specifically. See Hirschman, *The Passions*, 12–14, 32–34; Gunn, *Politics*, 36.

[34] Gunn, *Politics*, 36–38.

competed to define the category as they struggled to articulate what policies would benefit the nation, and even which authorities should lead it. Oliver Cromwell used the term with particular frequency, the insistence of a constitutional parvenu. "Interest" was confirmed, then, as a political matter.[35]

It was fragmented at the same time. One pamphleteer linked interest to the "people's principal," which had been swallowed up by abusive kings, and other authors tied it to the "natural rights" of those subjects. At about the same time, commentators began to emphasize the importance of people's "interests." To C. B. Macpherson, those interests had in fact created the conditions if not the necessity for the Civil War: the struggle occurred as men swept away the constraints of traditional morality in order to pursue the acquisition of wealth in a "fairly complete market society."[36] One mid-century writer maintains the singular use of the term, but his logic folds in a varied field. It also suggests the dawning respectability of the concept:

> Whatever it is that a man hath interest in, if that interest (as he conceived at least) be a just interest, shall he not have liberty to plead for it...And shall he have scornfull reflexions put upon him, for doing this so necessary a duty? Must he passe for a covetous worldling, a selfeseeker, a lover of his profit, and a carnale interest more than truth...because he askes for his owne?[37]

Gunn cautions against the conclusion that the salience of "interest" as a matter of statecraft naturally supported reference to private "interests." To be sure, few commentators reduced the public good to individuated interests.[38] As Gunn reminds us, "Generations of sermons and works on social morality had proclaimed the incapacity of ordinary citizens to deal with public policy." Their job was to be obedient, loyal, and surely God-fearing as well. In law and common morality, the stricture against self-dealing was embodied in the truism that no man should be judge in his own case. When they defined the public good, pamphleteers and political commentators commonly invoked the defense of the kingdom, the Protestant cause, national independence, and economic prosperity including work for the poor, as well as protection from arbitrary taxation and other abuses of the prerogative, and even (eventually) "freedom."[39]

But private interests did become important elements in political debate about the public good, as commentators began to push lines of thought that made individual concerns productive of public well-being. Political pamphleteers justified Parliament's representative role on the ground that its members shared

---

[35] Gunn, *Politics*, 40–41.   [36] Macpherson, *Possessive Individualism*, 66.

[37] *The Establishment or, a Discourse Tending to the Setling of the Minds of Men* (JG, 1653), 9–10.

[38] But see Richard Overton, *An Appeale from the Degenerate Representative Body the Commons of England Assembled at Westminster* (1647); letter written by R. Overton to Henry Marten (1646), as reprinted at LIBERTARIANISM.org, accessed June 20, 2014, <http://www.libertarianism.org/publications/essays/arrow-against-all-tyrants>.

[39] Gunn, *Politics*, 11–12, 17, 32–35.

both the interests of others in private property and the burdens of those coun-
trymen from taxation. As they were driven to protect their own affairs, office-
holders could act in ways good for the whole. The reasoning recognized self-
interest as conducive to public ends, suppressing intimations that the two could
conflict. More generally, the transformative thinkers of the times rooted the
raison d'être of civil society in the determination of people, each possessing
their own persons and labor, to protect themselves. As Macpherson argues,
that reasoning animated Hobbes in his defense of a unified sovereign and
Harrington in his ambition to create a balance between gentry and people. It
also supported critiques of the Crown and its attempts to make the "interest" of
the kingdom mysterious and unassailable to second-guessing. Rather, commentators put unprecedented emphasis on the particular concerns of men, dissatis-
fied by sweeping assertions that the sovereign preserved the people within a state
from enemies. The most populist thinkers went even further, emphasizing
the rationality and discernment of common people to know their own good.
Ranged against the trope that no man should act as his own judge, another
proverb gained currency as a political slogan during the Civil War. "Can any man
tell better than yourselves," wrote a pamphleteer, "where your shoe pincheth
you?"[40]

Commentators qualified the reach of the argument that shared interests
resulted in political action for the public good. Their claims focused on those
interests that affected public policy, particularly interests in property. The identity they suggested was generally implied rather than articulated, and drew power
from the exigent conditions of the Civil War. Skeptics noted the ambiguity that
attended efforts to define particular interests and resisted the suggestion that they
could amount to a generalized good. For example, the assertion that Members of
Parliament watched out for their property interests rationalized office-holding by
the propertied alone, neglecting the position of the poor. In the hands of radical
groups like the Levelers, the observation carried a democratic charge that challenged Parliament's own legitimacy. On the other side of the political spectrum,
Royalists resisted attempts to elevate individuated demands because they
detracted from the prerogative, even at the conceptual level.[41] And for religious
thinkers, the interests of people ultimately collapsed into divine purpose.

The political experience of England, however, had transformed attitudes
towards "interests" by the time of the Restoration. They did not, in aggregate,
amount to the public good—but the public good had to include them with
specificity. They no longer referred exclusively to the dubious proclivities of

---

[40] See *A New Found Stratagem Framed in the Old Forge of Machivilisme* (1647), 10–11; see also
Marchamont Nedham, *Mercurius Politicus*, No. 94 (March 18–25, 1652): 1474. See generally Macpherson,
Possessive Individualism, 263–271; Gunn, *Politics*, 3–35.

[41] Gunn, *Politics*, 3, 9–25, 29–32.

sinful men, but to the valid concerns of people.[42] And they had been invoked to promise unity rather than division; by the second decade of the Civil War, commentators were arguing that compromise would only come by securing the interests of all parties.[43]

Readied by those developments, the career of interest(s) expanded abruptly when the monarchy was re-established. It was there that the practice of individual interests (plural) would be directly reconciled to the national interest (singular): Charles II's innovation in public finance brought statecraft and private interests together. The campaign to create public credit, conducted during the 1660s, created common ground between the realpolitik of states and the materialist orientation of individuals. As in Hirschman's chronology, the harmony between the two priorities dates to that decade.[44]

As for the interest of the nation, Downing's priority was traditional—he invented Treasury Orders to raise money for the sovereign's defense of the kingdom. His advertising campaign emphasized the Crown's goal and its need for funds to address any exigencies. Charles II echoed that argument, stressing "the public service" provided by those lending to the government and the "public safety" secured by their contributions.[45]

But investing in bonds also brought monetary rewards to citizens. Like the Dutch, English officials had more latitude than those in Catholic countries to use material incentives and to promote them without ambivalence or qualification.[46] Downing, as we have seen, had actively promoted bonds as productive for lenders—he emphasized the compensation coming to them and dedicated particular revenue streams paying both principal and interest. Charles II likewise swore to keep the "respective interests" of lenders safe, despite wartime hostilities.[47]

Downing's program and the advertising campaign that accompanied it lauded calculating investment on the part of the general public as a worthy civic activity. It joined similar proposals, publishing and promoting the same logic. As William Killigrew put it when explaining his scheme for a tax-backed note that would circulate and bear interest, "This unites the King, and People, by the strongest bonds; I mean, *their interest*, to support each other." The author of another such project advocated it as "more for the benefit of the present and future owners of money, a prejudice to none, but a great convenience to many, and a public good."

---

[42] Likewise, they had moved beyond their technical legal meaning as an entitlement. See Gunn, *Politics*, 39–40.

[43] As Gunn develops this latter notion of "interest," it is conceptually distinct from the interest of agents in protecting their own concerns. Gunn, *Politics*, 43–52.

[44] Hirschman, *The Passions*, 31–42.

[45] See pp. 250–251 and n.77.

[46] See pp. 275–276. In fact, usury laws continued to limit the Bank of England's latitude to raise discounting charges through the period. The Bank of England instead discouraged borrowers by becoming more selective about which bills to accept. See N. J. Mayhew, *Sterling: The History of a Currency* (New York: Wiley, 2000), 129.

[47] See p. 251 and n. 77.

A government minister later recommended a form of interest-bearing paper money to merchants as "beneficial to trade in general, and their own private interest." The fanfare that the government made about the investors it had enlisted also suggested their patriotism.[48]

The innovation of public debt made citizen-investors out of subjects. Action in one's self-interest could further the public cause; the new institution of public credit thus legitimated private concerns as motivators. Indeed, we could go further. Public credit did more than suggest a world in which individual interests aggregated to amount to the common good—it designed that world. As Michel Callon has argued, intuitions are rarely independent of structures. Rather, they are powerfully supported when systems are built to reinforce them.[49]

In his analysis of political thought during the Interregnum, J. A. W. Gunn brilliantly delineates the power that the concept of interest held as a "social force," while insisting on its independence from "any notions of a right that might be possessed by an individual and equally unrelated to the ends of foreign policy."[50] But when he incorporated the orientation towards profit as the impetus that would fuel popular inclination to lend, Charles II harnessed that force. In that sense, institutionalizing the orientation was not distinct from the intellectual movement Gunn identified or that Macpherson made famous as "possessive individualism." Rather, when Charles II wrapped public finance around interest, he applied and entrenched that motivation. The intervention set England on its path towards the modern political economy by offering people a way to profit while furthering the public fisc.

A few decades later, one of the Bank of England's founders, Michael Godfrey, expressly equated matters of national interest and the personal interests of investors. For "interest" clearly had a precise and material private sense. Bank investors would be motivated "to lessen the interest of mony" for others because it was in "their own interest to do it." They more they lent the government, the more they could increase their own profit: the rate they had locked in from the government (8 percent) would be relatively higher than those others could gain and they would make even more when people stepped up borrowing as the common rate dropped. At the same time, "interest" had a clear (and also

[48] Sir William Killigrew, *An Humble Proposal Shewing How This Nation May Be Vast Gainers by All the Sums of Mony, Given to the Crown, without Lessening the Prerogative* (1663, republished 1690, 1696), 9; Thomas Neale, *A Way How to Supply the King's Occasions with Two Millions of Money* (1694, republished with attachment 1695), 2; Thomas Neale, *A Proposal for Raising a Million on a Fund of Interest* (1694), 2; Charles Montague, "A Document relating to the Establishment of Paper Credit (1696)," in *The Great Recoinage of 1696 to 1699*, ed. Ming-Hsun Li (London: Weidenfeld and Nicolson, 1963), 238. For the plans to publicize investors, see p. 250; see also Montague, "A Document Relating to Public Credit," 238; J. Keith Horsefield, *British Monetary Experiments, 1650–1710* (Cambridge, MA: Harvard University Press, 1960), 123.
[49] Callon, *Laws of the Market*.   [50] Gunn, *Politics*, 43–52.

material) meaning in the public realm. The more they provided money to the government, the more they served "the interest of the Nation."[51]

Beyond a simple identity of interests, the Bank's founder was articulating an entrancing new conception, one generative of an emerging liberalism. In fuller quote, his excitement becomes palpable:

> [T]he more they [the investors] serve the interest of the Nation, so much the more they serve their own, they being under this happy circumstance, *that they cannot do good to themselves but by doing good to others.*[52]

Perhaps the world was providentially organized so that, by attending to self-interest, people furthered the common good.

C. The legalities for liquidity II: the case of public debt

The promise of individual interests to mobilize lenders was tested just as the Bank of England was established. *The Case of the Bankers* arose out of the very success that the Treasury Orders achieved. By 1667, their popularity had induced the Crown to extend the promise of "in course" payment to Orders issued on the ordinary revenue.[53] But as the Crown entered hostilities with the Dutch, it failed its enlarged responsibility to repay. In what became known as the Stop of the Exchequer (1672), Charles II delayed payment on a large number of Treasury Orders, representing some £1,365,733 plus interest. Relative to annual Crown revenues that averaged somewhere short of £2 million, the debt was enormous. The Stuart government negotiated with its creditors, agreeing in 1677 to allocate an annual portion of a specified excise revenue to repay them. Over the next fifteen years, the Crown intermittently made payments on the obligation. When Parliament in 1690 appropriated the revenue it had previously dedicated to paying the creditors to the latest military exigency instead, the claimants despaired.[54] They sued the Crown in the Court of the Exchequer (see Fig. 7.3)—*The Case of the Bankers* was named after the profession most of them shared. It raised "a point of as great moment as ever came to be discussed in Westminster-hall," wrote John Somers, Lord Keeper of the Seal.[55]

---

[51] Godfrey, *A Short Account of the Bank of England*, 3–4.
[52] Godfrey, *A Short Account of the Bank of England*, 3–4 (italics in original).
[53] The action taken by royal proclamation was endorsed by Parliament (19 & 20 Car 2 c 4 (1667–1668)); Henry Roseveare, *The Treasury, 1660–1870: The Foundations of Control*, Historical Problems, Studies and Documents, no. 22 (London: Allen and Unwin, 1973), 32; see also p. 251.
[54] 2 W & M c 3 (1689); J. Keith Horsefield, "The 'Stop of the Exchequer' Revisited," *Economic History Review* 35 (2nd Series), no. 1982 (1982): 514–517; Bruce G. Carruthers, *City of Capital: Politics and Markets in the English Financial Revolution* (Princeton, NJ: Princeton University Press, 1996), 122.
[55] *The Case of the Bankers* (1690–1700) in T. B. Howell, *Cobbett's Complete Collection of State Trials and Proceedings for High Treason and Other Crimes and Misdemeanors from the Earliest Period to the Year 1783*, vol. 14 (London: R. Bagshaw, 1812), 1, 43.

Fig. 7.3 Court of Exchequer, Westminster Hall, from "The Microcosm of London," engraved by J. C. Stadler (fl. 1780–1812).

As Somers understood, the case went to the heart of the executive's prerogative to spend. Exactly how that power would be policed by Parliament after the Glorious Revolution was contested, but the Crown's traditional authority was in little doubt, and went far beyond repaying lenders.[56] The sovereign owed public creditors of many types, from suppliers to soldiers. Discharging its obligations amounted to distributing the public revenue. And distributing the public revenue was the core of governing, a matter that required latitude to respond to all demands in ways that were good for the public. "The treasure of the crown," as Somers put it, "is that upon which the safety of the king and kingdom must, in all ages, depend."[57]

According to that view, the sovereign needed to retain discretion to spend as the public good required, no matter if a legal settlement like the 1677 agreement

---

[56] The constitutional settlement brokered at the Glorious Revolution left spending authority with the Crown, while transferring authority over raising revenue to Parliament. The Commons could and did, however, contest the extent of executive control by working to develop oversight of executive expenditures. See Betty Kemp, *King and Commons, 1660–1832* (Westport, CT: Greenwood Press, 1984), 32–75; P. D. G. Thomas, *The House of Commons in the Eighteenth Century* (Oxford: Clarendon Press, 1971), 65–88.

[57] *The Case of the Bankers* (1690–1700), 43.

with the bankers dicated otherwise. That discretion had a profound institutional pedigree: Somers's seventy-page opinion, one of the longest ever delivered in the court, traced the intricate history of the sovereign's immunity from suit. Consistent with that practice, public creditors could enter the courts to demand payment only after obtaining the Crown's consent. The bankers had skipped that step when they sued in 1690.[58]

Compared to *The Case of Mixed Money*, Somers's argument was discreet in its defense of the prerogative, mindful of creditor demands, and judicious in its elaboration of the Crown's concerns. And indeed, the bankers' claim was clearly different—it demanded that the government pay money it had promised, not that it keep that money the same in content. At bottom, however, the Crown's authority to use the "treasure" it held was at issue in each case. Somers, like the Privy Council before him, put the barbarians at the gates of the kingdom and dared his opponents to take away the Crown's ability to make its own decision:

> So that suppose there was only 4,000l. in the exchequer, and we were threatened with a foreign invasion, how shall this money be disposed? Says the treasurer, to raise men to pay the army and our fleets, that by their assistance we may prevent the enemy from coming amongst us. No, say the barons [sitting as judges in the Court of the Exchequer], we must pay the bankers with this money, though at the same time we open the gates, and let in Hannibal to our utter ruin and destruction...[59]

There was no doubt about the gravity of the dilemma Somers illuminated. The depth of his research, the somber tone of his opinion, the warning that resonated in its conclusion—all underscored the stakes. Somers may have been motivated to protect William's regime at a time of fiscal crisis by staving off the huge burden of payment. As a committed Whig and patron of John Locke, however, he would have no ideological disposition to preserve the monarch's power. His opinion appears driven largely by the constraints of the common law he so painstakingly documented.[60]

---

[58] The opinion explored as well the alternate remedy usually employed by claimants, reliance on the administrative processes of the Treasury to pay as soon as circumstances allowed. For a summary of the complexities that attached to the "petition of right," the administrative remedy, and relevant scholarship, as well as a detailed analysis of the case, see Christine A. Desan, "Remaking Constitutional Tradition at the Margin of the Empire: The Creation of Legislative Adjudication in Colonial New York," *Law and History Review* 16, no. 2 (1998): 268–272. Chief Justice Holt, who opposed Somers's conclusion, agreed that the bankers had petitioned the barons of the Exchequer directly, rather than filing a petition of right with the king. See *The Case of the Bankers* (1690–1700), 35, 37. The issue was how much process was necessary, given the 1677 settlement that promised payment "without any further or other warrant to be sued for" (*The Case of the Bankers* (1690–1700), 11).

[59] *The Case of the Bankers* (1690–1700), 103.

[60] See William Searle Holdsworth, *A History of English Law*, 17 vols., vol. 7 (London: Methuen Sweet and Maxwell, 1982), 33–35; William L. Sachse, *Lord Somers: A Political Portrait* (Manchester: Manchester University Press, 1975), 74–76; Desan, "Remaking Constitutional Tradition," 268–272. For contrary assessments, see Horsefield, "The 'Stop of the Exchequer' Revisited," 272; Carruthers, *City of Capital*, 124–125.

The common law confronted a new phenomenon, however, in the institution that the Crown itself had created. Innovation had occurred on several levels, some practical and some conceptual. Downing had designed the logistics of public borrowing to induce easy and widespread participation. The value of the bonds depended in part on their ease of transfer, a claim that rested on popular belief that they would be reliably paid. Investors had been encouraged to think of themselves as stakeholders in a public project, to consult their own estimations of gain, and to consider those expectations as compatible with the greater good. The persuasive logic of the enterprise had been advertised by the Crown, performed for years before the breach, expanded over time, and acknowledged in negotiations. Moreover, public bonds created a resource, a new form of circulating credit, that offered great promise, as it were, to a society desperately attuned to the problems of liquidity. All these development wrapped government borrowing into the constitutional debates sweeping across England.[61]

During the first decade of constitutional settlement, *The Case of the Bankers* made its way up the judicial hierarchy—suit in 1691, an appeal in 1696, and determination by the House of Lords as ultimate judicial authority in 1700. Throughout the journey, arguments like Somers's confronted a new legal discourse. The bankers won at the first level, convincing a majority of the barons (the judges of the Exchequer's trial court) that their suit directly against the Crown was lawful.[62] At the appellate level, a majority of judges including Sir John Holt, Chief Justice of the King's Bench, accepted the bankers' procedural leap. Holt's tour through the case law was relatively brief. Implicitly, it acknowledged novelty in the bankers' effort and sought consonance if not precision in the precedent.[63] His real argument was substantive. Like the argument of the bankers, it rang in an idiom recognizably liberal.

Holt began with a premise that was at first glance unremarkable: the king had the right to alienate his revenue. But Holt's review gave him the occasion to locate the bankers as deserving claimants. They were like others who had benefitted the realm, a realm that operated on incentives. "And there ought to be a power in all governments to reward persons that deserve well; for rewards and punishments

---

[61] For the diversity of interests and constitutional thematics in the Glorious Revolution, see, e.g., Steven Pincus, *1688 The First Modern Revolution* (New Haven: Yale University Press, 2009); Hill, *The World Turned Upside Down*; Appleby, *Economic Thought and Ideology in Seventeenth-Century England*.

[62] The barons categorized the bankers' petition as one "of right," a conclusion denied by Somers. They also held that Charles II could alienate the excise revenue as he had in the 1677 settlement. See *The Case of the Bankers* (1690–1700), 6–7.

[63] See, e.g., *The Case of the Bankers* (1690–1700), 35 ("It is true . . . that the legitimation of any case may be suspected that has no case of kin to it . . . But I think I have found out some kindred to this present case"); *The Case of the Bankers* (1690–1700), 37. ([In a case of rent due] "it would be too hard to drive the grantee of the rent to his petition of right to the king. No, certainly, he may come to the court of the Exchequer . . .") The novelty lay in the path to the barons of the Exchequer for a money payment, without the approval of the king as by petition or right, or the treasurer. See *The Case of the Bankers*, 34–35.

are the supporters of all governments." The Crown had frequently used material recompense—revenues, pensions, estates—to recognize contributors.[64]

That was enough for Holt to connect earlier practice to the newly charged power of individuals and their interests. "We are all agreed that they have a right," continued Holt about the bankers, "and if so, then they must have some remedy to come at it too." The logic dissolved the differences that set the Crown apart from an individual:

> [T]he king himself, by reason of such his letters patents, hath obliged himself to make such payments. As in the case of an obligation where debt is brought upon it, and a recovery is had; it is not so much the judgment of the court as binds the property, as the obligor himself, who by his bond has subjected his property to be determined by the judgment.[65]

Likewise according to the bankers, the king was a party like all others, an argument that elevated the claim of the individual party even as it drained the power of the prerogative:

> indeed it would be a hard thing to say that the court of Exchequer can relieve the king against the subject, and not help and relieve that subject when he produces a legal title against the king.[66]

Recall that the sovereign in the traditional view, from the early days of *The Case of Mixed Money* to Somers's meticulous reconstruction of executive discretion, was essentially unique. As an authority identified with public ends, its determinations to allocate the public revenue could never be routinized. By contrast, Holt approached the Crown as a contracting party like other contracting parties ("as in the case of an obligation where debt is brought upon it..."). The king was analogous to an individual "obligor." Likewise, "his bond" was analogous to the bonds of private persons. As it did in their cases, his bond "subjected his property to be determined by the judgment." In Holt's hands, the bond's payment became an automatic matter, one triggered by the moment of commitment, without the possibility of second-guessing that Somers had emphasized.

The new approach identified as well the agents who would implement payment. In Holt's view, the judges responded appropriately to the bankers' request. Their action was remarkably mechanical. In mapping the logic of the king's obligation, Holt wrote "this determination of the barons in this case is not thus any judgment of their own," but that of the king, who had obliged himself to make payments. It was that original decision that bound the property, "not so

---

[64] *The Case of the Bankers* (1690–1700), 30.

[65] *The Case of the Bankers* (1690–1700), 55; see also *The Case of the Bankers* (1690–1700), 109 (Bankers' Brief): "A right and title without a remedy ... seems contrary to all laws, and to the rules of justice and reason."

[66] *The Case of the Bankers* (1690–1700), 109.

much the judgment of the court."[67] In this sense, the judges cast their attack on the prerogative as fidelity to the Crown's own command.[68]

Even as Holt portrayed the authority being transferred to judicial actors as minimal, they were gaining independence from the Crown as part of the Revolution's political settlement. As theories about the separation of powers developed, the courts claimed stature as a branch with an autonomous mandate.[69] Holt justified judicial decision-making by denying its potency; his judges acted primarily to effectuate the royal will in taking a loan. That conception was transitional, however. Over time, the judges would become more detached from the executive and its goals. They could then appear to act as arbitrators of private conflict and contract rather than ministers of public order.

By the end of the 17th century, the legal system had tracked the same direction where public authority over money was directly at issue. Monetary decrees setting the unit of account no longer threatened resistors with contempt, as if the offense was to the king's person. Penal sanctions, a remedy suited to maintain a public peace, also fell out of use to police exchange. Judicial enforcement of debt (and other damages) in private dispute resolution remained, now as the dominant way to enforce the official unit of account: the courts would require it as the mode of payment in cases between individuals.[70]

In this world, public ends did not have the status to trump private rights or perhaps, as suggested by the ascendance of interests, private rights had *become* public ends. If judicial officials in the Exchequer could not order that the king's revenue be used to pay his debts, "this would destroy all annuities, rent-charges, and other payments which the crown is obliged to make."[71] The solution was to secure the claims of those who held promises from the Crown, rather than to condition those promises on the Crown's determination of public needs.

Holt claimed to be looking backwards, but his argument swept in forms of finance that were young and experimental, as the bankers were quick to emphasize. "This cause in consequence must affect all persons claiming under the crown, or having any tallies or orders upon or payments out of the Exchequer." The failure of those financial innovations, rather than the barbarians at the gate,

---

[67] *The Case of the Bankers* (1690–1700), 55; see also *The Case of the Bankers* (1690–1700), 109 (Bankers' Brief). (The Lord Treasurer might be a "greater person" than others, but all subjects were "inferior to the courts.")

[68] Compare the traditional argument of the "king's two bodies," in one manifestation of which the ministers serving the true interests of the sovereign acted to restrain the deviant impulses of his or her human side. Ernst H. Kantorowicz, *The King's Two Bodies: A Study in Medieval Political Theology* (Princeton, NJ: Princeton University Press, 1957); Edmund Sears Morgan, *Inventing the People: The Rise of Popular Sovereignty in England and America*, 1st ed. (New York: Norton, 1988).

[69] M. J. C. Vile, *Constitutionalism and the Separation of Powers* (Oxford: Clarendon Press, 1967); Alfred F. Havighurst, "The Judiciary and Politics in the Reign of Charles II," *Law Quarterly Review* 66 (1950).

[70] Fox, "The Structures of Monetary Nominalism in the Pre-Modern Common Law." The kind of enforcement measures used during the Great Recoinage of 1696 invite investigation on this point.

[71] *The Case of the Bankers* (1690–1700), 37.

endangered "the public security."[72] If claimants under those instruments had not remedy, who would accept a pledge of public faith? And yet what else propelled the infant industry of the public funds forward? The advocates of the new order must have felt its foundations shake.

The end of *The Case of the Bankers* was both dramatic and opaque. While a majority of judges had agreed with Holt at the appellate level, Somers as appointing authority had a determining vote in the Court of the Exchequer Chamber. The House of Lords, however, retained appellate authority, and could reverse his holding.[73]

After four days of argument, the House of Lords did just that. The Lords determined that Somers's "judgment of reversal shall be, and is hereby, reversed." There was no substantive opinion, no elaboration of Holt's reasoning or the bankers' assertions. A handful of peers dissented on the ground that the precedents did not support the reversal. But in the face of Somers's argument—70 pages of precedent parsed—the Lords had reinstated the holding of the lower court. The bankers could sue for their money; indeed, they had sued and won.[74]

That conclusion changed the legal design of public debt. Moving with the momentum of the funds as they had been conceived and advertised, the courts now read into them a regime of judicially defined obligation. The revised law became an element in the way that investors approached public offerings, and the investors became a focal point for the revised law. An assumption that the courts could, and indeed should, protect their interests either for their own sake or for the larger good took root, shifting the relative positions of the sovereign, the courts, and the creditors. *The Case of the Bankers* thus articulated the legal workings of a fiduciary relationship as penetrating as the credit that moved hand to hand.

D. The practice of the public debt

If *The Case of the Bankers* was fertile in jurisprudential significance, its meaning was more cryptic in the larger context. Most immediately, the petitioners had a court order, but they still needed a payment. Shortly after the verdict, Parliament again appropriated the revenue stream dedicated to their payment—the only one committed by the Crown's order—to the war effort. The Treasury paid one

---

[72] *The Case of the Bankers* (1690–1700), 109 (Bankers' Brief). For contemporary arguments about the sanctity of the money due to pay off various public funds, see *A Letter to a Friend, Concerning the Credit of the Nation: And with Relation to the Present Bank of England*, printed for E. Whitlock, 1697, 5–6, and demands noted in Murphy, *English Financial Markets*, 61–63.

[73] The Court of Exchequer Chamber sat by the authority of the treasurer and chancellor, posts Somers represented as Lord Keeper. His conclusion was therefore dispositive. *The Case of the Bankers* (1690–1700), 3; John H. Baker, *An Introduction to English Legal History*, 3rd ed. (London: Butterworths, 1990), 158–159. For the authority of the House of Lords, see Sasche, *Lord Somers*, 76–77.

[74] *The Case of the Bankers* (1690–1700), 110–111.

creditor a limited amount in 1701 and then stopped, probably because the funds were exhausted. After all their efforts and a number of apparent victories, the bankers still had no money. Accustomed to petitioning Parliament, they returned to that body.[75] It finally reserved a portion of the incoming revenue to pay off the principal of the borrowing, but only at a much reduced rate of interest.[76]

The point is not that nothing had changed. It is rather that change in a complex constitutional landscape occurred in cross-cutting and sometimes surprising ways. That reality challenges the argument, powerfully asserted by Douglass North and Barry Weingast, that the structural change brought about by the Glorious Revolution—the rise of a representative Parliament and the diminution of Crown control over the courts—itself installed protection for "private rights." According to that hypothesis, Parliament and the courts checked "the state's ability to manipulate economic rules to the advantage of itself and its constituents."[77] Finance is supposed to epitomize the transformation.[78] The Stuart monarchs had frequently defaulted on creditors before the Revolution, an era that North and Weingast identify as one of sovereign debt unfunded by any dedicated revenue stream. According to their narrative, Parliament took control over the revenue after the Revolution and created the national debt when it dedicated specified revenue sources to repaying creditors. That guarantee was enforced through the courts. Before the end of the decade, lending to the Crown had increased enormously, a change that "must reflect a substantial increase in the perceived commitment by the government to honor its agreements." Economic development followed, facilitated by virtue of those "institutions that limit

---

[75] See, e.g., *Considerations Humbly Offered to the Great Councel of England in Parliament Assembled* (1699); *The Case of Many Thousands of His Majesty's Subjects* (1699–1700). For earlier petitions, see Anonymous, *The Deplorable Condition of the Assignees of Sundry Goldsmiths* (1697); *The Case of the Patentees and Their Assignees Who Are Intitled to Several Annual Payments out of the Hereditary Excise* (1695); *The Case of the Assignees of the Goldsmiths, for Their Interest Granted to Be Paid out of the Hereditary Revenue of Excise* (1689).

[76] 12 & 13 Will 3 c 12 (1700–1701); Horsefield, "The 'Stop of the Exchequer' Revisited," 522–523; see also Richards, *The Early History of Banking in England*, 66–67 (tracing final payment to 1723).

[77] Douglass C. North and Barry R. Weingast, "Constitutions and Commitment: The Evolution of Institutions Governing Public Choice in Seventeenth-Century England," *Journal of Economic History* 49, no. 4 (1989): 808. North and Weingast's 1989 article both inherited and modeled the basic narrative, stimulating a bevy of similar accounts and a set of critiques. See, e.g., Margaret Levi, *Of Rule and Revenue* (Berkeley: University of California Press, 1988); Hilton L. Root, *The Fountain of Privilege: Political Foundations of Marketes in Old Regime France and England* (Berkeley: University of California Press, 1994); Rafael La Porta, Florencio Lopez-de-Silanes, and Andrei Shleifer, "The Economic Consequences of Legal Origins," *Journal of Economic Literature* 46, no. 2 (2008). Less positively, see, e.g., Anne L. Murphy, *The Origins of English Financial Markets: Investment and Speculation before the South Sea Bubble*, Cambridge Studies in Economic History (Cambridge: Cambridge University Press, 2009), 53–58; Carruthers, *City of Capital*, 118–136; Nathan Sussman and Yishay Yafeh, *Constitutions and Commitment: Evidence on the Relation Between Institutions and the Cost of Capital*, CEPR Discussion Paper 4404 (2002); D. Stasavage, "Credible Commitment in Early Modern Europe: North and Weingast Revisited," *Journal of Law, Economics, and Organization* 18 (2002).

[78] North and Weingast, "Constitutions and Commitment," 810, 819, 824.

economic intervention [by the state] and allow private rights and markets to prevail in large segments of the economy."[79]

The North and Weingast frame sets an archetype of liberal economic development across a more unruly story, obscuring the dynamics that shaped the early modern political economy although it captures real changes. "Private rights" did not settle naturally on the English as they developed representative institutions, even if we consider the rights of public creditors as the exemplar. The developments in the design of the public debt attributed by those authors to the Glorious Revolution actually occurred before, arguably long before, that transformation. Both Treasury Orders and traditional tallies drew on specific revenue streams. In their original form, tallies anticipated a discrete revenue in named hands and had for centuries. And Downing had made the security of repayment central to his bonds.[80]

Conversely, the security that the Glorious Revolution was supposed to usher in did not appear in the 1690s, a decade of uncertainty for public creditors. When the bankers finally won in 1700, their award was delayed and reduced by Parliament, which had ignored petitions and entreaties since the Stop of the Exchequer itself.[81] Nor were the bankers alone. Pressed by war and economic difficulties, Parliament in 1696 allowed interest due the Bank of England to go unpaid, as also benefits on government annuities, and Million Adventure tickets. By 1697, the revenues dedicated to repay public debts fell short by more than £5 million. By the end of the next decade, more than £9 million in short-term government debt circulated at a heavy discount, reflecting pessimism over the prospects of repayment.[82] Indeed, Parliament's problems paying off the debt led it to a series of disastrous expedients like the chartering of the South Sea Company, the entity that ultimately engineered the most famous speculative

---

[79] North and Weingast, "Constitutions and Commitment," 805, 808, 814–817, 820–821. The nomenclature of "sovereign" and "national debt" is from Murphy, *English Financial Markets*, 54. For other examples of the vocabulary that locates government regulation as "rent-seeking" in contrast to court-enforced rights as non-regulatory, see North and Weingast, "Constitutions and Commitment," 814, 816 (identifying common law courts as traditionally "so favorable to property rights" and "so favorable to private rights"), 817–818, 819.

[80] See pp. 174–175, 178–179, 181, 248. Other authors also neglect the long development of debt funded by dedicated revenues, a matter emphasized by Roseveare, *The Treasury*; compare, e.g., Carruthers, *City of Capital*, 73. "Funded" and "unfunded" debts are misleading terms here; the latter meant "short-term." Such debt might or might not be financed by a particular revenue stream, but did not have a long-term or permanent fund dedicated to that purpose. Patrick K. O'Brien, "The Political Economy of British Taxation, 1660–1815," *Economic History Review* 41, no. 1 (1988): 2. For an argument on other terms that many property rights were secure by the early 17th century, see Gregory Clark, "The Political Foundations of Modern Economic Growth, 1540–1800," *Journal of Interdisciplinary History* 25 (1996): 564–565.

[81] See pp. 287–288; see also Thomas Turner, *The Case of the Bankers and Their Creditors Stated and Examined* (1674).

[82] Murphy, *English Financial Markets*, 56–57; Carruthers, *City of Capital*, 79. Even the Bank's originating and funding legislation (the Tonnage Act of 1694, known as the Bank of England Act) was repealed. H. Clapham, *The Bank of England: A History* (Cambridge: Cambridge University Press, 1970), 49. For Defoe's condemnation, see Daniel Defoe, "An Essay upon the Public Credit" (London: 1710).

bubble of the 18th century. Originally, the Company was given trading privileges, most notably to carry slaves to Latin America, in return for absorbing outstanding government debt from individuals who would accept South Sea stock in exchange. (The Company promised to absorb eight times the amount of debt previously assumed by the Bank of England, and the government was desperate enough to believe it.) Not all were converted. One contemporary asked straightforwardly, "Whether giving a fund of interest upon the debt, and then subjecting the whole to a hazardous and unlikely adventure may be properly called securing our debts?"[83]

More generally, developing a practice of reliably paying the public debt was a century-long project. Again, the South Sea Company furnishes an obvious example. The bubble that made it famous grew out of another scheme to sink government debt, this time in a swap for company shares that were artificially pumped up. In the end, the bust destroyed many lenders and left the government's credibility in tatters. Supporting public credit more effectively required a set of reforms that took time to develop, including regular government payments, the ability to estimate tax returns realistically, the willingness to impose the needed taxes, and the capacity to administer collections and payments efficiently.[84]

In short, some protections for public debt preceded the Revolution and others postdated it. Some event *other than* a constraint on that state's behavior attributed to the Revolution must explain the burgeoning industry and shifting legal architecture of public debt in the immediate period.

The event that catalyzed the growth in public debt and made the property rights of public creditors so compelling was the currency attached for the first time to public debt. When the government determined to popularize public bonds, it not only advertised them as safe but also endowed them with liquidity. Treasury Orders had changed hands only to a limited extent. But the forms of government debt that followed were all transferable. That quality was critical to the body of investors and that body of investors was critical to the government, even if it was relatively small at first. In turn, attaching the quality of currency to bonds multiplied the number of lenders involved and, perhaps as importantly, the number that the government projected to involve. State formation was indeed essential, but it was the turn to a new *medium* made by the Crown that pushed the new practice and legality of "rights."

---

[83] Carl Wennerlind, *Casualties of Credit: The English Financial Revolution, 1620–1720* (Cambridge, MA: Harvard University Press, 2011), 197–234. The quote is from the anonymous author of a 1711 pamphlet at p. 208. As the author coninues, "Whether a voyage to the *South-Sea* . . . and a voyage to the *world in the moon*, are not founded upon the same *phaenomena* of probabilities?" (italics in original).

[84] See generally P. G. M. Dickson, *The Financial Revolution in England: A Study in the Development of Public Credit, 1688–1756*, Modern Revivals in History (Aldershot: Greg Revivals, 1993), 348–355; John Brewer, *The Sinews of Power: War Money and the English State, 1688–1783* (New York: Knopf, 1988), 153–154.

As Anne Murphy shows, people holding different forms of government debt availed themselves increasingly of the ability to transfer it during the 1690s. Public lottery tickets and Bank of England stock changed hands at significant rates during the decade, as did government annuities to a lesser extent.[85] The exchange of public lottery tickets was significant enough that John Houghton offered a running price list. Murphy's argument is that the resilience of lenders— and thus the survival of the public funds as an industry—depended to a great extent on the secondary market that grew up to allow creditors to cash in their investments.[86] Murphy interprets the phenomenon as a sign that people had faith in "the financial market," rather than the government.

Murphy's evidence is compelling that the currency of bonds gave investors the latitude to lend to the public before rights had attached to protect them. But her conclusion that the "financial market" rather than the government was the catalyst for change mistakenly divides the government and the market. "The financial market" identified by Murphy was a *function* of the government and its decision to create a circulating debt. In the early years, it appears that people lent to the government in spite of the uncertainty attending repayment because the funds' liquidity made them easy to cash in, as well as the returns they offered and perhaps the patriotism of the act.[87]

The Revolution's settlement surely affected the process. In its light, the courts began articulating new theories of obligation, although they moved cautiously and their effectiveness was unsettled. Here, Chief Justice Holt is the best witness for the limits on his own power. "Cui bono?" (what good is it?) he asked bluntly if the bankers got a judgment, "what will it signify for them if they cannot come at any money?" His answer can be read doctrinally or more philosophically. "I do think," he wrote, citing statute and case, "that as soon as the writs are delivered to the officers of the exchequer...the property is altered, and the officers become debtors to the parties." Holt evidently hoped that the change in the parties' status created by the fact of the court's judgment could be meaningful, but he also acknowledged that it might not bring the claimants immediately into their money.[88]

---

[85] Murphy, *English Financial Markets*, 58–65; see also Larry Neal, *The Rise of Financial Capitalism: International Capital Markets in the Age of Reason*, Studies in Monetary and Financial History (Cambridge: Cambridge University Press, 1990); Carruthers, *City of Capital*, 81–83. For caution on the circulation of annuities, which was relatively difficult, see Dickson, *The Financial Revolution*, 459; Carruthers, *City of Capital*, 75–76. Note that Murphy is correct to categorize the Bank of England, established as a consortium of investors to lend to the government, as a vehicle for public borrowing. See pp. 296–322; see also Carruthers, *City of Capital*, 76 (noting public borrowing from other joint stock companies as a link between public and private finance).

[86] Murphy, *English Financial Markets*, 58–65. The bankers' original Treasury Orders were also transferable. See pp. 248–249, 251. When the Crown replaced those Orders with annuities in 1677, it facilitated the assignability of the annuities. Bruce Carruthers agrees on the importance of the assignability of early public bonds in their appeal to buyers, although he assumes bonds gained that quality before the early modern period. Carruthers, *City of Capital*, 121.

[87] Murphy, *English Financial Markets*, 55.

[88] *The Case of the Bankers* (1690–1700), 38.

Similarly, North and Weingast correctly point out that the rising power of Parliament eventually would allow it to protect more effectively its constituency. That constituency included the higher-income members of society, who were also disproportionately invested in the new public funds.[89] Those elites, like their Dutch counterparts, entered into alliance with public authorities over matters like tax enforcement, depreciation, and money creation. Public creditors would gain more leverage, if not a guarantee, as Parliament developed the public funds.

Here, however, the vocabulary that assumes an autonomy or universality of the market needs another adjustment. The rights of public creditors did not stand in for "private rights" insofar as that label implies a claim generally accessible to individuals, nor did their claims represent a self-defining body of "property rights."[90] Those who bought offices under the early Stuarts had claimed "private rights" to those sinecures and had those rights protected by the courts.[91] During the same period, those who held claims to common land protested for their own property rights, although with less success as the enclosures continued.[92]

More immediately, when the government in the figure of its judges directly prioritized the claims of government creditors, it diverted revenues and legal attention from the "private rights" of others, whether for better or ill. Thus the excise collection that produced funds to pay creditors was structured in a way that stripped those accused of tax evasion of traditional due process rights, including the right to a jury, the right to trial before an impartial decision-maker, and in many cases the right to an appeal.[93] Likewise, the government violated the private rights of those holding underweight coin when it demonetized that coin during the 1690s recoinage, a monetary intervention that would preserve full-weight coin for public creditors.[94] Similarly, those holding government debt convertible into South Sea stock derided the trade offered in 1711 as one that effectively coerced debt-holders by limiting the terms left to those holding the original public debt. Wasn't "obliging people to subscribe to this stocke, or else not admitting them to share the security given other for their debt" using as much "force as a high-way man demanding money with a pistol in his hand, seeing he does not take it by force, but only tells you what your condition may be if you refuse it?"[95] Those critics were notably silent about the most

[89] See Murphy, *English Financial Markets*, 137–160; North and Weingast, "Constitutions and Commitment," 814, 817, 829.

[90] North and Weingast, "Constitutions and Commitment," 817 (assuming that institutional changes protecting certain wealth-holders made "private rights...fundamentally more secure").

[91] Brewer, *Sinews of Power*, 17.

[92] Pincus, *1688*, 52.

[93] Brewer, *Sinews of Power*, 113. Brewer quotes jurist Sir William Blackstone as noting that "the rigour and arbitrary proceedings of excise laws seem hardly compatible with the temper of a free nation."

[94] See pp. 362–367.

[95] Wennerlind, *Casualties of Credit*, 197–203, 208. The quote is from an anonymous pamphleteer in 1711.

profound private right sacrificed in the whole project of protecting public creditors, the slaves who furnished the South Sea Company's stock in trade.

As a century of realist and critical legal scholarship has emphasized, "property," "contract," and other "private rights" are not self-defining absolutes. Rather, they are labels for a set of state interventions that are and have been used to protect very different people, ends, and capacities.[96] "Capital markets" cannot be "especially sensitive" indicators of "property rights" per se.[97]

In that case, the inclination to identify capital markets with property rights suggests an odd tilt in the modern imagination, one that equates a particularly defined set of rights with an abstract and unbiased standard. Those rights then appear outside of politics, in contrast to "regulatory restrictions . . . on the economy" imposed by policy-makers or legislators.[98] Neutralizing rights allows them to be cast as antithetical to regulation. In turn, the selectivity of the protection extended to certain groups disappears from view, leaving the illusion that the state has actually exited the frame or as North and Weingast put it, "limit[ed] economic intervention and allow[ed] private rights and markets to prevail."[99]

The early modern political economy was an altogether different matter. The Glorious Revolution did not divorce the state from "markets," or remove public interference from "private rights." Rather, it drew upon decades of experimentation and propelled the English towards a new vocabulary of governance. The constitutional drama affected the design of money and credit given their identity as matters of value created by collective orchestration. By 1690, public credit, vaunted to be secure, circulated to an unprecedented extent. That currency attracted creditors and gave them enough latitude to tolerate repeated public delays in payment and defaults. At the same time, the prevalence of public lending created the issue of creditors' rights. At the end of the century, the courts responded to that issue by rejecting a robust defense of executive discretion like that made in *The Case of Mixed Money* and emphasizing their own role as monitors of public commitment. Likewise, they replaced the earlier case's rhetoric of public utility with one identifying individual claims as primary, perhaps as a means of achieving public utility. Finally, the judiciary approached public debt

---

[96] The literature on this point is immense. For an introduction see Duncan Kennedy, "The Stakes of Law, or Hale and Foucault!," *Legal Studies Forum* 15, no. 4 (1991); Morton J. Horwitz, *The Transformation of American Law, 1780–1860*, Studies in Legal History (Cambridge, MA: Harvard University Press, 1977); Barbara Fried, *The Progressive Assault on Laissez Faire: Robert Hale and the First Law and Economics Movement* (Cambridge, MA: Harvard University Press, 1998); and as applied to money, Christine Desan, "The Market as a Matter of Money: Denaturalizing Economic Currency in American Constitutional History," *Law and Social Inquiry* 30, no. 1 (2005).

[97] North and Weingast, "Constitutions and Commitment," 819.

[98] North and Weingast, "Constitutions and Commitment," 814. North and Weingast actually go much farther, claiming that in their story, "the emergence of political and civil liberties was inextricably linked with economic freedom" (North and Weingast, "Constitutions and Commitment," 829). Given the fallacy of equating the development of public funds with economic freedom, that assertion is left aside here.

[99] North and Weingast, "Constitutions and Commitment," 808.

as if it were equivalent to private debt. It was a contract like others between individuals, not an agreement that had special status as a collective pact.

The revised legal vocabulary supported the government's experiment in using a fiduciary form—a promise of value—to create liquidity. The "constitutional commitment" of the new regime was not, then, to *exit* from the market; it was to *make* the market in another way. Even as critics warned contemporaries about its reach, the government developed an infrastructure that "put muscle on the bones of the British body politic," in John Brewer's words. That boom allowed it to shoulder its military commitments through "a radical increase in taxation, the development of public deficit finance (a national debt) on an unprecedented scale, and the growth of a sizable public administration devoted to organizing the fiscal and military activities of the state."[100]

We will add to that list perhaps its most important element—the invention of a new cash. Shortly after they structured public debt around selected private interests, authorities reconstructed money on the same design. In that experiment, the government would use public debt to bind the government to a set of investors willing to circulate their own promises in return for a profit. In the short run, the approach resolved the crisis of currency shortage. In the longer run, it ratcheted up the constitutional crisis suggested by the cases of the 17th century. Money, it turns out, still required periodic recalibration as a public medium. Those recalibrations now conflicted with the static commitments made to creditors. The "market" that resulted was not stable; it required continual intervention and maintenance, as the monetary dramas of the next century revealed.

[100] As Brewer notes, it would be more accurate to say that a stronger state replaced a more privatized one over the course of the 18th century than the other way around: Brewer, *Sinews of Power*, xvii–xviii.

8

Reinventing money

The beginning of bank currency

In 1663, William Killigrew drafted a proposal for Parliament. It claimed to explain "how this nation may be vast gainers by all the sums of money given to the Crown."[1] In the same decade, the English government began to borrow by issuing paper public debt that circulated and bore interest—the Treasury Orders promoted by George Downing. The idea that underlay both initiatives was similar: each suggested that the government take loans by way of a promise that was itself liquid. But Killigrew's proposal differed from Downing's in an important respect. Instead of a paper *public debt* that would circulate and bear interest, Killigrew suggested a paper *money* that would have the same qualities.

In the thirty years after Killigrew wrote, something like sixty projects were proposed by individuals who argued that it was possible to tap the present value of future government revenues to use as money.[2] Author after author claimed to have the perfect design. In fact, many of the proposals had bits and pieces of a mechanism, rather than conceiving exactly how to package value so as to mark and maintain it as the unit of account, as a mode of payment that held purchasing power, and as a medium that was current. But in retrospect, they had taken the critical turn towards modern cash.

That currency was a paper promise of value spent by the government in terms of the unit of account, allowed to circulate, and accepted back by it for taxes and other obligations. Sometimes the notes were promises of value made directly by the government (Exchequer bills); more often they were promises of value borrowed by the government from the Bank of England (Bank notes). The struggle to articulate the character of paper money and its relationship to coin would overflow the century.

When the government used those pledges to pay people, it distributed the value it had borrowed—a kind of public debt—among individuals, who exchanged it also among themselves. When the government took back the notes, it diminished the debt directly or by returning the pledges to the bank. Conceiving its action as a mode of borrowing whether immediately from individuals or from investors in the Bank of England, the government offered interest to the people who advanced value to

---

[1] Sir William Killigrew, *An Humble Proposal Shewing How This Nation May Be Vast Gainers by All Sums of Mony, Given to the Crown, without Lessening the Prerogative* (1663, republished 1690, 1696), A.

[2] J. Keith Horsefield, *British Monetary Experiments, 1650–1710* (Cambridge, MA: Harvard University Press, 1960), 114.

it. In contrast to the centuries during which it had charged for money, the government now paid for the currency it enabled.[3]

The next section considers the predicament that brought public authorities to act on the money supply in the 1690s and led to the political birth of the Bank. The chapter then explores the way that English officials, investors, and individuals structured the Bank's notes as money. The process took the better part of a decade and it left a radical redesign in place. "Capitalism" came when a government institutionalized interest in material profit as the engine—the pump—that made money as well as debt.

A. The turn towards paper money

England passed through the 16th and early 17th centuries in somewhat greater tranquility than her European counterparts, at least as military matters abroad were concerned. Warfare, John Brewer argues, had moved to a manpower-intensive style that left the island too costly to invade while the same setting made it difficult to launch a force. But over the same period, England turned more ambitiously towards the Atlantic, the Mediterranean, and the West Indian world. Its aims brought it increasingly into confrontation with other populations and powers. By the second half of the 17th century, that conflict made mobilizing its army, navy, and civil service into a constant challenge.

Financing government: debt or taxes

A government that urgently needs money—for war, in the English example—has two alternatives. It can tax or it can borrow. The alternatives might even overstate the options. At a fundamental level, the question is really how much to tax now, and how much to tax later in return for money borrowed up front.[4] Borrowing up front becomes the obvious choice in moments of exigency. Taxing is simply too slow and too laborious. In hard times, it produces more resentment than money. And in the currency-straitened circumstances of early modern England, it became particularly oppressive. "[T]here is no nation that is able to carry on

---

[3] As a conceptual matter, the new system raises an interesting issue, left aside here. It seems that the payment of interest on debt that is later canceled means that the system will never "clear." In that sense, there appears to be an inflationary aspect to the modern strategy of liquidity creation, all else equal.

[4] See, e.g., Patrick K. O'Brien, "The Political Economy of British Taxation, 1660–1815," *Economic History Review* 41, no. 1 (1988): 2. From David Ricardo to Robert Barro, a staple of economic debate concerns how the decision to tax versus borrow might affect economic growth, interest rates, and investment. See, e.g., Robert J. Barro, "Are Government Bonds Net Wealth?," *Journal of Political Economy* 82, no. 6 (1974). I am leaving aside here the time-honored expedient of depreciating the money supply, but that strategy can be conceptualized as an inflation tax.

war by the taxes which can be raised within the year," wrote an official worried about financing a later conflict—and England was no exception.[5]

Borrowing money assumes, however, that there is a money to borrow. Recall that something like £10–£14.5 million in coin circulated in England, perhaps two-thirds in silver, on the eve of the Glorious Revolution.[6] As that conflict ended, war with France began. During the combined reigns of William and Anne (1689–1714), England was at peace little more than five years.[7] War expenses drove up public spending from somewhat over £3 million in 1691 to more than £8 million in 1695.[8] In that decade, tax revenues averaged about £4.56 million per year. They were receivable only in coin through at least the middle of the decade, according to an Exchequer rule that required the verification of revenue intake by weight.[9] Some portion of the taxes recorded as received should reflect set-offs made by tally. But tallies aside, satisfying the Exchequer rule would have required an enormous amount of coin, given that silver circulated at approximately one half its official weight by 1695. Indeed, if the Exchequer rule was faithfully followed, netting £4.5 million would have swallowed the entire silver coin supply.[10] And silver would be the coin of choice to pay taxes insofar as people expected gold guineas to appreciate or found them appreciating relative to silver coin. Guineas traveled at a premium from 1693, and appreciated markedly near the end of 1694.[11]

Even as the government spent the money back into circulation, the collecting and processing of revenue in the early modern world slowed its return. During wartime, a significant part of the silver revenues went abroad in any case.

Under those circumstances, the government faced a difficult market for loans. As for the silver coin that still circulated, it was that eroded and underweight money remaining after taxes were paid—a weak reed for a war effort. As for

---

[5] John Adams made the observation about the American Revolution and its financing largely by tax anticipation notes. See John Adams, "Letter to the Comte de Vergennes," in *The Revolutionary Diplomatic Correspondence of the United States*, ed. Francis Wharton (Washington, DC: Government Printing Office, 1780, June 22), 810. For England's inability to support military actions by taxes alone, see O'Brien, "British Taxation," 2.

[6] See pp. 258, 264.

[7] The Nine Years War lasted from 1688 until 1697, and was followed by the War of the Spanish Succession (1702–1713). Anne died in 1714.

[8] See Bruce G. Carruthers, *City of Capital: Politics and Markets in the English Financial Revolution* (Princeton, NJ: Princeton University Press, 1996), 72. For the increase in annual parliamentary grants from £1.18 million in 1689 to £7.9 million in 1696, see Richard David Richards, *The Early History of Banking in England* (London: P. S. King, 1929), 144, and for the increase in fiscal totals from one fifteen-year period (1670–1685, £24.8 million) to another (1685–1700, £55.7 million), see Glyn Davies, *A History of Money: From Ancient Times to the Present Day*, 3rd ed. (Cardiff: University of Wales Press, 2002), 257 (citing Chandaman).

[9] 8 & 9 Will 3 c 28 (1696–1697). The statute exempted only Exchequer bills from the requirement.

[10] The average annual revenue is from Horsefield, *Monetary Experiments*, 9 (Table 1). The estimate of coin depreciation is from William Lowndes, *A Report Containing an Essay for the Amendment of Silver Coins* (London: Charles Bill & the Executrix of Thomas Newcomb, 1695), 106–107.

[11] Horsefield, *Monetary Experiments*, 10–12.

guineas, creditors with those stronger coin could claim a higher price for them. And insofar as the government could borrow the silver or gold coin that still circulated, its intervention would drive up interest rates and displace the credit available for individuals.

William Killigrew, republishing his proposals for paper cash with increasing urgency, captured the public dilemma. As he put it, the Crown needed money "immediately, without staying till the taxes come in, or being oblig'd to take up money, or buy stores at hard rates, and paying by uncertain assignments."[12] "When this war begun," concurred William Paterson:

> the credit of the Nation was low, and the wits on both sides, found no better nor honester way to supply the necessities of the Government, than by enhauncing the price and interest of money; the effect of which was, that the Government was obliged to pay from double to treble, or higher interest: The disease growing daily worse, men were tempted to draw their effects from trade and improvements, and found the best and securest gain, in making merchandise of the Government and the Nation.[13]

At mid-decade, a commentator was even more blunt. He estimated that the recoinage begun in 1695, when completed, would leave 3 million full-weight silver coin and 2 million gold coin circulating, while the levy would amount to 7 million pounds, "so that should trade totally stop, there is *not coin enough* to pay this year's taxes by *two millions.*" Nor would borrowing alleviate the problem because "if the money be advanced by way of loan by private persons, it must be *drawn out of trade*, and so trade ruined."[14]

The solution to the dilemma lay in improvising a way to borrow that created money as it operated. The English had the ingredients for such a solution. Tallies and circulating public debt both made current use out of the future value of public revenues, although neither could remedy the drastic cash shortfall.[15] Working with the logic they had made familiar, Killigrew, Paterson, and others were proposing another strategy (or parts of it): the government should borrow in the form of notes given the capacity to act as money.

---

[12] Killigrew, *A Proposal Shewing How This Nation May Be Vast Gainers by All the Sums of Mony, Given to the Crown, Without Lessening the Prerogative*, 12 (republished 1690, 1696).

[13] William Paterson, *A Brief Account of the Intended Bank of England* (Randal Taylor, 1694), 4. The link between the quantity of money and interest rates was widely noted. On the monopolistic practice of the goldsmith-bankers and others considered to drive up rates, see Davies, *History of Money*, 257; Andreas Michail Andreadìs, *History of the Bank of England, 1640 to 1903*, 4th ed., Reprints of Economic Classics (New York: A. M. Kelley, 1966), 33–35, 56. On the desire to induce interest rates to drop as "the highest interest of the government and people," see Paterson, "A Brief Account," 14–15; see also Paterson, *A Brief Account*, 1–2, 13; see generally Davies, *History of Money*, 256–257; Horsefield, *Monetary Experiments*, 102.

[14] *The Mint and Exchequer United* (1695), 2 (emphasis in original). For the circumstances of the recoinage, see pp. 364–367.

[15] By 1690, the traditional instrument of tax anticipation—the tally—had been weakened by its transformation under the Stuarts. Circulating public credit was also inadequate, given its inability to act as cash and the limited development of secondary markets for it. See pp. 259–262.

In fact, there were a variety of ways that the government could engineer a paper money based on the credit of the government. A multitude of proposals circulated. Some suggested public notes, instruments that would circulate like paper tallies but be good for taxes immediately. Others argued for notes privately issued, backed by landed security. The outpouring of monetary creativity illuminated the proposal that won, as we will see in coming chapters.

That proposal tapped the value of future public revenues by placing long-term debt with private investors and privileging the short-term instruments they issued as money.[16] Put in more familiar shorthand, the government would borrow from a "bank" in the form of its promises-to-pay. As William Paterson's proposal for the Bank of England put it, "a bank, or public fund" would be the means "by which the effects of the Nation, in some sort, might be disposed to answer the use, and do the office of money." Ironically, exactly how that would work was less clear to Paterson than to those proposing public bills. Indeed, how Bank notes came to acquire the capacities of money is the next part of the history here. By the end of the Bank's first decade, however, the basic dynamic was clear.

First, the government would use those promises-to-pay when it spent, thus assimilating them to the existing unit of account.[17] Both public officials and investors expressly assumed that the government would use Bank notes as currency: the loan was made up front by the investors in paper and the capital subscribed was not fully called in for several years, precisely because the notes could act as "fresh money brought into the nation."[18] Second, the government reciprocated the use it made of Bank notes when it spent by taking them back in payment when it taxed. That is a longer story, but, by 1695, a commentator who argued that public bills were a cheaper and fairer way to create cash nevertheless recognized that the notes issued by the Bank of England should be taken "in all the taxes and revenue" because their "foundation is on the Government."[19] Finally, Bank notes were from the start easily transferred between people. The core of the progenitors' idea was that paper promises-to-pay could "answer the use, and do the office of money."[20]

This sketch of the elements that came to animate Bank notes as money demonstrates how the strategy met the monetary dilemma facing the government.

---

[16] Paterson, *A Brief Account*, 2.

[17] I use "Bank notes" here to refer simply to the paper promises-to-pay that the government took, leaving aside for later the technicalities of Bank "bills" versus "notes." See pp. 308–311, 322–327. I capitalize when referring to the Bank of England notes.

[18] For the numbers of notes paid up, see Horsefield, *Monetary Experiments*, 267 (Table L). The quote is from Paterson's proposal. Paterson, *A Brief Account*, 14.

[19] *The Mint and Exchequer United*, 1.

[20] For Paterson, the idea seemed to be to gather resources from investors by publicly funding them with an ongoing interest stream. That would draw ever more of the nation's "effects" into use, as people offered them as security for transferable notes or "assignments upon the fund." The notes, meanwhile, would remain in circulation because they, like the capital itself, were interest-bearing. See Paterson, *A Brief Account*, 2, 4–5; see also *The Mint and Exchequer United*, 1–2.

The government could expand its funds immediately by lodging public debt with Bank investors and spending their promises-to-pay. When it took those promises back in satisfaction of taxes, it could return them to pay down its debt or, indeed, it could re-spend them and tax them in again.[21]

The sketch also documents the singularity of the partnership between the government and the bank from which it chose to borrow, the Bank of England. Purely private partnerships between borrowers and lenders were possible, but they could not produce money that would be universally accepted. An individual could borrow long-term from a goldsmith-banker and take the loan in the form of short-term demand notes on the goldsmith-banker. But neither the borrower nor the lender could be sure that other parties would accept the goldsmith-banker notes, let alone take and hold them instead of immediately cashing them. In particular, the largest creditor of all—the government—had no reason to accept the notes issued by myriad different bankers. It was not obligated to those issuers, and so had no debt that it needed to set off with their various notes. It incurred only inconvenience and risk in taking a stand-in for specie that a goldsmith-banker might or might not have on hand. And if the government did not take the banker's notes, no one could be sure that those notes would be accepted and held by others, aside from those who knew and trusted that banker or moved within a creditor community that used the bank.[22] In other words, goldsmith-banker notes could operate as credit, but not as that particular form of credit so universally accepted—money. And as credit less universally accepted, those notes would be cashed more often and so likely fail in a role *as* money.[23]

The distinction between the partnerships here matters: it makes clear that the development of "money" was not, as so often portrayed, a phenomenon that was accretionary out of private practice. The Bank notes that eventually became "money" resulted from an event that was structurally different. That event was the reconfiguration of value at the collective level.

---

[21] The strategy required the government to increase taxation to a degree sufficient to support demand for the new cash, all else equal, if it were to avoid depreciation. See pp. 385–389. The English government increased revenues during the 18th century to a greater degree than it increased money creation. For discussion, see pp. 45–46.

[22] As in medieval European practice, bankers who shared customers could accept each others' notes, regularly clearing balances owed each other. That practice did not create a private unit of account. Rather it expanded the public unit of account through the creation of reciprocal obligations that were periodically settled.

[23] Compare a contemporary account arguing that a number of conditions set the Bank apart from private competitors. The author advocated, among other differences, that the Bank could be given a monopoly as "general cashire" for "gentlemen, merchants, and traders" in London so that they all cleared their accounts at it, thus expanding the money supply. At another point, the author made the fascinating suggestion that the Exchequer pass (coined) revenues on collection through the Bank so that it could pay demands with that revenue as necessary. Instead (or before that arrangement came about), it seems that the Exchequer accepted Bank bills and notes and turned them over to the Bank of England: *A Letter to a Friend Concerning Credit and How It May Be Restor'd to the Bank of England* (Printed for Andr Bell, 1697), 4–5. An earlier version of the pamphlet is *A Letter to a Friend, Concerning the Credit of the Nation: and with Relation to the Present Bank of England* (Printed for E. Whitlock, 1697).

In fact, money was reinvented under much the same conditions as it was invented. A public imperative in a time of exigency catalyzed an arrangement to produce and spend in units of value that governing authorities soon recognized in satisfaction of (an expanding) tax liability and endorsed as a medium in interim exchange between individuals. In the modern moment, the units were created by borrowing long-term from a bank in the form of its short-term liabilities—its promises-to-pay, or bank notes. The government paid up front for its "borrowing" in note form: interest went to the investors for their provision of the specie security.[24]

The predicament that produced paper money reframes our expectations. If money had developed out of decentralized practices compounded over time, a product of individuals motivated in largely homogeneous ways, we might expect a largely horizontal topography. But because money issued from a political process, we find a much more surprising landscape. Although only lightly reconnoitred here, it is obviously one made of power disparately massed and deployed, arguments over privilege and national policy, and decisions about the way profits should flow.

The political birth of the Bank

The strange twist that brought public authority and private advantage together in the early 1690s had much to do with the ill fortunes that attended them each alone. The Stop of the Exchequer—Charles II's default on the Treasury Orders—had shaken investors' faith in the government and its fiscal expedients. The debacle remained very much in the news during the 1690s, when the Crown's responsibility to repay creditors was being litigated. As William Lowndes put it, "many people have still in their memories the loss they sustained," and the ongoing dispute was a source of "prejudice" against the proposals for a public paper currency.[25]

---

[24] As occurred in the Bank's early years, the bankers could choose to pass on some of the proceeds by making their own notes interest-bearing. See pp. 308–311. Note that, in the medieval world, those holding bullion went to the mint when coining it was cost-effective for them (or when coerced to do so by the sovereign). In that sense, they gained from the operation. They had paid with a portion of bullion, however, for the cash premium that attached to the coin they received. The modern arrangement presented a new form of profit. Investors got paid in money for their action contributing to the money supply, while the government attached a cash premium to their notes. As we will see, they were now receiving the fee (or part of the fee) that people had once been willing to give the government for its service in making money. Another comparison makes that point clear. The public bills alternative to Bank money, Exchequer bills, also carried interest. In that case, the government paid a widely diffused group of direct creditors, rather than the bankers, when it circulated those bills. In the latter case, the government's payment was concentrated and sent to the hands of those who, as intermediaries, would become a conduit to noteholders, now indirect creditors of the government. The issue then becomes to what extent the services provided by the bankers merited their fees.

[25] William Lowndes, "Remarks Upon the Proposal for Establishing a Fund to Raise Two Millions," in *The Writings of William Paterson* (London: Judd & Glass, 1859), xxvi; see generally pp. 281–294.

William III's administration was itself new, the result of an untested settlement. Rumors of Jacobite strength circulated, and evidence of Louis XIV's power abounded.[26] At the same time, the goldsmith-bankers and other money dealers evoked popular distrust and dislike. Contemporaries charged them as usurers and frauds, schemers who kept inadequate security and lent to unworthy borrowers.[27] Those private lenders ruined by the Stop had taken many of their depositors with them, which damaged their reputations still further.[28] Under those circumstances, a proposal to join public and private capacities or, perhaps, to thread between public and private vulnerabilities, had strong appeal.

The proposal by William Patterson to establish the Bank of England prospered when it garnered the support of influential English Whigs, including Charles Montague, a party leader who could promote it in Parliament, and Michael Godfrey, a wealthy Huguenot financier who could support it among his London peers.[29] From its oppositional roots in the 1680s, the Whig party had developed a broader political platform by the early 1690s. To its long-running antipathy to Catholicism and its adamant support for dissenters, members added vociferous support for measures that increased Parliament's independence and articulated an increasingly rich approach to economic development, identifying it with an environment that emphasized the support of labor as the source of property, the growth of manufacturing, and commerce between producers. Negotiations with William over the principle of legislative rule were difficult, but the Whig commitment to economic development pushed party strategists to favor war with France. That stance followed in part from their fear of Louis XIV, whose absolutism and Catholicism merged into what appeared a unified threat. But Whig militancy was also driven by the principle that trade between manufacturing countries promoted mutual wealth, a vision threatened by French imperialism on the Continent. In 1693 and 1694, William signaled his increasing interest in the party, appointing an array of Whig notables to high offices including Sir John Somers (Lord Keeper), Sir John Trenchard, Edward Russell, Thomas Wharton, and, Charles Talbot, Duke of Shrewsbury (Secretary of State), John Houblon, and Charles Montague (Chancellor of the Exchequer). City Whigs in London had been forthcoming with war financing and their parliamentary counterparts were similarly generous during the 1693–1694 session.[30]

---

[26] On the political uncertainty of the time, the limits on public legitimacy, and its effects on those conceiving the Bank, see Andreadìs, *History of the Bank*, 18–20, 57.

[27] See, e.g., *The Mystery of the New Fashioned Goldsmiths or Bankers* (1676); *Angliae Tutamen, or, The Safety of England* (sold by John Whitlock, 1695), 6 (denigrating financiers as "several sorts of blood-suckers, mere vermin, usurers and gripers, goldsmiths, tally-jobbers, Exchequer brokers, and knavish money-scriveners, and pawn-brokers, with their twenty and thirty per cent").

[28] See, e.g., *The Mystery of the New Fashioned Goldsmiths or Bankers*; see also Carruthers, *City of Capital*, 62–69; Andreadìs, *History of the Bank*, 33–35, 44.

[29] Horsefield, *Monetary Experiments*, 128.

[30] Steven Pincus, *1688 The First Modern Revolution* (New Haven: Yale University Press, 2009), 366–393; Henry Horwitz, *Parliament, Policy, and Politics in the Reign of William III* (Newark: University of Delaware

For Whig legislators, the Bank offered an alternative to the East India Company, an organization discredited by its earlier association with James II and dominated by Tory officers. In 1694, the Company was maneuvering to obtain an extension of its charter from Parliament in exchange for a £600,000 loan to the government. Paterson's Bank proposed to lend the government twice that amount, albeit at a higher interest rate.[31] Whig merchants, manufacturers, and others lined up to support the Bank for reasons both of interest and ideology. Investment in the Bank offered an inviting opportunity on its own terms. As critics emphasized, support for the Bank also opened the possibilities for profit in war insofar as the Bank helped to finance action against France. And as a matter of vision, the Bank beckoned those impatient with Tory arguments that trade must be monopolistically managed or frustrated by their exclusion from that field. As Steve Pincus has argued, the Bank drew on the developing Whig belief that England could build a vigorous political economy out of measures that promoted its internal productivity, particularly in manufactures, and its commerce abroad. That optimism contrasted with the Tory argument that a landed economy appropriately sorted the political power of inhabitants and that trade was a zero-sum competition based on the exchange of agricultural goods. For Tories, the Bank threatened to lower land values and increase interest rates. For Whigs, it represented a new means of finance. Although many were vague on the specifics, banks promised money and a means to pump it into circulation.[32] Finally, the Bank fit within the tradition of reciprocity that had long bound joint-stock companies to the Crown. The Bank's financial clout would assist both its investors and the king, while funding the defense of trade. Although Whig opinion was not uniformly in favor of the Bank, Whigs would strongly dominate its directorate, controlling its political maneuvering against rival institutions.[33]

Paterson proposed an institution that partnered public and private sectors. As the Bank's official historian would put it, the enterprise associated private investors with "what is almost the oldest and the most jealously guarded function of the state, the issue of money."[34] In that conjunction was the novelty. The government could borrow—and thus meet its need for finance. But it would borrow by drawing on a privately loaned "fund of credit" in the form of Bank

---

Press, 1977), 114, 116–117, 132–139; Dennis Rubini, "Politics and the Battle for the Banks, 1688–1697," *English Historical Review* 85, no. 337 (1970): 694.

[31] For a rich account of the ties between the East India Company, James II, and English Tories, see Pincus, *1688*, 372–381; Horwitz, *Parliament, Policy, and Politics*, 130–131.

[32] Pincus, *1688*, 390–393; Carruthers, *City of Capital*, 139–140; see also Rubini, "Battle for the Banks," 694–697.

[33] Carruthers, *City of Capital*, 76–77, 139–146 (including Table 6.2). For those of country persuasion, whether Whig or Tory, the Bank posed greater problems. See generally Rubini, "Battle for the Banks."

[34] See, e.g., H. Clapham, *The Bank of England: A History* (Cambridge: Cambridge University Press, 1970), 2.

notes—and thus engender a circulating medium. The proposal thus joined public debt at interest to the making of money.

B. The paradigmatic medium of the modern world: money from the Bank

The means of the bargain between public and private—its medium at the literal level—was the Bank note. Paterson's final proposal is focused almost entirely on the capacity of the arrangement to produce currency. "Whatever the groundless jealousies of men may be, none can reasonably apprehend any other consequences of this design to the government and nation, but that it will make money plentiful, trade easie and secure, raise the price of lands, draw the species of gold and silver into the hands of the common people..."[35] It will allow existing resources, Paterson continued, "at an easie and reasonable rate, to answer the end, and command the use of ready money."[36]

The emphasis on the need to "make coins go further," or replace coins with the "superior" medium of banknotes, as well as enlarge trade, drive down interest, and increase the national stock of money, dominated the debate of the early 1690s.[37] Unlike its predecessor public banks at Amsterdam, Venice or Genoa, Hamburg, Rotterdam, and elsewhere, which were essentially banks of deposit or exchange between current accounts, the Bank of England's "chief original function was that of a bank of issue"—the production of a cash medium.[38]

The innovation was effected, not articulated. One could read the entire authorizing statute, remarks the Bank's biographer, without realizing that "a new and experimental type of public bank was being created, a bank for 'Conveniency', and 'Income', and issue; *but in the first place for issue.*"[39] The 1694 Act, "An Act for granting to their Majesties several Rates and Duties upon Tunnage of Shipps" (today known as the Bank of England Act 1694), appears instead to be about the other part of the deal—the public debt.

---

[35] Paterson, *A Brief Account*, 14–15.

[36] Paterson, *A Brief Account*, 15; see also Paterson, *A Brief Account*, 1–2 (prioritizing aim of "facilitat[ing] the circulation of money"), 5 (noting attempt of proposers to get legal tender currency), 8 (considering effect on circulation of other securities), 9–10 (arguing that money must be based on specie), 13 (reviewing advantages of plentiful money), 17 (identifying Jacobites, usurers, and brokers of money as opponents).

[37] Horsefield, *Monetary Experiments*, 229–230. See, e.g., Godfrey, *A Short Account of the Bank of England*, 2–4, 5, 7. See pp. 340–341. For an earlier such argument, see Lambe, *Seasonable Observations Humbly Offered to His Highness the Lord Protector*, 7, 10.

[38] Margolein 'T Hart, Joost Johker, and Jan Luiten Van Zanden (eds.), *A Financial History of the Netherlands* (Cambridge: Cambridge University Press, 1997), 37, 46; Richards, *The Early History of Banking in England*, 136; Clapham, *Bank of England*, 2–4. The only European precedent appears to have been the brief example (1661) of the Bank of Stockholm. See, Sveriges Riksbank, accessed June 22, 2014, <www.riksbank.se/en/The-Riksbank/History/Money-and-power-the-history-of-Sveriges-Riksbank/Stockholms-Banco/>; Ian Wisehn, "Sweden's Stockholm Banco and the First European Bank Notes," in Virginia Hewitt, ed., *The Banker's Art Studies in Paper Money* (London: British Museum Press, 1995).

[39] Clapham, *Bank of England*, 3–4 (emphasis added).

The requirements of the government loan and the channel for subscribers' contribution claimed more attention in the statute than the logistics that would generate paper money. At first glance unrelated to the matter of a medium, they functioned critically to devise a mechanism that would produce money and do so with a very different dynamic than the old methods. As its title suggested, the Act levied a tax on ships, measured by the "tunnage" they could carry; it then dedicated those revenues to paying interest on a £1.5 million loan to the government. The major part of that loan, £1.2 million, was to come in the form of a "permanent fund" contributed by subscribers, consolidated and managed by a newly chartered "Bank of England."[40] The government was not to repay the principal, at least until 1706. Rather, it would pay interest of 8 percent or £100,000 annually on the fund, along with £4,000 for management costs.[41] Subscribers could contribute up to £20,000, 25 percent of which had to be paid up front at the time of the subscription.[42] The Act directed that the Bank could never lend more than the equivalent of its capital "unless it be by act of Parliament upon funds agreed in Parliament" or the debt would lie against subscribers personally in proportion to their share of capital.[43]

The Bank was subscribed within two weeks.[44] By the end of 1694, the loan had been fully advanced to the government.[45] Subscribed funds were called in over a schedule. By 1696, about 60 percent (£720,000) had been collected; another 20 percent followed by July 1697.[46] Parliament would authorize the Bank to increase its capital regularly over the next decades, up to £6,577,370 by 1709.[47] (As Bray Hammond explains, by the Bank's "capital," contemporaries assumed its basic assets, as opposed to the modern definition of capital as a liability representing

---

[40] See Bank of England Act 1694 (5 & 6 W & M c 20 s 19). The remaining £300,000 took the form of an annuity.

[41] Bank of England Act 1694 (5 & 6 W & M c 20 s 19). The government was to give a year's notice if it chose to repay the principal. Clapham, *Bank of England*, 18.

[42] Bank of England Act 1694 (5 & 6 W & M c 20 s 23).

[43] Bank of England Act 1694 (5 & 6 W & M c 20 s 26); Clapham, *Bank of England*, 18. Given the prohibition, the Bank's private lending was controversial from the start. Clapham, *Bank of England*, 22 (quoting complaint that the Bank was issuing unsecured notes); Horsefield, *Monetary Experiments*, 128–132. On the argument over the clause's interpretation, see pp. 310–311.

[44] Godfrey, *A Short Account of the Bank of England*, 2.

[45] See Horsefield, *Monetary Experiments*, 130, 266–267 (Table L); Clapham, *Bank of England*, 22 n.4.

[46] The first quarter of the subscription came in July 1694, according to the Bank's Cash Book A, while the second call that autumn netted only about 17 percent of the next quarter due, with somewhat less than another 10 percent coming in by end of year. By November 1696, the Bank had accepted bonds "reckoned as Cash" to make up its deficiency in the £720,000 due. See Clapham, *Bank of England*, 304–305 (Appendix F). The majority of the last 20 percent to be called in was submitted by July 1697, after an urgent appeal by the Bank directors who were facing a recoinage-related run on the Bank. See Clapham, *Bank of England*, 42–43. Horsefield reproduces the Bank accounts for March 1696 through July 1710 at Horsefield, *Monetary Experiments*, 264–265 (Appendix 6, Table J).

[47] See Horsefield, *Monetary Experiments*, 264–265 (Appendix 6, Table J); cf. 7 Ann c 30 (1708) (noting doubling of Bank stock to £4,402,343). Of the authorized capital, some £4,574,000 was subscribed. See also Clapham, *Bank of England*, 63–64; Horsefield, *Monetary Experiments*, 264–265 (Appendix 6, Table J). Subscribed funds were not always taken in specie, but included tallies, Bank notes, and bonds. See p. 307 n. 55.

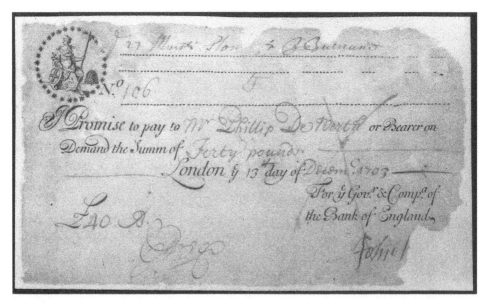

Fig. 8.1 Bank note for £40 from December 13, 1703, engraved by John Sturt with a figure of Britannia as reproduced in Derrick Byatt, *Promises to Pay: The First Three Hundred Years of Bank of England Notes* (London: Spink, 1994), 19.

the equity belonging to stockholders after all other corporate liabilities are satisfied.[48])

The melding of debt and cash creation, if understated, was essential to the whole scheme: the £1.2 million loan to the government was not made in specie, but in *promises-to-pay* specie—Bank bills or notes that the statute allowed the Bank to issue.[49] That device allowed the loan to be advanced to the government before the funds subscribed had been called in. "Yesterday," noted an observer less than six weeks after subscriptions began, "the new bank paid into the Exchequer £112,000, which they did by their bank bills, sealed with the seal of their corporation, being the Britannia sitting on a bank of money."[50] It was more than a temporary arrangement. The great majority of the loan was made in the same way, or by the less formal "Bank notes." See Fig. 8.1. As the Court Minute Books of the Bank document, £1.2 million had been authorized for advance to the Exchequer in Bank bills by November 28, 1694, along with £505,000 in notes. The last payment on December 19 was made in notes alone.[51]

[48] Bray Hammond, *Banks and Politics in Early America from the Revolution to the Civil War* (Princeton, NJ: Princeton University Press, 1957), 134.

[49] Bank of England Act 1694 (5 & 6 W & M c 20 s 28).

[50] Narcissus Luttrell, *A Brief Historical Relation of State Affaired from September 1578 to April 1714* (Oxford: Oxford University Press, 1857), 351. As suggested by the definition of "capital" above, the Bank's practice functionally created a fractional reserve ratio depending on the number of notes issued against subscribed capital actually paid in. See Hammond, *Banks and Politics*, 131–137.

[51] See Horsefield, *Monetary Experiments*, 130, 266–267 (Appendix 6, Table L); Clapham, *Bank of England*, 22, n. 4. As the numbers suggest, the Bank had already started to issue notes in a business discounting tallies and other securities. It had also received and was managing requests for additional advances to the government. See Horsefield, *Monetary Experiments*, 130, 267 (Appendix 6, Table M). All of

Payment in paper issues allowed the funds subscribed to be held by the investors, rather than transferred to the government as the substance of the loan. The progenitor of the Bank, Paterson, clearly recognized the innovative capacity of the arrangement:

> if the proprietors of the Bank can circulate their fundation of twelve hundred thousand pounds, without having more than two or three hundred thousand pounds lying dead at one time with another, this Bank will be in effect as nine hundred thousand pounds, or a million, that must have been employ'd in doing what the Bank will supply, may be employ'd to other purposes.[52]

Other supporters agreed: minimizing how much specie was immobilized was a public benefit "for the rest is left to circulate in trade."[53] The Bank's accounts suggest that many of the funds originally subscribed were fruitfully invested for several years, while a smaller cash reserve was used to redeem those paper notes, both from the original loan and subsequent advances made to the government.[54] In March 1696, the Bank had loaned some £2.767 million to the government of which at least £2 million remained outstanding in paper liabilities, against paid-up subscriptions of £701,913. Some £258,000 remained on hand in cash and bullion. Since almost a quarter of the £443,913 balance of funds had been subscribed in bonds, only some £342,158 had left the Bank's coffers in gold or silver coin.[55] In 1696, the Bank struggled to stave off a run by borrowing, expanding interest paid on its paper, and offering tallies in place of its own instruments. Reluctantly, the directors finally called in another 20 percent of the balance of capital (40 percent) due.[56] In later years, it ran a lucrative business "circulating" Exchequer bills for the government on a subscription of funds that was minimal.[57]

---

those activities raised the question how tightly it was bound by the limit on bill issues in the Bank of England Act, including how much the monarch could borrow without parliamentary authorization. See Horsefield, *Monetary Experiments*, 130–135; Davies, *History of Money*, 260.

[52] Paterson, *A Brief Account*, 13–14.   [53] Godfrey, *A Short Account of the Bank of England*, 8.

[54] For the Bank's subsequent lending, see Horsefield, *Monetary Experiments*, 130–135.

[55] See Horsefield, *Monetary Experiments*, 264–265 (Appendix 6, Table J). (Total note issue is taken from the sum of Fund of the Bank of England and Loans and Discounts on other Government Funds. The £2 million outstanding is taken from the Total Notes, including both Bank bills, specie, and running cash notes. £720,000 is the total of the initial call; Horsefield's larger total for "internal liabilities" includes dividends and salaries due. The lesser total for paid-up subscriptions is taken from Clapham's calculation that by November 1696, £600,158 had been paid in cash and £101,755 in bonds "reckoned as cash." It is possible some of the loan to government came from specie, but the amount would be limited to the liquid capital available, £342,158 which would also have covered redemption of any bills.) Clapham, *Bank of England*, 304–305 (Appendix F). The increase in subscriptions authorized in 1697 to £1,001,171 was also only partly liquid. It included "engrafted" tallies and Bank notes. See Davies, *History of Money*, 262–263. Later enlargements took Exchequer bills.

[56] Clapham, *Bank of England*, 36–38, 42–43. The Bank tried attaching interest to its notes and offered an interest-bearing "specie note" to bring in specie, promising to repay the note in the same hard money.

[57] Clapham, *Bank of England*, 58–72.

Commentators engaged in a small but steady debate over what cash reserve should be held by an institution like the Bank, and how liquid it should be. They suggested liquid reserves ranging from 10 to 33 percent. The Bank's own specie reserve generally fluctuated between 12.8 and 32 percent in its first decade, falling to a scant 2.7 percent during the short run on the Bank in 1696.[58]

Observers staged a much *larger* argument, however, over a different aspect, one easily assumed by later generations. As Paterson framed it above, the expansive capacity of the arrangement depended on the issue "*if* the proprietors of the Bank can circulate their fundation of twelve hundred thousand pounds" (emphasis added). Promises-to-pay would operate to multiply the money supply, to put it in the modern manner, only when they began to function as money. Contemporaries throughout the end of the century, proposing the plethora of funds they did—on land, on pawns, on future revenues—argued vociferously over how to make the notes issued on those funds acceptable as a currency.[59] The government and the Bank fumbled rather than theorized their way towards that end. Each took steps that made the system easier for them to operate in the short run—and moved towards monetizing the notes in the long run.[60]

The medium of exchange—bills and notes

The inventors of modern money began smoothly enough when they made the bills issued by the Bank of England easily assignable. According to the organizing statute, the bills could only be used if taken voluntarily.[61] They also remained "conditional" as payment, functioning to retire a debt only if the payee timely demanded payment from the Bank and those endorsing the bill.[62] But if the

---

[58] Horsefield, *Monetary Experiments*, 264–265 (Appendix 6, Table J); on the Bank's average cash ratio during the first decade of the 18th century, see Horsefield, *Monetary Experiments*, 143, 263. For an account of the run, see Clapham, *Bank of England*, 36–50.

[59] See, e.g., Sir Edward Forde, *Experimented Proposals How the King May Have Money to Pay and Maintain His Fleets with Ease to His People* (William Godbid, 1666), A2–A3; Robert Murray, *A Proposal for the Advancement of Trade, Upon Such Principles as Must Necessarily Enforce It* (AM and others, 1676); Charles Montague, "A Document relating to the Establishment of Paper Credit (1696)," in *The Great Recoinage of 1696 to 1699*, ed. Ming-Hsun Li (London: Weidenfeld and Nicolson, 1963), 237–238; see generally pp. 330–337.

[60] By dissecting the way that the early modern English institutionalized Bank paper to act as a medium, mode of payment, store of value, and unit of account, the following artificially separates arrangements that obviously inform each other. Out of some overlap, I hope the whole picture emerges.

[61] Bank of England Act 1694 (5 & 6 W & M c 20 s 28) (providing that "all and every bill or bills obligatory and of credit under the seal of the said corporation made or given to any person or persons shall and may, by indorsement thereon under the hand of such person or persons, be assignable and assigned to any person or persons who shall voluntarily accept the same, and so by such assignee, toties quoties, by indorsement thereupon; and that such assignment and assignments, so to be made, shall absolutely vest and transfer the right and property in and unto such bill or bills obligatory and of credit, and the monies due upon the same; and that the assignee or assignees shall or may sue for, and maintain an action thereupon in his own name.").

[62] See *Hill v Lewis* (1693) 1 Salk 132; 91 ER 124 (giving bill's drawer three days to pay before bill protested); see also *Ward v Evans* (1703) 6 Mod 36, 37; 87 ER 799, 800 (note written by debtor on insolvent party does not acquit debtor of money owed); see also James Milnes Holden, *The History of Negotiable*

contemporary witness to the widespread use of Bank issues is any indication, those caveats mattered little to most people offered the capacity of a convenient and secure medium.[63]

The way Bank paper became a medium offers more intrigue on second glance. Swept below the surface as cash flowed out was a switch in the kind of instrument issued by the Bank. The initiative that inaugurated Bank money had identified formal, sealed, and interest-bearing *bills* as the new currency. In fact, it was not those instruments that would come to travel so widely as cash but the unauthorized, informal, and non-interest-bearing Bank *notes*. The change would redefine both the medium that circulated and the cost it carried for holders.

According to the Bank of England Act, the Bank could issue "bills obligatory and of credit under the seal of the said corporation."[64] It began issuing the "bills" immediately. Bills, as opposed to notes, probably formed the majority of the original loan made to the government.[65] They were also used for some of the advances made (or receipts for deposits given) to private individuals.[66] Sealed bills of the period were issued to "A.B. or his assignes."[67] The Bank's bills bore interest of 2d. per £100 a day, or about 3 percent, and indeed, the Bank passed on a significant percentage to those holding its bills in the early years.[68]

The government accepted Bank bills and paid them to their creditors; the bills remained in use until 1716.[69] All the while, however, they circulated only to a limited extent. Holders deposited them and drew against them in the Bank, used them when paying the government, and chose them for other large transactions, including cross-country remittances. As the Bank's historian and earlier commentators noted, Bank bills offered "a short term investment."[70] They bore interest, after all, an attribute that may have been important to deter people

Instruments in English Law (Holmes Beach, FL: Gaunt, 1955), 85. For the fact that Bank notes still had to be accepted voluntarily in 1790, see *Wright v Reed* (1790) 3 TR 554; 100 ER 729.

[63] See, e.g., the complaints from Charles Davenant and the endorsement of Alexander Justice, quoted by J. K. Horsefield, "The Beginnings of Paper Money in England," *Journal of European Economic History* 117, no. 32 (1977): 127–128.

[64] Bank of England Act 1694 (5 & 6 W & M c 20 s 28).

[65] The records of bills and notes actually issued (as opposed to authorized) does not survive until 1696, after the Bank had made additional loans to the government. At that point bills comprised the better part (£1.124 million) of the paper still outstanding (£2.011 million) on the government's debt of £2.81 million (£2.767 million advance plus £43,000 interest due). See Horsefield, *Monetary Experiments*, 129–130, 264 (Appendix 6, Table J).

[66] See Richards, *The Early History of Banking in England*, 156–157.

[67] The text of the bills is not specified in the Act. Compare Clapham, *Bank of England*, 22 ("A.B. or his Assignes") and Richards, *The Early History of Banking in England*, 156 (maintaining that Bank bills were issued "to bearer").

[68] See Godfrey, *A Short Account of the Bank of England*, 10 (£36,000 paid per year to noteholders); Andreadis, *History of the Bank*, 84–85. Clapham reports that the first interest payments, covering only the first few months of circulation, amounted to £3,000. In later years, he finds payments for sealed bills outstanding. Clapham, *Bank of England*, 22, 24, 62 (1707, £17,000; 1708, £23,000).

[69] Clapham, *Bank of England*, 22–23.

[70] Clapham, *Bank of England*, 23; see, e.g., *The Reasons of the Decay of Trade and Private Credit* (printed for J. Morphew, 1707), 11–14.

from cashing them. That quality would make it easier to maintain a large issue of paper promises-to-pay specie with a limited reserve of gold and silver coin. In fact, the Bank in 1696 moved expressly to favor interest-bearing issues to reduce if not stave off a run on it triggered by the recoinage crisis of that year.[71] The same feature would, however, would make it more likely that people would hold bills instead of circulating them.

And why not, when a non-interest-bearing note was also circulating? From the start, the Bank had also issued "running cash notes." Four days after getting its Charter, the Bank ordered proofs for running cash notes in denominations of £5, £10, £20, £50, and £100.[72] After its first few years, the Bank would move away from its smaller denominations (below £50), probably in an attempt to staunch the cashing of those bills during the 1696 run on the Bank.[73] Over the course of the 18th century, however, the Bank moved progressively back into that niche, issuing £20 notes in 1725, £10 and £15 notes in 1759, £5 notes in 1793, and £1 and £2 notes in 1797.[74] Promises to pay specie on demand, running cash notes were to be issued to a named holder "or bearer," and generally bore no interest.[75]

The Bank's practice of issuing running cash notes tracked the activities of the goldsmith-bankers, just as the label picked up their language.[76] Initially, the Bank probably used the notes as those bankers had, in transactions with private clients. The notes were first identified as "for the use of the House," apparently a reference to the Bank's commercial lending business, although the Bank would soon turn to them in its dealings with the government as well.[77] Perhaps the Bank also used the logic of the goldsmith-bankers' practice to justify producing notes without the express endorsement of Parliament. If notes signified the value of a deposit, the Bank was arguably simply giving out receipts to its clients for their money, rather than conveying the value of a long-term loan in the form of short-

---

[71] Clapham, *Bank of England*, 36–38, 42; see also Horsefield, *Monetary Experiments*, 141.

[72] A. D. Mackenzie, *The Bank of England Note: A History of Its Printing* (Cambridge: Cambridge University Press, 1953), 5, 7 (noting later order for 12,000 such notes). The Bank was soon debating concerns about counterfeiting, and likely turned to handwritten running cash notes for several years instead. Mackenzie, *Bank of England Note*, 5–10, 20 and n.1. They continued to favor notes for round sums, generally a multiple of £5 or £10. Clapham, *Bank of England*, 22.

[73] The government issued Exchequer bills in small denominations to fill the gap. See Clapham, *Bank of England*, 21–22, 39 and n. 1, 40–42; Mackenzie, *Bank of England Note*, 10–11.

[74] See Mackenzie, *Bank of England Note*, 15–20. Feavearyear reviews the controversy over small notes and unregulated issues in the early 19th century. Albert Edgar Feavearyear, *The Pound Sterling: A History of English Money*, 2nd ed. (Oxford: Clarendon Press, 1963), 173–242.

[75] On the issue of notes "to bearer," see Mackenzie, *Bank of England Note*, 10; Richards, *The Early History of Banking in England*, 153. On the brief attachment of interest to the notes, see Clapham, *Bank of England*, 24; Richards, *The Early History of Banking in England*, 158.

[76] See Mackenzie, *Bank of England Note*, 1–4; Richards, *The Early History of Banking in England*, 158; Clapham, *Bank of England*, 20–22. See also *The Mint and Exchequer United*, 2, using term "Cashire's [sic] notes."

[77] See Horsefield, *Monetary Experiments*, 130, 136; Mackenzie, *Bank of England Note*, 4. For the use of running cash notes to pay portions of the £1.2 million loan to the government, see p. 306. Just as the Bank sometimes issued notes to the government, it sometimes used Bank bills in transactions with private clients. Richards, *The Early History of Banking in England*, 156.

term liabilities. By 1696, the Bank was issuing from 30 to 50 percent more notes than the £1.2 million authorized by the Bank of England Act.[78]

To operate as currency, however, the notes had to circulate and on that issue, they began with a status as ambiguous, at first glance, as that of the goldsmith-banker notes they copied. It would not be until 1704 that Parliament would make promissory notes "payable to X or bearer" assignable, and not until long after that, 1833 in fact, that Parliament would declare Bank notes legal tender.[79] But by the end of the 17th century, the Bank was already making out notes to standardized payees, one of its own employees such as a teller. The fiction apparently made the notes more secure because it maximized the chance that a holder could sue on the note.[80] More to the point here, the fact that the fiction was in wide use also indicates that notes were not functioning to pay specific people, a role largely taken over by the development of check-like drafts on the Bank.[81] By contrast, Bank notes that were not interest-bearing were operating as money—a new kind of cash had joined the currency stream. We will pick up their history after seeing why they might act as a mode of payment and unit of account.

The mode of payment, or how to make a fiat loop

Bank notes, like Bank bills, had been blessed from the beginning, or very close to it, by a second constitutional contrivance. Both public officials and individual holders cooperated to institutionalize them as a mode of payment by giving them a unique stature in exchange between the government and its citizens.

First, the Bank gave its paper issues to government agents who used them to pay public creditors. The Bank's loan had been made by December 1694 in the form of bills and notes. By 1696, it had advanced an additional £1.567 million, mainly if not completely in paper issues, to the government. The government injected them into circulation: in that year, more than £2 million notes were outstanding.[82] Amplifying the government's spending power was the idea from the start—William Lowndes begins his comments on an earlier proposal, there involving paper notes made legal tender, by considering the use of the notes to pay off Crown debts, including to the "navy, ordnance, army, or the like."[83]

---

[78] Horsefield, *Monetary Experiments*, 130. For the number of notes and bills issued, see Horsefield, *Monetary Experiments*, 264–265 (Appendix 6, Table J); Clapham, *Bank of England*, 43–44. In order to issue notes exceeding the £1.2 million, the Bank had to interpret the lending specified in the Act as applicable only to its governmental business, or to the issue of Bank bills as opposed to Bank notes, a matter on which even Bank officials were uncertain. See Horsefield, *Monetary Experiments*, 129–135.

[79] 3 & 4 Ann c 8 s 1 (1704); 3 & 4 Will 4, c 98 s 6 (1833). Goldsmith-banker notes were never declared legal tender.

[80] Mackenzie, *Bank of England Note*, 17–18.

[81] Mackenzie, *Bank of England Note*, 18.

[82] See pp. 306–307; Horsefield, *Monetary Experiments*, 264 (Appendix 6, Table J); Clapham, *Bank of England*, 23.

[83] Lowndes, "Remarks Upon the Proposal," xxiv, xxvii; cf. Killigrew, *An Humble Proposal Shewing How This Nation May Be Vast Gainers by All Sums of Mony, Given to the Crown, without Lessening the*

Second and after a somewhat more confused start, the government began to accept in payment what it spent in payment. Officials, having used Bank notes to pay those who served or supplied it, quite predictably felt compelled to take the notes back in payment of taxes or public fees. Individuals holding the Bank's issues agreed of course. It helped them to hold an instrument that they, or someone to whom they passed that note, could use to pay off a public obligation. The reciprocity may or may not have been intended—quite likely even the authors of the Bank of England Act held different expectations.

As it was conceived, the Bank of England was to lend a "perpetual fund" to the government in the form of Bank paper. That great mass, £1.2 million, would naturally pass through the hands of officials many times as it circulated. No clauses limited its use to private transactions. To the contrary, the Bank's progenitors and supporters emphasized that the Bank's issues would make taxes easier to collect and allow interest rates to fall. Many boosters may have imagined that paper issues would be treated as legal tender—a number of proposals for paper money advocated that end.[84] Others, however, imagined paper flowing as a supplementary medium; the Bank of England Act treated the Bank's bills as issues that could be taken voluntarily. Given that capacity, they could free up silver and gold coin for easier use.[85] Hypothetically, that coin could fill the government's coffers, while the paper circulated. William Paterson's final proposal is delicately worded to suggest such a possibility, if not limit the government to it.[86]

That belief may have been strained. It may even have been an artifice to offer opponents. But it avoided a controversy about making the Bank notes legal tender. Earlier proposals to establish the Bank, public bills, or other funds had antagonized those who feared that a paper instrument would be recognized legally as paying off outstanding debts at face value while circulating at values that were far less. Paterson's first proposal had in fact foundered on that very proposition. As he put it later:

Prerogative (proposing interest-bearing notes based on anticipation of taxes, as making money instantly available to government).

[84] See Paterson's earlier proposals, in W. Paterson, *The Writings of William Paterson... Founder of the Bank of England* (Effingham Wilson, 1859); and Lowndes's response, in Lowndes, "Remarks Upon the Proposal," xxiv, xxviii; see also pp. 336–337. On the aim of lowering interest rates, see sources cited at p. 298 n.13; see also *A Letter to a Friend Concerning Credit and How It May Be Restor'd to the Bank of England*, 6–7.

[85] See, e.g., *A Letter to a Friend Concerning Credit and How It May Be Restor'd to the Bank of England*, 4–5 (implying coined money collected in taxes).

[86] Paterson, *A Brief Account*, 4–5, 14–15; see also Godfrey, *A Short Account of the Bank of England*, 6. The closest that Paterson comes to suggesting that Bank notes may be taken for taxes is his suggestion that Bank notes may achieve the kind of currency that the "funds" have in "Holland, Genoua, and other places" where they "are accommodated to receipts and payments" (Paterson, *A Brief Account*, 15). Those models may have created circulating public debts that were receivable in local or state taxes. See 'T Hart, Johker, and Van Zanden, *Financial History*, 21 (tax receivers acted as managers of public debt).

[N]o sooner was this proposal stated by a society of considerable persons, but the notion of currency [legal tender] was started, and carried so far before it was well perceived or understood by some, that it then proved of pernicious consequence, to the success of this undertaking: some understood it ... [as] at the bottom intended, a downright force, the effect of which would have been, to turn the stomachs of mankind against it, coertion being of sufficient force, to marr a good thing of this nature, but never to mend a bad one.[87]

But if an explicit attempt to secure the status of paper as a mode of payment by making it legal tender was difficult, an indirect development to that end unfolded easily. Public officials could take the essential step with popular support because while private contracts separated parties into debtors and creditors, all individuals were debtors where public payments were concerned. Taxpayers had little reason to object to a practice that accorded value to the notes they held to pay off an obligation to a common creditor—the government. In that spirit, a flurry of proposals made throughout the 1690s replaced the stipulation that paper notes or bills have status as legal tender with the provision that the government accept those items for taxes.[88] Paterson may have calculated that a similar provision explicitly favoring Bank bills would draw political fire. Or he may simply have been wary of criticism, given the fate of his earlier proposal. Most likely perhaps, Paterson may not have understood that making Bank notes receivable for taxes would, effectively, persuade people to use them more broadly to make other payments. In any case, he did not so propose, nor did Parliament add the provision to the Bank of England Act. The practice would instead evolve de facto given the logic that the government should accept the same mode of payment it used.

John Clapham, the Bank's official historian, asserts without more detail that sealed bills were taken from the start by the government as cash. By 1696, other sources indicate that many officials were routinely accepting notes in place of specie, and citizens began to complain of those who did not.[89] When Treasury

---

[87] See Paterson, *A Brief Account*, 5.

[88] See Killigrew, *An Humble Proposal Shewing How This Nation May Be Vast Gainers by All Sums of Mony, Given to the Crown, without Lessening the Prerogative*, 8; Neale, *A Way How to Supply the King's Occasions with Two Millions of Money* (1694, republished with attachment 1695), 1; Neale, *A Proposal for Raising a Million on a Fund of Interest* (1694), 2; *The Mint and Exchequer United*, 1.; cf. Godfrey, *A Short Account of the Bank of England*, 1, 4; Anon., *A Review of the Universal Remedy for all Diseases Universal to Coin* (1696), 31. Charles Montague, Chancellor of the Exchequer in the mid-1690s, advocated this device to ensure the circulation of Exchequer bills. See Montague, "A Document Relating to Public Credit," 237 ("if his Majesty's officers accepted them in the publick receipts, every man might dispose of them without losse, and consequently receive them without prejudice"). Newton also implicitly endorsed tax receivability as influencing money's value (referring in that instance to coin), see Isaac Newton, "Isaac Newton Concerning the Amendment of English Coin (1696)," in *The Great Recoinage of 1696 to 1699*, ed. Ming-Hsun Li (London: Weidenfeld and Nicolson, 1963), 218.

[89] Clapham, *Bank of England*, 23. See the series of encounters set out in Horsefield, "The Beginnings of Paper Money in England," 128–131 (including practice in later years); see also Richard Kleer, "Fictitious Cash: English Public Finance and Paper Money, 1689–97," in *Money, Power and Print: Interdisciplinary Studies on the Financial Revolution in the British Isles*, ed. Charles Ivar McGrath and Christopher J. Fauske (Newark: University of Delaware Press, 2008), 92.

superiors equivocated about sanctioning the practice, aggrieved officials advised them to keep quiet about any decision that only specie was acceptable "lest those who had already accepted bank notes should raise what they called 'a clamour.'"[90] The Treasury backed down, perhaps recognizing how difficult it would be to assert that the medium used by the government would not be accepted by it.[91]

As the financial ties between the government and the Bank increased, it became more likely that the Exchequer would receive Bank bills or notes because it could return them to the Bank to settle the government's account there. Indeed, the logic echoed that which brought individuals to accept Bank issues from the government because they could return them in the form of tax payments. Eugen Von Philippovich, exploring the way that the Bank ultimately displaced the Exchequer as the depository for government funds, describes the reciprocal claims that the Exchequer and the Bank had on each other's funds. By 1696, the Bank often lent short-term to the government, at that point by taking its Exchequer bills; the government could pay off those bills in coin or by returning the Bank's paper.[92] The same reasoning suggests that the government would accept Bank issues from the start, as a medium it could use to pay off the interest due to the Bank on its original public loan.

In 1697, the Bank complied with the government's request to "engraft," or absorb as part of its capital, almost £1 million in tallies that were dragging down the government's credit. As part of the deal, Parliament allowed subscribers to make one-fifth of their contribution in Bank bills or notes taken at face value, although they were traveling at a significant discount. Raising the limit on the Bank's authority to issue bills, it also made the remarkable guarantee that the Exchequer would redeem those bills out of money due to the Bank, should the Bank be unable to do so.[93] In that case, the bills would effectively have been good for taxes to the amount of their face value. The same Act extended the monopoly status of the Bank to 1710, and provided that forgery of Bank bills and, remarkably, *Bank notes*, like the clipping of coin, would bring the death penalty—the provision did not extend to the notes of goldsmith-bankers, or any other entity.[94]

---

[90] Horsefield, "The Beginnings of Paper Money in England," 129, quoting a Prize Commissioners communication to the Treasury. It may be that much of the controversy was over the use of notes as opposed to bills, a possibility that would imply the earlier acceptance of bills.

[91] Horsefield, "The Beginnings of Paper Money in England," 129–130.

[92] See Eugen Von Philippovich, *History of the Bank of England and its Financial Services to the State*, trans. Christabel Meredeth, vol. 41, Senate Documents (1911), 178–179. For the initial advances on Exchequer bills, see Clapham, *Bank of England*, 38–39, 54–56, 58–72. The Bank injected Exchequer bills into circulation by paying them out in its discount business and by using them to pay dividends. It was also responsible for cashing Exchequer bills.

[93] 8 & 9 Will 3 c 20 s 30 (1696–1697); see also Horsefield, *Monetary Experiments*, 134. The Act even protected the stream of revenue that paid the Bank's interest from use for redeeming the notes.

[94] 8 & 9 Will 3 c 20 s 36 (1696–1697).

In 1698, Parliament again privileged the Bank's issues, although it did not act comprehensively. A series of statutory provisions stipulated that Bank "bills" should be accepted by the Treasury for public payments, although each time for a provisional period. In October of the same year, the Treasury confirmed that it would take non-interest-bearing bills as well.[95] At that point, a procedure that allowed Exchequer tellers to accept the same media as the tax collectors seemed likely. According to Von Philippovich, by the beginning of the 18th century, the tellers of the Exchequer "found themselves in possession of a large number of these notes every day."[96] The influx of notes initially created a predicament for Exchequer officials since their old rule about weighing all revenues, confirmed in 1697 by statute, made it impossible to take credit notes as cash payment.[97] But an off-the-record evasion was available to remedy the problem. Informally, the practice grew up of having an agent from the Bank attend daily at the Exchequer to verify that the notes were genuine. Set-offs in amounts owed between the government and the Bank were rising as the Bank became the regular agent which injected Exchequer bills into circulation in exchange for cash advances. According to a later House of Lords report, the Bank also simply held Exchequer bills as the securities denoting an advance to the government in anticipation of taxes.[98] Bank notes or bills accepted at the Exchequer would then be used to pay down the government's account. An elaborate system of clearing accounts between the Exchequer and the Bank developed.[99] That practice for accepting notes set them further apart from those of individual goldsmith-bankers.[100]

[95] 9 Will 3 c 44 s 79 (1697–1698); 10 Will 3 c 11 s 13 (1698); Horsefield, "The Beginnings of Paper Money in England," 131; "Warrants etc.: October 1698, 16–31," *Calendar of Treasury Books, Volume 14: 1698–1699* (1934), 161 (October 19, 1698), British History Online, accessed June 22, 2014, <http://www.british-history.ac.uk/report.aspx?compid=83003>. Neither directive covered "notes" as a literal matter, but the functional difference between non-interest-bearing bills and notes was itself fading, and would be further vitiated by the 1704 Act that made promissory notes assignable.

[96] Von Philippovich, *History of the Bank*, 178.

[97] See p. 297 n. 9.

[98] Testimony of Mr. Bosanquet, Bank of England, *Journal of the House of Lords*, vol. 41, 36 Geo III (1797), 196.

[99] According to the 1797 parliamentary report, the clearing of Exchequer bills for Bank notes had existed "time out of mind" (*Journal of the House of Lords*, vol. 41, 196). A later report (1831) suggested that the practice became established somewhat later, stating that the Bank of England "for nearly a century" had sent to the Exchequer "persons duly authorized to examine and receive its own notes." "Interrogation of the Head Cashier of the Bank," in First Report of the Commissioners of Public Accounts, House of Commons, October 10, 1831, 5. Von Philippovich estimates that the practice was institutionalized by the second decade of the 18th century. Von Philippovich, *History of the Bank*, 178, 180–181; see also Von Philippovich, *History of the Bank*, 178, 180–181 (considering suggestion in 1710 statute that particularly denominated Exchequer bills were being set aside for exchange with the Bank).

[100] See Von Philippovich, *History of the Bank*, 179–180. No broadly institutionalized reciprocation of notes existed between the goldsmith-bankers and the government; rather, the Exchequer appears occasionally to have accepted the notes it assumed could be easily cashed from specific goldsmith-bankers it deemed reputable. See Horsefield, "The Beginnings of Paper Money in England," 122–123 (citing 1680 and 1684 authorizations to tellers to accept notes of specific goldsmiths). The role of goldsmith-bankers as tax collectors may suggest a somewhat more significant practice of reciprocal clearing. See Andreadìs, *History of the Bank*, 35.

In 1708, Parliament extended an earlier Act giving privileged status to the Bank as a joint-stock company. Often overlooked but relevant here is how the statute actually operated. It accorded a specific role to the Bank by prohibiting any other joint-stock company larger than six persons from lending or borrowing "on their bills or notes, payable at demand, or at any less time than six months from the borrowing thereof." In other words, corporations could borrow and lend by issuing promissory notes or bonds with longer time horizons—but they could not issue notes that would represent immediate value, or compete with the currency constituted by the Bank's issue. (Notice that the statute prohibited the issue of "notes" as well as "bills," suggesting that Bank notes were well established as a medium by then.)[101] The 1708 Act thus confirmed that the arrangement undergirding the value of modern money was particular to the relation between the Bank and the government. The partnership would hold until the 19th century, when it was reaffirmed and extended.[102]

The closed system worked out between Bank, government, and individuals ensured that paper issues would have purchasing power (or act as a store of value) because it made predictable the outflow and withdrawal of that currency. It thus controlled the amount of money in ways holders could anticipate and calculate, allowing them to attribute value to the instruments and create real balances. Most obviously, the government and Bank had defined between themselves the amount of paper issued.[103] The Bank of England Act put a limit on the number of notes that could be issued—the ceiling imposed by Parliament on Bank issues. And while the proprietors apparently breached that ceiling quite often, they were constrained both by their personal liability under the statute for overlending and by their guarantee to cash all the notes they had issued.[104]

Once the government accepted Bank money to pay off public obligations, that currency was also predictably withdrawn from circulation. Financing its war with both short-term ("unfunded") and perpetual (funded) borrowing, the English imposed taxes to service its debt. Those taxes were sufficiently heavy, relative to the money supply, to ensure demand for all modes of payment receivable by the government. Between 1690 and 1695, taxes were almost double (£19.5 million) their total in the previous five years (£11.9 million). Between 1695 and 1700, they rose to £24.3 million. That was during a period in which the government

---

[101] 7 Ann c 30 s 66 (1708). For the earlier provision granting the Bank a monopoly, see 8 & 9 Will 3 c 20 s 28 (1696–1697). Private, as opposed to joint-stock, banks were not prohibited by the 1708 Act.

[102] Rondo E. Cameron, "England, 1750–1844," in *Banking in the Early Stages of Industrialization*, ed. Rondo Cameron et al. (New York: Oxford University Press, 1967), 20, 27–28.

[103] As the discussion below suggests, the stability of the arrangement depended on the government's determination to tax in paper issues and, in that sense, on the future value of government revenues. Paterson, by contrast, considered that the value of incoming revenues mattered only because it assured that the government would service its debt to the Bank. The latter effect (the promise of interest) kept the investors in the game, but the former assurance (the demand for notes) kept the game alive.

[104] See pp. 310–311. The same limits would also condition private lending.

conducted a comprehensive recoinage known as the Great Recoinage, the amount of coin in circulation actually fell, and a massive number of tallies were withdrawn from circulation.[105] Against that demand, a limited number of Bank notes circulated—some £1.74 million in 1698, for instance. Exchequer bills added a similar number of notes.[106]

When the government taxed so heavily, it brought Bank currency that it had sent into circulation back out of circulation again.[107] Like the Anglo-Saxon kings with their metal tokens and the medieval monarchs with tallies, the government was acting as stakeholder. Commenting on an early Paterson proposal, William Lowndes reproduced the logic precisely:

> As to the application of these bills to pay off the transport ships, and other debts of the crown, and the navy, ordinance, army, or the like, it is not doubted, but in these and other cases between the king and his subjects, these bills will be accepted, because hereby the creditors will have a plain and easy way to obtain their debts; that is to say, the paper which they, or any friends or assignees of theirs, especially merchants and brewers, may return again to the king for customs, excise taxes, and the like, for which these bills will certainly come into the exchequer.[108]

As Lowndes recognized, the value of such paper did not depend on a tangible asset, but on an operating system of public spending and withdrawing.[109]

What role, then, for the specie held by the Bank? At a formal level, the law subjected all promissory notes—Bank bills and notes like goldsmith-banker notes—to "encashment." Even after the category of promissory notes became easily transferable in 1704, that doctrine dictated that their transfer depended on their prompt presentation and cashing. The party who paid with such an

---

[105] Horsefield, *Monetary Experiments*, 245 (Table 11). O'Brien's numbers, based on five-year averages, are similar. O'Brien, "British Taxation," 2–4 (including Table 2, for five-year average tax levies). For the Great Recoinage of 1696, which took in some £10 million in coin and produced £6.8 million, see p. 366.

[106] For Bank notes, see Horsefield, *Monetary Experiments* (Table J, Appendix 6). Outstanding Exchequer bills are calculated as the difference between total bills created and redeemed from issue through 1698 (£1.5 million), as recorded in B. R. Mitchell, *Abstract of British Historical Statistics* (Cambridge: 1962), 404–405.

[107] As the models discussed in Chapter 1 [pp. 45–49] suggest, the value of Bank notes would depend on their expected future real value equal to their expected value in paying a tax. If the government capped the value of Bank notes so that they could not exceed 1:1 specie to bill, and taxed sufficiently to bring in all Bank notes, the value of Bank notes would remain at parity with specie. See Charles W. Calomiris, "Institutional Failure, Monetary Scarcity, and the Depreciation of the Continental," *Journal of Economic History* 48, no. 1 (1988) (modeling value of new issue as equal to aggregate specie value of tax obligation it extinguishes); see also Thomas Sargent and Neil Wallace, "Some Unpleasant Monetarist Arithmetic," *Federal Reserve Bank of Minneapolis Quarterly Review* (Fall 1981): 5. If a surfeit of Bank notes circulated on the basis of the same amount levied and the government accepted the notes at market value, people would use the notes to pay the government, but the notes would lose value relative to specie, given that they would all be used to extinguish the same aggregate specie value of the tax obligation. See Calomiris, "Institutional Failure."

[108] Lowndes, "Remarks Upon the Proposal," xxvii.

[109] As a contemporary proponent of paper credit money argued, once made current, such notes were "not liable to a postpone: for the Crown may as easily call back the mony paid out of the Exchequer, as stop what is given out for money" (Killigrew, *An Humble Proposal Shewing How This Nation May Be Vast Gainers by All Sums of Mony, Given to the Crown, without Lessening the Prerogative*, 6).

instrument (the transferor) could argue that the person who took the note (the transferee) could not protest payment belatedly, if the transferee had accepted the instrument, but had not presented it promptly for cashing. On the other hand, if the transferee did present the bill or note promptly and failed to get it cashed, he or she could reject it even after acceptance.[110]

At a practical level, however, the stature of the Bank's notes again set them apart from their competitors. Specie was not actually "backing" Bank issues in the sense that redemption was a significant part of the functioning system. According to the numbers in circulation, people held Bank notes rather than demanding specie. And indeed, if individuals had commonly cashed their bank issues, their concerted action would have abruptly contracted the paper money supply. Insofar as the encashment requirement was robustly enforced, in fact, it corroded the capacity of an instrument to act like currency; neither a transferee nor a transferor would neglect the "encashment" requirement if it alone secured the viability of a credit instrument. In the case of the Bank, those using bills or notes no longer needed to do so because they could use them to pay the government. In that sense, the government had reduced the risk of redemption to the Bank, diverting holders from the need to protect themselves by cashing the notes.[111] The government's imprimatur on Bank paper thus gave it a distinctive guarantee, practically if not formally.[112]

Freed from more laborious work, specie began assuming its modern role. First, it acted, as a kind of security, a default guarantee. If the Bank notes failed as money, people could claim specie as a back-up. (In other words, if the central premise of the system of public credit collapsed, people could harvest some of their savings. Note the similarity to the role of silver or gold where commodity money failed.)[113] Less directly, but more practically, specie was a legitimating

---

[110] See p. 308 n.62. Compare Horsefield, "The Beginnings of Paper Money in England," 124–125, to Holden, *The History of Negotiable Instruments in English Law*, 73–85.

[111] Indeed, even when presented with bills, the Bank apparently often exchanged them for new bills or running cash notes, instead of specie. Richards, *The Early History of Banking in England*, 156. That practice, if not protested, would suggest as well the currency of notes during this period.

[112] Courts would continue to hold the tender of Bank notes "conditional" until at least 1790, but only upon the objection of a party (*Wright v Reed* (1790) 3 TR 554; 100 ER 729). Notes clearly passed interchangeably with specie by mid-century, and the courts protected that practice with an eye towards widespread commercial reliance on it. See *Miller v Race* (1758) 1 Burr 452; 97 ER 398. Exchequer bills were probably not subject to this type of conditionality. Horsefield, reviewing all the media of the late 17th and 18th centuries for a currency accepted as money according to indicators like popular acceptance and legal status, found only Bank of England notes qualified, as opposed to country Bank notes, land Bank notes, goldsmith-banker notes, bills of exchange, tallies, mortgages, and annuity securities. See Horsefield, "The Beginnings of Paper Money in England."

[113] In the long term, the capital of the Bank was at least theoretically available, but the Bank habitually lent out a greater amount than its capital. Noteholders would presumably be reduced to suing Bank partners for personal liability. See 5 W & M c 20 s 26; Horsefield, *Monetary Experiments*, 128; Peter Temin and Hans-Joachim Voth, *Prometheus Shackled: Goldmith Banks and England's Financial Revolution After 1700* (Oxford: Oxford University Press, 2012), 44, 68–71. For contemporary criticism on the ground that personal suits would be difficult to bring, see *Some Considerations Offered against the Continuance of the Bank of England* (1694), 3–4.

device. The Bank's commitment to cash its demand instruments visibly limited the number it could issue.[114] And the image offered of gold or silver in the vault gave those holding paper the sense that an anchor existed—even if the anchor was actually elsewhere, in the sound functioning of the fiscal system.[115] As the next chapter suggests, Whig strategists were building an image of money as a tangible object, even as they developed paper money.

The security comprised by the loop made by Bank paper not only assisted holders, it also met the immediate needs of both the Bank and the government. The Bank gained because, as the government's virtual guarantee diminished demands for specie, it could lend its principal long term, but do so in the form of short-term liabilities, while holding only a fractional reserve.[116] And the government itself had become a player with an interest in the continued currency of the paper money. It could always return a portion of that money to the Bank to service interest on the "perpetual loan."[117] Otherwise, it could either cash the paper issues, which would reduce the money supply, or continue to use the notes returned to it by channeling them back into circulation.[118]

The latter strategy held enormous power. It would extend the lifetime of the currency by creating another issue and withdrawal—or another loop that animated paper promises with monetary value. That strategy reduced the need for fresh loans from the Bank while maintaining the higher level of liquidity represented by the paper money. Moreover, it allowed the government to spend anew in money that would hold value as long as the government matched its outlay with taxes. According to Michael Braddick's calculations, the government's spending power across the decade rose 34 percent.[119] Taxation, necessary to

---

[114] One way to put the point is that the device might have been essential in transmitting to participants an expectation about the dimension of the issue. Cf. Sargent and Wallace, "Some Unpleasant Monetarist Arithmetic," 5.

[115] See, e.g., Paterson, *A Brief Account*, 9–10 (identifying specie reserve as fundamental to the system); Killigrew, *An Humble Proposal Shewing How This Nation May Be Vast Gainers by All Sums of Mony, Given to the Crown, without Lessening the Prerogative,"* 2 (emphasizing need to avoid overissue). Compare Angela Redish, "Anchors Aweigh: The Transition from Commodity Money to Fiat Money in Western Economies," *Canadian Journal of Economics/Revue canadienne d'Economique* 26, no. 4 (November 1993) (interpreting public role in creating modern currency as a matter of policing reserve requirements).

[116] See Paterson, *A Brief Account*, 13–14. The Bank's directors clearly agreed, as demonstrated by their regular practice of exchanging incoming bills for new bills or cash. See p. 318 n. 111.

[117] For the constraints on repayment of the principal, see p. 305. The brake on repayment was consistent with the public goal of increasing the money supply.

[118] Officials made the logic of fiat currency remarkably clear in a parallel case, that of public Exchequer bills, which were a tax anticipation currency. In negotiations with the Bank over its management of the bills, the government originally required the Bank to redeem the bills for specie "upon the first issuing." The Bank later bargained for a delay in its obligation to redeem until the Exchequer bills had been collected for taxes and reissued. Only then, argued the Bank, had the bills really attained "a currency." See 6 Ann c 21 s 13 (1706); 7 Ann c 30 s 57 (1708); Clapham, *Bank of England*, 58–59, 64. Robert Murray, one of the promoters of Exchequer bills, identified the logic of the issue and retirement in Robert Murray, *The Manner and Method of an Exchequer Credit* (1695), 1.

[119] M. J. Braddick, *The Nerves of State: Taxation and the Financing of the English State, 1558–1714*, New Frontiers in History (Manchester: St. Martin's Press, 1996), 44. For the increase in annual revenues over a

sustain the purchasing power of the Bank notes, also rose abruptly during the period, as above. The same trend appears over the long term. Between 1670 and 1810, tax receipts in real terms increased by a factor of 16 and the English became among the most heavily taxed people in Europe.[120] That tax burden supported a significant expansion of paper money. In effect, the English had invented a fiat currency under the cover of a fiduciary one.

Once cash operated as a mode of payment between Bank, government, and individuals, it gained stability from the reciprocity of their obligation. But to call the system closed obscures one aspect in which it was radically open-ended. According to a variety of sources, the Bank early on pushed the boundaries of its authority by lending to private individuals.[121] Insofar as the Bank could make private loans in the form of short-term liabilities recognized as cash by the government, it could add to the money supply in times that credit was demanded. But while that development aided people who wanted more currency, it also disrupted the tie between issue and withdrawal that stabilized the amount of paper money in the system.

That development suggests the drama that lay ahead. The Bank itself remained conservative about lending to private parties, preferring to fund public debt in large measure. Unable to compete with the Bank on note issue, private banks slowly left the Bank to dominate in that role.[122] But commercial banks would return to the note industry in the future, finding ways to connect their own forms of credit to the system established by the government and the Bank and collapsing intermittently back to the stability of the money that partnership made on the basis of public debt.[123]

The unit of account, or the way sterling became paper

When the government accepted Bank paper to pay off specie obligations, it not only sanctioned the circulation of Bank of England currency, it effectively

---

slightly shorter period, from £4.11 million in 1691 to £5.84 million or about 42 percent in 1698, see Horsefield, *Monetary Experiments*, 9 (Table 1).

[120] The Dutch may have outmatched the English. O'Brien, "British Taxation," 4. During the same period, national income, also in real terms, increased by a factor of around three. For further discussion of increasing British taxes over the 18th century, see pp. 385–389.

[121] See, e.g., Godfrey, *A Short Account of the Bank of England*, 2–5 (discounting tallies, lending on mortgages, real securities, pawns, and privately held public funds). For the amount of discounting and similar lending according to the Bank's records, see Horsefield, *Monetary Experiments*, 264–265 (Appendix 6, Table J). The numbers indicate that the Bank's private business began early, and ebbed and flowed through its first 15 years. It grew through the 18th century to make up about 20 to 30 percent of its business. Cameron, "England, 1750–1844," 20–21.

[122] For the decline in private bank issues, see pp. 262, 321, 378–380, 396; see generally Iain Frame, "Country Rag Merchants and Octopus Tentacles: An Analysis of Law's Contribution to the Creation of Money in England and Wales, 1790–1844" (Harvard University, 2012), 230–245.

[123] See pp. 397–398.

equated those issues to silver and gold coin.[124] Without that equivalence, Bank bills and notes were demand instruments but not (quite) money: tender of Bank paper could be turned away for specie, or the value of the demand instrument discounted for the risk and burden that cashing them entailed. Those conditions disadvantaged the competing promises issued by other banks. Goldsmith-banks opened and closed rapidly during the 1690s, an evanescence that suggests how difficult it was to build a lending business that relied on the predictable acceptance of private notes, particularly once the Bank's issues became established.[125]

Assuming that the government was taking Bank currency for taxes by the late 1690s, the question remains whether it took those bills and notes for the same count at which it accepted the sterling unit of account.[126] The 1698 temporary statute providing that Bank bills were acceptable for taxes had limited that treatment to bills trading at par with specie. By the end of the previous year, Bank bills were passing at that rate, after a severe drop in value during the 1696 recoinage crisis. The drop occurred two days after the government had demonetized clipped coin, declining to take it at face value for taxes. As the need for cash skyrocketed, the Bank was pressed beyond its capacity; it suspended cash redemption of its issues for the first time. Their value reached its nadir at a 24 percent discount in early 1697.[127]

That suspension triggered a number of corrective actions. The government seems to have supported officials who had taken bills or notes without any discount; it may have recognized that those officials would have felt it proper to take Bank bills at the count at which the government had used them.[128] The government also agreed to allow the Bank, when it engrafted the tallies into its

---

[124] Appropriately, some contemporary observers began to include Bank issues in their estimates of the English money supply by the end of the 17th century. See Charles Davenant's estimates, reproduced by Horsefield, *Monetary Experiments*, 256 (Appendix 2).

[125] Although the Bank's historian downplays the hostility those competitors showed the Bank, there was surely good reason for it. Clapham, *Bank of England*, 29–33. The notes of private bankers circulated in numbers similar to that of the Bank's paper in its early years, but dropped to £0.7 million by the mid-18th century while the Bank's issues reached 20 times that number. Horsefield, *Monetary Experiments*, 14 (goldsmith-banker notes from £2–2.4 million from 1693 to 1698); Peter H. Lindert, "English Population, Wages, and Prices: 1541–1913," *Journal of Interdisciplinary History* 15, no. 4 (1985): 634. For the number of Bank issues, and the subsequent surge of note issuing by "country banks," see pp. 396–398.

[126] Silver coin, not gold coin, remained the unit of account. See Isaac Newton, "Observations on the State of the Coins of Gold and Silver" (1717); Feavearyear, *The Pound Sterling*, 154–155. Paper accepted by the government at face value, assimilated to the unit of account, might still travel at a discount between individuals if they preferred to hold coin. The case of early American bills of credit was analogous. See, e.g., James Madison, "Money," in *The Papers of James Madison*, ed. William T. Hutchinson and William M. E. Rachal (Chicago: University of Chicago Press, 1979), 302–310.

[127] Rogers uses Houghton's data to track the discount and its disappearance, while Clapham includes the measures by the Bank to raise cash. See James E. Thorold Rogers, *The First Nine Years of the Bank of England* (London: Macmillan, 1887), 170; Clapham, *Bank of England*, 36–37.

[128] The Treasurer of the Navy was thus held accountable for discounts on navy bills and then allowed money to recover for the loss. He had assumedly taken the bills at their nominal value when they were traveling at a discount, and was then protected from the loss given their lesser value. Horsefield, "The Beginnings of Paper Money in England," 130. American colonial legislatures apparently acted that way, taking their bills of credit back at face value as they had so issued them.

capital, to accept Bank paper at face value as part of subscriptions. That agreement helped support the paper's value. It would in turn have set the precedent for wider acceptance of the Bank's issues at count in order to avoid charges of favoritism. It was, of course, very much in the government's interest to take Bank notes at face value in order to keep the notes circulating. Assuming convertibility, the Bank notes' value could not fall far below that of specie without triggering demands for that medium. Holders could simply cash their notes to get specie for tax payments if they were given less than face value at the Exchequer for the notes.

As for the Bank, it kept its reserve at a relatively high ratio in the decade after the Great Recoinage (23–47.3 percent), notably above the level that contemporaries believed was necessary (10–33 percent).[129] The legitimacy offered by the reserve was likely critical during this inaugural period, until the government itself would commit to taking Bank notes by count.[130] Boosting the confidence of holders raised the value of notes, and the closer those notes came to full value for taxes, the less likely were holders to cash them—it was a virtuous cycle.[131] Finally, the fact that interest attached to Bank bills (and, during the run, to Bank notes) also supported their value relative to specie; it may have functioned to allow Bank of England issues to become established at face value.[132] Once Bank issues were established at that value, the government's acceptance of bills and notes interchangeably with specie would tend to sustain that parity.

By the end of the 17th century, the government and the Bank, in concert with individuals, had groped much of their way to a remarkable arrangement. They had inaugurated a paper currency that was tied to specie as the unit of account. The Bank, the government, and individuals used the paper to pay each other. It passed hand to hand and held purchasing power. Each side of the triangle benefitted from the arrangement. The remaining question is, how much?

Paying for money

The story comes back to Bank notes at this point to reveal how they—instead of Bank bills—become the paradigmatic paper of the modern world. Early in the 18th century, Bank notes began to displace Bank bills, the currency projected in the Bank's founding legislation. The Bank stopped issuing bills in favor of notes

---

[129] Compare Horsefield, *Monetary Experiments*, 143, 264–265 (Cash Ratio–Net), with 263 (Appendix 5).

[130] Bank notes were officially made acceptable for taxes at face value in 1816 (56 Geo 3 c 96 s 4 (1816)). The terms of legislation in 1811 and 1812 effectively accomplished that end. See 51 Geo 3 c 127 (1811); 52 Geo 3 c 50 (1812).

[131] As contemporaries noted, the convenience and safety of having a note rather than silver or gold also increased the value of Bank paper. See Feavearyear, *The Pound Sterling*, 215–216, for the vindication of this view during the 19th century.

[132] For the use of interest to undergird the notes' value, see Clapham, *Bank of England*, 36–37.

altogether in 1716.[133] That transition illuminates a last quality of the new currency: it reallocated the rewards for producing liquidity.

The desire of people for a medium with cash quality is the constant in the story. Many holders had once taken tallies from the government without interest, trading advances of goods or services for a currency with the capacity to circulate. They had acquired interest on the government bonds that replaced tallies. They continued to claim interest on the Bank bills innovated to act as the cash that bonds could not supply. Holders now returned to a medium stripped of interest once more, leaving that payment this time with the investors who issued paper notes. The handoff thus shifted the way benefits from creating currency flowed, channeling it to the Bank instead of the government. Individuals, it turns out, will pay for money; the modern system directed their contribution towards private rather than public hands.

Once again, the transformation occurred because it made sense to particular parties amid the short-term conditions, on the ground of a changing system; if it was theorized at a more abstract level, it remains hidden from the existing histories. At the outset, interest-bearing bills were probably the obvious expedient to use as the vehicle for a money-multiplying advance because the interest would help to get the bills—vehicles taken only voluntarily—established. As an advocate argued on behalf of an earlier scheme to issue public bonds as currency, attaching interest would make holders "prefer these bonds before any assignment of money itself, because these bonds will increase in their coffers."[134]

The desire to receive interest would make people less likely to cash the paper instrument, preserving the fractional quantity of specie allocated to redeem it.[135] It would also underscore the legitimacy of the bills and thus their value, perhaps essentially in a world skeptical of both public and private promises.[136] As Sir John Clapham later observed, the Stop of the Exchequer as well as the problems created by undisciplined use of tallies and Treasury Orders, had made "almost unthinkable" the notion that people would accept "a new sort of non-interest-bearing official promise to pay."[137] In fact, the main alternative to the circulating Bank bill initiated under William's reign, the Exchequer bill, was also interest-bearing.[138]

---

[133] Horsefield, *Monetary Experiments*, 264–265; Clapham, *Bank of England*, 22.

[134] The strategy would thus "make [silver and gold] more free and common amongst us," as men released specie to "hoard up these bonds." Killigrew, *An Humble Proposal Shewing How This Nation May Be Vast Gainers by All Sums of Mony, Given to the Crown, without Lessening the Prerogative*, 6, 8. Killigrew proposed a scheme quite like the one eventually adopted to produce Exchequer bills.

[135] The Bank employed that rationale explicitly during the 1696 run, temporarily attaching interest to its notes. See Clapham, *Bank of England*, 36–37. The Bank also invited the exchange of running cash notes for interest-bearing bills that holders would be less likely to cash. Clapham, *Bank of England*, 42.

[136] Clapham, *Bank of England*, 13 Those goals would implicate one to another; reducing the risk of runs on the Bank would help shore up its legitimacy and so make future runs less likely.

[137] Clapham, *Bank of England*, 13.

[138] For discussion, see pp. 339–341, 369–370.

In the early years, both types of paper money followed the same principle of paying holders for their forbearance from demanding specie.

Finally and more speculatively, the practice of attaching interest may have been consistent with the way contemporaries assumed that bills issued on a fractional reserve or portion of incoming revenue should be treated, economically and morally. Insofar as goldsmith-banker notes originally held status as literal receipts for deposit at the bank—insofar, that is, as they were issued on a full reserve and represented that reserve one-for-one in a more convenient form—no interest would be due anyone holding a note.[139] The note simply stood in for the immobilized specie.

The situation was very different when those issuing paper promises to pay coin were doing so while gainfully investing most of the specie that noteholders could hypothetically claim. The case was particularly clear in case of Bank promises: the investors could be expected to pass on some of the profit they were themselves getting on the funds loaned to the government. As a contemporary commented when the Bank issued non-interest-bearing notes instead of bills, that strategy was "never practiced before by any Corporation, and almost a fraud on the subject."[140] At least until the notion that a full reserve should back deposit notes faded, bills issued on less than that security shared something of the character of the government's Treasury Orders, the circulating stock of a cor-poration, or bonds, and would appropriately carry interest.[141] They were not obviously equivalent to coin or to the depositors' receipts given out by the goldsmith-bankers, both non-interest-bearing.[142]

That assumption would change as paper instruments were institutionalized as a currency that had immediate value as money without needing to be cashed. When that occurred, those holding bank paper may not have minded, indeed may even have preferred, the transition to a non-interest-bearing form. It was far

---

[139] See Mackenzie, *Bank of England Note*, 1 (goldsmith-bankers' practice rooted in notes signifying "depositor's 'running cash', that is to say, cash that should be immediately available for use" although goldsmiths could keep only a proportional amount as their "running cash"); Rogers, *The First Nine Years* (describing full reserve practice of European banks); see also *The Mint and Exchequer United*, 2 (criticizing Bank for issuing "cashire's notes" for amounts over £1.2 million in authorized lending as "never practiced before by any Corporation, and almost a fraud on the subject"); but see *A Letter to a Friend Concerning Credit and How It May Be Restor'd to the Bank of England*, 1 (attributing fractional reserve practice to private banks). Contemporaries periodically suggested that a full reserve requirement should attach to Bank of England: *The Mint and Exchequer United*, 2. In England, popular opinion appears to have moved away from the notion that a private banker had to hold a full reserve sometime after the mid-17th century, although the "encashment" obligation that required those receiving a bill or note to cash it immediately or lose the right to sue on it would have supported the practice of large or full reserves. For the development of fractional reserve banking, see pp. 389–401.

[140] *The Mint and Exchequer United*, 2.

[141] See pp. 245–254.

[142] The sequence suggested here—that noteholders may first have paid for the service of bailment, and then have shared in the profits when the bailor began using the funds and keeping only a fractional reserve—raises the question whether the idea that a bank should be paid for managing a reserve and assuming the associated risk was a still later development.

more convenient in everyday transactions to wash the endless calculations on daily interest out of the mix.[143] In economic terms, where liquidity is scant in the sense that people cannot make all the transactions they would like to facilitate in money, they will hold more money as it becomes available (demand will rise) without requiring interest as recompense. (They are, in effect, trading interest compensation for liquidity.)[144] The conditions we have seen in England would invite that decision.[145]

In fact, people's desire for money may have led some contemporaries not only to tolerate non-interest-bearing money, but to demand it. During the period, commentators expressed the fear that wealthy bankers or their like would hoard money, driving down prices and hurting debtors who were bound to repay at higher real values or buying the poor out of their land at low prices and then sending money back into the market to drive prices up once again.[146] That fear reverberated against the Bank. According to critics, one of the mechanisms that would induce hoarding and the deflationary wringer that it represented was the interest-bearing bill. (The interest-bearing *note*, issued occasionally when the Bank anticipated runs on its reserve, was even more suspicious.[147]) As individuals saved up interest-bearing bills for the profit they represented, they would drain liquidity out of the system. That is, a practice that would seem at first glance generous—the Bank's provision of interest to those holding its bills—was received as a technique with destructive capacities.

Critics leveled those very charges against the Bank after an economic depression and deflationary turn early in the 18th century.[148] According to pamphleteers, the Bank had encouraged hoarding by issuing interest-bearing bills or notes (its "running cash") while declining to discount bills of trade or other instruments. All the while, one observer claimed, directors in the Bank had colluded with some counterparts in the East India Company to store up money in order to

---

[143] For this sentiment, see Theodore Janssen, *A Discourse Concerning Banks* (1697), 7.

[144] Generally, compensation would come to those holding money only by a change in prices as opposed to getting interest on money. At stable prices, people are holding money because they want its liquidity. See pp. 46–48. The same inclination would make people willing to accept the transition from an interest-bearing to a non-interest-bearing form of money. Conversely, in modern financial markets, holders decide how much of their money to exchange for interest-bearing securities, depending on their demand for money.

[145] See pp. 254–259.

[146] See, e.g., *The Reasons of the Decay of Trade and Private Credit*; *Reasons Offer'd against the Continuance of the Bank* (1707), 10–12; *Some Queries, Humbly Offer'd to the Consideration of Both Houses of Parliament Relating to the Bank of England* (1707); cf. *A Short View of the Apparent Dangers and Mischiefs from the Bank of England* (printed for Benjamin Bragg, 1707), 9, 12–13. For an early warning of such effects, see *Some Considerations Offered against the Continuance of the Bank of England*, 9–11 (1694). (The pamphlet may have furnished the model for *Reasons Offer'd Against the Continuance*, published in 1707.) For a similar fear voiced in America, see *The Triumvirate of Pennsylvania. In a Letter to a Friend in the Country* (Andrew Bradford, 1725).

[147] *The Reasons of the Decay of Trade and Private Credit*, 5.

[148] See the charges made in the pamphlets cited at n. 146 see also Horsefield, *Monetary Experiments*, 140–141 (describing 1704 depression and 1706 deflation).

depress prices.[149] That drop ruined merchants and facilitated the predatory action of those with money in seizing the property of debtors. Non-interest-bearing notes resolved the problem, producing a currency that was the equal of specie, not its better.

The Bank, of course, would only be benefitted if it dropped the interest that it attached to its promises-to-pay.[150] Compensated 8 percent on its loan to the government, the Bank was advancing much of that money by way of instruments that carried from 3 to 4.5 percent interest.[151] The transfer of profits to holders would have been worth it when it operated actively to dissuade them from cashing Bank bills. But it was unnecessary insofar as people were willing to hold the Bank's paper as currency. The government, meanwhile, had facilitated that very development when it took Bank bills and notes in payment of public obligations and reduced the need people had to cash the promises they held.[152]

Finally, for public strategists, the transition to non-interest-bearing notes had appeal as well. First, the public currency established by the government (Exchequer bills) would be more competitive if it became the only cash paying interest. The government relied heavily on Exchequer bills as the War of the Spanish Succession dragged to a close; the Bank reduced its issues of interest-bearing Bank bills in just the same period.[153] Moreover, if the Bank was able to keep the profit on its advance without passing some on to the noteholders, it could lower the interest it charged on loans to the government. And, if the arrangement discouraged hoarding and put more money into circulation, that abundance would make it cheaper to borrow, further driving down interest rates— proponents of currency schemes had promoted them with that goal since the middle of the century.[154]

The basics of the Bank's movement towards displacing interest-bearing bills with non-interest-bearing notes can be traced in the records of issues made by the Bank. By March 1695, it had already sanctioned the issue of more than £1 million in notes, relative to a bit more than £1.5 million in bills. The Bank arrested its use

---

[149] *The Reasons of the Decay of Trade and Private Credit; Some Queries, Humbly Offer'd to the Consideration of Both Houses of Parliament Relating to the Bank of England.*

[150] For the quantity of bills issued from 1696 to 1710, see Horsefield, *Monetary Experiments*, 264–265. Bills, presumably all interest-bearing, made up the majority of issues every year but one before 1703; they were also the majority for several years afterwards. A significant majority of "specie" notes, lumped with running cash notes by Horsefield, were interest-bearing as well, at least when introduced. See Clapham, *Bank of England*, 37–38, 44.

[151] Interest on the bills ran about 2d.–3d./£100/day, or about £3.04–£4.56/£100/year, some 3 to 4.5 percent. See p. 309 n. 68.

[152] It is not clear how the government calculated interest due on bills when it accepted them for taxes, and whether it credited taxpayers for that interest. It may be that the Exchequer moved to regularly taking bank paper at face value when it became non-interest-bearing.

[153] Between 1709 and 1716, between £2.4 million and £4.3 million Exchequer bills were outstanding, calculated as the difference between bills created and redeemed, in Mitchell, *Abstract of British Historical Statistics*, 404–405; see also Feavearyear, *The Pound Sterling*, 159–160 (noting popularity of Exchequer bills).

[154] See pp. 304, 330, 335–337.

of notes shortly thereafter, however, probably because its directors began to fear that they were exceeding the authority to issue granted by the Bank of England Act.[155] The Great Recoinage soon confirmed the Bank in its newfound caution: as that reform drew in existing specie, individuals began cashing their Bank paper. That was the run in 1696 that drove the Bank's reserves to their lowest point and pushed Bank officials to call desperately for the remainder of the capital originally subscribed.[156] In the following year, the government authorized the Bank to expand its note issue in order to absorb public tallies that had been circulating at a discount.[157] Despite that invitation, the Bank continued warily where issuing notes was concerned. Or, according to its critics during the recessionary year 1707, the Bank favored interest-bearing bills as a way to induce hoarding, all to drive prices down and buy up assets cheaply before reversing that movement by beginning to lend freely again.[158] In any case, the outcry encouraged the Bank to step up its use of notes—those paper issues that did not bear interest—which began to outnumber bills in 1709.[159] With the support of those holding them, the Bank stopped paying interest on its paper issues altogether within the decade.

The transition changed the way the English paid for their money. For centuries, the government had charged people for money, piece by piece, as they bought coin from the mint or accepted tallies for specie. Now, the government used general revenue to borrow cash at interest from the Bank. The Bank kept the profits, no longer passing on a portion to noteholders. The shift was subtle, perhaps because Bank notes started small or because the government acted as middleman to the payment. One commentator on an early version of the Bank proposal flagged the change, however. "Who can think," wrote William Lowndes, "that posterity will be willing to pay a tax... not for the support of their own government, for the time being, but to go into the pockets of private men, strangers as well as natives, for money advanced to their ancestors...?"[160]

* * *

---

[155] See Horsefield, *Monetary Experiments*, 132–134, 266–267 (Appendix 6, Table L).

[156] The drama can be followed in the numbers of paper liabilities outstanding, which reflect a drop in both bills and notes outstanding, the inflow of capital, and the strain put on the reserve. See Horsefield, *Monetary Experiments*, 264 (Appendix 6, Table L).

[157] See Horsefield, *Monetary Experiments*, 264 (Appendix 6, Table L); see p. 305 n. 55.

[158] See p. 325 n. 146.

[159] Horsefield, *Monetary Experiments*, 264–265 (Appendix 6, Table L). Notes outstanding had occasionally outnumbered bills outstanding before that point, including during an unexplained bump up in note issues in 1703. Horsefield, *Monetary Experiments*, 264–265 (Appendix 6, Table L).

[160] Lowndes, "Remarks Upon the Proposal," xxv; see also Broughton, "Remarks upon the Bank of England" (1707-1708). For a more generalized condemnation of the profit ceded to banks by currency issue, see AD of Grey's Inn and Others, *Proposals to Supply His Majesty with Twelve or Fourteen Millions of Money: (or More If Requir'd) for the Year 1697, without Subscriptions or Advancing the Present Taxes* (printed for the author and sold by Peter Parker and others, 1697), 13, and discussion pp. 340–341. Lowndes came to work closely with the Bank as the government's agent. Clapham, *Bank of England*, 63–71.

An official statement that Bank notes were money would have to wait—until 1758 for judicial recognition, 1797 for the proposition that a tender of the notes would stave off arrest, 1816 for confirmation that Bank notes were unconditionally good for paying official obligations, and 1833 for formal status as legal tender[161]—but public officials, Bank agents, and individuals had constituted the notes as money in practice and significance long before. Those parties had incorporated bank notes into exchange between the government and individuals in ways that allowed them to pass it among themselves as the mode of payment interchangeable with the specie unit of account.

At the government's behest, the Bank would make additional advances in paper form to the government over the following years. Between 1696 and 1710, the number of Bank bills and notes in circulation ranged between £1 million to more than £2 million.[162] By the end of the century, £15 million Bank of England notes circulated. They had been joined by £10 million issued by "country banks"—small companies that issued notes for local use.[163] By that time, the money supply had increased more than 65 percent over its 1688 level and, through its newly refined instruments of public debt, the government borrowed at interest rates of about 4 percent, as compared with 12 percent a century earlier.[164]

Echoing the conventional creation story, a recent historian of money describes Bank money as produced "spontaneously and flexibly . . . in accordance with the vague but insistent demands of local trade and business." It was, the scholar continues, "substantially created, not ostentatiously and visibly by the sovereign power, but mundanely by market forces so vividly and aptly described by Adam Smith, as the 'invisible hand.'"[165] In fact, there was no invisible hand at work in the dawn of modern capitalism; the fingerprints of public authority, along with those of its business allies and the larger community, were all over the new medium. Bank currency had its impetus in an effort by the government to borrow in a form that multiplied liquidity, creating monetized promises-to-pay and enmeshing public officials and private lenders in a web of reciprocal relationships. The new medium circulated, had status interchangeable with specie as a

---

[161] See respectively 37 Geo 3 c 91 s 8 (1797) (Bank notes suffice to avoid arrest); 56 Geo 3 c 96 s 4 (1816) (Bank notes acceptable for taxes); 3 & 4 Will 4 c 98 s 6 (1833) (Bank notes legal tender). The courts first recognized Bank notes as "money" in *Miller v Race* (1758) 1 Burr 452, 453; 97 ER 398, 399 (Lord Mansfield C.J.). That recognition displaced the fact that Bank notes still had to be accepted voluntarily and, to support suit for non-payment, timely cashed. See *Wright v Reed* (1790) 3 D & E 45; Horsefield, "The Beginnings of Paper Money in England," 126–127.

[162] Horsefield, *Monetary Experiments*, 264–265. The Bank was authorized to issue up to £6,577,370 in 1709. See Davies, *History of Money*, 263.

[163] Cameron, "England, 1750–1844," 42.

[164] For figures on the money supply, see Lindert, "English Population, Wages, and Prices: 1541–1913," 624 (increase in money stock from £12 to £20 million). For interest rates, see Davies, *History of Money*, 281.

[165] Davies, *History of Money*, 282.

unit of account, and existed in a predictable amount all because of the arrangements they had worked out together.

One of the most remarkable aspects of the new medium was, however, that it made plausible a different assumption. While the practices that constituted the novel way of representing value were rooted in public debt, they licensed a new agent, an investment consortium, to issue notes at a profit. "Making money" thus depended directly on the decisions of investors. In those circumstances, the matter that later generations might call monetary policy seemed to be a function of the market, although it stood atop a public base.

In the new order, the government acquired the status of an individual, a party that consistently borrowed at interest to finance its expenses rather than a collective that used its distinctive capacity to anticipate taxes and dispense transferability in return. That activity, while animating the monetary system, seemed a separate matter. In consequence, even as people assumed that monetary policy belonged to the market, they identified fiscal policy as a political matter. As for the Bank, it brought specie to the deal. Although that value was itself created in concert with the larger community, it seemed to represent real money held by people independent of politics. The invisible hand, or rather the economic agent it represented, could thus become the star of a creation story crafted for it.

9

Re-theorizing money

The struggle over the modern imagination

As they remade money at the end of the 17th century, the English reconceptualized it. Each effort to resolve England's money problems raised the most basic issue: what *was* money? As Nicholas Barbon warned in an exchange with John Locke, "wherein the definition of money differs," prescriptions about how to reconstitute it would also disagree.[1]

Much of the commentary came from those proposing paper currencies. As they elaborated their designs, they justified them by explaining why their ideas would work. On the way, they produced accounts of money. To some, it was "a new specy" more secure than gold or silver. To others, it was a stand-in for coin because people could use it to "fetch their money for them." For still others, it was a means to "adjust contracts and accompts."[2] But most commonly, money was a kind of home-grown credit, a currency remarkably attainable, almost intoxicatingly so, should the public or some motivated group decide to create it for themselves.[3] Indeed, Bank of England currency was not the only paper money born in the 1690s. A purely public alternative, Exchequer bills, appeared a few years later. An instrument directly issued by the government and based on the anticipation of taxes, it depended solely on domestic public credit to hold value.

More commentary about money came from those concerned with rescuing coin. Battered and clipped, silver money lost value suddenly in the mid-1690s, when England was at war. Those seeking to restore it needed to map the problem and solution. They needed to explain, in other words, what made coin operate as money. Here, John Locke contributed a powerful account, one that offered a

---

[1] Nicholas Barbon, *A Discourse Concerning Coining the New Money Lighter* (printed for Richard Chiswell, 1696), A2.

[2] Sir William Killigrew, *An Humble Proposal Shewing How This Nation May Be Vast Gainers by All the Sums of Mony, Given to the Crown, Without Lessening the Prerogative* (1663, republished 1696), 8 (a modified version of this proposal was published in 1690); Godfrey, *A Short Account of the Bank of England* (1695), 6; Sir Edward Forde, *Experimented Proposals How the King May Have Money to Pay and Maintain His Fleets with Ease to His People* (William Godbid, 1666), 1.

[3] The coverage here includes about twenty-five pamphlets, a robust sample of those who proposed to make money out of the anticipated public revenue. Keith Horsefield identifies thirty-eight pamphlets advocating the anticipation of taxes in paper money; a number of those are variations on a theme by the same authors. J. Keith Horsefield, *British Monetary Experiments, 1650-1710* (Cambridge, MA: Harvard University Press, 1960), 116. For a review of proposals assuming other valuables as a base, including land and lumbard (or lombard) banks (those lending on the basis of pawned goods), see Horsefield, *Monetary Experiments*, 104–210. Only proposals to monetize government revenue came to fruition and did so in the form of notes issued by the Bank of England and Exchequer bills.

striking counterpoint to the notion of money as home-grown credit. Money, argued Locke, was instead like traders' silver, a natural resource that society recognized rather than engineered.

Both positions diverged from the approach taken by *The Case of Mixed Money* a century earlier. Written after almost a millennium of English experience with commodity money, *The Case of Mixed Money* represented traditional thinking. It had emphasized the Crown's power over coin: the king alone could make money and his prerogative to define its value was absolute. He acted, as *The Case of Mixed Money* continued, for the public good. That was a matter identified with both governmental and civic ends. Money provided the medium for the work of war and the defense of the kingdom; it also allowed for commensurable and thus just exchange between individuals. Finally, *The Case of Mixed Money* confirmed that commodity money was a political medium, consistent with its sovereign source. The value of money was an "extrinsic good." Its "shape and stamp," its political identity gave silver value as money.[4]

By contrast, the arguments elaborated by credit theorists and by proponents of a fixed metallic standard in the 1690s tested new vocabularies. Minted in a changing world, they recast the long-standing challenge of making money and articulated strategies they believed to be better. They aimed to explain and induce, persuade and gain momentum; if they succeeded in convincing an audience that could act, they could capture the future.

For Nicholas Barbon was entirely correct: the way people understood money affected the way they made it. He had entered the debate himself because he feared that Locke's approach led to a monetary strategy that would be "fatal" to the nation, "no less than the want of the species of money, a stop of trade, and a general complaint and poverty all over."[5] And Locke—along with luminaries like Christopher Wren and Isaac Newton—wrote at the request of government authorities determining how they should resurrect the country's coin.[6] Conceptual commitments had material impact in the project of making money.

A. Money as home-grown credit

If Bank of England notes later seemed the very epitome of sterling, they were contenders among a crowd in late 17th century England. Both private individuals and government officials proposed a variety of paper moneys that relied, directly or indirectly, on the anticipation of taxes for their value. Eventually, they produced a purely public alternative to Bank money.

---

[4] See pp. 267–274.

[5] Barbon, *A Discourse Concerning Coining the New Money Lighter*, A4.

[6] Horsefield, *Monetary Experiments*, 51; Ming-Hsun Li, *The Great Recoinage of 1696 to 1699* (London: Weidenfeld and Nicolson, 1963), 100–101.

Their theorizing drew on a long tradition. The structural dimensions of *The Case of Mixed Money* reappear in their writing, but those dimensions have been revised and updated, ventilated in a world with a changed constitutional atmosphere. As for the source of money's value, it remained domestic and political, but it now took a specific relational shape. The money imagined by the projectors depended on credit, the promise of a resource that was anticipated or was elsewhere. Money's current value thus remained "extrinsic," far exceeding the negligible "intrinsic" value of the paper on which it was written. As for purpose, the effort to establish credit currencies led to a particular emphasis on functionality. Those proposing such cash took pains to demonstrate it would "answer all the uses" of money.[7] Theirs was a pragmatic approach, offered to meet the familiar needs of government and private exchange. And as for the sovereign author of money, it too had shifted. Parliament took its place as the source of the revenues that would fund the promise of credit. It produced the new public medium—Exchequer bills—on its own authority.

A paper promise as value: the idea of credit

Two early pamphlets suggest the moment in 17th century England when people began turning towards "credit" as a matter that could be made into money with immediate value. We met Samuel Lambe above, expressing the view in 1658 that individuals should serve the public good as a way to benefit all. Lambe was a modern enough man to argue that the English should establish "banks" to "augment their stocks" of money. But when Lambe explained how banks would accomplish that, he cast banks as clearinghouses, rather than institutions issuing notes that could circulate as cash:

> as for example, [a] merchant buys cloath of a cloathier, for 100 l. value more or less, and goes with him to the Bank, where he is debtor so much money as he takes up, and the clothier is made creditor in account for so much as he sold for to the said merchant, then such cloathier having occasion to pay money to a stapler or wool-monger for wool, he doth buy of him, so the said clothier is made debtor, and the woolmonger creditor in account; the said woolmonger hath bought his wool of a countrey farmer, and must pay him for it, so the woolmonger is made debtor, and the farmer creditor. The farmer must pay his rent to his landlord, with the proceeds of the said wool, so the farmer is made debtor, and such landlord creditor. The landlord for his occasion, buys goods of a mercer, grocer, vinener, or the like, then he is made debtor, and such mercer, or other tradesman creditor. Then peradventure such mercer, or other tradesman, buys goods of the same merchant that took up the first credit in Bank, and stands yet debtor there, but upon sale of good to the mercer, or other tradesman, both clear their account in Bank, and such mercer, or other

---

[7] W. Van Laitz, *A Proposal to Ease the Subject, and to Restore the Credit of the Nation* (1696), 2.

tradesman is made debtor, and the said merchant creditor. Thus every mans account is cleared.[8]

By 1666, Edward Forde presented a very different conception. Noting that "bills, bonds, book accompts, and even verball promises" passed between men, he concluded that if value could be secured, many things could act as money: "for who would not rather have a straw, or a piece of paper, than a hundred pounds, if he were sure it would at all times yield him as much as he took it for."[9] Forde suggested that the king could anticipate taxes ten years into the future and "by making currant bills thereon, may have it all presently without any deductions."[10]

William Killigrew had proposed "Office-bonds" a few years earlier on the same theory. The bills were "currant credit," based on security a hundred times better than ever offered—"all the revenues of the Crown," and the trade and consumption that generated it.[11] Killigrew, like a number of later projectors, emphasized that the paper bills should not only "be transferable, but currant, as money, in all payments whatsoever, even into the *Exchequer*."[12] Indeed, with a flourish, the author noted:

> ☛ On this paragraph depends the whole proposal . . . This causes the bills, or tallies, to be a new specy of money, superior to money, made of gold or silver.[13]

In the next decades, writers embroidered on the same logic. Invoking the value of future revenues, they advocated bills with "the same credit as banker notes" but

---

[8] Samuel Lambe, *Seasonable Observations Humbly Offered to His Highness the Lord Protector* (1657), 10, 12–13.

[9] Forde, *Experimented Proposals How the King May Have Money to Pay and Maintain His Fleets with Ease to His People* (William Godbid, 1666), A2–A3. Forde claimed that the transfer of promissory notes was approved by law, a conclusion that was somewhat premature. See pp. 262–263. Both Lambe and Forde cite the Dutch as their model, suggesting a variety of Dutch initiatives.

[10] Forde, *Experimented Proposals How the King May Have Money to Pay and Maintain His Fleets with Ease to His People*, 2.

[11] Killigrew, *A Proposal Shewing How This Nation May Be Vast Gainers by All the Sums of Mony, Given to the Crown, Without Lessening the Prerogative*," 10, 8–9. As Killigrew put it, "This makes the security a hundred times more than ever was proposed or given; because all the revenues of the Crown, all our trade and consumption, is security, as well as the taxes, set to pay the principal and interests, and charges."

[12] Killigrew, *An Humble Proposal Shewing How This Nation May Be Vast Gainers by All Sums of Mony, Given to the Crown, Without Lessening the Prerogative*, 8; Thomas Neale, *A Way How to Supply the King's Occasions with Two Millions of Money* (1694), 1; Thomas Neale, *A Proposal for Raising a Million on a Fund of Interest* (1694), 2; *The Mint and Exchequer United*, 1. Neale appended a draft bill to a publication made February 6, 1695, providing that the notes "will be taken for one hundred pounds by the King in all payments for customs, or excise." More mysteriously, the draft also was receivable "in the places writ about it." See Thomas Neale, *A Way How to Supply the King's Occasions with Two Millions of Money* (1694, republished with attachment 1695), 3. The anonymous *Mint and Exchequer United* noted that only the issues of the Bank of England and the Million-Bank should likewise be receivable, because they were also founded "on the government" (*The Mint and Exchequer United*, 1).

[13] Killigrew, *A Proposal Shewing How This Nation May Be Vast Gainers by All the Sums of Mony, Given to the Crown, Without Lessening the Prerogative*," 8; see also Neale, *For Raising a Million*, 2. As Robert Murray put it, the "fund is in reason superior to all others, because the Nation itself is lyeable to make good the revenue, the revenue being a rent-charge or quit-rent issuing out of the whole Nation, and charged upon it by law" (Robert Murray, *The Manner and Method of an Exchequer Credit* (1695), 1).

payable when sums granted by Parliament came into the Exchequer or bills that offered "a safe credit and ease" on a similar fund.[14] One suggested bills that would "supply the want of coin by credit," calling public revenues "so true a foundation" that it would be as good as coin, while another lauded "publick bills of credit" that would provide a "true National universal credit throughout all the kingdom."[15] As Thomas Neale put it, "In short, as the King pays out silver and gold, and takes it again for just the same as he paid it out; so . . . he should take again these bills (*viz.*) as 100 l. 50 l. or 20 l. as he paid them out."[16] Other authors suggested credit based on a tangible resource as evident security—land, pawns, or specie. William Paterson claimed that Bank of England bills were superior given their redeemability in coin—but it was by no means necessary.[17]

The logic reached even further. Some authors conceptualized coin itself as a kind of credit. At pains to point out the inability of most people to know the amount of silver in a coin, Nicholas Barbon turned upside down the suggestion that the government's stamp on coin documented the quantity of metal in it. To the contrary, Barbon acerbically observed, the government used alloys apparently "that the quantity of silver in each piece, and the mystery of the mint," would be preserved.[18] Barbon's reasoning took him to the argument that the value of coin depended on the government's obligation to receive it—that is, on its status as a public liability:

> The stamp upon the money is the seal of the government; so that if there was not a law to make it current, and had only the King's seal or stamp upon it, it ought rather to have a better, or at least the same value as a bank note, or any private person's bond or seal; which only shews, that the person whose note or seal it is, is oblig'd to pay or

---

[14] EW, *A Speedy Way to Supply Their Majesties Occasions* (1691), 1; Neale, *For Raising a Million*, 2.

[15] See, respectively William Atwood, *A Safe and Easy Method for Supplying the Want of Coin, and Raising as Many Millions as the Occasions of the Publick May Require* (printed for Roger Clavel, 1695), 1; AD of Grey's Inn and Others, *Proposals to Supply His Majesty with Twelve or Fourteen Millions of Money: (or More If Requir'd) for the Year 1697, without Subscriptions or Advancing the Present Taxes* (printed for the author and sold by Peter Parker and others, 1697), 13, 18. To his suggestion that Parliament provide a £500,000 fund per year to redeem the bills of credit he proposed, Atwood added that any deficiencies should be made up by any money that was in the Exchequer or "the *next publick tax.*" See Atwood, *A Safe and Easy Method for Supplying the Want of Coin, and Raising as Many Millions as the Occasions of the Publick May Require*, 2. See also *A Proposal for the King's Supply, and for Quieting the People, and to Prevent the Loss of Our Wealth to Foreigners* (1696) (proposing note issue by public lender); Thomas Houghton, *A Plain and Easie Method for Supplying the Scarcity of Money and the Promoting of Trade* (E. Whitlock, 1696) (proposing "parliamentary notes"); Van Laitz, *A Proposal to Ease the Subject*, 1 (proposing "bills of credit"); Charles Montague, "A Document relating to the Establishment of Paper Credit (1696)," in *The Great Recoinage of 1696 to 1699*, ed. Ming-Hsun Li (London: Weidenfeld and Nicolson, 1963), 237 (noting consensus on need for "paper credit").

[16] Neale, *A Way How to Supply*, 1.

[17] Dr. Hugh Chamberlen, John Briscoe, John Asgill, and Dr. Nicholas Barbon were the main progenitors of land banks, including the proposal briefly endorsed by Parliament. For review, see Horsefield, *Monetary Experiments*, 156–217. For credit issued on pawns, see, e.g., Robert Murray, *A Proposal for the Advancement of Trade, Upon Such Principles as Must Necessarily Enforce It* (AM and others, 1676). For Paterson's advocacy of the security for Bank bills, see William Paterson, *A Brief Account of the Intended Bank of England* (Randal Taylor, 1694), 10.

[18] Barbon, *A Discourse Concerning Coining the New Money Lighter*, 22.

exchange it. And if there were no other obligation from the King's stamp than to show that the King would take it in his revenue, it would give it a sufficient currency, tho' there were no law to make it current.[19]

When those conceptualizing money as credit applied their logic to coin, they arrived at the understanding of the ancients who had mapped the working of money in their city-states as a currency that depended on its political identity as sovereign debt. The jurists deciding *The Case of Mixed Money* had invoked Seneca given his observation that "Both the man who owes gold coins and the man who owes leather imprinted with an official stamp is said to be in debt."[20] Barbon and contemporary credit theorists updated the logic to equate coins and paper.

The modern touchstone: functionality

As Barbon's argument suggested, conceiving money as credit opened up a host of possibilities. The range of proposals alone demonstrated that credit might be conceived on a variety of securities.[21] And as a number of authors recognized more or less clearly, if monetized value could be created out of credit, the money supply could be expanded with the deliberate engineering of reciprocal obligations.[22] The debates indicate the breadth of choices that people now saw implicated by how money might be made.

Orthodoxy receded in the face of their inventiveness. For the point, as author after author emphasized, was to make something *that worked*. The momentum of their thought, along with the need they perceived for currency, had taken them beyond the singularity of coin to whatever could function in its stead. At times, that purpose was stated with great sophistication: Nicholas Barbon arguably captured the price of money as a matter in part dependent on its premium as cash ("the great use of it").[23] At other times, the advantages of money to finance

---

[19] Barbon, *A Discourse Concerning Coining the New Money Lighter*, 28–29.

[20] See *The Case of Mixed Money* (1605) in T. B. Howell, *Cobbett's Complete Collection of State Trials and Proceedings for High Treason and Other Crimes and Misdemeanors from the Earliest Period to the Year 1783*, vol. 2 (London: R. Bagshaw, 1809), 114, 124 (quoting Seneca).

[21] Claims and counterclaims about those securities and their strength runs like a thread through their proposals. See, e.g., Van Laitz, *A Proposal to Ease the Subject*, 1; Neale, *For Raising a Million*, 3; Killigrew, *A Proposal Shewing How This Nation May Be Vast Gainers by All the Sums of Mony, Given to the Crown, Without Lessening the Prerogative*, 10–11.

[22] See, e.g., AD of Grey's Inn, *Proposals to Supply His Majesty with Twelve or Fourteen Millions of Money: (or More If Requir'd) for the Year 1697, without Subscriptions or Advancing the Present Taxes*, 6; Montague, "A Document Relating to Public Credit," 237; Neale, *A Way How to Supply*, 1; Neale, *For Raising a Million*, 3; Murray, *A Proposal for the Advancement of Trade, Upon Such Principles as Must Necessarily Enforce It*, 10–12.

[23] As Barbon argued: "Now if it be true in itself, that nothing has a value or price; That the value of all things arises from their use, it will be no strange consequence that money should have a value, from the great use of it, above the price of bullion…And that the government should have power to set and fix a value or price upon their money, as well as the merchant and trader upon their goods and wares." Barbon, *A Discourse Concerning Coining the New Money Lighter*, 27.

the war (any war), facilitate trade, lower the interest rate, increase employment, and fund public works were simply listed.[24] In either case, the point was to make something that was *equal to* money in its effects, whether or not it *was* money. The sensibility of the projectors reads in retrospect as one belonging to the transitional figures they were.

On the one hand, commentators did not dislodge coin from its stature as the prototype of money; rather, they assimilated paper notes to it. Bills of credit, wrote a projector, would "be as useful as money" and "equivalent to ready-money" at low interest rates.[25] Parliamentary bills would be "as good as ready money to the king upon all accounts" and "pass from hand to hand" to pay for purchases or debts, argued another advocate.[26] Thomas Neale suggested that the interest attached to notes anticipating taxes would "make these bills 'twixt man and man much better than ready money."[27] William Atwood, Thomas Houghton, and William Paterson all agreed with other authors—bills based on valuable funds could "supply the want of coin, and answer all the uses of it."[28]

On the other hand, their focus on creating an equivalent for coin induced projectors to map very deliberately how money could be made to work. They attended to each of the attributes of money—its roles as a mode of payment, a unit of account, and a medium of exchange. On the first, theorizing paper as credit that would be received back by its issuer ensured that it would act as a mode of payment. According to one of Thomas Neale's proposals, for example, 2 million pounds could be "paid out by the King as so much ready money, to those his Majesty has occasion to pay money to, and are ready to receive it."[29] Here gather all the proposals that emphasized that paper issued on the anticipation of

---

[24] See, e.g., AD of Grey's Inn, *Proposals to Supply His Majesty with Twelve or Fourteen Millions of Money: (or More If Requir'd) for the Year 1697, without Subscriptions or Advancing the Present Taxes,* 5; Montague, "A Document Relating to Public Credit," 237; Houghton, *A Plain and Easie Method for Supplying the Scarcity of Money and the Promoting of Trade,* 5–6, 11; Atwood, *A Safe and Easy Method for Supplying the Want of Coin, and Raising as Many Millions as the Occasions of the Publick May Require,* 2; Forde, *Experimented Proposals How the King May Have Money to Pay and Maintain His Fleets with Ease to His People,* 3–4; Killigrew, *A Proposal Shewing How This Nation May Be Vast Gainers by All the Sums of Mony, Given to the Crown, Without Lessening the Prerogative,* 12–14.

[25] Robert Murray, *An Account of the Constitution and Security of the General Bank of Credit* (John Gain, 1683), 6–7; see also Murray, *A Proposal for the Advancement of Trade, Upon Such Principles as Must Necessarily Enforce It,* 4 (credit written on a substantial fund would "in all respects answer the use of money"). In the same pamphlet, Murray ventures a definition of money as "being not more than a deposit given for such commodities as men part withal" (Murray, *A Proposal for the Advancement of Trade, Upon Such Principles as Must Necessarily Enforce It,* 4).

[26] EW, *A Speedy Way to Supply Their Majesties Occasions,* 1.

[27] Neale, *A Way How to Supply,* 1. See also Neale, *A Way How to Supply,* 2 (comparing bills favorably in function to Bank bills or goldsmiths' notes); Neale, *For Raising a Million,* 2–4 (similar).

[28] Van Laitz, *A Proposal to Ease the Subject,* 2; see Houghton, *A Plain and Easie Method for Supplying the Scarcity of Money and the Promoting of Trade,* 7; Atwood, *A Safe and Easy Method for Supplying the Want of Coin, and Raising as Many Millions as the Occasions of the Publick May Require,* 2; Paterson, *A Brief Account,* 2; AD of Grey's Inn, *Proposals to Supply His Majesty with Twelve or Fourteen Millions of Money: (or More If Requir'd) for the Year 1697, without Subscriptions or Advancing the Present Taxes,* 6.

[29] See Neale, *A Way How to Supply,* 1; see also Neale, *For Raising a Million,* 2. Neale frequently republished his work. See, e.g., Neale, *A Way How to Supply* (1694, 1695).

taxes to come.[30] Projectors reached money's identity as a unit of account when they discussed the use of paper bills to pay creditors or to give investors. That would make the bills act as "money immediately" because the currency could be used interchangeably with specie.[31] Finally, so that bills could be used along the way, those proposing them provided that they be easily transferable or "easie assignable," whether made payable as a creditor dictated, made payable to "bearer," or in a way left unspecified.[32] Some authors suggested that the bills be issued in denominations as small as 5 pounds "for the lesser the bonds are, the better they will pass in trade."[33] The discussion amounted to a tutorial on money as a constitutional project.

The ingenuity of projectors even reached beyond the traditional dogma that money must be made by the sovereign. A set of pamphlets promoted private collective action by merchants, tradesmen, and landowners, any of which could bind themselves to accept paper notes they issued as a collective.[34] Local or trade currencies had circulated intermittently in England. They would continue throughout the 18th century. But those efforts, launched without the comprehensive or coercive powers of government, were always more fragile affairs. If they represented the fresh stirrings of civil society, they did not make significant inroads into the sovereign's territory. Sovereignty had, however, changed since the early 17th century.

Sovereignty and money

Conceiving money (or its equivalent) as the credit produced by a group for its own purposes, most projectors of new currencies reached the last dimension identified in *The Case of Mixed Money*—that of money's authorship. They assumed, as did the jurists there, that the sovereign created money. But late

---

[30] See pp. 333–335; compare pp. 45–46.

[31] Killigrew, *An Humble Proposal Shewing How This Nation May Be Vast Gainers by All Sums of Mony, Given to the Crown, without Lessening the Prerogative*, 7, 12 (including reference to Crown use of bills for "purchase of stores"); see also Killigrew, *An Humble Proposal Shewing How This Nation May Be Vast Gainers by All Sums of Mony, Given to the Crown, without Lessening the Prerogative,*" 10 (defending ability of Crown to obligate men to take "proposed current credit"); Murray, *The Manner and Method of an Exchequer Credit*, 1 ("credit be taken and current in all manner of payments to and from the Crown"); *The Mint and Exchequer United*, 1.

[32] Killigrew, *An Humble Proposal Shewing How This Nation May Be Vast Gainers by All Sums of Mony, Given to the Crown, without Lessening the Prerogative*, 7; *The Mint and Exchequer United*, 1; Neale, *A Way How to Supply*, 1 (notes would travel "'twixt man and man much better than ready money" because they were interest bearing).

[33] Killigrew, *An Humble Proposal Shewing How This Nation May Be Vast Gainers by All Sums of Mony, Given to the Crown, without Lessening the Prerogative,*" 7; Neale, *A Way How to Supply*, 1; *The Mint and Exchequer United*, 1.

[34] Murray, *A Proposal for the Advancement of Trade, Upon Such Principles as Must Necessarily Enforce It*; Van Laitz, *A Proposal to Ease the Subject*. For private land bank plans, see Horsefield, *Monetary Experiments*, 156–217. Some of these projects actually assumed some public support or involvement; Murray, for example, refers to "public repositories" for pawned materials. Murray, *A Proposal for the Advancement of Trade, Upon Such Principles as Must Necessarily Enforce It*, 6.

17th century credit theorists reflected the constitutional turmoil of the century. In the 1660s, Sir Edward Forde had felt it necessary to append an "Additional Defence of Bill-Credit," to his proposal, showing how the revenue collected in silver coin to pay the bills could be secured from the monarch's reach. "Nor do I think we get by screwing any of His rights from Him," noted Forde, "whom we must preserve potent and able to defend us, or all come to speedy and certain ruin."[35]

After the Glorious Revolution, William Paterson would rehearse the point only in passing. In light of the settlement between William III and Parliament, he was as much if not more concerned to refute the contention that banks naturally led to "republicks." In the course of debate about establishing the Bank of England, Tory and country critics had raised the danger that the democratic tendency might go too far:

> That the very establishing of a bank in England, will of course alter the Government, for that is to entrust the fund of the nation in the hands of subjects, who naturally are, and will always be sure to be of the popular side, and will insensibly influence the Church and State.[36]

The skirmish was serious—for Tory opponents, the Bank threatened to empower men whose wealth was unconnected to the land and the bond to England that land represented. Money had become a matter that empowered a new group of political actors.

The dispute revealed a larger area of agreement. By the 1690s, those proposing paper currencies had turned their attention to Parliament as the active source of the credit to support it; no longer did the power to make money "inhere in the bones of princes," as it had for the jurists early in the century.[37] Paterson was one of many who preached little constitutional homilies on the security of the incoming revenue "that cannot fail, but with the nation." It had been "settled by Parliament for the uses thereby limited and appointed," he continued, "there being no country in Christendom where property hath been more sacred and secure for some ages past, notwithstanding all our Revolutions."[38] William Atwood looked to Parliament to provide the revenue, even as he lauded the (apparently refortified) foundations of the monarchy, "which can never be

---

[35] Forde, *Experimented Proposals How the King May Have Money to Pay and Maintain His Fleets with Ease to His People*, B1–3.
[36] Paterson, *A Brief Account*, 8. For a more substantial critique of the Bank as inconsistent with monarchy, see *Some Considerations Offered against the Continuance of the Bank of England*, 2–3.
[37] See p. 270 (quoting *The Case of Mixed Money*).
[38] Paterson, *A Brief Account*, 12; see also, e.g., Killigrew, *A Proposal Shewing How This Nation May Be Vast Gainers by All the Sums of Mony, Given to the Crown, Without Lessening the Prerogative*, 5, 12 (noting approval of "several Parliaments" for proposal, republished in 1696, to "the Wisdome of the King and both Houses of Parliament"); AD of Grey's Inn, *Proposals to Supply His Majesty with Twelve or Fourteen Millions of Money: (or More If Requir'd) for the Year 1697, without Subscriptions or Advancing the Present Taxes*, 6–8 (attributing to Parliament ability to settle "an inexhaustible fund...the whole revenue of the kingdom").

Fig. 9.1 An interest-bearing Exchequer bill for £100 issued in 1704 to raise funds for the South Sea Company. © Trustees of the British Museum.

moved, but by such a calamity as should leave us no visible means of continuing a protestant nation, or free people."[39]

The capacity of Parliament to make money was generative. It had established the Bank of England in its major creative enterprise. The logic rolled out by credit advocates led as well to the public alternative: Exchequer bills.[40] See Fig. 9.1.

Exchequer bills were designed to travel easily as "bearer" notes in relatively small denominations, £5 and £10.[41] The idea came to fruition in the mid-1690s as a way to ease the currency shortage that the Great Recoinage would produce. In fact, the Bank moved away from issuing small denomination notes just as Exchequer bills were issued in 1696; the timing suggests that the division of

---

[39] Atwood, *A Safe and Easy Method for Supplying the Want of Coin, and Raising as Many Millions as the Occasions of the Publick May Require*, 8.

[40] See the National Land Bank Act 1696 (7 & 8 Will 3 c 31 s 67) (authorizing £1.5 million Exchequer bills or "indented bills of credit"); 8 & 9 Will 3 c 6 (1696–1697) (authorizing additional £1.5 million Exchequer bills); see also 8 & 9 Will 3 c 20 ss 64, 66 (1696–1697) (adjusting compensation for those holding and circulating bills). Parliament also experimented with lottery tickets and other credit instruments, some of which had limited currency.

[41] The National Land Bank Act authorized bills in "even" numbers from 10 to 100 pound denominations and other such sums as were "convenient." The bills were to "pass in payment from any person or persons to any other persons that shall be willing to accept and take the same" (National Land Bank Act 1696 (7 & 8 Will 3 c 31 s 70); see also H. Clapham, *The Bank of England: A History* (Cambridge: Cambridge University Press, 1970), 38.

labor was coordinated.[42] The government put Exchequer bills into circulation by paying them to creditors who would take them or selling them to investors who lent to the state. The bills could be cashed on demand at the Exchequer, assuming funds there from the same revenue measure. After the first year, Exchequer bills could also used for public payments, notably taxes.[43]

Like Bank bills, Exchequer bills were interest-bearing.[44] The fact that interest attached here, an initiative taken by the government not the Bank, suggests that attitudes about sovereign power over money had indeed changed. Credit theorists had commonly argued that interest was due on the issues they advocated. For them, money was indeed borrowing rather than a trade of liquidity for an advance of resources, the older conception. As one put it, while the bills would act as "redy money" for "merchants and others" as well as the king, they were not to be imposed on people. Their acceptance would depend on the recognition that they were "a safe credit and ease." "Let credit be given to the person receiving such bills for the money for which those bills were then given," proposed Neale with interest as the reward he had in mind.[45] As the form of public borrowing that was finally institutionalized, Exchequer bills carried a like reward.

The focus on interest expressed, as well, an awareness that making money was a profitable enterprise. The entity that could issue promises-of-value paid off only in the future held a valuable franchise. For some, the lucrative nature of that power warranted a second look at the Bank. In 1697, an anonymous advocate of parliamentary bills posed the issue directly whether the public was being short-changed by its private agents:

> Now forasmuch as the currency of bills is so vast a booty, as that all banks have labour'd so strenuously to keep the same out of the hands of the King and Government, endangering the ruin of both, they have (surely) the best right and most reason

---

[42] Even with Exchequer bills, the main medium for smaller transactions remained coin throughout the first half of the 18th century. See Albert Edgar Feavearyear, *The Pound Sterling: A History of English Money*, 2nd ed. (Oxford: Clarendon Press, 1963), 160.

[43] For receivability in taxes, see 8 & 9 Will 3 c 20 s 63 (1696–1697). Contrary to Clapham's assertion, the first bills were in fact "payable upon demand" at the Receipt of the Exchequer, assuming that there were funds at the Exchequer from amounts advanced under the Act's provisions for borrowing by payment order or Exchequer bill. See National Land Bank Act 1696 (7 & 8 Will 3 c 31 ss 69, 70); compare Clapham, *Bank of England*, 39. Subsequent issues, of which specimens survive, were acceptable in public payments. See Richard David Richards, *The Early History of Banking in England* (London: P. S. King, 1929), 142–143 (including specimens); Clapham, *Bank of England*, 38–39, 123–124 (including specimens).

[44] See the National Land Bank Act 1696 (7 & 8 Will 3 c 31 ss 67, 69) (interest up to maximum of 3d. per day per £100); see also 8 & 9 Will 3 c 20 ss 64, 66 (1696–1697) (interest of 5d. per day per £100, and authorizing Treasury to compensate Bank of England or others assisting circulation of bills). See generally Li, *The Great Recoinage of 1696 to 1699*, 130–134.

[45] See Neale, *For Raising a Million*, 2 (6 percent); Neale, *A Way How to Supply* (6 percent). Others also attached interest to the bills they proposed. Killigrew, *An Humble Proposal Shewing How This Nation May Be Vast Gainers by All Sums of Money, Given to the Crown, without Lessening the Prerogative*, 7–8 (6 percent); *The Mint and Exchequer United*, 1 (a bit more than 4 percent).

to take it [the currency of bills] themselves to preserve both the one and the other, from penury by them, and desolation by France.[46]

The government continued to issue Exchequer bills into the 19th century, although it never accepted the proposal to use them broadly.[47] As we will see, Exchequer bills instead became a medium most used in times of banking crisis: as legislatively issued instruments that depended directly on government credit, they could be deployed to stabilize the currency supply. The visibility of a public alternative transparently based on incoming revenues gradually faded, along with the energetic theorizing that had produced it.[48] It appears that the notion of money as credit was overtaken by an alternative.

B. Money as traders' silver

The debate over money's definition reached silver money in the 1690s because that is when coin fell apart. The decade was something like the perfect monetary storm for commodity money from start to (as it would turn out) finish.

Since the Restoration, the government had failed to procure a strong flow of metal to the mint. Silver, the content of everyday coin, was chronically under-valued relative to gold; much of it was melted and exported. War had repeatedly disrupted trade; after 1689, the hostilities against France radically depressed exports, reducing the amount of bullion coming to England. Foreign remittances to pay military expenses added to the outflow of specie. Both routine use and regular abuse had eroded the remaining currency. Wear and tear deteriorated coins and "clippers" shaved off additional bits of metal.[49] Prices had been rising

[46] AD of Grey's Inn, *Proposals to Supply His Majesty with Twelve or Fourteen Millions of Money: (or More If Requir'd) for the Year 1697, without Subscriptions or Advancing the Present Taxes*, 13; see also William Lowndes, "Remarks Upon the Proposal for Establishing a Fund to Raise Two Millions," in *The Writings of William Paterson* (London: Judd & Glass, 1859), xxv; *Some Queries, Humbly Offer'd to the Consideration of Both Houses of Parliament Relating to the Bank of England*," 2; *A Short View of the Apparent Dangers and Mischiefs from the Bank of England*, 21–22.

[47] In the mid-1710s, for example, something like £4.4 million Exchequer bills were outstanding. See data from B. R. Mitchell, *Abstract of British Historical Statistics* (Cambridge: Cambridge University Press, 1962), 404–405. The estimate reflects the total of Exchequer bills created less the number of bills redeemed, but may overstate the number of bills actually circulating if many had been used to pay taxes rather than redeemed. See Li, *The Great Recoinage of 1696 to 1699*, 133–134. For estimates of the number of bills held by the Bank of England, see Horsefield, *Monetary Experiments*, 135. For the use of Exchequer bills during banking crises, see pp. 369–370, 406.

[48] The credit-theory tradition does crop up regularly in later writing, if not as vigorously. Charles Jenkinson, 1st Earl of Liverpool, whose passion was to see England safely attached to a coinage system built on a single unit of account with supplemental token money that held value because it was convertible (see pp. 377–381 for discussion), seems at times close to articulating an approach to money that understands it as fiscally driven. See Charles, Earl of Liverpool, *A Treatise on the Coins of the Realm in a Letter to the King* (London: Oxford University Press, 1805), 77–79; see also S. Dana Horton, *The Silver Pound and England's Monetary Policy since the Restoration; Together with the History of the Guinea* (London: Macmillan, 1887), 76–77 (theorizing support for the guinea's value to flow from government spending and taxing).

[49] See Horsefield, *Monetary Experiments*, 5–12; Li, *The Great Recoinage of 1696 to 1699*, 8–13; C. E. Challis, "Lord Hastings to the Great Silver Recoinage, 1464–1699," in *A New History of the Royal Mint*, ed. C. E. Challis (Cambridge: Cambridge University Press, 1992), 379–381.

since the beginning of the war, first for imported goods including raw materials, and then in 1692–1693 for consumer goods.[50] As prices rose with the war and coins lost value, the flow of silver to the mints dropped precipitously; it was virtually non-existent after 1690.[51] By the middle of the decade, prices in silver coin were up between 20 and 30 percent; gold and guineas gained value abruptly. By 1695, the silver currency carried only half the weight it had when issued, according to Exchequer accounts.[52] Even that coin seemed to be fast disappearing.

Although circumstances in the middle of the decade were dire, they were not unprecedented. England had weathered such storms before, from the episode of the "imitation pennies" in the 1290s on. As early as 1690, a House Committee had reported on the problems. It began with traditional diagnoses, including the French king's increase in the mint price he offered for silver. It continued with familiar suspicions; the Committee scapegoated Jews as particularly likely to export the metal, if not alone in doing so. And it came to the conventional conclusion: the government should prohibit the export of silver and "enhance" or devalue the silver coin.[53] Perhaps the only surprising aspect of the Committee's report is that its recommendation for devaluation was not immediately adopted.

The case for devaluation was strong. Given the low value of coined silver money and the significant demand for silver abroad, it no longer rewarded people to bring bullion to the mint. In this case, the long-standing problem captured as Gresham's Law had been exacerbated by a more modern circumstance, the public subsidy of money's cost in place since the Restoration. On the first, recall that when coins with the same count but different commodity contents circulated, people would use the low-content coin at face value but hoard the full-content coin, melt it, or export it. Because a low-content coin passed at face value, the bullion in the full-content coin rose in price. That bullion could be used for non-monetary purposes or sent abroad. Indeed, the sterling exchange rate would fall, as diminished silver coin bought fewer foreign counterparts. Silver bullion, by contrast, would hold its metal value and thus bring a higher price in foreign exchange or foreign goods. It paid to export full-weight coin or bullion.

The public subsidy of coin worsened the differential between silver coin and the market price for silver. When the Crown picked up the cost for coin, it effectively invited anyone holding bullion to bring it to the mint in full exchange for coin, whenever coin was worth more than bullion. People would accept the

---

[50] Li, *The Great Recoinage of 1696 to 1699*.

[51] See Horsefield, *Monetary Experiments*, 3–12; Li, *The Great Recoinage of 1696 to 1699*, 53–59.

[52] William Lowndes, *A Report Containing an Essay for the Amendment of Silver Coins* (London: Charles Bill & the Executrix of Thomas Newcomb, 1695), 106–107; Li, *The Great Recoinage of 1696 to 1699*, 56–57, 112.

[53] "House of Commons Journal Volume 10: 8 May 1690," *Journal of the House of Commons*: volume 10: 1688–1693, British History Online, accessed June 22, 2014, <http://www.british-history.ac.uk/report.aspx?compid=29027>; Li, *The Great Recoinage of 1696 to 1699*, 54–55.

invitation as long as they desired the cash qualities of coin, taking silver to the mint to get coin until coin's added value over the same amount of bullion was zero. In that way, full-weight coin freely available from that government lost the evident premium that had traditionally boosted its value above that of bullion. In earlier days, even as coin lost commodity content, its superior face value—perhaps 5 to 10 percent above the value of bullion—delayed the point at which people would seek the bullion in full-weight coin by hoarding, melting, or exporting it.[54] Now, as coin depreciated in content (but continued to pass at face value), its full-weight counterpart was immediately worth culling out for different use.[55]

According to William Lowndes, the gap between the mint price and the market price of silver in the 1690s created opportunities for arbitrage across England's border. It was not the only problem created by the possibility that the mint's prices in the unit of account could be played off of market values. The mint was also offering mint prices for silver and for gold that undervalued silver, given the market ratios of the two metals.[56] Nor were all of the problems with the money supply the result of count/content discrepancies. Most importantly, there was a war drawing silver to foreign lands; remittances made for supporting troops abroad created an unfavorable exchange rate for English coin.[57] But the problem created by the gap between the mint and market price of silver was exacerbating every other challenge. As people siphoned silver bullion out of the country, it became more valuable still in terms of the domestic unit of account—but the government's low mint price for coin remained fixed.[58]

---

[54] See p. 238.

[55] In fact, as we have seen, publicly subsidized coin was never worth more than an equivalent amount of silver, but it could be worth less: while people could convert silver into coin without a fee, they could only convert coin into silver by paying to melt it and incurring other expenses, like evading any restrictions on its export. That burden sometimes made coin of a particular content less desirable for certain purposes than the same amount of silver bullion. See pp. 238–239. This contingency would be a particular problem after the Great Recoinage, when full-bodied coin circulated. Before the Great Recoinage, it was mitigated insofar as coin of low content still passed at face value. In that case, it would cost more silver at the mint to replace the existing coin.

[56] Insofar as coin traveled at its face value at home, people preferred to save silver coin for use at its bullion value in international exchange and use gold coin at home. Lowndes also argued that, as people fled clipped silver coin and turned to gold, they drove the price of guineas higher, making it yet more overvalued compared to silver. That price would further encourage gold imports to England. Lowndes, *Amendment of Silver Coins*, 110–111.

[57] See Li, *The Great Recoinage of 1696 to 1699*, 12–13. Absent the gap between the mint and market prices of silver, a trade imbalance could be expected to correct itself. If English and Dutch pennies contained the same amount of silver, their exchange rate would be approximately 1:1. But if demand rose among the English for Dutch goods, the price for bills of exchange in London paying Dutch coin to be used for purchases in Amsterdam might rise to 1.5 English:1 Dutch penny. Cf. Lowndes, *Amendment of Silver Coins*, 72–73, 79–80. At some point it became worth it for purely monetary gain (i.e., independent of the balance of trade) to take English pennies to Holland, melt them, mint them into Dutch money, and offer them for 1.5 English pennies at home. But that circumstance should simply hasten the rebalancing of trade that would occur as the lower value of the English pound raised the cost of imports and cheapened exports.

[58] Lowndes thus distinguished the falling supply of silver because of balance of payment problems from the fact that, once silver was undervalued, it would be exported because it bought more abroad, arguing that

The predicament brings us back to the Committee's recommendation. In order to cure the problem haunting coin, its count or face value had to be brought closer to the market value of silver.[59] Devaluation was the time-honored solution in England (and Europe): diminishing the silver content of new coin brought it down to the level of existing coin. Assuming that the diminished standard approximated the existing currency, prices could be expected to remain stable. Rather, the change would effectively increase the mint price for silver, as the public unit of account "bought" less bullion. The remedy thus avoided the difficult effects of deflation and minimized the costs visited on those holding old coin during the transition.[60] That would be particularly beneficial in wartime, when a drop in the money supply would wreak even more havoc. A revaluation, by contrast, brought the content of all coin, including the worn and eroded stuff that circulated widely, up to the existing standard. All things equal, prices could be expected to fall and the value of coin increase (coming up to the value of silver), as the money supply decreased. Both alternatives would bring the mint and market prices of silver together, then, but they would do so in very different ways: devaluation would act by bringing up prices for silver at the mint; revaluation by driving down prices for commodities in general.

Whether or not contemporaries understood the choice clearly,[61] political support for a devaluation was impressive. Between the House Report of 1690 and the escalation of prices in 1695, a series of bills to devalue silver money was introduced although not passed. By August of that year, the Board at the Treasury was sufficiently convinced to order William Lowndes, Secretary of the Treasury, to produce a report elaborating the case for devaluation.[62] As Richard Kleer

---

a fix for the latter problem through a devaluation would not exacerbate any trade imbalance (Lowndes, *Amendment of Silver Coins*, 77–78). Indeed, it could improve that imbalance, rasing the price for imports and making exports cheaper.

[59] Adjustment of the government price of coin was also needed to address bimetallic problems. When silver was mispriced by the mint relative to gold, it paid traders to export silver bullion and import the relatively overvalued gold. Lowndes, *Amendment of Silver Coins*; see, e.g., Thomas J. Sargent and Francois R. Velde, *The Big Problem of Small Change*, The Princeton Economic History of the Western World Indexes (Princeton, NJ Princeton University Press, 2002), 271–290.

[60] See pp. 120–125. Likewise, if those supporting devaluation were correct about general price inflation, the exchange rate already assumed the diminished silver content of coin. If they were wrong, devaluation would make bills of exchange more expensive, worsening England's problem accumulating silver. For the argument that it was not only unwise but anomalous to revalue during wartime, see Barbon, *A Discourse Concerning Coining the New Money Lighter*, 94.

[61] Richard Kleer argues that contemporaries did not clearly evaluate the effects of revaluation or devaluation and doubts that a general price inflation had actually occurred. He attributes the high prices to the extraordinary demand for English commodities induced by arbitrage trading in gold, pointing out that significant price inflation only occurred in the summer of 1695. See Richard A. Kleer, "'The Ruine of their Diana': Lowndes, Locke, and the Bankers," *History of Political Economy* 36, no. 3 (2004): 543–544. Ming-Hsun Li finds prices rising in both imported and a variety of consumer goods by 1692–1693 through August of 1694, falling considerably between September 1694 and July 1695 before beginning to rise sharply again. Li, *The Great Recoinage of 1696 to 1699*, 8.

[62] I follow Patrick Hyde Kelly's evaluation here, given his exhaustive parsing of the political record. See Patrick Hyde Kelly, *Locke on Money*, 2 vols., vol. 1 (Oxford: Clarendon Press, 1991), 17–24, 29, 106–109. By early 1695, Charles Montague, Chancellor of the Exchequer, several other Treasury Commissioners

points out, the role of such a report was to ensure support in the Commons for the requisite Bill.[63]

John Locke and the debate over the definition of money enter the story at this point. Or actually, somewhat earlier—from 1690 on, a number of Whig politicians, including Sir John Somers (Solicitor-General, Lord Keeper, and Lord Chancellor in succession) and Sir Edward Clarke (a Member of Parliament and eventually party manager in the Commons) mobilized to oppose devaluation. John Locke was integral to that effort, although he was not alone in the case he made—he would both draw from and influence contemporaries.[64] Indeed, it is not clear whether the political motivations of the group drew from its intellectual convictions or the other way around. Locke, a figure with close connections to Clarke, Somers, and other Whig politicians, was the figure who increasingly theorized money in a way that brought those aspects together.[65] As Patrick Kelly reconstructs events, the philosopher produced each of his major works on money in response to contrary initiatives in Parliament.[66]

In order to make the case against devaluation, Locke offered a cohesive definition of money, one that broke with tradition. According to Locke, money was the same as traders' silver, the commodity that traveled in international

including Sir Stephen Fox and Sydney Godolphin, and a number of House members apparently at first favored devaluation. Kelly, *Locke on Money*, 17–24, 29, 107–108. By contrast, a number of historians citing Feavearyear or following Lord Liverpool's narrative assume Montague resisted devaluation. See, e.g., Horsefield, *Monetary Experiments*, 51; Liverpool, *A Treatise on the Coins of the Realm in a Letter to the King*, 72. As Kelly documents, Montague came to that position later, after negotiations with John Somers and Locke. See pp. 362–363. Extensive accounts of the Great Recoinage and the debate leading up to it are also given by Horsefield, *Monetary Experiments*, 37–70, and Li, *The Great Recoinage of 1696 to 1699*. In early 1695, another Committee reported its recommendation in favor of a devaluation, and action stalled again. For the Committee's report, see "House of Commons Journal Volume 11: 12 March 1695," *Journal of the House of Commons*: volume 11: 1693–1697, British History Online, accessed June 22, 2014, <http://www.british-history.ac.uk/report.aspx?compid=39126>.

[63] Kleer, "Lowndes, Locke, and the Bankers," 547–551.

[64] For arguments that resembled Locke's in some aspects, see e.g., Sir Dudley North, *Discourses Upon Trade, Principally Directed to the Cases of the Interest, Coynage, Clipping, Increase of Money* (printed for Tho. Basset, 1691), as reprinted in <http://avalon.law.yale.edu/17th_century/tradenor.asp>, accessed June 22, 2014; James Houblon, "Observations on the Bill Against the Exportation of Gold and Silver," ed. Historical Manuscripts Commission 17 (London, 1690).

[65] Locke was a close friend of Clarke's. He had influence on other members in the House, including Sir Walter Yonge, Sir Francis Masham, Lord Ashley, and Maurice Ashley. Among the peers, Lords Monmouth and Pembroke respected Locke, while influential merchants like the Houblon brothers had known Locke since their days as associates of Lord Shaftesbury. John Houblon would become Governor of the Bank of England in 1694. Another well-connected lawyer, John Freke, kept in touch with Locke and others: Kelly, *Locke on Money*, 13–15, 19, n. 2; Peter Laslett, "John Locke, the Great Recoinage, and the Origins of the Board of Trade: 1695–1698," *William and Mary Quarterly*, 3rd Ser. 14, no. 3 (1957): 378–382.

[66] Locke's pamphlet, *Some Considerations of the Consequences of the Lowering of Interest, and Raising the Value of Money*, aimed to halt the progress of the Devaluation Bill in 1691. *Short Observations on a Printed Paper, Intituled, for Encouraging the Coining Silver Money*, originally targeted an influential pro-devaluation broadsheet in 1693; it was published to shape the House debate and action in 1694. *Further Considerations Concerning Raising the Value of Money* followed in late 1695 to promote recoining at the existing standard: Kelly, *Locke on Money*, 16–19, 21–23, 30–31. The 1693 broadsheet *For Encouraging the Coining of Silver Money in England* was apparently authored by Thomas Neale, author of many credit-theory proposals, in support of a Bill for devaluation introduced by Sir Richard Temple. The broadsheet is reprinted in Kelly, *Locke on Money*, 613–616.

exchange. Later, that definition would be cast as old-fashioned, a simple statement of the commodity nature of money. But commodity money—as indicated
by centuries of medieval practice and the bedrock of English law, all neatly
recapitulated by Lowndes's report—bore no resemblance to the money in Locke's
imagination. As Kelly concludes, compared to Lowndes, "it was Locke who was
enouncing [*sic*] a new, and in the circumstances revolutionary, doctrine in
insisting on the sacrosanctity of the monetary standard."[67] Compared to the
jurists in *The Case of Mixed Money*, the same conclusion follows. In their view,
traditional coin was a money given "extrinsic" value by sovereign authority,
produced for public as well as private ends, and intended to nurture a domestic
community. Locke turned around each dimension of money. Money became a
commodity with intrinsic (metallic) value, engendered as a medium by the
consensus of traders, for their use in international exchange. The next three
sections follow Locke through each dimension.

Defining money: the medium of "all the civilized and trading parts of the world"

In the first lines of his major work on the money crisis, Locke defined the terms of
his argument. "Silver," wrote Locke, "is the instrument and measure of commerce
in all the civilized and trading parts of the world." Launched on a world stage,
silver "considered as money" loitered there. Silver worked "as money" because it
offered "intrinsick value." That value attached by the "common consent" of those
using silver as an instrument of "the universal barter or exchange."[68] "I have
spoken of silver coin alone," he rehearsed later, "because that makes the money of
account, and measure of trade, all through the world."[69]

The surrounding pages describe silver as money in terms that generalize across
polities. Locke considered the alloys included with silver and the stamp set on
silver "by the public authority of [a] country," as if money were merely silver of
certified amount. "The coining of silver, or making money of it, is the ascertain-
ing of its quantity by a public mark, the better to fit it for commerce," he
continued. The argument put sovereigns in a place peripheral to international
trade. Their role followed: "It would perhaps have been better for commerce in
general," Locke observed, "if the princes every where, or at least in this part of the
world," would have agreed to use the same purity of silver across coinage
systems.[70]

---

[67] Kelly, *Locke on Money*, 29.
[68] John Locke, "Further Considerations Concerning Raising the Value of Money," in *Locke on Money*,
ed. Patrick Hyde Kelly (Oxford: Clarendon Press, 1991), 410. For similar arguments by Locke's colleagues,
see, e.g., Houblon, "Observations on the Bill Against the Exportation of Gold and Silver"; North, *Discourses
Upon Trade*, 1.
[69] Locke, "Further Considerations Concerning Raising the Value of Money," 422.
[70] Locke, "Further Considerations Concerning Raising the Value of Money," 410, 411–413, 422.

Contemporaries were quick to point out that coin often traveled at its face value, not its commodity content. Money must be different, then, from the silver it contained. Those observers were undeniably correct—except for one situation: international trade. Between countries, coin traveled at its value in silver. "[A]ll foreigners that deal with us," agreed William Lowndes, "regard the intrinsick value more than the extrinsick denomination, and exchange with us accordingly." Foreign exchange ran "at par" when the currencies of each country traded for each other in the amount that reflected the quantity of silver they contained.[71]

The anomaly was not so mysterious. The reason coins traveled across foreign borders according to their silver content was that, in precisely that circumstance, they were *not* "money." Money was a domestic affair, a political project based on the institutions of minting, spending, taxing, adjudicating, and enforcing that made it work as a way to count value, settle debts, and circulate value at home. Stripped of that infrastructure—outside of the engineering that made it circulate *as money*—coin was, in fact, bullion. European polities had long settled external accounts in silver or gold, given the value those metals held for money-making within their bounds.

But conflating the shared content of moneys—bullion—with the domestic measure itself was not hard to do. After all, silver and gold *did* move between countries as a means of lubricating trade. That point of reference was enormously attractive, especially for those unfamiliar with the way communities engineered money internally.[72] For Locke, it produced a powerful simplicity of vision, one that discarded coin as a shell and recurred to its content:

> Men in their bargains contract not for denominations or sounds, but for the intrinsick value; which is the **quantity** of silver by publick authority warranted to be in pieces of such denominations. And 'tis by having a greater **quantity** of silver, that men thrive and grow richer, and not by having a greater number of denominations; which when they come to have need of their money will prove but empty sounds, if they do not carry with them the real **quantity** of silver is [*sic*] expected.[73]

The point that "it is only the **quantity** of the silver in [coin] that is, and will eternally be, the measure of its value," would become a trope in Locke's writing.[74] And while the metaphor of contract drew upon the notion of transactions made and supported within a community's legal jurisdiction, Locke was imagining

[71] Lowndes, *Amendment of Silver Coins*, 32; Locke, "Further Considerations Concerning Raising the Value of Money." As contemporaries recognized, this is not quite right—the par depended more precisely on the bullion content of money priced in the domestic unit of account. See Barbon, *A Discourse Concerning Coining the New Money Lighter*, 19–25; Li, *The Great Recoinage of 1696 to 1699*, 15. Because the domestic price of bullion depended in part on monetary demand for silver, the "intrinsic" value of bullion depended on the "extrinsic" value of the home currency.

[72] See, e.g., the confusion of terms in Appleby's discussion of the balance of trade. Joyce Oldham Appleby, "Locke, Liberalism, and the Natural Law of Money," *Past & Present*, no. 71 (1976): 56–59.

[73] Locke, "Further Considerations Concerning Raising the Value of Money," 415 (emphasis in original).

[74] Locke, "Further Considerations Concerning Raising the Value of Money," 416.

a wider space. As he summarized his argument defining money, it was silver that "mankind" had agreed to take and give "for all other commodities, as an equivalent." Locke invoked a universal in order to set the standard for local practice.[75]

A comparison makes the salience of Locke's choice clear. In the report that made the most elaborate case for devaluing coin, William Lowndes conveyed an orientation that was emphatically domestic. He vowed to learn about "silver and gold moneys" by reviewing the English archives on money, and he produced an extensive history of past practices in England. His goal was just as tuned to the national. As he put it there and elsewhere, it was to discover "the most practicable methods for new coining" money and supplying "sufficient coins to pay the kings taxes and revenues, and to carry on the publick commerce."[76] A few pages on, he would condemn the proclivity of "gentlemen" to consider the use of coin only "as it hath relation to foreign exchanges or remittances whereas," he noted, "it serves principally the inland commerce."[77]

Locke did attend to the domestic situation, but he did so by extrapolating from his model. Having described bullion but called it money, Locke then assimilated the latter to former. According to his argument, domestic money and its denominations existed to guarantee a particular quantity of silver. Recall his argument above that "princes every where" should have agreed to use the same standard. "The standard once settled by publick authority, the **quantity** of silver establish'd under the several denominations, (I humbly conceive) should not be altred, till here were an absolute necessity shewn of such a change, which I think can never be."[78] Indeed, if money traveled only by weight and could be identified with weight, there would be no need for more than information about how much silver any token held. Locke had arrived at a point that was diametrically opposed to Barbon's reasoning that a domestic authority need not convey the content of coin. For Locke, certifying the content of coin was the only reason for the

[75] Locke, "Further Considerations Concerning Raising the Value of Money," 423; see also Locke, "Further Considerations Concerning Raising the Value of Money," 447. Another example of Locke's tendency to assume that internal exchange existed according to the rules of world trade occurs when he considers an island country, "Bermudos," with a limited amount of silver. Inhabitants trade commodities for silver, but the values of each are treated as independent, leaving some people to barter because the value of the commodities far exceeds that of the available silver. Locke's scenario would be coherent if the value of both were set in a world market. But in a closed economy, silver as a medium would rise in value to capture the commodities exchanged in it. See Locke, "Further Considerations Concerning Raising the Value of Money," 451–452; see also Locke, "Further Considerations Concerning Raising the Value of Money," 420 (identifying amount of silver gained in trade (here 400,000 oz) with amount of money gained (£100,000 at 4 oz/pound)).

[76] Lowndes, *Amendment of Silver Coins*, 3–4. See, e.g., Lowndes, *Amendment of Silver Coins*, 10–11 (identifying coin as *firmamentum belli* and *orna[mentum] pacis*/the sinews of war and the ornament of peace, as well as a medium for the king's subjects "with relation not only to their trade and commerce, but also to all other ordinary means of livelihood.") Similarly, see Lowndes, *Amendment of Silver Coins*, 109–110.

[77] Lowndes, *Amendment of Silver Coins*, 74.

[78] Locke, "Further Considerations Concerning Raising the Value of Money," 415 (emphasis in original).

monetary authority. The project that public authorities had long pursued to create a working medium for public as well as private purposes disappeared from his view.

Locke had, however, conceived money according to the terms he knew. He had come of age in a country as revolutionized by the expansion of overseas trade as by the rise of Parliament. Debates over balances of payment, mercantilism, and the sources of wealth crowded the pamphlet literature of the century. Locke's political experience was powerfully inflected by his engagement with England's colonizing adventure in America. That exposure tied him back into an obsession with trade; as Lord Shaftesbury's advisor, he had tracked the literature on trade and economic policy.[79]

The desperate state of England's money supply in the 1690s followed from factors both "monetary" and not. In the first category were outflows due to the arbitrage opportunities caused by count/content disparity across different silver coins and by a similar disparity across silver and gold coins.[80] In the second category were changes in foreign exchange value that depended on the country's balance of payments and would occur even when money's count and content lined up perfectly across all coins. The latter category was a perennial object of concern for politicians but especially so in times when silver seemed to be flowing out of the kingdom. By 1695, William III's ministry had brought together men it considered experts of public import, including Locke, Wren, Newton, Sir Josiah Child, and others. As Peter Laslett recounts, the connection between trade, the balance of payments, and the silver supply was an important theme in the group's discourse. By winter of that year, Locke had produced *Further Considerations Concerning Raising the Value of Money*, his most sustained contribution on the Great Recoinage. He had also been appointed to the Board of Trade, a royal commission newly established by his allies in the ministry. Locke would hold the post until 1700.[81] For him, exchange was an international matter, and he evidently assumed that money was as well.

Socializing money: exchange as agency and origin

Locke's focus on international exchange did more than define money as silver, it also informed his view about the way that metal became a medium. Silver was money because of "that estimate which common consent has placed on it." That acclaim made it "equivalent to all other things," "the universal barter or exchange which men give and exchange." While silver was clearly the material "fittest" to be used as a medium, asserted Locke, "It is enough that the world has agreed on it,

[79] Laslett, "Origins of the Board of Trade," 377–378; Li, *The Great Recoinage of 1696 to 1699*, 15–25.
[80] See pp. 110–116, 120.
[81] Laslett, "Origins of the Board of Trade," 378–389.

and made it their *common money.*" As he concluded, even "the *Indians* rightly call it, *measure.*"[82]

Locke's contention that social convention created money located him at one extreme of the historical debate over what money was. He could draw upon those who naturalized the utility of silver or gold for money, most famously Aristotle, who had speculated that money had its start in a metal passed hand to hand because it had durability and appeal that different groups would value. But Aristotle's speculation fit within a larger theory that conceptualized money as a public construct.[83] In his most extended treatment of money, he located the value of money in "law," as had his teacher before him. Both Plato and Aristotle conceived money as actually constitutive of political justice within a community.[84]

In similar fashion, medieval commentators who protested the debasement of coin lived in regimes that emphasized the sovereign authorship of money. Even Nicholas Oresme, perhaps most focused on the rights of private individuals in coin, argued that money legitimately belonged to a community, not the Crown. That realignment was intended to limit the Crown's authority to manipulate coinage to the occasions necessary for the good of the community, but it did not deny the dependence of money on political agency.[85] That understanding accorded with the high constitutional rhetoric used by the English Privy Council earlier in the 17th century in *The Case of Mixed Money.*

As Secretary of the Treasury, William Lowndes in 1695 recognized political agency in contemporary English terms. Coining money was "a right of regality" that tied sovereign and citizens together, especially in times of war. Money was, basically, nation-building:

> [Rescuing the coinage has become] indispensably necessary, to render effectual the very ways and means, which in Parliament may be resolved upon, in reference to aids or supplies for carrying on of the [current] war, and to produce a species of money that may be useful and serviceable for the upholding of the commerce, and for

---

[82] Locke, "Further Considerations Concerning Raising the Value of Money," 410, 423. But see the implication in the Second Treatise that silver may not have been so universally embraced as money. John Locke, *Two Treatises of Government*, in *The Works of John Locke* (Rivington, 1824, 12th ed., 1691), Bk II, Chap. XVI, sec. 184.

[83] See Aristotle, *Politics*, written 350 B.C.E., trans. Benjamin Jowitt, Internet Classics Archive, accessed June 22, 2014, <http://classics.mit.edu/Aristotle/politics.html> Book I, Part IX; Barry J. Gordon, *Economic Analysis before Adam Smith: Hesiod to Lessius* (London: Macmillan, 1975), 47–48.

[84] See Aristotle, *Nichomachean Ethics*, written 350 B.C.E., trans. W. D. Ross, Book V, sec. 5, Internet Classics Archive, accessed June 22, 2014, <http://classics.mit.edu/Aristotle/nicomachaen.html>; Gordon, *Economic Analysis*, 43–48; see pp. 271–272.

[85] For England, see pp. 169–170. For Oresme's recognition of money's utility to the state as well as individuals, the prince's role producing coin (and right to claim "tribute" in it), and the community's ownership of it along with individuals' ownership, see, Charles Johnson, trans./ed., *The De Moneta of Nicholas Oresme and English Mint Documents* (London: Thomas Nelson, 1956; repr., Ludwig von Mises Institute, 2009), 4–5, 9–11, and discussion, pp. 70–78.

answering not only of the publick, but also of all private revenues, rents, debts, and other occasions, which concern *the very existence of the great political body*.[86]

By contrast, Locke took social agency to imperial lengths. It was "mankind," rather than a king or even a political community, that had first produced money.[87]

Locke's argument about the social origins of money comported with his larger theoretical project. By the time the Great Recoinage crisis broke, he had already conceptualized money as an essential element to liberal development. According to his work in *Two Treatises of Government*, money was a matter made "out of the bounds of society, and without compact." It was a means created by "mutual consent"—an act of agreement prior *even* to the political consent that created civil society.[88] Indeed, Locke's creation story was pristine. It told of individuals who moved acorns and apples "out of the state that nature hath provided" by the work of their hands, each person appropriating the fruit of the earth as property insofar he "mixed his labour" with it. "No man's labour could subdue, or approriate all," Locke noted. Natural capacity limited an individual's accumulation, beyond a bit of barter that allowed him to trade items that would otherwise spoil for those with a longer shelf life.

And there, in the easy assumption of exchange within any man's reach, an echo of barter itself, was the origin of money. It would also, it turns out, be the origin of unlimited accumulation, a matter made possible by money. In the key passage, political authority has no place:

> And if he also bartered away plums, that would have rotted in a week, for nuts that would last good for his eating a whole year, he did no injury; he wasted not the common stock; destroyed no part of the portion of the goods that belonged to others, so long as nothing perished uselessly in his hands. Again, if he would give his nuts for a piece of metal, pleased with its colour; or exchange his sheep for shells, or wool for a sparkling pebble or a diamond, and keep those by him all his life, he invaded not the right of others, he might heap as much of these durable things as he pleased; the exceeding of the bounds of his just property not lying in the largeness of his possession, but the perishing of any thing uselessly in it.

Rather than political authority explaining the genesis of money, the agency of parties in exchange—social agency—was critical. As Locke continued:

> And thus came in the use of money, some lasting thing that men might keep without spoiling, and that by mutual consent men would take in exchange for the truly useful, but perishable supports of life.

In Locke's narrative, the creative work done in those early days, before the pact that created the state, occurred in decisions proximate to the labor that produced

---

[86] Lowndes, *Amendment of Silver Coins*, 109–110.

[87] Compare more modest "metallist" arguments, pp. 129–133.

[88] Locke, *Two Treatises*, Bk II, Chap. V, sec. 50, 47; C. B. Macpherson, *The Political Theory of Possessive Individualism: Hobbes to Locke* (Oxford: Clarendon Press, 1969), 208–209.

property and personal to each of those making them. The "tacit agreement of men to put a value" on the metal made it money.[89]

The same move stripped the government of any essential agency, reducing it to an administrative actor facilitating private trade. According to Locke, its money differed from silver "only in this ... the stamp it bears." In fact, if that stamp did not act as a "publick voucher" that certified the silver content of coin, then "coining is labor to no purpose."[90] Locke thus marginalized government, even as he reasoned his way into direct opposition to English law.

Locke's reasoning collided with English law because his agents operated independently of an institutional mesh holding them in relationship to one another. *The Case of Mixed Money* had settled a dispute between parties who made a deal in the Queen's money by way of a contract enforced through the common law. By contrast, Locke abstracted contract from the political regimes and legal vocabularies that created it. Contracts were "every where made, and accounts kept in silver coin," Locke wrote, or at least "I am sure they are so in England, and the neighboring countries."[91] In Locke's argument, they were agreements between individuals to transact in a medium of their own choosing, silver. Given that reading, any deficit in the amount of silver due a creditor counted as a default. "Men are absolved from the performance of their legal contracts, if the **quantity** of silver, under settled and legal denominations be altred."[92]

Whether or not Locke realized that he was out of step with at least five centuries of English law (and very probably pre-Norman, Anglo-Saxon practice), he was true to the postulates of his argument. As we have seen, nominalism created a rule system that locked parties into a domestic monetary relationship: all parties owed and claimed in the polity's unit of account. Should the government need to change that unit of account, the change occurred in constant terms across the community because all items were owed, claimed, and priced in that unit of account. In a very real sense, then parties holding money were treated equally when it was devalued.[93] Lowndes and other commentators correctly articulated nominalism's logic.[94]

---

[89] Locke, *Two Treatises*, Bk II, Chap. V, sec. 46–47, 36.

[90] Locke, "Further Considerations Concerning Raising the Value of Money," 414, 423. MacPherson argues that Locke understood government more generally as fundamentally ministerial—the recipient of those powers that men exercised in a pre-political space and now transferred to a civil authority that could better protect their natural rights. See Macpherson, *Possessive Individualism*, 218.

[91] Locke, "Further Considerations Concerning Raising the Value of Money," 422.

[92] Locke, "Further Considerations Concerning Raising the Value of Money," 415–416; see also Locke, "Further Considerations Concerning Raising the Value of Money," 437–442. For Liverpool's recognition that Locke here transferred the "right of seting a rate or value on the coins" from the sovereign to the individual, see Liverpool, *A Treatise on the Coins of the Realm in a Letter to the King*, 177.

[93] See pp. 126–133.

[94] Lowndes, *Amendment of Silver Coins*, 81–82 (noting required passage of money by count); Barbon, *A Discourse Concerning Coining the New Money Lighter*, 28–34 (noting count as essential term in contracts). Lowndes reaffirmed the English antipathy to changing the fineness of metal because making changes in its weight allowed more transparent adjustments. Lowndes, *Amendment of Silver Coins*, 31–32.

But while all those holding money might be treated equally, creditors due money after a change could find themselves with a lesser amount of silver, as opposed to money, when the government decreased the metal content of coin.[95] That mattered less for those making domestic deals in the unit of account (trading in money, not silver) than for those settling international deals (trading in silver, not money). As if on cue, Locke made it clear that he was, in fact, thinking about the losses that a devaluation would bring those wishing to deal with *foreigners*. Indeed, he made those losses, with all their evocative power to English elites, exemplary of losses that must occur on the domestic side:

> The salt, wine, oyl, silk, navel-stores, and all foreign commodities, will none of them be sold us by foreigners for a less quantity of silver than before, because we have given the name of more pence to it, is I think demonstration. All our names (if they are any more to us) are to them but bare sounds; and our coin, as theirs to us, but meer bullion, valued only by its weight. And a Sweede will no more sell you his hemp and pitch, or a Spaniard his oyl, for less silver; because you tell him silver is scarcer now in England, and therefore risen in value one fifth; than a tradesman of London will sell his commodity cheaper to the Isle of Man because they are grown poorer, and money is scarce there.[96]

Locke's collision with legal nominalism—a doctrine that identified the value of money as a domestic matter of governance—revealed just how deeply his commitment went to read money's foundations as not political, not legal, but social.

By locating agency over money in the consensus of strangers or people without politics, Locke offered the image of a medium that needed no collective engineering. It would service the exchange of commodities like those passed in international trade. For those purposes, governments were ministerial (at best) and contracts were material, not legal. The gathering vision was of a real economy that operated in the convergence of autonomous individuals according to an elemental logic. The "market" in the medieval world was an event inaugurated by the sovereign. In Locke's hands, it became a matter separate altogether, introduced from outside as an imperative.

Naturalizing money: from count to weight

Throughout the long life of commodity money, users identified money with its silver or gold content. Sometimes a shorthand, sometimes an argument, it was an intuition made easy by the evident value of the metal that coin contained and it gained particular strength when the government assumed the cost of making

---

[95] See pp. 126–127, 130–133.

[96] Locke, "Further Considerations Concerning Raising the Value of Money," 442; see also Locke, "Further Considerations Concerning Raising the Value of Money," 417–418. Note the admission in this context that money moving across borders is "meer bullion."

coin. Coming of age at such a time, Locke could imagine a world in which silver and money were literally interchangeable.[97] Once Charles II had, by subsidizing coin, effectively equated full-bodied coin and its silver content, the unit of account, which had a fixed commodity content, shared an intrinsic value with that amount of silver and traveled at the same price.[98]

Following that logic, a measure of silver—weight, if one held fineness constant—could serve as well as count in Locke's model. The same reasoning explained how Locke could conclude that "princes every where" would have better accommodated "commerce in general," if they had agreed to use the same purity for their silver coin. In that case, weight itself could stand in for the unit of account.[99]

The conclusion was upside down, both historically and conceptually. Historically, the quality for which people had been willing to pay for centuries and which the government now subsidized was the quality that distinguished coin from metal—its capacity to mark value, transfer it in payment, and carry it from hand to hand. Money in turn allowed silver to be priced, supporting its sale as bullion. "Silver would no more pass for *Money* than Gold," wrote Barbon, "unless the price of each piece were fixt by Publick Authority."[100] In fact, the demand for silver across borders depended in significant part on the fact that silver had become the common commodity content of coin. It was therefore an attractive way to settle accounts: bullion held value as a "liquidity put," as it were—a material that held heightened value not because it was money, but because it could be *turned into* money in another polity.[101] Conceptually, the quality of liquidity that set coin apart from bullion identified the count of coin as a prior accomplishment to bullion's easy transfer; it was the matter that engendered the market in silver by weight. Weight could only be imputed a natural liquidity in a world where liquidity had become cheap. And that had occurred through the successful production and financing of money by public authorities.

The historical and conceptual irony had a practical edge. The equivalence that Locke drew between money and silver disregarded the fact that the liquidity of

[97] The difference between "money" and "bullion" is elaborated above. See pp. 43–50, 70–97. As sketched there, money entails material value as a unit receivable for public obligations and is enhanced by the cash premium it offers in the meantime. When governments chose to make money out of silver, they identified silver coin as the item that satisfied public obligations. (Citizens submitting taxes and the like in silver rather than coin would have to pay a larger amount of bullion to satisfy their obligations.) The distinction between coin and silver does not suggest that silver did not continue to have great value to those holding coin. The fact that coin held both monetary and non-monetary values is what made it an unstable medium. See pp. 110–120.
[98] For discussion, including the possibility that full-bodied coin would be worth slightly less than bullion under certain circumstances, see pp. 238–239.
[99] Locke, "Further Considerations Concerning Raising the Value of Money," 410, 411–413, 422.
[100] Barbon, *A Discourse Concerning Coining the New Money Lighter*, 26.
[101] James Tobin, "Money," in *The New Palgrave Dictionary of Economics*, ed. by Steven N. Durlauf and Lawrence E. Blume (London: Palgrave Macmillan, 2008), 9. I thank Nadav Orion Peer for the modernist turn-of-phrase that captures bullion's value so well.

coin continued to furnish the means of exchange. That is, even if people did not pay (directly) for the cash quality of coin, that quality mattered. In particular, the penny as the unit of account carried a capacity that distinguished it from silver insofar as people took it at face value, despite ambiguities across coins by their silver content. As Barbon continued:

> Or else there could be no bargain made upon an equal foot, there being such a certain difference in the quantity of the silver in the several coins, which could never be remedied unless publick authority had fixt the *value* to their *money,* by which all those fractions and inequalities in the several coins are even'd.[102]

Money, in other words, created the domestic economy. And that brought the irony full circle. The domestic economy was basic to the trade that Locke coveted. In other words, international exchange depended, in a very direct way, on a quality—the special capacity that coins peculiar to a community held within that economy—that disrupted the simplicity of Locke's vision.

The final problem for Locke was that the quality of coin as cash required constant maintenance—the debate of the 1690s followed from the litany of troubles that had long destabilized coin as a commodity money. Old coin, clipped coin, silver coin priced at a rate that misvalued it relative to gold coin—all invited people to distribute their use of money in ways that played count against content.[103] And yet, if one disregarded coin's identity as money and imagined that it moved only by weight, the difficulties would vanish: by obviating the count of coin—its face value—there would be no discrepant point of reference against which coins of different commodity contents could be compared.

Locke's response was twofold—he started with fireworks and followed up with a prescription. Coined silver could not, Locke insisted again and again, be worth less than uncoined silver, the silver that Lowndes claimed was being taken abroad because the mint price was too low. Silver was silver, ounce for ounce, the philosopher continued, ignoring the monetary unit of account that offered a way to price the content of money. If so, then raising the mint price of silver to bring it closer to the market price was just a word game that claimed to work a substantive change:

> I will take the boldness to advise His Majesty to buy, or to borrow any where so much bullion ... as is equal in weight to twelve hundred pound sterling of our present mill'd money. This let him sell for mill'd mony. And according to [Mr. Lowndes's] rule, it will yield fifteen hundred pounds. Let that fifteen hundred pound be reduc'd into

---

[102] Barbon, *A Discourse Concerning Coining the New Money Lighter*, 26–27.

[103] The bimetallic problem, theoretically independent of the problems with silver's mint/market ratio, was worsened as people fled silver because of its depreciation, driving up the price of gold. See p. 343 and n. 56. Further compounding the problem was the early modern subsidy of coin, which removed the premium that had protected coin from being cannibalized for its metal content as soon as some coin was undervalued.

bullion, and sold again, and it will produce eighteen hundred and sixty pound; Which
eighteen hundred and sixty pound of weight money being reduc'd to bullion, will still
produce one fifth more in weight of silver...

Eventually, Locke mocked, the King will turn around the bullion "as fast as he
receives it," until he had brought all the money in England into his hands.[104]
Obviously, the strategy was futile. No more successful would a boy be in cutting
his small cloth into more pieces to make it cover a greater area, nor would a sailor
be in patching a boat with a board of 12 inches that he now called 15 inches long.
Only if sounds gave weight to silver would the "noise of a greater number of
pence" create a larger supply of money.[105]

The argument glibly obscured the phenomena that both created commodity
money and rendered it unstable. It was neither sleight of hand nor mystery that
drove the mint price of money lower than its market price, but the concerted
action of people splitting their use of money by count in domestic exchange from
their use of its silver content across the border. In an odd way, money's stubborn
capacity to move by count, even when worn and clipped, bore witness to the
unique stature that money claimed as a domestic medium. Given that reality,
Locke's invitation to the Crown was inapposite. As Richard Temple observed, no
one bought silver with silver—or as in Locke's example, full-weight coin.[106] But
the Lockean argument slowed people who no longer thought about the cash
premium and how it changed money from bullion.

Second, the prescription. Locke argued that coin should travel by weight
whenever its content diverged from the amount it was publicly certified to
contain. That parameter furnished the condition under which Locke's "money"
would work. Note that it also assumed the very quality of cash that was created by
count. Locke did not explain how bullion attained the quality that English
sovereigns had secured only within the polity and that the English people,
individually and collectively, had for centuries paid to acquire.

Rather, Locke proposed that coin was, effectively, traveling by weight already.
It must be that bullion cost so much because it was purchased by clipped coin.
Because people valued money only by silver, they appropriately paid many more
of the lightweight, worn, and clipped coins, driving up the prices of things.[107]
That would lead reasonable men to hoard full-weight coin. The same erosion of
silver content in coin would affect the exchange rate; it would rise in terms of
English units of account because those held less silver.[108] Here, Locke's reasoning

---

[104] Locke, "Further Considerations Concerning Raising the Value of Money," 445.

[105] Locke, "Further Considerations Concerning Raising the Value of Money," 450–451.

[106] Sir Richard Temple, *Some Short Remarks Upon Mr. Lock's Book, in Answer to Mr. Lounds, and
Several Other Books and Pamphlets Concerning Coin* (printed for Richard Baldwin, 1696), 4.

[107] Locke, "Further Considerations Concerning Raising the Value of Money," 444, 445–446.

[108] As all agreed, once tale and weight values were significantly discrepant, the presence of underweight
coin traveling at face value dissuaded people from coming to the mint and prices from falling. Some,

led him back to clipped coin as the archvillain, the evil that drove face value of coin away from the value of silver by weight. "Clipping is the great leak, which for some time past has contributed more to sink us, than all the force of our enemies could do. 'Tis like a breach in the sea-bank, which widens every moment till it be stop'd."[109]

Locke's assumptions carried him part of the way—after all, silver content had considerable value and was pushing the value of full-weight coin up, above lesser coin with the same face value. But Locke's prescription was writ so broadly that it went beyond the pathology of clipped and worn coin; it denied the basic advantage that separated the value of coin as cash from the value of bullion. Locke responded by elaborating deviations from the uniform treatment of silver money by weight, treating them as lapses from an ideal system. For example, people "who know not how to count but by current money" took gold for a higher face value in silver than they should.[110] They were supported by the lamentable practice of the Exchequer, as well as bankers, landlords, and others, to take coin by tale or close to its face value, when it actually contained less silver.[111] In turn, people's mistakes in valuing coin created opportunities for unwarranted profits by others.

People should be required to act otherwise. "'Tis no *difficulty to conceive*," Locke wrote (italics his), "that clip'd money, being not lawful money, should be prohibited to pass for more than its weight."[112] There is something remarkable about Locke's own italics here; they seem to underscore the feat of conceptualization that produced his vision. Money, in Locke's image, held value only according to its silver content. Should the weight of coin vary for whatever reason, it could still be used, innately prorated as it were. In fact, treated as bullion, clipped or worn coin would be readily brought to the mint, because it had no remaining advantage over full-weight coin.[113] Or at least that is what should happen, Locke noted, extending his prohibition on taking clipped coin except by weight: the government itself should not take back its own coin at face value. That practice supported underweight coin at a higher value, disturbing the discipline

however, argued that clipping, at least radical clipping, occurred as a *result* of the discrepancy, rather than as its *cause*: when silver was very undervalued, it was particularly worth clipping.

[109] Locke, "Further Considerations Concerning Raising the Value of Money," 472–473; see also Locke, "Further Considerations Concerning Raising the Value of Money," 418, 475–476.

[110] Locke, "Further Considerations Concerning Raising the Value of Money," 469–470. Two years after the Recoinage, Locke also recognized the effect that the government's willingness to receive guineas had on keeping up their value. See Report of the Commissioners of Trade, reprinted in Li, *The Great Recoinage of 1696 to 1699*, 126–128.

[111] Locke was dogged about tracing the effects of tale valuation through the system. Liverpool would make similar calculations, while accepting the propensity of people to use money by count as a feature that distinguished money from a commodity. Compare Locke, "Further Considerations Concerning Raising the Value of Money," 468–470 with Liverpool, *A Treatise on the Coins of the Realm in a Letter to the King*, 77–78.

[112] Locke, "Further Considerations Concerning Raising the Value of Money," 466–467.

[113] Locke, "Further Considerations Concerning Raising the Value of Money," 466–467.

that would make money work according to its silver content.[114] Indeed, if all coin passed at only the value of the silver it contained, the government need not rush to recoin its money supply.[115] A similar logic would reform problems with gold coin as well. The government could coin gold "to ascertain its weight and fineness," and let that token be used as a commodity with which people could trade.[116]

By the time Locke got to the question of the money supply, there was little work left to do. Making money meant obtaining silver, and obtaining silver depended on the balance of trade. "The true and only good reason that brings bullion to the mint to be coin'd," pronounced Locke, "is the same that brings it to England to stay there, viz. The gain we make by an over-balance of trade."[117] By the same token, tinkering with denominational values would be ineffectual. "[T]he coining, or not coining our money, on the same foot [standard] it was before, or in bigger or less pieces, and under whatsoever denominations you please, contributes nothing to, or against its melting down or exportation."[118]

In modern terms, the prescription disallowed recalibrating the money supply in ways that left the costs for depreciation where they lay. Political judgment about distributive consequences—an evaluation that would be appropriate if the money supply were a public entity—had no place in the matter. The solution must lie instead in a return to the fundamentals—trade that brought bullion to England's shores.

At the end of the day, Locke had produced a theory that cleared money of the very qualities that distinguished it from silver. Those qualities were the same ones

---

[114] Locke, "Further Considerations Concerning Raising the Value of Money," 470–471.

[115] By the fall, 1696, Locke did agree that a recoinage was necessary; see Kelly, *Locke on Money*, 26.

[116] In stipulating that gold would pass as a commodity, Locke targeted the problems caused when market prices for silver and gold changed against a constant public mint price, stipulating that gold should not serve as the money of account. There could only be one unit of account, against which gold must float. The government could mint gold at a certain price and let it pass current at whatever value it would. As long as the mint's price was lower for gold than the market price, gold would not flow to the mint just because the ratio of market values (silver to gold) had changed. Locke, "Further Considerations Concerning Raising the Value of Money," 422–423.

[117] Locke, "Further Considerations Concerning Raising the Value of Money," 449; see also Locke, "Further Considerations Concerning Raising the Value of Money," 424. As Locke continued:

> When our merchants carry commodities abroad, to a greater value than those they bring home, the over-plus comes to them in foreign coin or bullion, which will stay here, when we gain by the balance of our whole trade. For then we can have no debts beyond sea to be paid with it: In this thriving posture of our trade, those to whose share this bullion falls, not having any use of it whil'st it is in bullion, choose to carry it to the mint to have it coin'd there, whereby it is of more use to them for all the business of silver in trade, or purchasing land; the mint having ascertained the weight and fineness of it: So that on any occasion, every one is ready to take it at its known value, without any scruple; a convenience that is wanting in bullion. But when our trade runs on the other side, and our exported commodities will not pay for those foreign ones we consume, our treasure must go; and then it is in vain to bestow the labour of coining on bullion that must be exported again. To what purpose is it to make it pass through our mint, when it will away?

Locke, "Further Considerations Concerning Raising the Value of Money," 449–450.

[118] Locke, "Further Considerations Concerning Raising the Value of Money," 433.

instilled by the collective relations effected by a domestic community and the ones that made it work as money. They included identifying a unit of account, supporting it by making it the mode of payment used by the public with its members, and enforcing its easy transfer between individuals in the meantime. The consequence of Locke's consistency was striking: it read money as a politic-ally contrived resource out of the course of exchange. The stakes of losing money followed: one had to imagine a world that worked on the basis of real exchange alone.

Locke's political argument built a bridge for the leap. He had already offered the platform—trade between national communities, understood as if it occurred independently of those communities. Locke had also substantiated the action of people outside of governance—in that space, people made deals in commodities that came to hand and law depended on convention, much like the customs that drew longtime trading partners together. Groups, including the public, did not appear and voice any need as collectives for a medium. Information—not political relation—created exchange in this vision. The market followed: it was generated by the diffuse and constant exchange of dealers who used information, rather than a public medium. Locke had updated the paradigm of barter. We might even say that an auction, rather than the interaction of people within a political architecture, seemed a realistic reference point for markets.

10

The 18th century architecture of modern money

At the end of 17th century, the English resolved the debate over money they had conducted since the Restoration. For the first time, bank currency written against public debt circulated. It could be redeemed for silver or gold coin. That traditional medium—coin—would be reformed according to the notably non-traditional theory that it was a static amount of metal. An auxiliary kind of currency expressly based on the government's own issue and promise of revenues, Exchequer bills, also began to circulate. The new order was a work in progress. In ways its authors only vaguely anticipated, the design was powerfully productive of modern capitalism.

The key was the odd conjunction that Parliament fashioned from the conflicting imperatives before it. On the one hand, the influence of the Lockean argument was apparent. The theory that money was a matter freely produced by private exchange reordered priorities. The government's role recalibrating coin lost its stature as a public service. Instead, the government's critical office became guaranteeing coin of a particular content. That commitment legitimated bank money, casting it as a fiduciary rather than fiat medium. Just as importantly, insistence on a Lockean approach had another, more ironic, impact. It actually undid "commodity money," which could not function according to the fiction that coin was simply an amount of metal and thus did not require regular adjustment. The ladder of silver denominations that had existed since the medieval period fell apart. The gold guinea took the place of the sterling penny in representing the unit of account. Rather than one rung among others of proportional metal content, the guinea became a kind of pivot or point of reference for fractional and multiple currencies that were convertible into it. New moneys—tokens and bank currencies—began to fill in the denominational space left open.

On the other hand, money in the 18th century proliferated according to a practice incompatible with the Lockean conception of money. Consistent with the arguments advanced by the credit theorists, the government deployed its power over the public debt to engineer currencies that moved by count. That was as true of coin as it was of later moneys—the silver penny had been contrived when the Crown recognized it as a sovereign liability that the government both spent and took back, enforced in its own courts, and endorsed as a medium. In turn, it was the government's support for the gold guinea through its fiscal activities, support untheorized but effective, that displaced the silver penny as the English unit of account. Bank of England notes were entrenched by the same fiscal engineering.

By accident and innovation, the modern money made after the 1690s flowed much more liberally than earlier moneys had. Most remarkable was the development of commercial bank currencies. These promises-to-pay circulated as private parties extended credit, denominated in the public unit of account. They depended on that unit, as well as the peculiarities of English common law, and the anchoring operation of the Bank of England. That combination produced fractional reserve banking, a legal institution that entitled bankers to use funds left with them as if they were their own while maintaining a debt to depositors. Licensed by the common law and the government's support via the Bank of England, private entrepreneurs now provided currency for sale to individuals.

Strange as it may seem, banks acted analogously to the medieval mint insofar as they supplied cash to individuals for a fee. The mint had issued coin in return for silver. Banks now issued notes, and eventually checkable deposits, on a commitment of future productivity. But if the structures of medieval and modern money were analogous, the monetary dynamics put into play by the new arrangement were unprecedented. Bank currencies carried enormous capacity to nourish growth—consider how much easier it was to proffer a promise of future productivity than a pound of silver bullion. Bank currencies also imported a startling fragility into the money supply—consider how much more difficult it was to cash out a promise of productivity than the metallic content of a coin.

Despite its oddities, the English approach produced an answer to the constitutional dilemma created when they adopted individuated incentives as the pump used to expand the amount of money that circulated. Money would be public in practice—the government's authority to determine debt remained the linchpin of the system and was deployed continuously to define money, to maintain it, and often, to rescue it. But money would be private in theory—the legitimacy of the government's actions would depend on how effectively it protected the individuated incentives of those now pumping money into circulation. That settlement was sealed in the early days of the 19th century, as an epilogue to the chapter explores.

A. Resolving the debate: the Whig alliance over Bank currency and coin

The monetary experiments of the 1690s overflowed the boundaries of political party. Individuals advocated principles at odds with their political fellows in the ongoing effort to understand the currencies they were making. The Whig Charles Montague, for example, initially disagreed with John Locke's formulations on coin. Later he would parrot that dogma on hard money while advocating the obviously fiat alternative of Exchequer bills.[1] The Whig and Tory parties, or country and court tendencies, were themselves fluid, factions still in the process of formation.[2]

Nevertheless, the major monetary events of the 1690s—the Bank of England, the Great Recoinage, and the advent of Exchequer bills—were firmly identified with the Whig party and supported by its authority. Products of the political process in which they unfolded, they represented an answer to the long debate over money that the English had conducted over the course of the 17th century. Along the way, party strategists both rejected competing institutions and shaped the way their own candidates functioned. The sequence legitimated a set of monetary alternatives as orthodox.

The Bank began the chain of Whig interventions. As mapped above, it produced money that depended on anticipated revenues to hold value. Bank money circulated as the representation of a loan to the government; it was accepted by the government as its own liability. It was thus well within the family of credit-based currencies suggested by modern strategists.

Despite that genealogy, its authors stoutly denied any kinship. The only "credit" they understood as relevant to the Bank's paper was its own promise of redeemability. According to their argument, the foundation for money was "the universal species of gold and silver." As Godfrey emphasized, only "specie" was "money." Bank bills were demand notes immediately redeemable for specie.[3] That claim set them apart from notes that lacked the material security of coin.

As for coin, English officials adopted an approach that guaranteed its content as a static amount of metal. By the time the Bank was established in 1694, the debate that culminated in the Great Recoinage of 1696 was well underway. The Whig ministry was at first split over how the reform should proceed. Charles Montague, Chancellor of the Exchequer, favored diminishing new silver coin's content so that those issues would carry the same amount of metal as the worn coin that currently circulated and set prices. In the summer of 1695, William Lowndes, Secretary of the Treasury, produced his report making the case for devaluation.[4] The Bank's governor, John Houblon, and leading directors including Gilbert Heathcote supported strengthening coin or revaluation, an alternative

---

[1] Charles Montague, "A Document relating to the Establishment of Paper Credit (1696)," in *The Great Recoinage of 1696 to 1699*, ed. Ming-Hsun Li (London: Weidenfeld and Nicolson, 1963), 238.

[2] Dennis Rubini, "Politics and the Battle for the Banks, 1688–1697," *English Historical Review* 85, no. 337 (1970). Pincus finds party visions more firmly articulated, but party allegiance shifting. Steven Pincus, *1688 The First Modern Revolution* (New Haven: Yale University Press, 2009), 398.

[3] William Paterson, *A Brief Account of the Intended Bank of England* (Randal Taylor, 1694), 10; Michael Godfrey, *A Short Account of the Bank of England* (1695), 6.

[4] In 1694, Montague turned towards the plan to devaluate the silver coin. Opponents within the planning committee included Edward Clarke and Sir Francis Masham, a Member of Parliament whose family had hosted Locke at their residence in the country since 1691. See Patrick Hyde Kelly, *Locke on Money*, 2 vols, vol. 1 (Oxford: Clarendon Press, 1991), 14–15, 21–22; see also pp. 342–346.

that required calling in old coin and reminting it.[5] Locke had been arguing for that end since 1691. His arguments captured the views of Somers among others and moved the Whigs towards recoinage at the original standard.[6] At a critical moment in late 1695, William III agreed to the strategy. As William recognized, he could implement the solution that strengthened the silver penny simply by enforcing existing law. In other words, the reform could proceed without involving Parliament—William's desire to exclude the legislative authority here gave shape, if only selectively, to the vision that money was not a matter of political authorship.[7]

By late October 1695, the ministry had coalesced around Locke's proposal that coin be reminted at the original standard, that all current eroded coin be taken only by weight, and that the loss lie on those holding such coin. Acting on the ministry's orders, Lowndes drew up a proposal tracking Locke's prescriptions in lieu of his own conclusions. Eventually, the Council of Lords Justices, a group sitting to assist William III during periods that took him abroad, would soften the purity of its prescriptions somewhat, rejecting Locke's contention that clipped money be accepted only by weight and opting to compensate current holders partially with the proceeds of a public tax. The Council and king also agreed that Parliament must be consulted.[8]

As members of the Whig government mobilized to move a Revaluation Bill through Parliament, they turned to Locke once again, pleading that he complete and publish his major intervention, *Further Considerations*. "Very many gentlemen" sought him out, wrote a friend, "to have been set right in their notions what is fit to be done at this time with respect to the coin." Although Locke condemned the modifications that the Council had made to his proposal, he allowed his work to be published for the cause.[9] Members of Parliament and other government officials would recur repeatedly to his arguments. Montague himself would use Locke's logic in a later proposal for paper bills, invoking as the legitimacy he sought for paper money the naturalized support that Locke imputed to coin as a money created by "the consent of all people which at first made gold and silver

---

[5] See Ming-Hsun Li, *The Great Recoinage of 1696 to 1699* (London: Weidenfeld and Nicolson, 1963), 78–80.

[6] Locke's submissions included "Propositions Sent to the Lords Justices," and "Answer to my Lord Keeper's Queries." (Locke developed the latter into *Further Considerations*.) See Kelly, *Locke on Money*, 27–32. According to Kelly's reading of contemporary material, the Lords Justices only seriously considered the submissions by Locke and Christopher Wren, despite having invited a much broader group of notables to respond. Kelly, *Locke on Money*, 29–30. See pp. 345–346.

[7] The Exchequer was obliged to turn over lightweight coin to the mint for recoining. Technically, a revaluation could take place without more than effective dispatch of that mandate. For that consideration, the material in front of William, the sequence of decision, and the language that William appears to have adopted from Locke, see Kelly, *Locke on Money*, 27–28.

[8] Kelly, *Locke on Money*, 30. For William's concession to involve the Commons on a matter "of so general concern, and of so very great importance," see Li, *The Great Recoinage of 1696 to 1699*.

[9] Freke to Locke, December 5, 1695, as cited in Kelly, *Locke on Money*; Kelly, *Locke on Money*, 30–32.

the medium of commerce."[10] Pamphleteers for the opposition targeted Locke as the spokesperson who must be refuted, while contemporaries witnessed to his influence on political officials and the public.[11] Nor did Locke write alone; his argument flowed from and reinforced that of allies.[12]

Parliament resolved the issue as directed by its Whig managers. An Act for Remedying the Ill State of the Coin became law on January 21, 1696.[13] It provided that new coin would hold the content officially set in the existing mint indentures "which weight and fineness are hereby declared to bee and shall remain to bee the standard of and for the lawful silver coin of this kingdom." Since 1601, one troy ounce of sterling silver had produced 5 shillings 2 pence.[14] Under the Act of 1696, a coin supply 50 percent lighter would be reminted to that standard.[15] Describing Locke, Albert Feavearyear noted that he had newly sanctified "the mint weights." Following Locke, Parliament now did the same.[16]

The Great Recoinage marked the first time since the episode of the imitation pennies in 1299 that the English reformed their money supply by strengthening weak coin to standard rather than altering the standard to align with the de facto commodity content of the coin.[17] We have seen that under the medieval system in which people paid for coin, recalibrating money by leveling it down was by far more common. Depreciating the content of coin amounted to raising the price for silver, which operated to draw money to the mint: holders of coin would bring in their battered supplies because the higher price for its content meant that they were likely to get back as many or more units of account as they currently held.[18] By contrast, the same people would be hurt if they brought in old coin for

[10] Kelly, *Locke on Money*, 15 and n. 2; Montague, "A Document Relating to Public Credit," 238.
[11] Pamphlets aimed expressly at Locke included those by Nicholas Barbon and Sir Richard Temple. Barbon, *A Discourse Concerning Coining the New Money Lighter* (printed for Richard Chiswell, 1696), A3; Sir Richard Temple, *Some Short Remarks Upon Mr. Lock's Book, in Answer to Mr. Lounds, and Several Other Books and Pamphlets Concerning Coin* (printed for Richard Baldwin, 1696); see also Henry Layton, *Observations Concerning Money and Coin and Especially Those of England* (Peter Buck, 1697), Preface 2, 11; *A Review of the Universal Remedy for All Diseases Incident to Coin* (printed for A. & J. Churchill, 1696); Hodges to Locke, February 8, 1696/7, cited by Kelly, *Locke on Money*, 35; Kelly, *Locke on Money*, 36–37.
[12] See, e.g., Sir Dudley North, *Discourses Upon Trade, Principally Directed to the Cases of the Interest, Coynage, Clipping, Increase of Money* (printed for Tho. Basset, 1691), as reprinted in <http://avalon.law.yale.edu/17th_century/tradenor.asp>, accessed June 25, 2014; James Houblon, "Observations on the Bill Against the Exportation of Gold and Silver," ed. Historical Manuscripts Commission 17 (London, 1690).
[13] 7 & 8 Will 3 c 1 (1695–1696). For continuing skirmishes over the decision, see Kelly, *Locke on Money*; Li, *The Great Recoinage of 1696 to 1699*.
[14] 7 & 8 Will 3 c 1 s 1 (1695–1696). Sterling fineness was 11 oz and 2 dwt silver, 18 dwt alloy to the troy (12 oz) pound with an allowance of 2 pence in weight or fineness. A troy pound of silver therefore would be minted into £3 2s. in silver coin, or 5s. 2d./oz at the mint. See Li, *The Great Recoinage of 1696 to 1699*, 47.
[15] It would continue to do so until 1816, when it was displaced (and devalued) in favor of a new, golden identity for the unit of account. Angela Redish, *Bimetallism: An Economic and Historical Analysis*, Studies in Macroeconomic History Index (Cambridge: Cambridge University Press, 2000), 146.
[16] Albert Edgar Feavearyear, *The Pound Sterling: A History of English Money*, 2nd ed. (Oxford: Clarendon Press, 1963), 148.
[17] See pp. 144–149; Feavearyear, *The Pound Sterling: a History of English Money*, 146. On that occasion, Edward I had effectively appreciated the metal content of foreign pennies by "calling down" their face value.
[18] For discussion, see pp. 121–122.

revaluation: they would receive back fewer units of account, a real loss given the continued operation of those units of account in stating prices and current obligations. To surmount that difficulty, the government paid up front for much of the costs of strengthening the coin. It carried that expense by taxing the community, distributing the burdens of the Great Recoinage through the fiscal system. To move the process, officials also added a more familiar stick; they prohibited the continuing use of old money.

During the spring of 1696, the government took old and worn coin at face value for taxes and for the purchase of bonds, netting about £4.7 million. Including costs due to the shortfall in coin's weight and minting, the government swallowed a bill of about £2.3 million. Public expenses were driven up by clipping, which flourished because the government for a period accepted the damaged coins in taxes and loans advanced to it. Authorities also paid a premium for silver plate. In due course, the bill for the process came to the taxpayers. The government imposed a levy on houses to run seven years, apportioned according to the number of windows per house. The tax fell on inhabitants, not owners, an approach therefore regressive. Legislation lightened that burden a bit, extending the policy of accepting payments in old coin at face value. Parliament supplemented the house tax further with revenues from diffuse sources. The total public bill for the Great Recoinage eventually came to about £2.7 million.[19]

Individuals holding money bore the brunt of the later phases of the Recoinage. Beginning that summer (July 1696) for the following year and a half, the government accepted coined silver by weight, with a slight premium at the mint and a somewhat greater premium from tax collectors, receiving more than £4.9 million.[20] Considering the period to July 1697, Sargent and Velde estimate that the old coin was minted into £3.3 million at the standard silver content. The new approach thus meant a gross loss of coin to money holders of £1.6 million, less a fraction (£0.25 million) returned by the government by way of

---

[19] See C. E. Challis, "Lord Hastings to the Great Silver Recoinage, 1464–1699," in *A New History of the Royal Mint*, ed. C. E. Challis (Cambridge: Cambridge University Press, 1992), 383–384 (including Table 55); Li, *The Great Recoinage of 1696 to 1699*, 114–119; Thomas J. Sargent and Francois R. Velde, *The Big Problem of Small Change*, The Princeton Economic History of the Western World Indexes (Princeton, NJ: Princeton University Press, 2002), 286. The house tax was anticipated to raise about £1.2 million. A tax on paper followed in 1697 and 1698. Challis, "Lord Hastings to the Great Silver Recoinage, 1464–1699," 385, 390. Lord Liverpool's estimates of the total cost to the public are taken as authoritative by recent scholarship. See Charles, Earl of Liverpool, *A Treatise on the Coins of the Realm in a Letter to the King* (London: Oxford University Press, 1805), 73–76; Challis, "Lord Hastings to the Great Silver Recoinage, 1464–1699," 397, n. 420.

[20] The procedure was apparently an extension of a program that induced people to turn plate in to the mint for coining until November 4, 1696 (7 & 8 Will 3 c 19 (1695–1696)). The withdrawal of coin after November 4, 1696, was more formally provided for by legislation enacted that fall. See Challis, "Lord Hastings to the Great Silver Recoinage, 1464–1699," 389–390. The estimate of £4.9 million is taken from Sargent, although it should undercount the amount received at the mint because it concerns the period July 1696 to July 1697. Sargent and Velde, *Big Problem of Small Change*, 286 (source unspecified). Compare the estimate of £4.84 million turned in by November 1696, according to Challis. Challis, "Lord Hastings to the Great Silver Recoinage, 1464–1699," 389 (starting date unspecified).

the premium it offered. That was an enormous amount in the prices of the day. (Tax revenue in 1696–1697 amounted to £3.4 million.)[21] After December 1697, old coin was completely demonetized. The government took in a last £0.5 million as bullion.[22]

The hardships from the Great Recoinage were felt throughout society, but fell disproportionately on the poor and middling. First, the reform targeted only silver coin as opposed to the gold guineas held by the wealthier part of the population. And, while everyone holding silver coin was affected, people with taxes to pay or the ability to lend the government money were able to put their coin to use at face value. The government also invited those owing certain taxes to anticipate future payments in order to get face value for their coin. Those without that channel found the value of their money discounted at the beginning; if they did not pay taxes, they had no choice but to exchange it at a loss with those who did. Even those who did owe some tax or public levy were often not organized to turn in their money when it was still accepted at face value, so the last coin was demonetized in their hands.[23]

The total collected by the government amounted to about £10 million. The amount of new coin produced from old coin augmented by plate and other sources was £6.8 million.[24] The Great Recoinage thus abruptly contracted the amount of money in circulation. Officials managed the recoinage ineptly, causing even more hardship. The mints took in coin but were much slower to produce it. In 1696, some £2.3 million in face value was lost to circulation. No alternative medium was issued, despite proposals for a substitute paper currency. Prices for a majority of 22 non-agricultural commodities fell sharply in the spring of 1696 until 1697. Interest rates skyrocketed, reaching 16 to 17 percent, despite legal prohibitions.[25] Demands for silver triggered the first run on the Bank of England, which partially stayed cash redemptions. Protest, unrest, and threats of insurrection occurred around the country. The diarist John Evelyn reported that money was "exceeding scarce" in May 1696, not to be had for paying or receiving. In the

[21] See Sargent and Velde, *Big Problem of Small Change*, 286. Challis, considering coin received before November 4, 1696, finds a net of £2.56 from £4.84 old coin. Challis, "Lord Hastings to the Great Silver Recoinage, 1464–1699," 389 (Table 58).

[22] Sargent and Velde, *Big Problem of Small Change*, 286. For private losses, annual tax revenue, and the conditions of the Great Recoinage, see Sargent and Velde, *Big Problem of Small Change*, 286. These estimates do not count the losses incurred by ordinary people as they sought to do business without coin throughout the process.

[23] See Challis, "Lord Hastings to the Great Silver Recoinage, 1464–1699," 382–390, 397; Li, *The Great Recoinage of 1696 to 1699*, 119–121; Keith J. Horsefield, *British Monetary Experiments, 1650–1710* (Cambridge, MA: Harvard University Press, 1960), 62.

[24] Challis, "Lord Hastings to the Great Silver Recoinage, 1464–1699," 388.

[25] William Lowndes, *A Report Containing an Essay for the Amendment of Silver Coins* (London: Charles Bill & the Executrix of Thomas Newcomb, 1695), 119–120, 139–145, 152–153 (proposing paper substitute money); Horsefield, *Monetary Experiments*, 6–9, 12, 18. Horsefield uses the unweighted commodity prices given by John Houghton, noting some discrepancy with the Phelps-Brown and Hopkins index. He also attempts to measure changing velocity of circulation and concludes that the use of credit rose significantly during the Recoinage. Horsefield, *Monetary Experiments*, 13–18.

following month he noted the "[w]ant of money to carry on the smallest concerns, even for daily provisions in the markets...tumults are every day feared."[26] In July, an observer in Ipswich catalogued the dismal situation:

> Our tenants can pay no rent. Our corn factors can pay nothing for what they have at hand and will trade no more, so all is at a stand. And the people are discontented to the utmost; many self murders happen in small families for want, and all things look very black.[27]

As discontent and economic distress mounted, Parliament again considered devaluation. In the fall of 1696, the House of Commons rejected that course. "This House will not alter the standard of gold and silver," it resolved, "in fineness, weight or denomination."[28]

The consequences of the Great Recoinage disturbed politicians, party strategists, and observers within the Whig coalition, as well as without. William III most famously would regret his compliance.[29] Their concern was warranted for longer than they realized—the Great Recoinage set a precedent of revaluation that legitimated a string of harsh interventions in the 19th century.[30] But the economic catastrophe caused by the Great Recoinage also had a more immediate and somewhat ironic consequence. It destroyed the main competitor to the monetary order that the Whig officials were creating.

For decades, credit theorists had proposed money based on the security of land. Their designs varied: a number suggested paper money that capitalized future rents while others advocated money subscriptions to provide a cash reserve for mortgage loans. As the logic of credit theorists indicated, a specie reserve was not an essential element in the making of money. Tallies had operated effectively on the basis of tax anticipation alone and land banks without specie reserves would soon proliferate in the American colonies, producing stable currencies when they were well managed.[31] By 1696, however, proposals for monetizing rental streams were non-starters in England. Instead, supporters converged on proposals quite like the Bank of England; they advocated a land bank that would hold a specie reserve and issue notes backed by public debt and the income stream it represented.[32] The hardening orthodoxy likely followed in

[26] John Evelyn, May 13, 1696; June 11, 1696, reproduced in Li, *The Great Recoinage of 1696 to 1699*, 136–137.

[27] Edmund Bohun, July 31, 1696, as quoted in Challis, "Lord Hastings to the Great Silver Recoinage, 1464–1699," 387.

[28] Li, *The Great Recoinage of 1696 to 1699*, 120.

[29] William's reversal in Kelly, *Locke on Money*, 37. Rubini details the Whig country opposition to the orthodoxy that increased during the Great Recoinage period. Rubini, "Battle for the Banks."

[30] See pp. 408–416.

[31] On tallies, see pp. 178–180; on land banks, see Leslie V. Brock, *The Currency of the American Colonies, 1700-1764, A Study in Colonial Finance and Imperial Relations*, Dissertations in American Economic History (New York: Arno Press, 1975).

[32] National Land Bank Act 1695 (7 & 8 Will 3 c 31). For this consensus, see Richard Kleer, "Fictitious Cash: English Public Finance and Paper Money, 1689-97," in *Money, Power and Print: Interdisciplinary*

part from the Lockean vision, confirmed in the Great Recoinage, that fetishized money as a matter of instrinsic metal content.

According to the plan accepted by Parliament that year, a National Land Bank would lend the government £2 million at 7 percent, later increased to more than £2.5 million—just the amount that officials desperately needed to meet wartime expenses. The advance would be based on cash subscriptions to that amount and accompanied by land subscriptions with a capitalized value of another £2.8 million: those investing cash got interest dividends while those subscribing land had access to low-cost mortgages. A portion of the money lent by the Land Bank, up to £2.8 million (later much reduced), would be in the form of paper, allowing it to profit from the fractional arrangement while keeping a cash reserve.[33]

Scholars have divided over the dominant political color of land bank supporters. But the National Land Bank's authors, its most active promoters in Parliament, and its public advocates were men with a deepening attachment to the Tory cause.[34] Bank of England officials, clearly associated with the Whig party, launched a series of attacks against the proposed competitor.[35] But the National Land Bank was already primed for failure by that other Whig initiative: the Great Recoinage made it almost impossible for the newcomer to gather a specie reserve.

According to its authorizing legislation, the Land Bank's cash subscription of £2 million had to be completely pledged and a quarter paid in before August 1, 1696, for incorporation to proceed.[36] At that point, the Recoinage was drying up coin by the day and interest rates were steep. "The wonder is," wrote Keith Horsefield, that any group of officials even attempted "so Herculean a task" as collecting cash. In the end, the commissioners trolling for £2 million in subscriptions received only £2,100 in individual commitments; an even lower amount was

---

Studies on the Financial Revolution in the British Isles, ed. Charles Ivar McGrath and Christopher J. Fauske (Newark: University of Delaware Press, 2008), 86–97; cf. Horsefield, *Monetary Experiments*, 204–205.

[33] In the Act, mortgages were limited to a total value of £500,000 and the role of land subscription was moderated. Rather than a security for the loan, it became simply an option for borrowers who could borrow against mortgaged land. See the National Land Bank Act of 1695 (7 & 8 Will 3 c 31 s 29). Kleer's analysis of the proposals and the shifting relationship of projectors is the most comprehensive. Kleer, "'Fictitious Cash,'" 92–97. See also Horsefield, *Monetary Experiments*, 202–206. Rubini's rendition is more confused. Rubini, "Battle for the Banks," 698–701.

[34] Steve Pincus and Alice Wolfram, "A Proactive State? The Land Bank, Investment and Party Politics in the 1690s," in *Regulating the British Economy, 1660-1850* (Farnham: Ashgate, 2011), 45–54; H. Clapham, *The Bank of England: A History* (Cambridge: Cambridge University Press, 1970), 34; see also Bruce G. Carruthers, *City of Capital: Politics and Markets in the English Financial Revolution* (Princeton NJ: Princeton University Press, 1996), 141–142. By contrast, Dennis Rubini argues that Land Bank supporters most notably shared a country orientation. According to Ann Murphy, Land Bank proponents came from all political parties. See Rubini, "Battle for the Banks"; Anne L. Murphy, *The Origins of English Financial Markets: Investment and Speculation before the South Sea Bubble*, Cambridge Studies in Economic History (Cambridge: Cambridge University Press, 2009), 57–58.

[35] See pp. 301–304; Clapham, *Bank of England*, 34.

[36] See the National Land Bank Act 1695 (7 & 8 Will 3 c 31 ss 16–17).

paid up. Stranded at low monetary tide, the National Land Bank went out with a whimper.[37]

Far from rendering the Land Bank any assistance, the Whig ministry planned for its demise. It refused requests to mitigate the subscription requirements imposed and took no action to issue a paper currency during most of the Recoinage.[38] In the spring of 1697, the directors of the Bank of England capitalized on the National Land Bank's failure. Demanding relief from future competition, they obtained legislation that granted the Bank monopoly stature as long as its charter lasted.[39]

In the same legislation that authorized the Land Bank, Whig politicians took a last step to institutionalize their monetary vision. They included provisions for Exchequer bills up to a value of £1.5 million.[40] Montague, ever the monetary pragmatist, had gotten the idea from Thomas Neale, one of the most prolific of the projectors proposing credit-based issues.[41]

Recall that Exchequer bills were issued on the promise of future revenue. They were payable at the Exchequer only to the extent it held funds reserved for that purpose from money advanced by the bills to the government. In other words, Exchequer bills were notes quite like the Bank's—they simply lacked the private intermediary. Over the next two years, the government took several steps to strengthen the bills' ability to circulate. First, it made the bills receivable for taxes. That change jump-started their popular acceptability. Subsequently, it garnered enough subscriptions from merchants to publicize cash-on-demand for redemption. By mid-1697, more than a million Exchequer bills had been issued; by November 1702, the number was over £3 million. And while the bills could be redeemed for cash, more than £2.5 million had been cancelled by being used for taxes instead. Even as money became identified with silver, an enormous proportion transparently operated according to the predictions of the credit theorists.[42]

That potential, however, Whig strategists left both unarticulated and underdeveloped. In a memorandum that argued for the reforms—including tax receivability—that had so effectively strengthened Exchequer bills, Montague merely noted that the bills might thereby win "the consent of all people which

---

[37] Horsefield, *Monetary Experiments*, 95; see also Kleer, "'Fictitious Cash,'" 95. The final total was £7,100, including a royal commitment of £5,000.

[38] See Li, *The Great Recoinage of 1696 to 1699*, 78–80; Rubini, "Battle for the Banks," 708.

[39] See 8 & 9 Will 3 c 20 s 28 (1696–1697); Clapham, *Bank of England*, 46–47.

[40] See pp. 339–340.

[41] Montague sought and obtained support for the bills from a broad range of people. Montague, "A Document Relating to Public Credit," 237–239; Clapham, *Bank of England*, 38–39. For Neale's contributions to the credit theories, see pp. 336–337.

[42] See 8 & 9 Will 3 c 20 s 63 (1696–1697); Montague, "A Document Relating to Public Credit," 237–239; Li, *The Great Recoinage of 1696 to 1699*, 130–134. Note that Lowndes's report identifies amounts issued by 1702 as slightly greater than the amounts created according to B. R. Mitchell, *Abstract of British Historical Statistics* (Cambridge: 1962), 404–405.

at first made gold and silver the medium of commerce." Assimilated to those metals, Exchequer bills might suit *temporarily* to "supply their place while the silver is recoyning."[43]

Exchequer bills would in fact have a long career, but always as an apparently temporary expedient. They took their place as supporting players to the monetary stars of the decade, money made by the Bank of England and specie of "sound" content. Those currencies, installed by an enormously effective political party, became the repertory cast, the trusted company, of the next century. Those monetary initiatives distinguished the court Whigs as more adept than their Tory competitors at financing war, enlisting the aid of the manufacturing and commercial classes, and developing the industry of public and private credit.[44] Whig political success in turn confirmed the currencies they had authored. The issue that remains is to understand exactly what that combination of moneys, conceptualized as they were, meant for the modern world.

B. The liberal turn to "gold"

Constitutional reorganization

Scholars considering the Great Recoinage of the 1690s widely agree that it disrupted the economy. Likewise, many fault Locke for his prescriptions.[45] The economy would recover and the philosopher would retire—but Parliament's determination to treat money as a matter outside of political control was far from transient. To the contrary, the approach had constitutional impact. As it put the new array of currencies into circulation, the government shifted the way it responded to the claims of creditors, taxpayers, and citizens more generally. Its policy comported with liberal arguments that elevated the concerns of traders as agents of economic development. Indeed, the new policy was so concerted as to be destabilizing—the monetary turn taken in the 1690s unintentionally reorganized the 18th century monetary landscape.

The Great Recoinage aimed at problems endemic to the conduct of commodity money. That practice, as it was traditionally managed, maintained domestic

---

[43] Montague, "A Document Relating to Public Credit," 238.

[44] See Pincus, *1688*, 366–399; Pincus and Wolfram, "A Proactive State?"; Steve Pincus, "Addison's Empire: Whig Conceptions of Empire in the Early 18th Century," *Parliamentary History* (2012); Carruthers, *City of Capital*, 142; see also Rubini, "Battle for the Banks" (court Whigs). For the future success of Exchequer bills, see Feavearyear, *The Pound Sterling: A History of English Money*, 159–160.

[45] Sargent and Velde, *Big Problem of Small Change*, 286–290; Challis, "Lord Hastings to the Great Silver Recoinage, 1464–1699," 379–397; Horsefield, *Monetary Experiments*, 62; cf. Li, *The Great Recoinage of 1696 to 1699*, 135–140 (considering war as a major cause of "great losses" from recoinage). Even David Hume, contemplating a recoinage 50 years later, would disavow the revaluation chosen in 1696 on the ground that an increase in the money supply that followed a devaluation could have stimulating effects. David Hume, "Discourse III: Of Money," in *Political Discourses* (London: R. Fleming, 1752), 32, n. 1. By contrast, Locke and the Great Recoinage enjoyed acclaim during the 19th century. For a description of Thomas Macaulay's celebratory reception, see Sargent and Velde, *Big Problem of Small Change*, 287–288.

exchange as a priority. That priority explains why the English had generally chosen devaluation to cure eroded coin.[46] Insofar as coin had lost value because it had lost silver content, the costs had been spread long-term over many debtors and creditors and across many shorter-term transactions. Revaluation, by contrast, imposed the consequences of deflation abruptly on current debtors when it upgraded the amount of silver represented by obligations denominated in the unit of account. As at the Great Recoinage, a revaluation predictably drove prices lower as the coin supply decreased. The drop was intended; it brought the rising value of coin up and the market price of silver down. However, it also made debts that had been incurred when coin was less valuable more difficult to repay. The policy both erased the argument that problems in the money supply had long-running origins and created short-term economic turmoil.

At the same time, the Great Recoinage elevated the dimension of coin that made it useful outside England's boundaries. When it paid for the strengthening of coin, a government that had not abusively depreciated the money supply determined to reimburse the current generation of creditors in a monetary unit that held additional silver. That additional silver did not change the relative terms of current domestic exchange. Prices still moved together; creditors passed on coin of higher value for domestic objects as well as receiving it. The silver did, however, convey to creditors more material that had independent value for transactions across the English border. In that sense, it tied the internal touchstone that had always controlled—the unit of account—to an external touchstone—the static silver content demanded by those working across the border.[47]

Comparing arguments against nominalism in previous English administrations, like the one posed by the creditor in *The Case of Mixed Money*, suggests the impact of the new government policy. Earlier arguments against nominalism claimed that the metal content of coin should control the amount that debtors owed current creditors, no matter what the nominal value of the unit of account. In the case of a state-authored devaluation, debtors should repay creditors in a constant amount of silver, although that meant overpaying them in the nominal unit of account. Metallist arguments thus protected a set of existing creditors for a limited period, insulating them from the effects of the devaluation. Metallist arguments did not, however, prevent a sovereign's determination to depreciate

---

[46] See pp. 121–123; see also Sargent and Velde, *Big Problem of Small Change*, 289–290 (summarizing argument for devaluation at the Great Recoinage).

[47] Compare the argument by some advocates of liquid capital that it disciplined the government by allowing wealth to be spirited away from government authorities. The dynamic here, which may ground that more abstract argument, is instead that government authorities affirmatively privileged the claims of those concerned about a loss of a non-monetary resource regionally valued because of its use as an ingredient in domestic currencies.

its money supply more generally.[48] Rather, those depreciations had occurred regularly, a product of political judgments about the domestic economy.

In that light, the work by Locke and others to elevate the rights of creditors takes on new significance. Creditors had always objected to devaluations. And English creditors, more than most, had effectively minimized the occasions of their loss. Locke articulated the claims of creditors with particular vehemence, arguing that any alteration of the monetary standard amounted to a "publick failure of justice" and operated "arbitrarily to give one man's right and possession to another . . . without any the least advantage to the publick." His logic took him even farther, to the conclusion that governmental action on coins was worse than clipping by common thieves. "[B]y clipping the loss is not forced on anyone" who did not wish to take the coin, Locke noted, while public devaluations operated coercively, forcing a new standard on everyone.[49] But the stakes went deeper than a transient loss to creditors.

In the liberal theory that Locke and his colleagues were developing, money was transformative. More, its transformative character depended on its identity as a medium made outside of the state. Before money, individuals appropriated to themselves the riches of the earth through labor. It was the "*labour* of his body, and the *work* of his hands" that allowed a man to claim a portion of the common bounty and make it his property.[50] That measure left more than enough for others because "no man's labour could subdue, or appropriate all; nor could his enjoyment consume more than a small part."[51] The observation was also an

---

[48] See pp. 267–274. The arguments of Continental metallists were more aggressive. Thus Nicholas Oresme condemned all changes in the metal content of coin engineered by a prince for his own profit, although Oresme excepted from that rule changes made necessary by a significant change in supply or bimetallic value. Charles Johnson, trans./ed., *The De Moneta of Nicholas Oresme and English Mint Documents* (London: Thomas Nelson, 1956; repr., Ludwig von Mises Institute, 2009), 13–14, 15–17, 20–22. Assumedly, such change could include wear, although Oresme did not so acknowledge. He also accepted alterations made by a community "if it needs a large sum of money for war or for the ransom of its prince." In fact, Oresme noted that altering the money was "more fair or proportional" than other methods of collecting money from people "since he who can afford most pays most." Oresme did, however, require that money altered for the community's good be restored to "its due and permanent state" as quickly as possible. Johnson, *De Moneta/English Mint Documents*, 36–37.

[49] Locke, "Further Considerations Concerning Raising the Value of Money," 416; see also Locke, "Further Considerations Concerning Raising the Value of Money," 437–442. The Lockean position thus picked up the most aggressive vein of Continental metallist argument (see previous note), while omitting that approach's concession to necessary devaluations. See also, e.g., Houblon, "Observations on the Bill Against the Exportation of Gold and Silver"; North, *Discourses Upon Trade*, 7; see also Daniel Defoe, *The Master Mercury* (Los Angeles: William Andrews Clark Memorial Library University of California, 1977 [1704]), 24. Kelly emphasizes that Locke also attended to the concerns of poorer folk, fearing that the continued circulation of clipped coin at face value allowed speculators to hoard it. Kelly, *Locke on Money*, 26–27; see also Richard A. Kleer, " 'The Ruine of their Diana': Lowndes, Locke, and the Bankers," *History of Political Economy* 36, no. 3 (2004): 543–544.

[50] John Locke, *Two Treatises of Government*, in *The Works of John Locke* (Rivington, 1824, 12th ed., 1691), Chap. V, sec. 27.

[51] Locke, *Two Treatises*, Chap. V, sec. 36.

injunction. According to Locke, the duty to avoid waste meant that an individual could appropriate only as much as he or she could use.[52]

Money intervened into that egalitarian but modest economy: it lifted the limit imposed by the injunction against waste. When men could trade plums for a store of value that operated as a medium of exchange, they could acquire and accumulate without letting anything spoil. More than that, they could acquire to produce. As C. B. Macpherson so acutely elaborated, Locke made money into capital. Money allowed those who were industrious to appropriate more property than they alone could work. Instead, they hired help, made improvements, and sold surplus. In that fashion, money induced investment, trade, and productivity. In the philosopher's words, "he who appropriates land to himself by his labour, does not lessen, but increase the common stock of mankind: for the provisions serving to the support of human life, produced by one acre of enclosed and cultivated land, are ... ten times more than those which are yielded by an acre of land of an equal richness lying waste in common."[53]

In this ecology, the definition of money as pre-political mattered. Locke had identified money with "a piece of metal" that a man "pleased with its color" took in return for the nuts he had gathered or "a sparkling pebble" he took in return for the wool he had produced. If that was right, then it was beyond the state's ability to interfere.[54] As Locke put it, "This partage of things in an inequality of private possessions, men have made practicable out of the bounds of society, and without compact, only by putting a value on gold and silver, and tacitly agreeing in the use of money."[55] Money's very identity as a commodity chosen by individuals making deals set it apart, assuring its emancipatory role, its power as an agent of economic development. The mutual agreement on money in turn insulated the disparity in wealth it enabled as a necessary attribute of growth.

Given that import, the stakes of defining money as a particular amount of metal moved up in the world. The agreement that created coin *must* be classified as "private" and the purpose of creditors *must* be accorded a kind of sanctity. They made the activity that set Europe, with its civilization and sophistication, apart from the New World, with its savages and untapped abundance. "In the beginning all the world was America," Locke famously claimed, "for no such thing as money was any where known."[56] In the Great Recoinage, Parliament bowed to the argument and the economic concerns it privileged.

---

[52] Locke, *Two Treatises*, Bk II, Chap. V, sec. 31 ("The same law of nature, that does by this means give us property, does also *bound* that *property* too ... As much as any one can make use of to any advantage of life before it spoils, so much he may by his labour fix a property in: whatever is beyond this, is more than his share, and belongs to others.").

[53] Locke, *Two Treatises*, Bk II, Chap. V, sec. 37; C. B. Macpherson, *The Political Theory of Possessive Individualism: Hobbes to Locke* (Oxford: Clarendon Press, 1969), 203–221.

[54] See the discussion of Locke's definition of money, pp. 330–331, 346–349. The quote is from Locke, *Two Treatises*, Bk II, Chap. V, sec. 46.

[55] Locke, *Two Treatises*, Bk II, Chap. V, sec. 51.

[56] Locke, *Two Treatises*, Bk II, Chap. V, sec. 48–49.

The liberal turn to an external touchstone for value and the "right" that it imputed to creditors had an impact yet wider because Parliament's logic did more than identify coin as a constant amount of metal. It bestowed a material guarantee on the paper promises that increasingly supplemented coin. By the time of the Great Recoinage, the English administration had come to rely heavily on negotiable public credit. The "financial revolution" was underway; it supplied major funding for the war effort.[57] Parliament's decision to revalue likely drew from the need to legitimate public credit and the new paper form of currency, Bank money. As creditors saw it, if the government could devalue the coin promised by current credit, it could depreciate the amount it owed claimants and mint the silver it recouped, multiplying the units of account that functioned to pay off outstanding promises.

Opponents raised the other side to the argument. If coin lost silver content over the course of decades, the government's intervention to recoin at a lower content recognized the reality that silver had been worn or clipped. It was the toll on coin that drove mint prices apart from market prices, discouraging people from bringing any more silver to the mint and bringing those hard times when flows of metal to the mint were scant. The government was not allocating silver to itself; indeed, there *was* no silver to be recouped—it had long since disappeared. Rather than gaining an illicit benefit, the government was recalibrating the machinery that made coin. Devaluing coin relieved the harsh consequences that came when silver stopped flowing to the mint, while strengthening coin at such a moment imposed too heavy a cost.

The deadlock revisited the issue that bondholders litigated across the same decade. As we have seen, *The Case of the Bankers* raised the question whether loans taken by Charles II had to be repaid as a matter of right to creditors. If they did, then similarly, those who lent expecting to be repaid in coin at the original standard could make that claim as a matter of right.[58] Recall Justice Holt's argument that allowing a delay in payment "would destroy all annuities, rent-charges, and other payments which the crown is obliged to make." By contrast, Lord Somers in his post as judge of the Exchequer Chamber had defended sovereign discretion to subordinate the demands of creditors to the needs of the larger polity. In that view, contractual rights could only be determined within the wider context of public need. Intervening after the appellate decision, the House of Lords had opted for Holt's position. Acting as the high court of the

---

[57] See pp. 251–254.

[58] If this is right, it would be worth exploring whether the emergence of the "will theory" of contracts followed from a changed understanding of contract for commercial uses. See Morton J. Horwitz, *The Transformation of American Law, 1780–1860*, Studies in Legal History (Cambridge, MA: Harvard University Press, 1977), 180–188.

realm, the Lords had confirmed the bankers' claim and elevated their rights as creditors.[59]

The Bank of England's bills and notes gained legitimacy under shelter of that imperative. The government's commitment to the original standard for coin strengthened the promise made by the Bank: those holding its paper gained a guarantee that they could redeem it for a particular amount of silver, no matter what cost to the public. After noting that men would only leave their money "safe in a bank" if they knew it would be paid them, an early critic of the Bank continued:

> ...the only way to make the Bank of England capable to supply the Nation's want of real species by their notes and bills, is first to ascertain to that Bank the funds upon which they are established, and have or shall hereafter lend any money to the government, by the strongest ties and obligations of security, that the wisdom of the Parliament can invent, so that the generality of men may be satisfied therewith.[60]

The Bank's projectors went even further. For years, they had pointed to "the universal species of gold and silver" as the only true money; in their view, Bank money held value only because it promised gold and silver, not because of the relationship between the Bank and the government that created demand for the Bank's issues.[61] Money, insofar as it was produced through the intermediary of the Bank, was a contract that got stronger the further it was distanced from public discretion. By casting Bank notes as promises of guaranteed material content, the Great Recoinage gave them a genealogy like the one that defined coin as an amount of metal. Both were ideally independent of the government and both were tied to an external touchstone for value. In the next century, those defining the Gold Standard would understand Bank notes as a medium that must be convertible into a fixed amount of metal.[62] Their determination came to seem a matter of law and right. Conflicting claims appeared to be political or humanitarian in comparison. That conceptual difference structured debates over the conditions that justified allowing banks to suspend redemption of notes. The claims of creditors gained particular sanctity against arguments that depended on the health of the domestic economy and the working individuals who populated it.

---

[59] *The Case of the Bankers* (1690–1700) in T. B. Howell, *Cobbett's Complete Collection of State Trials and Proceedings for High Treason and Other Crimes and Misdemeanors from the Earliest Period to the Year 1783*, vol. 14 (London: R. Bagshaw, 1812), 37, 106–110 (Lords' holding). Note that, as above, the practical value of the Lords' guarantee depended on the cooperation of Parliament to fund the award. See pp. 287–288.

[60] *A Letter to a Friend Concerning Credit and How It May Be Restor'd to the Bank of England* (printed for Andr Bell, 1697) 4; see also *A Letter to a Friend, Concerning the Credit of the Nation: And with Relation to the Present Bank of England* (printed for E. Whitlock, 1697), 7–8.

[61] Paterson, *A Brief Account*, 10; Godfrey, *A Short Account of the Bank of England*, 6.

[62] See, e.g., Select Committee on the High Price of Gold Bullion, *Report*, ed. House of Commons (London: Richard Taylor and Co., 1810), 47–49, 53–54, 74; see also Liverpool, *A Treatise on the Coins of the Realm in a Letter to the King*, 146, 220.

The end of "commodity money" and the installation of a gold pivot

The linked developments had a last, unforeseen, and deeply ironic effect, one that takes us to "gold" even more literally. Parliament's intransigence on the question of recalibrating coin effectively destroyed commodity money as a working proposition. Commodity money failed because it could not be maintained according to the Lockean theory. The loss confounded contemporaries in the 18th century—but it also, quite accidentally, released the English from the strictures that the commodity money system had long imposed. Silver coin—the traditional "sterling" unit of account—failed first. In turn, the English wrapped the gold coin that now represented the unit of account in a plethora of token moneys, both large and small. As a recent account by Thomas Sargent and Francois Velde emphasizes, the conversion to the new, composite set of moneys ultimately resolved the "big problem of small change" that had haunted the earlier world.[63] As importantly, the modern denominational array would also provide unparalleled liquidity to the English economy.

The history of commodity money, so often overlooked, provides the baseline for the shift. As it had been practiced for centuries, commodity money was a medium that delivered liquidity by linking coins with proportional amounts of metallic content—a ladder of denominations—to a scale of value in exchange. That project was a demanding one: the limits on metal as a natural resource, the struggles to keep old, worn, or clipped coin in circulation, the difficulty of generating currency at the right scale for everyday exchange, the sovereign competition over silver and gold, the difficulty of getting the bimetallic ratio between two metals right—all these and more made commodity money a delicate medium. It could not be maintained by insisting inflexibly on a particular price and content for coin while disregarding the dynamics that chronically destabilized flows of metal to the mint. But that is, in effect, what Parliament's approach did. As it happened, the price for silver that the mint set in 1696 undervalued it compared to gold. The metal hierarchy that earlier generations had worked so hard to sustain fell apart. After some eight centuries, the silver penny disappeared as the unit of account.[64] Over the next century, the English unit of account became defined by the guinea, with a value rated at 21 shillings and a fixed gold content.

---

[63] See Sargent and Velde, *Big Problem of Small Change*; see also Carlo M. Cipolla, *Money, Prices, and Civilization in the Mediterranean World, Fifth to Seventhteenth Century* (New York: Gordian Press, 1967), 27–37. As the history below suggests, filling out the denominational array took decades. The breakthrough, however, had occurred. It was the move to a unit of account supplemented by token moneys.

[64] The treatise on money packaged as the *Letter to the King* written by Charles Jenkinson, 1st Earl of Liverpool was, in many respects, an effort to document the drama. See Liverpool, *A Treatise on the Coins of the Realm in a Letter to the King*. See also Sargent and Velde, *Big Problem of Small Change*, 291–305; Cipolla, *Money, Prices, and Civilization*, 27–37; Feavearyear, *The Pound Sterling*, 150–172.

The guinea provided a measure, but was inadequate to service smaller and larger exchange. The smallest gold coin was the quarter-guinea or a bit more than 5 shillings. Prices rose during the 18th century, but even in 1774, a laborer earned only about £25 annually, or slightly more than £2 a month. A quarter-guinea represented, then, two days of work or more. Lower-value silver coin had previously acted to allow smaller, everyday trades. As it disappeared, people turned to credits, book accounts, and set-offs. But those strategies shut out more episodic, or less reciprocated exchange. Most obviously, England needed a currency to pay wages. "[T]he monthly (or longer) settlements and bills of exchange that would do for other traders would not suit most workers," wrote an historian of the period. They needed "regular payment in readily acceptable money of low denomination."[65] Even at the high end, people sought out alternatives to the guinea. As Lord Liverpool reported at the end of the century, London bankers preferred bank notes over coin 30 to 1 at the least, and 140 or "much greater" to 1 at the most. "The higher orders of paper currency" were "very convenient" in carrying on "the trade of a country so wealthy as Great Britain."[66]

The predicament prompted a spate of innovations to answer people's demand for cash. The English government would spend decades experimenting with copper coin to fill the void at the bottom, abandoning the effort at mid-century only to pick it up again at the end when it unsuccessfully contracted out the production of tokens. The mint also sought to attract silver for lower-value coin, although, over the course of the century, that flow of silver only amounted to something like 1/20th the amount that came to the mint in the century and a half before the Bank was established. In 1821, authorities effectively institutionalized token coinage that held little value as metal but was convertible into the gold unit of account. That kind of currency would eventually fill out the lower rungs of the denominational ladder.[67]

---

[65] L. S. Pressnell, *Country Banking in the Industrial Revolution* (Oxford: Oxford University Press, 1956), 16. But see Liverpool, *A Treatise on the Coins of the Realm in a Letter to the King*, 147–149, who was at pains to justify the gold unit of account as a unit of account of relatively convenient value for much exchange.

[66] Liverpool, *A Treatise on the Coins of the Realm in a Letter to the King*, 177–178, 220. On token coin, see G. P. Dyer and P. P. Gaspar, "Reform, the New Technology and Tower Hill, 1700–1966," in *A New History of the Royal Mint*, ed. C. E. Challis (Cambridge: Cambridge University Press, 1992), 434–436; Redish, *Bimetallism*, 153–161; Sargent and Velde, *Big Problem of Small Change*.

[67] See Dyer and Gaspar, "Reform, the New Technology and Tower Hill, 1700–1966," 434–436; Sargent and Velde, *Big Problem of Small Change*, 271; Redish, *Bimetallism*, 153, 154–161; Liverpool, *A Treatise on the Coins of the Realm in a Letter to the King*, 166, 171–172, 185–200 (including tables showing metal loss to rise as denomination size drops). Using Dyer's data, Mayhew estimates that the government issued something like 100 million copper halfpennies and farthings by the mid-18th century before ceding much small exchange to privately produced trade tokens in the next decades. N. J. Mayhew, *Sterling: The History of a Currency* (New York: Wiley, 2000), 104. The mint would resume production of copper coins in 1821. Redish, *Bimetallism*, 161. The proportion of silver coin minted is from Feavearyear, *The Pound Sterling: A History of English Money*, 158.

Fig. 10.1 A token issued by the Anglesey Copper Mine bearing a druid and promising the holder a halfpenny in value. From Lawrence Chard, <http://www.chards.co.uk>.

In the interim, tradesmen and industrialists across the country issued their own cash substitutes. The Anglesey Copper Mine began producing tokens in 1787, "not being able to procure good halfpence for the payment of their labourers." Like bank notes in metal, ACM tokens were engraved "We promise to pay the bearer one penny" on one side and "On demand in London, Liverpool, Anglesea" around the other. A druid's portrait graced the face of the token, apparently to evoke "the ancient residence of the Druids in the island."[68] See Fig. 10.1.

Notes, small and large, would become even more important. "Private individuals," writes L. S. Pressnell, "endeavoured to fill a gap left by the failure of the Mint and of the Bank of England to supply money for everyday needs." Notes, as opposed to checks or other instruments, became "the principal way in which this was done." Early notes had been payable after a certain date and sometimes carried interest; they had failed when competing against the notes issued by the Bank of England. In the late 1780s, bearer notes payable on demand became common and the payment of interest less common. As we will see, they now depended on the Bank as an anchoring institution.[69] As Pressnell documents, note issue often segued into full-blown country banking. That sector blossomed in the second half of the 18th century, induced in significant part by the government's failure to provide "an adequate currency."[70]

---

[68] The company's initials (P.M.C. for the Paris Mountain Company) appeared on the reverse. "New Anglesey Coin," *Gentleman's Magazine* 57 (1787): 1160–1161. For the context, see Pressnell, *Country Banking*, 14–36.

[69] Pressnell, *Country Banking*, 136, 138–140. For strategies other than note issue, see Pressnell, *Country Banking*, 153. For the Bank of England's anchoring role, see pp. 394–397.

[70] Pressnell, *Country Banking*, 14.

Those in the mining and metalworking industries, textiles, and brewing were particularly prolific. In crises, municipalities and groups of merchants also took action—at critical moments, they organized collective support for local notes.[71] Industrial areas had a special need for currencies; payment of wages was a "major use for notes" along with their role in everyday exchange by "labouring men."[72] Small notes were particularly inviting for both those purposes. They were also very easily abused—and so triggered even more tinkering with the media on offer. Businesses could, for example, make redeeming small notes more difficult than it was worth and then overissue them with confidence that they would not be cashed.[73] Notes below £1 and £5 were prohibited in the last quarter of the 18th century, but allowed during much of the period after 1797, the period of inconvertibility. When small notes were unavailable, employers paid workmen jointly, "it being their own responsibility sometimes to break [a single note] up amongst themselves."[74]

The moneys meant to supplement the gold pivot kept flowing. By the early 19th century, country banks were widespread outside London; every English county (and all but one Welsh county) boasted at least one licensed to issue notes. By the end of the 18th century, country bank notes added perhaps £10 million to circulation. By 1809, they supplied something like £14.5 million. They expanded to about £15 to £30 million as estimated by observers in the following years.[75]

The supply of country bank notes, extraordinary as it was, never quite equaled those issued by the Bank of England. By the end of the 18th century, the Bank's notes amounted to some £15 million. They increased during the period of inconvertibility, and would greatly outstrip private note issues after 1825.[76] Bank of England notes circulated nationally, but were generally of larger denomination. They filled in the upper rungs of the denominational ladder.

The developing money market also contributed forms of credit that were useful for large transactions.[77] Private bankers in London, limited by the terms of the

---

[71] Iain Frame, "Country Rag Merchants and Octopus Tentacles: An Analysis of Law's Contribution to the Creation of Money in England and Wales, 1790–1844" (Ph.D. Dissertation, Harvard University, 2012), 40–129.

[72] Pressnell, *Country Banking*, 148, 153–156. The spread of Bank of England notes into industrial areas, along with the prohibition of small value (under £5) notes reduced the prevalence of private notes in industrial areas after 1829. By contrast, note issue rose in agricultural areas. See Pressnell, *Country Banking*, 148–153.

[73] A hearing in 1774 castigated businesses for attaching oppressive conditions to the redemption of small notes as small as sixpence: they were payable on demand "if the holder brings with him change in silver for a guinea" (Pressnell, *Country Banking*, 16).

[74] Pressnell, *Country Banking*, 140–144, 153. Pressnell estimates that small notes made up less than 50 percent of country note issues for most of the first two decades of the 19th century; in one year, 43 percent of notes were £2 2s. or less in size. Pressnell, *Country Banking*, 147–148.

[75] Rondo E. Cameron et al. (eds.), *Banking in the Early Stages of Industrialization: A Study in Comparative Economic History* (New York: Oxford University Press, 1967), 42–43; Pressnell, *Country Banking*, 145–152.

[76] Pressnell, *Country Banking*, 159–161.   [77] Pressnell, *Country Banking*, 15, 138.

Bank of England's monopoly, could not compete in issuing their own notes. Increasingly, however, bankers and brokers there provided credit that moved money more quickly between those furnishing and those using capital. Private credit, including inland bills of exchange that were discounted by banks and often traveled hand to hand, represented as much as another £100 million in circulation by the end of the 18th century.[78] Finally, public bonds and other forms of negotiable public credit, including publicly issued Exchequer bills, supplied another medium. It was valued at up to £245 million by the end of the American war.[79]

By contrast, the English recoinage in 1774 produced some £16.5 to £19 million in gold coin.[80] Even assuming an increase of several million in the next years, that amount was more than matched by paper currencies and was positively dwarfed by paper credit. Gold coin did not circulate widely in the countryside; increasingly, it would be held as a reserve by the Bank of England.

The denominations stripped away when the traditional coinage fell apart had been recreated in moneys that were *not* commodity-based, including the paper money recently invented. Rather than providing a ladder of metal scaled to provide proportionate values, the new hierarchy pivoted on a central unit of account defined in terms of an amount of gold. Moreover, the modern array was expanding. Eventually, moneys transparently based on credit—whether token coin or paper bank money—would displace gold coin at the center.

But in an echo of the theory that had destabilized commodity money, the English conceptualized money as they had installed it during the Great Recoinage. Gold coin was the standard; copper and silver coins were "subordinate," "subservient to," and "representative of" that coin. Likewise, paper money could operate as "a substitute" for gold coin, which could "be represented by notes, or paper currency." Coin remained "the principal measure of property and instrument of commerce."[81] And coin, according to Locke's project, was a natural product, one that could not legitimately be (re)constituted by political

---

[78] Mayhew, *Sterling*, 107–111. On the Bank of England's monopoly, see pp. 369, 396. Tallies, a significant credit medium at the beginning of the century, had declined in importance by the end.

[79] John Brewer, *The Sinews of Power: War Money and the English State, 1688–1783* (New York: Knopf, 1988), 114–115. The issue of Exchequer bills varied according to need, and it is difficult to know how many circulated at any one time. Nevertheless, the government created an average of £8 million annually in the last quarter of the century, although it may have *circulated* far fewer. In emergencies, that number rose significantly; in 1793 alone, the government injected £2.2 million as currency to avert a run on the banks. See Feavearyear, *The Pound Sterling*, 178. Calculation of outstanding Exchequer bills using the data from Mitchell to sum up the total of Exchequer bills created less those redeemed over the years suggests a circulation in the neighborhood of £10 million in the early 1790s. Mitchell's data may not include bills cancelled, however. See Mitchell, *Abstract of British Historical Statistics*, 404–405.

[80] Feavearyear, *The Pound Sterling*, 168.

[81] Liverpool, *A Treatise on the Coins of the Realm in a Letter to the King*, 160, 166. Liverpool roundly condemned low-quality paper currency, by contrast: Liverpool, *A Treatise on the Coins of the Realm in a Letter to the King*, 219–229.

authorities. That returns us to the question how gold coin and the currencies burgeoning around it actually took effect.

C. Money as a domestic process

The Great Recoinage in the near term, the disappearance of commodity money in the long term, the elevation of creditors' rights over the dangers to local economic exchange—all can be attributed to the radical commitment that the English Parliament made toward the Lockean vision. The ideological consequences of the approach would capture the classical economic commentaries of the next century. But at another level, Parliament never took the liberal argument seriously. Doing so would have meant allowing—or rather requiring—coin to circulate by weight, as if silver naturally composed money. Locke was willing to make that move, if only where clipped coin was concerned. Parliament, by contrast, held fast to the sovereign authority to make money. Public practice animated each of the moneys in the new English architecture, from the silver penny that was on its way out to the expanding array of new moneys that would take its place. Even banks, the modern engines of currency creation, made money through the domestic process authorized and organized at the center.

Units of account: the silver penny, the gold guinea, and the Bank of England pound

Most basically, sovereign authority consistently defined the unit of account, first in terms of silver coin and then gold coin. Despite the arguments for change advanced before the Great Recoinage, Parliament acted true to tradition when it distinguished coin from silver per se. Parliament continued to use the penny and its multiples as the unit of account that it both spent and required in payment, a circumstance no less momentous for all its mundanity.[82] Indeed, the importance of ordaining the official "money" was daily on display during the Great Recoinage. The government had repeatedly to change the pace at which it demonetized old coin; people otherwise panicked as they worried that old coin would no longer travel by count.[83] Parliament also continued to support the provision of coin, subsidizing its minting expenses as the government had since Charles II's time.

To the dismay of officials, the system never reached the equilibrium that should have occurred when the government made coin costless for individuals

---

[82] When the Act for Remedying the Ill State of the Coin provided that the mint should "press into the current money of this realm" silver recovered from old coin, it was maintaining the system of count that had long existed. Coin of certain denominations would be "the lawful silver coin of this kingdom," ensuring its use by the spending departments and its requirement by the Exchequer (7 & 8 Will 3 c 1 ss 1–2 (1695–1696)).

[83] Li, *The Great Recoinage of 1696 to 1699*, 115–119.

Fig. 10.2 Detail of a gold guinea. © Trustees of the British Museum.

to procure. After the Great Recoinage was complete, silver failed to flow robustly to the mint, despite popular commentary and complaint that confirmed the widespread demand for liquidity. Although the account here is tentative, it appears that the obstacle to silver's flow was itself a product of the government's capacious ability to produce money, deployed at cross-purposes to support the gold guinea.[84] The effect would be to displace the silver unit of account and install the gold unit of account we met above.

The story of the transition turns on the guinea, a coin often stamped with a small African elephant and called after the homeland of the gold it contained.[85] See Fig. 10.2. Like the penny, the guinea contained a specified amount of metal, 129.4 grains of gold to be exact. First minted in 1670, the guinea had generally traveled at stable value, floating against the sterling unit of account at a value slightly above 21 shillings.[86] At times in the mid-1690s, however, the guinea reached a market value as high as 30 shillings; the coin was eagerly taken in lieu of clipped and worn silver.[87]

---

[84] The following paragraphs largely follow Albert Feavearyear's analysis. See Feavearyear, *The Pound Sterling*, 154–158.

[85] The guinea first issued in 1663. See Feavearyear, *The Pound Sterling*, 97–98. The denomination was formalized in 1670, according to the mint indentures reprinted by Challis. See C. E. Challis, *A New History of the Royal Mint* (Cambridge: Cambridge University Press, 1992), 745–746 (App. 2).

[86] See Challis, *A New History of the Royal Mint*, 745–746 (App. 2). The guinea traveled at values between 21s. 2d. and 21s. 10d. Horsefield, *Monetary Experiments*; Feavearyear, *The Pound Sterling*, 130–131.

[87] Traditionally, gold coin had been current at a value in the unit of account defined by authorities, who struggled to adjust its official value relative to silver coin so that the ratio of gold to silver value matched the market ratio as closely as possible. In the period immediately before the Great Recoinage, officials had allowed guineas to pass at a much higher value than their mint price; the pattern apparently reflected an escalating demand for gold coin in the face of the ever-weaker silver coinage. Speculators also brought gold to the mint as the guinea's value rose above that of its gold content. See, e.g., Feavearyear, *The Pound Sterling*, 30–31, 130–131.

In 1696, the government had capped the exchange value of the guinea. The action came at the demand of merchants who complained about the artificially high value of the guinea as the Great Recoinage ended and speculative activity by hoarders continued. The government agreed; it also collected less in taxes paid in guineas when guineas were traveling at 30 shillings. The government lowered the ceiling it imposed on the guinea by successive amounts to 22 shillings. While there were ways to trade around the price limit, the market rate of the gold coin started to fall.[88] Gold was, however, still overvalued. In response to an official report, the Exchequer in 1699 began to take the guinea at 21 shillings and 6 pence.[89] In turn, the government had to pay public creditors at the same rate: goldsmiths owed money by the government refused to take guineas rated at 22 shillings, even though the guinea was passing at a higher value in other exchange. It was manifestly unfair, they argued, to pay debts to a party at a rate that counted each of their coins low and receive payment from the same party at a rate that counted each of the coins high. After the discrepancy was corrected, the guinea's value fell to 21 shillings and 6 pence.[90]

At that value, the gold guinea remained overvalued compared to the silver penny. Because the value of the guinea floated, the comparison depended on the domestic purchasing powers of the guinea and silver coin respectively, relative to the value of gold and silver bullion.[91] If the guinea lost shilling value over time, the imbalance in the mint prices would be remedied. Using that logic, Isaac Newton predicted in 1717 that silver would flow out of England, driving the value of silver and silver coin up.[92] Gold would lose relative value and the purchasing power of the guinea would fall in terms of the silver unit of account.

Newton had noted in his report that instead of waiting for silver's scarcity to drive down the guinea's value, the government could simply receive the guinea at

[88] See 7 & 8 Will 3 c 10 s 18 (1696) (26s.); 7 & 8 Will 3 c 19 s 12 (1696) (22s.); Horsefield, *Monetary Experiments*, 80–82; Sargent and Velde, *Big Problem of Small Change*, 296.

[89] As a member of the official review, Locke theorized that the government could take the guinea at a determinate exchange rate to silver coin without displacing the latter as the unit of account, as long as the rate was below the guinea's market value. See John Locke et al., "Report from the Council of Trade to the Lords Justices in Council on the Guinea, 22 Sept. 1698," in *The Great Recoinage of 1696–1699*, ed. Ming-Hsun Li (London: Weidenfeld and Nicolson, 1963); Horsefield, *Monetary Experiments*, 82. The problem that developed was, however, that the public rating effectively propped up the guinea's market value.

[90] When the Treasury enforced its directives by limiting the rate at which tax collectors could take guineas in 1697 and lowering that rate in 1699, the market price of guineas fell to the tax-driven value. See Liverpool, *A Treatise on the Coins of the Realm in a Letter to the King*, 49–53, 68–78; see also Sargent and Velde, *Big Problem of Small Change*, 278, 295–296 (including Fig. 16.3).

[91] See the table of values, including value of guinea-by-piece, recorded by Li. Li, *The Great Recoinage of 1696 to 1699*, 10–11 (Table III). For Newton's analysis demonstrating that the guinea in England was passing a higher value compared to coined silver than its equivalents by weight in most Continental currencies, see Isaac Newton, "On the Value of Silver and Gold in European Currencies and the Consequences on the World-Wide Gold- and Silver-Trade," in *Select Tracts and Documents Illustrative of English Monetary History 1626–1730*, ed. William A. Shaw (London: Wilsons and Millne, 1717; reprint, 1896), available at Editions Marteau, accessed March 12, 2014, <http://www.pierre-marteau.com/editions/1701-25-mint-reports/report-1717-09-25.html>.

[92] See Newton, "On the Value of Gold."

a lower value for taxes. That alternative was more imperative than Newton assumed, however, because the government significantly affected the purchasing power of money when it placed a value on obligations it owed and collected. The government's influence acted both to bring value of a coin down—but also to keep it up. As Albert Feavearyear has argued, the early modern government conducted a "great volume of public financial transactions," enough to direct the market's valuation of coin. Businessmen had adopted the guinea as their coin of choice by the 1690s, given the ravaged state of silver coin. After 1698, people making commercial contracts could write them in guineas with assurance, given the government's policy on receiving them for a stated value at tax time.[93]

In 1717, the Crown took one more step to defend the sterling penny, confirming the guinea "to be current" at 21 shillings. At the same time, the gesture advertised the government's commitment to take the guinea at that rate; the government did not lower the guinea any further.[94] With the gold coin at that rate, silver remained undervalued. It kept flowing out of the country and gold kept flowing in.[95] Over the course of the century, the mint produced less than £5,000 in silver coin per year, with slightly more than that amount again added by infrequent events like the capture of enemy bullion during wartime.[96] In effect,

---

[93] Feavearyear, *The Pound Sterling*, 153–154, 156–157; see also Horsefield, *Monetary Experiments*, 81–83.

[94] Proclamation of December 22, 1717, see *Cobbett's Parliamentary History of England*, vol. VII (London: Printed by T. C. Hansard, 1811), 524–525; see also Liverpool, *A Treatise on the Coins of the Realm in a Letter to the King*, 23, 84, 139. That rate was written into Newton's next indenture, a change that actually increased by a shilling the official rating of the guinea in that document. See the Mint Indenture of May 6, 1718, in Challis, *A New History of the Royal Mint*, 750 (Appendix 2). The government's failure to lower the guinea's value may have been due to the fact that each such modification would increase the number of guineas that the government owed to public creditors, if it paid them in that coin. At the same time, each change drew protests from taxpayers, whose burden in guineas increased. Indeed, the public had apparently resisted the revaluation of the guinea in 1717—speakers in the House of Lords took notice of "the great ferment that was in the nation." *Cobbett's Parliamentary History of England*, 530, 533.

[95] Feavearyear points out that when the guinea became the unit of account, silver coin should have gained purchasing power relative to it, as silver coin became scanter. See Feavearyear, *The Pound Sterling*, 155. However, assuming that the government continued to take silver for taxes at its mint price and not more, silver coin would remain undervalued. Here, see Redish, *Bimetallism*, 162, n. 40 (noting that silver would not be exported from England because of undervaluation if it traveled at a premium). As Redish points out, the refusal of the government to "call up" the value of the silver coin (or raise its unit of account value) was "as much a forerunner of the stability of the pound as the recoinage of 1696" (Redish, *Bimetallism*, 67). It is also clear that good coin was often exported by those knowledgeable, while bad silver coin that cost more to melt and export passed at face value—a de facto premium given its silver content. Redish, *Bimetallism*, 67. Isaac Newton noted that the government took unmilled money at face value in the 1690s, effectively supporting the tale value of underweight coin. Newton, "Amendment of Coins," 218.

[96] There were four years in which such events brought in significant amounts of silver—1701, 1709, 1723, and 1746. Redish, *Bimetallism*, 67. For annual outputs, see Dyer and Gaspar, "Reform, the New Technology and Tower Hill, 1700–1966," 434 (Table 64). A recoinage of gold in 1774 exposed just how drastic the bimetallic flow had been. The Great Recoinage of 1696 had produced almost £9 million in silver against some £4 million in gold. The recoinage in 1774 produced about £800,000 in silver against £18.2 million in gold. Feavearyear, *The Pound Sterling*, 153–154; Mayhew, *Sterling*, 106–107. For English undervaluation of silver to gold compared to their prices in the rest of Europe, see Sargent and Velde, *Big Problem of Small Change*, 296–298; Li, *The Great Recoinage of 1696 to 1699*, 49–50.

the government had displaced the old standard based on the silver penny (since 1601, £5s. 2d. per ounce of silver) with a new one based on the gold guinea at 21 shillings (£3 17s. 10½d. per ounce of gold).[97]

Ironically, then, it was the importance of the count, deployed in a way that favored gold coin, that disrupted England's ability to create a robust supply of silver coin. In turn, Parliament's ability to define the count converted the guinea into the coin anchoring the unit of account. That fixed value became the gold pivot that served as a point of reference for the new rafts of "representative" money, token coins and paper, that soon filled out the denominational hierarchy.

Like the silver penny and the gold guinea, Bank of England notes also depended on the domestic process for their stature as the English unit of account. By 1776, it was abundantly clear to Adam Smith that silver and gold coin were "a very valuable part of the capital of the country which produce[d] nothing to the country." A banking system could provide a currency just as effective, reducing the expense of coin's metal content by substituting paper for "a great part of this gold and silver." As he put it in a metaphor fabulously mixing futuristic and old world elements:

> The gold and silver money which circulates in any country may very properly be compared to a highway, which, while it circulates and carries to market all the grass and corn of the country, produces itself not a single pile of either. The judicious operations of banking, by providing, if I may be allowed so violent a metaphor, a sort of waggon-way through the air, enable the country to convert, as it were, a great part of its highways into good pastures and corn-fields, and thereby to increase very considerably the annual produce of its land and labour.[98]

Smith ultimately argued that coin made of metal was important to maintain but his conclusion was a pragmatic one, based on the notion that commerce and industry were less secure "suspended upon the Daedalian wings of paper money as when they travel about upon the solid ground of gold and silver."[99]

By that time, however, the English were deep into a century of experimentation with paper money and Smith acutely captured the fiat logic that underlay the medium. The sovereign's demand for a certain paper in taxes marked it as a unit that "counted" (literally) as money and furnished currency in the place of gold or silver coin:

---

[97] Feavearyear, *The Pound Sterling*, 154; Sargent and Velde, *Big Problem of Small Change*, 293.

[98] Adam Smith, "Chapter II: On Money Considered as a Particular Branch of the General Stock of the Society, or of the Expense of Maintaining the National Capital," *An Inquiry into the Nature and Causes of the Wealth of Nations* (1937 [1776]). As Smith continued, "Over and above the accidents to which they are exposed from the unskillfulness of the conductors of this paper money, they are liable to several others, from which no prudence or skill of those conductors can guard them." For the developing conviction that the quantity of money should be tied to external trade, see pp. 408–412.

[99] Smith, "On Money."

A prince who should enact that a certain proportion of his taxes should be paid in a paper money of a certain kind might thereby give a certain value to this paper money, even though the term of its final discharge and redemption should depend altogether upon the will of the prince. If the bank which issued this paper was careful to keep the quantity of it always somewhat below what could easily be employed in this manner, the demand for it might be such as to make it even bear a premium, or sell for somewhat more in the market than the quantity of gold or silver currency for which it was issued.[100]

The sound functioning of a fiscal system, not treasure valued in an external market, created money with real purchasing power.

The amount of money spent and taxed by the English government rose enormously over the course of the 18th century. According to John Brewer's calculations, aggregate net revenue grew sixfold between the reign of Charles II and the American Revolution.[101] The ever-increasing flow of taxes went to pay public creditors whose loans fed the state's rising expenditures. Despite some lulls and periods when it was paid down, public debt rose over the course of the 18th century from £16.7 million in 1697 to £50 million in 1720, £76 million in 1748, £133 million in 1763, and £245 million in 1783. As Brewer demonstrates, the rise in taxes and credit were intimately linked. The Financial Revolution, so famed as the genesis of British power during the 18th century, depended critically on the rise in the taxing power of the English government because creditors demanded regular payment.[102]

The insight that taxes secured public credit applies at a yet more basic level, consonant with the way Smith conceptualized the value of money. As the history of the Bank of England reveals, its notes were a form of public debt. They were paper promises of value advanced by the Bank on behalf of the government. The government confirmed their value when it accepted them from holders as valid to extinguish a tax obligation. The entire operation could be carried out without recourse to gold redeemability. Rather, when the government accepted Bank notes, it could return them to the Bank and pay down its debt. Alternatively, it could spend the notes and tax it in again. A domestic political relation made money, more and more obviously. And insofar as it did so reliably, it did so successfully. The Financial Revolution was not just about the credibility of *credit* (although it was), but also about the credibility of *money*, which was likewise based on a promise of future events.

---

[100] Smith, "On Money." For the modern theory relevant here, see pp. 43–50.
[101] Brewer, *Sinews of Power*, 89. By the 1780s, Britons were paying 46 livres to every 17 livres paid by their French counterparts. Another study found the share of British per capita income appropriated in taxes rising over in the century after 1716 from 16 percent to 20 percent (1760) to 23 percent (1783) and finally to 35 percent during the Napoleonic Wars (Brewer, *Sinews of Power*, 89–91).
[102] Brewer, *Sinews of Power*, 89–91, 114.

In fact, the level of Bank money increased with constraint compared to the pace of taxation over the course of the 18th century, reaching almost £5 million by mid-century, almost £10 million after another quarter-century, and finally £15 million by the century's end. That injection of paper probably kept prices in England from dropping severely relative to those in 1688, but deflation did recur regularly, including in the early 1700s, the 1720s, and the 1730s, and by some measures, the 1770s.[103] Money demand would be affected by a number of factors, including levels of economic activity and credit innovations. But given how modestly the English at first enlarged their money stock, the high rates at which they taxed must have generated significant demand for both the paper issued by the Bank and the coin that circulated.

Thus paper money rose on the power of the revenue-raising machinery that the English developed during the 18th century. According to Rondo Cameron, Bank of England notes were receivable for excise and customs taxes during the 18th century. Pressnell confirms that excise collections were channeled through London bankers who submitted them to the Exchequer "probably by Bank of England paper"—that was certainly the cash medium they used most frequently.[104] Land taxes, according to Adam Smith, were ultimately taken in Bank paper. According to Pressnell, receivers in the countryside probably collected those revenues initially in local media, and remitted them to London in Bank of England notes.[105] Those collections—the excise, customs, and land taxes—comprised the main sources of public revenue during the period, providing some 90 percent of it.[106] Improving the revenue-raising machinery was a major governmental goal during the period; the movement from the direct tax on land to indirect taxes (excise and customs) was itself driven by the fact that the latter were easier to collect.[107]

By century's end, the excise had become the most important source of revenue. The reality of its operation configured domestic relations. There were some 1,000 excise officers in 1690; by 1780, almost three times that number. The department was the largest in the government, and it reached deep into the daily life of most citizens. The excise tax applied to sales of malt, beer, hops, soap, salt, candles,

---

[103] For Bank issues, see Cameron, "England, 1750–1844," 42–43. For prices, see Nicholas Mayhew, "Prices in England, 1170–1750," *Past & Present* 219 (2013): 5 (Phelps Brown-Hopkins and Allen indices).

[104] See Cameron, "England, 1750–1844," 12; Pressnell, *Country Banking*, 56, 60, 77 n. 5.

[105] Smith, "On Money" ("[The Bank] . . . advances to government the annual amount of the land and malt taxes, which are frequently not paid up till some years thereafter. In those different operations, its duty to the public may sometimes have obliged it, without any fault of its directors, to overstock the circulation with paper money"). Land taxes were often collected in country bank notes and remitted to London by bill of exchange for Bank notes held there. See Pressnell, *Country Banking*, 56–58, 61–62, 77, n. 5.

[106] For the dominance of these revenue sources, see Brewer, *Sinews of Power*, 94–95. Bank notes were receivable for both ordinary and extraordinary revenues by 1801 and after coin payments by the Bank were restricted. See Walter Boyd, "A Letter to the Right Honourable William Pitt, on the Influence of the Stoppage of Issue in Specie at the Bank of England" (1801), in *Foundations of Monetary Economics*, ed. D. P. O'Brien (London: Pickering & Chatto, 1994), 13, 25–26.

[107] Brewer, *Sinews of Power*, 99–100.

leather, tea, wine, and tobacco; those collecting it visited 33,000 brewers and food sellers, 36,000 establishments licensed to sell alcohol, and 35,500 tea and coffee dealers, along with "several thousand" chandlers and smaller numbers of those printing cloth and making paper. According to the popular view, the Excise was a monster with "ten thousand eyes." Its officers were "watchful to excess."[108]

In fact, enforcement of the excise tax was legendary. The department was organized around a system of internal checks and controls that put to shame the wobblier methods used to collect revenues on land or customs. A highly trained crew of gaugers assessed commercial transactions. Evasions were rigorously punished without benefit of common law protections and conviction rates were high, between 79 and 85 percent in 1789–1790.[109]

Bank of England notes, substantiated by such a fiscal juggernaut, represented value as solid as any lump of gold. If not paid in paper, the tax obligation would be exacted in-kind: the government would take commodities in lieu of currency from those who defaulted. Bank currency sufficed because the government recognized that paper as its own liability, a debt owed since the moment the government had used the note to make purchases. In that sense, paper money, like coin, embodied a material value enhanced by liquidity: individuals could pay their taxes with notes or with a contribution of goods or services that the government would otherwise seize from them. In the latter case, the government surely took enough to cover the costs of converting the contribution to money as necessary to use in the public interest. Money entailed both "real" value, in other words, and a premium that came with its liquidity.

The power of domestic demand and obligation to support money was not inconsistent with the fact that Bank notes carried a promise of redeemability for gold coin, so long as that promise was not routinely cashed out. The system, most obviously as it operated by the late 18th century, could not have functioned in that case. The fact that people refrained from demanding gold coin for Bank notes was not accidental or conventional, but structural: Bank notes held all the advantages of coin as long as the government accepted them interchangeably with it and used a critical number to set off its own debt, rather than redeem them for specie. Notes were also far easier to carry, store, and count, especially at large denominations. Given the institutionalized equivalence of gold coin and paper money in a functioning polity, the value of paper money was not "based on" the value of gold. Rather, the price level depended on the total money stock (including both coin

[108] Brewer, *Sinews of Power*, 102, 113. The quote is from Ezekial Polsted, *The Excise Man, showing the Excellency of his Profession* (London, 1697), 45.

[109] Brewer, *Sinews of Power*, 101–114 Blackstone himself apparently doubted the compatibility of the procedures used to resolve excise cases with "the temper of a free nation." Sir William Blackstone, *Commentaries on the Laws of England*, 9th ed., vol. 1 (London: printed by A. Strahan, 1783), 319.

and Bank notes) that people anticipated, relative to their demand for money, as informed by the tax burden and the desire to make additional (private) transactions.[110]

Multiplying money: commercial banking as a source of liquidity

The plethora of bank currencies that came to multiply the English money supply fit within this domestic architecture. The history of the institutions that issued them has been richly explored elsewhere.[111] The narrower task here is to connect that history to this narrative about money because commercial banks would come to replace the mints as the dominant purveyors of cash to individuals. The banks' role depended on the public unit of account and the peculiarity of the common law, as well as the credit arrangements individuals made between themselves, ultimately cleared through the Bank of England. That architecture created a distinctive currency, one both powerful in its reach and fragile in its engineering.

In early modern England, banking was an amorphous term. Goldsmiths and financiers held money for safekeeping, engaged in money exchange, extended loans to private and sovereign borrowers, and, after the Civil War, began acting as brokers in the public funds.[112] According to Peter Temin and Hans-Joachim Voth, however, early banking was a weak industry: rather than relying on it, most enterprises expanded on the basis of reinvested profits until well into the 18th century.[113] It was only after about 1720 that private banks in London effectively provided resources to individuals for business initiatives. The key was their accumulating experience in fractional reserve lending.[114]

As Temin and Voth note, lending to private individuals financed by deposits was a relatively new idea in the late 17th century, one that took decades to refine. Goldsmiths and others had specialized "almost exclusively" on trade finance or sovereign lending; extending credit outside those tight circles was pioneering economic activity.[115] That estimate comports with other evidence that lending to individuals on a partial reserve—what we might call "retail" lending as opposed to the extension of credit among merchant networks—was not highly developed on the Continent. As Raymond de Roover reconstructed the medieval history of

---

[110] For reasoning by bullionists that arguably comports, see pp. 405–407; see also pp. 43–50.

[111] Peter Temin and Hans-Joachim Voth, *Prometheus Shackled: Goldsmith Banks and England's Financial Revolution after 1700* (Oxford: Oxford University Press, 2012); Michael Collins, *Money and Banking in the UK: A History* (London: Croom-Helm, 1988); Cameron, "England, 1750–1844"; Pressnell, *Country Banking*; Richard David Richards, *The Early History of Banking in England* (London: P. S. King, 1929).

[112] Temin and Voth, *Prometheus Shackled*, 19, 32, 39–40; James Steven Rogers, *The Early History of the Law of Bills and Notes: A Study of the Origins of Anglo-American Commercial Law*, Cambridge Studies in English Legal History Index (Cambridge: Cambridge University Press, 1995), 117–124; Richards, *The Early History of Banking in England*, 36.

[113] Temin and Voth, *Prometheus Shackled*, 35.

[114] Temin and Voth, *Prometheus Shackled*, 43–72.

[115] Temin and Voth, *Prometheus Shackled*, 43.

banking in Bruges, it depended on the transfer of deposit accounts, a technique that allowed fractional reserve lending but limited its reach. The Bank of Amsterdam, in many ways the successor to the Flemish model, provided credit by clearing the accounts of merchants with mutual indebtedness rather than writing loans on consolidated deposits.[116]

Temin and Voth approach the development of fractional reserve banking as a financial matter—the evolution of effective intermediation.[117] And, indeed it was. The process brought the capital of savers to the enterprise of entrepreneurs. But fractional reserve banking as it emerged in England was also and emphatically a monetary matter—the innovation of "maturity transformation" that would enlarge the money supply. As textbooks on the subject later elaborated, banks engineered a mechanism to fund their lending that expanded the currency denominated in the public unit of account available for use. Banks operated by borrowing money on a short-term basis that was effectively rolled over continuously, allowing them to advance money over a longer term to new and existing customers. Neither aspect can be taken for granted.

First, London bankers loaned "long" in the form of cash. That was obviously the case when they made gold coin available to borrowers for a length of time. Bank of England notes were a currency almost as good. As we have seen, the government fairly early accepted Bank notes for public obligations. Bank currency could easily be handed on: according to the Bank's authorizing legislation, its bills were assignable by endorsement. While still subject to encashment, they obligated the Bank directly; it was liable to redeem its paper issues to the new holder.[118] By the mid-18th century, Lord Mansfield confirmed, in a case involving a Bank of England note, that "bank notes...are as much money, as guineas themselves are; or any other current coin, that is used in common payments, as money or cash."[119] Bankers were, in other words, providing money, not only credit, when they lent to borrowers in coin or Bank notes.

As private banking developed, the capacity of fractional reserve banking to create money expanded. When the country bankers issued local notes and the joint-stock bankers created checkable deposits, they were conveying claims to a

---

[116] Raymond De Roover, *Business, Banking, and Economic Thought in Late Medieval and Early Modern Europe* (Chicago: University of Chicago Press, 1974), 229–236, 345–354; see also Jongchul Kim, "How Modern Banking Originated: The London Goldsmith-bankers' Institutionalisation of Trust," *Business History* 53, no. 6 (2011): 939–940, 954, 958, n. 31.

[117] Temin and Voth, *Prometheus Shackled*, 33–34, 42–43.

[118] For assignability of bills, see Bank of England Act 1694 (5 & 6 W & M c 20 s 28), and generally pp. 308–309. By 1698, Bank notes that changed hands without endorsement were likely considered to convey ready cash, like the bill of exchange that changed hands without endorsement and therefore by "sale" in a case determined that year. See *Bank of England v Newman* (1698) 12 Mod 241; 88 ER 1290; see also Rogers, *Law of Bills and Notes*, 146–147. On the inability of goldsmith-bankers to compete with the Bank of England on note issue, see pp. 321, 378–380; see also Temin and Voth, *Prometheus Shackled*, 32.

[119] *Miller v Race* (1758) 1 Burr 452; 457, 97 ER 398, 401; see also pp. 311–317. For comparisons to other transferable instruments, see Kim, "How Modern Banking Originated," 942–945; Rogers, *Law of Bills and Notes*, 97–100; Pressnell, *Country Banking*, 89–90, 170–171.

reserve that functioned as cash. Other bankers did the same, creating a set of reciprocal promises to the money on reserve. Those promises in local notes or deposits were "cashed" at particular banks. The banks in turn cleared the claims each held against the claims each owed. Rather than requiring cash to fund each claim, the system could operate soundly as long as each banker had enough reserve to pay off any balance owing from his bank.[120] The reciprocity both economized on the cash that had to change hands—money could exist as an obligation that would be recognized at a particular time—and depended ultimately on cash as the eventual means of settlement.

Second, London bankers borrowed "short" in the form of deposits. The term "borrowed" is a legal one with significant consequence. Bankers acquired funds from depositors and claimed to have those funds available for them, while at the same time extending cash or a claim to cash to new clients. As Jongchul Kim points out, descriptions of banking often assume without reflection that bankers naturally had the capacity to convey funds or claims to the funds they held to new borrowers.[121] But if English bankers had been considered persons charged with safeguarding the specific property of their depositors, their action extending cash to others would have been an illegal or fraudulent act.[122] Cash was, after all, the sovereign's unit of account and, as the medieval experience made clear, a matter of intense public concern. Successful administrations continuously policed representations of money by prosecuting counterfeiters, patrolling the way people settled monetary debts, and by other means. The legality of lending on less than a 100 percent reserve was likewise contested. On the Continent, the practice emerged in certain places and was restricted in others, as the tolerance of its risks varied.[123] More clearly, in England from sometime in the 17th century, bankers were authorized to convey depositors' funds or claims to the funds because they were considered the bankers' own.

The common law category of debt appears to have produced the legal permission that allowed bankers to use or promise that money, money that otherwise appeared to belong to depositors. Recall that the common law action for money due under certain conditions ("debt") was distinguished early on from the action for all other articles ("detinue"), including non-fungibles like a horse or

---

[120] See pp. 378–380, 394–397. Insofar as the London bankers earlier used book accounts or running accounts to promise cash to borrowers, their practice would have anticipated the creation of checkable deposits. Those book or running accounts may not, however, have been accepted as widely as checkable deposits, a practice that effectively "retailed" accessibility to cash.

[121] Kim, "How Modern Banking Originated," 948.

[122] As Benjamin Geva argues, the remedy available against a bailee (someone receiving money to be used or kept for another) who had failed in his duty required sorting out which common law writ—detinue, debt, or account—applied. See Benjamin Geva, *Bank Collections and Payment Transactions: Comparative Study of Legal Aspects* (Oxford: Oxford University Press, 2001), 76–77.

[123] See, e.g., De Roover, *Money, Banking and Credit in Medieval Bruges*, 293–354; Martijn Konings, *Development of American Finance* (Cambridge: Cambridge University Press, 2011), 18; Kim, "How Modern Banking Originated," 946–947.

a plow but even including other fungibles like wheat. Common law debt, with its emphasis on money as a special entity, effectively set money as the unit of account apart from the silver or gold it contained. If money *was* the unit of account, then payment according to the official unit of account ruled: current coin sufficed to pay off a debt, regardless whether the sovereign had changed the intrinsic value of a coin.[124] The action of debt made money distinctive as a form of payment or matter claimed.

The power of that identification may have invited the courts to conclude, conversely, that where money was the matter claimed, the action should be debt. Beginning in the late 14th century, courts allowed parties suing to recover money "bailed" or left with another for a particular purpose to use the action of debt. In a late 16th century case, a plaintiff who had delivered money to another "to be redelivered" on demand sued when the person holding the money refused. The judges rejected the argument that the plaintiff should have used the equitable action of "account," an action designed to confirm the correct use of funds in trust. The court held instead that an action for debt was appropriate because delivery of money that "cannot be known" had "altered" the property. (Money that "cannot be known" was money that was not "earmarked," for example by being in a sealed bag.) The defendant presumably *owned* the funds after the delivery, although he *owed* the plaintiff the same amount of money on demand.[125]

A permissive attitude towards bankers' use of funds likely gained strength from other circumstances as well. R. D. Richards suggests that the English practice of leaving funds on deposit became established just before or during the Civil War of the mid-17th century, as the insecurity engendered by the conflict pressed people to safeguard their wealth. At the same time, the goldsmith-bankers gained from financial activity delegated to administrative units outside the Exchequer by Parliament and by the opportunities for lending to the government during the first Dutch War (1651-1654).[126] In his view, most goldsmith-bankers remained custodians of the money they held until early years of the Restoration, when they began to use the funds, setting aside what they anticipated their depositors would demand.[127] Alternatively, the English movement to give bankers latitude with

---

[124] See pp. 83–97, 133–138. For the conditions that limited the obligation of debt in the early common law, see Geva, *Bank Collections*, 76–77.

[125] *Bretton v Barnet* (1598) Owen 86; 74 ER 918; see also *Core's Case* (1537) 73 ER 42. For the 14th century developments, see Geva, *Bank Collections*, 76–77, 79–80. As Geva points out, the fungibility of money may justify the mixing of moneys together without "necessarily explain[ing]" a keeper's right to use the money. Geva, *Bank Collections*, 67, 81. At the same time, the ability to mix moneys was a precondition to a banker's use of them.

[126] See Richards, *The Early History of Banking in England*, 35–38.

[127] See Richards, *The Early History of Banking in England*, 223–225; see also North, *Discourses Upon Trade*, 20. In Richard's view, time demand notes allowed invited bankers to use funds held before payment was due, as did "running cash notes." Richards assumes an evolution of notes' currency over the period. Richards, *The Early History of Banking in England*, 226–230.

customers' funds may have drawn from the spirit if not the letter of trust doctrine.[128]

The practicalities of the arrangement seem to have been the strongest argument for Lord Mansfield, an eminent jurist renowned for his reforming approach to commercial law. In a mid-18th century case involving the theft of Bank of England note from the mail, the judge took pains to approve the practice of fractional reserve banking. In an aside gratuitous to the main issue, Mansfield emphasized the bankers' ability to use bank notes they held. Rejecting the argument that bank notes were less fungible than cash, he observed that "this reasoning would prove (if it was true . . .) that if a man paid to a goldsmith 500l. in bank notes, the goldsmith could never pay them away."[129] Implicitly, but obviously in Mansfield's world, the opposite was the case.

By the early 19th century, a series of cases confirmed that funds transferred to a banker became his own; they were not the property of the depositor, although that party had the right to the same amount of money on demand. As the court put it in *Carr v Carr*, "money had no ear-mark . . . when money is paid into a banker's, he always opens a debtor and creditor account with the payor. The banker employs the money himself, and is liable merely to answer the drafts of his customer to that amount."[130] The argument evoked the traditional line distinguishing debt from detinue, suggesting the power of common law categories—in particular, the old common law category of debt—to configure argument.[131] By the mid-19th century, it was abundantly clear that money left with a bank became owned by the banker and was his to use, rather than remaining the possession of the depositor:

> Money, when paid into a bank, ceases altogether to be the money of the principal; it is then the money of the banker, who is bound to return an equivalent by paying a

---

[128] For the trust argument, see Kim, "How Modern Banking Originated." While banking was never categorized as a trust per se, that theory developed contemporaneously and may have suggested that money held for a depositor, analogous to a beneficiary, could be used by the banker, analogous to a trustee. Bankruptcy law may also have influenced the evolving doctrine.

[129] *Miller v Race* (1758) 1 Burr 452, 459; 97 ER 398, 402.

[130] See *Carr v Carr* (1811) 1 Mer 625; 35 ER 799, 800; see also *Sims v Bond* (1833) 5 B & AD 389; 110 ER 834 ("Sums which are paid to the credit of a customer with a banker, though usually called deposits, are, in truth, loans by the customer to the banker" (citing *Devaynes v Noble* (1816) 1 Mer 529, 568; *Carr v Carr* (1811) 1 Mer 625, 625). I am indebted to Zach Howe for his analysis of the cases.

[131] Facing the issue in a related case whether liability for money owed from a depositor's current account could be allocated to different partners of a banking house, the judge determined that "all the sums paid in form one blended fund, the parts of which have no longer any distinct existence:" *Devaynes v Noble* (1816) 1 Mer 529, 608; 35 ER 767, 793. The reasoning arguably carries forward an approach that depends on the indistinguishable nature of the unit of account. Cf. Geva, *Bank Collections*, 118–122. In a series of cases involving theft of Bank notes, Exchequer bills, and other paper forms in the late 17th and 18th centuries, the English courts debated whether those forms should be treated as less fungible than coin, given the presence of identifying numbers and marks on paper issues. Their concern went, however, to the liability of a bank to pay a stolen note, not to the question whether the bank had the power to issue notes on its own account. In any case, Lord Mansfield authoritatively identified Bank of England notes with cash in *Miller v Race* (1758) 1 Burr 452, 457; 97 ER 398, 401.

similar sum to that deposited with him when he is asked for it. The money paid into the banker's, is money known by the principal to be placed there for the purpose of being under the control of the banker; it is then the banker's money; he is known to deal with it as his own; he makes what profit he can, which profit he retains to himself.[132]

The legal permission to extend credit on a fractional reserve allowed the London bankers to expand the money supply. According to a recent study, goldsmith-bankers first offered money against jewelry, using their comparative advantage to assess the silver, gold, and diamonds that customers brought in and catering to the significant demand for their funds as long as there was "solid collateral." After experimenting with a range of borrowers in the late 17th century, goldsmith-bankers retreated to a more elite clientele for much of the 18th century. While their caution, as well as the relatively small number of London banking firms, would keep their effect on the money supply modest, the structure of their operations multiplied the number of pounds in use.[133]

Merchant bankers in the City of London operated more dynamically, support-ing traders and connecting them with producers in the countryside. These banks lent cash on short-term commercial paper; the bill of exchange was their instru-ment of choice. Bills of exchange had functioned throughout the medieval period as a method of moving funds between traders in different lands. Their design allowed a party with distant funds who wanted money near at hand to swap his distant funds with another who had money near at hand but wanted it in the distant site.[134] The swap of funds could also be used to extend credit or to speculate on changes of rates in foreign exchange.[135] By the mid-17th century,

---

[132] *Foley v Hill* (1848) 2 HL 28, 38–39; 9 ER 1002, 1006–1007.

[133] The bankers were responding to a variety of circumstances, including the caps imposed by remaining restrictions on usury and unlimited liability for default. They offered mortgages and invested in government securities. See Temin and Voth, *Prometheus Shackled*, 46–94, 125–147; see also Pressnell, *Country Banking*, 265. For a portrait of the vigorous activity of late 17th century goldsmith-bankers, see Richards, *The Early History of Banking in England*, 23–64. On unlimited liability, see Temin and Voth, *Prometheus Shackled*, 71. There were two dozen bankers in the West End in 1700 and not an enormous number more in 1770. Temin and Voth, *Prometheus Shackled*, 40.

[134] As James Rogers explains, the bill of exchange developed with the rise of trade that produced profits for merchants in remote places. For example, an English wool exporter might accumulate money in Flanders. Once he began to work with a regular representative or agent in Flanders, he could make deals with another merchant, e.g. a Flemish lace dealer, who was accumulating profits in London. The wool dealer with funds afar (the "drawer") wrote a bill directing his agent in Flanders to pay his funds there to the lace dealer or his agent. The wool dealer then gave the bill to a lace dealer (the "receiver" or "drawee") in return for payment of money in London. The lace dealer sent the bill to his agent, who cashed it with the drawer's agent for money in the distant location. See Rogers, *Law of Bills and Notes*, 94–100.

[135] The drawee of a bill extended credit insofar as he gave cash immediately to a local drawer, but only cashed the bill, a kind of IOU, later; bills were generally written as time-dated instruments payable at a date in the future. Rogers, *Law of Bills and Notes*, 115. Credit could also flow from the drawer of a bill, if he gave the bill on credit and received payment for it later. Rogers, *Law of Bills and Notes*, 114–115. Parties to a bill speculated on shifting values of foreign exchange when they fixed the amounts of the swap; a party would profit if the currency he offered at a particular rate lost value against the sum in the currency he gained. See Rogers, *Law of Bills and Notes*, 95–96.

the bill of exchange had acquired a domestic presence in England. Farmers or producers in the provinces who accumulated funds in London wrote "inland bills" on those funds. The bills could be used to move money in the traditional way, when the farmer sold a bill locally for funds he directed to be paid in London to the buyer of the bill. By the 18th century, bills were also simply written and transferred for value to a party "or bearer" on the promise of funds in London. Endorsing the bill, the party receiving it could pass it on, also by endorsement, to another party in the provinces. Bills of exchange sometimes carried long lists of endorsements, a testament to their success in circulating.[136]

Bills of exchange written to "bearer" provided an ideal instrument against which London bankers could lend cash. In return for an amount of money less than face value, bankers acquired bills and collected the payment they produced when they matured. The difference between the amount advanced by the bankers and the face value of bills represented the "discount," effectively an interest charge on the amount advanced. Bankers also began to offer a reciprocal service: for a fee, they "accepted" bills, guaranteeing their payment on behalf of a factor or on the basis of funds held by the bank. Bills might be accepted before they were due, increasing their value as credit instruments that could circulate and transmit value themselves.[137]

The industry of discounting and accepting bills created a deepening market for money in London. Banks coordinated the money they harvested from discounted bills at maturity with the money they owed on bills they accepted. In the 19th century, bill brokers would open even more specialized businesses making a profit on that practice. The English economy functioned on the credit provided; merchants bought supplies on the basis of bills, and accepted bills in promise of payment of their own goods. Bills circulated before and after acceptance, providing additional liquidity.

The edifice of credit was impressive on its own terms, as a number of historians emphasize.[138] But that edifice depended, at its base, on the provision of cash. The merchant banks and bill brokers survived insofar as they produced cash when it was needed, both to pay off bills when they matured and to buy (or "discount") other bills that would pay them in turn.[139] Like their more genteel cousins in the West End, the merchant banks and brokers were engaged in creating money on the basis of a fractional reserve: they rolled over incoming funds from the maturing bills, as well as deposits from savers and factors, and lent out money in discounts and early acceptances.

---

[136] Rogers, *Law of Bills and Notes*, 99, 111–112; Pressnell, *Country Banking*, 170–171.
[137] Rogers, *Law of Bills and Notes*, 111–114; Perry Mehrling, *The New Lombard Street: How the Fed Became the Dealer of Last Resort* (Princeton, NJ: Princeton University Press, 2011), 18–21.
[138] See, e.g., Rogers, *Law of Bills and Notes*, 124.
[139] Mehrling, *New Lombard Street*, 18–21.

Fig. 10.3 One pound bank note issued by the Vale of Aylesbury Bank in 1810. © Trustees of the British Museum.

The London bankers catered to a clientele that formed the final and outer tier to England's monetary architecture. "The business of the banker in London," testified one of them in the early 19th century, "is to pay the notes of the country banker for whom he is agent, to accept his drafts, and pay them, to execute his stock orders, and do any other business that he may wish to have done in London in the way of money transactions."[140] The country banks by their activities supplemented the money supply produced at the center; they created the currency that dominated outside of London.

The country banks ascended in the latter part of the 18th century. The London bankers had given up writing their own notes much earlier, after the Bank of England had gained a monopoly over note issue as a joint-stock company in 1708. (Until 1826, note-issuing banks could contain no more than six partners.)[141] As silver coin declined, however, the great demand for currency rose in the provinces. Bankers there found that issuing local notes saved them the significant expense of procuring Bank of England notes and gold coin to circulate. See Fig. 10.3. It was "the grand source of profit," as one treatise put it; another local banker estimated note issue as "at least one-half" of his living.[142] Lastly, note issue represented stature, a claim of wealth and respectability; it lent a "sort of éclat to the establishment," claimed an enterprising member of the profession.[143]

---

[140] Pressnell, *Country Banking*, 80 (quoting Loyd's testimony to the House of Commons in 1819). Lewis Loyd was a partner in both Manchester and London: Pressnell, *Country Banking*, 106, 109, 301.

[141] 7 Ann c 30 s 66 (1708); Pressnell, *Country Banking*, 4–6; see also Temin and Voth, *Prometheus Shackled*, 40–41 (documenting low survival rate for late-17th century goldsmith banks).

[142] Pressnell, *Country Banking*, 157.   [143] Pressnell, *Country Banking*, 157.

Like their contemporary counterparts in London, country banks lent on the basis of bills of exchange. They too could arrange to dispense cash and take it in, advancing cash on bills by discount while taking in cash from maturing bills.[144] Their ability to issue notes, however, set them apart in an important way. Country bankers were not limited in the cash they could dispense by their holdings of Bank of England notes. Assuming sound lending practices, they were constrained instead by their borrowers' prospects for the future productivity, along with precautions against strong demand for conversion of their notes into guineas or Bank of England notes. Country bankers could issue local notes on a bill drawn by a producer, who would pay wages in the local notes and promise a sum of Bank of England notes in London. The banker could take in local notes in turn, selling a bill drawn on London to a tax receiver or someone else who needed Bank funds there. Country banks also cleared note issues locally, reciprocally recognizing each others' issues and extending their shared ability to support currencies that circulated regionally. In addition, country notes were taken by shopkeepers and other locals, who returned them to pay off debts to the local bankers, often wholesalers who supplied the retail sellers.[145]

The English system of money-making thus developed "as a three-tiered structure." The Bank of England anchored the system, producing Bank notes and holding most of the gold reserve. The London money market operated within the Bank's ambit; London banks and bill brokers used Bank of England paper for large payments and cleared their balances in that medium. In turn, the country banks depended on the London money market. They kept their reserves there and depended on that market for credit when necessary. As L. S. Pressnell put it, when money was scarce, "country banks in general turned to London, much as London firms turned to the Bank of England, as lender of last resort."[146]

The banking system in modern England followed from that basic design. In the second half of the 19th century, the joint-stock banks would gradually displace the country banks. Legal restrictions, imposed as evidence accumulated that the note-issuing practice of those older banks rendered the money supply more

[144] Pressnell, *Country Banking*, 171–179. Variations on the theme often suggested themselves. Bankers could, e.g., allow borrowers to take on credit bills drawn on the bankers' own accounts in London. The modern practice of checkable deposits was not common until sometime near the mid-19th century. Pressnell, *Country Banking*, 162–170.

[145] Pressnell, *Country Banking*, 14–36, 126–135. As wholesalers and industrialists, early country bankers also often issued notes directly to people for pay. They then took them back from cooperating shops which had accepted them as payment. As for revenues, land and stamp taxes were accepted in local notes by receivers who remitted them to London by buying bills of exchange maturing there; payment to the Exchequer was likely made in Bank of England notes. Tax receivers themselves often went into banking, given the large balances of funds they carried. See Pressnell, *Country Banking*, 56–74.

[146] Pressnell, *Country Banking*, 75–76, 195–197; see also Pressnell, *Country Banking*, 210–212, 217–224; Rogers, *Law of Bills and Notes*, 121. For the importance of the country's cash needs to the London banks, see Pressnell, *Country Banking*, 79–80. Against their issues, country bankers kept cash reserves made up of both local notes and coin and Bank notes; the proportion of each varied according to conditions, as did the total reserve that bankers maintained. Pressnell, *Country Banking*, 193–200.

volatile, had weakened them.[147] In 1833, joint-stock banks were authorized to operate in London and beyond by the Bank Charter Act, as long as they did not issue notes.[148] Joint-stock banks would flourish—in part because the reform of money creation attempted by the Act was notoriously short-lived. As the joint-stock banks soon learned, checkable deposits functioned analogously to private notes to extend currency in the public unit of account. Creating checkable deposits—accounts on which borrowers could draw on demand—effectively reproduced the activity of making money by issuing local notes that country banks had pioneered.[149] Commercial banking in England thus matured on the infrastructure constructed during the 18th century.

Commercial banking would develop to dominate modern money creation: it was the new method of putting cash up for sale to individuals. Under the medieval system, the public mints made coin available for people to buy, beyond that needed for the government's fiscal needs. In exchange for silver sufficient to supply the content for coin and cover the charge for its manufacture, the mint returned a certain number of pennies that carried the quality of cash. The government supported the system because it produced tokens identified as sufficient to meet the tax obligation and, more broadly, expanded the medium enough to service increasing economic exchange. Likewise, the modern system allowed people to buy cash. In exchange for a promise of future productivity that would yield money in the future, secured by collateral if required, commercial bankers issued notes denominated in the public unit of account. Assuming no default, those notes were cancelled when the borrowers repaid the advance, including interest.[150] The government supported the system insofar as it allowed these private promises, issued and repaid, to act as money and to clear through the Bank of England.

In both cases, medieval free minting and modern commercial banking, people were converting a resource—silver or future productivity—into a unit that could be used in the present as cash. In that sense, each system made money available to people at a price—whether the mint charge or the interest advanced to the bank. Modern theories of endogenous credit creation capture the logic of commercial banking in ways that resemble, to a significant extent, the theory of free minting. According to that logic, credit creation expands the money supply available to meet the demand for money generated by new economic activity. Although

---

[147] For the regulatory initiatives that disempowered the country banks, see Pressnell, *Country Banking*, 158–159.

[148] 3 & 4 Will 4 c 98 (1833). The Act responded in part to claims that the terms of the Bank of England's charter should be read to allow joint-stock banks to operate as long as they did not issue notes. See Frame, "Country Rag Merchants," 215–278.

[149] For the structural analogy between bank notes and deposits in modern credit theory, see Marc Lavoie, *Post-Keynesian Economics: New Foundations* (Cheltenham: Edward Elgar, 2014).

[150] The borrower could also repay in gold coin; that coin would redeem any notes outstanding.

inflation may occur because of the complex mix of factors that affect prices (particularly wages), including distributional conflicts and resources scarcities, the supply of money should remain linked to demand.[151]

If there were great similarities between free minting and commercial bank lending, there were also enormous differences. Perhaps the most obvious was the dynamism of modern money-making. If money could be made on a promise of future productivity (and collateral if required), then anyone with that promise— as opposed to an amount of silver or gold—could obtain money. With the development of deposit banking in the middle third of the 19th century (1831–1865), the money supply corrected for inflation in Britain expanded almost fivefold.[152] Walter Bagehot, speaking in the salad days of commercial banking, captured the spirit of the new system perfectly. "We have entirely lost the idea," he wrote, "that any undertaking likely to pay, and seen to be likely, can perish for want of money; yet no idea was more familiar to our ancestors, or is more common now in most countries."[153]

The corollary of money's new accessibility was its fragility. Silver coin capitalized a resource that held value based on past earnings and was immediately accessible. By contrast, modern bank currencies capitalized a resource, future productivity, that depended on time—along with the use of cash in the interim— to come to fruition. The system worked beautifully as long as the banks could roll over their short-term liabilities (deposits or bank notes). But it ran into trouble if those holding such promises wanted to cash them in. A borrower might transfer a country bank note or, later, write a check, to someone who wanted a gold guinea or Bank of England note immediately. The bank issuing the commercial currency would cash it out of the liquid balances it held. But if many people demanded the public unit of account all at once, the commercial bank would quickly exhaust its

---

[151] See Lavoie, *Post-Keynesian Economics: New Foundations*, Chapter 4. Older "real bills" theories abstracted the argument more simply, assuming that supply would never exceed demand for money. See, e.g., Pressnell, *Country Banking*, 216; Perry Mehrling, "Retrospectives: Economists and the Fed: Beginnings," *Journal of Economic Perspectives* (2002). Indeed, the system is mildly deflationary, all things equal, insofar as interest due would mean that a borrower would owe slightly more than he or she borrowed.

[152] The calculation is based on Rondo Cameron's figure for money supply in England and Wales (1831, £99 million, 1865, £367 million), deflated according to the price index offered by Hills, Thomas, and Dimsdale (Sally Hills, Ryland Thomas, and Nicholas Dimsdale, "The UK Recession in Context—What Do Three Centuries of Data Tell Us?," *Bank of England Quarterly* Q4 (2010)) to produce a 4.5-fold increase. By 1885, according to Cameron's figures (£594 million), the money supply was more than 7.6 times that of 1831. Per capita, real balances remained approximately constant from 1831 to 1865, assuming the population figures in Mitchell, *Abstract of British Historical Statistics*, 5–6. In nominal terms, the increase is even more striking. From 1800 to 1913, the money stock in Britain (England and Wales) would expand from £50 million to £1,264.2 million, a 2,528 percent increase. See Samuel Knafo, "The Gold Standard and the Origins of the Modern International System," *Review of International Political Economy* 13, no. 1 (2006): 84. The nominal increase should not be dismissed—it would shift the denominational reach of the currency in ways that alleviated the difficulty of small purchases. See pp. 192–200.

[153] Walter Bagehot, *Lombard Street: A Description of the Money Market* (New York: John Wiley, 1999, first published 1873), 7.

reserves. Bank runs began occurring in the third quarter of the 18th century, just as country banking became established.[154]

Bank runs could occur even if the banks had been lending soundly and none of their borrowers were headed for default. It was the very logic of the system to make money available on a promise and assume that most people would be content with that representation, rather than demanding the official unit of account from the commercial banking system. If people demanded cash at the same time, even banks with assets that over time would match their liabilities, were in trouble. The demand by those holding commercial bank currencies (local notes or, later, deposits) could only be met by handing them guineas or Bank of England notes, a far smaller proportion of the effective money stock.

That reality turned the banks towards the Bank of England at times of crisis; the system would collapse inward, retrenching to depend on public help. As the government's bank, the Bank was distinct from the commercial banking system. Outside of its small private practice, its notes issued to the government in return for public debt. The future revenue of the nation, not the predicted profits of a private borrower, comprised the resource dedicated to pay off Bank notes. That difference allowed the Bank to act as lender of last resort, just as it would empower later central banks in the same capacity.

Barring support from the Bank of England, the effort by banks in crisis to get cash would have disastrous consequences. Commercial bank currencies supported an economy built on credit flows—entrepreneurs depended on wholesalers who depended on producers. All of them borrowed to make their outlays and counted on reaping profits to meet their payment obligations. A banking crisis threw a wrench into the interlocking promises and pay-offs of the business world. As banks called in loans, those parties failed to make deliveries to others who failed to meet their commitments in turn. Bagehot famously described the cascade of failures that followed; his account would be borne out again and again.[155]

Bagehot made another observation about the character of commercial bank currency that would turn out to be prescient. While bankers could practice sound lending and remain perfectly solvent, the nature of bank currency invited them to make riskier loans. After all, when times were good, promises of future productivity seemed particularly persuasive. Bankers looked for loans to fund, and their competition drove them to expand the opportunities they offered borrowers. As

---

[154] Carmen Reinhart and Kenneth Rogoff, *This Time Is Different: Eight Centuries of Financial Folly* (Princeton, NJ: Princeton University Press, 2009), 141–173. Busts occurred in 1763, 1772, 1778, 1783, 1793, and 1797. The initial attempts to prevent them relied on policing fragile issuers and prohibiting low-denomination notes as paper more likely to be held by less sophisticated individuals. Mayhew, *Sterling*, 126–131; Feavearyear, *The Pound Sterling*, 173–175.

[155] Bagehot, *Lombard Street: A Description of the Money Market*, 122–125; see also Mehrling, *New Lombard Street*, 19–21; Roy Kreitner, "When Banks Fail," *Common-Place* 10, no. 3 (2010). The presence of collateral did not necessarily solve the problem. Collateral needed to be sold to produce money. That strategy might fail if, as many people scrambled to sell collateral, the market for it collapsed.

bankers extended more tenuous loans, the prospects for defaults that under-mined the credibility of the banking system rose. In addition, as cash flowed into the economy, it became more likely that the amount of money circulating would exceed the demand for it. Prices would begin to rise. Ironically, that would only stimulate more lending—rising prices meant that estimates of future productivity could be raised as well and the value of the collateral securing bank loans appeared to increase. In other words, the way commercial banks "made money" fueled credit bubbles—here, Bagehot famously prescribed the Bank's duty to raise interest rates, dampening economic activity and drawing in bullion from abroad.[156] For once a bubble inflated, a bust was bound to follow. The spiral down, driven by runs on the banking system and the collapse of the currencies they supplied, would be just as dramatic as the credit boom that preceded it.[157]

The complexity of the modern system was evident as soon as its elements came together. The 18th century ended with a bank run, an ironic counterpoint to the Great Recoinage that began the era with the reification of money's value. In 1797, the Bank of England stopped redeeming its notes. It acted in concert with the government and, indeed, as ordered by it. The Bank's reserve had dropped in previous years, drained by public borrowing to finance the war against France and by the efforts of the country banks to build up their own reserves by drawing on money in London. In the spring of 1797, rumors of invasion triggered a run on banks in several regions; contagion threatened the Bank itself. And so, on a Sunday in late February, by a public Order in Council, the pound sterling became an inconvertible paper currency.

Within a week, Parliament had authorized the issue of Bank notes down to £1 pound, making it a currency that reached much smaller exchange. Within a month, Parliament had begun debate on legislation confirming the Order in Council; it was passed before the spring was out. The Act was periodically extended until the end of hostilities with the French. In 1797, the cartoonist James Gillray produced a picture of Pitt as a Midas in reverse: rather than turning all into gold, Pitt here turned all gold into paper. The Restriction period would last more than two decades, through the Napoleonic Wars and until a difficult transition back to convertibility in 1821.[158] See Fig. 10.4.

---

[156] Bagehot, *Lombard Street: A Description of the Money Market*, 46–62.

[157] Bagehot, *Lombard Street: A Description of the Money Market*, 116–117, 137–156. The rich literature here includes R. G. Hawtrey, *Currency and Credit*, 3rd ed. (London: Longmans Green, 1930); Hyman P. Minsky, "The Financial Instability Hypothesis," *Working Paper* No. 74 (May 1992); Hyman P. Minsky, "Capitalist Financial Processes and the Instability of Capitalism," *Journal of Economic Issues* 14, no. 2 (1980); Mehrling, *New Lombard Street*; Steve Keen, *Debunking Economics*, Revised & Expanded ed. (London: Zed Books, 2011); Morgan Ricks, "Regulating Money Creation after the Crisis," *Harvard Business Law Review* 1 (2011).

[158] For the authorization of small Bank notes, see 37 Geo 3 c 28 (1797). For the Restriction Act, see 37 Geo 3 c 45 (1797), which provided that Bank notes would be deemed "payments in cash if made and accepted as such." Pitt was apparently not sufficiently secure politically to make the inconvertible notes legal tender. Feavearyear, *The Pound Sterling*, 179–224. That occurred in 51 Geo 3 c 127 (1811); 52 Geo 3 c 50 (1812). For the return to convertibility, see 1 and 2 Geo IV, c 26. The Gillray reference is thanks to Nicolas Mayhew. Mayhew, *Sterling*, 137.

Fig. 10.4 James Gillray, *MIDAS, Transmuting all into Gold [Gold crossed out] PAPER.* Published by Hannah Humphrey: March 9, 1797. © National Portrait Gallery, London.

The era of inconvertibility turned a generation raised to sanctify gold into the reluctant pioneers of a medium that was undeniably fiat. Those developments were linked. The British had, over the course of the 18th century, destroyed the country's traditional monetary system. Their insistence that "money" be defined as a finite amount of metal left them unable to recalibrate the hierarchy of full-weight silver and gold denominations sufficiently to maintain them in circulation. Instead, the amount of gold represented by the guinea came to establish a reference point for the unit of account. That mint weight became the golden promise made on the face of Bank notes and public bonds, country bank notes and bills of exchange. Over the course of the 19th century, those paper media branched through the political economy, intimately structuring exchange after exchange. It may be that the sheer volume of cash available to the British jump-started economic dynamism more effectively than any other development.

At the same time, the golden promise periodically invited action that led the entire edifice to collapse. When it did, it revealed the fiscal engineering that, all along, rendered the machinery viable. The government with its collective capacity stood at the center of the British monetary system. That public actor would rescue and reset that system again and again. Each time, it acted in compliance with the constitutional compromise worked out over the century: money might be a public practice, but it should be managed as if private incentives alone "made money."

11

Epilogue to the 18th century
The Gold Standard in an era of inconvertibility

The era of inconvertibility stripped the promise of gold coin out of British money, leaving bank currency to circulate on the strength of demand for it as England's medium and mode of payment. The situation was anomalous for a people committed to a specie standard, and it pushed observers to evangelize their approach to money. Those whose ideas prevailed ultimately articulated a constitutional compromise. They recognized that a domestic process "made" money; indeed, they would deploy that domestic process intensively. But they argued that the process should be tied to the touchstone of private exchange, not public need more broadly. That settlement came to characterize modern money.

The monetary order known as the Gold Standard was the vehicle for the compromise. Its earliest architects accepted bank currency as an important part of modern exchange, and effectively acknowledged the government's orchestrating role. At the same time, those theorists denigrated money's character as a process expressive of collective dynamics, rather than individual exchange alone. To them, public involvement in making money posed a threat to the vision of economic development that Locke had offered. The solution they advocated continued the local and political character of money, but installed a particular compass for it. Money creation should be tied to the needs and profits of commerce, a matter deliberately defined as outside of political control. That drama deserves its own account—but many of its ingredients came from the history that is closing here.

Recognizing the fiat reality of money

Officials and advisors charged with making British money in the early 19th century recognized the efficacy of paper money. They had little choice: soon after the crisis in 1797, the value of the Bank note stabilized. More slowly, people began to use country bank notes again and guineas returned to circulate interchangeably with paper. After an inflationary crisis in 1799, prices returned close to earlier levels for a decade. Significant inflation returned after that point, although the conditions invited far worse. Both the Bank of England and the country banks fed the money supply by discounting notes freely during a speculative boom in 1809–1810. Neither acknowledged that their paper issues might be contributing to the depreciation. A collapse in credit subsequently pulled prices down, but wartime spending in excess of revenues drove them up again in late 1813 or early 1814. According to a variety of indexes, prices approximately doubled their height. They fluctuated at lower levels until Napoleon's final defeat in 1815 and a serious credit collapse in the fall of 1815. After expanding during the last boom, a number of country banks had failed again. As for the Bank of England, its directors still operated without a clear monetary policy. Nevertheless, the country had survived and, indeed, emerged victorious from an enormously expensive war.[1]

Contemporaries acknowledged Bank money as the dominant medium in England after 1797. The Select Committee on the High Price of Gold Bullion, appointed by the House of Commons in 1810, would produce what became the leading treatise for a return to convertibility. The "Bullion Report" openly doubted whether "gold has in truth continued to be our measure of value," or "whether we have any other standard of prices than that circulating medium, issued primarily by the Bank of England and in a secondary manner by the country banks." At the very least, gold had been rendered "variable" in value "in consequence of being interchangeable for a paper currency which is not at will convertible into gold."[2] That paper currency—and the Bank of England note in particular—obviously operated as the unit of account; it determined prices, according to influential commentators including David Ricardo, Henry Thornton (a member of the Bullion Committee), Walter Boyd, and Lord Peter King. As Thornton argued in 1802, Bank notes had long been "interchanged" for gold coin; the amount of paper issued had therefore driven up the price of the gold contained in the coin.[3] By 1810, the Bullion Committee wrote in terms suggesting that the gold in coin was no longer at issue:

> [I]n the present situation of the Bank, intrusted as it is with the function of supplying the public with that paper currency which forms the basis of our circulation, and at the same time not subjected to the liability of converting the paper into specie, every advance which it makes of capital to the merchants in the shape of discount, becomes an addition also to the mass of circulating medium.[4]

[1] See, e.g., P. J. Cain and A. G. Hopkins, *British Imperialism: Innovation and Expansion: 1688–1914* (London: Longman Pearson Education, 1993), 76–83.

[2] Select Committee on the High Price of Gold Bullion, *Report*, ed. House of Commons (London: Richard Taylor and Co., 1810), 16.

[3] Henry Thornton, "An Enquiry into the Nature and Effects of the Paper Credit of Great Britain" (1802), in *Foundations of Monetary Economics*, ed. D. P. O'Brien (London: Pickering & Chatto, 1994), 65–67; see also Lord Peter King, "Thoughts on the Effects of the Bank Restrictions" (1804), in *Foundations of Monetary Economics*, ed. D. P. O'Brien (London: Pickering & Chatto, 1994), 150–155; Walter Boyd, "A Letter to the Right Honourable William Pitt, on the Influence of the Stoppage of Issue in Specie at the Bank of England" (1801), in *Foundations of Monetary Economics*, ed. D. P. O'Brien (London: Pickering & Chatto, 1994), 5–6; David Ricardo, "The High Price of Bullion" (1810) in *The Works of David Ricardo*, vol. 3, ed. Piero Sraffa (Cambridge: Cambridge University Press, 1951), 51–52, 54–55.

[4] Bullion Committee, *Report*, 55. The Committee continued on to describe the way that Bank notes affected the money stock in terms of the quantity theory: "The necessary effect of every such addition to the

Commentators were not clear about exactly what established Bank notes as the unit of account, but their prescriptions drew on the domestic nature of that currency. Lord Peter King, a commentator endorsed by Ricardo as having anticipated his own arguments in the letters to the *Morning Chronicle*, noted that paper money had "a mere local value, confined to the country within which it circulates."[5] *The Times* had exhorted people to take Bank notes for patriotic reasons when they were first made inconvertible. Hundreds of merchants and bankers had publicly affirmed that they would use and accept them. The Bank had advertised and emphasized its soundness as an institution.[6] And the government, creditor to every taxpayer in the nation, reliably received the Bank notes in payment of debts.[7]

There was consensus as well on the necessity of paper. Henry Thornton staked out the imperative relatively early, writing that to deny a country its "old and accustomed system of paper credit," if not excessive issues, would "deprive [it] of the means of recovering itself which it naturally possesses." Ricardo soon after endorsed Adam Smith's argument about the productivity of using paper bills, and Lord Liverpool agreed that merchants benefitted from the convenience of Bank notes.[8]

More striking still, paper money backed by the public faith alone proved effective at critical moments. Exchequer bills, instruments issued since the days of the Great Recoinage to anticipate taxes, had been used to save the monetary system from collapse during the bank run of 1793 and when the speculative bubble in 1809 burst. It was an incongruity for those who believed that only coin was real money: currency based purely on a public pledge was used to save a system built on money that broke because of its fiduciary nature, which had been developed to expand a unit of account epitomized by gold coin.[9]

In 1811, Lord King provoked an official answer to the question whether paper money was effectively operating the English economy. He threatened to call in all outstanding debts to him in gold coin on the ground that it was the only "good and lawful money of Great Britain." According to King, the fact that people took

mass, is to diminish the relative value of any given portion of that mass in exchange for commodities" (Bullion Committee, *Report*, 56).

[5] Lord Peter King, "Thoughts on the Effects of the Bank Restrictions," in *Foundations of Monetary Economics*, ed. D. P. O'Brien (London: William Pickering, 1804 [1994]), 148; Ricardo, "The High Price of Bullion," 3, 51–52.

[6] Albert Edgar Feavearyear, *The Pound Sterling: A History of English Money*, 2nd ed. (Oxford: Clarendon Press, 1963), 182–183.

[7] See pp. 311–317.

[8] Thornton, "An Enquiry," 80; Ricardo, "High Price of Bullion," 55; Charles, Earl of Liverpool, *A Treatise on the Coins of the Realm in a Letter to the King* (London: Oxford University Press, 1805), 220. Chapter 5 of Thornton's *An Enquiry into the Nature and Effects of the Paper Credit* defends paper currency by deftly demonstrating how it might be deployed to avoid the recessions that would otherwise trouble a country with a temporary imbalance of trade.

[9] The government loaned more than £2.2 million in Exchequer bills in 1793, and stood ready with more. In 1811, it issued more than £6 million. See Feavearyear, *The Pound Sterling*, 178, 208–209.

"bank paper in payment or satisfaction of a lawful debt" had been used to support the proposition that "in point of fact, there existed no difference in value between paper and gold." King overstated his argument, asserting that authorities were denying the existence of depreciation. Not so, as the Bullion Committee made clear. But King was correct that the government had, by privileging "bank paper" as money, put England onto a fiat standard, one that did not include recourse to a gold veto over an expanding money supply.[10]

When authorities scrambled to defend Bank money, they confirmed that they believed it essential. Their action also dispelled any lingering doubt that it acted as the unit of account. Confronting King immediately, Parliament enacted legislation that disallowed anyone from accepting or paying gold coin at a higher rate than its "true lawful value"—whether that value was paid in "lawful money, or in any note or notes, bill or bills of the Governor and Company of the Bank of England." Conversely, Bank notes could not be valued "for less than the amount of lawful money expressed therein."[11] In effect, if not exactly in word, the legislation equated Bank notes with legal tender. A later Act confirmed that the courts would enforce Bank notes as a mode of payment.[12]

The development continued the odd pairing that characterized modern money. Since the Great Recoinage had "sanctified the mint weights" and introduced a century of turmoil for coin, Bank notes, Exchequer bills, and other paper credit had functioned as increasingly important currency. See Fig. 11.1. Once the panic and run in 1797 had ended gold redeemability, those paper currencies provided England's de facto money. Now officially assimilated to gold coin and enforced as a transferable mode of payment both public and private, the Bank note became England's money in all but name. As the English fetishized gold coin, they expanded—and eventually embraced—the paper moneys they issued on the evidently fiat basis of a domestic process.

---

[10] Lord Peter King, "On the Second Reading of Earl Stanhope's Bill Respecting Guineas and Bank Notes," in *A Selection from the Speeches and Writings of the Late Lord King*, ed. Earl Fortescue (London: Longman, Brown, Green, and Longmans, 1844 [1811]), 232, 233.

[11] An Act for making more effectual provision for preventing the current gold coin of the Realm from being paid or accepted for a greater value than the current value of such coin..., 51 Geo III c 127 (July 24, 1811).

[12] An Act...to continue...and amend...an Act...for making more effectual provision for preventing the current gold coin of the realm from being paid or accepted for a greater value than the current value of such coin..., 52 Geo III c 50 (May 5, 1812). In a provision responding to King yet more specifically, the statute even made it "lawful" for tenants—the debtors that King had targeted—to tender Bank notes in payment. That, of course, left an intransigent creditor to refuse the paper anyway. Perhaps that is what Lord King did because a subsequent act followed close on the passage of the first. It provided that any payment made according to a court order would be deemed to settle the outstanding debt; creditors had no recourse but to take Bank notes and to take them at face value. Later Acts continued the arrangement until the Bank resumed payments. See 53 Geo 3 c 5 (1812); 54 Geo 3 c 52 (1814).

Fig. 11.1 A set of troy mint weights dating from 1707 and Isaac Newton's tenure as Master of Mint. © Royal Mint Museum.

The private as compass

The irony was not completely lost on contemporaries. Even as they strengthened the fiat design of money, a set of critics decried the dangers that money transparently based on a domestic process represented. Sons of the Great Recoinage, they saw certain dangers more clearly than others. Their attention went to the falling value of money rather than other problems, including the fragility of the banking structure or its distributive consequences, currency shortages at the bottom, or, as it would turn out, the harsh effects of deflation.[13] They lacked a theory that established how large the money supply should be, but, by the light of "experience and observation," they identified excessive issue of paper as the most relevant threat.[14]

---

[13] As for the distributive consequences of Bank currency, the Committee did make the arresting observation that the expansion of the money supply by inconvertible notes was highly profitable to the Bank; see Bullion Committee, *Report*, 71–72. As for attending to currency shortages, Liverpool was a notable exception. His prescriptions were formally institutionalized in 1816. Liverpool, *A Treatise on the Coins of the Realm in a Letter to the King.*

[14] King admitted that no "safe or satisfactory opinion [could] be formed concerning the proper limits of a paper currency, except what is derived from experience and observation of the effects produced" (King, "Bank Restrictions," 156–157). For the Bullion Committee's recognition of the wide variety of factors determining an appropriate money supply, see Bullion Committee, *Report*, 63–64.

The circumstances invited a return to gold coin or, more attractive yet, gold itself as the touchstone of value. John Locke had written that mankind commonly chose a "piece of metal, pleased with its color" and called it money. David Hume picked up the assumption, using "gold" and "money" interchangeably, and his contemporaries did the same.[15] Fifty years later, Walter Boyd easily asserted "the currency of gold and silver or . . . of paper always convertible into . . . and therefore truly and faithfully performing the functions of those metals." And the Bullion Committee set the terms for its analysis by asserting that "gold being thus our measure of prices, a commodity is said to be dear or cheap according as more or less gold is given in exchange for [it]."[16]

The architects of the Gold Standard were not recurring to a naïve approach, one that denied the difference between coin and bullion. Indeed, the difference between the monetary unit of account and its metallic content would become the touchstone of their system. While it came to be called the "Gold Standard," the system actually aimed to discipline the amount of *bank currency* in circulation by tying it, as a unit of account, to gold *coin*. Given that link, changes in the price of the commodity contained in coin—gold—could affect the amount of money in circulation: when prices for gold rose, those holding paper notes would be moved to cash it in for coin and those holding coin would melt or export coin for its content. The design created a way for those holding British money to contract its supply when the unit of account lost value relative to its worth as a traded commodity.

If high theorists understood and deployed to specific effect the difference between money and metal, the informal equation of gold coin and gold was nevertheless relevant. It supported the notion that a traded commodity, gold, was the proper compass for the monetary system while obscuring the collective work that allowed a metal to work as a currency in the first place. The Bullion Committee defined the "real price of gold" as "the quantity of commodities given in exchange for it."[17] Familiar from Locke's era, the trope had long obscured that one could not obtain a price at all until money made of gold had installed that metal as the common content of coin and created demand for it.

---

[15] See, e.g., David Hume, "Discourse V: Of the Balance of Trade," in *Political Discourses* (London: R. Fleming, 1752), 80, 90, 99. The change in vocabulary was common. See, e.g., Malachy Postlethwayt, "Great-Britain's True System," in *Great-Britain's True System* (A. Millar and others, 1757). Hume, like Locke, assumed that silver and gold became "the common measures of exchange" organically, like "languages gradually establish'd by human conventions without any promise." See David Hume, *A Treatise of Human Nature*, Project Gutenburg Ebook, 1739–1740, Book III, Part II, sec. II, accessed June 25, 2014, <http://www.gutenberg.org/files/4705/4705-h/4705-h.htm>. The character of convention in Hume's work is complex. It invites analysis as a locus for his theorizing about the nature of reciprocal commitment and contract. See Carl Wennerlind, "An Artificial Virtue and the Oil of Commerce: A Synthetic View of Hume's Theory of Money," in *David Hume's Poltical Economy*, ed. Carl Wennerlind and Margaret Schabas (London: Routledge, 2008), 106–108.

[16] Boyd, "A Letter," 9; Bullion Committee, *Report*, 10–11.

[17] Bullion Committee, *Report*, 11.

The market price of bullion in 19th century England—and the prices of commodities that could be extrapolated from it—depended on the mint price in a unit of account and the subsidy that produced coin, now embedded in a system of government-supported paper currency.[18] Bullion with a market price flowed readily across borders under those circumstances, particularly demanded throughout the region as the material of money. Referring to the "real price of gold" as a quantity of commodities was thus a material omission. But accomplishing it, gold as it traveled outside of political boundaries appeared to be the primal touchstone for value.

Bank money fit easily into the category of the private. As the resolutions produced by the Bullion Committee declared, Bank notes were "promises to pay gold." "Every Bank note was a true and faithful representative of gold and silver" wrote a supportive commentator, oblivious to the complicated reciprocity of debt between government and Bank that made the Bank's notes into money. Henry Thornton's discussion distinguished Bank notes from bills of exchange and other instruments because of the "high credit" they offered. Far more sophisticated than other expositions, his account nevertheless suggested that the difference between paper instruments was a matter of degree: Bank notes offered a more secure promise, but one that could be conceptualized within the frame of private mercantile credit.[19] Indeed, the Bank claimed to operate as a private entity; its directors argued long into the era of inconvertibility that they properly focused only on commercial demands. The Bullion Committee would only slowly persuade the Bank to take responsibility for the money supply more broadly. And even (or especially) there, the Committee prescribed a return to "the ordinary system of banking" and "true principles of banking." That is, the Bank would best serve the country by making the determinations the bankers would make using commercial judgment to defend their issues given convertibility.[20]

Readied with a compass made of gold and the motive force of business decision-making, the gathering orthodoxy advocated a mechanism that tied Bank money to commerce outside of national borders as a means to test and secure its value. Supporters pointed to the declines in the value of England's money that had occurred in 1797, during the speculative boom of 1809–1810,

[18] Liverpool, ever more precise, recognized "gold coins," not gold, as "the principle measure of property" and noted that any public charge for liquidity, if levied on individuals, would prevent that measure from being "perfect." Liverpool, *A Treatise on the Coins of the Realm in a Letter to the King*, 154.

[19] See *Report of the Bullion Committee*, Mr. Horner's Resolutions, Hansard, HC Deb., May 6, 1811, vol. 19, cols. 798–919, accessed June 25, 2014, <http://hansard.millbanksystems.com/commons/1811/may/06/report-of-the-bullion-committee-mr> (Resolution 8); Boyd, "A Letter," 27–28; Thornton, "An Enquiry," 43–45. See also Thornton's argument that privately created credit would replace Bank notes, should they be "annihilated." The analogy that paired private credit with Bank money would become standard; see, e.g., Richards, *The Early History of Banking in England*, 40–43, although Thornton sketched real differences between Bank money and credit substitutes without specifically theorizing their source (Thornton, "An Enquiry," 50–52).

[20] See, e.g., Bullion Committee, *Report*, 54–57, 77–78.

and in the last years of the Napoleonic War. The danger of depreciation dictated measures that compared the value of sterling with international indicators, including the price in sterling of foreign currency and of gold.[21]

The design of the system required a return to convertibility. Under those conditions, coin, unlike bullion, was fixed to the value of Bank notes; both functioned as the unit of account. At the same time, coin also held value as bullion, and could be exported and used as bullion if its value as bullion exceeded its domestic value as the unit of account. That external touchstone of value thus functioned as a point of comparison for the paper units of account. Holders of Bank notes could cash them in when they deviated too far from the value of gold.[22]

When they embraced rather than condemned international trade in bullion, the architects of the Gold Standard exposed how far they departed from the customary approach to commodity money. In medieval practice, communities sought to create a domestic measure out of an uncommon resource (bullion) and struggled to protect access to that resource—and thus their money supplies— from competition for bullion from abroad.[23] Those constructing the modern monetary system assumed instead that international trade in bullion—rather than domestic exchange—represented the real market. In turn, they argued that the value of gold as an internationally traded commodity constructively and consistently informed the value of domestic currency.

Here, the liberal tendency to think of money as the gold it contained invited theorists to assume an organic connection between the unit of account as a domestic product and the value of gold on external markets. So long as Bank money was convertible, bankers would find it "returned upon themselves in demand for specie," should the English pound on the foreign exchange markets fall far below the par value of gold coin or should the price of gold at home rise. The decentralized activity of many decision-makers, each attending to his or her private advantage, would regulate the system. As the Bullion Committee saw it:

---

[21] Those two values were closely related given the widespread use of gold for money's content in Europe. The par value of gold coin was measured by considering the monetary value of a pound of gold. Assuming a guinea at 129.4 grains of gold (.9166 fine), the par value for a pound of standard gold (at 5760 grains) was 44.5 times the content of the guinea. Thomas J. Sargent and Francois R. Velde, *The Big Problem of Small Change* (Princeton, NJ: Princeton University Press, 2002), 295, n. 8. Its par value as a monetary matter was thus £46.725 or £46 14s. 6d. (After 1816, the gold sovereign worth 20 shillings took the place of the shilling.) See G. P. Dyer and P. P. Gaspar, "Reform, the New Technology and Tower Hill, 1700–1966," and Appendix 2, in C. E. Challis, ed., *A New History of the Royal Mint* (Cambridge: Cambridge University Press, 1992), 480–481, 756–757, At par, the English pound held that value against the domestic monetary value of currencies with the same gold content.

[22] Bullion Committee, *Report*, 47–48.

[23] Free minting left room, in theory, for those holding metal to use it for domestic purposes if they valued those more than the liquidity that coin brought. But the loss of metal beyond borders brought only problems, as it increased the likelihood of deflation with all its problems. See pp. 110–120.

If at any time, [the bankers] incautiously exceeded the proper limit of their advances and issues, the paper was quickly brought back to them, by those who were tempted to profit by the market price of gold or by the rate of exchange. In this manner the evil soon cured itself.[24]

Advocates cast the choice as a means that would predictably diminish paper issues after they exceeded a certain threshold, the value at which people no longer wanted to hold it.

The availability of "cash payments" thus furnished a "natural and true control," wrote the Bullion Committee. "No safe, certain, and constantly adequate provision against an excess of paper currency, either occasional or permanent, can be found, except in the convertibility of all such paper into specie."[25]

Advocates of convertibility rejected the notion that lending on the prospect of productivity with good security provided a safeguard.[26] They also dismissed the possibility that credit paper could be policed according to another touchstone other than an externally traded commodity. Finally, they refused to consider the public capacity to control the money supply, as asserted by Adam Smith, although some acknowledged the importance of fiscally driven demand.[27] The Gold Standard alone had the allure of a self-equilibrating model, one easily assimilated to the model of an ideal commodity money or Hume's price-specie flow theory.[28]

For all its beauty, the image was internally inconsistent. The mechanism understood as the Gold Standard was not free-standing: it was part of a domestic system of money production. That system was integral to the production of "gold" as a touchstone; paper media and token coin acted in crucial roles to scale up and down the gold pivot. The fiat extension of currency was essential, in other words, to a regime that identified the unit of account with a fixed amount of

[24] Bullion Committee, *Report*, 47–48.

[25] Bullion Committee, *Report*, 53–54, 73; see also Boyd, "A Letter," 10–11 (considering the par of gold coin the "natural level" of the exchange). As commentators pointed out, a deficit in the balance of payments could depress the English exchange rate, but because merchants would ship gold when it became more expensive to buy foreign currency on the market, sterling would not fall further than the costs of transporting gold. The amount of value that sterling would lose because of trade imbalance was thus limited, unlike the amount it might lose if paper units of account were issued to excess. See King, "Bank Restrictions," 152–153.

[26] According to the doctrine that would become known as "real bills," lending was safe if done on real commercial bills that were short-term and ideally self-liquidating. The doctrine was an endogenous credit theory, advocated with less recognition of the danger of credit-driven inflationary bubbles than later advocates developed.

[27] For the rejection of what would become known as the real bills doctrine, see Bullion Committee, *Report*, 50, 56–59. For the rejection of currency based on the credit of land or other resources, see, e.g., Liverpool, *A Treatise on the Coins of the Realm in a Letter to the King*, 227–228. For references to the government's authority to control demand, see Boyd, "A Letter," 25–26; Liverpool, *A Treatise on the Coins of the Realm in a Letter to the King*, 227–228.

[28] See Bullion Committee, *Report*, 58. Hume's price-specie flow model did not attend to money creation, but assumed a flow of gold according to the balance of trade that dictated a natural level for the money supply.

metal. But a new challenge inhered in that credit-based structure—the booms and busts of money expanded on a fractional reserve. As it turned out, while nothing made the anodyne path of a self-modulating money supply impossible, nothing made it automatic either.

A system based on a reserve easily valued internationally but multiplied by credit-based units of account created the conditions for asset bubbles. Good economic times promoted additional borrowing in money, money made available by lenders who accepted the promises of productivity made to them. Both the money supply and economic activity expanded, encouraging yet more borrowing. Under the circumstances, particular asset classes could become overvalued without prices rising overall in the society. Eventually, a bubble fed by credit-based money would burst, whether because the bubble was driving up costs of borrowing elsewhere, evidence of unwise investment or fraud, or an external shock that decreased demand in the particular asset classes that were overvalued. Just as the bubble had been inflated by monetary means (expansion of credit-based units of account available on promises of productivity), the collapse was also a monetary matter. Depositors, fearing that their banks may have made loans that would not be repaid, would rush to withdraw their deposits. International creditors would do the same. In those circumstances, money based on future promises of productivity—credit-based moneys produced by banks—could not satisfy depositors. The gold reserve would be under sudden pressure for reasons structured into the very design of the system.[29]

In a fascinating excursion, the Bullion Committee attempted to explain panics by extending the dichotomy it drew between domestic treacheries and the disciplined dynamics of international commerce. According to the argument, bank runs occurred because confidence failed at home creating "demand" for coin that could be "sometimes a very great and sudden one." By contrast, "an unfavorable state of the foreign exchanges" created a "drain upon the Bank for gold."[30] According to that argument, the foreign exchange rate would transmit signals so as steadily to constrain issues by degrees.[31]

The diagnosis obscured the fact that the Gold Standard itself constructed domestic and international values as alternatives that affected the money stock. Demand for the domestic medium of money could support its value against

[29] See Perry Mehrling, *The New Lombard Street: How the Fed Became the Dealer of Last Resort* (Princeton, NJ: Princeton University Press, 2011), 18–21; Farley Grubb, "The U.S. Constitution and Monetary Powers: An Analysis of the 1787 Constitutional Convention and the Constitutional Transformation of the U.S. Monetary System," *Financial History Review* 13 (April 2006): 70–71. A classic diagnosis of the system's basic fragility is Walter Bagehot, *Lombard Street: A Description of the Money Market* (New York: John Wiley, 1999, first published 1873).
[30] Bullion Committee, *Report*, 64–66, 77.
[31] As the Bullion Committee put it, "the serious expectation of this event [a return to convertibility] must enforce a preparatory reduction of the quantity of paper, and all other measures which accord with the true principles of banking." See Bullion Committee, *Report*, 78.

international touchstones during a boom—but collapse during a bust. At that point, redeemability for a commodity valued in international exchange would expose the banks to more danger than they would experience in a system with inconvertibility. A series of studies focused on later crises suggests that they have occurred more frequently in periods of high international capital mobility. Although many conditions contribute to the finding, the ability of money holders to flee a troubled currency by relocating wealth to an international commodity is surely significant.[32] The Gold Standard made that logic formative.

Constitutional compromise

The new orthodoxy supplied an answer to the constitutional dilemma created when the English adopted individuated incentives as the pump at the heart of the public medium of money. As they rationalized the system, the English came to cast governmental power to define the economy as legitimate only insofar as it furthered decentralized interests. The modern monetary order, so obviously public in practice, became conceptualized as an enterprise for commercial rather than civic purposes.

That conclusion dictated the way the monetary machinery would be operated by the government, as well as supporting actors. First, it justified the imperatives of the Gold Standard as a system, one that produced money by pairing convertible bank currency and a gold reserve of fixed content. In terms of monetary governance, the resolution defined the contractual expectations of those holding money as matters of right and located the claims of the domestic community as matters of policy. Second, the settlement rationalized the rescue of banks within the terms of the new system, identifying the legal exceptions made and costs incurred in those events as necessary. Third, it appointed the banks as the agents that would "make money" for the larger society and appropriately reap the rewards for doing so.

As for the imperatives of the Gold Standard as a system, the impact on the government's role was direct. The importance attached to the mechanism for modulating money led advocates to defend "the permanency of that common standard" dogmatically. Within the world projected by believers, devaluation would be a "breach of public faith and dereliction of a primary duty of government."[33] A change in the monetary standard was therefore impossible as a remedy for any problems, including the effects of long-running and cumulative changes like the after-effects of war finance or the distortions brought by bank rescues. The terms omitted any uses that the polity as a collective might make of

---

[32] Carmen Reinhart and Kenneth Rogoff, *This Time Is Different: Eight Centuries of Financial Folly* (Princeton, NJ: Princeton University Press, 2009), 155–156 (summarizing data from studies).

[33] Bullion Committee, *Report*, 74; see also King, "Bank Restrictions," 150–151.

money. It was a remarkable assertion, given traditional sanctities such as the government's duty to provide for national defense. The Napoleonic Wars themselves demonstrated that the prescription was overly broad, but its normative direction was clear. If the most exigent purposes of the public were passed over, more quotidian needs, like the government's responsibility for the well-being of its citizenry, did not register. The new vocabulary thus buried nominalism's ancient if often forgotten promise that communal needs could trump narrower interests. Rather, the government's essential job was to "secure to the people a standard of determinate value, by affixing a stamp... to pieces of gold."[34]

In such a system, "the substantial justice and faith of monied contracts and obligations between man and man" were properly paramount.[35] Bank notes were, after all, only a private credit device, once their public infrastructure became invisible. "One of the greatest practical improvements" that a state could make in its political economy—a fully convertible currency—had to be brought under the law's unerring protection of "property and the securities of every description by which it [property] is represented."[36] Advocates were not oblivious of the impact on individuals. The Bullion Committee had picked out the damage that depreciation visited upon "common country labour," as "by far the most important portion" of the harm. But in that case and others, the theory trained attention on the status of individuals as creditors alone, without considering their likely indebtedness. Indeed, the largest creditor in the country was classified with debtors ("government and all other debtors") in the Committee's focus on private investors.[37] As above, the core blueprints of the Gold Standard paid negligible attention even to the classic needs of the government to finance defense or the civil sphere.

Given the imperative that the government protect the private, commentators dismissed on principle alone a series of possible remedies, short of a return to convertibility, "even if their efficacy could be made to appear": they would be "objectionable as a most hurtful and improper interference with the rights of commercial property."[38] To Walter Boyd, when Parliament had suspended convertibility, it had wrongfully displaced a system based on "pure, unmixed

---

[34] Bullion Committee, *Report*, 12.   [35] Bullion Committee, *Report*, 74.

[36] Bullion Committee, *Report*, 72.

[37] As the Bullion Committee put it: "The effect of [an] augmentation of prices upon all money transactions for time; the unavoidable injury suffered by annuitants, and by creditors of every description, both private and public; the unintended advantage gained by Government and all other debtors; are consequences too repugnant to justice to be left without remedy." See Bullion Committee, *Report*, 73–74; see also Bullion Committee, *Report*, 75; Boyd, "A Letter," 22–24. By contrast to the Committee, Boyd also recognized the expenses depreciation brought the government as a purchaser. See Boyd, "A Letter," 12–13, 16–18.

[38] Bullion Committee, *Report*, 75; see also Liverpool, *A Treatise on the Coins of the Realm in a Letter to the King*, 227–229 (rejecting other approaches to paper money). For an earlier exhortation that government leave money alone unless action was necessary to protect "its people and manufactures," see Hume, "Discourse V: Of the Balance of Trade," Book II, Part V, sec. 39.

confidence" with one based on "authority or necessity." The currency of Bank notes should always be "free, not forced," wrote Boyd, who found the government's determination to receive taxes and pay annuities in Bank notes to be coercive. The conclusion unwittingly identified the very activity that defined money—fiscal activity performed in money—and recommended its abolition.[39]

The resolutions of the Bullion Committee tracked its theory. Initially unsuccessful, they gained adherents over the next decade. By the time Sir Robert Peel chaired another parliamentary committee in 1819, witnesses in favor of resuming convertibility far outnumbered opponents. Peel's resolutions aggressively promoted that program, including a provision that £10 million in outstanding government debt be repaid to the Bank.[40] As the money supply contracted suddenly and the price of gold fell, the Bank built up its reserves. Despite warnings by Ricardo among others that restoring convertibility at the current standard without mitigating measures would bring disastrous deflation, the Bank resumed redemptions with the government's permission in 1821.

Economic circumstances had been precarious since the end of the Napoleonic Wars. When prices fell suddenly in 1822, the rural population lost its fragile hold on subsistence. Urban distress also rose to frightening levels. The harshness contrasted sharply with the benefits brought to those holding government bonds—having purchased funds with paper, they were paid off in gold coin. The amounts were extraordinary, upwards of £30 million a year. Later commentators would concur that the official decision sacrificed the domestic well-being of many to deflationary ravages.[41]

The emerging orthodoxy generated a second prescription. Even as the Gold Standard dictated contractions in the money supply brought by convertibility, it legitimated discretionary measures to rescue the banks in times of crisis. The Bullion Committee was studiously restrained about the remedies used to manage banking panics. But in a side comment delivered as it defended a return to convertibility, the Committee noted that domestic panics might warrant qualification of that convertibility guarantee in the future. As the Committee clarified, the deflationary pressure of normal times was tonic, but exceptions to the rule

[39] Boyd, "A Letter," 25–26.
[40] See *Report of the Bullion Committee*, Mr. Horner's Resolutions, Hansard, HC Deb., May 6, 1811, vol. 19, cols. 798–919, accessed June 25, 2014, <http://hansard.millbanksystems.com/commons/1811/may/06/report-of-the-bullion-committee-mr>. The Bank's defenders, strengthened by concerns about action taken during wartime, led the opposition to the Resolutions. See Feavearyear, *The Pound Sterling*, 198–201. Peel's speech and resolutions are found at Hansard, HC Deb., May 24, 1819, vol. 40, cols. 676–748, accessed June 25, 2014, <http://hansard.millbanksystems.com/commons/1819/may/24/bank-of-england-resumption-of-cash>. The legislation, which became known as Peel's Act, is at 59 Geo 3 c 49 (1819).
[41] See, e.g., Angus Whiteford Acworth, *Financial Reconstruction in England, 1815–1822* (London: P. S. King & Son Ltd., 1925); Feavearyear, *The Pound Sterling*, 220–231; Mayhew, *Sterling*, 147–152; see also Larry Neal, "The Financial Crisis of 1825 and the Restructuring of the British Financial System," *Review of the Federal Reserve Bank of St. Louis* May/June (1998) (arguing that the recessionary difficulties produced beneficial institutional reform).

might be necessary to protect the "Banking establishment."[42] The contrast was explicit, as the Committee distinguished contractions due to "the foreign exchanges" from alarms at home that it would be "impossible for any banking establishment to provide against." As the system was structured, the provision of money and credit by the banking industry was indeed essential.[43] At the same time, it was characteristic of the new order that public action protected the larger system by securing commercial interests.

As panics recurred over the course of the 19th century,[44] the English slowly institutionalized the Bank's ability to act as a "lender of last resort." That capacity drew upon the government's power in a number of ways. Most evident was the public capacity to expand the money supply through the Bank. Its small private lending excepted, the Bank's notes issued on the basis of public debt. Public debt memorialized the promise of taxes to come; notes that held value on the nation's revenue stream could always be invoked in a crisis. Commercial bank notes held value, by contrast, on the promise of productivity that a crisis betrayed. At the domestic level, the government could rescue the commercial banks by making more Bank money available as necessary.[45] Public action was somewhat more difficult when foreign creditors were involved; they generally insisted on gold coin. There, the government deployed a different panoply of tactics to stave off demands, including channeling gold home to the Bank from its colonies.[46]

The costs of public action to rescue the banking sector were significant. Considering both the direct costs of a crisis and the consequential costs that follow an economic crash, a recent study suggests that the fiscal burden in terms of real government debt rises 86 percent in the three years after a banking crisis.[47] Ironically, however, the increasing centrality of the Bank validated the orthodox logic. As a conceptual matter, developing the Bank's capacity increased the salience and reach of the banking sector. In that sense, it performed the

---

[42] Bullion Committee, *Report*, 77.

[43] See, e.g., Thornton's scholarly embrace and lecture to the uncomprehending about the importance of restoring credit. Thornton, "An Enquiry," 45–49.

[44] See Reinhart and Rogoff, *This Time Is Different*. The fragility of the banks before 1797 is well established. Reduced to 320 after the crash of 1793, the number of banks increased to more than 750 by 1810. Resurgent after Peel's Act of 1819, they crashed again in 1825. Feavearyear, *The Pound Sterling*, 185–186, 234–237. Banking crises occurred in 1836, 1839, 1847, 1857, and 1866.

[45] Bagehot, *Lombard Street*, 28–29, 203–204; see also Mehrling, *The New Lombard Street*, 18–21. Ideally, the Bank acted to avert panics in the first place, by raising the discount rate to reduce demand at home and draw in bullion from abroad. See Bagehot, *Lombard Street*, 46–62.

[46] For the debate over the methods the British government used to stave off demand by foreign creditors, see Samuel Knafo, "The Gold Standard and the Origins of the Modern International System," *Review of International Political Economy* 13, no. 1 (2006); Barry Eichengreen, *Globalizing Capital: A History of the International Monetary System*, 2nd ed. (Princeton, NJ: Princeton University Press, 2008); Roy Kreitner, "The Standard Which Is Not One: Gold and Multiple Liquidity Regimes," in *Inside Money*, ed. Christine Desan (Philadelphia: University of Pennsylvania Press, forthcoming 2015). For the role of imperial gold, see Marcello De Cecco, *The International Gold Standard: Money and Empire* (New York: St. Martin's Press, 1984).

[47] Reinhart and Rogoff, *This Time Is Different*, 142, 162–173.

conviction held by advocates of the Gold Standard that decisions about private investment, here in the figure of the banking industry including a lender of last resort, best determined the money supply.[48]

Finally, the design of the Gold Standard appointed the Bank of England and, in time, the commercial banks it served, as the agents of money creation. They were the appropriate decision-makers to manage a system set up on the logic of trade. The theorists of the Gold Standard put it in terms that, in that now familiar turn, collapsed the difference between money as a domestic unit of account and bullion as a commodity, to make the whole relation seamless instead of arbitrary:

> When the currency consists entirely of the precious metals, or of paper convertible at will into the precious metals, the natural process of commerce, by establishing exchanges among all the different countries of the world, adjusts in every particular country, the proportion of circulating medium to its actual occasions, according to that supply of the precious metals which the mines furnish to the general market of the world.[49]

In this paradigm, the "general market of the world" determined the appropriate "proportion of circulating medium to its actual occasions" within each country.[50] Bankers as the experts in commercial affairs should have their hands on the levers of the machinery that made money, not politicians.[51]

In fact, that reasoning discredited the public medium that had long circulated. Exchequer bills were issued according to decisions made by political authorities. In addition, they transparently carried value because they anticipated future revenues, instead of holding it for the apparent reason that they were tied to external trade. The same logic made inconvertible Bank money suspect as well, because it violated the precept that only trade could determine the amount of money that should circulate. As the *Bullion Report* had asserted:

> The proportion, which is thus adjusted and maintained by the natural operation of commerce, cannot be adjusted by any human wisdom or skill. If the natural system of currency and circulation be abandoned, and a discretionary issue of paper money substituted in its stead, it is vain to think that any rules can be devised for the exact exercise of such a discretion...[52]

---

[48] See the formulations by the Committee that anticipated the Bank's lender of last resort function and its insistence on a Bank-centered regime. Bullion Committee, *Report*, 49, 65–67, 75–76.

[49] Bullion Committee, *Report*, 58. Similar statements are at Ricardo, "On Foreign Trade"; Hume, "Discourse V: Of the Balance of Trade," 83–85; see also Hume, "Discourse V: Of the Balance of Trade," 99 (gold flowing through canals "of which we have no notion nor suspicion").

[50] Bullion Committee, *Report*, 58, 64; see also Bullion Committee, *Report*, 74 (considering circulation for a "great commercial country" like England); Liverpool, *A Treatise on the Coins of the Realm in a Letter to the King*, 228–229 (similar).

[51] Bullion Committee, *Report*, 58; see also Bullion Committee, *Report*, 49–50, 75 (rejecting other means of regulating paper as "objectionable as a most hurtful and improper interference with the rights of commercial property").

[52] Bullion Committee, *Report*, 58. For the structure analogously linking country bank notes to Bank of England issues, see Bullion Committee, *Report*, 67.

Given the theory, the government stopped issuing Exchequer bills as currency and left banks alone in the field.[53] The government would create the unit of account by minting specie and borrowing cash from the Bank of England, and by licensing commercial banks to lend and expand those units on a fractional reserve.

The era of inconvertibility made the benefits of that arrangement more conspicuous. In a fascinating detour, the Bullion Committee demanded to know why the banks should get the profits—the private seignorage—that came from multiplying the money supply. "These parties," wrote the Committee about the country banks, "have been enabled under the protection of the law, which virtually secures them against such demands [to redeem the notes], to create...at a very trifling expense, and in a manner almost free from all present risk to their respective credits as dealers in paper money, issues of that article to the amount of several millions." The notes they created "operat[ed] in the first instance and in their hands, as capital for their own benefit." In addition, they increased the money supply, the new paper entering with higher value but diminishing that value:

> when used by them, falling into and in succession mixing itself with the mass of circulation of which the value in exchange for all other commodities is gradually lowered in proportion as that mass is augmented.[54]

In the Bullion Committee's view, the situation was "so unnatural, and teeming, if not corrected in time, with ultimate consequences so prejudicial to the public welfare."[55]

The Committee was speaking about banks allowed to expand the money supply without incurring the responsibility to redeem the notes they issued. As long as they could stay in business, those banks would be particularly profitable and particularly irresponsible. But the basic insight that banks profited from expanding the money supply held, even after the era of inconvertibility had ended, independent of over-abundant lending, and in times of stable prices. Given their demand for cash, people were often willing to hold money without demanding interest. Insofar as demand for liquidity persisted as the banks injected new money into circulation, prices would not rise (although a fall that otherwise would have occurred might be avoided), but the banks would benefit from the structure of cheap funding they had discovered for longer-term lending.[56]

"Maturity transformation" was a lucrative business, an opportunity that linked the country banks of the late 18th century to the shadow banks of the late 20th

---

[53] In the crisis of 1825, the government asked the Bank to discount Exchequer bills, rather than issuing them as currency to quell the panic. Feavearyear, *The Pound Sterling*, 237–238.

[54] Bullion Committee, *Report*, 71.   [55] Bullion Committee, *Report*, 72.

[56] See Morgan Ricks, "Regulating Money Creation after the Crisis," *Harvard Business Law Review* 1 (2011): 90–95.

century. In the second half of the 19th century, commercial banks established themselves as powerhouses of money creation when they created checkable deposits in the unit of account.[57] In the modern world, the currency made by the banking sector would comprise over 95 percent of the money stock.[58] Given the dimension of money creation by commercial banks, the Bullion Committee's concern about the compensation going to the agents who "made money" for the new order was prescient. "Some mode ought to be devised of enabling the state to participate much more largely in the profits accruing from the present system," it wrote.[59]

As money issued, however, its financial impact rather than the profits or process entailed in its creation claimed the spotlight. As Bagehot put it, England was the "greatest moneyed country in the world," an attribute it claimed because its money was banked and therefore "borrowable." "Our people are bolder in dealing with their money than any continental nation," he wrote, and even if they had not been:

> the mere fact that their money is deposited in a bank makes it far more obtainable. A million in the hands of a single banker is a great power; he can at once lend it where he will, and borrowers can come to him, because they know or believe he has it. But the same sum scattered in tens and fifties through a whole nation is no power at all; no one knows where to find it or whom to ask for it.[60]

A fervent reformer driven by concern about the "economical delicacy" that attended England's enormous "economical power," Bagehot astutely mapped the intricacies of money creation. But his analysis emphasized the banking industry as "a sort of standing broker between quiet saving districts of the country and active employing districts." Later commentators picked up disproportionately on Bagehot's appreciation of Lombard Street as the "great go-between."[61] Rather than discussing banks as motors of money creation, scholars cast them as intermediaries who linked savers and borrowers.[62] Bankers became renowned for the principles of commercial judgment that guided their work.

---

[57] Michael Collins, *Money and Banking in the UK: A History* (London: Croom-Helm, 1988); Michael Collins and Mae Baker, *Commercial Banks and Industrial Finance in England and Wales, 1860–1913* (Oxford: Oxford University Press, 2003); Timothy L. Alborn, *Conceiving Companies: Joint-stock Politics in Victorian England* (London: Routledge, 1998). On the shadow banking system as one of maturity transformation, see, e.g., Ricks, "Money Creation"; Gary Gorton, "Bank Regulation When Banks and Banking Are Not the Same," *Oxford Review of Economic Policy* 10, no. 4 (1994).

[58] Josh Ryan-Collins et al., *Where Does Money Come From?* (London: New Economics Foundation, 2011), 23 (commercial bank notes constituted more than 98 percent of money stock, according to Bank of England figures for broad money to base money).

[59] Bullion Committee, *Report*, 71. For a current appeal, see Martin Wolf, "Strip Private Banks of their Power to Create Money," *Financial Times*, April 24, 2014.

[60] Bagehot, *Lombard Street*, 4, 5–6.   [61] Bagehot, *Lombard Street*, 4, 11.

[62] Bagehot, *Lombard Street*, 11; see, e.g., Peter Temin and Hans-Joachim Voth, *Prometheus Shackled: Goldsmith Banks and England's Financial Revolution after 1700* (Oxford: Oxford University Press, 2012), 33–34; James Tobin, "Commercial Banks as Creators of 'Money'," in *Banking and Monetary Studies*, ed. Dean Carson (U.S. Treasury: Richard D. Irwin, 1963); Paul Krugman, "Commercial Banks as Creators of

The monetary structure of that financial dynamo, an architecture that its own engineers had never admired, was neglected in the process. Rather than considering how money was made, commentators imagined it as an extant stock that flowed between countries as independent producers, according to the demands of exchange. The fact that credit-based moneys obviated the denominational problems of the Middle Ages, a fortuitous but emancipatory effect, made the model all the more plausible. Economists who came after that time could imagine that the stock was infinitely divisible. In that case, a static resource could service all exchange; changes in price functioned to draw money to and from countries as their balance of payments with trading partners changed. Price changes, rather than money creation, became the most interesting aspect of money. Put another way, money creation reduced to price changes; the identity of exchange ($MV = PT$) seemed to capture all the important monetary dynamics.

Under those circumstances, there was no reason to attend to the fact that people still purchased and paid for liquidity, or that the modern purveyors of money profited from that reality. Likewise, there was no reason to consider the government's unique role in the system or its transformative decision to institutionalize the investment calculus at its core. Finally, there was no reason to think that domestic monetary policy was anything other than short-term manipulation, since money at a basic level simply contracted and expanded in incremental expression of the needs generated by the real economy. In those circumstances, money could assume its modern definition as a means engendered by the activity of trading individuals, and the market could claim its stature as a space independent of politics.

'Money'," in "The Conscience of a Liberal," *The New York Times*, August 24, 2013, accessed June 25, 2014, <http://krugman.blogs.nytimes.com/2013/08/24/commercial-banks-as-creators-of-money>. Compare Ricks, "Money Creation," 101–103 (approaching banks as money creators, not financial intermediaries).

Conclusion

From blood to water

During a parliamentary debate in the Commons of 1621, a speaker drew on a peculiar analogy to describe money making. "I heard a wise man compare the hammers of the Mint in the state unto the pulses in a natural body," he announced, "For as if these beat strongly, it argues health, but if faintly, weakness in the body is natural."[1] From the medieval through the early modern period, metaphors casting money as blood or another bodily fluid were common in Europe. (It was early days, after all, in the science of the body and notions varied about exactly how blood, humors, or other vital flows worked.[2]) "Money... is to the body politic what blood is to the human body," the French Estates General noted in a 1484 communication to King Charles VIII.[3] In the same century and with a similar turn of phrase, the Franciscan preacher Bernardino of Siena berated the accumulation of money and wealth. It is as dangerous, the priest wrote, as "when the natural warmth of the body abandons the extremities and concentrates only in the heart and the internal organs." An abscess and "deadly hemorrhage" were bound to follow.[4] The formulations fit beautifully within the medieval tendency to conceptualize the polity as an organic whole, a body whose health depended on its complex and interconnected workings.[5] In the next century, Bernardo Davanzati embroidered on the image. Money, the Italian economic writer suggested, was properly considered "the second blood" because "as blood is the sap and the nutritive substance in the natural body," so money "maintains the body of the republic."[6]

---

[1] C. E. Challis, "Lord Hastings to the Great Silver Recoinage, 1464–1699," in *A New History of the Royal Mint*, ed. C. E. Challis (Cambridge: Cambridge University Press, 1992), 307–308 (quoting debate in 1621 Commons).

[2] See, e.g., Domenico Ribatti, "William Harvey and the Discovery of the Circulation of the Blood," in *Journal of Angiogenesis Research* (National Institutes of Health: U.S. National Library of Medicine, 2009).

[3] Charles Mayer, *Les Etats Généraux et Autres Assemblées Nationales*, 18 vols., vol. 10 (Paris: 1789), 60.

[4] Bernardino of Siena, *Opera Monia*, as cited in Cary Nederman, "Body Politics: The Diversification of Organic Metaphors in the Later Middle Ages," *Pensiero Politico Medievale* 2 (2004): 86; see also Oresme's formulation at Charles Johnson, trans./ed., *The De Moneta of Nicholas Oresme and English Mint Documents* (London: Thomas Nelson, 1956; repr., Ludwig von Mises Institute, 2009), 43–44.

[5] That tendency followed in turn from both classical sources and Christian imagery of the Church. See, e.g., Nederman, "Body Politics," 59–60.

[6] Bernardo Davanzati, as quoted in Jerah Johnson, "The Money=Blood Metaphor, 1300–1800," *Journal of Finance* 21, no. 1 (1966): 120; compare Toland's more contemporary but less graceful translation, Bernardo Davanzati, "A Discourse Upon Coins," (1588), in *The Avalon Project* (New Haven: Yale Law School, 2008). As Davanzati noted, "grave and famous authors" also cast money as the sinews or nerves of the state. Davanzati, "A Discourse Upon Coins." Cicero's formulation of a limitless supply of money as the "sinews of

The English and French political economists of the early 17th century ran with the metaphor; it captured their belief in the importance of money's ability to infuse wealth across a kingdom. Just as William Harvey was documenting the circulatory route of blood, their advocacy promoted money's currency as a way to maintain harmonious activity in a society. A "general want of money in the kingdome" was a terrible deficiency, wrote Edward Misselden, for money was "the vitall spirit of trade, and if the spirits faile, needs must the body faint."[7] Thomas Hobbes, ever sensitive to the sovereign's defining influence, focused the image to distinguish money used domestically from gold and silver. While metals moved country to country as carriers of value, "mony" was "the bloud of [the] Common-wealth." Money, as Hobbes put it, "of what soever matter coyned" by the sovereign:

> ...is a sufficient measure of the value of all things else, between the Subjects of that Common-wealth...and the same passeth from Man to Man, within the Common-wealth; and goes round about, Nourishing (as it passeth) every part thereof; In so much as this Concoction, is as it were the Sanguification of the Common-wealth: For naturall Bloud is in like manner made of the fruits of the Earth; and circulating, nourisheth by the way, every Member of the Body of Man.[8]

At the end of the century, a critic of the Bank of England used the traditional understanding to sound an alarm. "A wise state," wrote the observer, "should constantly discourage a monopoly of cash and credit, they being to trade what the blood and spirits are to the body, which then thrives best, when every part receives its proportion, and there is a free unrestrained circulation throughout the whole..."[9] The money as blood metaphor, "virtually a stock-in-trade for five hundred years," lingered through the 18th century. According to a scholar tracing its genealogy, it "has seldom been used since."[10]

A new metaphor has replaced the old one. Money, wrote David Hume in 1752, would remain proportionate to the art and industry of a nation just as "water, wherever it communicates, remains always at a level." Hume deployed the image

---

war," is probably the best known. M. Tullius Cicero, "The Fifth Oration of M.T. Cicero against Marcus Aurelius," in *The Orations of Marcus Tullius Cicero*, ed. C. E. Yonge (London: George Bell and Sons, 1903); online at Perseus Digital Library, accessed June 25, 2014, <http://www.perseus.tufts.edu/hopper/text?doc=Cic.+Phil.+5&fromdoc=Perseus%3Atext%3A1999.02.0021l>. See also Jean Bodin, *The Six Bookes of the Commonweale*, trans. Richard Knolles (London: 1576), Book VI, Chap. ii.

[7] See Edward Misselden, *Free Trade or, the Meanses to Make Trade Flourish* (London: John Leggatt for Simon Waterson, 1622), Chap. II; Ludovic Desmedt, "Money in the 'Body Politick': The Analysis of Trade and Circulation in the Writings of Seventeenth-Century Political Arithmeticians," *History of Political Economy* 37, no. 1 (2005): 86.

[8] Thomas Hobbes, *Leviathan, or the Matter, Forme, and Power of a Common-wealth, Ecclesiasticall and Civil* (London: Andrew Crooke, 1651); online at Project Gutenburg Ebook, accessed June 25, 2014, <http://www.gutenberg.org/files/3207/3207-h/3207-h.htm>.

[9] *A Short View of the Apparent Dangers and Mischiefs from the Bank of England* (printed for Benjamin Bragg, 1707), 10–11.

[10] Johnson, "Money=Blood," 119.

to suggest money's flow between nations despite barriers artificially erected by any of them. Should the market or the real economy be in place—"people and industry" in his words—"the money always finds its way back again, by a hundred canals, of which we have no notion or suspicion."[11] Prices for domestic goods, rising or falling if the money supply "miraculously" expanded or diminished, would invite imports or exports. The money supply would equilibrate just as water would:

> Ask naturalists the reason; they tell you, that, were it to be raised in any one place, the superior gravity of that part not being balanced, must depress it, till it meet a counterpoise.[12]

Hume's formulation became iconic. Walter Bagehot used it to describe the interregional movement of capital. "Thus," as he put it, "English capital runs as surely and instantly where it is most wanted, and where there is most to be made of it, as water runs to find its level."[13] The same motif figured in popular and political thought.[14]

Later economists analyzed the flow of market forces as hydraulic in character. Money became articulated more abstractly: it provided the terms of value on which people acted, although the "watery metaphors" continued as an informal usage.[15] For many purposes, money was identified simply as a commodity that measured other commodities—the conflation echoed that of the early Gold Standard advocates, who collapsed gold coin into gold itself. Arguably, that displacement of money with a commodity numeraire rendered money unnecessary, while certain illustrations—Irving Fisher's equilibrium-producing system of cisterns and vessels among them—continued vividly to evoke water. In either case, money was a

---

[11] David Hume, "Discourse V: Of the Balance of Trade," in *Political Discourses* (London: R. Fleming, 1752), II.V.11, II.V.38. For an early use, see *A Letter to a Friend, Concerning the Credit of the Nation: And with Relation to the Present Bank of England*, printed for E. Whitlock, 1697, 9–10.

[12] Hume, "Discourse V: Of the Balance of Trade," II.V.11, II.V.38. Water is not the only model employed to explain money. For the argument that economics more generally is based on late 19th century physics, see Philip Mirowski, *More Heat than Light: Economics as Social Physics, Physics as Nature's Economics*, Historical Perspectives on Modern Economics (Cambridge: Cambridge University Press, 1989).

[13] Walter Bagehot, *Lombard Street: A Description of the Money Market* (New York: John Wiley, 1999, first published 1873), 13.

[14] See, e.g., Testimony of Rep. Simeon Fess, quoted in Herman Kroos and Paul A. Samuelson, *Documentary History of Banking and Currency in the United States*, vol. 2 (New York: Chelsea House Publishing, 1969), 359 ("Money does not leave the country for the centers because of statutory enactment, nor for the lack of statutory enactment. It flows with the ease of the current from the country when it does not find employment to the centers where it does find employment...I admit that growth can be impeded by unwise legislation as it can be augmented by wise laws, but after all you cannot make water run up hill be declaring it shall do so by law"); *McConnell v F.E.C.*, 540 U.S. 93, 224 (2003) ("Money, like water, will always find an outlet").

[15] Willie Henderson, "Metaphor, Economics, and ESP: Some Comments," *English for Specific Purposes* 19 (2000): 172. See, e.g., Marcia Stigum and Anthony Crescenzi, *Stigum's Money Market*, 4th ed. (New York: McGraw Hill, 2007), 501–502 ("In the fed funds market now, regional banks buy up funds from even tiny banks, use what they need, and resell the remainder in round lots in the New York market. Thus, the fed funds market resembles a river with tributaries: money is collected in the many places and then flows through channels into the New York market").

material that flowed between bodies rather than circulating within one organism. In that guise, money supplied the information (price) that induced arbitrage in real goods between people according to their preferences. Goods moved accordingly or, perhaps, irresistibly.[16]

Images of money are purely suggestive. Medieval officials struggling to get mint prices right made calculations that took them far beyond notions about the "blood" of the kingdom. The architects of Britain's 19th century monetary system intimately explored the intricacies of their bank-based architecture. They too approached money with the sophistication of designers. But if the images of blood and water are not analytic or comprehensive, neither are they accidental. The products of their times, they capture contemporary assumptions about money. Their commonalities are remarkable. Both blood and water appear as essential, life-giving liquids, organic fluids that nurture growth. Both direct attention to flow, blood driven by a circulatory system and water returned by gravity to the sea level or the water table. But within that shared territory, it is their differences that are arresting. Each image tells a different story about money, one grounded in the circumstances of its manufacture.

Making money in the medieval world was a difficult task, one essential to the survival of the sovereigns who undertook it. Charged by the center to individuals, coin by coin, money was a precious resource highly identified with the political community. The emphasis fell on money's particularity to the organism that produced it; it was conspicuously a domestic medium. That focus illuminated the public claim to money as a medium for its own use: in England, sovereign authority over the money supply was uncontested. That included public power to ordain its use in exchange and to recalibrate the content of coin to maintain its circulation. Imagining money as blood suggested as well a role for money between individuals. It located them as participants in an animate community who could (or, often, must) procure the silver penny from its center for private exchange as well as public obligation. The medium nourished commercial activity at the daily level, often by configuring credit sought and contested in the unit of account.

Money in the medieval world remained a scant and costly item. Keeping money in circulation—despite the loss of metal to wear, the counterfeits, the sovereign competition, the shifting values of silver and gold—was a consuming political task. Spreading it throughout the body of the kingdom was more difficult still. Bernardino spoke as a theologian when he warned that money, like the "natural warmth" of the body, must travel back to the peripheries (or "life is

---

[16] See, e.g., Irving Fisher, *Mathematical Investigations in the Theory of Value and Prices* (New York: Cosimo, Inc., 2007 [1892]). For the numeraire, see Mark Blaug, *Economic Theory in Retrospect*, 5th ed. (Cambridge: Cambridge University Press, 1996), 143–151; James Tobin, "Money," in *The New Palgrave Dictionary of Economics*, ed. Steven N. Durlauf and Lawrence E. Blume (London: Palgrave Macmillan, 2008), 14.

slipping away, and that person is soon to die").[17] Authorities from the early Anglo-Saxons to the Plantagenets surely held expectations richly inflected through their religious beliefs about the moral dimensions of matters economic. But they also experienced Bernadino's imperative in a more profane space: the security of their rule depended on making and maintaining money adequate to keep order and defend their borders.

The image of money as blood leaves the medium's relation to the outside world untheorized. The implication is, at one level, misleading. Those designing medieval money were profoundly aware that they made money from material held precious outside (and for that matter, within) their borders. Their struggle to acquire and control the bullion content of coin pervasively informed their strategies at the mint, not to mention their foreign relations, military decisions, and colonizing efforts. As for individuals, they calculated the benefits of bullion as opposed to money when they could, producing many of the instabilities that undermined medieval coin. But if money was always a matter affected by the outside world, it was in many ways, antagonistic to that environment. Money as the medieval English made it was a medium designed by public authority to mobilize goods within its control, to effectuate the safekeeping of the realm, and to nurture local exchange. On that basis, the kingdom would engage its neighbors and greater ambitions.

The image of water is distinctive, consonant with the fundamental change to money in the modern era. The metaphor became common only after the English government began picking up the cost of making money, both coin (1666) and bills based on public debt from the Bank of England (1694). Indeed, it appears when the English were well into constructing money that turned for the first time on a static guarantee of metal. That golden pivot could be identified as money, abstracted into innate value. It was a remarkable equation, in part because the very identity made essential a proliferation of currencies that would do the real work of money. As for those currencies, they flowed according to a logic that put commercial calculation in charge of making money. The government created units of account by borrowing for interest from the Bank of England, as well as maintaining the mint. Individuals enlarged the supply by borrowing from commercial banks, which loaned according to their assessment of the future productivity of borrowers.

The pump that made modern money at the behest of borrowers and bank lenders produced a flood. The very abundance of money could make liquidity seem routine. Although it took decades to fill out the denominational space above and below the gold unit of account, the English had broken out of the strictures

---

[17] Bernadino of Siena, *Opera Monia*, as cited in Nederman, "Body Politics," 86.

that had haunted their medieval predecessors. That accomplishment diffused money to many hands.

Water was an apt analogy for money under the circumstances. It suggested a new coherence, one that located the source of money outside the sovereign. Money, to most of those using it, irrigated their material efforts and, in the best of circumstances, their expanding productivity. Beneath the flow of modern money remained a powerful public engine. Wholly redesigned from its medieval predecessor, it retained certain principles of operation. Fiscal forces ultimately undergirded demand and ensured supply. Legal practices supported money's operation as a unit of account, mode of payment, and medium; they gave money the cash quality that enhanced its value. Those public dynamics were obvious, however, only when the great proliferation of money collapsed. At other times, money appeared to be a matter produced by private arrangement, one that expanded and contracted with the needs of the market. Increasingly, money seemed colorless and universal—the generic accomplishment of exchange. Money could be imagined as information alone despite the enormous infrastructure necessary to produce it.

To modern eyes, the image of money as blood advertises an antiquarian sensibility. Money, in an earlier world, may have had political, moral, even religious implications. But the image of money as water or as an abstract numeraire is no more neutral. In particular, modern approaches to money leave unexplored a set of issues that are exposed by money's history. Three are particularly salient.

First, while water is (or may appear) free, money is not. There is a distributive drama wrapped into the history of money. As that history reveals, money is a medium that is collectively made. The costs and rewards of making it have been allocated in different ways over time. The transformation mapped in this book is only one example, although it is major to our world. But exactly how the material burdens and benefits of making money were reapportioned there, or in other cases, have never been adequately analyzed.

For centuries, the English government charged people individually for the quality of cash. The government could impose that charge because it held a virtual monopoly over the creation of money as the stakeholder with the ability to define and manage the monetary unit. The charge was heavy: it included the allocation of a precious resource, silver or gold, to use as money and a fee for the minting of that metal into coin. In return for that charge and public taxes more generally, the government provided the systems of law, civil service, and defense that supported money as a domestic process.

There were many reasons to move away from the traditional practice. It escalated the cost of money by dedicating gold and silver to monetary use. It hampered money production by tying it to the determinations of users singly calculating their expenses rather than a government creating a public resource. It was likely more amenable to abuse than systems less complacently monopolized. Beyond its direct costs of production, commodity money exacted other tolls, including the competition for gold and silver that drove European states into destructive relations and catalyzed the devastating colonial quest for precious metals.

While reform to the old system brought relief, it is much less clear the British ever considered the distributive implications of their innovation when they made it. According to the new structure, the government paid investors for producing promises that held value, ultimately, on the anticipation of public revenues. There were many catalysts for the government's action—the exigencies of war, the desire for the credibility that arguably came with private lenders, the advantages to creating a class of public creditors. But the arrangement nevertheless granted an astonishing privilege to the Bank of England: the Bank now benefitted from money creation based on public debt, a monopoly the state shared for the first time.

The British government eventually reclaimed the profits from the Bank, nationalizing it in the mid-20th century.[18] By that time, however, the British government had bestowed the license to create money on another set of private actors. Since the 18th century, commercial banks have effectively charged individuals for enlarging the money supply, accommodated by the Bank of England and recognized as money creators in English law.[19] There are tremendous strengths to the arrangement. The country banks, like the joint-stock banks that followed, met the enormous popular demand for currency. They increasingly refined their skills as lenders, gaining expertise that would set them apart from less specialized actors. They decentralized money creation, providing sources for funds in locales across the country. Those functions are today reproduced by modern commercial banks.

At the same time, the government decision to distribute its monopoly and to subsidize an industry happened almost improvisationally: the advent of country note issue and the expansion of checkable deposits both occurred without debate about the extent of official support they assumed. To the contrary, those designing the English system were, in many ways, ideologically opposed to public authority over money. Given their commitments, they were more interested in disciplining that authority than in documenting the advantages it bestowed. The rise of money creation by commercial actors diverted from government to private

[18] See the Bank of England Act 1946 (9 & 10 Geo 6 c 27). Central banks today commonly return to state treasuries the profits they make on the public debt that creates base money. See generally Charles Goodhart, *The Evolution of Central Banks* (Cambridge: Cambridge MIT Press, 1988).

[19] See generally pp. 394–400, 419–420. For the articulation of the "charter value" held by modern banks, see Gary Gorton, *Slapped by the Invisible Hand: The Panic of 2007*, Financial Management Association Survey and Synthesis Series (New York: Oxford University Press, 2010), 160–162.

coffers revenues that would otherwise have come from the public provision of money, as by the Exchequer bills or even the tallies of old. The grant to banks displaced as well other uses for the funds, an alternative of inchoate consequence perhaps most striking for the fact that it went unnoticed.

As for the road taken, we lack scholarly estimates of the benefits accruing from money creation that came and continue to come to commercial banks—the extent of private seignorage. Even without that work, it is clear that few obligations initially conditioned the profits of commercial banks. Banking regulation was a reactive affair from the start, and Parliament scrambled to keep up with the creative abuses of the industry.[20] The cost of bank rescues may have been the largest public grant of all. As the modern architecture of money indicates, panics are not independent of the system or accidental within it, but structural to it.[21] Scholars have debated the way that various reforms, including central bank support and the deposit insurance, allocate costs. The point here is simpler: banks themselves are not an evolutionary event; they are a distributive decision about monetary design.

The 2008 Financial Crisis underscores the point in a modern context. As it revealed, the government's monopoly on money creation can be disseminated beyond the commercial banking sector. An increasing number of accounts identify the Crisis as a run on the shadow banking industry, a set of financial actors that fund their lending with short-term borrowing.[22] That funding structure leaves the industry vulnerable to panics and renders it dependent on public authority and the contribution of taxpayers for rescue. The parallel extends beyond extraordinary events. Just as in commercial banking, shadow banking makes use of a public system for clearing transactions, sovereign units of account, national legal systems that enforce their transactions, and public lenders of last resort.

Old arguments about design are suddenly relevant again. One position suggests withdrawing the legality of fractional reserve banking altogether; the approach would effectively revoke the license that allows banks to create money in the sovereign unit of account.[23] Other proposals defend the monopoly that commercial banking enjoys as a practice insured or adequately structured to

---

[20] See, e.g., L. S. Pressnell, *Country Banking in the Industrial Revolution* (Oxford: Oxford University Press, 1956), 501–510.

[21] Attention to the heavy costs of panics is increasing. Charles Calomiris and Stephen Haber, *Fragile by Design: The Political Origins of Banking Crises and Scarce Credit* (Princeton, NJ: Princeton University Press, 2014); Gary Gorton, *Misunderstanding Financial Crises: Why We Don't See Them Coming* (Oxford: Oxford University Press, 2012); Carmen Reinhard and Kenneth Rogoff, *This Time IS Different: Eight Centuries of Financial Folly* (Princeton, NJ, Princeton University Press, 2009).

[22] Morgan Ricks, "A Simpler Approach to Financial Reform," *Vanderbilt Public Law Research Working Paper No. 13–42* (2013); Gorton, *Misunderstanding Financial Crises*; Mehrling, *New Lombard Street*; Gorton, *Slapped by the Invisible Hand*, 13–154.

[23] Martin Wolf, "Strip Private Banks of their Power to Create Money," *Financial Times*, April 24, 2014; John Cochrane, "Stopping Bank Crises Before They Start," *Wall Street Journal*, June 23, 2013; Andrew Jackson and Ben Dyson, *Modernizing Money: Why Our Monetary System Is Broken and How It Can Be Fixed* (London: Positive Money, 2012); Laurence Kotlikoff, *Jimmy Stewart Is Dead* (Hoboken, NJ: John

reduce risk, while warning against further delegations to the financial indus-try.[24] Another approach accepts the expansion of money creation by the shadow banks, and advocates retooling central bank support to strengthen the new structure.[25] Each proposal concerns the changing shape of banking as money creation. In that way, they all reconsider the justice of an order that confides so much to the private creation of a public resource. They are governance proposals, and the way wealth is distributed in the next century will depend on the results.

Money's history suggests a second aspect obscured by modern approaches to it. Conceptions of money as a matter that moves goods hydraulically or abstractly to enable the real economy miss the very quality that separates money from water or gold. Overlooking the identity of money as a unit of account eclipses the public determinants of money's operation. That tendency has old roots but contemporary relevance.

When Hume and Ricardo described the balance of international trade, they conflated money with gold. That shorthand drew on the particularity of their monetary system. Gold, priced in the English unit of account, would flow in or out of England if the English unit of account, pegged to a certain amount of gold, rose or fell in value.[26] Expanded for precision, their claim was a prediction about the behavior of gold, but it was the unit of account, as opposed to the gold it contained, that created the possibility of easily priced exchange. In the world created by the English penny, shilling, and pound, the commodity that Hume and Ricardo dreamed as liquid could become exactly that.

Identifying money with the gold it contained comported with the 18th century liberal commitment to emphasize private agency in making money, along with much else in the world. Hume's conflation, if we can call it that, is matched today by the tendency to collapse money and the material value it represents. The numeraire in the Walrasian auction invites the same move. That measure, as James Tobin pointed out, is *not* money, "although it is tempting to identify *numeraire* prices as money prices." The numeraire is, instead, an hypothesized commodity that provides the measure for other commodities in the barter

Wiley & Sons, 2010). For the older proposals, see, e.g., Ronnie J. Phillips, *The Chicago Plan & New Deal Banking Reform* (Armonk, NY: M. E. Sharpe, 1995).

[24] Gary Gorton does not trace the government's monopoly to make money back in time, but he picks up the thread in the mid-19th century. As he frames the issue, commercial banks long enjoyed "a monopoly on an important source of firm finance" because the government restricted entry into banking. As Gorton notes, the restriction takes effect both formally, given requirements that banks hold state or federal charters, and informally, given the vital support banks receive in access to the public lender of last resort. In protection of that monopoly, they policed their own propensity for risk-taking (Gorton, *Slapped by the Invisible Hand*, 155–173). Morgan Ricks is more explicit about the singular nature of "maturity transform-ation," arguing that it should be permitted only by issuers adequately policed and insured. Morgan Ricks, "A Regulatory Design for Monetary Stability," *Harvard John M. Olin Discussion Paper Series*, Discussion Paper No. 706 (2011).

[25] Mehrling, *New Lombard Street*.   [26] See pp. 408–414.

economy we might imagine.[27] But if Tobin can resist the temptation to call that commodity "money," others cannot. As Mark Blaug describes it, the numeraire is an "accounting money," if not money kept as a store of value.[28]

Blaug's description locates "accounting money," as opposed to money kept for transactional purposes, as a matter coherently identified with a commodity. The English history of the unit of account discredits that equation. Analogizing the unit of account to a commodity, insofar as it implies determinations about the way money should be managed, distorts the prescriptions based on it. Thus the monetary policies recommended by Locke, like those advocated by the architects of the early Gold Standard, selectively sighted the power of private enterprise. Those theorists could accept Hume's conflation because of their conviction that commercial exchange across borders provided an accurate compass for the market. In turn, the market became defined by the compass of commercial exchange. The possibility, so richly suggested by their own history, that money followed from public capacity and had long flowed towards public needs did not occur to them.[29]

Or if it did, they could not give their recognition voice. The demands of the public order had, after all, no natural boundary. After law, defense, and sovereignty, there were claims without limit—poor relief, education, health care, employment. The terms quickly become modern. Then, as now, the prospect yawned that monetary policy should be shaped to support the community in ways that required debate and public decision. That eventuality erased the bright line Locke had drawn to protect the accumulation of capital as a matter clearly deserved.

The 18th century alternative was to define the public as a sphere that ideally supported individual exchange. The government became the administrator that standardized money and stabilized it, rather than making money for ends politically determined. That approach remains a vital part of contemporary discourse. According to many, it represents the macroeconomic orthodoxy.[30] It also confines modern attempts to think about money as a more complicated commitment, a public resource underwritten by collective contributions as well as a medium expanded by individuals for their own use. Engaging that commitment would suggest that we define money and democracy in ways that strengthen each.

---

[27] The thought experiment associated with Leon Walras imagines a frictionless barter economy in which one good serves to price others. Tobin, "Money," 9; see also Blaug, *Economic Theory in Retrospect*, 144–145.

[28] Blaug, *Economic Theory in Retrospect*, 144–145.

[29] Thomas Hobbes is a striking exception here. He can be read to propose a fiscal theory of money. See Hobbes, *Leviathan, or the Matter, Forme, and Power of a Common-wealth, Ecclesiasticall and Civill*, Chap. XXIV ("The Conduit and Way of Money to the Public Use").

[30] See generally pp. 31–32.

The image of money as water supports a third implication that is central to modern conceptions of money but at odds with its history. Water advertises transparency: it is colorless and tasteless. In the language of economics, it is neutral. Money, according to the classical dichotomy, has no long-term impact on the real economy. Like the hypothetical commodity described above, it supplies information only.

The claim of neutrality is incongruous to money's practice. According to that record, money is created by a political intervention: it carries material value by changing the way people relate to resources and it distributes costs and profits as it does so. Unique in its ability to entail material value recognized as a standard and in its currency as that standard, money enables exchange selectively as it operates.

The process is made literal in money's history: money changed the possibilities for governance and individual exchange alike in very particular ways. By that circumstance, money's design influences the relative value of goods priced in it. The same logic applies to money's continued creation—its entry into circulation and withdrawal. Changes in money's quantity therefore also logically affect the long-term prices of goods in ways that are not neutral.

The history recounted here began with money's invention. According to that account, money appeared when a stakeholder, using its singular location at the hub of a community, began to mark the disparate contributions of individuals in a common way. Sovereign units of accounts were receipts first of all, claims that a resource due to the stakeholder had already been surrendered. But in that very fact, they were unique: they represented material value that had relevance to everyone who owed the stakeholder. That was a novelty that allowed them to act as a standard of measure and gave them a premium as cash.[31]

That story staged the drama that followed—a history of how the making of money changed the way that governments and individuals mobilized, measured, and exchanged resources. The theme of that drama is basic: making money set the terms of the market, just as it responded to them. As a mode of governance, money created new value for authorities. They used it to establish and defend their own boundaries, an elemental requirement for a domestic economy. With money, they compelled compliance with the obligations to the center—tithes, taxes, fees, and debts—that determined money's very viability. Officials estab- lished systems to resolve disputes over sales, debts, and other deals; moneyed exchange enforced by the center furnished the occasion for defining legitimate transactions. That included what counted as "money" and when it could be changed. In fact, governing action taken with money determined what items

---

[31] See pp. 43–50.

counted as "commodities" at all—and thus as matters that should be priced relative to others.[32]

As that process unfolded, it created a new interaction over material value within the community. Money entered society only through certain channels— the government had created money as a technology that allowed authorities to spend to a narrower group than the one from which they taxed. Their expend- itures went disproportionately for specific goods and services, privileging certain individuals from the start. Even when people bought cash directly, the mode of its manufacture made it more available to some than to others. Merchants in bullion, for example, had easier access to the medieval mint than those without wealth in gold or silver, and so more coin to send on in return for the commod- ities they favored.

The process obviously outruns the past tense. In the modern day, entrepre- neurs with good security can borrow at commercial banks and send the money on more easily than others, students with human capital, for example. All the peculiarities of the way money is made—its material content; its denominations; its susceptibility to change; the fragility of finance it imports, even the politics it implies—affect the way that people value items in the market. Likewise, the determinations that build the monetary system more broadly, including money's connection to personal credit, negotiable instruments, public debt, and other forms of finance, influence the way prices came or come to be settled. As a monetary matter alone, medieval exchange in England, shaped around the powerful penny and riven by consumption credit, would produce a different set of relative prices from the exchange of the mid-19th century, with its plentiful token currencies and commercial paper. Nor can we set some number of those contingencies aside in order to assume an abstract environment. There *is* no abstract way of making money, at least not one capable of representing the real world. Money cannot, in other words, be divorced from the material exchange it produces.

What about the claim, apparently more modest, that an increase in money's quantity is neutral, an intervention that will leave relative prices constant? It asks whether, if we took all the conditions of a monetary system as given and simply raised the water level, prices would rise in proportion. As David Hume put it, "suppose that all the money of Great Britain were multiplied fivefold in a night," would not the relations of the real economy immediately be restored?[33] In modern parlance, wouldn't a helicopter drop of money leave real values constant?

Perhaps it would. But in light of money's practice, the claim is not a cognizable reality. In that light, just as the advent of money radically changed the

---

[32] See, e.g., Christine Desan, "Money as a Legal Institution," in *Money in the Western Legal Tradition* (Oxford: Oxford University Press, 2014).

[33] Hume, "Discourse V: Of the Balance of Trade," 10.

possibilities for government and individuals, the expansion of money changes those patterns continually. According to the process of making money, it enters inevitably through certain channels that matter—whether the silver coin spent on soldiers, the creation of more checkable deposits, or the proliferation of money-like claims by the shadow banks. Likewise, money leaves circulation in peculiar ways with an impact on the system—by drain in certain taxes from particular people, by wear on the fragile body of commodity coin, or by financial actors canceling balances through access to a centralized system for denominating the unit of account. In that course, money affects relative values in lasting ways by providing profits in its creation, empowering certain institutions disproportionately, reaching some individuals before others, raising particular legal issues only, fueling changes in political culture, and setting off different financial dynamics. The opportunities presented and the obstacles imposed are not simply undone as people adjust their expectations to match the larger money supply. History's answer to Hume's question is straightforward: there is no such thing as an expansion that occurs "miraculously," a helicopter drop, or rain on a reservoir of money.

Imagining money as a matter that was separate from the market, Hume could also imagine a market produced by decentralized decisions. Arguably, capitalism is distinctive in that very combination: it constructed a money tuned by individual exchange for profit, institutionalizing that motive as the heart of productivity. And it identified that money as neutral, locating all value and judgments about value in the "real economy" it facilitated.

So capitalism wrote the account of money's reinvention. The breadth of the project in the modern day vanished, along with the wealth of ways that communities have engineered money and the human relations that give it value. Looking at its history does not suggest that money was more fairly made in another era nor does it counsel for or against "the market." There is no romantic baseline to the coming of capitalism. But looking at the history of money does suggest that the market is a matter of constitutional design, a political and legal creation. It is a governance project all the way down, starting with its money. That enterprise, rather than the space outside it, makes the economy real.

Primary Sources

A.D. *Proposals for a National Bank*. London: Printed for Richard Cumberland, 1697.

AD of Grey's Inn, and Others. *Proposals to Supply His Majesty with Twelve or Fourteen Millions of Money: (or More If Requir'd) for the Year 1697, without Subscriptions or Advancing the Present Taxes*. Printed for the author and sold by Peter Parker and others, 1697.

Adams, John. "Letter to the Comte De Vergennes." 1780. In *The Revolutionary Diplomatic Correspondence of the United States*, edited by Francis Wharton. Washington, D.C.: Government Printing Office, 1889.

Angliae Tutamen, or, the Safety of England. Sold by John Whitlock, 1695.

Arcedeckne, R. *A Short View of the Practice of Giving Money at Interest*. 1734.

Aristotle. *Nichomachean Ethics*. Written 350 B.C.E. Translated by W. D. Ross. Internet Classics Archive, <http://classics.mit.edu/Aristotle/nicomachaen.html>.

Aristotle. *Politics*. Written 350 B.C.E. Translated by Benjamin Jowitt. Internet Classics Archive, <acceshttp://classics.mit.edu/Aristotle/politics.html>.

Asgill, John, Nicholas Barbon, and John Briscoe. *Proposals Made to the Honorable House of Commons, by the Land Bank United, for Raising Two Million, or More*. London: 1696.

Atwood, William. *A Safe and Easy Method for Supplying the Want of Coin, and Raising as Many Millions as the Occasions of the Publick May Require*. Printed for Roger Clavel, 1695.

Baker, J. H. and S. F. C. Milsom, eds. *Sources of English Legal History: Private Law to 1750*. London: Butterworths, 1986.

Barbon, Nicholas. *A Discourse Concerning Coining the New Money Lighter*. Printed for Richard Chiswell, 1696.

Bentham, Jeremy. *An Introduction to the Principles of Morals and Legislation*. 1789. Oxford: Clarendon Press, 1907.

Blackstone, Sir William. *Commentaries on the Laws of England*. 9th ed. Vol. 1. London: printed by A. Strahan, 1783.

Bodin, Jean. *The Six Bookes of the Commonweale*. Translated by Richard Knolles. London: 1606.

Boyd, Walter. "A Letter to the Right Honourable William Pitt, on the Influence of the Stoppage of Issue in Specie at the Bank of England." 1801. In *Foundations of Monetary Economics*, edited by D. P. O'Brien. London: Pickering & Chatto, 1994.

Bracton, Henry de. *Bracton on the Laws and Customs of England*. Translated by Samuel E. Thorne. Vol. 1. Buffalo, NY: William S. Hein & Co., Inc., 1997.

Britton. Translated by Morgan Francis Nichols. London: Macmillan and Co., 1865.

Caenegem, R. C. van. *Royal Writs in England from the Conquest to Glanvill*. Publications of the Selden Society. Vol. 77. London: Bernard Quaritch, 1959.

The Case of the Assignees of the Goldsmiths, for Their Interest Granted to Be Paid out of the Hereditary Revenue of Excise. 1689.

The Case of Many Thousands of His Majesty's Subjects. 1699–1700.

The Case of the Patentees and Their Assignees Who Are Intitled to Several Annual Payments out of the Hereditary Excise. 1695.

Charles II. *His Majesties Declaration to All His Loving Subjects to Preserve Inviolable the Securities by Him Given for Moneys: And the Due Course of Payments Thereupon in the Receipt of the Exchequer*. John Bill & Christopher Barker, 1667.

Cicero, M. Tullius. "The Fifth Oration of M. T. Cicero against Marcus Aurelius." In *The Orations of Marcus Tullius Cicero*, edited by C. E. Yonge. London: George Bell and Sons, 1903.

Cobbett's Parliamentary History of England. Vol. VII. London: Printed by T. C. Hansard, 1811.

Considerations Humbly Offered to the Great Council of England in Parliament Assembled. London: 1699.

Coss, Peter, ed. *Thomas Wright's Political Songs of England: From the Reign of John to That of Edward II.* Cambridge: Cambridge University Press, 1996.

Crook, David, ed. *Curia Regis Rolls.* Woodbridge: Boydell Press, 2002.

Davanzati, Bernardo. *A Discourse Upon Coins.* 1588. In *The Avalon Project.* New Haven: Yale Law School, 2008.

Davenant, Charles. *Discourses on the Publick Revenues and on Trade.* 1698.

A Declaration of the Christian-Free-Born Subjects of the Once Flourishing Kingdom of England. 1659.

Defoe, Daniel. *An Essay Upon the Public Credit.* London: 1710.

Defoe, Daniel. *The Master Mercury.* 1704. Los Angeles: William Andrews Clark Memorial Library University of California, 1977.

De Haas, Elsa, and G. D. G. Hall, eds. *Early Registers of Writs.* Selden Society, 1970.

The Deplorable Condition of the Assignees of Sundry Goldsmiths. 1697.

The Establishment or, a Discourse Tending to the Setling of the Minds of Men. Printed by JG, 1653.

EW. *A Speedy Way to Supply Their Majesties Occasions.* 1691.

Felt, Joseph B. *An Historical Account of Massachusetts Currency.* Microform. 1839.

Fitz-Herbert, Anthony. *The New Natura Brevium.* 1534. London: Eliz. Nutt and R. Gosling, 1743.

fitz Nigel, Richard. *Dialogus de Scaccario.* Circa 1179. In *English Historical Documents, 1042–1189,* edited by David C. Douglas and George W. Greenaway. London: Eyre & Spottiswoode, 1953.

Fleta. Vol. 2. Translated by H. G. Richardson and G. O. Sayles. In *Publications of the Selden Society.* Vol. 72. London: Bernard Quaritch, 1953.

Forde, Sir Edward. *Experimented Proposals How the King May Have Money to Pay and Maintain His Fleets with Ease to His People.* London: William Godbid, 1666.

Godfrey, Michael. *A Short Account of the Bank of England.* 1695.

Great Britain, Deputy Keeper of the Records, ed. *Calendar of the Patent Rolls.* Vol. 3, 1292–1301, London: Her Majesty's Stationery Office, 1895.

Great Britain, Deputy Keeper of the Records, ed. *Calendar of the Close Rolls.* Vol. 4, 1296–1302. London: His Majesty's Stationery Office, 1906.

Great Britain, Deputy Keeper of the Records, ed. *Calendar of the Close Rolls.* Vol. 10, 1256–1259. London: His Majesty's Stationery Office, 1932.

Great Britain, Parliament, House of Lords, ed. *The History and Proceedings of the House of Lords.* London: Timberlake, Ebenezer, 1742.

Great Britain, Parliament. *Journal of the House of Lords.* Vol. 41. Testimony of Mr. Bosanquet, Bank of England. 1797.

Great Britain, Parliament. Select Committee on the High Price of Gold Bullion. *Report.* Ordered by the House of Commons. London: Richard Taylor and Co., 1810.

Great Britain, Parliament, 1 *The Statutes of the Realm,* 219–220 (London: G. Eyre and A. Strahan, 1810–1828), available online at HeinOnline English Reports (Buffalo, NY: W.S. Hein, 1993).

Hale, Sir Matthew. *Historia Placitorum Coronae [The History of the Pleas of the Crown].* 1672. 2 vols. Vol. 1, London: E. Rider, Little-Britain, 1800.

Hall, G. D. G., ed. *The Treatise on the Laws and Customs of the Realm of England Commonly Called Glanvill,* Oxford Medieval Texts. Oxford: Clarendon Press, 1993.

Hamilton, Alexander. "Report of the Secretary of the Treasury, Dec. 14, 1790." In *Documentary History of the First Federal Congress of the United States of America,* Vol. 4, edited by Charlene Bangs Bickford and Helen E. Veit, 174–210. Baltimore: Johns Hopkins University Press, 1986.

Harrington, James, *The Commonwealth of Oceana; and, a System of Politics.* Edited by J. G. A. Pocock, Cambridge Texts in the History of Political Thought. Cambridge: Cambridge University Press, 1992.

Hobbes, Thomas. *Leviathan; or, the Matter, Forme and Power of a Common-wealth, Ecclesiasticall and Civil.* London: Andrew Crooke, 1651. Online at Project Gutenburg Ebook.

Horton, S. Dana. *The Silver Pound and England's Monetary Policy since the Restoration; Together with the History of the Guinea.* London: Macmillan and Co., 1887.

Horwood, A. J., ed. *Year Books of the Reign of King Edward the First, Michaelmas Term, Year 33, and Years 34 and 35*. London: Longmans, 1879.

Houblon, James. "Observations on the Bill against the Exportation of Gold and Silver." In *The Manuscripts of the House of Lords, 1690–1691*, 13th Report, App. Part 5. edited by Historical Manuscripts Commission. London: Her Majesty's Stationery Office, 1892.

Houghton, Thomas. *A Plain and Easie Method for Supplying the Scarcity of Money and the Promoting of Trade*. Printed by E. Whitlock, 1696.

Hume, David. "Discourse III: Of Money." In *Political Discourses*. London: R. Fleming, 1752.

Hume, David. "Discourse V: Of the Balance of Trade." In *Political Discourses*. London: R. Fleming, 1752.

Hume, David. *A Treatise of Human Nature*. 1739–1740. Online at Project Gutenberg Ebook.

Janssen, Theodore. *A Discourse Concerning Banks*. 1697.

Jenkinson, Hilary, and Beryl E. R. Formoy, eds. *Select Cases in the Exchequer of Pleas*. Publications of the Selden Society, Main Series 48. London: Bernard Quaritch, 1932.

Johnson, Charles, ed. and trans. *The De Moneta of Nicholas Oresme and English Mint Documents*. London: Thomas Nelson and Sons, Ltd., 1956. Ludwig von Mises Institute, 2009.

Killigrew, William Sir. *An Humble Proposal Shewing How This Nation May Be Vast Gainers by All Sums of Mony, Given to the Crown, without Lessening the Prerogative*. 1663, republished 1696.

Killigrew, William, Sir. *An Humble Proposal Shewing How This Nation May Be Vast Gainers by All Sums of Mony, Given to the Crown, without Lessening the Prerogative*. 1690.

King, Lord Peter. "On the Second Reading of Earl Stanhope's Bill Respecting Guineas and Bank Notes." 1811. In *A Selection from the Speeches and Writings of the Late Lord King*, edited by Earl Fortescue, 231–259. London: Longman, Brown, Green and Longmans, 1844.

King, Lord Peter. "Thoughts on the Effects of the Bank Restrictions." London: William Pickering, 1804. In *Foundations of Monetary Economics*, edited by D. P. O'Brien. Pickering & Chatto (Publishers) Ltd., 1994.

Kroos, Herman, and Paul A. Samuelson. *Documentary History of Banking and Currency in the United States*. Vol. 2. New York: Chelsea House Publishing, 1969.

Lambe, Samuel. *Seasonable Observations Humbly Offered to His Highness the Lord Protector*. 1657.

Layton, Henry. *Observations Concerning Money and Coin and Especially Those of England*. Printed for Peter Buck, 1697.

A Letter to a Friend Concerning Credit and How It May Be Restor'd to the Bank of England. Printed for Andr Bell, 1697.

A Letter to a Friend, Concerning the Credit of the Nation: And with Relation to the Present Bank of England. Printed for E. Whitlock, 1697.

Liber Quotidianus Contrarotulatoris Garderobae. Anno regni regis Edwardi primi vicesimo octavo [1299–1300]. Edited by the Society of Antiquaries of London. London: J. Nichols, 1787.

Liverpool, Charles, Earl of. *A Treatise on the Coins of the Realm in a Letter to the King*. London: Oxford University Press, 1805.

Locke, John. *Further Considerations Concerning Raising the Value of Money*. 1695. In *Locke on Money*, edited by Patrick Hyde Kelly. Oxford: Clarendon Press, 1991.

Locke, John. *Some Considerations of the Consequences of the Lowering of Interest and Raising the Value of Money*. 1692. In *Locke on Money*, edited by Patrick Hyde Kelly. Oxford: Clarendon Press, 1991.

Locke, John. *Two Treatises of Government*. 1691. In *The Works of John Locke*. 12th ed. London: Rivington 1824.

Locke, John, Ph. Meadows, John Pollexfen, and Abr. Hill. "Report from the Council of Trade to the Lords Justices in Council on the Guinea, 22 Sept. 1698." In *The Great Recoinage of 1696–1699*, edited by Ming-Hsun Li, 126–128. London: Weidenfeld and Nicolson, 1963.

London Gazette, Thursday, February 28–Monday, March 4, 1666.

Lowndes, William. "Remarks Upon the Proposal for Establishing a Fund to Raise Two Millions." 1691. In *The Writings of William Paterson*, xxiv–xxviii. London: Judd & Glass, 1859.

Lowndes, William. *A Report Containing an Essay for the Amendment of Silver Coin*. London: Charles Bill & the Executrix of Thomas Newcomb, 1695.

Luttrell, Narcissus. *A Brief Historical Relation of State Affaired from September 1578 to April 1714*. Oxford: Oxford University Press, 1857.

Madison, James. "Money." 1779. In *The Papers of James Madison*, edited by William T. Hutchinson and William M. E. Rachal, 302–310. Chicago: University of Chicago Press, 1962.

Madox, Thomas. *History and Antiquities of the Exequer of the Kings of England*. 2nd ed. London 1769. Reprinted 1969.

Magens, Magens Dorrien. *An Inquiry into the Real Difference between Actual Money... And Paper Money*. London: J. Asperne, 1804. Reprint, Bristol Selected Pamphlets.

Marx, Karl. *Capital: A Critique of Political Economy*. Pelican Marx Library. Harmondsworth, U.K.: Penguin, 1976.

Marx, Karl. *Economic and Philosophic Manuscripts of 1844*. New York: International Publishers, 1964.

Mayer, Charles. *Les Etats Généraux Et Autres Assemblées Nationales*. 18 vols. Vol. 10. Paris: 1789.

The Mint and Exchequer United. 1695.

Misselden, Edward. *Free Trade or, the Meanses to Make Trade Flourish*. London: John Legatt, for Simon Waterson, 1622.

Mommsen, Theodor, and Alan Watson, eds. *The Digest of Justinian*. Philadelphia: University of Pennsylvania Press, 1985.

Montague, Charles. "A Document Relating to the Establishment of Paper Credit (1696)." In *The Great Recoinage of 1696 to 1699*, edited by Ming-Hsun Li. London: Weidenfeld and Nicolson, 1963.

Murray, Robert. *An Account of the Constitution and Security of the General Bank of Credit*. Printed by John Gain, 1683.

Murray, Robert. *The Manner and Method of an Exchequer Credit*. 1695.

Murray, Robert. *A Proposal for the Advancement of Trade, Upon Such Principles as Must Necessarily Enforce It*. Printed by AM and others, 1676.

Myers, A. R. "Some Household Ordinances of Henry VI." *Bulletin of the John Rylands Library* 26 (1954): 449–467.

The Mystery of the New Fashioned Goldsmiths or Bankers. 1676.

Neale, Thomas. *A Proposal for Raising a Million on a Fund of Interest*. 1694.

Neale, Thomas. *A Way How to Supply the King's Occasions with Two Millions of Money*. 1694, republished with attachment, 1695.

Neale, Thomas D. *For Supplying Five Millions of Money*. London, 1696.

Neale, Thomas D. *A Way to Make Plenty of Money for All Sorts of Occasions, and to Pay the Debts of the Publick...* 1696.

Nedham, Marchamont. *Mercurius Politicus*, No. 94. March 18–25, 1652.

A New Found Stratagem Framed in the Old Forge of Machivilisme. 1647.

Newton, Isaac. "Isaac Newton Concerning the Amendment of English Coin (1696)." In *The Great Recoinage of 1696 to 1699*, edited by Ming-Hsun Li, 217–223. London: Weidenfeld and Nicolson, 1963.

Newton, Isaac. "Observations upon the State of the Coins of Gold and Silver." 1717. Online at the Newton Project.

Newton, Isaac. "On the Value of Silver and Gold in European Currencies and the Consequences on the World-Wide Gold- and Silver-Trade." 1717. In *Select Tracts and Documents Illustrative of English Monetary History 1626–1730*, edited by William A. Shaw. London: Wilsons and Millne, 1896.

North, Sir Dudley. *Discourses Upon Trade, Principally Directed to the Cases of the Interest, Coynage, Clipping, Increase of Money*. Printed for Tho. Basset, 1691.

O'Callaghan, Jeremiah. *Usury or Interest Proved to Be Repugnant to the Divine and Ecclesiastical Laws, and Destructive to Civil Society*. London: C. Clement, 1825.

Oresme, Nicolas. *The De Moneta of Nicholas Oresme and English Mint Documents.* Translated by Charles Johnson. Medieval Texts. London; New York: Thomas Nelson and Sons, 1956.

Overton, Richard. *An Appeale from the Degenerate Representative Body the Commons of England Assembled at Westminster.* 1647.

Paterson, William. *The Writings of William Paterson ... Founder of the Bank of England.* London: Effingham Wilson, 1859.

Paterson, William. *A Brief Account of the Intended Bank of England.* Printed by Randal Taylor, 1694.

Pepys, Samuel, Mynors Bright, and Henry Benjamin Wheatley. *The Diary of Samuel Pepys.* London: G. Bell, 1924.

Postlethwayt, Malachy. *Great-Britain's True System.* Printed for A. Millar and others, 1757.

A Proposal for the King's Supply, and for Quieting the People, and to Prevent the Loss of Our Wealth to Foreigners. 1696.

The Reasons of the Decay of Trade and Private Credit. Printed for J. Morphew, 1707.

Reasons Offer'd against the Continuance of the Bank. 1707.

A Review of the Universal Remedy for All Diseases Incident to Coin. Printed for A & J Churchill, 1696.

Ricardo, David. "The High Price of Bullion." 1810. In *The Works of David Ricardo,* vol. 3, edited by Piero Sraffa. Cambridge: Cambridge University Press, 1951.

Ricardo, David. "On Foreign Trade." 1817. In *The Works and Correspondence of David Ricardo,* I, Principles of Political Economy and Taxation, edited by Piero Sraffa. Cambridge: Cambridge University Press, 1951. Online at the Liberty Fund.

Riley, Henry Thomas, ed. *Liber Custumarum.* Vol. II. London: Longman, Green, Longman, and Roberts, 1860.

Scott, S. P., ed. *The Civil Law, Including ... The Enactments of Justinian.* Cincinnati: The Central Trust Company, 1932.

Seipp, David J., ed. *Medieval English Legal History: An Index and Paraphrase of Printed Year Book Reports, 1268–1535.* Database Legal History: The Year Books at <http://www.bu.edu/law/seipp/>. Boston: Boston University, 2013.

Shakespeare, William. *The Merchant of Venice.* 1596.

A Short View of the Apparent Dangers and Mischiefs from the Bank of England. Printed for Benjamin Bragg, 1707.

Smith, Adam. "Chapter II: On Money Considered as a Particular Branch of the General Stock of the Society, or of the Expense of Maintaining the National Capital." *An Inquiry into the Nature and Causes of the Wealth of Nations.* New York: The Modern Library, 1937.

Smith, Adam. *The Essential Adam Smith.* Edited by Robert L. Heilbroner and Laurence J. Malone. Oxford: Oxford University Press, 1986.

Smith, Adam. *The Theory of Moral Sentiments.* Edited by Ryan Patrick Hanley. 250th anniversary ed. New York: Penguin Books, 2009.

Some Considerations Offered against the Continuance of the Bank of England. 1694.

Some Queries, Humbly Offer'd to the Consideration of Both Houses of Parliament Relating to the Bank of England. 1707.

A State of the Case, between Furnishing His Majesty with Money by Way of Loan, or by Way of Advance of the Tax of Any Particular Place, Upon the Act for the £1250000. 1666.

Temple, Sir Richard. *Some Short Remarks Upon Mr. Lock's Book, in Answer to Mr. Lounds, and Several Other Books and Pamphlets Concerning Coin.* Printed for Richard Baldwin, 1696.

Thomas, A. H., ed. *Calendar of Early Mayor's Court Rolls, 1298–1307.* Cambridge: Cambridge University Press, 1924.

Thornton, Henry. *An Enquiry into the Nature and Effects of the Paper Credit of Great Britain,* 1802. In *Foundations of Monetary Economics,* edited by D. P. O'Brien. London: William Pickering, 1994.

The Triumvirate of Pennsylvania. In a Letter to a Friend in the Country. Andrew Bradford, 1725.

Turner, G. J. *Brevia Placitata.* The Publications of the Selden Society. Vol. 66. London: Quaritch, 1951.

Turner, Thomas. *The Case of the Bankers and Their Creditors Stated and Examined.* 1674.

United States. Commission, Financial Crisis Inquiry. *The Financial Crisis Inquiry Report.* Washington, D.C.: Government Printing Office, 2011.

Van Laitz, W. *A Proposal to Ease the Subject, and to Restore the Credit of the Nation,* 1696.

Vaughan, Rice. *A Discourse of Coin and Coinage.* London: Printed by T. Dawks, 1675.

Viner, Charles. *A General Abridgment of Law and Equity.* 2nd ed. Vol. 20. Cornhill: George Stahan, 1793.

Whitelock, Dorothy, ed. *English Historical Documents.* 2nd ed. Vol. 1. London: Eyre Methuen, 1979.

Secondary Sources

Abdy, Richard. "After Patching: Imported and Recycled Coinage in Fifth- and Sixth-Century Britain." In *Coinage and History in the North Sea World, c. AD 500–1250*, edited by Barrie Cook and Gareth Williams, 75–98. Leiden: Koninklijke Brill NV, 2006.

Abdy, Richard, and Gareth Williams. "A Catalogue of Hoards and Single Finds from the British Isles c. AD 410–675." In *Coinage and History in the North Sea World, c.AD 500–1250*, edited by Barrie Cook and Gareth Williams, 11–74. Leiden: Koninklijke Brill NV, 2006.

Acworth, Angus Whiteford. *Financial Reconstruction in England, 1815–1822*. London: P. S. King & Son Ltd., 1925.

Agnew, Jean-Christophe. *Worlds Apart: The Market and the Theater in Anglo-American Thought, 1550–1750*. Cambridge: Cambridge University Press, 1986.

Alborn, Timothy L. *Conceiving Companies: Joint-Stock Politics in Victorian England*. London: Routledge, 1998.

Allen, Martin. *Ecclesiastical Mints in Thirteenth-Century England*. In *Thirteenth Century England VIII: Proceedings of the Durham Conference, Durham Conference 1999*, edited by R. Britnell, R. Frame, and M. Prestwich. Woodbridge, 2001.

Allen, Martin. *Mints and Money in Medieval England*. Cambridge: Cambridge University Press, 2012.

Allen, Martin. "The Proportions of the Denominations in English Mint Outputs, 1351–1485." *British Numismatic Journal*, no. 77 (2007): 190–209.

Allen, Martin. "The Volume of the English Currency, 1158–1470." *Economic History Review* 54, no. 4 (2001): 595–611.

Allen, Robert C. "The Great Divergence in European Wages and Prices in the Middle Ages to the First World War." *Explorations in Economic History* 38 (2001): 411–447.

Alsop, J. D. "The Exchequer of Receipt in the Reign of Edward VI." Thesis. Cambridge University, 1978.

"America's Stalling Recovery Crisis." *Financial Times*, July 8, 2012.

Andreadìs, Andreas Michaïl. *History of the Bank of England, 1640 to 1903*. Reprints of Economic Classics. 4th ed. New York: A. M. Kelley, 1966.

Appadurai, Arjun. *The Social Life of Things: Commodities in Cultural Perspective*. Cambridge: Cambridge University Press, 1986.

Appleby, Joyce Oldham. *Economic Thought and Ideology in Seventeenth-Century England*. Los Angeles: Figueroa Press, 2004.

Appleby, Joyce Oldham. *Inheriting the Revolution: The First Generation of Americans*. Cambridge: Belknap Press of Harvard University Press, 2000.

Appleby, Joyce Oldham. "Locke, Liberalism and the Natural Law of Money." *Past and Present*, no. 71 (1976): 43–69.

Ashton, Robert. *The Crown and the Money Market, 1603–1640*. Oxford: Clarendon Press, 1960.

Ashton, Robert. "Deficit Finance in the Reign of James I." *Economic History Review* 10, no. 1 (1957): 15–29.

Ashton, Robert. "Revenue Farming under the Early Stuarts." *Economic History Review* 8, no. 3 (1956): 310–332.

Bagehot, Walter. *Lombard Street: A Description of the Money Market*. 1873. New York: John Wiley and Sons, Inc., 1999.

Baker, John H. *An Introduction to English Legal History*. 3rd ed. London: Butterworths & Co., Ltd., 1990.

Barro, Robert J. "Are Government Bonds Net Wealth?" *Journal of Political Economy* 82, no. 6 (November–December 1974): 1095–1117.

Barron, Caroline M., and Anne F. Sutton, eds. *Medieval London Widows, 1300–1500*. London: Hambledon Press, 1994.

Bell, Stephanie. "The Role of the State and the Hierarchy of Money." *Cambridge Journal of Economics* 25, no. 2 (2001): 149.

Bernholz, Peter. "Inflation, Monetary Regime and the Financial Asset Theory of Money." In *Kyklos* 41, 1 (1988): 5.

Biéler, André. *Calvin's Economic and Social Thought*. Translated [from the French, 1961] by James Greig. Edited by Edward Dommen. Geneva: World Alliance of Reformed Churches, 2005.

Bisson, Thomas N. *Conservation of Coinage: Monetary Exploitation and Its Restraint in France, Catalonia, and Aragon (c.A.D.1000–c.1225)*. Oxford: Clarendon Press, 1979.

Blair, John, and Nigel Ramsay. *English Medieval Industries: Craftsmen, Techniques, Products*. London: Hambledon Press, 1991.

Blaug, Mark. *Economic Theory in Retrospect*. 5th ed. Cambridge: Cambridge University Press, 1996.

Bloomfield, Morton W. *The Seven Deadly Sins: An Introduction to the History of a Religious Concept*. East Lansing: Michigan State College Press, 1952.

Blyth, Mark. *Great Transformations: Economic Ideas and Institutional Change in the Twentieth Century*. New York: Cambridge University Press, 2002.

Bolton, J. L. *Money in the Medieval English Economy: 973–1489*. Manchester: Manchester University Press, 2012.

Bordo, Michael, and Lars Jonung. *The Long Run Behavior of the Velocity of Circulation: The International Evidence*. Cambridge: Cambridge University Press, 1987.

Bouton, Terry. *Taming Democracy: "The People," the Founders, and the Troubled Ending of the American Revolution*. Oxford: Oxford University Press, 2007.

Boyer-Xambeu, Marie-Therese, Ghislain Deleplace, and Lucien Fillard. *Private Money and Public Currencies: The 16th Century Challenge*. Translated by Azizeh Azodi. Armonk, NY: M. E. Sharpe, 1994.

Braddick, M. J. *The Nerves of State: Taxation and the Financing of the English State, 1558–1714*. New Frontiers in History. Manchester: St. Martin's Press, 1996.

Brantlinger, Patrick. *Fictions of State: Culture and Credit in Britain, 1694–1994*. Ithaca: Cornell University Press, 1996.

Braudel, Fernand. *Afterthoughts on Material Civilization and Capitalism*. Johns Hopkins Symposia in Comparative History. Baltimore: Johns Hopkins University Press, 1979.

Breen, T. H. *The Marketplace of Revolution: How Consumer Politics Shaped American Independence*. Oxford: Oxford University Press, 2004.

Brennan, Thomas. "Peasants and Debt in Eighteenth-Century Champagne." *Journal of Interdisciplinary History* 37, no. 2 (Autumn 2006): 175–200.

Brewer, John. *The Sinews of Power: War, Money, and the English State, 1688–1783*. New York: Knopf, 1988.

Briggs, Chris. "The Availability of Credit in the English Countryside, 1400–1480." *Agricultural History Review* 56 (2008): 1–24.

Briggs, Chris. "Credit and the Peasant Household Economy in England before the Black Death: Evidence from a Cambridgeshire Manor." In *The Medieval Household in Christian Europe, c.850–c.1550: Managing Power, Wealth, and the Body*, edited by C. Beattie, A. Maslakovic, and S. Rees Jones. Turnhout: Brepols, 2003.

Briggs, Chris. *Credit and Village Society in Fourteenth-Century England*. British Academy Postdoctoral Fellowship Monograph. Oxford University Press, 2009.

Britnell, R. H. *The Commercialisation of English Society, 1000–1500*. Manchester Medieval Studies. 2nd ed. New York: Manchester University Press, 1996.

Britnell, R. H. "The Proliferation of Markets in England, 1200–1349." *Economic History Review*, 2d ser. 34 (1981): 209–221.

Brock, Leslie V. *The Currency of the American Colonies, 1700–1764, A Study in Colonial Finance and Imperial Relations*. Dissertations in American Economic History. New York: Arno Press, 1975.

Brooke, George C. "Quando Moneta Vertebatur: The Change of Coin-Types in the Eleventh Century; Its Bearing on Mules and Overstrikes." *British Numismatic Journal* 20 (2d ser., vol. 10) (1929–30): 105–116.

Burgess, Glenn. *The Politics of the Ancient Constitution*. University Park, PA: Pennsylvania State University Press, 1992.

Byatt, Derrick. *Promises to Pay: The First Three Hundred Years of Bank of England Notes*. London: Spink, 1994.

Cain, P. J. and A. G. Hopkins. *British Imperialism: Innovation and Expansion: 1688–1914*. London: Longman Pearson Education, 1993.

Callon, Michel, ed. *The Laws of the Markets*, Sociological Review Monograph. Oxford: Blackwell Publishers/*The Sociological Review*, 1998.

Calomiris, Charles W. "Institutional Failure, Monetary Scarcity, and the Depreciation of the Continental." *Journal of Economic History* 48, no. 1 (March 1988): 47–68.

Calomiris, Charles, and Stephen Haber. *Fragile by Design: The Political Origins of Banking Crises and Scarce Credit*. Princeton, NJ: Princeton University Press, 2014.

Cameron, Rondo. "England, 1750–1844." In *Banking in the Early Stages of Industrialization*, edited by Rondo E. Cameron, Olga Crisp, Hugh T. Patrick, and Richard Tilly, 15–59. New York: Oxford University Press, 1967.

Cameron, Rondo E., Olga Crisp, Hugh T. Patrick, and Richard Tilly. *Banking in the Early Stages of Industrialization: A Study in Comparative Economic History*. New York: Oxford University Press, 1967.

Campbell, James. "Observations on English Government from the Tenth to the Twelfth Century." *Transactions of the Royal Historical Society* 25 (1975): 39–54.

Carruthers, Bruce G. *City of Capital: Politics and Markets in the English Financial Revolution*. Princeton, NJ: Princeton University Press, 1996.

"Central Banks: Don't Give Up." *The Economist*, June 28, 2012.

Challis, C. E. *Currency and the Economy in Tudor and Early Stuart England*. New Appreciations in History. Edited by Gareth Elwyn Jones. Vol. 4, London: Historical Association, 1989.

Challis, C. E. "Lord Hastings to the Great Silver Recoinage, 1464–1699." In *A New History of the Royal Mint*, edited by C. E. Challis. 1992.

Challis, C. E. *A New History of the Royal Mint*. Cambridge: Cambridge University Press, 1992.

Challis, C. E. "Spanish Bullion and Monetary Inflation in England in the Later Sixteenth Century." *Journal of European Economic History* 4, no. 2 (1975): 381–392.

Challis, C. E. *The Tudor Coinage*. Manchester: Manchester University Press, 1978.

Chandaman, C. D. *The English Public Revenue, 1660–1688*. Oxford: Clarendon Press, 1975.

Chrimes, S. B. *An Introduction to the Administrative History of Mediaeval England*. 3rd ed. Oxford: B. Blackwell, 1959.

Cipolla, Carlo M. "Currency Depreciation in Medieval Europe." *Economic History Review* 15, no. 3 (1963): 413–422.

Cipolla, Carlo M. *Money, Prices, and Civilization in the Mediterranean World, Fifth to Seventeenth Century*. New York: Gordian Press, 1967.

Clapham, J. H. *The Bank of England: A History*. Cambridge: Cambridge University Press, 1970.

Clark, Elaine Gravelle. "Debt Litigation in a Late Medieval Vill." In *Pathways to Medieval Peasants*, edited by J. A. Raftis, 247–279. Toronto: Pontifical Institute of Mediaeval Studies, 1981.

Clark, Gregory. "The Political Foundations of Modern Economic Growth, 1540–1800." *Journal of Interdisciplinary History* 25 (1996): 563–588.

Cochrane, John. "Stopping Bank Crises before They Start." *Wall Street Journal*, June 23, 2013.

Collins, Michael. *Money and Banking in the U.K.: A History*. London: Croom Helm, 1988.

Collins, Michael, and Mae Baker. *Commercial Banks and Industrial Finance in England and Wales, 1860–1913*. Oxford: Oxford University Press, 2003.

Comaroff, Joan, and John L. Comaroff. "Millennial Capitalism: First Thoughts on a Second Coming." *Public Culture* 12, no. 20 (Spring 2000): 291–343.

Courtenay, William J. "Token Coinage and the Administration of Poor Relief During the Late Middle Ages." *Journal of Interdisciplinary History* 3, no. 2 (1972): 275–295.

Cust, Richard, and Ann Hughes. *Conflict in Early Stuart England: Studies in Religion and Politics, 1603–1642*. London: Longman, 1989.

Dark, Kenneth. *Britain and the End of the Roman Empire*. Stroud: Tempus Publishing Group, Ltd., 2000.

Davies, Glyn. *A History of Money: From Ancient Times to the Present Day*. 3rd ed. Cardiff: University of Wales Press, 2002.

De Cecco, Marcello. *The International Gold Standard: Money and Empire*. New York: St. Martin's Press, 1984.

De Cecco, Marcello. "Monetary Theory and Roman History." *Journal of Economic History* 45, no. 4 (1985): 809–822.

De Haas, Elsa. "General Introduction." In *Early Registers of Writs*, edited by Elsa de Haas and G. D. G. Hall, xii–xvi. Selden Society, 1970.

De Roover, Raymond. *Business, Banking, and Economic Thought in Late Medieval and Early Modern Europe*. Chicago: University of Chicago Press, 1974.

De Roover, Raymond. *Early Banking before 1500 and the Development of Capitalism*. Geneva: Librairie Droz, 1971.

De Roover, Raymond. *Money, Banking and Credit in Medieval Bruges: Italian Merchant-Bankers, Lombards, and Money-Changers—A Study in the Origins of Banking*. The Rise of International Business. London/New York: Routledge/Thoemmes Press, 1999.

De Roover, Raymond. "Scholastic Economics: Survival and Lasting Influence from the Sixteenth Century to Adam Smith." *Quarterly Journal of Economics* 69, no. 2 (May 1955): 161–190.

Desan, Christine. "Beyond Commodification: Contract and the Credit-Based World of Modern Capitalism." In *Transformations in American Legal History—Law, Ideology, and Method*, edited by Daniel W. Hamilton and Alfred L. Brophy, 111–142. Cambridge: Harvard Law School, 2010.

Desan, Christine. "From Blood to Profit: Making Money in the Practice and Imagery of Early America." *Journal of Policy History* 20, no. 1 (2008): 26–46.

Desan, Christine. "The Market as a Matter of Money: Denaturalizing Economic Currency in American Constitutional History." *Law and Social Inquiry* 30, no. 1 (Winter 2005).

Desan, Christine. "Money as a Legal Institution." In *Money in the Western Legal Tradition*, edited by Wolfgang Ernst and David Fox. Oxford: Oxford University Press, forthcoming 2015.

Desan, Christine. "Remaking Constitutional Tradition at the Margin of the Empire: The Creation of Legislative Adjudication in Colonial New York." *Law and History Review* 16, no. 2 (Summer 1998): 257–317.

Desan, Christine, ed. *Inside Money*. Philadelphia: University of Pennysylvania Press, forthcoming 2015.

Desmedt, Ludovic. "Money in the 'Body Politick': The Analysis of Trade and Circulation in the Writings of Seventeenth-Century Political Arithmeticians." *History of Political Economy* 37, no. 1 (2005): 79–101.

Dickson, David. "Catholics and Trade in Eighteenth-Century Ireland: An Old Debate Revisited." In *Endurance and Emergence, Catholics in Ireland in the Eighteenth Century*, edited by T. P. Power and K. Whelan, 85–100. Dublin: Irish Academic Press, 1990.

Dickson, P. G. M. *The Financial Revolution in England: A Study in the Development of Public Credit, 1688–1756*. Modern Revivals in History. Aldershot, U.K.: Gregg Revivals, 1993.

Dietz, Frederick C. *English Public Finance, 1558–1641*. Vol. 2. 2nd ed. New York: Barnes & Noble, 1964.

Dolley, R. H. M., and D. M. Metcalf. "The Reform of the English Coinage under Eadgar." In *Anglo-Saxon Coins: Studies Presented to Sir Frank Stenton on the Occasion of His 80th Birthday*, edited by R. H. M. Dolley. London: Methuen, 1961.

Dowd, Kevin. "The Invisible Hand and the Evolution of the Monetary System." In *What Is Money?*, edited by John Smithin, 139. London: Routledge, 2000.

"Downing, Sir George." In *Encyclopaedia Britannica*, edited by Hugh Chisholm, 458. Cambridge: Cambridge University Press, 1911.

Dyer, Christopher. *Making a Living in the Middle Ages*. New Economic History of Britain. New Haven: Yale University Press, 2002.

Dyer, G. P., and P. P. Gaspar. "Reform, the New Technology and Tower Hill, 1700–1966." In *A New History of the Royal Mint*, edited by C. E. Challis, 398–606. Cambridge: Cambridge University Press, 1992.

Dykes, D. W. "The Coinage of Richard Olof." *British Numismatic Journal* 33 (1964): 73–79.

Editorial Desk. "Time for Bankers to Intervene." The New York Times, June 27, 2012.

Eichengreen, Barry. *Globalizing Capital: A History of the International Monetary System*. 2nd ed. Princeton, NJ: Princeton University Press, 2008.

Elton, G. R. *The Tudor Revolution in Government: Administrative Changes in the Reign of Henry VIII*. Cambridge: Cambridge University Press, 1953.

Ernst, Wolfgang. "The Glossators' Monetary Law." In *The Creation of the Ius Commune: From Casus to Regula*, edited by J. W. Caims and Paul J. du Plessis, 219–246. Edinburgh: Edinburgh University Press, 2010.

Esmonde Cleary, A. S. *The Ending of Roman Britain*. London: B. T. Batsford, 1989.

Evans, Allen. "Some Coinage Systems of the Fourteenth Century." *Journal of Economic and Business History*, no. 3 (1931).

Farmer, D. "Prices and Wages." In *The Agrarian History of England and Wales*, edited by H. E. Hallam, 716–817. Cambridge: Cambridge University Press, 1988.

Feavearyear, Albert Edgar. *The Pound Sterling: A History of English Money*. Edited by E. Victor Morgan. 2nd ed. Oxford: Clarendon Press, 1963.

Ferguson, E. James. "Currency Finance: An Interpretation of Colonial Monetary Practices." *Willam and Mary Quarterly* 10, no. 2 (April 1953): 153–180.

Ferguson, Niall. *The Cash Nexus: Money and Power in the Modern World, 1700–2000*. New York: Basic Books, 2001.

Fisher, Irving. *Mathematical Investigations in the Theory of Value and Prices*. 1892. New York: Cosimo, Inc., 2007.

Fox, David. "Money and Monetary Obligations in Early Modern Common Law." In *Money in the Western Legal Tradition*, edited by Wolfgang Ernst and David Fox. Oxford: Oxford University Press, forthcoming 2015.

Fox, David. "The Structures of Monetary Nominalism in the Pre-Modern Common Law." In *Money in the Western Legal Tradition*, edited by Wolfgang Ernst and David Fox. Oxford: Oxford University Press, forthcoming 2015.

Frame, Iain. "Country Rag Merchants and Octopus Tentacles: An Analysis of Law's Contribution to the Creation of Money in England and Wales, 1790–1844." Cambridge, MA: Harvard University, 2012.

Fried, Barbara. *The Progressive Assault on Laissez Faire: Robert Hale and the First Law and Economics Movement*. Cambridge, MA: Harvard University Press, 1998.

Friedman, Milton. *The Optimum Quantity of Money: And Other Essays*. Chicago: Aldine Publishing Company, 1969.

Frug, Gerald E. *City Making: Building Communities without Building Walls*. Princeton, NJ: Princeton University Press, 1999.

Fryde, E. B. "Materials for the Study of Edward III's Credit Operations, 1327–48." *Bulletin of the Institute of Historical Research* 22 (1949): 105–138.

Gannon, Anna. *The Iconography of Early Anglo-Saxon Coinage*. Oxford: Oxford University Press, 2003.

Geva, Benjamin. *Bank Collections and Payment Transactions: Comparative Study of Legal Aspects*. Oxford: Oxford University Press, 2001.

Gillingham, J. B. "Chronicles and Coins as Evidence for Levels of Tribute and Taxation in the Late 10th and Early 11th-Century England." *Economic History Review* 105 (1990): 939–950.

Goodhart, Charles. *The Evolution of Central Banks*. Cambridge, MA: MIT Press, 1988.

Goody, Esther N. *From Craft to Industry: The Ethnography of Proto-Industrial Cloth Production*. Cambridge: Cambridge University Press, 1982.

Gordon, Barry J. *Economic Analysis before Adam Smith: Hesiod to Lessius*. London: Macmillan, 1975.

Gorton, Gary. "Bank Regulation When Banks and Banking Are Not the Same." *Oxford Review of Economic Policy* 10, no. 4 (1994): 109–119.

Gorton, Gary. *Misunderstanding Financial Crises: Why We Don't See Them Coming*. Oxford: Oxford University Press, 2012.

Gorton, Gary. *Slapped by the Invisible Hand: The Panic of 2007*. Financial Management Association Survey and Synthesis Series. New York: Oxford University Press, 2010.

Green, J. A. "The Last Century of the Danegeld." *English Historical Review* 96, no. 374 (April 1981).

Grice-Hutchinson, Marjorie. *The School of Salamanca: Readings in Spanish Monetary Theory, 1544–1605*. Oxford: Clarendon Press, 1952.

Grierson, Philip. *The Origins of Money*. London: Athlone, 1977.

Grierson, Philip. "Sterling." In *Anglo-Saxon Coins*, edited by R. H. M. Dolley, 273. London: Methuen, 1961.

Grierson, Philip. "The Purpose of the Sutton Hoo Coins." *Antiquity* 44 (1970): 14–18.

Grierson, Philip, M. A. S. Blackburn, Lucia Travaini, and Fitzwilliam Museum. *Medieval European Coinage: With a Catalogue of the Coins in the Fitzwilliam Museum, Cambridge*. Cambridge: Cambridge University Press, 1986.

Grubb, Farley. "Is Paper Money Just Paper Money? Experimentation and Local Variation in the Fiat Monies Issued by the Colonial Governments of British North America, 1690–1775." In *NBER Working Papers*, no. 17997. Washington, D.C.: National Bureau of Economic Research, 2012.

Grubb, Farley. "Specie Scarcity and Efficient Barter: The Problem of Maintaining an Outside Money Supply in British Colonial America." In *Inside Money*, edited by Christine Desan. Philadelphia: University of Pennsylvania Press, forthcoming 2015.

Grubb, Farley. "The U.S. Constitution and Monetary Powers: An Analysis of the 1787 Constitutional Convention and the Constitutional Transformation of the U.S. Monetary System." *Financial History Review* 13 (April 2006): 43–71.

Gunn, J. A. W. *Politics and the Public Interest in the Seventeenth Century*. Studies in Political History. London: Routledge & Kegan Paul, 1969.

Hahn, Frank. *Money and Inflation*. Oxford: Basil Blackwell, 1982.

Hall, Hubert. *The Antiquities and Curiosities of the Exchequer*. London: E. Stock, 1891.

Hammond, Bray. *Banks and Politics in America, from the Revolution to the Civil War*. Princeton, NJ: Princeton University Press, 1957.

Harper, W. Percy. "The Significance of the Farmers of the Customs in Public Finance in the Middle of the Seventeenth Century." *Economica* 25 (April 1929): 61–70.

Harris, W. V. "A Revisionist View of Roman Money." *Journal of Roman Studies* 96 (2006): 1–24.

Harriss, G. L. *King, Parliament, and Public Finance in Medieval England to 1369*. Oxford: Clarendon Press, 1975.

Harriss, G. L. "Fictitious Loans." *Economic History Review* 8, no. 2 (1955): 187–199.

Hart, Keith. "On Commoditization." In *From Craft to Industry: The Ethnography of Proto-Industrial Cloth Production*, edited by Esther N. Goody, 38–49. Cambridge: Cambridge University Press, 1982.

Hartz, Louis. *The Liberal Tradition in America: An Interpretation of American Political Thought since the Revolution*. 1st ed. New York: Harcourt Brace, 1955.

Harvey, P. D. A. "The English Inflation of 1180–1220." *Past and Present* 61 (1973): 3–30.

Harvey, S. "Royal Revenue and Domesday Terminology." *Economic History Review*, 20, no. 2 (1967): 221–228.

Havighurst, Alfred F. "The Judiciary and Politics in the Reign of Charles II." *Law Quarterly Review* 66 (1950): 62–78, 229–252.

Hawtrey, R. G. *Currency and Credit*. 3rd ed. London: Longmans Green, 1930.

Henderson, Willie. "Metaphor, Economics, and ESP: Some Comments." *English for Specific Purposes* 19 (2000): 167–173.

Hendy, Michael F. "From Public to Private: The Western Barbarian Coinages as a Mirror of the Disintegration of Late Roman State Structures." In *Viator Medieval and Renaissance Studies* 19, 29–78. 1988.

Henretta, James A. *The Origins of American Capitalism: Collected Essays*. Boston: Northeastern University Press, 1991.

Hill, Christopher. *The World Turned Upside Down; Radical Ideas During the English Revolution*. London: Temple Smith, 1972.

Hill, David. "The Construction of Offa's Dyke." *The Antiquaries Journal* 65 (1985): 140–142.

Hills, Sally, Ryland Thomas, and Nicholas Dimsdale. "The UK Recession in Context—What Do Three Centuries of Data Tell Us?" *Bank of England Quarterly* Q4 (2010).

Hirschberg, Eliyahu. *The Nominalistic Principle*. Ramat-Gan, Israel: Bar-Ilan University, 1971.

Hirschman, Albert O. *The Passions and the Interests: Political Arguments for Capitalism Before Its Triumph*. Twentieth Anniversary ed. Princeton, NJ: Princeton University Press, 1997.

Hoffman, Philip T., Gilles Postel-Vinay, and Jean-Laurent Rosenthal. *Priceless Markets: The Political Economy of Credit in Paris, 1660–1870*. Chicago: University of Chicago Press, 2000.

Holden, James Milnes. *The History of Negotiable Instruments in English Law*. Holmes Beach, FL: Gaunt, 1955.

Holdsworth, William Searle. *A History of English Law*. 17 vols. Vol. 7. London: Methuen Sweet and Maxwell, 1982.

Horsefield, J. Keith. "The Beginnings of Paper Money in England." *Journal of European Economic History* 117, no. 32 (1977): 36.

Horsefield, J. Keith. "The 'Stop of the Exchequer' Revisited." *Economic History Review* 35 (2nd Series), no. 1982 (1982): 511–528.

Horsefield, J. Keith. *British Monetary Experiments, 1650–1710*. Cambridge, MA: Harvard University Press, 1960.

Horsefield, J. Keith. "Copper v. Tin Coins in Seventeenth-Century England." *British Numismatics Journal* 52 (1982): 161–180.

Horwitz, Henry. *Parliament, Policy, and Politics in the Reign of William III*. Newark: University of Delaware Press, 1977.

Horwitz, Morton J. *The Transformation of American Law, 1780–1860*. Studies in Legal History. Cambridge, MA: Harvard University Press, 1977.

Hurst, James Willard. *Law and the Conditions of Freedom in the Nineteenth-Century United States*. Madison: University of Wisconsin Press, 1967.

Ibbetson, D. J. *A Historical Introduction to the Law of Obligations*. Oxford: Oxford University Press, 1999.

Ingham, Geoffrey. "On the Underdevelopment of the 'Sociology of Money.'" *Acta Sociologica* 41, no. 1 (1998): 3–18.

Jackson, Andrew, and Ben Dyson. *Modernizing Money: Why Our Monetary System Is Broken and How It Can Be Fixed*. London: Positive Money, 2012.

Jaffe, Louis L. "Suits against Governments and Officers: Sovereign Immunity." *Harvard Law Review* 77, no. 1 (1963): 1–39.

Jenkinson, Hilary. "Exchequer Tallies." *Archaeologia* 62 (1911): 367–380.

Jenkinson, Hilary. "Medieval Tallies, Public and Private." *Archaeologia* 74 (1925): 289–351.

Jenkinson, Hilary. "Note Supplementary to 'Exchequer Tallies.'" *Proceedings of the Society of Antiquaries* 25 (1913): 29–46.

Jenkinson, Hilary. "An Original Exchequer Account of 1304." *Proceedings of the Society of Antiquaries* 26 (1913): 36–41.

Jenkinson, Hilary, and Charles H. Haskins. "William Cade." *English Historical Review* 28, no. 112 (October 1913): 730–732.

Johnson, Jerah. "The Money=Blood Metaphor, 1300–1800." *Journal of Finance* 21, no. 1 (1966): 119–122.

Johnson, Simon, and James Kwak. *13 Bankers: The Wall Street Takeover and the Next Financial Meltdown.* New York: Pantheon Books, 2010.

Jones, Charles I. *Introduction to Economic Growth.* New York: Norton, 1998.

Jones, Robert A. "The Origin and Development of Media of Exchange." *Journal of Political Economy* 84, no. 4 (1976): 757–775.

Jones, S. R. H. "Devaluation and the Balance of Payments." *Economic History Review* 44, no. 4 (1991): 594–607.

Kantorowicz, Ernst H. *The King's Two Bodies: A Study in Medieval Political Theology.* Princeton, NJ: Princeton University Press, 1957.

Katzner, Donald W. "Unity of Subject Matter in the Teaching of Intermediate Microeconomic Theory." *Journal of Economic Education* 22, no. 2 (1991): 154–163.

Kaye, Joel. *Economy and Nature in the Fourteenth Century: Money, Market Exchange, and the Emergence of Scientific Thought.* Cambridge Studies in Medieval Life and Thought; 4th Ser., 35. New York: Cambridge University Press, 1998.

Keen, Steve. *Debunking Economics.* Revised & Expanded ed. London: Zed Books, 2011.

Kelly, Patrick Hyde. *Locke on Money.* 2 vols. Vol. 1, Oxford: Clarendon Press, 1991.

Kemp, Betty. *King and Commons, 1660–1832.* Westport, CT: Greenwood Press, 1984.

Kennedy, Duncan. "The Stakes of Law, or Hale and Foucault!" *Legal Studies Forum* 15, no. 4 (1991): 327–365.

Kent, J. P. C. "From Roman Britain to Saxon England." In *Anglo-Saxon Coins,* edited by R. H. M. Dolley. London: Methuen & Co., Ltd., 1961.

Kerridge, Eric. *Trade and Banking in Early Modern England.* Manchester: Manchester University Press, 1988.

Keynes, John Maynard. *The General Theory of Employment, Interest, and Money.* New York: Harcourt Brace, 1936.

Keynes, John Maynard. "A Self-Adjusting Economic System?" *The New Republic,* February 20, 1935, 35–37.

Kim, Jongchul. "How Modern Banking Originated: The London Goldsmith-Bankers' Institution-alisation of Trust." *Business History* 53, no. 6 (2011): 939–959.

Kirby, J. L. "The Issues of the Lancastrian Exchequer and Lord Cromwell's Estimates of 1433." *Bulletin of the Institute of Historical Research* 24, no. 121–151 (1951).

Kishlansky, Mark. "The Emergence of Adversary Politics in the Long Parliament." *Journal of Modern History* 49 (1977): 617–644.

Kleer, Richard. "Fictitious Cash: English Public Finance and Paper Money, 1689–97." In *Money, Power and Print: Interdisciplinary Studies on the Financial Revolution in the British Isles,* edited by Charles Ivar McGrath and Christopher J. Fauske, 70–103. Newark: University of Delaware Press, 2008.

Kleer, Richard A. "'The Ruine of Their Diana': Lowndes, Locke, and the Bankers." *History of Political Economy* 36, no. 3 (2004): 533–556.

Knafo, Samuel. "The Gold Standard and the Origins of the Modern International System." *Review of International Political Economy* 13, no. 1 (2006): 78–102.

Knapp, Georg Friedrick. *The State Theory of Money.* Translated by H. M. Lucas. London: MacMillan, 1924.

Konings, Martijn. *Development of American Finance.* Cambridge: Cambridge University Press, 2011.

Kotlikoff, Laurence. *Jimmy Stewart Is Dead.* Hoboken, NJ: John Wiley & Sons, 2010.

Kowaleski, Maryanne. *Local Markets and Regional Trade in Medieval Exeter.* New York: Cambridge University Press, 1995.

Kreitner, Roy. "The Jurisprudence of Global Money." *Theoretical Inquiries in Law* 11 (2010): 177.

Kreitner, Roy. "The Standard Which Is Not One: Gold and Multiple Liquidity Regimes." In *Inside Money,* edited by Christine Desan. Philadelphia: University of Pennsylvania Press, 2014.

Kreitner, Roy. "When Banks Fail." *Common-Place* 10, no. 3 (April 2010).

Krueger, Anne. "Brief for Amicus Curiae Anne Krueger in Support of the Republic of Argentina and Reversal." April 1, 2013.

Krugman, Paul. "Commercial Banks as Creators of 'Money'." In *The Conscience of a Liberal. The New York Times*, August 24, 2013.

Krugman, Paul. "The Market Mystique." *The New York Times*, March 26, 2009.

Kulikoff, Allan. *The Agrarian Origins of American Capitalism.* Charlottesville: University Press of Virginia, 1992.

La Porta, Rafael, Florencio Lopez-de-Silanes, and Andrei Shleifer. "The Economic Consequences of Legal Origins." *Journal of Economic Literature* 46, no. 2 (2008): 285–332.

Langholm, Odd Inge. *Wealth and Money in the Aristotelian Tradition: A Study in Scholastic Economic Sources.* New York: Columbia University Press, 1983.

Lapidus, Oresme. "Metal, Money, and the Prince: John Buridan and Nicholas Oresme after Thomas Aquinas." *History of Political Economy* 29, no. 22 (1997): 25–27.

Laslett, Peter. "John Locke, the Great Recoinage, and the Origins of the Board of Trade: 1695–1698." *William and Mary Quarterly,* 3rd Ser. 14, no. 3 (1957): 370–402.

Lavoie, Marc. *Post-Keynesian Economics: New Foundations.* Cheltenham: Edward Elgar, 2014.

Lawson, M. K. "Danegeld and Heregeld Once More." *Economic History Review* 105 (1990): 951–961.

Lerner, Abba P. "Functional Finance and the Federal Debt." *Social Research* 20, no. 1 (1943), reprinted in D. Colander, ed., *Selected Economic Writings of Abba Lerner.* New York: New York University Press, 1983.

Levi, Margaret. *Of Rule and Revenue.* Berkeley: University of California Press, 1988.

Levine, Ross. "Financial Development and Economic Growth: Views and Agenda." *Journal of Economic Literature* 35, no. 2 (June 1997): 688–726.

Li, Ming-Hsun. *The Great Recoinage of 1696 to 1699.* London: Weidenfeld and Nicolson, 1963.

Lindert, Peter H. "English Population, Wages, and Prices: 1541–1913." *Journal of Interdisciplinary History* 15, no. 4 (1985): 609–634.

Lipietz, Alain. *The Enchanted World: Inflation, Credit and the World Crisis.* Translated by Ian Patterson. London: Verso, 1985.

Lipsey, Richard. *An Introduction to Positive Economics.* London: Weidenfeld and Nicolson, 1975.

Loveluck, Christopher. "A High-Status Anglo-Saxon Settlement at Flixborough, Lincolnshire." *Antiquities* 72 (1998): 146–161.

Loveluck, Christopher, Keith Dobney, and James Barrett. "Trade and Exchange—The Settlement and the Wider World." In *Rural Settlement, Lifestyles and Social Change in the Later First Millenium AD: Anglo-Saxon Flixborough in Its Wider Context.* Excavations at Flixborough. Oxford: Oxbow Books, 2007.

Loyn, H. R. "Boroughs and Mints, A.D. 900–1066," in Michael Dolley, ed. *Anglo-Saxon Coins; Studies Presented to F. M. Stenton on the Occasion of His 80th Birthday, May 17, 1960.* London: Methuen, 1961.

Luke, Timothy W. Review of Charles Perrow, Organizing America: Wealth, Power, and the Origins of Corporate Capitalism. Princeton, NJ: Princeton University Press, 2002. *Theory and Society* 33 (2004): 117–129.

Mackenzie, A. D. *The Bank of England Note: A History of Its Printing.* Cambridge: University Press, 1953.

Macphail, Richard I., Henri Galinie, and Frans Verhaeghe. "A Future for Dark Earth?" *Antiquity* 77, no. 296 (2003): 349–358.

Macpherson, C. B. *The Political Theory of Possessive Individualism: Hobbes to Locke.* Oxford: Clarendon Press, 1969.

Maddicott, John Robert. "The English Peasantry and the Demands of the Crown 1294–1341." *Past & Present,* Supplement 1 (1975).

Mankiw, N. Gregory. *Macroeconomics.* 5th ed. New York: Worth Publishers, 2003.

Mankiw, N. Gregory. *Macroeconomics.* 4th ed. New York: Worth Publishers, 2000.

Mann, Bruce H. *Neighbors and Strangers: Law and Community in Early Connecticut.* Studies in Legal History. Chapel Hill: University of North Carolina Press, 1987.

Mann, F. A. *The Legal Aspect of Money.* 2nd ed. Oxford: Clarendon Press, 1953.

Marglin, Steve A. *Raising Keynes: A 21st Century General Theory.* Manuscript on file with author.

Marshall, Richard K. *The Local Merchants of Prato: Small Entrepreneurs in the Late Medieval Economy.* Baltimore: Johns Hopkins University Press, 1999.

Mate, Mavis. "Monetary Policies in England, 1272–1307." *British Numismatic Journal* 41 (1972): 34–79.

Mayhew, N. J. "Numismatic Evidence and Falling Prices in the Fourteenth Century." *Economic History Review* 27, no. 1 (1974): 1–15.

Mayhew, N. J. "Population, Money Supply, and the Velocity of Circulation in England, 1300–1700." *Economic History Review* 48, no. 2 (May 1995): 238–257.

Mayhew, N. J. *Sterling Imitations of Edwardian Type.* London: The Royal Numismatic Society, 1983.

Mayhew, N. J. *Sterling: The History of a Currency.* New York: Wiley, 2000.

Mayhew, N. J., and Peter Spufford. *Later Medieval Mints: Organisation, Administration and Techniques.* B.A.R. International Series. Vol. 389. Oxford: British Archaeological Reports, 1988.

Mayhew, N. J., ed. *Edwardian Monetary Affairs (1279–1344).* Vol. 36. Oxford: British Archaeological Reports, 1977.

Mayhew, N. J., ed. "From Regional to Central Minting, 1158–1464." In *A New History of the Royal Mint,* edited by C. E. Challis, 83–178. Cambridge: Cambridge University Press, 1992.

Mayhew, N. J., and D. R. Walker. "Crockards and Pollards: Imitation and the Problem of Fineness in a Silver Coinage." In *Edwardian Monetary Affairs (1279–1344),* edited by N. J. Mayhew, 125–146. Oxford: British Archaeological Reports, 1977.

Mayhew, N. J. "Prices in England, 1170–1750." *Past & Present* 219 (2013): 3–39.

McFarlane, K. B. "Loans to the Lancastrian Kings: The Problem of Inducement." *Cambridge Historical Journal* 9, no. 1 (1947): 51–68.

McIntosh, Marjorie Keniston. *Autonomy and Community: The Royal Manor of Havering, 1200–1500.* Cambridge Studies in Medieval Life and Thought, 4th Ser., 5. Cambridge: Cambridge University Press, 1986.

Mehrling, Perry. "Minsky and Modern Finance: The Case of Long Term Capital Management." *Journal of Portfolio Management* 26, no. 2 (2000): 81–88.

Mehrling, Perry. *The New Lombard Street: How the Fed Became the Dealer of Last Resort.* Princeton, NJ: Princeton University Press, 2011.

Mehrling, Perry. "Retrospectives: Economists and the Fed: Beginnings." *Journal of Economic Perspectives* (2002).

Menger, Carl. *Principles of Economics.* Translated by James Dingwall and Berthold Frank Hoselitz. The Institute for Humane Studies Series in Economic Theory. New York: New York University Press, 1981.

Merrill, Michael. "The Anticapitalist Origins of the United States." *Fernand Braudel Review* 13 (1990): 465–497.

Metcalf, D. M. *Thrymsas and Sceattas in the Ashmolean Museum Oxford.* 3 vols. Vol. 1 and vol. 3, London: Royal Numismatic Society and Ashmolean Museum, 1993 and 1994.

Miller, Edward. "Farming of Manors and Direct Management: Rejoinder." *The Economic History Review* 26, no. 1 (1973): 138–140.

Milsom, S. F. C. *Historical Foundations of the Common Law.* 2nd ed. London: Butterworth & Co. Ltd., 1981.

Minsky, Hyman P. "Capitalist Financial Processes and the Instability of Capitalism." *Journal of Economic Issues* 14, no. 2 (1980): 505–523.

Minsky, Hyman P. "The Financial Instability Hypothesis." *Working Paper* No. 74 (May 1992).

Mirowski, Philip. *More Heat Than Light: Economics as Social Physics, Physics as Nature's Economics.* Historical Perspectives on Modern Economics. Cambridge: Cambridge University Press, 1989.

Mishkin, Frederic S. *The Economics of Money, Banking, and Financial Markets*. The Addison-Wesley Series in Economics. 9th ed. Boston: Addison-Wesley, 2010.

Mitchell, B. R. *Abstract of British Historical Statistics*. Cambridge: Cambridge University Press, 1962.

Monroe, Arthur Eli. *Monetary Theory Before Adam Smith*. Cambridge, MA: Harvard University Press, 1923.

Moorhead, T. S. N. "Roman Bronze Coinage in Sub-Roman and Early Anglo-Saxon England." In *Coinage and History in the North Sea World, c. AD 500–1250*, edited by Barrie Cook and Gareth Williams, 99–109. Leiden: Koninklijke Brill NV, 2006.

Morgan, Edmund Sears. *Inventing the People: The Rise of Popular Sovereignty in England and America*. 1st ed. New York: Norton, 1988.

Mossman, Philip L. *Money of the American Colonies and Confederation: A Numismatic, Economic and Historical Correlation*. Numismatic Studies, No. 20 Index. New York: American Numismatic Society, 1993.

Muldrew, Craig. *The Economy of Obligation: The Culture of Credit and Social Relations in Early Modern England*. New York: Macmillan, 1998.

Muldrew, Craig. "'Hard Food for Midas': Cash and Its Social Value in Early Modern England." *Past & Present* 170 (2001): 78–120.

Muldrew, Craig. "Interpreting the Market: The Ethics of Credit and Community Relations in Early Modern England." *Social History* 18, no. 2 (1993): 163–183.

Munro, John. "Deflation and the Petty Coin Problem in the Late-Medieval Economy: The Case of Flanders, 1334–1484." In *Bullion Flows and Monetary Policies in England and the Low Countries, 1350–1500*, edited by John Munro. Farnham: Variorum, Ashgate Publishing Ltd., 1992.

Murphy, Anne L. *The Origins of English Financial Markets: Investment and Speculation before the South Sea Bubble*. Cambridge Studies in Economic History. Cambridge: Cambridge University Press, 2009.

Naismith, Rory. *Money and Power in Anglo-Saxon England: The Southern English Kingdoms 757–865*. Cambridge: Cambridge University Press, 2012.

Neal, Larry. "The Financial Crisis of 1825 and the Restructuring of the British Financial System." *Review of the Federal Reserve Bank of St. Louis*. May/June (1998).

Neal, Larry. *The Rise of Financial Capitalism: International Capital Markets in the Age of Reason*. Studies in Monetary and Financial History. Cambridge: Cambridge University Press, 1990.

Nederman, Cary. "Body Politics: The Diversification of Organic Metaphors in the Later Middle Ages." *Pensiero Politico Medievale* 2 (2004): 59–87.

Nesvetailova, Anastasia. "The Crisis of Invented Money: Liquidity Illusion and the Global Credit Meltdown." *Theoretical Inquiries in Law* 11, no. 1 (2010): 125–145.

"New Anglesey Coin." *Gentleman's Magazine* 57 (1787): 1160–1161.

Nightingale, Pamela. "Monetary Contraction and Mercantile Credit in Later Medieval England." *Economic History Review* 43, no. 4 (November 1990): 560–575.

Nightingale, Pamela. "'The King's Profit': Trends in English Mint and Monetary Policy in the Eleventh and Twelfth Centuries." In *Trade, Money, and Power in Medieval England*, 61–75. Farnham, U.K.: Ashgate Variorum, 2007.

Nightingale, Pamela. *A Medieval Mercantile Community: The Grocers' Company and the Politics and Trade of London, 1000–1485*. New Haven: Yale University Press, 1995.

Nightingale, Pamela. "Money and Credit in the Economy of Late Medieval England." In *Medieval Money Matters*, edited by Diane Wood. Oxford: Oxbow Books, 2007.

Noonan, John Thomas. *The Scholastic Analysis of Usury*. Cambridge, MA: Harvard University Press, 1957.

North, Douglass C., and Barry R. Weingast. "Constitutions and Commitment: The Evolution of Institutions Governing Public Choice in Seventeenth-Century England." *Journal of Economic History* 49, no. 4 (1989): 803–832.

North, Douglass Cecil. *Structure and Change in Economic History*. 1st ed. New York: Norton, 1981.

O'Brien, P. K., and P. A. Hunt. "The Rise of a Fiscal State in England, 1485–1815." *Historical Research* LXVI (1993): 129–176.

O'Brien, Patrick K. "The Political Economy of British Taxation, 1660–1815." *The Economic History Review* 41, no. 1 (1988): 1–32.

O'Rourke, Kevin H., and Jeffrey G. Williamson. "When Did Globalization Begin?" *European Review of Economic History* 6, no. 1 (2002): 23–50.

Ormrod, W. M. "Edward III and the Recovery of Royal Authority in England." *History* 72, no. 234 (1987): 4–19.

Ostroy, Joseph M., and Ross M. Starr. "Money and the Decentralization of Exchange." *Econometrica* 42, no. 6 (1974): 1093–1113.

Peacock, Mark S. "Accounting for Money: The Legal Presuppositions of Money and Accounting in Ancient Greece." *Business History* 55, no. 2 (2013): 280–301.

Petersson, H. Bertil A. *Anglo-Saxon Currency, King Edgar's Reform to the Norman Conquest*. Bibliotheca Historica Lundensis 22. Lund: Gleerup, 1969.

Phelps Brown, E. H., and Sheila V. Hopkins. "Seven Centuries of Building Wages." *Economica* 22, no. 87(1955).

Phillips, Ronnie J. *The Chicago Plan & New Deal Banking Reform*. Armonk, NY: M. E. Sharpe, 1995.

Pincus, Steve. "Addison's Empire: Whig Conceptions of Empire in the Early 18th Century." *Parliamentary History* (2012): 99–117.

Pincus, Steve, and Alice Wolfram. "A Proactive State? The Land Bank, Investment and Party Politics in the 1690s." In *Regulating the British Economy, 1660–1850*. Farnham: Ashgate, 2011.

Pincus, Steven. *1688: The First Modern Revolution*. New Haven: Yale University Press, 2009.

Plucknett, Theodore F. T. *A Concise History of the Common Law*. 5th ed. Boston: Little, Brown and Co., 1956.

Polanyi, Karl. *The Great Transformation: The Political and Economic Origins of Our Time*. 2nd ed. Boston: Beacon Press, 2001.

Poole, Reginald Lane. *The Exchequer in the Twelfth Century*. Oxford: Clarendon Press, 1912.

Poovey. *A History of the Modern Fact: Problems of Knowledge in the Sciences of Wealth and Society*. Chicago: University of Chicago, 1998.

Postan, M. M. *Medieval Trade and Finance*. Cambridge: Cambridge University Press, 1973.

Postan, M. M., ed. *The Cambridge Economic History*. Vol. 1. *The Agrarian Life of the Middle Ages*. Cambridge: Cambridge University Press, 1966.

Pressnell, L. S. *Country Banking in the Industrial Revolution*. Oxford: Oxford University Press, 1956.

Prestwich, J. O. "War and Finance in the Anglo-Norman State." *Transactions of the Royal Historical Society* 4 (1954): 19–43.

Prestwich, Michael. "Edward I's Monetary Policies and Their Consequences." *Economic History Review* 22, no. 3 (December 1969): 406–416.

Prestwich, Michael. *Plantagenet England: 1225–1360*. Oxford: Oxford University Press, 2005.

Priest, Claire. "Colonial Courts and Secured Credit: Early American Commercial Litigation and Shays' Rebellion." *Yale Law Journal* 108, no. 8 (1999): 2413–2450.

Priest, Claire. "Currency Policies and Legal Development in Colonial New England." *Yale Law Journal* 110, no. 8 (June 2001): 1303–1405.

Purcell, Edward A. *Litigation and Inequality: Federal Diversity Jurisdiction in Industrial America, 1870–1958*. New York: Oxford University Press, 1992.

Radford, R. A. "The Economic Organisation of a P.O.W. Camp." *Economica* 12, no. 48 (November 1945): 189–201.

Reddy, William M. *Money and Liberty in Modern Europe: A Critique of Historical Understanding*. Cambridge: Cambridge University Press, 1987.

Redish, Angela. "Anchors Aweigh: The Transition from Commodity Money to Fiat Money in Western Economies." *Canadian Journal of Economics/Revue canadienne d'Economique* 26, no. 4 (November 1993): 777–795.

Redish, Angela. *Bimetallism: An Economic and Historical Analysis.* Studies in Macroeconomic History Index. Cambridge: Cambridge University Press, 2000.

Redish, Angela, and Warren E. Weber. "A Model of Commodity Money with Minting and Melting." *Federal Reserve Bank of Minneapolis Research Dept. Staff Report* No. 460 (2011).

Reece, R. "Models of Continuity." *Oxford Journal of Archaeology* 8, no. 2 (1989): 231–236.

Reed, Clyde G., and Terry L. Anderson. "An Economic Explanation of English Agricultural Organization in the Twelfth and Thirteenth Centuries." *Economic History Review* 26, no. 1 (1973): 134–137.

Reinhart, Carmen, and Kenneth Rogoff. *This Time Is Different: Eight Centuries of Financial Folly.* Princeton, NJ: Princeton University Press, 2009.

Ribatti, Domenico. "William Harvey and the Discovery of the Circulation of the Blood." *Journal of Angiogenesis Research* 1 (2009). National Institutes of Health: U.S. National Library of Medicine.

Richards, Richard David. *The Early History of Banking in England.* London: P.S. King & Son, 1929.

Ricks, Morgan. "Regulating Money Creation after the Crisis." *Harvard Business Law Review* 1 (2011).

Ricks, Morgan. "A Regulatory Design for Monetary Stability." *Harvard John M. Olin Discussion Paper Series* (2011): Discussion Paper No. 706.

Ricks, Morgan. "A Simpler Approach to Financial Reform." *Vanderbilt Public Law Research Working Paper No. 13–42* (2013).

Riley, James C. and John J. McCusker. "Money Supply, Economic Growth, and the Quantity Theory of Money: France, 1650–1788." *Exploration in Economic History* 20 (1983): 274–293.

Robertson, D. H. *Money.* Chicago: University of Chicago Press, 1959.

Rogers, James E. Thorold. *The First Nine Years of the Bank of England.* New York: Macmillan and Co., 1887.

Rogers, James Steven. *The Early History of the Law of Bills and Notes: A Study of the Origins of Anglo-American Commercial Law.* Cambridge Studies in English Legal History Index. Cambridge: Cambridge University Press, 1995.

Romer, Christina D. "It's Time for the Fed to Lead the Fight." *The New York Times,* June 9, 2012.

Root, Hilton L. *The Fountain of Privilege: Political Foundations of Markets in Old Regime France and England.* Berkeley: University of California Press, 1994.

Roseveare, Henry. *The Treasury, 1660–1870: The Foundations of Control.* Historical Problems, Studies and Documents, 22. London: Allen and Unwin, 1973.

Rothenberg, Winifred Barr. *From Market-Places to a Market Economy: The Transformation of Rural Massachusetts, 1750–1850.* Chicago: University of Chicago Press, 1992.

Rothschild, Emma. *Economic Sentiments: Adam Smith, Condorcet, and the Enlightenment.* Cambridge: Harvard University Press, 2001.

Rubini, Dennis. "Politics and the Battle for the Banks, 1688–1697." *English Historical Review* 85, no. 337 (1970): 693–714.

Ruding, Rogers. *Annals of the Coinage of Great Britain and Its Dependencies: From the Earliest Period of Authentic History to the Reign of Victoria.* 3rd ed. London: printed for J. Hearne, 1840.

Rufner, Thomas. "Money in the Roman Law Texts." In *Money in the Western Legal Tradition,* edited by Wolfgang Ernst and David Fox. Oxford: Oxford University Press, forthcoming 2015.

Russell, Conrad. *The Crisis of Parliaments: English History, 1509–1660.* The Short Oxford History of the Modern World. Repr. (with corrections) ed. Oxford: Oxford University Press, 1974.

Russell, Conrad. *Parliaments and English Politics, 1621–1629.* Oxford: Clarendon Press, 1979.

Ryan-Collins, Josh, Tony Greenham, Richard Werner, and Andrew Jackson. *Where Does Money Come From?* London: New Economics Foundation, 2011.

Sachse, William L. *Lord Somers: A Political Portrait.* Manchester: Manchester University Press, 1975.

Sahlins, Marshall. *Stone Age Economics.* New York: Aldine de Gruyter, 1972.

Samuelson, Paul, and William D. Nordhaus. *Economics.* 9th ed. New York: McGraw-Hill, 1973.

Sandel, Michael J. *What Money Can't Buy: The Moral Limits of Markets.* New York: Farrar, Straus, and Giroux, 2012.

Sargent, Thomas J. "The Ends of Four Big Inflations." In *Conference on Inflation*. Washington, D.C.: National Bureau of Economic Research, 1981.

Sargent, Thomas J., and Francois R. Velde. *The Big Problem of Small Change.* The Princeton Economic History of the Western World Indexes. Princeton: Princeton University Press, 2002.

Sargent, Thomas, and Neil Wallace. "Some Unpleasant Monetarist Arithmetic." *Federal Reserve Bank of Minneapolis Quarterly Review* (Fall 1981): 1–17.

Sawyer, P. H. *The Wealth of Anglo-Saxon England: Based on the Ford Lectures Delivered in the University of Oxford in Hilary Term 1993.* 1st ed. Oxford: Oxford University Press, 2013.

Sawyer, P. H. "The Wealth of England in the Eleventh Century." *Transactions of the Royal Historical Society* 15 (1965): 145–164.

Scheidel, Walter. "Coin Quality, Coin Quantity, and Coin Value in Early China and the Roman World." *Princeton/Stanford Working Papers in Classics* (2010).

Schofield, Phillipp R. "Access to Credit in the Medieval English Countryside." In *Credit and Debt in Medieval England C.1180–C.1350*, edited by N. J. Mayhew and Phillipp R. Schofield. Oxford: Oxbow Books, 2002.

Schofield, Phillipp R. "Dearth, Debt and the Local Land Market in a Late Thirteenth-Century Village Community." *Agricultural History Review* 1997, no. 45 (1997): 1–17.

Schofield, Phillipp R. "The Social Economy of the Medieval Village in the Early Fourteenth Century." *Economic History Review* 61, no. 1 (2008): 38–63.

Schumpeter, Joseph Alois. *History of Economic Analysis.* Edited by Elizabeth Boody Schumpeter. New York: Oxford University Press, 1994.

Screen, Ellen. "Anglo-Saxon Law and Numismatics: A Reassessment in the Light of Patrick Wormald's *The Making of English Law*." *British Numismatics Journal* 77 (2007): 148–172.

Sellers, Charles Grier. *The Market Revolution: Jacksonian America, 1815–1846.* New York: Oxford University Press, 1991.

Shaw, William A. "The Treasury Order Book." *Economic Journal* 16, no. 61 (March 1906): 33–40.

Shell, Marc. *The Economy of Literature.* Baltimore: Johns Hopkins University Press, 1978.

Simmel, Georg. *The Philosophy of Money.* Edited by David Frisby. 3rd enl. ed. London: Routledge, 2004.

Simpson, A. W. B. *A History of the Common Law of Contract.* Oxford: Clarendon Press, 1975.

Smith, Bruce D. "American Colonial Monetary Regimes: The Failure of the Quantity Theory and Some Evidence of an Alternate View." *Canadian Journal of Economics* 18, no. 3 (1985): 531–565.

Smith, Bruce D. "Money and Inflation in Colonial Massachusetts." *Quarterly Review (Federal Reserve Bank of Minneapolis)* 26 (Fall 2002): 3.

Smith, Bruce D. "Money and Inflation in the American Colonies: Further Evidence on the Failure of the Quantity Theory." Ontario: Centre for the Study of International Economic Relations, 1987.

Sommerville, J. P. *Royalists and Patriots: Politics and Ideology in England, 1603–1640.* 2nd ed. London: Addison Wesley Longman, 1999.

Spufford, Peter. *Money and Its Use in Medieval Europe.* Cambridge: Cambridge University Press, 1988.

Stasavage, D. "Credible Commitment in Early Modern Europe: North and Weingast Revisited." *Journal of Law, Economics, and Organization* 18 (2002): 155–186.

Steel, Anthony. "The Negotiation of Wardrobe Debentures in the Fourteenth Century." *English Historical Review* 44, no. 175 (July 1929): 439–443.

Steel, Anthony Bedford. *The Receipt of the Exchequer, 1377–1485.* Cambridge: Cambridge University Press, 1954.

Stewart, Ian. "The English and Norman Mints, c. 600–1158." In *A New History of the Royal Mint*, edited by C. E. Challis, 1–82. Cambridge: Cambridge University Press, 1992.

Stigum, Marcia, and Anthony Crescenzi. *Stigum's Money Market.* 4th ed. New York: McGraw-Hill Co., 2007.

Sumner, Scott. "Colonial Currency and the Quantity Theory of Money: A Critique of Smith's Interpretation." *Journal of Economic History* 53, no. 1 (March 1993): 139–145.

Sussman, N. "The Late Medieval Bullion Famine Reconsidered." *Journal of Economic History* 58 (1998): 126–154.

Sussman, Nathan, and Yishay Yafeh. *Constitutions and Commitment: Evidence on the Relation between Institutions and the Cost of Capital.* CEPR Discussion Paper 4404, 2002.

'T Hart, Margolein, Joost Johker, and Jan Luiten Van Zanden, eds. *A Financial History of the Netherlands.* Cambridge: Cambridge University Press, 1997.

Temin, Peter, and Hans-Joachim Voth. *Prometheus Shackled: Goldsmith Banks and England's Financial Revolution after 1700.* Oxford: Oxford University Press, 2012.

Thayer, Theodore. "The Land-Bank System in the American Colonies." *Journal of Economic History* 13, no. 2 (1953): 145–159.

Thomas, P. D. G. *The House of Commons in the Eighteenth Century.* Oxford: Clarendon Press, 1971.

Thomas, A. H., ed. *Calendar of Early Mayor's Court Rolls, 1298-1307.* Cambridge: Cambridge University Press, 1924.

Titow, J. "Evidence of Weather in the Account Rolls of the Bishopric of Winchester 1209-1350." *Economic History Review* 12, no. 3 (1960): 360–407.

Tobin, James. "Commercial Banks as Creators of 'Money'." In *Banking and Monetary Studies,* edited by Dean Carson. U.S. Treasury: Richard D. Irwin, 1963.

Tobin, James. "Money." In *The New Palgrave Dictionary of Economics,* edited by Steven N. Durlauf and Lawrence E. Blume. London: Palgrave Macmillan, 2008.

Usher, Abbott Payson. *The Early History of Deposit Banking in Mediterranean Europe.* Cambridge, MA: Harvard University Press, 1967.

Valenze, Deborah M. *The Social Life of Money in the English Past.* Cambridge: Cambridge University Press, 2006.

Van Caenegem, R. C. *Royal Writs in England from the Conquest to Glanvill.* Publications of the Selden Society. Vol. 77. London: B. Quaritch, 1959.

Vile, M. J. C. *Constitutionalism and the Separation of Powers.* Oxford: Clarendon Press, 1967.

Von Philippovich, Eugen. *History of the Bank of England and Its Financial Services to the State.* Translated by Christabel Meredeth. Senate Documents. Vol. 41. 1911. Book reprinted as congressional document.

Wallace, N. "Whither Monetary Economics." *International Economic Review* 42, no. 4 (November 2001): 847.

Watson, Andrew M. "Back to Gold-and Silver." *Economic History Review* 20, no. 1 (1967): 1–34.

Weber, Max. *The Protestant Ethic and the Spirit of* Capitalism. 1930. Translated by Talcott Parsons. London: Routledge Classics, 2001.

Wennerlind, Carl. "An Artificial Virtue and the Oil of Commerce: A Synthetic View of Hume's Theory of Money." In *David Hume's Poltical Economy,* edited by Carl Wennerlind and Margaret Schabas, 105–126. London: Routledge, 2008.

Wennerlind, Carl. *Casualties of Credit: The English Financial Revolution, 1620-1720.* Cambridge: Harvard University Press, 2011.

Wickham, Chris. *Framing the Early Middle Ages: Europe and the Mediterranean, 400-800.* Oxford: Oxford University Press, 2005.

Willard, James F. "The Crown and Its Creditors, 1327-1333." *English Historical Review* 42, no. 165 (January 1927): 12–19.

Willard, James F. *Surrey Tax Returns.* London: Roworth and Co., 1922.

Willard, James F. "An Early Exchequer Tally." *Bulletin of the John Rylands Library* 7, no. 2 (1923): 269–278.

Williams, Gareth. "The Circulation and Function of Coinage in Conversion-Period England, c. AD 580–675." In *Coinage and History in the North Sea World, c. AD 500–1250,* edited by Barrie Cook and Gareth Williams, 145–192. Leiden: Koninklijki Brill NV, 2006.

Wisehn, Ian. "Sweden's Stockholm Banco and the First European Bank Notes," In *The Banker's Art Studies in Paper Money,* edited by Virginia Hewitt. London: British Museum Press, 1995.

Wolf, Martin. "Strip Private Banks of their Power to Create Money." *Financial Times*, April 24, 2014.

Wolffe, Bertram Percy. *The Royal Demense in English History*. London: George Allen & Unwin Ltd, 1971.

Wood, Gordon S. *The Radicalism of the American Revolution*. 1st Vintage Books ed. New York: Vintage Books, 1993.

Wordie, J. R. "Deflationary Factors in the Tudor Price Rise." *Past & Present* 154 (1997): 33–70.

Wormald, Patrick. *The Making of English Law: King Alfred to the Twelfth Century*. 2 vols. Vol. 1: Legislation and its Limits. Oxford: Blackwell Publishers Ltd., 2001.

Wray, L. Randall. "Alternative Approaches to Money." *Theoretical Inquiries in Law* 11, no. 1 (January 2010): 29–49.

Wray, L. Randall. *Understanding Modern Money: The Key to Full Employment and Price Stability*. Cheltenham, U.K.: Edward Elgar, 1998.

Wray, L. Randall. "Modern Money." In *What Is Money?*, edited by John Smithin. 42–66. New York: Routledge, 2000.

Zelizer, Viviana A. Rotman. *The Social Meaning of Money*. Princeton, NJ: Princeton University Press, 1997.

communities (or groups):
  communal function of money 1, 6, 7, 346, 359
  communal or sovereign power over money 169
  economic organization in 41–3, 60
  effect of money on 1, 60, 110, 346, 425
  money as property of 350
  money creation in 1, 6–7, 24, 106–7, 359, 425
compound value of coins, *see under* coins
constitutional project, money as 69
  authority over taxation and money in 152–3,
    168–9, 192, 282 and n56
  defining authority 1
  distributing resources 1, 106
  and Gold Standard system 20, 404, 414–15
  in governance of material resources 1, 7, 69,
    106, 192
  governmental power for commercial
    purposes 20, 414
  individual interests and 20, 266, 293–4, 361
  and Locke's theory of money 349, 370, 404
  market shaped by 293–4, 434
  political community, money as product of 106–7
  political decisions in money creation 7–8, 293–4
  private interests and public authority in 20,
    293–4, 361, 403, 404, 414
  private theory and public practice in modern
    money 20, 361, 403, 404
  public–private interaction in 8, 106–7, 293–4
  relations between sovereign and subjects
    in 152–3
  strong money, high taxation system as 152–3
  and Whig liberal policy 370–5
contracts:
  bank money as a contract 375
  Crown as contracting party 285
  between government and creditors 13, 285,
    293–4
  in Gold Standard system 414, 415
  in law and in Locke's theory, compared 352, 353
  public debt as a private contract 293–4
convergence theory 24, 28–9, 37–8
  critique of 38
copper, in "black money" 202
copper coins:
  in 18th century 377 and n67
  farthings 237, 257, 263, 377n67
  halfpennies 257, 377n67
  issued by Stuarts 257
  subordinate to gold coin 380
  tokens, copper 171n65, 257n94
corporate stock, circulating 324
counterfeiting 18, 32, 52, 81, 82, 96, 105, 112, 178,
    257, 263, 391
country banks, *see under* banks
Court of Common Pleas 136
courts (generally):
  increasing independence of 286, 287, 288
  on legal status of paper money 328 and
    n161, 407
  obligations defined by 285–6, 287, 291, 293
  on ownership of bank deposits 393
  protection of private interests 286, 287, 288–9,
    293–4
  see also law

credit:
  Bank notes as private credit 410, 415
  bills of 45n64, 47, 49, 179, 321nn126 and
    128, 336
  boom and bust cycles of 401, 404–5
  cash loans in 211, 216
  circulating credit 69, 235, 245, 284, 293
  coins as a form of 334
  collective creation of 293
  and commodity money 206
  as complement to strong money system 10, 105,
    206, 207, 215
  consumption credit 10, 105, 191–2, 207–14,
    216–27, 262–3, 433
  credit to coin ratio in London 259
  credit bubbles 401
  credit currencies 232, 243, 332, 362
  credit theorists 16, 340, 331, 367, 369
  dependence of, on law 206
  domestic credit, money and 330, 331–41, 386
  in England and Europe, compared 192, 205,
    211–12, 214
  European experiments in public credit 246
  and financial revolution 374, 386
  historiography on 214–15
  horizontal and vertical 212, 213–14, 218
  in international exchange 228–9
  investment credit 192, 211, 213, 214
  land-based 367
  mercantile credit 224, 228–9, 244 and n48, 410
  money as a form of 16, 17, 60, 254, 300, 330, 337,
    341, 410
  and money, compared 206, 254, 300
  and money supply 105n120, 206, 224–7, 228,
    254–5, 263, 335, 379–80
  "peasant credit" 212
  personal and official, compared 60
  private, compared to public 95–6, 300
  private credit innovations, in 17th
    century 244–5, 262
  public and private interests in 279–81, 415
  public credit currencies 171, 172, 232, 243,
    290, 293
  revolution of public credit 178
  sales credits 207, 209, 211, 223
  securities as basis for, variety of 334, 335
  and shortage of small change 191–2, 206, 207
  stratification of 192, 206, 212–13, 227–8, 229
  in village exchange 216, 223, 227
  see also creditors; debt; debt, public; paper
    money; tallies
creditors:
  claims of, against the government 12, 281–2,
    287, 292, 301, 374–5
  in consumption credit system 212–13, 216,
    220–1, 223, 225–6, 227
  effect of deflation on 218n75, 225
  effect of recoinages on 132
  and gold coin 298
  Gold Standard and 16, 415
  government's alignment with 12–13, 190,
    292, 415
  interests of, and government authority 287, 292
  judicial protection of 287, 292

and money supply management 407, 412
paper money, fiat logic of 319–20, 385–6
tallies as 172
fiduciary currency 320, 360, 406
fiduciary orders 260
financial revolution 374, 386
fiscal value of money 14–15, 17, 22, 24, 44, 45, 46,
  49, 189, 360–1, 386, 388, 416, 427
Fisher, Irving 424
Flanders 124, 194
Florence 10, 246
  banking and credit in 224
  florin of 124, 168
  municipal bonds of 240
  small coins of 194, 203
florin (English) 113n9
Forde, Edward 333, 338
foreign coins (in England):
  and competition for silver and minting 108,
    142, 149
  galley-halfpennies 202
  imitation pennies 76n24, 108–9, 138, 142–9,
    203, 272, 364n17
  and shortage of English small change 199, 202–3
  use or exclusion of, in England 76n24, 80, 94, 96,
    105, 108–9, 142–9, 199, 202–3
foreign trade, *see* international trade
forgery, penalty for 314
France 159, 245
  coinage and competition for silver by 124, 142,
    151, 225, 342
  credit in 205, 246
  debasements in 142, 151, 162, 166, 168n55,
    169, 225
  devaluation in 122n40
  England's conflicts with 142, 225, 297, 302, 341
  Estates General on money 422
  recoinage in 121, 123
  use of money in 97, 102n114

Germany 98n100, 155, 159n24, 167, 246
Gillray, James 401
Glanvill, Ranulf de 86–8, 270
Glorious Revolution, *see under* England
Godfrey, Michael 266, 280–1, 302, 362
gold:
  in bimetallic system 115, 116, 196, 344n59, 376
  competition for, in Europe 116, 376
  development of coins from 27–8, 29, 52–3, 70
  dilution of, in coin 123
  equated with gold coin 19, 409, 411
  gold and silver at mint, compared 116, 140,
    196, 199, 226, 234, 237, 257, 343,
    344n59, 376
  and gold coin, in Gold Standard system 19,
    409, 411
  House of Commons committee on 405
  in international trade and credit 19, 229n113,
    347, 411, 430
  in Locke's theory of money 358 and n116
  as raw material 21, 52, 70, 229n113, 382
  scale of exchange with 116, 237
  shortage of 119
  as tangible value in coin 110

value of, compared to silver 9, 115, 196, 237, 341,
  376, 383, 384
see also gold coins; Gold Standard; silver
gold coins:
  Anglo-Saxon 51, 53, 54
  arbitrage between gold and silver coins 115, 349
  in bimetallic system 115, 116, 196, 297, 349,
    355n103
  as bullion, in trade 138
  Christian and Roman iconography in 53, 54
  as commodity money 112–13, 116, 353, 358
  copper and silver coin subordinate to 380
  count and content of 82, 83
  debasement of 53, 232
  dilution of gold content in 123
  dominance of, compared to silver 116, 376, 380
  equated with gold 19, 409, 411
  face value mandate for 94n93
  fetish regarding 407
  and gold, in Gold Standard system 19, 409, 411
  gold penny experiment 113n9, 140
  in international trade 10, 53, 83, 124, 127n61
  introduction of, in 14th century 112–13, 196
  as lawful money, and value of 406, 407
  in Locke's theory of money 358 and n116
  low-value coins proposed 106n124
  in money supply 99n102, 102, 116, 226, 236,
    297–8, 380, 384n96
  nonmonetary uses of 53
  origins of 27–8, 29, 52–3, 70
  "pale" gold coins 53
  as a reserve 380
  and royal authority 53, 54
  and silver coin, in money supply 54–5, 99n102,
    102, 116, 205, 226, 297–8, 384n96
  and silver coin, relative value of 9, 10, 115, 122,
    297, 342, 343n56, 355, 382n87, 383, 384–5
  in stratified exchange 83, 116, 195, 205
  transition from silver to gold coin 17, 376, 380,
    382, 384–5
  as unit of account 17, 18, 364n15, 376, 381,
    382, 409
  valuation of, in trade 10, 19, 83, 138
  see also coins; florin; gold; Gold Standard; guinea;
    noble; sovereign; thrymsas
gold reserve 11, 31, 380, 397, 413
goldsmith-bankers, *see under* banks
Gold Standard 5, 29, 32, 238, 375
  Bank of England in system of 416–18
  and bank rescues 20, 414, 416–17
  as constitutional compromise 16, 20, 404, 414
  gold, gold coin, and bank currency in 19–20,
    409, 411
  government's role under 19, 20, 414–15
  international trade as basis of 19, 410–11,
    413, 431
  and liberalism 411, 430
  in management of money supply 20, 409,
    412, 413–14
  as private touchstone for money
    creation 20, 404
  role of banks in 20, 416–17, 418
  as a system 16, 19–20, 414–15
  see also gold; gold coins

Horsefield, J. Keith 257, 262, 264, 318n112, 366n25, 368–9
Houblon, John 302, 362
Houghton, John 291, 366n25
Houghton, Thomas 336
Hovenden's chronicle 93
Hume, David 29, 274, 370n45, 409, 412, 423–4, 430, 431, 433, 434

iconography, *see* design and iconography
individuals:
 compared to group organization 41–2
 and the Crown, as contracting parties 285
 as focus of conventional theory 14, 20, 24–5, 27, 29, 171, 404, 421, 434
 government's status equated with 329
 incentives of, compared to community interest 101 and n109
 interests of, aligned with public interest 12–13, 266, 277–9, 280
 interests of, in modern theory 20, 274, 361, 414, 434
 in Locke's theory of money 16, 351, 353, 404
 medieval views of individual self-interest 274–5
 possessive individualism 280
 profit motives of 11, 12–13, 14, 266, 434
 in Protestantism 275
inflation, *see under* prices
information:
 as basis of exchange 359
 money as 35, 36, 425, 427, 432
interest (financial):
 Bank bills, interest-bearing 309–10, 322–4, 325, 326, 340
 Bank of England and interest rates 280, 312, 328, 401
 bonds, interest-bearing 12, 231, 247, 248, 250, 295, 323
 Catholic doctrine on 275–6
 in consumption credit 223–4
 early loans at interest 240–1, 242–3
 effective interest in prices 188
 Exchequer bills, interest-bearing 323, 326, 340
 government reliance on, and profit seeking 295–6, 340
 government's payment of, to Bank of England 289, 295–6, 305, 319, 326, 328
 introduced in Stuart system 186, 240–1, 242, 246, 247, 260, 295
 liquidity–interest trade-off 325
 money supply and interest rates 298 and n13, 304, 326, 328, 366
 participation and interest rates 248, 250
 as payment for commercial bank money 398
 Protestants' validation of 275–6
 role of, in stabilizing modern money 401
 and transition to interest-free paper money 322–7
 and usury prohibition 224, 226, 275
interests:
 capitalism and 5
 concept of, in Civil War 12, 276–9
 judicial protection of 287, 293–4
 and liberalism 12, 250, 266

medieval view of 274–5, 276
in modern theory 20, 274
as a political matter 276–9
private interests and money creation 265, 294, 361
profit motive in 265, 266, 274
public and private aligned 12–13, 250, 266, 277–81, 286
and rights, in law 266
self-interest, generally 5, 266, 274, 280, 281
statecraft and national interests 276, 277, 279
see also self-interest
international trade:
 balance of payments and foreign exchange 349, 358, 421, 430
 bimetallic system and 10, 115, 124
 coin as bullion in 347, 354
 credit relations in 228–9
 dependence on domestic economy 355
 domestic and international use of money, compared 132, 346–9, 355, 359
 and English monetary policy 19, 349, 358, 430, 431
 flow of bullion from Europe 119
 gold and silver coins in 10, 53, 83, 115, 124, 127n61, 138, 229 and n113, 346–7
 Gold Standard keyed to 19, 410–11, 413, 431
 growth of, in 17th century 256–7, 302, 349
 in Locke's theory of money 16, 346, 349, 358, 431
 and money supply 358, 424
 and nominalism or metallism 132
 traders' silver in 16, 345–6, 347, 353
 undervalued coin in 114
 valuation of gold in 19, 410–11
 in Whig political economy 302, 349
investment (and investors):
 Bank bills as 309–10
 in Bank of England 266, 280, 303, 305
 calculus of, as pump for money creation 235
 citizen-investors 235, 250, 280
 and European coinage 10
 investment credit 192, 211, 213, 214
 investors in public debt 2, 13, 250–1, 279–80, 287, 428
 investors' rights and government authority 13–14, 287
 in joint-stock enterprises 257, 261–2
 and money creation 14, 235, 329, 428
 and national interest 12–13, 266, 280
 public bonds as 235, 247–8, 250, 254
Ireland:
 bartering in 200
 debasement of coinage in 137, 170, 268, 273
 shortage of coin in 204
Italy:
 credit and money in 224, 229n114
 gold and silver coin in 10, 123, 124, 159
 Italian bankers in England 144
 Roman law in 85

James I:
 gold and silver under 236
 revenue of 235